GENERAL MANAGERS IN ACTION

GENERAL MANAGERS
IN ACTION

FRANCIS JOSEPH AGUILAR

New York   Oxford
OXFORD UNIVERSITY PRESS
1988

Oxford University Press

Oxford   New York   Toronto
Delhi   Bombay   Calcutta   Madras   Karachi
Petaling Jaya   Singapore   Hong Kong   Tokyo
Nairobi   Dar es Salaam   Cape Town
Melbourne   Auckland

and associated companies in
Beirut   Berlin   Ibadan   Nicosia

Published by Oxford University Press, Inc.,
200 Madison Avenue, New York, New York 10016

Oxford is a registered trademark of Oxford University Press

Library of Congress Cataloging-in-Publication Data
Aguilar, Francis Joseph
General managers in action.
Includes index.
1. Chief executive officers—Case studies.
2. Management—Case studies. I. Title.
HD38.2.A39   1987   658.4   87-12503
ISBN 0-19-504083-X

2 4 6 8 10 9 7 5 3 1

Printed in the United States of America
on acid-free paper

To
Gillian, Bruce, John, Kim,
and Anne-Marie

PREFACE

This book is about those things general managers know and do. My objective in preparing *General Managers in Action* has been to provide a means for learning about the job of the general manager with an appreciation for its complex and dynamic character and for its rich human dimension.

The book combines introductory chapters that discuss the general manager and issues of general management with cases that explore real situations where concepts can be tested and shaped and where the discovery of new ideas can take place. Twenty years in the classroom with MBA students and executives has convinced me that the case method is a particularly effective way to learn about the ill-defined, multi-dimensional issues of general management. For two years, I had an unusual opportunity to devote full-time to developing cases that would be rich in the administrative complexities faced by general managers. This book contains the best materials of the collection.

The introductory chapters present concepts and ideas, derived from and related to the cases, which have proved helpful to students in learning about the job of the general manager. While the cases were written for the purpose of classroom discussion, it can also be instructive just to read their descriptions of industries, organizational problems, and management practices. The executive or student interested in strategic planning can learn about the origin of many of the currently widespread concepts and practices associated with it in reading General Electric's Strategic Planning: 1981. Those interested in the workings of corporate culture could benefit from reading Johnson & Johnson (A). Asset redeployment, business in China, the health care industry, division-corporation relationships, and leadership are just some of the other topics of interest emphasized in one or more cases.

To bring to life the general managers involved in the cases, many were videotaped in the classroom as they discussed their thinking and their actions either with M.B.A. students or executives. These commentaries, edited to focus on case-related issues with the executive's choicest comments, have been packaged on four tapes for use with this book.

It would be difficult to exaggerate the added dimension to teaching that these tapes provide. The general managers I have come to know over the years as a casewriter, management consultant, and director were invariably interesting people. Many were quite impressive. Some were genuinely extraordinary individuals. On many occasions as a teacher I have found myself frustrated in straining to give my students a feeling for the people in the case—their character and their demeanor. Without this insight the classroom analysis lacked a vital dimension, for any course or program about general management is really a study about general managers, individual men and women. This limitation was clear every time we were fortunate enough to have the general manager whose case was being studied attend class and answer questions. The increase in students' interest, involvement, and learning was almost palpable. These classes would usually be voted among the more popular sessions in any course-end poll.

Though the book can certainly be used alone, the videotapes can bring an immediacy into any classroom, providing the students with information about the general manager which would be difficult or impossible to convey in words on paper. The Johnson & Johnson case can certainly describe Jim Burke's engaging presence as a CEO and the passion of his feelings about the company's Credo, but for many readers the man himself remains muted. In contrast, his intensity and charm virtually leap out of the video presentation for all to see.

The videotape format makes it possible for the teacher to use it in whole or in part at any point in the session where it can best fit the flow of discussion. The four tapes are organized around the following topics:

> Corporate Culture
> Strategic Planning
> Management of Rapid Growth
> Managing the Operating Unit

Information about the tapes is available from the publisher.

A final word. This book represents a tribute to the general manager. The American businessman and public official David E. Lilienthal observed in his book, *Management: A Humanist Art,*

> This I believe, and this my whole life's experience has taught me: the managerial life is the broadest, the most demanding, by all odds the most comprehensive and most subtle of all human activities. And the most crucial.

I also believe this to be true, especially for the general manager.

Boston, Massachusetts   F.J.A.
June 1987

ACKNOWLEDGMENTS

My greatest debt of gratitude is owed to the general managers who made this book possible. They were gracious with their time and almost without exception desirous of contributing to management education. They were also very busy people, which made their involvement so much more appreciated.

I am also indebted to those gifted people who shared with me the burden of writing the cases: James Austin, Arvind Bhambri, Carolyn Brainard, Dong Sung Cho, Dwight Crane, Richard Hamermesh, Jian-Sheng Jin, Paul Lawrence, and Robert Massey. To this list I must add the many doctoral candidates who provided invaluable suggestions in critiquing case drafts as part of a case writing seminar and my faculty colleagues who showed me what the cases could do in the classroom.

A word of thanks is also owed to Jay Lorsch for inviting me to spend two years developing teaching materials for Harvard's Advanced Management Program, to Dean John McArthur for his support of the project, and to the many other people who helped me to prepare this book.

CONTENTS

I

THE GENERAL MANAGER

1

The General Manager's Job

Imagine that you are attending a business conference dinner and are seated at a table with five strangers. At someone's suggestion, everyone in turn introduces himself or herself.

The woman on your left says that she is the vice president of marketing for a consumer product company. You would have a good idea about what she does for the most part. The job would typically involve decisions about pricing, channels of distribution, sales, advertising, and perhaps customer service and even product design. The man next to her describes himself as a vice president of manufacturing, and you conjure up an image of someone involved with plants, equipment, materials, and workers. Job titles of chief financial officer and vice president of personnel evoke equally descriptive mental images. But when the fifth person at the table says, "I'm a general manager," your understanding of what that meant might not be nearly so clear.

In real life, of course, no one uses the title *general manager* unadorned. Rather, your table companion would be more likely to specify a title such as division general manager, country manager, group vice president, president, or chief executive officer, and all at the table would nod their heads in acknowledgment. But even so, most people's understanding of the general manager's job would still be fairly limited, seldom going much beyond the vague notion of being the boss.

The General Manager Defined

Kenneth R. Andrews' seminal book on corporate strategy opens with the following definition of general management:

> Management may be defined as the direction of informed, efficient, planned and purposeful conduct of complex organized activity. General management is in its simplest form the management of a total enterprise or of an autonomous subunit. Its diverse forms in all kinds of businesses always include the integration of the work of functional managers or specialists.[1]

3

The notions of "total" and "integration" in this definition are essential characteristics of this job. John P. Kotter defines general managers as "individuals who hold positions with some multifunctional responsibility for a business (or businesses)."[2] And Peter F. Drucker observes, "There are a number of tasks which are top-management tasks . . . because they are tasks that can be discharged only by people who are capable of seeing the whole business and of making decisions with respect to the whole business."[3]

Since our view of the general manager emphasizes action, the following definition might serve us better as a starting point:

> The general manager is the person in charge of an enterprise (a relatively autonomous operating organization) with responsibility for the timely and correct execution of those actions promoting the successful performance and well-being of the unit.

The chief executive officer of a corporation, the president of the League of Women Voters, and the mayor of Boston are all general managers of relatively autonomous entities for whose overall health and development they are directly responsible. All three share a significant opportunity for deciding what needs to be done and for ensuring that it gets done.

To develop a fuller understanding of what the general manager's job entails, we turn to a brief case history. Although the tasks each general manager must do differ significantly in detail and emphasis, the following account is representative of a chief executive officer's position and applies in large part to other, more restricted general management positions as well.

A General Manager in Action

In April 1982, fifty-five-year-old C. Robert Powell, executive vice president at Diamond Shamrock in charge of chemical operations, accepted an offer to head Reichhold Chemicals. This manufacturer of industrial chemicals, with sales approaching a billion dollars, was experiencing a seriously declining profit performance, and Powell was recruited to take corrective actions.

The first thing Powell did as Reichhold's new chief executive officer was to take stock of the situation. He had already concluded from his initial assessment of the company that it had parted from its specialty-chemicals origin to become a volume-driven commodity-chemicals producer. A review of the product lines uncovered a "hodgepodge, with some pretty decent technology in the portfolio and some duds."

"I thought that I knew Reichhold Chemicals pretty well when I joined it," Powell later remarked. "It had been one of my important customers for years, and the board gave me access to all information during our negotiations. However, I found out one thing in a hurry—you never really know what's going on in a company until you work there." A cover story in *Chemical Week*, July 10, 1985, noted:

> he was "appalled" at the lack of organization structure and personnel management. From what Powell could determine when he came on board, there

wasn't any. There were four executive vice-presidents, but no organization chart. Everybody reported to the founder-chairman, and he was the only one with profit-loss responsibilities.

Powell soon concluded that Reichhold was in need not just of a fine tuning, but of a major overhaul. First, though, he would have to convince the board of the necessity for the company to change its strategy, its structure, and its people, and complicating this task was the membership of the board. A majority comprised incumbent senior managers, including the firm's founder and sole previous CEO for over fifty years, and his protégé and former heir apparent, the company's president.

Powell moved quickly on three fronts. He took various steps to gain greater independence from his predecessor's pervasive influence. He decided to focus the company's efforts on building its good-technology products and to divest its other lines. And he lured an up-and-coming personnel manager from Diamond Shamrock to launch and direct human-resource development for Reichhold.

The tailspin Reichhold had been experiencing played itself out in 1982. Sales declined as a result of depressed economic conditions, and divestiture of several unprofitable operations produced nonoperating losses. The financial results for the year, as shown in Table 1.1, were dismal, but Powell pointed to the strengthening of the company as the measure to watch. The investing community appeared to agree: The common-stock share value rose from the $10 to $12 range at the time Powell joined Reichhold to an all-time high of $19⅝ by the end of the year.

Progress occurred on many fronts in 1983. Several unattractive facilities were sold or shut down, and several small operations were acquired to strengthen the company's principal product lines. To support the growing emphasis on asset redeployment, Powell seized the opportunity to attract GAF's former chief financial officer and recently appointed president when he fell victim to an unfriendly takeover action.

Recognizing the need for people who could formulate Reichhold's business strategies as well as carry them out, Powell gave high priority to strengthening the management team. He carefully assessed the quality of his people as he worked with them on operating and planning problems. Managers showing promise were given additional responsibilities; others were encouraged to leave.

Table 1.1 Reichhold Chemicals' financial results, 1979–82 ($ millions).

	1979	1980	1981	1982
Sales	844	854	916	786
Net income	12.2	16.1	14.7	4.7
Return on sales	1.4%	1.9%	1.6%	0.6%
Return on equity	5.7%	2.8%	6.8%	1.0%
Share price: high	16½	15	16	19⅝
low	10⅞	9⅝	11⅛	10

A new participatory style of management was introduced to stimulate management initiative and teamwork. As Powell was later to remark, "In the past,
managers were rewarded for loyalty and punished for mistakes. In contrast,
we reward achievement. We do not punish mistakes, only people not doing
anything."

With two audiences in mind—the financial community as well as his management team—Powell announced ambitious financial goals for 1987. The principal objective was to achieve a 20 percent return on shareholder's equity. This
figure was compared in the annual report with a fourteen percent average ROE
for all U.S. manufacturing companies in 1982 and with Reichhold's historical
return of 6 percent to 7 percent.

Financial goals were only one vehicle by which Powell sought to set new
standards for performance. As the year opened, he also made a formal decla-
ration as to the kind of company he wanted Reichhold to be. As can be seen
from the new statement of corporate philosophy contained in Exhibit 1.A, emphasis was to be placed on creativity, reasonable risk taking, delegation, and
teamwork. This proposed management style stood in marked contrast to the
centralized decision making and relatively static atmosphere that had come to
characterize Reichhold's management in recent years.

Leading the company in new directions occupied Powell's attention, but he
was not unmindful of the need to consolidate his own position. To this end,
three departing "inside" directors on the board were replaced by three outsiders friendly to Powell's aims.

The financial results for 1983 also helped Powell to consolidate his position.
Earnings were up almost fivefold to $21.7 million, and return on equity climbed
from 1 percent to 10.8 percent. The financial community took note, and the
stock price rose from around $20 to over $38 per share.

With favorable results confirming the validity of his approach, Powell turned
his attention to developing the organization. His letter in the 1984 *Annual Report* noted:

> We also instituted team-building and participative management activities
> that are reaching virtually all levels of the organization.
> Of course, a reward system is one of the best personal motivators avail-
> able. Reichhold now has in effect programs whereby virtually every salaried
> employee is eligible for some form of incentive bonus to reward outstanding
> individual effort, including a sales incentive compensation plan—a rarity in
> the industry.

Powell also set out to strengthen the company's financial structure and to
engage his managers in developing the corporate strategy. Common stock was
issued to retire bank debt, and a decision to enter the adhesives business
launched a search for a suitable acquisition. When Beatrice Chemicals was put
up for auction, Powell gained board approval to bid for this sizable property.
According to the press, Reichhold was prepared to pay up to $600 million, but
was outmatched by Imperial Chemicals Industries' $750 million offer.

Financial results for 1984 again showed marked improvement over the pre-

Exhibit 1.A The Reichhold philosophy.

The pursuit of excellence in all phases of our corporation—our goals, our products and services, our people and our life styles.

Our corporate goal is to become a high-technology, specialty chemical company with a 20% return on equity.

Quality is essential—in our products, our working environment and our people. Economy comes from high value not from low cost.

Professional management will be practiced throughout our organization—people act and are treated as professionals. Trust is implicit: creativity and reasonable risk taking are encouraged.

Decisions should be made at the lowest possible level with responsibility and authority clearly defined.

Dedication to the principle of honesty and openness is expected. Attainment of goals requires the action of a team. The free flow of information and ideas is essential to the team effort.

We want people to be able to say that Reichhold is a fun place to work and that it supports and recognizes individual achievement.

To this end:

- Pursue your own standards of excellence
- Share responsibility well and be a good team player
- Plan and work to make things better
- Enjoy the difficult tasks
- Learn from mistakes
- Believe your efforts can make a difference

January 1983

ceding year. But even while the good news was being celebrated, telltale signs of a weakening market were evident as Reichhold sailed into 1985.

The year began on a high note as Reichhold consummated two major expansion moves: purchase of the majority holdings of its Canadian subsidiary for $55 million; and acquisition of Eschem, a worldwide adhesives and coatings business, for $54 million. These purchases were to be financed in part with funds made available from several major divestitures. Delays in selling off these properties forced the company to incur more temporary debt than anticipated and to carry money-losing operations on its books for most of the second quarter. That predicament, along with a general business slump, raised a red flag as

Exhibit 1.B   The Reichhold strategy.

Reichhold Chemicals has developed a broad range of specialty polymers serving a multitude of industries. The focus of our business is on customer responsiveness and flexibility of design based on technology and the economics of changing raw material bases. Our mission is to perpetuate this specialty nature by—

(1) Increased penetration of adhesives, paper chemicals, coatings and plastics markets through new product development and through niche acquisition of companies, product lines or technology.

(2) Providing applications research and customer service to preserve the specialty nature of the business.

(3) Continued infusion of capital for plant modernization to maintain cost efficient production.

(4) Adjusting the technology of the business by exiting stagnating product lines.

(5) Expansion into niche markets of the world where Reichhold's technology can be exploited.

(6) Targeting a financial strategy that creates a single A debt rating but allows flexibility to take advantage of special business opportunities.

(7) Completing investment in a participative management philosophy which develops achievement-oriented, agile people.

November 1985

second-quarter earnings fell below the year-earlier period. By midyear, it had become clear that Reichhold was facing a difficult period.

While pressure was put on the operating divisions to improve current performance, Powell continued to invest in long-term development. Product- and management-development programs were maintained. Strategic planning efforts were also continued, resulting in a statement of corporate strategy. This statement, contained in Exhibit 1.B, indicated the company's emerging focus on supplying specialty polymers to the adhesives, paper chemicals, coatings, and plastics markets.

During the course of the year, two additional outside members were added to replace the founder and another long-standing member of the board. In January 1986, the former president resigned from the company and board. His place was filled by another outsider, leaving Powell as the only inside director.

Table 1.2 Reichhold Chemicals' financial results, 1982–85 ($ millions)

	1982	*1983*	*1984*	*1985*	*1987 goals*
Sales	786	747	801	822	—
Operating income	14.5	34.5	43.6	8.2	—
Net income	4.7	21.7	25.7	(27.8)	—
Return on sales	0.6%	2.9%	3.2%	negative	5%
Return on equity	1.0%	10.8%	13.3%	negative	20%
Share price: high	$19\frac{5}{8}$	$38\frac{7}{8}$	$35\frac{5}{8}$	$43\frac{1}{4}$	
low	10	$18\frac{1}{4}$	23	$31\frac{7}{8}$	

By the end of 1985, Reichhold had disposed of eighteen businesses, with total yearly sales of about $300 million, and acquired five businesses with roughly equivalent total sales. While the newly acquired properties performed better than expected, Reichhold's core businesses continued to slide. As a result, the fourth quarter produced operating losses. A $50 million provision for losses associated with the disposition of unwanted assets resulted in a net loss for the year of $27.8 million. The share price dropped from a midyear high of $43\frac{1}{8}$ to the low 30s. Table 1.2 reviews the company's financial performance during Powell's tenure.

Powell commented to the board on the poor showing as follows:

> The market was tough this year, but I've got to say that we could have done a better job than we did. As a result, I've decided to award no bonuses, including my own, except for a few lower-level individuals who did outstanding work.
>
> It would have been easy to avoid the low operating results by cutting back on R&D and management development. But I refuse to mortgage the future in this way. It's important to show our people and Reichhold watchers that management is truly committed to long-term improvement and to excellence.
>
> In some ways I regret the easy accomplishments in 1983 and 1984. They lulled us into a false sense of security. As a result, we tried to do more than we had the talent to do. As business got tough, we still had too many people sit back and wait for instructions, just like they used to do.
>
> If I've learned anything over the past three-and-a-half years, it's this: It is much easier to change strategy than culture.

Powell's outlook for the future was generally optimistic, as reflected in his remarks on January 11, 1986, to the Conference Board:

> I've got to admit that I feel a little like the general and his troops who find themselves surrounded. The troops ask, "What should we do?" There's only one answer, "Attack!"
>
> One of our primary objectives this year is to instill in our people a sense of urgency, a bias for action. The only way we can fail is for our people to lose faith and give up. My main job is to see that that doesn't happen.

In February 1986, management's yearly planning conference was entitled "Countdown 22," to highlight the number of months remaining for the company to achieve its 1987 financial goals. By late February, as the Dow Jones industrial index broke the 1700 level for the first time, Reichhold's share price rose to $36\frac{5}{8}$.

Key Tasks for the General Manager

In this account, we see Powell dealing on many fronts as he strives to consolidate his position, to set a strategic direction for the firm, to build its capabilities in line with this direction, and to carry out day-to-day operations. The specific tasks he performed can be classified in various ways, but the following list provides a comprehensive basis for describing the general manager's job:

1. Creating and maintaining organizational values and norms;
2. Setting strategic objectives and direction;
3. Negotiating with stakeholders;
4. Marshaling, developing, and allocating people and other resources;
5. Organizing the work;
6. Attending to on-going operations.

A word of caution is in order as we examine these key tasks. This list and the following discussion might suggest an orderliness of process. But in practice, as demonstrated by Powell's experience, a general manager seldom has the luxury of addressing key tasks in an orderly and leisurely manner. Problems requiring the attention of general management intrude from any and all quarters, and at any and all times, with the result that the general manager's day is usually fragmented, as he or she shifts attention from one pressing issue to another. In these encounters, problems are rarely solved. The general manager is usually involved at any one time with a host of issues and problems, taking positive steps on this one now, studying that one next, regrouping on another one after that, all the while trying to make sure that all the right actions get done in time. Rather than a sense of completion, one has a sense of work in process.

We should also keep in mind that these six tasks, as part of a whole cloth, interrelate and overlap in many ways. For example, setting strategic objectives cannot be separated from negotiating with important stakeholders, if only to set practical limits to what is feasible. Likewise, the way the general manager attends to ongoing operations has a direct bearing on how organizational values and norms are maintained. And the general manager's concerns with establishing and raising standards of performance, as we shall see, appertain to all six tasks.

Creating and Maintaining Organizational Values and Norms

The basic belief system or philosophy of a firm, encompassing the values and norms important to it, serves as a unifying force to define the kind of business a company is in, the kind of people it wants associated with it, and how these people operate.

In discussing IBM, Thomas J. Watson, Jr., stressed the critical role values and beliefs play in achieving success over time:

> Consider any great organization—one that has lasted over the years—and I think you will find that it owes its resiliency, not to its form of organization or administrative skills, but to the power of what we call beliefs and the appeal these beliefs have for its people.
>
> This, then, is my thesis: I firmly believe that any organization, in order to survive and achieve success, must have a sound set of beliefs on which it premises all its policies and actions.
>
> Next, I believe that the most important single factor in corporate success is faithful adherence to those beliefs.
>
> And finally, I believe that, if an organization is to meet the challenges of a changing world, it must be prepared to change everything about itself except those beliefs as it moves through corporate life.[4]

In practice, the top executive or executives set the basic tone and character of the firm. This essential spirit reveals itself in various ways. For example, a company's basic approach to doing business might be characterized as one of being lean and mean, classy or prestigious, innovative, bureaucratic, or professional. Or as a place to work, a company can be known for steady and secure employment, for personal challenge and development, or for high pressure, high rewards, and survival of the fittest. Style of operation can be formal or informal, hierarchical or participative. And ethical considerations can serve as the overriding decision criteria or be subordinated to pragmatism. Although these labels are not precise, they can portray the essence of the underlying spirit of the firm, reflecting the values of its leaders.

Although it was nine months before Powell articulated Reichhold's philosophy, his views on what kind of company he wanted to run were undoubtedly firmly in place when he took the job. His basic beliefs and values shaped every major decision and action from the moment he took charge.

Setting Strategic Objectives and Direction

In long-range planning, there is a saying, "If you don't know where you're going, any road will do." Obviously, what needs to be done depends on what one wants to accomplish. Knowing what an enterprise is to be and is to do—its strategy—serves as a prerequisite for taking purposive actions.

Rarely does a general manager have the luxury of setting objectives and direction from scratch. As we saw with Reichhold, firms or divisions are normally engaged in on-going business activities with many attending personal and organizational commitments. The economic costs associated with change, comfort with the familiar, and vested interests are all inertial forces favoring the status quo.

As the principal agent of change for an enterprise, the general manager has to ensure (1) that developments which threaten to undermine the effectiveness of the organization's strategy and opportunities to improve it are perceived; (2) that the necessary economic and competitive analyses are well done; and (3) that a strategy suitable to the company and to the circumstances is selected. (A "suitable" strategy reflects the spirit and philosophy of the firm, the resources and skills the firm has or can obtain or develop, and the opportunities and threats the firm does, might, and will face over time.)

For most complex business situations, the general manager must involve others to help formulate strategy. For example, Powell could not possibly know each of Reichhold's major businesses well enough to conceive and evaluate alternative strategies for them. He had to rely on other people capable of assisting him in these efforts. The need to involve others in strategic planning introduces many difficult administrative decisions, such as who should be involved and in what manner. Powell decided to rely on Reichhold managers rather than on outside consultants. But not all of his key people were capable of undertaking strategic analysis. He had to decide whom to involve, how to help them to do the best job, and what outside people to bring in for business operations not otherwise covered.

Once strategy making is under way, the general manager must juggle the counterpressures implicit in a process that is creative, practical, timely, and thorough. At the same time the process should respond adequately to the interests of various key parties (stakeholders).

Negotiating with Stakeholders

The task most often associated with general management is that of ensuring that the interests of the various important stakeholders are met. Stakeholders here are defined as parties with a claim on benefits arising from the firm's operations and the value of its assets and as parties with power—operational or latent—to affect the firm's abilities to function. Even the self-employed professional or artisan must balance his or her personal interests with those of client or customer and with societal expectations as reflected in laws and norms. For the general manager of a large publicly owned corporation, stakeholders include customers, suppliers, creditors, shareholders, employees, communities, and even the nation in matters of military security or international relations.

For our purposes, negotiating with stakeholders should be interpreted in its broadest sense, involving positioning as well as discourse. Changes in Reichhold's board membership was as much a part of Powell's negotiations with that body as were the many discussions he undoubtedly held with board members concerning specific decisions.

In their excellent book, *Decision Making at the Top*, Gordon Donaldson and Jay Lorsch point to top management's desire to remain free from the power of the product market, the capital market, and the employees as a major driving force for decision making. In discussing the myths and realities of strategic choice, the authors note:

> Those realities begin with the fact that there are important constraints on the choices the corporate managers of these companies can make. Contrary to popular myth, these top executives do not have great latitude in their strategic choices. Instead the constraints on their choices are several, and they are both psychological and objective. . . .
>
> Operating within the limits of their unique belief system, corporate managers strive, with varying degrees of urgency, to relax the objective constraints imposed on them; to minimize the potential for dominance by major constituencies; to increase the potential for managerial discretion; and to assure personal and corporate success. Pragmatically, this means they are trying to be as financially self-sufficient as possible to reduce their dependence on the capital market. They are seeking diversification to reduce their dependence on one industry. And they are striving to develop a committed and loyal employee force to minimize the chance of dominance from this quarter.[5]

In practice, balancing stakeholder's interests involves constant adjustments as changes in circumstances and performance alter the assumptions and expectations of the various constituencies involved.

Marshaling, Developing, and Allocating People and Other Resources

A firm needs human, information, material, and financial resources to carry out its strategy. The general manager has to ensure that these resources are available when and where they are needed in an organization.

The keystone resource for most enterprises is human. There is a need for people who can discover specific business opportunities, who can figure out how to exploit the opportunities, and who can carry out the job successfully. As a result, most general managers are called on to devote considerable attention to the various tasks associated with building and utilizing human resources; recruiting, training, evaluation, compensation, job assignments, and terminations. When Jack Welch, soon after becoming CEO of GE, was asked what he considered to be his most important activity, he responded:

> The people process! I am the ultimate believer . . . [in] people first, strategy second. I spend my time managing the people equation. I am involved in the selection, the compensation of some 125 in detail and 500 with a pass-off. Everyone knows when they put their slate of five together for job X, Y, and Z, that I will review it. . . .[6]

Information is another important resource to be marshaled and allocated. There is an obvious connection between information and human resources. But not all important information resides, or needs to reside, in an organization's knowledge bank. Organizations might have to rely on outside parties for information about dynamic developments outside the firm (such as shifts in defense procurement priorities or political developments in South Korea) and about specialized considerations (such as the arcane case law connected with take-over practices). Concern with marshaling critical information extends beyond the information itself to include the enterprise's ability to obtain such information when needed or when needed information first comes into being. Reliable information sources are another important resource.

Plant, equipment, and money are obvious supporting resources. Other resources—such as brand recognition, trade relations, or raw material access—can also be critical for conducting certain businesses and need to be developed or acquired.

The call for resources in an enterprise usually exceeds its availability, and the general manager must devote considerable attention to allocating what is available. Scarcity is not the only reason for allocating resources within an organization. Sensitive information might have to be disseminated selectively to preserve its confidentiality. Whatever the reason, since resources translate into power within an organization, this process requires considerable sensitivity to internal politics as well as to economics. Various organizational mechanisms—such as long-range plans, staffing plans, operating budgets, and capital budgets—are typically employed to carry out the resource-allocation process.

Organizing the Work

Where success depends on the energy and initiative of more than one person, the general manager must assign work and motivate employees to act in the best interests of the company. Questions of organizational structure and work assignments typically occupy a great deal of a general manager's time as he or she tries to marry the work to be done with the capabilities and interests of the available people. This job can become particularly difficult as the organization is changing its strategy, is growing rapidly in size, is adding many new employees, or, as is often the case, is experiencing some combination of the three.

Planning, budgeting, control, compensation, communications, and other management systems serve as important organizing mechanisms. Staff specialists are often heavily involved in designing and implementing such systems. Nonetheless, since the purpose of these systems is to enable line managers to develop organizational capabilities and to manage on-going operations, the general manager plays a special role in ensuring their appropriateness to the specific needs of the organization as well as overseeing their proper use. Taken together, these systems are the machinery that keeps a business operating effectively.

Attending to On-Going Operations

Good thinking and planning are important elements of a general manager's job, but they are not enough. As Peter Drucker has so aptly noted, "If objectives are only good intentions, they are worthless. They must degenerate into work."[7] Ultimately, changes in strategy have to translate into ongoing operations, and the general manager bears responsibility for that conversion.

The general manager is also responsible for the improvement and the continued success of ongoing operations. This task might be less glamorous or exciting than those of changing strategy and structure, but it is no less important. It is where operating profits are finally realized.

In managing operations, the general manager typically gets involved in such activities as staffing, coordinating, controlling, enforcing standards, trouble shooting, arbitrating, and giving commands. There are few rules to how he or she should go about these activities. Involvement can be direct and explicit or suggestive, continuous or on an as-needed basis, decisive or flexible. Whatever the approach, the general manager must be committed and sufficiently knowledgeable about operations to make the right things happen at the right time and in the right way.

Since ongoing operations involve the most people and the most resources for most established enterprises, their direction typically places heavy demands on the general manager. For this reason, in many large corporations, this task is separated from the others so that it can receive the attention it requires. The chief operating officer carries this burden for the chief executive officer.

Key Roles for the General Manager

In dealing with the six key tasks, the general manager must play several important roles. He or she must ensure that decisions are made and actions taken when called for, that important items take precedence, that the myriad initiatives undertaken form a cohesive whole, and that the organization continually strives for superior performance. In effect, the general manager has to be an instigator, a priority setter, an integrator, and a taskmaster.

The General Manager as Instigator

However valid a program of change might be, it is bound to encounter moments of apathy, pockets of resistance, or a loss of interest because of fatigue or distraction. As a result, vital deliberations and actions are not initiated or lose momentum, and progress falters or comes to a standstill. It is up to the general manager to ensure that there is enough push behind each vital element in the program to carry it through these obstacles in timely fashion.

As instigator, the general manager has to goad thinking and action wherever needed in the organization. This can be done in various ways—for example, by direct involvement or by involving others—once the need is recognized. But recognizing the need for initiative or push can pose problems. For a general manager attempting change on many fronts, the difficulty of keeping track of the numerous efforts under way or still to be undertaken poses serious practical limits to timely intervention. The difficulty in recognizing a need for added push can be exacerbated if the general manager receives feedback that is unwarrantedly favorable, either because of mistaken optimism or by subordinates' reluctance to admit failure.

Providing sufficient impetus to each move at the outset, before resistance or apathy can build up, has obvious benefits. Doing it right the first time can spell the difference between success and failure, especially in those cases where the general manager is operating at the limits of his or her resources. But it is in just such circumstances that the general manager will find it most difficult to follow this approach. Although preventing fires is better than fighting fires, it would be foolhardy to disperse all firefighters to inspecting facilities and instructing the public about fire prevention and not to have a force available to fight the inevitable fire. For the same reason, general managers with limited resources have to choose carefully where to invest their time and how much to invest in specific activities and how much to keep in reserve. They must set priorities.

The General Manager as Priority Setter

Although general managers must concern themselves with all of the key tasks described above, they need not, and indeed normally should not, devote equal attention to each. The importance of being selective and of setting priorities is underscored in the following comment by Andrall E. Pearson, former president of Pepsico:

> [A] primary skill of general managers is to pick the specific areas where their involvement will have the greatest impact on business results. As we have seen, the scope of the job is such that a GM nearly always faces many more problems and opportunities than he or she can possibly deal with personally. So at one time the GM may decide to put greater emphasis on strategy and superior execution; at another time the focus will be on people development or the working environment. Knowing what to emphasize, when to emphasize it, what and when to delegate and to whom to delegate are crucial decisions.[8]

At Reichhold, Powell emphasized different tasks at different times, sometimes moving on several fronts, other times focusing heavily on one. See Figure 1.1. His decisions regarding his priorities and the emphasis he placed on them were no doubt influenced in part by the particular course of events at Reichhold as well as by his own personal style and preferences. But a major consideration for making these decisions was the basic nature of the situation in which he found himself. Another person in Powell's place probably would have acted similarly, and Powell in another situation probably would have acted differently.

Reichhold was a mature, multibusiness corporation with a well-entrenched management experiencing operating difficulties and under shareholders' pressure (through declining stock price) to change. Powell's initial attention to setting broad direction, to building management capabilities, and to dealing with the board (negotiating with stakeholders) would seem correct for that situation.

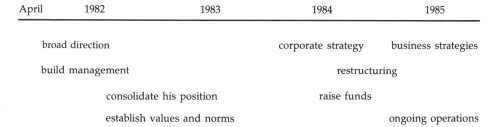

April	1982	1983	1984	1985
	broad direction		corporate strategy	business strategies
	build management			restructuring
		consolidate his position	raise funds	
		establish values and norms		ongoing operations

Figure 1.1　Tasks emphasized by Powell at Reichhold over time.

His subsequent decisions to emphasize building a new culture, formulating business strategies, and restructuring (buying and selling businesses) in se-quence over the ensuing three years would also seem in keeping with the situation.

Had Powell been called on to take charge of a company experiencing rapid growth, he would have followed a quite different course of action. Marshaling resources—people and skills as well as funds and other assets—would have been prominent among the tasks receiving his emphasis and priority. Such a situation might also have called for increased attention to changes in organizational structure and management support systems.

In effect, we can identify a number of prototypical situations calling for certain responses. For example, start-up situations typically have many problems in common and tend to have a similar profile with respect to which tasks need to be emphasized and in what order. The same is true of troubled enterprises requiring turnaround actions. (A general manager, naturally, stresses different tasks in dealing with a start-up compared to a turnaround.) Rapid growth of an established firm and a plateauing mature business each impose their own requirements for action. With respect to complexity, a company with many related businesses poses different challenges to a general manager from one predominantly in a single business or one in many unrelated businesses (conglomerate). The general manager of a subsidiary unit (a division or a strategic business unit, SBU) must approach problems and act differently from a chief executive officer. And a general manager trying to make major changes where strong external pressures are in play faces a different challenge from one where such pressures are absent.

In reality, any situation must involve a combination of the above prototypes: An enterprise can be start-up, rapid growth, mature, or failing; it can be single-business, related multibusiness, or conglomerate; the general manager can be at the top or in the middle of a firm; and clear pressures for change might or might not be present. This simple list of governing characteristics would result in forty-eight prototypical combinations, and the list can easily be enlarged. What we must conclude is that any attempt to provide comprehensive guidelines for general managers is likely to meet with failure. We and they can gain some insight about how to deal with a situation from an understanding of similar situations, but most circumstances are sufficiently complex to resist simple solutions. In setting priorities, the general manager must discern what is distinctive about his or her situation and what is typical and respond accordingly.

The General Manager as Integrator

The general manager by definition has multifunctional responsibilities, and often multibusiness responsibilities as well. As such, he or she bears a special responsibility for meshing the many organizational activities into a cohesive whole. This responsibility has both horizontal and vertical dimensions, requiring an integration of efforts across the organization and over time.

In a single business enterprise, the general manager must ensure the consonance of different functional policies. To leave marketing, manufacturing, engineering, finance, and the other functional areas on their own, however competent the department managers might be, is a little like a woman asking a milliner, a dressmaker, and a leather stylist to furnish her with their greatest creations. The individual hat, dress, bag, and shoes might be extraordinarily beautiful, but as an ensemble, they might draw attention for the wrong reasons, with clashing colors, textures, and designs. The most effective marketing plan probably will clash with the best manufacturing plan, and both might be at odds with the most advantageous engineering approach or with optimal financial maneuvering. The need for functional policies to relate to each other as well as to competitive and market forces is discussed in the next chapter, as are the ways in which a general manager with multibusiness responsibilities can consider the relationships between and among business units.

The general manager also has to be concerned with the pattern of efforts over time. Attention must be given to the order (first things first), consistency, and continuity (no key steps missing) of sequential actions. As author or sponsor of an organization's game plan, the general manager must monitor the plan's implementation to ensure that it makes as much sense in action over time as it did in concept. This is not to say that modifications should not be made as events change or as the organization learns how to respond better. But the general manager must assure everyone concerned, outside stakeholders as well as employees, that the enterprise knows what it is doing and that its efforts make good business sense. A general manager can undermine support very quickly by projecting an image of confused and erratic actions.

The General Manager as Taskmaster

Several studies about America's best-run companies thrust the word *excellence* into some prominence in the business jargon of the 1980s. One of their conclusions, not surprisingly, is that the person in charge (the general manager) has to care about the quality of accomplishment and has to promote it constantly for excellence in performance to occur.

Caring about excellence has its origins in a person's basic beliefs and values. On the foundations of such values, challenges and standards of performance must be defined and enforced. But in striving for excellence, it is the underlying values that provide the energy, the tenacity of purpose, and the inspiration needed to achieve superior performance, as Thomas J. Watson, Jr., argues in his discussion of IBM's success:

> Men who have accomplished great deeds in large organizations might have done less if they had been challenged with less, and they would have realized less of their potential and their individuality. . . .
> *We believe that an organization should pursue all tasks with an idea that they can be accomplished in a superior fashion.* . . . An environment which calls for perfection is not likely to be easy. But aiming for it is always a goal to progress.
> In addition to this persistent striving for perfection, we believe an organization will stand out only if it is willing to take on seemingly impossible tasks. . . . T. J. Watson used to tell our people, "It is better to aim at perfection and miss than it is to aim at imperfection and hit it."[9]

Specific challenges and standards of performance are defined in various ways: the mission statement, the strategic plan, the budget, departmental plans, and in setting the individual's objectives. These challenges and standards are in turn interpreted and enforced in the feedback of reviews (approval and disapproval) and through the reinforcement of rewards and punishments. The kind of people advanced and supported in an organization is a vital element in raising standards of performance and in upholding high standards. In his biographical sketch of Jean Riboud, the late CEO of Schlumberger, Auletta touched on this connection:

> On several occasions, he has said that the company's goals should be "to strive for perfection." To this end, he searches for fighters, for independent-minded people who don't, in his words, "float like a cork." In 1974, when he appointed Carl Buchholz his vice president of personnel, it was largely because Buchholz was not afraid to speak out. Riboud recalled first seeing Buchholz at a Schlumberger management conference in Geneva. "All the people were reciting the Mass, and suddenly Buchholz said, 'You're full of it!' I said, 'This is a fellow who speaks his mind.' "[10]

Expediency is to excellence as friction is to motion. Without constant pressure, momentum will be lost. The danger for a struggling-to-succeed organization to cut corners and to go for the sure and easy payoff is easy to understand. Lacking confidence in its abilities to achieve superior performance, the organization is conditioned to accept less. Indeed, in such cases, the general manager may have to start with modest challenges and standards, raising them over time in line with improved results and increased confidence.

The force of expediency is also a menace for organizations that dominate their field. The general managers of enterprises enjoying monopolistic powers must constantly fight apathy and disregard. But so too must those responsible for enterprises that have succeeded through excellent performance. Auletta noted, "One of Riboud's preoccupations is that Schlumberger will lose its drive as a company and grow complacent. . . ."[11] Thomas Watson, Jr., of IBM, also expressed concern about this peril:

Unless management remains alert, it can be stricken with complacency—
one of the most insidious dangers we face in business. In most cases it's
hard to tell that you've even caught the disease until it's almost too late. It
is frequently most infectious among companies that have already reached
the top. They get to believing in the infallibility of their own judgments.[12]

The quest for superior performance is a never-ending battle. The general
manager must constantly set the high standards for excellence and goad performance to meet them.

Evaluating the General Manager

Boards of directors have a responsibility for evaluating the performance of the
CEO. Investors have good reason for so doing as well. Senior-level general
managers must evaluate lower-level general managers. Even subordinates will
evaluate their general manager in deciding their level of commitment to the
enterprise.

Where an organization's performance improves or deteriorates markedly
over time, evaluating the general manager may be a relatively simple and
straightforward matter. But for those critical occasions where a general manager is just starting out, or where unforeseen events suddenly invalidate an
established strategy or render proven practices obsolete, such evaluation becomes much more difficult. In situations such as these, an evaluation of the
general manager must rest on an assessment of what he or she is doing or not
doing. But these situations are usually sufficiently complex and the relationships between cause and effect sufficiently obscure to frustrate any definitive
evaluation. There will remain considerable room for doubt and opposing opinions. It is something like judging a pudding while it is still cooking. The only
proof is in the eating. Still, the cook cannot suspend judgment until that moment, at least if the pudding is not to be burned.

Figure 1.2 attempts to summarize the description of the general manager's
job. It can be a helpful reference for evaluating the general managers described
in the cases to follow and for thinking about the job in practice. But as was
cautioned earlier, any suggestion of conceptual completeness or orderliness of
process should be rejected. In particular, a proper evaluation of a general manager must include consideration of what is not acted upon as well as what is.
This chapter has stressed the action side of the general manager's job—doing
something, directing action, making decisions. But there is also an important
realm of positive inaction, where the general manager consciously or instinc-
tively decides not to act. In discussing executive decision making, Chester Barnard stresses the importance of decisions not to decide, concluding:

> *The fine art of executive decision consists in not deciding questions that are not
> now pertinent, in not deciding prematurely, in not making decisions that cannot be
> made effective, and in not making decisions that others should make.* Not to decide
> questions that are not pertinent at the time is uncommon good sense. . . .
> Not to make decisions that cannot be made effective is to refrain from de-
> stroying authority. Not to make decisions that others should make is to
> preserve morale, to develop competence, to fix responsibility, and to pre-
> serve authority.[13]

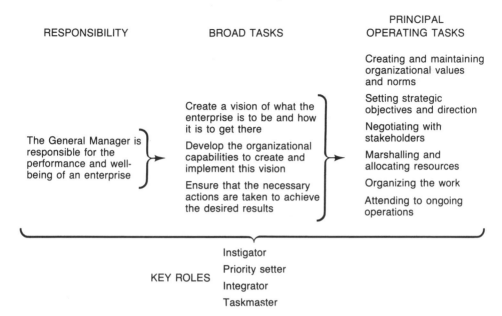

Figure 1.2   The job of the general manager.

By now it should be apparent just how complex and how challenging the general manager's job can be. It is not a job everyone can do or would want to do. The job calls for such personal qualities as intelligence, high energy, self-assurance, a willingness to take big risks, adaptability, and good character. Above all, it calls for insightfulness and good judgment. For there is still a great deal of art and spontaneity in the general manager's job.

Notes

1. Kenneth R. Andrews, *The Concept of Corporate Strategy* rev. ed. (Homewood, IL, 1980), p. 2.
2. John P. Kotter, *The General Managers* (New York, 1982), p. 2.
3. Peter F. Drucker, *Management* (New York, 1973), p. 609.
4. Thomas J. Watson, Jr., *A Business and Its Beliefs* (New York, 1963), p. 5.
5. Gordon Donaldson and Jay W. Lorsch, *Decision Making at the Top* (New York, 1983), pp. 6, 7, 10.
6. "General Electric Company: Dr. John F. Welch, Jr.," Harvard Business School videotape 882–024, 1982.
7. Drucker, *op. cit.*, p. 101.
8. "Role of the General Manager," Harvard Business School publication 0–386–041, 1985, p. 11.
9. Watson, *op. cit.*, pp. 27 and 34.
10. Ken Auletta, "A Certain Poetry," *The New Yorker*, June 6, 1983, p. 89.
11. *Ibid.*
12. Watson, *op. cit.*, pp. 63, 64.
13. Chester I. Barnard, *The Functions of the Executive* (Cambridge, MA, 1960), p. 194.

2

Strategy and
the General Manager

Setting strategic direction ranks among the more dramatic and visible acts of the general manager. If Reichhold succeeds, Bob Powell will be remembered primarily for repositioning the company in growth specialty chemical businesses. The importance attached to strategic direction can be more fully appreciated when we are mindful of the central role strategy plays among the general manager's tasks. As a vision of what the enterprise is to be and how it is to get there, strategy represents a practical embodiment and articulation of an organization's basic values and norms. It serves to steer the development of organizational capabilities and to guide day-to-day operations. It is the nexus for negotiating with stakeholders.

The Concept of Strategy

The word *strategy* has its origins in military science. It is defined in the dictionary as the "science and art of employing the armed strength of a belligerent to secure the objects of war, especially the large-scale planning and directing of operations in adjustment to combat area, possible enemy action, political alignments, etc." As used in business, the meaning of strategy includes the character and purpose of an enterprise. According to Andrews:

> Corporate strategy is the pattern of decisions in a company that determines and reveals its objectives, purposes, or goals, produces the principal policies and plans for achieving those goals, and defines the range of business the company is to pursue, the kind of economic and human organization it is or intends to be, and the nature of the economic and non-economic contribution it intends to make to its shareholders, employees, customers, and communities.[1]

Let us return to Reichhold Chemicals' statements of strategy and corporate objectives to illustrate Andrews' definition:

Business to be in

To develop, manufacture, and sell specialty chemicals.

Objectives

(1) To achieve a 20 percent return on average common stockholder's equity.

(2) To be a firm highly regarded by its customers, employers, investors, suppliers, and the communities in which it operates.

Policies

Markets: focus on adhesives, paper chemicals, coatings, and plastics; global coverage

Products: develop broad range of specialty polymers; drop products that have become commodities

Product development: acquisition and application research

Marketing: intensive interaction with the customers

Manufacturing: modern plant for cost-effective production

Finance: single A debt rating with a willingness to go lower to take advantage of special investment opportunities; 20–25 percent dividend payout ratio

Organizational structure: decentralized divisional operations

Management style: participative interaction

Kind of company it is to be

The polymer chemical supplier known for its responsiveness to customers' special needs and its ability to provide competitively priced alternative formulations that allow customers to modify their products in line with changing raw materials' prices and availability.

This strategy makes clear Reichhold's intention to emphasize earnings and shareholder value by focusing on four industrial markets, so that it can develop the capabilities and the relationships necessary to provide its customers the specialty polymer chemicals they need at an attractive price. Whether or not this strategy will provide Reichhold with the distinctive competitive advantage it needs to achieve its objectives will depend on the quality of its analysis as to what the customers want and as to what the firm in practice can offer.

Corporate and Business Strategy

Corporate strategy, as defined above, applies to the whole enterprise. How a firm intends to compete in a particular business is called a business strategy. For a single business corporation, corporate strategy is essentially equivalent to business strategy. For a multibusiness firm, a distinction must be made between the two. In this situation, the focus of corporate strategy is on managing a business mix to achieve corporate goals. Here attention is given to such matters as selecting which businesses to enter or exit, allocating resources among businesses, and deciding what the relationships should be between and among the operating units.

The distinction between corporate and business strategy takes on practical importance, because each of these activities typically involves different people, different managerial processes, and different conceptual tools. Corporate strategy is usually the responsibility of the chief executive officer, and business strategies of the divisional general managers.

The strategy-making process differs in several respects. The principal audience for the CEO is likely to be outsiders (analysts, creditors, etc.) with limited access to information and limited means for intervention. The divisional general manager, in contrast, must face an audience of superiors with full access to information. Moreover, the CEO has fewer constraints than the divisional general manager, and in a reasonably healthy firm, also less personal risk. The division general manager's fortunes typically ride on one horse, or a few at most. The CEO has a stable of horses, and only some have to be winners.

The analytical models used for developing business and corporate strategies differ in multibusiness firms. For business strategy, the conceptual tools generally focus on the structure of an industry and on the dynamics of doing business in that industry. Central to the analysis of corporate strategy are the cash flow, earnings, and other financial consequences associated with alternative combinations of business strategies. The following discussion relates primarily to strategy for a single business enterprise.

Strategic Analysis

To prepare for battle, the commanding and staff officers must take into account the strength and readiness of the enemy, its position and deployment, and its will to fight. They must examine their own forces in similar fashion. Weather, terrain, and other local conditions also have to be considered. Only when these factors have been carefully analyzed can the command devise a strategy of battle—whether, where, when, and how to fight. Rightly or wrongly, the commanding officer's decision can be strongly influenced by such personal considerations as his willingness to risk death and his desire for power and glory.

Business has its counterparts to the military situation. The general manager is commanding officer. Competitors are the enemy forces. The enterprise represents the general manager's forces. The economy, laws and regulations, and technology correspond to weather, terrain, and other ambient conditions. The military analogy begins to break down when we consider customers and products, but it is sufficiently close and vivid to suggest a basis for business strategy analysis.

For our purposes, we can reorder slightly the earlier breakdown in our analysis of military strategy to focus on the battle environment (enemy and local conditions), one's own forces, and the commanding officer's will. For business, these three cornerstones of strategic analysis translate into competitive environment, company capabilities, and management values.

Competitive Environment

Identifying and assessing opportunities and risks in a business environment calls for a wide-ranging view and considerable ingenuity. At the center of this analysis is an understanding of who the customers are and what they want or might want, and who the competitors are and what they provide. Strategic analysis seeks gaps between what is wanted and what is provided. These gaps represent potential business opportunities for the firm. Gaps always exist, since customers will always welcome lower prices, higher quality, and better service. Moreover, compromises usually have to be made, as the following notice on the customer's counter in a printshop so well illustrates:

```
PRICE

QUALITY

SERVICE

Pick any two
```

In this instance, the customer gets to select what he or she has to give up. In most cases, it is the supplier who makes that selection, not the customer. McDonald's is organized to compete on price and delivery, with acceptable quality. But its limited selection of foods and its ambiance will not satisfy the person seeking haute cuisine or a romantic setting. These limitations provide opportunities for other eating establishments.

Strategic analysis has to extend beyond customers, suppliers, and the immediate competitive arena. Changes in technology, laws and regulations, international affairs, and any of a multitude of other factors can lead to new opportunities and risks. As described in the Johnson & Johnson Hospital Services case, improved information technology allowed American Hospital Supply to redefine the nature of the hospital-supply business to its advantage. As a result, it was able to transform itself from a distributor of hospital supplies to one of the largest producers. In another example, when deregulation of air travel fractured a long-standing, entrenched oligopoly, Continental, TWA, PanAm, and Eastern soon fell victims to the onslaught of the new low-cost carriers that seemed to sprout from the turbulence.

American Hospital Supply's accomplishment highlights the dynamic character of strategy. A firm's strategy is not bound by any configuration of existing and prospective customers' demands and competitors' supplies, as the following reference to Akio Morita, Sony's CEO, illustrates:

Morita frequently tells a story about two shoe salesmen who, in their travels, find themselves in a rustic, backward section of Africa. The first salesman wires back to his head office: "THERE IS NO PROSPECT OF SALES SINCE ALL THE NATIVES ARE BAREFOOT." The other, reflecting Morita's concept of marketing, reports: "NO ONE WEARS SHOES HERE. WE CAN DOMINATE THE MARKET. SEND ALL POSSIBLE STOCK."

"We don't believe in market research for a new product unknown to the public," says Morita. "So we never do any. We are the experts. . . . Sony's philosophy is to develop a product when there is *no* market—and then create one."[2]

Opportunities for an enterprise to redefine the competitive environment, altering the situation to play to its strengths, are not limited to new product introductions. In the case studies, we shall see how Cray Research has created a new business involving supercomputers for industrial use and how Dr. Pelz was attempting to restructure the European elevator industry to DAAG's advantage. Obviously, restructuring a competitive environment is not your everyday garden-variety type of strategy. It can involve big risks and considerable resistance. But as American Hospital Supply and Cray Research demonstrate, the rewards from its success can be generous.

Industry Structure

Michael Porter, in his work on competitive strategy, points to the importance of analyzing the dynamics and structure of the industry context. He notes:

The first fundamental determinant of a firm's profitability is industry attractiveness. . . . Industry profitability is not a function of what the product looks like or whether it embodies high or low technology, but of industry structure. Some very mundane industries such as postage meters and grain trading are extremely profitable, while some more glamorous, high-technology industries such as personal computers and cable television are not profitable for many participants.[3]

To analyze the inherent attractiveness of an industry, Porter devised a simple and powerful construct (see Figure 2.1) with five driving forces: competitors, buyers, suppliers, potential entrants, and substitutes for the product or service. In industries where these forces are strong, he argued, profitability is likely to be low; in industries where weak, a firm could reasonably expect high profitability.

In assessing the forces associated with competitors and potential entrants, consideration needs to be given to entry and exit barriers. High barriers to entry—such as might result from high required investments, proprietary technology, and established brands—clearly diminishes the threat of potential entrants to further crowd the field of competitors. Low barriers to exit for firms already in the industry also adds to an industry's attractiveness. If troubled firms can exit easily, fewer survivors remain to divide the pie. If exit is difficult, troubled firms can disrupt the market in their struggles to avoid collapse. Not unlike the new breathable waterpoof fabrics that allow body moisture to pass

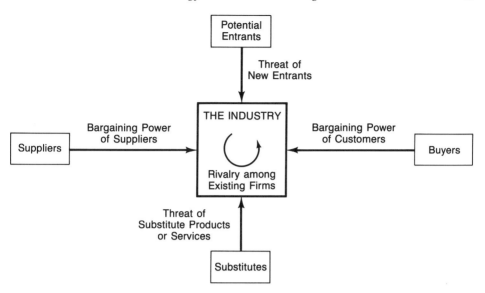

Figure 2.1 Forces driving industry competition. *Source:* Michael E. Porter, *Competitive Strategy* (The Free Press, New York: 1980), p. 4.

out and block rain water from coming in, "easy out" and "difficult in" contribute to industry attractiveness.

The tin-can and pharmaceutical industries provide two examples to illustrate. As described in the American Can Company case, can suppliers faced the following situation: (1) struggling competitors who were unable to exit because of large investments in plant and large unfunded pension liabilities; (2) large and powerful customers, such as Anheuser Busch and Campbell Soup, who could and did self-manufacture cans as a way of applying pressure on the merchant can suppliers; (3) large and powerful suppliers, such as U.S. Steel, who could set and hold raw material prices high; and (4) an increasing number of substitute products as packaging and food technology changed. Little wonder that those can companies who could afford to diversify into other fields did so.

The pharmaceutical industry stands in marked contrast to the can industry. The long-standing record of high industry profitability is largely attributable to several favorable industry features. First, pharmaceuticals really comprise many different and distinctive medication groupings, such as cardiovascular, analgesics, respiratory, antiinfective, and internal medicine. Pharmaceutical firms tend to specialize in one of these groupings, thereby reducing direct competition among themselves. This specialization is carried to the point where many pharmaceutical firms generate most of their profits from one or two individual drugs. Over the past twenty years, the bulk of Hoffman-LaRoche's worldwide profits came from the antidepressants Valium and Librium. The antiulcer drug Tagamet has made an important contribution to SKF's recent profits, as has

Feldene, an arthritis drug, to Pfizer's. For good reasons, each of these firms invests a great deal of its resources to retain supremacy in its particular field.

Second, raw materials represent an almost insignificant cost for most drug companies, giving suppliers little bargaining power. Third, buyers also have limited leverage. That doctors prescribe and patients pay certainly weakens the buyers' position. The threat of generics is blunted by the feeling or well-being that established brand names give to both doctors and patients. Fourth, high R&D costs and long delays in drug approval discourage entry. Fifth, there are few substitutes for conventional medicines. Genetic engineering is more an integral part of pharmaceutical technology than a substitute. With all five industry forces greatly attenuated, there is little wonder as to why successful pharmaceutical companies are content to stick to their knitting.

Most industries fall somewhere between these two examples with respect to industry attractiveness. Obviously, in selecting an industry—such as Peter Grace did for W. R. Grace in picking chemicals as a replacement for the moribund South American shipping business, or as more commonly happens in decisions concerning the relative emphasis to be given to different businesses in a firm—the general manager usually will do well to favor the more attractive industry. That freedom of choice, however, may be limited or unavailable for many general managers. They are obliged to do the best they can in their industries.

Whatever the level of attractiveness an industry might hold, some firms will do better than average, and some might even do better than firms in more attractive industries. For years, Crown Cork and Seal made attractive returns as a can manufacturer, while American, Continental, and National struggled. Although it is more difficult for a general manager to develop a star performer in an unattractive industry than in an attractive one, it has been done.

Company Capabilities

The second cornerstone of strategic analysis concerns the company's ability to devise and carry out a program of action. If an assessment of the competitive environment addresses the question of what is possible, an assessment of a company's capabilities addresses the question of what it can do. These capabilities involve skills and competencies, physical assets, business relationships, and proprietary rights and knowledge.

Skills and competencies have to do with human resources. A firm needs people capable of setting strategic direction, of making the products or performing the services, of selling, of organizing people and activities, and of marshaling the other resources needed. The specific skills and competence needed will, of course, depend on a company's business, its strategy, and its particular makeup.

Physical assets include money, plant and equipment, office space, and the like. Although money can resolve many physical asset problems, it has its limits. A paper manufacturing firm that decides to expand its coated paper operations with state-of-the-art equipment in order to take advantage of high market demand will require about two years to build the plant and another several years to bring it up to full speed. Throwing money at the problem will not speed up this timetable very much.

A firm's capabilities also depend on the relationships it enjoys with suppliers, customers, and the investment community. Good relationships with unions, government regulatory bodies, the leadership of communities in which it operates, and with the general public can also be of critical importance to successful performance, as is access to reliable information sources. Many of these relationships can require years of careful nurturing. Since important business relationships typically are not cost free, the general manager has to give careful thought to the priority and emphasis each should receive, just as if he or she were developing a firm's other capabilities.

Patents, copyrights, brands, confidential proprietary information, and customer lists also represent important resources for a firm. We have only to observe the zealousness with which J&J protects its BandAid registered mark and Polaroid its patents to appreciate the concern a general manager must devote to such matters.

Management Values

Even while addressing questions of what is possible (the competitive environment) and of what the enterprise can do (company capabilities), general managers must consider what they and other key managers would like it to do. Here we encounter the values the leader brings to the situation. The critical role such values can play in shaping a general manager's expectations and demands is well illustrated in the following account by Thomas J. Watson, Jr., former chairman of IBM:

> My father was the son of an upstate New York farmer. He grew up in an ordinary but happy home where the means, and perhaps the wants, were modest and moral environment strict. The important values, as he learned them, were to do every job well, to treat all people with dignity and respect, to appear neatly dressed, to be clean and forthright, to be eternally optimistic, and above all, loyal.
>
> There was nothing very unusual about this. It was a normal upbringing in rural nineteenth-century America. Whereas most men took the lessons of childhood for granted, however, and either lived by them or quietly forgot them, my father had the compulsion to work hard at them all his life. As far as he was concerned, those values were the rules of life—to be preserved at all costs, to be commended to others, and to be followed conscientiously in one's business life.[4]

The general manager's attitudes toward work, taking risks, public attention, prestige, social responsibility, ethical behavior, social interaction, and other similar considerations bear on strategy in important ways, as can be seen in several of the cases. Chairman Kim's sense of duty to Korea, his philosophy of hard work, and his attitude toward risk did as much to shape the Daewoo Group as did the competitive environment. General Robert Wood Johnson's beliefs about human behavior let to J&J's family-of-companies' approach to competing in the marketplace and to the company's highly praised responsiveness to the public's needs so dramatically exemplified in the two Tylenol incidents. That Seymour Cray's values would set the tone for his new company, Cray Research, is not surprising. But the general manager need not be the founder nor the firm a fledgling for the general manager to leave a deep personal imprint. Jack Welch's forceful personality will undoubtedly alter the character of General Electric in fundamental ways.

It is wrong to protest that personal preferences are extraneous to professional management. Business is fundamentally a human endeavor, and as such it can never be divorced from the human spirit. When the stakes are high and success in question, a person has to believe in what he or she is doing. For a general manager to promote a strategy that goes counter to his or her values and beliefs can lead only to frustration and discomfort. Either the strategy or the person will have to be changed.

Business Strategy

A sound analysis of the competitive environment, company capabilities, and management values will suggest directions to follow and directions to avoid. However strong these indicators might be, the general manager still has to make difficult judgments in defining the objectives, policies, and plans for an enterprise. As shown in Figure 2.2, objectives, policies, and plans make up a business strategy.

Objectives

An enterprise's objectives define what management intends it to achieve. Publicly owned corporations invariably employ financial performance objectives, such as return on equity, return on net assets, profit growth, debt rating, and shareholders' value. Industry ranking along various dimensions is also common. For example, Jack Welch demands that each of G.E's businesses should be or should become the number one or number two profitmaker in its industry. Examples of more qualitative objectives are Cray Research management's intention to retain its leadership in supercomputer design and chairman Kim's aim for Daewoo to contribute to Korea's ascendancy as a global economic power.

Objectives can be specific and results-oriented, or they can be broad and inspirational. In all cases, their role is to provide impetus and guidance for action.

Specific objectives can be used to disaggregate a strategy into its manageable components, prescribing the results to be accomplished and the timing for each. These objectives enable subordinates to concentrate on specific actions with the knowledge that their efforts are in line with the efforts of others and will contribute to the broad strategic direction of the enterprise. For the general manager, such objectives are a means for dividing the total undertaking into

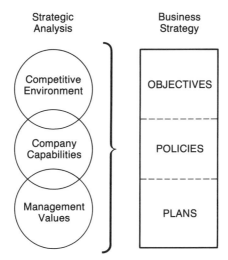

Figure 2.2 Strategic considerations.

smaller and simpler assignments, for tracking progress with measures appropriate to each task, for setting standards of performance, and for targeting intervention when performance appears inadequate.

Business is sufficiently complex and dynamic to defy precise planning. Unanticipated events can invalidate specific targets or can call for new actions not covered by established targets. To deal intelligently with the unexpected, an organization needs to understand the spirit and broad thrust of the basic intentions underlying specific objectives. Only then can an organization avoid a slavish adherence to specific objectives that are or have become unsuitable. The important validating reference is provided in broadly stated objectives that stress the principle of the matter rather than the details of execution. Cray Research's explicit commitment to offer the most powerful commercially available supercomputer in existence was the litmus test for all of the company's specific decisions and targets.

Even more broadly encompassing are those objectives that articulate the organizational values driving strategy. These objective provide the most fundamental and enduring guidelines for action. Their potential to inspire derives from their readily identifiable association with important human values and aspirations.

In effect, the general manager employs a hierarchy of objectives—ranging from specific targets to broader guidelines and finally to fundamental imperatives—in order to guide and motivate the organization in sufficiently diverse ways so as to be as comprehensively relevant as possible with respect to situations and audience. The Johnson & Johnson Hospital Services case provides a good example of this hierarchy of objectives. The plan for the new hospital-services unit specified a three-phase roll-out for involving the various J&J companies in the proposed marketing services, starting with supplies, then moving to pharmaceuticals, and finally to equipment. For Pete Ventrella, the newly appointed general manager of Hospital Services, this timetable governed his organization's activities in many ways. These targets, however, were valid only insofar as they continued to serve the broader strategic objective of positioning J&J to provide an effective integrated service to hospitals. This objective was in turn driven by the company's enduring commitment to serve the customer, as articulated in the Johnson & Johnson credo. As this situation illustrates, there is a need for specific objectives to guide and motivate actions, and a need for broad objectives to validate the continuing suitability of the specific targets.

One important function that objectives serve is in setting standards of performance. They provide a reference by which the general manager signals to subordinates as well as to investors and other outsiders what is acceptable and what is not. The difficulty for the general manager in setting standards is in finding that point where the objective is ambitious enough to be challenging and is still realistically achievable. If objectives fail to be taken seriously—because they are too easily achievable, unrealistically difficult, or for any other reason—they lose their effectiveness in motivating performance.

Policies

Individual policies serve as guidelines for action. Business policies collectively define the way in which an enterprise has chosen to compete. To promote a consistent and coordinated program of action, specific policies should be articulated for each important aspect of doing business. The resulting list of important policies can be long, covering various aspects of the products offered (selection, quality), research and engineering, manufacturing, marketing, finance, relations with important external parties (unions, government, the public), personnel, organization, and administration. In the absence of specific policy guidelines, immediate operating pressures can more easily lead to decisions that undermine the integrity of a firm's efforts and that put into question management's strategic concepts and its command of the situation.

To be effective, individual policies must meet three tests. First, they should make sense in the competitive environment. Second, they should be consistent with each other. Third, they should reflect management's objectives and underlying values. Reichhold Chemicals' policies as stated in the beginning of this chapter can be reexamined to show how they demonstrate these propositions.

The essence of Reichhold's competitive strategy is "to provide attractive alternative formulations [of specialty polymer chemicals] which allow customers to modify their products in line with changing raw material prices and availability." This strategy requires a broad range of products. To be responsive to changing needs, Reichhold people interact closely with the customers' technical people. Both applications research and acquisitions are emphasized as means for adding new products. To be able to price competitively, the company is committed to investing in cost-effective manufacturing facilities. The financial policies concerning debt rating and dividend payout aim to hold down the cost of capital needed to support the investments in plant and product. Reichhold's focus on four industrial markets enhances close customer relations and helps to limit investment requirements. Quick and innovative responsiveness to customers' needs requires that initiative be taken in the field. The firm's decentralized divisional structure and its emphasis on participative management is consistent with such behavior. These policies are also in line with Powell's personal style of management.

Understanding how each policy fits within the total scheme is essential in formulating strategy. Of course, not all policies are of equal importance. Usually, one, two, or at most several policies play a dominant role in a business strategy. For these policies, good fit with the key requirements of the competitive environment, with the general manager's objectives and values, and with each other should be stressed. Other policies play a supporting role, and care should be taken to ensure their fit with the dominant policy or policies.

For many organizations, the passage of time or the immediacy of pressures from on-going events can obscure which policies are critical to success and which are only of secondary importance. The general manager must not only keep this distinction in mind, he or she should ensure that everyone concerned also knows the difference.

Plans

To make strategic concepts and business policies actionable, a general manager has to make decisions with respect to priorities, timing, individual assignments, responsibilities, and other important administrative considerations. These decisions as to who does what, when, where, and how provide the grist for strategic plans.

Since plans, as compared to objectives and policies, tend to be more vulnerable to circumstances, they are more susceptible to change. If a key person gets sick, if a competitor makes a surprise move, or if a new relevant bill is enacted in Congress, plans may need to be revised, even when objectives and policies remain unchanged.

Circumstances can change at any time. Judgments and assumptions can be mistaken. For these reasons, plans should not be applied rigidly or followed blindly. Managers should have room for maneuver and be encouraged to do so. Jack Welch remarked on this world of action soon after he took over leadership of General Electric, "In business, you don't get from her to there in a straight line. The good manager has to be a broken field runner, weaving and bobbing in response to the independent forces of competition, technology and customers."[5]

Corporate Strategy for Multibusiness Firms

In a multibusiness firm, corporate strategy focuses on the relationship between and among business units. At one end of the spectrum, businesses are viewed as a portfolio of independent units, to be acquired, built, pared, or divested as circumstances change. In this setting, cash flow and earnings performance become the key considerations. With respect to cash flow, the general manager seeks a mix in which the more mature business units can throw off sufficient excess cash to nourish the growth businesses. At the same time, these businesses collectively should generate steadily growing earnings. Corporations following this strategy—such as Textron, Gulf & Western, and other conglomerate firms—are characterized by lean corporate staffs and free-standing business units.

At the other end of the spectrum is the related multibusiness corporation where management seeks synergistic relationships between and among businesses. In this setting, corporate strategic planning seeks to strengthen businesses by recombining organizational units, by acquiring operations to fill gaps, and by divesting operations that do not fit. Corporations following this strategy—General Electric, for one—are characterized by large corporate staffs and by frequent organizational reshuffling to accommodate new business concepts.

A Winning Strategy

Military strategy aims to engage in battle, so that the outcome increases the likelihood of winning the war. So too, at the heart of business strategy, is the idea of achieving a sustainable competitive advantage. Basically a firm can gain such advantage in one of two ways. First, it can price lower than the competitors for a similar product or service. To do this over time, the firm must have a cost advantage. Second, it can offer the customer something not readily obtainable elsewhere. Special product features, delivery, and service are common ways of differentiating industrial products. Many consumer items gain advantage through brand recognition, where brand is perceived to ensure quality or to enhance a user's status. In his writings on competitive strategy, Michael Porter argues that a firm failing to achieve *cost leadership* or *differentiation* will compete at a disadvantage. He terms such firms as being "stuck in the middle."

Beyond these sound but rather broad prescriptions, the general manager still faces infinite possibilities. The purpose of strategic analysis is to uncover opportunities and constraints, to define a firm's strengths and weaknesses, and to indicate the risks and rewards associated with various courses of action. There are limits to what any firm can accomplish, but these are ultimately defined by the general manager's imagination, ingenuity, and daring. We have only to look at how William Woodside went about maneuvering American Can from its lackluster can-manufacturing business into financial services and specialty retailing to appreciate the freedom of action open to those who have the vision and nerve to strike out in new directions. Few people thought that Lee Iacocca would succeed in saving moribund Chrysler. His bold and unconventional plan, ingenious in retrospect, met with widespread incredulity. His success, in certain respects, redefined American business practice.

The opportunity to redefine business practice is always present. Business is a sufficiently complex undertaking, involving so many factors and so much chance, that no body of experts can ever model a "best strategy" for a firm. There is always room for insight and invention. The general manager might well consider the words of Ogden Nash's shortest poem, "In the land of mules, there are no rules."[6] Business might not reside in the land of mules, but it is within walking distance.

Notes

1. Kenneth R. Andrews, *The Concept of Corporate Strategy*, rev. ed. (Homewood, IL., 1980), p. 18.
2. Nick Lyons, *The Sony Vision* (New York, 1976), pp. 110, 128.
3. Michael E. Porter, *Competitive Advantage* (New York, 1985), pp. 4, 5.
4. Thomas J. Watson, Jr., *A Business and Its Beliefs* (New York, 1963), p. 12.
5. "General Electric Company: Dr. John F. Welch, Jr.," Harvard Business School videotape 882–024, 1982.
6. Ogden Nash, *The Private Dining Room and Other Verses* (Boston, 1953), p. 60.

3

Managing the Quality of Strategic Thinking

In all too many companies, strategic planning efforts produce little more than window dressing for poor thinking. Even in cases where considerable management time and energy are devoted to the task, where a good strategic planning system is in place, and where the chief executive officer is an enthusiastic supporter, the output is often characterized by insipid ideas and flawed strategies. In time, the managers involved become disappointed, frustrated, and even scornful of strategy and strategic planning.

Some indication of the pervasiveness of this problem was given in an article reviewing the state of strategic planning in 1979:

> The consultants share a somewhat dirty little secret: most believe that over 90 percent of American companies, their clients included, have so far proved incapable of developing and executing meaningful corporate strategies.[1]

Although this assessment may be exaggerated, the general manager still faces, and will always face, a difficult challenge in managing the quality of strategic thinking.

Strategy Making in Complex Settings

Setting strategic direction is an inherently difficult task. It can involve considerable organizational effort and typically requires making decisions with a limited understanding of the forces at work, challenging established views, and facing an uncertain chain of events and outcome. It can mean upsetting established relationships with suppliers and customers, established approaches to manufacturing and marketing products, and the power and influence of individual managers. In general, the intended benefits of a strategic move are far more uncertain than are the associated costs, so there are always strong reasons for maintaining the status quo or for making small adjustments at most.

The singular accomplishments of inspired leaders in conceiving and carrying out powerful strategies, such as Edwin Land for Polaroid and Lee Iacocca for Chrysler, are impressive. They are even more so when the major inputs come from the contributions of many people—often separated by age, experience, and rank.

To enact a strategic change involves both insight and commitment. Someone has to come up with an idea for change. Someone has to commit company resources. In complex corporate settings, these "someones" are not likely to be the same person. The someone generating new business strategies typically resides at the middle-level ranks of management, where the industry knowledge and operating responsibility are to be found. The someone committing corporate resources is likely to belong to senior general management at the corporate level. The less connected they are in terms of trust and confidence, the more difficult will be the marriage of insight and commitment. This difficulty reflects the uncertainties and risks associated with most strategic changes. Conclusions rest on judgments and conjecture and are vulnerable to doubts and to contradiction. Under these circumstances, one person's considered opinion can easily be another's idea of nonsense.

Necessary Conditions for Developing Good Strategies

To develop a good strategy requires a person or persons with the ability to understand the underlying concepts of strategy, with strong diagnostic skills, and with good business judgment. A manager has to be able to generate new strategic ideas before he or she can propose or promote them, in the same way a senior manager has to be able to evaluate new strategic ideas before approving or rejecting them.

In view of the difficulties and uncertainties associated with strategy, coupled with its visibility and importance, it is understandable how a manager might perceive an element of personal risk in playing too active a role in this planning process. Apprehensions of this nature can dampen a manager's willingness to promote or to approve new ideas that depart from established practice or that run counter to entrenched commitments. Managers, able as they might be, also have to be *willing* to create and advocate new strategic ideas. And a senior-level manager has to be willing to commit resources to attractive but unproven, and usually unprovable, new strategic moves.

We now have two basic elements in the strategy-development process—conceiving good ideas and approving them—and two necessary human attributes—ability and willingness. When put together, as shown in Figure 3.1, we can identify four enabling conditions for effective strategy formulation: (1) an ability to conceive and to advocate new, effective strategic ideas; (2) a willingness to conceive and to advocate new, effective strategic ideas; (3) an ability to evaluate the new strategic ideas and to commit the necessary resources; and (4) a willingness to evaluate the new strategic ideas and to commit the necessary resources. These four elements might involve only one person, as is often

PERFORMER(S)' ATTRIBUTES

		Ability	Willingness
	Insight	able to conceive and advocate new concepts	willing to conceive and advocate new concepts
TASKS	Commitment	able to evaluate new concepts and to commit resources	willing to evaluate new concepts and to commit resources

Figure 3.1   Enabling conditions for developing strategy.

the case for a small enterprise, or they might involve many people at different levels of authority, as is typical for a large, complex enterprise.

The distinctions between ability and willingness and between insight and commitment have practical significance for the general manager. Little is gained in sending a divisional manager to a management course on strategy if that person is holding back new ideas because of an unwillingness to confront a perceived reactionary corporate review. Likewise, little is gained in eliciting business strategies from managers if the corporate reviewer is incapable of evaluating the resulting proposals. For each of the four conditions, the reasons for inaction and ineffectiveness are likely to differ, as are the corrective actions needed to deal with the problems.

The Problem of Inability

Not surprisingly, lack of ability is a widespread reason for poor strategic planning. According to an unpublished study on strategic planning, many of the general managers responsible for setting corporate or business direction do not understand the underlying concepts of strategy, and some do not possess the analytical skills needed to do this kind of work.[2] Just because a person is good at running an ongoing operation does not ensure that he or she is also good at conceptualizing new strategic approaches.

The reasons for limited abilities and the possible corrective actions are neither straightforward nor simple. The individual manager's intellectual capacity and his or her developed skills for dealing with strategic concepts are obviously relevant. But a manager's abilities to think about new strategic moves are also influenced by contextual considerations.

Experience and conventional wisdom are valuable assets for a manager, but they can also be liabilities, stifling innovative thinking. A general manager who has performed successfully in an industry for twenty years can find it very difficult to think along fresh lines. A cohesive and detailed concept of how things work, reinforced by the proof of long experience, is a powerful mental anchor. Moreover, the more strongly one's respected colleagues share these established views, the more inhibiting this conventional wisdom is likely to be to new ideas. The "repressive powers of corporate mythology" was the way one senior executive put it.

The kind of information that the general manager normally receives also affects his or her ability to conceive or to commit to new strategic ideas. The information most line managers receive tends to be heavily skewed toward operational considerations.[3] Information from conventional sources—such as industry publications, industry association meetings, an individual's network of industry-related personal contacts—can suffer from inbred myopia. Information from unconventional sources not related to the industry carries the extra burden of having to be proved relevant or urgent. The more distant in time or substance an issue is to current industry concerns, the more difficult it is for managers to establish that it applies to their business in some significant way (relevancy) and that it should be addressed now (urgency).

Ironically, a formal process of strategic planning often does more to inhibit than to enhance innovative conceptual thinking. The study on strategic planning referred to above uncovered several reasons for this outcome. For example, many managers became confused and distracted by the mechanics and terminology (jargon) of the elaborate planning systems increasingly in vogue. This was especially true in companies where the planning system was in a continual state of revision. More time went into trying to figure out what was wanted than into thinking about the business.

Also, managers often became enamored with specific planning concepts, employing them with a fervor that inhibited sensitivity to special considerations and that diverted attention from other important issues. In such cases, planning degenerated into mechanical routines or into exercises in sophistry as the focus of attention shifted from the underlying business issues to the conceptual constructs in use. In this connection, planning concepts created new corporate myths as repressive as the old. For example, in several large industrial firms where portfolio planning approaches had been firmly implanted, senior managers complained that operating managers had become so conditioned by their assigned "cash cow" business role that they were insensitive to possible growth opportunities in segments within the overall charter of their unit.

The most deleterious situations were those where general managers abdicated their responsibility for setting strategic direction to staff planners. The trappings of a well-packaged planning system, supported by consultants and an aggressive planning staff, would be taken as evidence that strategic planning was in good hands, leaving the general manager free to take on other tasks more to his or her liking. In the absence of top-level involvement, subordinate managers would soon accord planning lower priority. In companies where the CEO failed to participate, divisional general managers typically considered the planning effort as just another instance of corporate staff intrusion and responded accordingly. For example, planning forms were viewed as a nuisance and were relegated to lower level divisional personnel for completion. Or the resistance was more overt, sometimes leading to heated confrontations between line and staff employees.

Even when a general manager engages in the planning effort, form can be mistaken for substance. A well-structured planning system and a detailed, comprehensive plan can give managers the illusion of having done good planning when no constructive imaginative thinking has actually taken place. This pitfall is well illustrated by the CEO who came to my office to inquire about his experience with strategic planning:

> I don't really know whether or not I have a problem. We used the [consulting firm] planning system, the division managers prepared strategic plans for each of our businesses, the corporate officers reviewed and approved these plans, and we now have a corporate strategic plan. Everything seems in order. The only thing that bothered me was that I felt no sense of excitement about the whole affair.

Little wonder. It was old wine in a new bottle. The strategic plans were little more than optimistic expansions of the company's ten existing businesses. A subsequent, more spirited and challenging rethinking of the strategy eventually led management to push two businesses more aggressively and to exit from six of the other businesses.

Based on a study of nine large companies, James Brian Quinn made the following assessment of formal planning as a tool for strategic decision making:

> Although the formal planing approach is excellent for some purposes, it tends to focus unduly on measurable quantitative forces and to underemphasize the vital qualitative, organizational, and power-behavioral factors that so often determine strategic success in one situation versus another. It can easily become a rigid, cumbersome routine, used primarily as a basis for financial control, rather than a creative direction-setting challenge.[4]

Senior-level general managers responsible for committing corporate resources face several problems with respect to their ability to assess the quality and appropriateness of new business strategies. First is their limited knowledge and understanding of the facts. A business general manager who moves up to corporate responsibilities can quickly lose touch with his or her former industry. The problem of limited knowledge is intensified in multibusiness companies for those businesses where the senior managers have not had direct experience. Fred Borch, while CEO of General Electric, gave a clear indication of just how severe this problem can be:

> With hundreds of products ranging from electric pencil sharpeners to diesel engines and nuclear plants, it is difficult to do an effective job of planning. It is, in fact, impossible for management to have a direct, personal feeling and knowledge about so many business environments.[5]

Second is the extent to which a senior general manager is systematically or even deliberately excluded from the decision-making process. William Wommack, deputy chairman of the board of directors for the Mead Corporation, described this problem:

> The idea that the organization will present strategic alternatives to top management is a fiction. If alternatives are ever generated, they get eliminated as they move up the organization. Top management is then faced with accepting or rejecting the one proposed plan that survives the organizational screening.[6]

When senior managers feel the way Wommack did, they are likely to be cautious in their support of new and different strategic moves.

With limited ability to evaluate the business situation directly, a senior manager's decision to commit resources often rests heavily on his or her assessment of the person or persons making and carrying out the proposed strategy. A division president's record of successful accomplishments can be far more reassuring to a CEO than the logic of the strategy, especially if any of these accomplishments are related to the proposed course of action.

Although an assessment of the proposer can serve as a legitimate proxy for an assessment of the proposal, this substitution can also distort the evaluation. The senior general manager can be strongly influenced by the charm, guile, appearance, and other qualities of the proposor that might have little bearing on the merits of the proposal.

The problems just discussed have to do with a senior general manager's limited knowledge about an individual business. This person must also be able to assess how each business strategy fits into the total range of concerns for the corporation. How does each proposed move relate to the other known corporate business activities and concerns in terms of importance and possible interactions? How might a specific move enhance or constrain the corporation's overall future opportunities? Are there other issues of importance to the corporation being overlooked? These are questions not easily answered.

The Problem of Willingness

Some people are gamblers, and others feel comfortable only when dealing with givens and knowns. Some people want to stand out and lead the pack, others prefer to avoid conflict and are content to follow. In like manner, managers differ greatly with respect to their desire for recognition, their tolerance for ambiguity, and their willingness to bear personal risks. Although there is probably relatively little that can be done to alter an individual's innate proclivities in this regard, general managers can still influence employees' willingness to engage in strategic planning in several important ways.

The priority a general manager assigns to strategic redirection is probably the most important factor motivating people. In companies where strategic change was constructively under way, the general manager's clearly perceived determination to have strategies improved was most often singled out as the principal reason for its success.

Willingness to undertake the rigors and stresses associated with developing new strategies and practices also depends on other pressures. Evidence of poor financial results, loss in market share, or mounting customer dissatisfaction can help to overcome an organization's natural inertia in favor of the status quo. Threats to a company (and to a lesser extent, opportunities) can also provide strong incentives for strategic redirection.

Even a CEO bent on improving strategy-making, but not "blessed" with threats or crises, can face an uphill battle in trying to obtain serious organizational involvement. As one senior executive of The Coca-Cola Company once put it during its heady days of industry dominance: "The very on-going success of this company works against its planning for change." The unwelcomed inroads by Pepsi Cola probably did as much as anything else to help Coca-Cola to change its ways. Figure 3.2 shows how the general manager's commitment to improve strategies and the firm's economic situation or prospects combine to set a climate for strategic planning.

The clarity of senior management's goals for change has a major effect on strategy making. The healthiest situations are those where the CEO and other senior managers have a clear idea of the desired direction and urgency of strategic change, and where this thinking is clearly promulgated to the line and staff managers responsible for business strategies. In these situations, middle managers are able to calibrate the personal risks attached to strategic change and can feel some security in advocating changes that are in line with senior management's goals. Where top management is unclear and vacillating in its position with respect to strategic change, the risks of advocating new ideas escalates for operating managers.

New strategic ideas are often in need of modification and almost always vulnerable to second-guessing. The way senior managers react to strategic ideas greatly affects the way their subordinates perceive the risks of advocacy. No one cares to be embarrassed or punished. How ideas and proposals are corrected or rejected is a vital consideration with respect to encouraging or discouraging further participation, not only by the business managers directly affected, but by all his or her peers who are likely to experience the same treatment. In one company, the CEO had a habit of firing division managers when new strategies did not work out. It came as no surprise to find business managers throughout the company most reluctant to advocate any changes. Admittedly, how to deal with a manager who has advocated a strategic move that proves a flop is not a simple matter.

The formal measurement and reward systems also influence the climate for change. In most companies, great attention and effort go into budgeting. Managers are evaluated and often compensated by how well they do with respect to yearly profits. This stress on short-term results can act as a deterrent to good strategic thinking. Management's concern for "making budget" often leaves little time for thinking ahead. Moreover, this pressure for current performance tends to give disproportionate importance to moves that produce near-term profits.

To realign the measurement and reward systems so as to encourage the

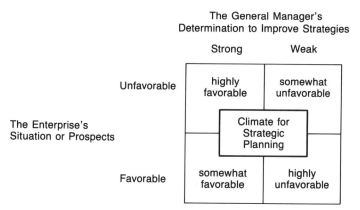

Figure 3.2 The influence of the general manager and circumstances on the climate for strategic change.

development of good strategies is not easy. These systems in large companies are ponderous and deeply rooted. To change them requires great effort and time and can be upsetting to an organization. Moreover, management still has to run the company's operations, and the requirements for this task do not necessarily coincide with the requirements for encouraging new strategic moves.

Improving on Enterprise's Strategy-Making Capabilities

For the CEO or division general manager intent on improving corporate or business strategy, a good place to start is with an assessment of the enterprise's strengths and weaknesses with respect to each of the four enabling conditions noted earlier in Figure 3.1. This kind of diagnosis enables the general manager to focus corrective actions on specific deficiencies—a practice likely to be far more effective and efficient than one of promoting whatever happens to be currently fashionable in the management literature, or one of blindly adopting a consulting firm's packaged approach to strategic planning.

People and Sense of Urgency

The sine qua non for effective strategy making is to have people able and willing to generate and advocate good, new ideas and people able and willing to make good resource-allocation decisions with respect to these proposed changes. The general manager has two basic ways to get such people: one is to improve the necessary abilities and attitudes on the part of a manager who already holds a position with strategic responsibility; and the other is to replace this manager with another person who already has the desired abilities and attitude. The choice between these two courses of action depends on the expected ease of improving the manager in place, on the availability of a more qualified candidate, and on the administrative problems such a change might entail. On this last point, even when a replacement is called for, violating precedence or a policy favoring internal development and job continuity might demoralize staff. Or a CEO might decide to leave in place a well-entrenched, powerful general manager who is near retirement to avoid disruptive infighting in the management ranks.

Ostriches have a reputation for sticking their heads in the sand to avoid seeing danger. Ostriches might not deserve this reputation, but many managers do. Even in companies staggering into collapse one can find managers who prefer to believe that everything will work out for the best, given time. Whether these persons fail to appreciate the problems, or whether they fear change more than the known difficulties, the general manager's task is to convince them of the necessity and urgency of change, if it is ever to take place.

Without a strongly established sense of dissatisfaction with the status quo, the general manager will have difficulty in coping with the self-doubts that are bound to arise as the risks associated with specific strategic moves become apparent. In view of these difficulties, the strongest possible case for strategic change needs to be developed at the outset. Where the enterprise has been experiencing difficulties or is facing significant dangers, this task might be a relatively straightforward one of highlighting and emphasizing these problems at every opportunity. Where circumstances fail to provide obvious compelling grounds for strategic redirection, the general manager might have to search for less obvious, compelling reasons to serve this purpose.

A thoughtful examination of possible future developments for the industry can usually uncover such reasons. For example, through informal discussions and formal strategic-planning workshops, the CEO of a successful major newsprint company emphasized the emerging threats posed by the increasing concentration of newspaper chains (buyers) and by the impact of interactive electronic media on future newspaper usage to challenge his managers and board of directors to reconsider the firm's strategy.

To motivate strategic change, the general manager must in effect undermine management's confidence in the strategy already in place. Its inadequacy or vulnerability must be made clear. The more relevant and urgent the reasons for change can be made to appear, the more power they will have to motivate managers to search for and to adopt a new strategy.

Creating dissatisfaction with the status quo and a sense of urgency are important conditions for reconsidering strategy, but they are not enough by themselves. Managers also need time and often need help for good strategic thinking to take place.

Time to Think

Developing good strategic ideas is a creative act. Sometimes it comes as the result of an explosive insight. More often, it is the result of careful thinking and rethinking of the business situation and of the many possible ways in which the enterprise might deal with it.

Such thinking requires time. As James March and Herbert Simon have warned, "Daily routine drives out planning."[7] Strategic thinking is certainly one of the most vulnerable aspects of planning in this regard. It needs to be constantly nurtured and protected. Otherwise, it risks being stunted or still-born.

There are many ways in which the general manager can increase the time devoted to strategic thinking. One common practice is to have the managers involved set aside one or several days for discussing strategic issues. The purpose of such meetings can range from one of stimulating thinking and identifying relevant issues to one of analyzing specific developments or possible courses of action. While some structure is usually advisable for such deliberations, if only to provide a sense of discipline and purpose, there should also be ample opportunity for exploratory thinking and "noodling around."

As the following remarks by a CEO indicate, getting quality time devoted to strategic thinking depends on the general manager's ingenuity and persistence: "I give a lot of thought on how to keep my people thinking about strategy. I try to get together with each of them in an informal setting to kick around ideas. Sometimes we'll do this at lunch, or we may have an impromptu meeting at some other time of day when we have some free time. Traveling together, a round of golf, anyplace where we can have a little time to think and talk."

Another way to increase attention to strategic concepts is to schedule enough time for a thoughtful interchange between middle and senior managers in the review process. The all-too-common practice of scheduling an annual marathon of planning reviews tends to be self-defeating. Almost always, there is too much ground to cover in the time available.

In order to get thoughtful and thorough reviews in the Norton Company, business-strategy review sessions were spread throughout the year so that only one business would be reviewed at a time. In this way, senior managers had time to become deeply engrossed with a particular strategic proposal. If more time was needed for discussion, there was no "next planning item" to rush closure.

A newcomer to Norton's top management ranks gave his impression of this practice.

> I really like the idea of holding strategic review meetings for different businesses at different times during the year. By looking at one business at a time, we get a chance to focus our thoughts and to concentrate on the distinctive aspects of that business. The opportunity to go into depth in a given business has also helped us to gain new insights into some of our other businesses.[8]

Concepts and Coaching

The ability to conceptualize strategies is not a natural and commonplace skill. Most managers need to develop this skill sometime in their career. As with most skills, development typically depends on some mix of theory (analytical concepts), instruction, and hands-on experience.

Analytical concepts, such as those described in Chapter 2, can help people to think about strategy. Even simple concepts can provide a helpful structure for analysis. For example, the management of a large company manufacturing industrial products employed a "test for winning strategies." The idea was that a strategic proposal must show a clear competitive advantage with respect to at least one of the following considerations: input factors (raw material/labor); process; product; selling/distribution; service; or special. "Trying harder" was explicitly ruled out as a basis for a winning strategy. With this simple checklist, management was able to shift some consideration from the content of a strategy to its merits.

Providing analytical concepts is not enough for most managers. They also need help in using them. The planning memoranda and manuals on which many companies rely for instruction are grossly inadequate. In at least one respect, strategic thinking might be likened to tennis: Some people might be able to learn good tennis from a book, but most need coaching, and lots of it. The need for coaching seems to hold true for strategic thinking as well, for all levels of management.

Lowering Personal Risk

As we noted earlier, where managers perceive a great deal of personal risk associated with strategic planning, they are less likely to engage fully in the process. Clear concepts and good coaching can go a long way to give managers some reassurance that they are doing the right things and will not be made to look foolish. The general manager would be well advised to consider what else could be done to lessen anxiety about strategic planning.

An intermediary between corporate and divisional general management— such as a corporate staff planner or an outside consultant—can play a valuable role in reducing the perceived risks inhibiting innovation. A division manager in a large insurance company gave some idea why he valued such an arrangement.

> Having someone from the corporate planning staff work with us in depth is valuable. I appreciate the opportunity to try out new ideas on one of these people rather than to spring a full blown new idea on top management without this earlier testing. Not only can the staff coordinator help me to shape my ideas in a way that will be most convincing to senior managers, he also can be very helpful in explaining to senior managers what we are doing.

In effect, such an intermediary can serve as an informed and nonthreatening sounding board for the divisional manager and as a "friend in court" in arguing the merits of the strategic plan with senior managers. In this liaison role, the corporate staff planner also can contribute to senior managers' confidence in the new ideas by having served as a corporate agent in the process.

Another way for the middle-level general manager to reduce the risk of having a proposal cut to pieces by or before his or her superiors is to be able to test the ideas early in their formation with senior managers. When this is possible, a manager can "try out a new idea for size," and can then drop it, modify it, or push it, depending on the nature of the response received.

These early and repeated exchanges also serve to give senior managers confidence in a new idea. By being exposed to a new idea as it grows over time, the senior executive has an opportunity to shape it and to become comfortable with it. In practice, managers will make every effort to test ideas and to check for support as strategy is developed, whether or not explicit mechanisms have been created for this purpose. In his book on strategic decision making, Quinn gives an excellent account of how and why senior executives behaved in this way:

> Even under extreme pressure, effective top executives often consciously delayed initial decisions, or kept such decisions vague, to encourage subordinates' participation, to gain more information from specialists, or to build commitment to solutions. They were extremely sensitive to organizational and power relationships and consciously managed decision processes to improve these dynamics. Even when a crisis tended to shorten time horizons and make decisions more goal-oriented than political, these executives consciously tried to keep their options open until they understood how the crisis would affect the power bases and needs of their key constituents.[9]

This description of top-management behavior would also apply for general managers at operational levels.

Incremental vs. Fundamental Strategic Change

Strategic changes can be incremental or bold. With reference to Japanese automotive manufacturers, Richard Pascale argues the virtues of responsive, incremental adaptations involving many people in the firm:

> Contrary to myth, the Japanese did not from the onset embark on a strategy to seize the high-quality small car market. They manufactured what they were accustomed to building in Japan and tried to sell it abroad. Their success, as any Japanese automotive executive will readily agree, did not result from a bold insight by a few big brains at the top. On the contrary, success was achieved by senior managers humble enough not to take their initial strategic positions too seriously. What saved Japan's near-failures was the cumulative impact of "little brains" in the form of salesmen and dealers and production workers, all contributing incrementally to the quality and market position these companies enjoy today. Middle and upper management saw their primary task as guiding and orchestrating this input from below rather than steering the organization from above along a predetermined strategic course.
>
> The Japanese don't use the term "strategy" to describe a crisp business definition or competitive master plan. They think more in terms of "strategic accommodation," or "adaptive persistence," underscoring their belief that corporate direction evolves from an incremental adjustment to unfolding events. Rarely, in their view, does one leader (or a strategic planning group) produce a bold strategy that guides a firm unerringly. Far more frequently, the input is from below. It is this ability of an organization to move

information and ideas from the bottom to the top and back again in continuous dialogue that the Japanese value above all things. As this dialogue is
pursued, what in hindsight may be "strategy" evolves.[10]

But the need for a bold strategic move, however rare, cannot be ignored.
Such responses are in order when the firm encounters major opportunities or
life-threatening events. The idea of logical incrementalism, as Quinn labels the
adaptive approach to making strategic decisions, should not be equated with
incremental strategies. In developing his thesis, Quinn cites numerous cases
involving major strategic changes. Still, logical incrementalism can lead to incremental strategies, even when conditions call for radical responses.

Jack Welch, General Electric's chief executive officer, warned of this danger:

> Most bureaucracies—and ours is no exception—unfortunately still think in
> incremental terms rather than in terms of fundamental change. . . .
>
> We've seen huge chunks of entire industries preside over their own orderly
> death, while making what could be called incremental progress.[11]

The challenge for the general manager is to create a strategy-making process that allows bold moves—when these are called for—to be conceived and
implemented in ways that foster interactive learning and opportunities for adjustment and change.

Notes

1. "Playing by the Rules of the Corporate Strategy Game," *Fortune*, September 24, 1979.
2. This unpublished study by the author, conducted in the late 1970s, focused on the problems
   of strategy making in complex, corporate settings where insight and commitment involved
   different people. The information was gathered primarily through unstructured interviews with
   general managers who were responsible for corporate or business strategies and with staff
   managers responsible for various aspects of the planning process. About 150 managers in
   twenty firms participated in the study.
3. Francis J. Aguilar, *Scanning the Business Environment* (New York, 1967), p. 43.
4. James Brian Quinn, *Strategies for Change: Logical Incrementalism* (Homewood, IL, 1980), pps. 14,
   15.
5. "Norton Company: Strategic Planning for Diversified Business Operations," Harvard Business
   School case number 377–044, 1976, p. 2.
6. "The Mead Corporation," Harvard Business School case number 9–379–070, 1978, p. 7.
7. James March and Herbert Simon, *Organizations* (New York, 1958), p. 185. The authors go on
   to explain this point: "When an individual is faced both with highly programmed and highly
   unprogrammed tasks, the former tend to take precedence over the latter. . . ."
8. "Norton Company," *op. cit.*
9. Quinn, *op. cit.*, p. 21.
10. Richard T. Pascale, "Perspectives on Strategy: The Real Story Behind Honda's Success," *Cali-
    fornia Management Review*, Vol. XXVI, No. 3 (Spring 1984), pp. 63, 64.
11. John F. Welch, Jr., "Competitiveness from Within—Beyond Incrementalism," Hatfield Fellow
    Lecture, Cornell University, April 12, 1984.

4

Implementing Strategy

Creating a vision of what the enterprise is to be and how it is to get there is only one of the general manager's broad tasks. He or she also has to develop the organizational capabilities needed to implement this vision. After all, a brilliant strategy is empty without people able and willing to carry it out. In considering the need to provide for an enterprise's readiness and capacity to act, the general manager might well heed the words of Edward Gibbon: "The winds and waves are always on the side of the ablest navigators."

Clearly, even Gibbon's navigators could not master wind and waves without the special instruments of that craft, sextant and chronometer. So too, must the general manager ensure that his people have the "instruments" needed to perform their duties. Raising funds in the capital market (or securing corporate funds for a division) and marshaling other necessary assets are serious and challenging tasks. Even more complex and challenging are the tasks of ensuring that the navigational instruments get used to full advantage as the enterprise strives to follow its plotted course. It is to this second challenge of employing one's people effectively that we now turn our attention.

The General Manager's Means of Influence

The general manager has a variety of means at his or her disposal to influence how well an enterprise carries out its strategy. They can be broadly grouped along the following lines:

Organizational structure: The definition of responsibilities and reporting relationships for employees.

Planning and allocation of resource systems: The mechanisms and processes for deciding in concept and in practice who will do what with what. Planning represents intended commitments of company resources for specific purposes; the allocation of resources involves the actual commitments of money, assets, and people.

Information and control systems: The collection and dissemination of information for analysis and operations.

Reward systems: The various rewards and punishments that can be meted out to members of the organization to influence their behavior.

Staffing and people development: The various activities connected with the selection and recruitment of people, their placement and movement in the organization, and the development of their managerial and technical skills.

Leadership: The manner in which the general manager relates to his people to inspire their involvement and commitment to the enterprise and its purpose.

Each of these considerations commands its own field of study and discourse. It is not feasible in this volume to cover any of these topics in depth. Nor is it necessary for our purposes. The case studies touch on all of these organizing elements, but always in the context of a broader set of general management issues, rather than as a central focus.

A general familiarity with the way organizations function and with the major alternative approaches to organizing, planning, compensating, and so on is all the reader needs. For example, in the Johnson & Johnson Hospital Services case, the general manager of the newly formed Hospital Services Company is trying to decide whether to organize his unit as a cost center or a profit center. Neither he nor the reader has to be expert in management control to decide the issue. Obviously, some familiarity with the motivational effects associated with each approach, as well as an awareness that a unit can also be organized as a revenue center or an investment center, provide further perspective to such analysis.

Similarly, in the Daewoo Group case, the chairman espouses a policy of lifelong employment. In contrast, General Electric and American Can both implemented major reductions of work force. In assessing these practices, one should have some idea of the general effects that alternative approaches to employment relationships—such as lifelong, up-or-out, or in-and-out (employees can enter at any level in the organization and may be asked to leave at any level)—can have on employee morale, organizational flexibility, costs, and other strategic considerations.

The General Manager's Perspective

Rarely will the general manager be expert in any one of these organization-related fields. He or she will have to rely on the expertise of specialists as well as on his or her general experience with the workings of an organization. But there is an important, even critical, perspective that the general manager must bring to the consideration of these organizational structures and processes: that of the strategy of the enterprise.

No single organizational structure, no particular compensation scheme, no specific planning system is intrinsically superior to all others, whatever their proponents might claim. The merits of each depend on what the general manager is trying to accomplish and on the nature and complexity of the enterprise itself. The driving forces of strategy—competitive environment, strengths and weaknesses of the enterprise, and management's values—are also the driving forces for organizing the enterprise. On this point, Kenneth Andrews concludes:

> [T]he chief determinant of organizational structure and the processes by which tasks are assigned and performance motivated, rewarded, and controlled should be *the strategy of the firm*, not the history of the company, its position in its industry, the specialized background of its executives, the principles of organization as developed in textbooks, the recommendations of consultants, or the conviction that one form of organization is intrinsically better than another.[1]

Emphasis and Priorities

While the general manager needs to be concerned with each of the means to influence implementation and how they relate to the firm's strategy and to each other, he or she must also be sensitive to possible priorities of importance. Various circumstances can call for special attention to one or another of these elements. For example, when a firm is in need of people with special expertise who are in short supply, such as software designers or merger and acquisition deal makers, recruiting activities and compensation systems are likely to be of particular importance.

The stage of an organization's development also affects the relative importance of the various elements. Managers starting up an enterprise tend to experience many similar implementation problems. The same can be said for managers in firms experiencing rapid growth, relatively stable conditions, or serious decline.

A brief look at the special problems faced by rapidly growing companies can serve to illustrate this point. Marshaling and assimilating resources is typically of critical importance in such situations. Where this growth requires a rapid expansion in the number of employees, the general manager has to pay special attention to how good people can be identified and attracted and to how the newcomers can be assimilated as quickly as possible. What makes this difficult is that the people already on board are usually under pressure to deal with the expanding work load and have little time to help acclimate the new people. Moreover, the responsibilities of key people are often in flux as ad hoc arrangements are made to cover new tasks until new people can be added and as the support systems are quickly outgrown. Figure 4.1 depicts the problems characteristic of this situation.

As we can see, for the general manager in charge of a rapidly growing enterprise, the various activities connected with the selection and recruitment of people, their placement and movement in the organization, and the rapid alignment of their managerial and technical skills to the immediate needs of

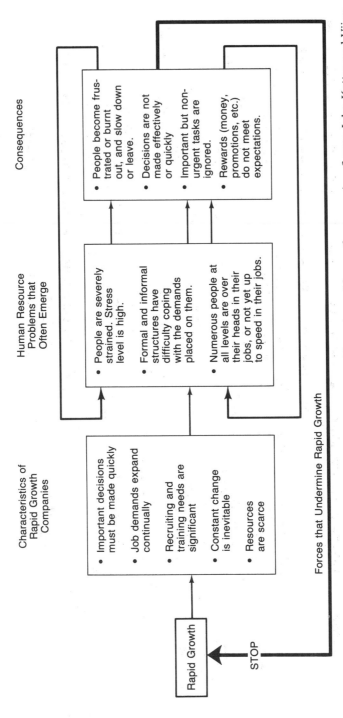

Figure 4.1 Consequences of unattended human resource problems in rapid growth companies. *Source:* John Kotter and Vijay Sathe, "Problems of Human Resource Management in Rapidly Growing Companies," *California Management Review* (Winter 1978, Vol. XXI, No. 2).

the organization are likely to merit precedence over other organizing activities. In sharp contrast is the firm experiencing a severe business downturn, where survival is at stake. Here, cash flow is likely to be of critical importance, and attention is likely to be placed on controlling costs, allocating resources, and possibly reducing the work force.

Contextual Fit

We saw in Chapter 2 how business policies, to be effective, had to fit with the firm's environment, with the firm's nature, with management's values, and with each other. In like manner, each organizing vehicle must fit with these strategic cornerstones and with each other.

The earlier discussion of Reichhold Chemicals can help to illustrate. Powell's decision to decentralize operations and decision making reflected the distinctive technical and marketing requirements associated with each of the several markets the company had chosen to serve and the importance of responding quickly to the ever-changing customer requirements for specialty chemicals. This decision also reflected Reichhold's new policy to enter and exit businesses as particular chemicals enjoyed increased specialty usage or degenerated into commodity items. In line with these requirements and with a decentralized structure was Powell's decision to encourage a participative style of management. This style also fit with his personal preference on how to relate with his key people.

A more detailed examination of contextual fit can be made in connection with the Johnson & Johnson (A) case. Long dedicated to providing health-care supplies and equipment, J&J management had come to recognize the need to serve distinctive subelements of this market in different ways. To increase its responsiveness to these needs, J&J adopted a multibusiness, decentralized organizational structure. Generous incentive compensation based on individual unit performance, a bottoms-up approach to planning, and divisionally based information systems reinforced this attention to individual market requirements and to the need for productivity and creativity. A strong financial reporting and control system, close supervision by the Executive Committee, and an explicit statement of basic values (the Credo) served as guards against possible abuse or serious error and provided some balance and connection among the firm's many operations and initiatives.

The ideal overall situation toward which a general manager should strive is to have the strategy of the firm, its organizational structure and managerial processes, and the skills and values of its people all fit with each other and with the world in which the firm competes. With good management and reasonably stable conditions, firms can achieve this powerful alignment, where every element reinforces every other element in line with purpose.

AT&T in the 1960s and early 1970s provides a classical example of this achievement. In an environment somewhat frozen for some fifty years by regulation, the company achieved a remarkable degree of fit among its strategy, structure, processes, people, and the world in which it operated. Its strategy

focused on providing superior telephone communications for people throughout the land (rural as well as urban). The successful accomplishment of this
mission gained the popular and political support the company needed to deal
with the regulatory authorities. A functional organizational structure ensured
well-organized operations throughout the vast and complex system. An emphasis on engineering and field service aimed to maximize the quality and
reliability of telephone service. Customer satisfaction, a key measure of performance, was tracked through monthly interviews. For most of AT&T's more
than one million employees, the fond reference to Ma Bell reflected a sense of
family and lifelong commitment. Pride lay behind the AT&T's employees' self-
deprecating admission to having bell-shaped heads, an allusion to a corporatewide mentality prizing competence and service. Their working world was indeed bell-shaped during those golden years.

In considering organizational fit with strategy and the environment, Raymond Miles and Charles Snow point to its effect on performance:

> Corporate excellence requires more than minimal fit. Truly outstanding per-
> formance, achieved by many companies, is associated with tight fit—both
> externally with the environment and internally among strategy, structure,
> and management process. In fact, tight fit is the causal force at work when
> organizational excellence is said to be caused by various managerial and
> organizational characteristics. . . .
>
> > In short, the causal dynamic of tight fit tends to operate in four stages:
> > First, the discovery of the basic structure and management processes
> > necessary to support a chosen strategy create a *gestalt* that becomes so
> > obvious and compelling that complex organizational and managerial de-
> > mands appear to be simple.
> >
> > Second, *simplicity* leads to widespread understanding which reinforces
> > and sustains fit. . . .
> >
> > Third, simplicity *reduces the need for elaborate coordinating mechanisms.* . . .
> >
> > Fourth, as outstanding performance is achieved and sustained, its *asso-
> > ciation* with the process by which it is attained is reinforced and this
> > serves to further simplify the basic fit among strategy, structure, and
> > process.
> >
> > It should be emphasized that we do not specify "finding the right strat-
> > egy" as an important element of this causal linkage. In fact, finding
> > strategy-structure-process fit is usually far more important and problematic.
> > It may be that there is less to strategy than meets the eye. . . .[2]

Responding to Changes in Circumstances

An enterprise experiencing major change in its circumstances normally encounters new requirements for conducting its business successfully. Such changes
in circumstance can occur in a firm's environment or in the firm itself. Where
established strategy, organizational structure, administrative practices, and people
were particularly well suited to the earlier conditions, the general manager
likely has to make changes to some or all of these elements to have them
conform to the changed requirements.

External Causes. The travails of AT&T and the Bell system since 1980 provide a good example of how disruptions in the environment can set off a chain reaction of accommodative changes in strategy, structure, and people.

Successive waves of new technologies for transmitting electronic signals (microwave, satellites, and fiber optics), the convergence of communications and data processing, and a general move toward deregulation in the United States combined to undermine the erstwhile placid world of telephone service. As the forces battling to dismantle AT&T and its near-monopolistic hold on telephone communication approached victory, management turned its attention to how the surviving enterprises would compete once the restructuring came into effect.

New strategies changing the emphasis from engineering to marketing and aiming to provide new services were devised reasonably quickly. More slowly, management adopted new organizational structures, new planning processes, new information systems, new reward systems, and new leadership styles. But the people were still "bell-shaped," with bell-shaped mentalities and bell-shaped values. And the more senior the individual in rank, the stronger his or her commitment to this perspective was likely to be. After all, Judge Green and the judicial system notwithstanding, these values were responsible for one of the best-run enterprises in the world and for the successful careers of these managers.

This history is depicted in Figure 4.2. As the left column shows, the original Bell system was designed to fit its regulated bell-shaped world. The new arrangement defined by the courts exposed the newly formed seven regional companies and AT&T (retaining the long-line operations, Bell Labs research center, and Western Electric manufacturing facilities) to an openly competitive, market-driven world, represented by a square. As indicated in the right-hand column, the strategy could be "squared" to fit the new world and the organizational structure and processes "squared" to fit the new strategy, but the people's skills and attitudes could not be so radically transformed. While established managers and staff might "square" their appearances and while new "square" talent could be recruited, the dominant shape of skills and attitudes would remain bell-shaped.

Imposing such a radically different strategy and structure at the outset could prove unworkable, given the degree of misfit with the skills and attitudes in place. Figure 4.3 depicts how strategy and structure might be modified to bridge the gap between the new square world and the bell-shaped people. The modified strategy would still emphasize the introduction of new products and services for existing and new markets, but might give priority to those moves where engineering and field services are most valued. In this way, management would avoid the dangers associated with a sudden status diminution for the powerful technical-functional units, as well as an excessive reliance on the newly enhanced and still-unproved marketing function. In like manner, management would position the organizational systems to serve as a bridge between the mostly square strategy and the largely bell-shaped people. For example, the marketing department might be put on a par with the engineering and operations units in the organizational hierarchy, marketing information

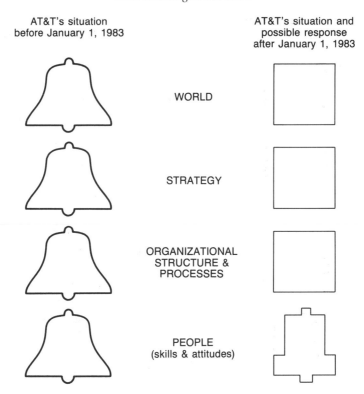

AT&T's situation
before January 1, 1983

AT&T's situation and
possible response
after January 1, 1983

WORLD

STRATEGY

ORGANIZATIONAL
STRUCTURE &
PROCESSES

PEOPLE
(skills & attitudes)

Figure 4.2   Fit and change for AT&T, radical response.

might be given some prominence, market penetration might accompany service reliability as a key performance measure, and highly qualified marketing managers might be recruited at all levels.

The various compromises would reflect management's recognition of the need to make an orderly transition from one strategy to another and its desire to retain the best features of the firm's traditional bell-shaped approach to doing business. In time, training, new recruits, and retirements would transform the skills and attitudes of the people to fit the new requirements, and strategy and structure could be further squared. Of course, the world is also likely to change in the intervening years, further complicating the general manager's already formidable undertaking.

Internal Causes. The stimulus for changing an enterprise's mode of operations can also arise from internal causes. For example, a general manager might need to introduce a more elaborate organizational structure, increasingly formalized management systems, and people with different administrative skills in a firm that has experienced considerable growth. All of these changes may be required, even when the strategy remains ideally suited to a relatively static environment.

Changes in internal conditions can also lead to new strategies, which in

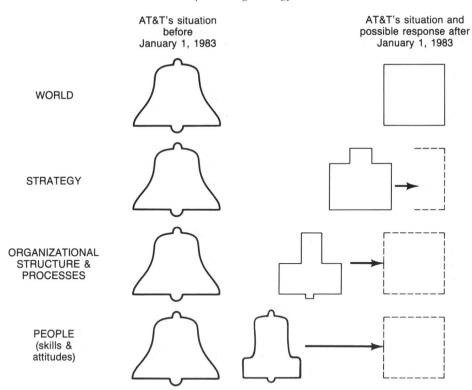

Figure 4.3 Fit and change for AT&T, transitional adaptation.

turn might require organizational changes. For example, as a successful single-business company serving the domestic market increases its human and financial resources, management might favor exploiting opportunities with moves the firm could not have afforded earlier, such as expanding operations abroad or into related products and services. To implement either of these moves, the general manager might have to replace a functional organization with a divisionalized structure and place more emphasis on formalized planning and resource allocation to deal with the increased complexity of doing business with the new strategy.

Earlier we discussed how each stage of organizational development (start-up, growth, maturity, decline) had its own characteristics and requirements. Moving from one organizational stage to another (which could result from internal or external causes) almost always involves considerable difficulties in adjustment.

The well-publicized changes in Apple Computer provide a good case in point. Steve Jobs, Steve Wozniak, and a small coterie of other pioneers were extraordinarily successful as they shared the early heady experience of almost unfettered rapid growth. IBM's entry into the personal-computer field soon slowed Apple's growth. No longer could Apple simply do its own thing. The freedom it enjoyed with respect to technical design, product introductions, pricing, service, and almost every other activity would henceforth be severely constrained by the pressure of IBM's attack. In time the company came to recognize the need to introduce more structure and discipline into its operations. John Scully was recruited from Pepsico to help Apple to function in an environment of slower growth and tough competition. As anyone who followed the news accounts in 1985 would already know, the transition was not accomplished without considerable turmoil and pain.

The Difficulty of Responding to Changes in Circumstances

Dramatic discontinuities of the kind AT&T encountered or the clear and undeniable pressures for change that Apple faced are exceptions rather than the rule. Most enterprises experience a gradual drift of circumstances. Customers' needs, technologies, relationships, and a host of other factors may change imperceptively month by month, like a young child growing up. And just as this child will soon outgrow its clothing, the enterprise will find its strategy and practices increasingly ill-fitting over time.

The general manager dealing with unobtrusive change faces a difficult challenge. The unwelcomed initial signs of pending trouble are no match for the eagerly sought-after signs of accomplishment in competing for management's attention. And even when noticed, they are easily rebuffed. The attitude many managers are likely to adopt can be characterized by the saying, "Don't fix it if it ain't broken." In time, as evidence of trouble mounts, defenders of the status quo fall back on the reassuring argument, "This approach has a proven track record. All we have to do is to work harder at it." And finally, as Peter Drucker observed, when the need for change can no longer be denied, "they often set up beautiful mechanics, 'decentralize' their organization chart, preach a 'new philosophy'—and go on acting just as before."[3]

One of the most difficult challenges a general manager faces is in sensing when a successful approach to doing business is beginning to lose its appropriateness and power and needs to be changed. This challenge involves a difficult dilemma. On the one hand, there are serious risks associated with abandoning practices that have worked successfully in favor of an untried, new approach. A premature or wrong move can be quite costly. On the other hand, the best time to make such changes is when the enterprise is healthy and strong. While it is the best time, it is not the easiest time to make major changes. The evidence pointing to weakness is often tenuous and debatable; the internal resistance to change is likely to be strong and entrenched. The general manager must have genius and courage to recognize emerging problems and to act while the firm is still doing well.

Business Needs versus the Individual's Needs

Business decisions can be viewed from the perspective of the business's requirements or from the perspective of the individual's needs. The needs of the business and those of its employees often differ and can even be in conflict. It is vital that the general manager be aware of these differences and consciously attempt to find a proper balance in satisfying the requirements of each.

In their book on managing human assets, Michael Beer and his coauthors stress this point in discussing human-resource flows. They argue that "human resource flow [comprising inflow (recruitment), internal flows (promotion, lateral transfers, demotions), and outflows (terminations and retirement)] must be managed strategically so as to match organizational needs with the career aspirations of employees."[4] Their ensuing discussion on managing outflows illustrates well the kind of issues the general manager must consider:

> A company may attempt to improve its mix of competencies rapidly by increasing the outflow of personnel through early retirement programs and/or layoffs of the lowest performers. Early retirement increases the percentage of younger personnel who management often believes are more flexible in adjusting to a changing business future than older, more entrenched employees. At the same time, personnel reductions allow for a rapid lowering of payroll costs, which can improve profitability in the short term. In the United States, this scenario has been used by companies in many industries as a response to recession and competition. . . .
>
> The central strategic dilemma for managers is how to balance the needs and rights of employees for employment security with the requirements of the corporation to use personnel outflow as a means of cost reductions and renewal. Research evidence and experience demonstrate that employees who become insecure because of work force reductions are less productive and less committed to the organization.[5]

The need to balance business-driven needs and those of individual employees applies to the other organizational processes as well. To the economic and the motivational considerations noted above, the general manager must also add his or her own values concerning efficiency of operations and respect for the individual.

The Evolution of Common Practice

As complicated as the equation might already be for the general manager in trying to balance the business-driven and people-driven requirements in line with his or her values, the calculus is further complicated by major undercurrents of change. There are forces at work that profoundly affect each of these variables (business requirements, employee's expectations, and the general manager's values) and that could redefine common and acceptable organizational practices. Some of these forces, according to a recent essay on the history of human resource management in American industry, are the impact of increasingly powerful microprocessors on the deployment of people, the pressure of intense international competition, and emerging new values and expectations of a better educated populace.[6] A newspaper article on the U.S. economy pointed to an important demographic occurrence as a force for changing accepted practices over the next decade: "Because of the earlier 'baby bust'—the sharp, twenty-year decline in the birth rate that started in 1957—today's labor force is increasing slowly. . . . Over the long term, personnel policies will be a greater factor in success or failure than in the past."[7] Rampant merger and takeover activities and the increasing pressure on boards of directors to play a more active governance role might also alter the equation by redefining management's hegemony.

Richard Walton speculates on some of the consequences of these forces on management practices. Identifying mutuality as the dominant theme for future policies, he anticipates radical changes in how managers will organize and motivate people.[8] Table 4.1 compares his predictions of emerging practices with traditional practices.

Whether this particular pattern of emerging practices is correct and imminent or just how these changes will play themselves out are open to question. Moreover, as with any management practices, the general manager must judge how they fit with the organization's strategy and the values of its people. But

Table 4.1　Human resource management models.

Policy Areas	Traditional Control Model	New Commitment Model
Job design principles	Individual attention limited to performing individual job Job design "deskills" and fragments work and separates doing and thinking Accountability focused on individual Fixed job definition	Individual responsibility extended to upgrading system performance Job design enhances content of work, emphasizes whole task, and combines doing and thinking Frequent use of teams as basic accountable unit Flexible definition of duties contingent on changing conditions
Performance expectations	Measured standards define minimum performance Stability seen as desirable	Emphasis placed on higher, "stretch objectives," which tend to be dynamic and oriented to the marketplace
Management organization: structure, systems, and style	Structure tends to be layered, with top-down controls Coordination and control rely on rules and procedures	Flat organization structured with mutual influence systems Coordination and control based more on shared goals, values, and traditions

Policy Areas	Traditional Control Model	New Commitment Model
	More emphasis on prerogatives and positional authority Status symbols distributed to reinforce hierarchy	Management emphasis on problem solving and relevant information and expertise Minimum status differentials to deemphasize inherent hierarchy
Compensation policies	Variable pay where feasible to provide individual incentive Individual pay geared to job evaluation In downturn, cuts concentrated on hourly payroll	Variable rewards to create equity and to reinforce group achievements: gain sharing, profit sharing Individual pay linked to skills, mastery Equality of sacrifice
Employment assurance	Employees regarded as variable costs	Assurance that participation will not result in job loss High commitment to avoid or assist in reemployment Priority for training and retaining existing work force
Management philosophy	Management's philosophy emphasizes management prerogatives and obligations to shareowners	Management's philosophy acknowledges multiple stakeholders: owners, employees, customers, and public

Source: Adapted from Richard E. Walton, "Toward a Strategy of Eliciting Employee Commitment Based on Policies of Mutuality," in *HRM Trends & Challenges* (Boston, 1985), pp. 37–40.

the point is that, for the general manager, familiarity with established practices is not sufficient. He or she must also be on the lookout for, and open to, new thinking for new times and new circumstances and must learn to distinguish between catchy management fads and valid progress.

Organization Shapes Strategy

This chapter began with a premise that structure follows strategy, where structure was shorthand for organizational structure, managerial processes, and people's skills and attitudes. Simply put, the general manager should put into place the combination of structure, processes, and people that would be best suited for carrying out the strategy of an enterprise.

This prescription is sound, but the relationship between strategy and structure is not so simple. Consider the following three points: (1) organizational structure and processes strongly influence the way people think and act with respect to their jobs; (2) the kind of people an enterprise employs affects what gets considered and how; and (3) strategy is a product of what and how people think. If you agree with these assertions, then you would have to conclude that strategy is also an offshoot of structure.

In Reichhold Chemicals we saw one example of this reverse relationship. With only a broad and tentative definition of strategic direction in mind, Powell decentralized operations and moved in people with experience in the different specialty chemical businesses, giving them the responsibility for defining new business strategies. General Electric, in the Strategic Planning 1981 case, provides another vivid example of restructuring to bring about new strategies. The creation of strategic business units, the introduction of new analytical concepts, and the hiring of people experienced with strategic planning proved to be powerful inducements for developing new business strategies.

The interplay between structure and strategy can often be subtle and unintentional. An account of what happened at the operating level when Monsanto introduced a zero-based budgeting system to control and redirect its marketing, administrative, and technical expenditures is instructional in this regard. The following scene took place at a divisional meeting of business and staff managers to rank requests for resources in order of priority:[9]

> John Coulson, manager of Commodities Chemicals, defending his interest, threw up his hand like at traffic cop to confront Joe Roboh, R&D manager, on the ranking of R&D projects.
>
> "Wait a minute Joe, your next four increments all involve basic research aimed at consumer products."
>
> "Well that's where the future is, John."
>
> "But we're in the present and won't ever reach the future unless we pay our bills," Coulson said adamantly. "There's no support for my stuff!"
>
> "Calm down. If we want to get to the future, we have to start now. Besides, we have applications research and production service for Commodity Chemicals in the threshold."
>
> "But, that's just a tiny bit. Hell, my products pay the salaries around here, and we deserve a fair shake. I want those increments that have my stuff in them ranked now, before we spend all we've got on a future we're not sure exists."
>
> At this point Fred Ellis, manager of Consumer Chemicals, broke in. "John, demand in your markets isn't growing, and competition may soon start to drive your margins down. I know you are producing most of the cash generated by Queeny, but we ought to use that cash to support the best opportunities we've got, and right now those opportunities are in Consumer. Besides, when you consider . . ."
>
> Coulson interrupted, "That's bull! Our demand continues to grow and our competition won't change all that much. The fact of the matter is, Commodity Chemicals continues to be the mainstay of this division, and we would be crazy to weaken it. Process improvements, and that means R&D,

and hard-driving marketing are what it will take to keep this cash cow pro-ducing."

Later in the same meeting, the following dispute occurred with respect to advertising:

> "Right now I've got 90 percent of current advertising expense in the budget," Brewster, manager of Oil Additive Chemicals, said. "Rates will go up at least 15 percent, and if we take my next increment, I'll be just short of my current level in advertising purchase power. If we take Consumer's increment, Fred will be at 160 percent of current. I don't even understand why we're wasting time talking about it."
>
> "Maybe it's time to start cutting your advertising," responded Chris Hubbard, division general manager. "You've been spending at high levels, but you dominate the market now and you keep telling me you get terrific word-of-mouth. You haven't convinced me that this advertising increment will have much effect on either your share or profitability."
>
> "I'm the one who needs the advertising," Fred Ellis interrupted. "Consumer, is right where you were a few years ago. We are at 'take-off.' We have terrific products in a growth market, and we have to get out there and establish a dominant position. Right now, getting more awareness and sup-porting our distributors is critical." Brewster looked straight at Chris Hub-bard, speaking in a slow, deliberate voice. "If our ad budget gets cut, I can't promise the profits we've delivered in the past. We've been damn success-ful, and our advertising has been an important part of our marketing pro-gram. It doesn't make sense to change a successful strategy."

These managers are ostensibly discussing budget allocations, but what they are really arguing about is strategy. These disputes reflect two areas of confu-sion about business strategies. First are the differences of opinion as to the prospects for each unit. Figure 4.4 indicates how the different managers seem to view the various business situations.

The second source of difficulty reflects the different judgments the man-agers have concerning the effects of specific moves in implementing the strat-egy. Conceivably, Coulson's arguments relate less to the issue of whether or not Commodity Chemicals should serve as a "cash cow" than to the issue of "how much fodder to feed the cow to keep it healthy for milking." Coulson is arguing that Hubbard is cutting back too fast and too far.

Brewster's resistance is of a similar nature. Hubbard wants to cut fat from a unit whose growth is beginning to slow down. Brewster argues that the cuts will sever muscle and not fat. The necessary judgments undoubtedly involve a great deal of conjecture, since the business appears to be entering a state of transition.

Someone can argue that the disputes reflect the need for more hard data and a clearer statement of strategy. While this argument has some merit, no amount of data or elaboration of strategy can remove the need for judgments with respect to specific actions. Since the information available in practice is far from perfect, differences of opinion are to be expected and encouraged, not rejected. The new budgeting system forced the conflicting judgments to be

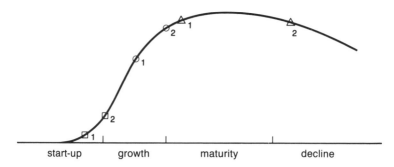

□₁	Consumer Chemicals as viewed by Coulson.
□₂	Consumer Chemicals as viewed by Ellis.
○₁	Oil Additive Chemicals as viewed by Brewster.
○₂	Oil Additive Chemicals as viewed by Hubbard and Ellis.
△₁	Commodity Chemicals as viewed by Coulson.
△₂	Commodity Chemicals as viewed by Ellis and Hubbard.

Figure 4.4   Managers' differing views of business situations.

"placed on the table" where they could be weighed. As with case law, where specific court decisions interpret and give shape to the law, so the specific budget commitments at Monsanto interpreted and gave shape to strategies.

The events at Monsanto were driven in part by competitive considerations. They were also driven by the kind of people involved, their values, and the general approach being followed in introducing the new system to the company. In their comparative study of Japanese and American management practices, Richard Pascale and Anthony Athos point to the success of firms where management not only recognizes the importance of each of these considerations, but purposely shapes them in a coordinated and cohesive manner:

> Executives have only a limited number of "levers" to influence complex large organizations. We have explored seven—superordinate goals [including human values], strategy, structure, systems, skills, style, and staff. . . . All of our outstanding companies are very advanced in their grasp of strategy, structure, and systems, but, unlike less successful firms which rely primarily on these S's, the best companies also have great sophistication on the four "soft" S's. Thus the best firms link their purposes and ways of realizing them to *human values* as well as to economic measures like profit and efficiency. . . . [I]t is probably the least publicized "secret weapon" of high-performing American firms.[10]

The Importance of People

Well-designed organizational structures and processes can bring out the best in an enterprise's people. But these administrative mechanisms can help only to shape the clay; the quality of the clay itself is a vital factor in achieving excellence. Developing people with superior skills and attitudes is of paramount importance for the general manager.

While most general managers would agree unreservedly with this counsel, its implementation is often disappointing. As a staunch and successful advocate of people development, Andrall Pearson, former president of Pepsico, noted, in an unpublished speech in 1986, that:

> Despite the importance attached to people development, and the effort expended, very few companies—a handful, at best—succeed in assembling a dynamic cadre of accomplished managers.
>
> In the many companies that fail to get high marks for people development, there are, of course, many reasons for their lack of success. To begin with, there is no short-term payoff to emphasizing people development. Progress comes slowly, in contrast to shorter-term levers like strategy, or promotions or new products. So it is tempting to allow current volume pressures to overwhelm people development activities. . . . Also, people development is a detail-driven function, with few "home runs." So busy CEOs too often decide they're too busy to get deeply involved. And in many companies, the key managers have never seen first-hand the impact talented managers can exert on a business.

To these reasons can be added an understandable reluctance on the part of less talented managers to recruit or develop people who might outperform them.

As with improving the quality of strategic thinking, general managers must clearly signal their commitment to improving the quality of the organization's human resources in order to get others to support this effort. And as with so many other human endeavors, actions speak louder then words. The amount of attention and support the general manager devotes to this quest will be a prime motivator for subordinates. Powell's unabated involvement in people development and his announcement that the sizable investments associated with these efforts would continue despite losses in 1985 and an anticipated difficult 1986 put his managers on notice as to the importance he placed on building the Reichhold organization.

Some of the principal areas for attention include recruiting, setting standards, performance reviews, job assignments, and training. The common reference point for all of these activities should be the kinds and levels of abilities and the attitudes the organization needs to succeed. These attitudes have to do with commitment to quality performance, willingness to take risks, and adherence to other basic organizational values and aspirations.

The question of who should play what role in people development poses operational issues for the general manager to consider. As with conceptualizing new strategies, not everyone is equally gifted in developing people. Although the general manager should attempt to raise everyone's awareness of this process, the major burden will invariably rest on the shoulders of some line and staff managers. The roles that the personnel or human-resources staff and individual line managers should play will depend on the skills and interests of the specific people involved.

Pearson pointed out in the same speech the importance of setting higher performance expectations across the organization, using challenging job assignments, adjusting the work environment to help motivate talented managers, establishing a process for infusing talent at each organizational level, getting key line managers deeply involved, and making the personnel department a key player:

> The system I've just described takes a full-court press, over an extended period of time—and it affects nearly every aspect of running the business—strategy, work environment, resource allocation, operations and organization. That's why it's so hard to do it well.
>
> Personally, I found this whole process of people development to be the single most exciting, rewarding and important part of my job. I saw first-hand how this approach makes a difference—a tremendous difference—in the bottom line; in the strategic success; and in the fun people have when they come to work in the morning.
>
> That's why I'm convinced that building a dynamic management is top management's biggest challenge—and its best guarantee that the company will continue to be a leader, no matter how the competitive climate changes.

Success in upgrading people's skills and attitudes depends on a clearly thought-out approach and a determined, even dogged, effort to overcome inevitable organizational resistance, discouragement, and relaxation over time. Success also depends on the general manager's abilities as a leader to inspire others in this difficult task.

Notes

1. Kenneth R. Andrews, *The Concept of Corporate Strategy* (Homewood, IL, 1980), p. 109.
2. Raymond E. Miles and Charles C. Snow, "Fit, Failure and the Hall of Fame," *California Management Review*, Vol. XXVI, No. 3 (Spring 1984), pp. 14–15. See also Miles and Snow, *Organizational Strategy, Structure, and Process* (New York, 1978).
3. Peter F. Drucker, *The Practice of Management* (New York, 1954), p. 247.
4. Michael Beer, Bert Spector, Paul R. Lawrence, D. Quinn Mills, Richard E. Walton, *Managing Human Assets* (New York, 1984), p. 92.
5. *Ibid.*, pp. 91, 92.
6. Paul R. Lawrence, "The History of Human Resource Management in American Industry," in *HRM Trends & Challenges* (Boston, 1985), p. 15.
7. *The Wall Street Journal*, April 14, 1986, p. 1.
8. Richard E. Walton, "Toward a Strategy of Eliciting Employee Commitment Based on Policies of Mutuality," in *HRM Trends & Challenges* (Boston, 1985).
9. "Monsanto Company: The Queeny Division (A)," Harvard Business School case number 9–380–048, 1979.
10. Richard T. Pascale and Anthony G. Athos, *The Art of Japanese Management* (New York, 1981), pp. 202., 206.

5

The General Manager
as Leader

The general manager is responsible for the overall performance and well-being of an enterprise. Whether this enterprise is the whole firm, an operating division, or some lesser, relatively autonomous unit within it, the general manager must ensure that there are people in the organization able and willing to conceptualize a sound strategy and to carry it out in a timely and forceful fashion. These accomplishments, taken as a whole, constitute organizational leadership. They have to do with giving an organization its vision of the future and its impetus to translate that vision into reality.

Earlier chapters focused on *what* the general manager should consider and do. Still missing is a look at *how* the general manager breathes life and enthusiasm into the organization as its leader.

Leaders

"Managers are people who do things right; leaders are people who do the right things." This catchy definition make the important distinction between efficiency (doing things right) and effectiveness (doing the right things). But it is not wholly acceptable in light of this book's treatment of the general manager. First, the opposite of the leader in our sense is the bureaucrat, not the manager. In our view, the job of the general manager is to lead *and* to manage. Second, the general manager is responsible for ensuring that the right things happen, not necessarily for doing them.

What sets general managers apart from many other kinds of leaders is the presence of authority and power. According to James MacGregor Burns:

> Executive leaders have effective power (rather than merely formal authority) to the degree that they can activate the need and motivational bases of other leaders and subordinates in the organization. This power in essence is the traditional power to reward and penalize—but what do the respon-

dents or power recipients consider to be rewards and penalties? In a large organization these motivations are likely to be as varied as human needs can be—not only for security, higher income, and better working conditions but for affection, recognition, deference, esteem, and for both autonomy toward and dependence on the executive leader, for both conformity and individuality—traits that can exist in the same person. Other things being equal, the stronger the motivational base the leader taps, the greater control over that person the leader can exercise.[1]

But even if leaders have authority and power, Burns views authentic executive leadership as a collective process, involving a mutuality of interests. In their study of organizational leadership, Louis Barnes and Mark Kriger also advise against equating leaders with formal authority. In their view, anyone taking initiative in defining and fostering change is a leader, be that anyone boss, subordinate, or one of several people interacting with each other: "Managers inevitably occupy *both* leadership and followership positions due to the very nature of organizational hierarchies. All bosses, including CEO's, are also subordinate to other people or pressures."[2] They go on to define organizational leadership as a multiperson phenomenon, "where leader roles overlapped, complemented each other and shifted from time to time and from person to person."

From this perspective, the general manager's role as leader could be seen as fostering leadership by others. This is not to say that general managers can simply sit back and wait for the right things to happen. In their leadership capacity, they must, at the very least, create conditions conducive to making the right things happen, be prepared and able to recognize when the right things are happening, and support these initiatives with the power and influence of their office. In effect, then, *general managers as leaders are people who ensure that the right things get done.*

Leadership

An important distinction can be made between a general manager who gets people to achieve specific goals and one who get people to achieve specific goals *and* develops a self-actualizing belief system or culture. Both are exercising leadership. But, to borrow Burns' terms, the first is dealing with *transactions*, the second is *transforming* the character of the organization.[3] A political leader who forms an alliance of several nations to counter a military threat, a corporate executive who organizes a coalition of companies to partition a takeover target, or an individual who hires casual laborers to harvest a crop are all engaged in transactional leadership. When the task is completed, participation ceases. In contrast, the leaders of American Can, Daewoo, and General Electric, as the cases illustrate, are largely engaged in transformational leadership. Although both forms of leadership are valid undertakings for the general manager, the remainder of this chapter will focus primarily on transformational leadership, since it is the more complex and comprehensive of the two, and ultimately the more important.

Philip Selznick argues that the most vital mission of the leader is to infuse an organization with values so that it becomes prized for its own sake. Distinguishing between an organization as a technical instrument for achieving specific goals and an organization as an institutional fulfillment of group integrity and aspiration, he defines the leader as an agent of institutionalization:

> [T]he task of building values and a distinctive competence into the organization is a prime function of leadership. . . . The task of leadership is not only to make policy but to build it into the organization's social structure. This, too, is a creative task. It means shaping the "character" of the organization, sensitizing it to ways of thinking and responding, so that increased reliability in the execution and elaboration of policy will be achieved according to its spirit as well as its letter.[4]

Burns echoes Selznick:

> Some define leadership as leaders making followers do what followers would not otherwise do, or as leaders making followers do what the leaders want them to do. I define leadership as leaders inducing followers to act for certain goals that represent the values and the motivations—the wants and needs, the aspirations and expectations—of both leaders and followers. And the genius of leadership lies in the manner in which leaders see and act on their own and their followers' values and motivations.[5]

And Edgar Schein makes the strongest case for transformational or institutional (Selznick's term) leadership, *"the only thing of real importance that leaders do is to create and manage culture."*[6] He goes on to describe mechanisms for institutionalizing values:

> The most powerful primary mechanisms for culture embedding and reinforcement are (1) what leaders pay attention to, measure, and control; (2) leader reactions to critical incidents and organizational crises; (3) deliberate role modeling, teaching, and coaching by leaders; (4) criteria for allocation of rewards and status; (5) criteria for recruitment, selection, promotion, retirement, and excommunication. . . .
>
> The most important secondary articulation and reinforcement mechanisms are (1) the organization's design and structure; (2) organizational systems and procedures; (3) design of physical space, facades, and buildings; (4) stories, legends, myths, and parables about important events and people; (5) formal statements of organizational philosophy, creeds, and charters.
>
> I have labeled these mechanisms "secondary" because they work only if they are consistent with the primary mechanisms discussed previously. When they are consistent, they begin to build organizational ideologies and thus to formalize much of what is informally learned at the outset. If they are inconsistent, they either will be ignored or will be a source of internal conflict. But the operating cultural assumptions will always be manifested first in what the leaders demonstrate, not in what is written down or inferred from designs and procedures.[7]

Indeed, almost any administrative procedure might have a bearing on the distinctive role and character of the enterprise. The institutional leader has to be sensitive to the possible impact any proposed changes might have on the maintenance or enhancement of desired values.

Leading

There are many different ways in which a general manager can lead, but they all seem to share certain common elements, including espousing a vision of purpose, gaining organizational commitment to this vision of purpose, and providing the wherewithal to carry it out.

Vision. In their book on leaders, Warren Bennis and Burt Nanus write:

> [A] vision articulates a view of a realistic, credible, attractive future for the organization, a condition that is better in some important ways than what now exists. . . . With a vision, the leader provides the all-important bridge from the present to the future of the organization.[8]

The power of such vision is in its ability to energize the emotional and spiritual resources of the organization. When Chairman Kim described his dreams for the Daewoo Group, he spoke with a passion. Other general managers in the case studies—Burke of J&J, Welch of GE, Das of Richardson Hindustan, and Pelz of DAAG—also had clear and strongly held visions of where they wanted to take their organizations. The enthusiasm each held for his vision, probably more than its inherent soundness, energized others.

For these leaders, rank and formal authority were not necessary conditions. Neither Das nor Pelz was in the upper echelons of his corporation. And while Das enjoyed the explicit support of his superiors at headquarters, Pelz lacked even that advantage. (Whether Pelz's vision would or could result in a "condition that is better than what exists" will be considered in the DAAG case.)

Sheer enthusiasm, of course, is not enough. A vision must be understandable, credible, and uplifting. The vision Thomas J. Watson, Sr., had for IBM to become a dominant force in the information-processing field certainly met these requirements, as the following account testifies:

> Preachers know good sermons make at most three points, and the Watson philosophy was simple, too. One, give the best service of any company in the world. Two, strive for superior performance. Three—the one IBMers think is most important—respect the individual.[9]

The message was clear and straightforward. Its credibility rested on the good business sense of the practices espoused. Its power to inspire derived from the appeal to basic human values favoring respect for each other and excellence of performance.

As Bennis and Nanus observed:

> Great leaders often inspire their followers to high levels of achievement by showing them how their work contributes to worthwhile ends. It is an emotional appeal to some of the most fundamental human needs—the need to be important, to make a difference, to feel useful, to be a part of a successful and worthwhile enterprise.[10]

In our view of organizational leadership, such inspiration may be directed upward to include superiors, sideways to peers, downward to the ranks of workers, and outward to members of the board of directors, to shareholders, and even to union, governmental, and other social leaders.

Vision is viewed as a basic building block in our examination of leadership, and if we increase the magnification of our analytical microscope and train it on vision itself, we can see that it too has its own stages of development. A vision that is valid, understandable, credible, and uplifting is an end product in its own right. Occasionally, such a vision may spring full blown from the mind of an individual in a flash of inspiration, as Eve from the rib of Adam. More often, it evolves over time, taking on substantive changes and polish with the growth of insight and eloquence. In its earliest stages, vision might be no more than a nagging feeling that something is wrong (a dissatisfaction with the status quo). Yet even a vision as fuzzy and vestigal as "We seem to be headed for trouble and need to do something different" can serve as a catalyst for change. This was essentially Borch's state of mind in the late 1960s as he viewed the General Electric Company. Fifteen years later Jack Welch articulated the resultant vision:

> A decade from now I would like General Electric to be perceived as a unique, high-spirited, entrepreneurial enterprise . . . a company known around the world for its unmatched level of excellence. I want General Electric to be the most profitable highly diversified company on earth, with world-quality leadership in every one of its product lines.[11]

Commitment. A general manager must become an impassioned spokesman for his or her vision in order to get others in the organization to understand, agree with, and finally to identify with it. Of course, we chuckle at the wry inconsistency of an executive admonishing his subordinates, "I want you to adopt a participative management style, or else." But the CEO who unabashedly accepts a big bonus while preaching the need for others to cut costs and tighten belts deserves the cynical response he or she is likely to receive. More likely to succeed is the way John Connelly went about getting commitment to cost cutting and customer service as the means to save Crown Cork and Seal Company from bankruptcy in 1957. He not only preached this message, he lived it:

> At Crown, all customers' gripes go to John Connelly, who is still the company's best salesman. A visitor recalls being in his office when a complaint came through from the manager of a Florida citrus-packing plant. Connelly assured him the problem would be taken care of immediately, then casually remarked that he planned to be in Florida the next day. Would the plant manager join him for dinner? He would indeed. As Crown's president put the telephone down, his visitor said that he hadn't realized Connelly was planning to go to Florida. "Neither did I," confessed Connelly, "until I began talking."[12]

Consistency of word and deed on the leader's part is absolutely necessary if others are to commit themselves to the personal and business risks associated with new and unproven courses of action. The general manager who runs hot and cold on issues will fail to encourage confidence in others—superiors and peers as well as subordinates. Nobody wants to go out on a limb and risk being abandoned at the first sound of cracking wood.

Although the consistency and forcefulness of a leader's articulation of vision and its inherent soundness are of critical importance, they will not guarantee commitment. The audience also has to be receptive to its consideration if commitment is ever to occur. This receptivity is a function of an organization's belief system.

All organizations depend on the existence of shared beliefs and ways of interpreting ideas and events to cope with complexity and ambiguity. A well-developed belief system provides powerful guidelines and impetus for organizational action. But such beliefs, when no longer appropriate to changed conditions, can become just as harmful to an organization's functioning. The following observation about basic organizational beliefs by Gordon Donaldson and Jay W. Lorsch really applies to all the organization's members:

> These beliefs are often a major barrier to strategic change because top executives have become so emotionally committed to them that they are unwilling—or unable—to alter practices that have been successful in the past. Events that transform the conditions under which a particular industry or firm operates are therefore difficult to accommodate. . . . Consequently, we argue that the ability to manage these psychological constraints is an important key to the success of individual companies and to the economy as a whole.[13]

The importance of managing the belief system is also made by Bennis and Nanus, who define social architecture as the norms and values that shape behavior in any organized setting:

> Social architecture, as we have continually emphasized, provides *meaning*. The key point is that if an organization is to be transformed, the social architecture must be revamped. The effective leader needs to articulate new values and norms, offer new visions, and use a variety of tools in order to transform, support, and institutionalize new meanings and directions.[14]

The general manager, at the very least, has to discredit established beliefs inimical to the new vision. Better yet, of course, is to institutionalize supportive beliefs.

Empowerment. A person committed to a new vision can do little if he or she does not have the necessary wherewithal to carry it out. To enable an organization to convert vision into reality, the general manager must assure that the change agents (the general manager and/or others) are provided with what Rosabeth Kanter describes as the " 'three basic commodities' that can be invested in action: *information* (data, technical knowledge, political intelligence, expertise); *resources* (funds, materials, space, time); and *support* (endorsement, backing, approval, legitimacy)."[15]

With vision, commitment, information, resources, and support, the scene is set for things to happen. We look next at how the general manager can go about energizing these ingredients.

Leadership Styles

People can perform the vital functions of leadership in very different ways. Each of the general managers in the case studies that follow went about "getting the right things done" in his own manner. Some appeared more leaderlike than others, but such appearances can be deceiving. It is important not to confuse form with substance in evaluating the general manager as leader. What good this individual accomplishes is the true measure, not the manner in which he or she goes about the task.

The style of leadership a general manager adopts depends on the situation and on his or her personality traits. The interplay between these two factors is complex. Some situations may favor one style; other situations may be largely indifferent to style. Some individuals can vary their style to accord with the situation; others cannot.

Leadership styles are complex and varied, depending as they do on many behavioral details. One way to consider leadership style is to look at how an individual goes about influencing others. Leaders can rely on their charisma as the prime force for change, on their mission or goals, on organizational processes, or on negotiating with key participants (those who are to carry out the mission and those who must approve). This delineation of leadership approaches or styles, however, is a matter of emphasis only. Rarely, if ever, in complex situations will a leader not employ multiple avenues of influence, often concomitantly.

Leading Through Charisma. For many people, the word leader evokes a romantic picture of a towering figure on a white horse, pointing the way to victory and projecting strength and wisdom. In a more contemporary vein, Winston Churchill, Charles de Gaulle, Eleanor Roosevelt, Mahatma Ghandi, Mao Tse Tung, John F. Kennedy, Pope John XXIII, and Martin Luther King, Jr., might be mentioned as examples of great leaders. And in the world of business and commerce, the names Ford, Wallenberg, Olivetti, Honda, Wristen, and Iacocca are synonymous with leadership.

Leaders often have a special magnetic charm or appeal, qualities arousing loyalty and enthusiasm. While the leader's appeal is often linked with an inspiring vision, this need not be so. Mae Tse Tung is a good example of a leader who changed directions frequently in his later years, without impairing the hold he had on his followers. Supporters of the charismatic leader often become disciples, motivated by a deep, at times blind, personal trust of the individual.

Leading Through Mission and Goals. What characterizes these leaders is the emphasis they place on their mission or on specific goals, to motivate others. The cause or target serves as the fulcrum for change and action. "Being number one or number two in your industry" and "Making the world's most powerful computers," compelling rally cries for Jack Welch of General Electric and John Rollwagen of Cray Research, provide a basis for inspiring and guiding action.

In his Pulitzer prize-winning account of the development of a new computer, John Kidder provides an excellent illustration of the enormous motivational power a mission can have on people. The challenge of designing a computer that could outperform the successful model of the archrival Digital Equipment Corporation as well as the in-house officially sanctioned Data General computer development project drove Tom West and his ad hoc engineering team to work day and night. Their goal-oriented behavior is captured in the following comments. West recruited the team:

> We had the best high-energy story to tell a college graduate. They'd all heard about VAX. Well, we were gonna build a thirty-two-bit machine less expensive, faster and so on. You can sign up a guy to that any day of the year. And we got the best there was.

For months during the project, Rasala, one of the hardware engineers, would come home and tell his wife he had had a terrible day.

> But as he went on describing the day's events, his wife noticed, he became increasingly excited.
> "Maybe it's masochism," Rasala said, "But I guess the reason I do it fundamentally is that there is a certain satisfaction in building a machine like this, which is important to the company, which is on its way to becoming a billion-dollar company. There aren't that many opportunities in this world to be where the action is, making an impact." It struck him as paradoxical, all this energy and passion, both his own and that of the engineers around him, being expended for a decidedly commercial purpose. But that purpose wasn't his own. . . .
> Rasala said, "I was looking for"—he ticked the items off on his fingers—"opportunity, responsibility, visibility."
> What did these words mean to him, though?
> Rasala shrugged his shoulders. "I wanted to see what I was worth," he explained.[16]

Leaders espousing a mission or goal tend to confront key issues directly and openly. Within legal and ethical limits, anything that contributes to the desired end is sanctioned; anything that impairs its accomplishment is repudiated. Since a sense of right versus wrong prevails, this approach can involve organizational conflicts resulting in winners and losers.

Leading Through Process. In his penetrating analysis of the Cuban missile crisis, Graham Allison identified organizational features and procedures as one possible explanation for the behavior observed and the decisions taken. In support of this view, he argued that the "preeminent feature of organizational activity is its programmed character: the extent to which behavior in any particular case is an enactment of preestablished routines."[17]

Organization structure and management systems are powerful instruments for directing behavior. A general manager can promote and guide action by orchestrating the organizational context. In describing his reasons for reorganizing General Electric's sector structure, Jack Welch gives a dramatic illustration of this approach to leadership:

> Why did we reorganize this time? G.E. Information Services with all their networking and G.E. Credit were in two different places, under two different sector executives. We were convinced there was synergy in tieing networking to financial services. The best way to do it . . . crash them together. Let the new sector head figure it out.[18]

Goals, compensation schemes, information networks, and approval structures are other aspects of an organization that can be modified and orchestrated by a general manager to promote and guide action in desired directions. Decisions in such matters as who is to be involved in key activities, timing, and the openness of debate can influence thinking and swing support one way or another.

General managers who are effective in structuring and using organizational context as a primary means of motivating people are sensitive to the limits of this approach. While rules, structures, and systems guide actions in general, situations calling for exceptional treatment are bound to arise. In his sociological study of bureaucratic organizations, Michel Crozier argues that a manager imposing rules must retain some freedom of action:

> To achieve his aims, the manager has two sets of conflicting weapons: rationalization and rule-making on one side; and the power to make exceptions and to ignore the rules on the other. His own strategy will be to find the best combination of both weapons, according to the objectives of the unit of which he is in charge and to the degree to which members of the unit are interested in these objectives. Proliferation of the rules curtails his own power. Too many exceptions to the rules reduce his ability to check other people's power.[19]

Crozier's reference to other people's power and his reasoning that a manager be open to making exceptions to the rules in order to accommodate such power touches on another approach to leading.

Leading Through Negotiations. With this approach, a leader seeks to achieve accord by accommodating those people with power to affect the organizations' ability and willingness to change. The vision, which might be explicit or vague, serves more to guide the leader than to inspire others.

In their writings on leadership, Joseph Badaracco and Richard Ellsworth give the following rationale for this leadership style:

> Companies are rarely harmonious communities of benign, cooperating individuals who pursue broad strategic goals determined by rational analysis. Much more commonly, they are political arenas in which individuals

jockey and bargain to advance their own interests and those of the organizational units for which they are responsible. . . . Executives who can maneuver astutely within and gently nudge the complex, often intense politics
of a company can gain leverage over the centrifugal forces of politics and
can focus company efforts on strategic objectives—without running roughshod over the autonomy and decentralization that their capable subordinates demand.[20]

This comment relates to senior-level executives. Clearly, the need to maneuver
astutely in such an environment becomes even greater for lower-level general
managers who lack the power to force their ideas on others, let alone run
roughshod.

The principal skill for this approach is in finding and exploiting commonalities of interest as a means of gaining support, or at least of reducing opposition. This can be a slow and fragmented process as the leader probes for such
commonalities of interest or waits for opportune occasions. This approach is
characterized by negotiations, compromise, opportunism, incremental advances, and hidden agendas.

Personal Qualities of a Successful General Manager

In examining the general-management function and the general manager as
manager and leader, we covered a wide range of considerations concerning
responsibilities and concepts. But what about the person? As the cases make
clear, there is no optimal model to describe the successful practitioner. He or
she can be outgoing or private, dynamic or reflective, conceptual or empirical,
tough or compassionate. Successful general managers defy any precise specifications, but they do seem to share certain personal characteristics: knowledge
and skills, commitment, integrity, concern for others, resiliency, presence, and
judgment.

Knowledge and Skills. Successful general managers typically have bright and
facile minds. Although intellectual brilliance is not necessary—and might even
be a hindrance if not tempered with action-oriented qualities—a general manager must reason well, make decisions in uncertain circumstances, and adapt
as circumstances change—all of which call for above-average general intelligence.

Being well-informed about one's industry—its technology, customer expectations, and competitive practices—and about one's company—its culture,
practices, and key people—is also valuable for the general manager. Admittedly, there is some controversy as to whether a good general manager can be
effective in any setting or must rely on industry- and company-specific experience. The transferability of the general manager's capabilities to manage and
lead in different settings probably depends on the specific situation and on the
nature of his or her experiences.

The broad responsibilities of the general manager's job call for a breadth
and diversity of managerial experience. Reporting on a study comparing successful senior executives with promising managers who plateaued or failed at

high levels, Morgan McCall and Michael Lombardo pointed to characteristic differences in their track records:

> Derailed executives had a series of successes, but usually in similar situations: they had turned a business around more than once, or they had managed progressively larger jobs, but in the same function. By contrast, the arrivers had more diversity in their successes—they had turned a business around *and* successfully moved from line to staff and back; or they had started a new business from scratch *and* completed a special assignment with distinction. . . . They showed a breadth of perspective and interest that resulted (over 20 to 30 years) in detailed knowledge of many parts of the business, as well as first-hand experience with *different kinds* of challenges.[21]

Since the general manager must work through others, he or she also must have command of important administrative skills—such as how to organize work and people, how to assemble a strong staff, and how to delegate. For most complex business situations, no individual, no matter how brilliant and energetic, can achieve as much as a well-trained and well-organized group of talented people under gifted leadership.

Commitment. Senior executives devote long hours to their work. The enormous challenges general managers face in directing large, complex organizations invariably require hard work and a strong commitment to purpose. Ambition and self-sacrifice are common traits contributing to success. Good physical and mental health is another invaluable asset for the general manager working under pressure over time and facing inevitable obstacles, inertia, and setbacks.

Integrity. Trust plays a greater role in organizational life as one moves up the management hierarchy, reflecting the increasing complexity and imprecision of the work and relationships. For this reason, integrity—a generally desirable human quality—takes on special importance for the general manager. McCall and Lombardo stress this point:

> One senior executive . . . said that he thought only two things differentiated the successful from the derailed—total integrity and understanding other people.
> Integrity seems to have a special meaning to executives that is vastly different from its mom-and-apple-pie image. The word does not refer to simple honesty, but embodies a consistency and predictability built over time that says, "I will do exactly what I say I will do when I say I will do it. If I change my mind, I will tell you well in advance so you will not be harmed by my actions." Such a statement is partly one of ethics, but more, it may be one of deadly practicality. This seems to be the core method of keeping a large, amorphous organization from collapsing in its own confusion.[22]

Concern for Others. The most frequent cause for derailment, according to the McCall and Lombardo report, was insensitivity to others.[23] A general manager's genuine respect and concern for others—subordinates, peers, superiors, customers, and suppliers—form the basis for the cooperative interaction so vital to his or her functioning. Self-serving and manipulative behavior is bound to cause resentment among victims and even onlookers. Being empathic and tactful can work as much to a general manager's advantage as being cold, aloof, or arrogant can to his or her disadvantage.

Resiliency. Everyone makes mistakes, and successful general managers are no exceptions. What separates these people from others is their ability to learn from their mistakes, to work on correcting the problems rather than on fault-finding, and to move on. Iacocca rebounding from his painful fall from grace at Ford is the contemporary exemplar of resiliency.

Setbacks and failures, distressing as they may be, have their benefits. They can often be more powerful learning experiences than successful endeavors. And they can help the successful manager gain humility—a trait far preferable to arrogance in dealing with others.

Presence. General managers must ask a lot of their staffs and of others. People respond because they have confidence in the general manager's ability to handle the situation and to achieve purpose. To gain and hold this confidence, a general manager has to project personal maturity and competence. This is true especially in times of adversity. Falling apart, lashing out, or withdrawing are examples of behavior bound to undermine the grounds for trust.

Judgment. If knowledge and skill are the foundation of essential qualities for a person to perform well as a general manager, good judgment is the capstone. It is this quality to which Jack Welch, GE's chief executive officer, referred in extolling "street smarts" as critical to a general manager's effectiveness.

The general manager typically has to deal with an overwhelming array of demands, including problems that are messy, confusing, and insolvable. As such, he or she must be able to distinguish between what is important and what is not, what to do and what not to do. The kinds of judgment called for suggest a foundation in native good sense coupled with intellectual qualities that enable one to discern facts or conditions that are not obvious, to comprehend the significance of those facts and conditions, and to draw correct unbiased conclusions from them. To paraphrase Coleridge, judgment is common sense to an uncommon degree.

Success for the General Manager

In the case studies, we shall see general managers in action, dealing with a wide variety of issues in a wide variety of situations. The one common concern of all these studies is how well the individual performed as general manager.

To answer this question, we must consider how well the general manager has discharged his or her responsibility for the performance and well-being of the enterprise. Has he or she created a vision of what the enterprise is to be and how it is to get there? Has he or she developed the organizational ability and willingness to carry out this vision? Has he or she ensured timely and proper actions?

In accomplishing these broad tasks, the general manager ensures the achievement of purpose. This is one measure of success for the general manager. But beyond the achievement of purpose is the creation of an organization valued for its own sake. Selznick notes the following measure of success: "Successful institutions are usually able to fill in the formula, "What we are proud of around here is . . ."[24] What better accolade could the general manager want?

Notes

1. James MacGregor Burns, *Leadership* (New York, 1978), p. 373.
2. Louis B. Barnes and Mark P. Kriger, "The Hidden Side of Organizational Leadership," *Sloan Management Review* (Fall 1986), pp. 15–25.
3. Burns, *op. cit.*, p. 4. Strictly speaking, Burns uses the concept of transformational leadership in connection with the effects on the individuals involved.
4. Philip Selznick, *Leadership in Administration* (New York, 1957), pp. 27, 62–63.
5. Burns, *op. cit.*, p. 19.
6. Edgar H. Schein, *Organizational Culture and Leadership* (San Francisco, 1985), p. 2.
7. *Ibid.*, pp. 224, 225, and 237.
8. Warren Bennis and Burt Nanus, *Leaders.* (New York, 1985), pp. 89, 90.
9. "Behind the Monolith: A Look at IBM," *The Wall Street Journal*, April 7, 1986, p. 25.
10. Bennis and Nanus, *op. cit.*, p. 93.
11. "General Electric: 1984," Harvard Business School case number 9–385–315, 1985.
12. *Fortune*, October 1962, p. 164.
13. Gordon Donaldson and Jay W. Lorsch, *Decision Making at the Top* (New York, 1983), p. 8.
14. Bennis and Nanus, *op. cit.*, p. 139.
15. Rosabeth Moss Kanter, *The Change Masters* (New York, 1983), p. 159.
16. John Tracy Kidder, *The Soul of a New Machine* (Boston, 1981), pp. 64 and 153.
17. Graham T. Allison, *Essence of Decision* (Boston, 1971), p. 81. Allison proposes three models of cause and effect to serve as possible explanations for the way in which U.S. authorities handled the Cuban missile crisis: (1) the rational-actor model, in which decisions were made on the basis of calculated choices to serve national interests; (2) the organizational-process model, in which decisions reflected the outputs of established procedures for participation (protocols as to who would be involved and how); and (3) the political model, in which decisions were a result of various bargaining games among players in the national government. These three models bear some resemblance to the leadership styles under discussion.
18. "General Electric Company: Dr. John F. Welch, Jr.," Harvard Business School videotape 882–024, 1982.
19. Michel Crozier, *The Bureaucratic Phenomenon* (Chicago, 1964), pp. 163, 164.
20. Joseph Badaracco and Richard Ellsworth, "Incremental Leadership," Harvard Business School publication 0–385–106, 1984, p. 2.
21. Morgan W. McCall, Jr., and Michael M. Lombardo, "Off the track: Why and How Successful Executives Get Derailed" (Greensboro, NC, Center for Creative Leadership, Technical Report 21, January 1983), p. 9.
22. *Ibid.*, p. 11.
23. *Ibid.*, p. 5.
24. Selznick, *op. cit.*, p. 151.

II
CASES

THE CASE METHOD

. . . the root of the true practice of education must start from the particular fact, concrete and definite for individual apprehension, and must gradually evolve towards the general idea.

Alfred North Whitehead[1]

It can be said flatly that the mere act of listening to wise statements and sound advice does little for anyone. In the process of learning, the learner's dynamic cooperation is required.

Charles I. Gragg[2]

In these two statements are the educational underpinnings of the case method: inductive reasoning (from the particular to the general) and active participation. The validity of this approach for the study of the general manager rests on the nature of the subject matter and on the objectives of management education.

As the text has underscored and the cases will demonstrate, general management is an enormously complex subject, and the general manager has an enormously complex job. To rely on principle for either the study or the practice of general management is to stand on shaky ground for several reasons. First, any important challenge a general manager faces typically involves too many critical factors to yield to simple recipes. Several principles are likely to apply to a given situation, and they will often be at odds with one another. Second, innovative managerial actions repeatedly vitiate or alter the significance of business precedents and principles. Accepted routines and conventions are successfully broken every day in practice as enterprising managers find ingenious new ways to deal with obstacles and opportunities.

While these limitations to the use of principles as the basis for studying general management are severe, even more compelling is the lack of definition and clarity the general manager typically faces. As experience shows, one of the general manager's most critical challenges is to identify and define problems and opportunities. It does little good to act in accordance with principles in dealing with the wrong problem. As you will discover in reading the case studies, the problem is seldom exactly what you thought it to be. And a single modification in the definition of a problem can change the whole analysis and call for a radically different course of action. Only a skillful selection and analysis of the many facts and conjectures about a given situation can provide the general manager with the diagnosis effective action requires.

The case study approach is similar to the approach used in legal, medical, and other professional training, in which the aim is to develop practitioners skilled in diagnosing situations and acting accordingly. Arthur Dewing captures the essential nature of management education as preparation for the manager "to meet in action the problems arising out of new situations in an ever-changing environment."[3]

Drawing on some forty years of experience as a dedicated practitioner of case-method instruction, C. Roland Christensen connects these educational objectives to the need for students to participate actively in the learning process:

> In education for management, where knowledge and application skills must be related, student involvement is essential. One does not learn to play golf by reading a book, but by taking club in hand and actually hitting a golf ball, preferably under a pro's watchful eye. A practice green is not a golf game, and a case is not real life. Fortunes, reputations, and careers are not made or lost in the classroom. But case discussion is a useful subset of reality. It presents an opportunity for a student to practice the application of real-life administrative skills: observing, listening, diagnosing, deciding, and intervening in group processes to achieve desired collaboration.[4]

He goes on to describe some of the specific in-class experiences good case discussions should provide:

- a focus on understanding the specific situation;
- a focus on the total situation, as well as on the specific;
- sensitivity to interrelationships; the connectedness of all organizational functions and processes;
- examining and understanding any administrative situation from a multidimensional point of view;
- approaching problems as one responsible for the achievements of the organization; and
- an action orientation.[5]

Amplifying his last point, he characterizes "action orientation" as the following:

- an acceptance of institutional conflict;
- a sense for the possible;
- a sense for the critical, "the jugular";
- a willingness to make firm decisions;
- the skill of converting desired objectives into a program of action;
- an understanding that obtaining the commitment of personnel to the accomplishment of any plan is crucial;
- an appreciation of the limits of management action.[6]

Rarely, if ever, is there one correct solution to any major problem that the general manager faces. As Dewing points out, it would be surprising if any group of experienced businesspeople could offer an unequivocal solution with unanimous accord. He concludes:

> Cases should be used with the clear consciousness that the purpose of business education is not to teach truths—leaving aside for a moment a discussion of whether there are or are not such things as truths—but to teach men to think in the presence of new situations.[7]

In any learning experience, there is usually a direct relationship, in accordance with intelligence and aptitude, between a person's efforts and the learning that takes place. Unlike most lecture courses, the case method requires such efforts before and after classroom discussions as well as during.

How to Prepare a Case[8]

The starting point is individual preparation. You have to read the case, figure out what is at issue, do the necessary analysis, and draw whatever conclusions the assignment calls for.

While no single preparation method works best for everyone, you should consider the following generally useful guidelines:

1. Try to anticipate what is at issue by reviewing the assignment questions and by taking into account what major topic or topics your course is currently trying to address.
2. Skim the case quickly to ascertain the general nature of the situation and the kinds of information it provides for analysis.
3. Read the case carefully with respect to the issues under consideration, noting specific problems and the data germane to each.
4. Analyze each problem and issue, taking into account all the relevant data in the case and noting explicitly your assumptions.
5. Develop a set of recommendations supported by your analysis.

The next preparation step, when feasible, is to meet with about six other students to discuss the case. (Discussion groups may be formally organized.) This discussion, which typically might last thirty minutes to an hour, is an opportunity to get assistance on technical points that you might not understand or on other confusing matters, to present your arguments and test your reasoning, and to hear other viewpoints. This exchange is an important preparatory step for class discussion.

The purpose of the discussion group meeting is *not* to develop a consensus or a "group" position. Rather, it is to help each member refine his or her own thinking. It is not necessary, nor is it even productive, to continue spending time trying to convince the others to agree with your position once you have made it clear. The most constructive procedure is to exchange ideas on as many of the important issues as time permits, not to beat one to death.

Classroom Discussion

The guidelines for classroom discussion are few and simple. The first is to participate, participate, and participate. The second is to make a conscious effort to contribute to classroom discussion by adding new ideas to the debate and by introducing new dimensions and new issues at opportune moments.

Active participation is critical to case-method study not only because your comments can help your classmates learn, but also because it is one of the most effective ways for you to learn. Each of us has powerful defense mechanisms to protect our ego from getting bruised. One of these mechanisms is a proclivity to hear what we want to hear.[9] A student who only listens in class may hear only what reinforces his or her preconceptions, especially if they are broad and fuzzy. Taking a position and exposing your thinking to the questions and challenges of others is one of the best ways to discover inconsistencies or gaps in your understanding and flaws in your reasoning and judgment. This discovery can be a painful experience at times—after all, no one likes to be shown wrong—but it is undoubtedly better to make your mistakes in the classroom than on the job.

Participation works best for all concerned when the comments relate to the flow of the classroom discussion, adding new information and insight. Challenging or supporting recent speakers with different facts and new interpretations stimulates thinking and learning. The student who repeats earlier comments or simply recites case facts deadens the learning process. So does the student whose comment is off the point.

Introducing a new topic of discussion can be a constructive move at times, but runs the risk of being disruptive to the group's learning process. Inexperienced case students might do well to rely on the instructor for such transitional moves.

Debriefing

A good case discussion can generate a lot of intriguing ideas. These ideas do not always make their appearance in a logical sequence, nor are they always entirely consistent with each other. The student needs to take a little time after class to sort them out. Moreover, with normal classroom time pressures, rarely will a class cover all of the important implications of the key points. Thinking about these implications, particularly as they might relate to your own interest and experience, can be very productive.

You might ask yourself the following two general questions to get your debriefing started:

- What did I learn in class?
- What did I not learn that I wish I had?

In answering these questions, be modest in your expectations and reasonably charitable in your assessments. After all, much of the responsibility for what you learn in class is yours.

Notes

1. Alfred North Whitehead, *The Aims of Education* (New York, 1929), p. 97.
2. Charles I. Gragg, "Because Wisdom Can't be Told," in Malcolm P. McNair, ed., *The Case Method at the Harvard Business School* (New York, 1954), p. 6.
3. Arthur Stone Dewing, "An Introduction to the Use of Cases," in Cecil E. Fraser, ed., *The Case Method of Instruction* (New York, 1931).
4. C. Roland Christensen, *Teaching by the Case Method,* (Boston, 1981), p. 10.
5. *Ibid.,* p. 13.
6. *Ibid.,* pp. 13, 14.
7. Dewing, *op. cit.*
8. The content of this section was derived in part from a paper by E. Raymond Corey, "The Use of Cases in Management Education," Harvard Business School Publication 9–376–240.
9. Communication theory has something to tell us about unintentional distortions that arise from cognitive limitations to the human reception of information. As noted in Donald T. Campbell, "Systematic Error on the Part of Human Links in Communication Systems," *Information and Control* (December 1958), pp. 334–369:" This tendency to distort messages in the direction of identity with previous inputs is probably the most pervasive of the systematic biases. . . . It is also one of the most typically 'human' error tendencies."

GUIDE TO THE CASES

The cases presented here are comprehensive in nature and can be used in various sequences to emphasize different aspects of general management. Since the order of their use will depend on the design and objectives of the course and on the instructor's personal preference and judgment, they are arranged in alphabetical order. For most of the cases, comments by the general managers involved are available on videotape.

American Can Company, 1984

During the early 1980s American Can Company was engaged in what was called the most massive redeployment of assets in the history of American business. The company had set out to reduce its dependence on mature, capital-intensive industries (packaging and paper products) and to build a strong position in profitable, fast-growing businesses (financial services and specialty retailing). As of early 1984, the transformation was in midstream. While early performance indications had seemed favorable, the long-term success of the strategy was still in question. Top management faced difficult decisions concerning both strategy and organization. With respect to strategy, it had to decide exactly what specific services to pursue in each field and how fast to move. With respect to organization, it had to consider how to relate the new perspectives associated with merchandising and financial services with the traditional culture associated with a mature manufacturing operation. The Chief Financial Officer's concerns with cash flow added a vital financial dimension to the situation, and the CEO's intention to retire in two years introduced the issue of succession.

Bard MedSystems Division

A middle-level general manager battles to turn around a troubled division. By 1987, he has finally achieved initial success, but still faces several major challenges. This case examines general management from two perspectives. The first deals with the divisional manager in considering how he was able to devise a business strategy, build an organization, and create an up-beat divisional spirit against formidable odds. The second perspective concerns how the corporate culture might have influenced the division manager's performance. Senior management's attitudes and a number of corporate practices and systems are described for this purpose.

Bowater Computer Forms, Inc.

Bowater Computer Forms—the rapidly growing sole subsidiary of the large U.S. paper company, Bowater—was at a point of organizational transition as its management continued to implement a strategy of geographic roll-out with a goal of national coverage by 1990. The case describes the business operations of this dedicated forms manufacturer and the problems its general manager faced in trying to professionalize the organization as it became increasingly large and dispersed. His challenge was complicated by the need to deal with pressures from corporate management to accelerate expansion and to decentralize operations.

British Petroleum Company, p.l.c.

The British Petroleum Company case involves a major strategy decision concerning the future direction of the company in a situation where financial considerations were of vital importance. The initial focus of the case on a possible BP move to acquire the minority shareholding interests in Sohio invites discussion on a broad range of possible moves and investments under consideration by Sir Peter Walters and BP senior management.

To provide some insight into BP's personality, the case presents in some detail a history of its activities over the years. Analysis of the data shows BP as a company with major financial constraints as it attempts to chart a future course.

Cray Research, Inc.

The Cray Research case focuses on the problems facing corporate-level general managers in a rapidly growing high-technology company. It presents a rich mix of strategic, organizational, and administrative issues that can be analyzed from the perspective of the company's CEO, John Rollwagen.

The strategic issues center around Cray's choice between continuing to focus on state-of-the-art supercomputers for sophisticated government and university users (Cray's "classic customers") versus increasing emphasis on industrial markets with their larger sales potential. The organizational issues include the difficulties associated with preserving the entrepreneurial spirit and small-company atmosphere, which in Rollwagen's judgment contributed so vitally to the company's successful growth, in an ever larger and increasingly complex organizational entity.

The growing relative importance of software and marketing also poses problems for Rollwagen as he tries to increase the prominence of these functions without antagonizing the vitally important reigning stars, the supercomputer design engineers. Getting Cray's management to decide these issues and to implement the strategic and organizational changes needed to carry Cray Research forward presents a severe test to Rollwagen's administrative skills.

DAAG Europe

This classic case goes directly to the heart of managing change in a large multinational organization. The head of DAAG Europe is somewhere midstream in his unpopular effort to standardize elevator construction as a means of entering the large market for low-rise buildings. The company's traditional business has been in supplying high-performance elevators for high-rise buildings. What further complicates the situation is that the principal advocate for change is a middle-level general manager, newly placed in charge of a restructured European organization, and located 4,000 miles from an international headquarters staff that is becoming increasingly uncomfortable with the poor financial results of a questionable new strategy. The case allows a broad consideration of headquarters-subsidiary or corporate-divisional relationships under stress. The process of negotiating with multiple constituencies having conflicting interests, so important to middle-level general managers, can also be highlighted in the discussion.

Daewoo Group

The Daewoo Group is one of several remarkable Korean firms that have experienced explosive growth, coming from nowhere in 1967 to emerge as a giant trading and manufacturing business empire. The case invites discussion about how this company was able to accomplish so much so quickly, about the problems and opportunities it faced in 1984, and about the actions management should take. Government-business relations, the limits and allocation of resources, corporate strategy, the role of Korean firms with respect to Japanese and Western businesses, and the leadership qualities of Chairman Kim Woo-Choong are salient issues for consideration. An invitation to purchase a government-owned large-scale integrated-circuit manufacturing plant serves to focus attention on the company's strategic direction as a unifying theme for the discussion.

General Electric's Strategic Planning: 1981

General Electric is widely acknowledged to be a world leader in strategic planning. The case, in describing the origins of some of today's most commonly employed planning concepts—such as the strategic business unit and the port-folio investment grid—invites discussion about the function of these particular planning constructs and what top management must do to operationalize them. Tracking Reg Jones's activities during the 1970s gives students an opportunity to assess the job of the chief executive in a large diversified company. The decision to have Jack Welch succeed Jones as CEO enables them to reconsider the role of planning in GE for the 1980s and to examine how a new chief executive following in the footsteps of the *Fortune* 500's "CEO of the Year" award winner for 1981, should take charge of a successful company.

General Electric: 1984

The General Electric: 1984 case chronicles events at GE from the time Jack Welch became CEO in April 1981 until the end of 1984. At the broadest level, the objective of the case is to facilitate an evaluation of Welch's performance as CEO. If the case is used in conjunction with General Electric's Strategic Planning: 1981, comparisons can be made between Jack Welch's leadership and accomplishments and those of Reginald Jones. In addition, the evolutionary nature of change at General Electric can be analyzed. The case also raises issues dealing with entrepreneurship in large companies, the appropriate role of planners vis-à-vis general managers in the planning process, and the impact of financial systems on managerial behavior.

Gold Star Co., Ltd.

Gold Star, the largest and most profitable firm in the Korean electronics indus-try, was a part of the giant Lucky-Goldstar group. The case issues are well summarized in its opening paragraph:

> On April 6, 1984, Mr. Chung Jang-Ho, the recently appointed executive managing director for exports for Gold Star, was informed of the U.S. Inter-national Trade Commission's determination that an "industry in the United States is materially injured by reason of imports of color television receivers from the Republic of Korea which are sold at less than fair value." The resulting antidumping penalty added another obstacle to an already difficult course for establishing Gold Star as a major premium brand name in the U.S. for home electronics products. In a climate of growing protectionism in Europe and the U.S., Mr. Chung had to resolve the somewhat conflicting pressures from two even more pressing developments. One was an appar-ent effort by U.S. and Japanese electronics firms to dislodge Gold Star from its U.S. beachhead. The other, which had direct repercussions on export strategy, was a major challenge in Korea to Gold Star's domestic leadership position in home electronics products.

The situation can be analyzed from the perspectives of the U.S. general manager, the executive managing director for exports in Korea, and the Gold

Star general manager—thereby permitting consideration of subsidiary-parent relationships and the special problems of a middle-level country manager.

Gurney Seed & Nursery Corp.

Gurney is a venerable mid-Western seed catalog and mail-order firm with sales of $35 million. The case examines a new management team's actions and plans shortly after its purchase of the troubled company through a leveraged buy out. Improving operations and setting a new strategic course for the company are vital issues for consideration. The company's cash flow is of particular importance because of the severe seasonal swings and the large bank loans outstanding.

Johnson & Johnson (A)

Johnson & Johnson is a successful company. Its chief executive officer, James Burke, credits the corporate culture for this success. The two J&J cases are designed to examine the power and limitations of a strong corporate belief system and how such a culture might be managed.

The thrust of the first case is to understand how a corporate culture is implanted and managed and how it can serve as a powerful motivational force in guiding and inspiring people. The second case introduces the dysfunctional consequences of a prized belief system—J&J's long delay in responding to a major competitive threat and the difficulty it has had in implementing a response—and focuses on the potential Achilles heel of a strong corporate culture: its power to limit organizational flexibility. When used in sequence, the apparent contradiction between the lessons associated with each case provides a powerful learning experience.

The principal topics of the (A) case include:

- the importance of a corporate culture or belief system in shaping and directing a firm;
- how culture works in J&J: the interplay between beliefs and management process;
- the dynamics by which a strong culture develops in a company: the role of executive leadership, symbolic actions, and external stimuli (e.g., Tylenol) in institutionalizing values.

Johnson & Johnson (B): Hospital Services

This case builds directly on the issues raised in the Johnson & Johnson (A) case, relating culture and management process. The source of the hospital-services problem has to do with the incompatibility of the environmental requirements for strategy and the cultural constraints on organization. The case describes the internal resistance to the proposed changes and top management's efforts to resolve the contradictory requirements of strategy and culture. A major case issue concerns the challenges facing a middle-level general manager who has been given responsibility for operationalizing the forced solution.

Monsanto Company: The Queeny Division

The Monsanto Company: The Queeny Division case focuses on the administrative actions of a general manager, Chris Hubbard, as he attempts to implement strategic changes for his division through a newly imposed corporate administrative system. The problem he faced was to determine the activities supporting the division's strategy and to develop a budget accordingly. His difficulty was increased by his and his colleagues' lack of familiarity with the new priority resource budgeting (PRB) system, a variation of zero-based budgeting.

National Medical Enterprises

Only fifteen years after its founding, NME, one of the several for-profit hospital-management companies that benefited from Medicare funding, reported 1984 sales in excess of $2.5 billion. The case examines management's attempts to cope with this rapid growth and to deal with the pressures from increased competition and the severe tightening of government payments. The situations for two newly formed divisions are described to allow for an in-depth consideration of the problems facing divisional general managers as they deal in a large corporation with the complex interactions among related businesses.

Nike in China

From its inception, off-shore sourcing has been central to Nike's strategy for supplying high-quality running and sports shoes. When faced with a rapid growth in demand and increasing costs in its established source countries, Nike decided to enter China and develop a major low-cost source of shoes for world export. The case describes this experience from Nike's perspective and allows the class to evaluate the company's entry strategy and to recommend a course of action.

Nike in China: 1985

This case continues the Nike-in-China account, covering an additional year's experience. This time we also see the Nike experience through the eyes of the Chinese managers and government bureaucrats.

This case ends on a note of urgency for the young general manager in charge of the China venture, as operating problems and reduced world demand combine to produce a net annual loss of close to $1 million for his operation. Nike Corporation's first quarterly losses in November 1984 and February 1985 result in increased pressures at headquarters to curtail the company's activities in China.

Richardson Hindustan Limited

The Richardson Hindustan Limited case deals with the job of a "country manager"—a general manager in charge of a foreign operation. It was written to highlight the problems in serving multiple constituencies with different and often opposing interests. This typical middle-management issue is complicated by distance (about 10,000 miles between Bombay, India, and Wilton, Connecticut), a difference in cultures, the significance of government-business relationships and, in this instance, outside ownership. Two specific projects call for decisions that help to sharpen the different perspectives.

American Can Company, 1984

American Can is attempting one of the most ambitious asset redeployments in the history of U.S. business. [In April 1981], recognizing that the company was engaged in two capital-intensive businesses—cans and paper products—with slim profit margins and low growth potential, American Can's board approved Mr. Woodside's plan to abandon the paper business, which provided about a quarter of the company's sales, and plunge into the financial-services market.

Wall Street Journal, October 10, 1983

With each passing quarter, American Can Co.'s name becomes more glaringly anachronistic. Its impending annual report is expected to show that production of cans contributed only about one-fourth of 1983 earnings, with recently acquired financial services and specialty retailing operations accounting for the rest. Armed with a cash hoard that could soon top $600 million, American Can is positioning itself to make another big acquisition or two—continuing its three-year-old campaign to restructure itself.

"We're only a little over halfway there," says William S. Woodside, chairman and chief executive of American Can, which has already invested at least $750 million in acquisitions, mainly of insurance companies. . . . Woodside discloses that AmCan is now screening a dozen more acquisition candidates in financial services and an additional ten in specialty retailing: "We are trying to speed up the process of acquisitions."

Business Week, February 27, 1984

If nothing else, William Woodside had managed to improve American Can's press image. One had only to compare the above remarks with those in a *Forbes* article of March 1, 1982, featuring American Can with the scathing title, "A company with two left feet"; a lead sentence, "Some companies, like some people, just can't seem to do anything right"; and the conclusion that "CanCo investors want out. They have seen it fall on its face too often, and few seem inclined to wait around to see whether miracle man Gerry Tsai and financial services will finally get CanCo moving again."

By 1984 most observers would have readily conceded that American Can had done much more than merely improve its image. Substantial assets had been redeployed from businesses that held little promise for the company—

either because they were in decline or because they required investments in fixed assets the company could no longer afford—to businesses with more favorable characteristics. Moreover, management had articulated a strategy for growth in financial services, specialty retailing, and packaging that gave purpose to the company's many acquisitions and divestitures.

Nonetheless, the outcome of American Can's turnaround was still a matter of debate. Some people questioned, for example, whether the company could successfully enter financial services. Did the individual acquisitions make sense as a whole? Could American Can run them successfully? The preliminary returns, as reported in *Business Week*, appeared cautiously favorable: "Most analysts who follow the company agree that so far AmCan's restructuring has met the most basic criterion of success: The companies it has bought are far more profitable than the ones it sold."

In Woodside's view, American Can had clearly turned the corner and was on its way. His message to the shareholders in the 1983 annual report revealed his optimism:

> The redirection of your company began to pay off with significantly improved performance during 1983. We dramatically improved our portfolio of businesses, earnings recovered to $3.75 per share, we strengthened our overall financial position and our common stock price rose more than 50 percent. . . . We are confident that our 1983 accomplishments are just the beginning of American Can's turnaround story.

But even those who were pleased about the company's moves recognized that major issues loomed ahead: What should be the balance of investment for future growth between financial services and specialty retailing? Should the company continue acquiring financial service businesses? If so, what kind? Should it take some time to consolidate its present portfolio? Who should succeed Woodside when he retired in 1987?

These were some of the broad issues facing management and the watchful investment community in 1984 as American Can continued to make headlines in its efforts to transform itself from its erstwhile position as America's number-one can maker.

American Can

In the early years of metal can production, two large firms—American Can and Continental Can—dominated the market. Competition was scarce in such a capital- and labor-intensive business. By offering volume discounts, the two giants of the industry held a hammer lock on the large accounts for food and beverage packaging.

Can manufacturers prospered until a 1950 federal antitrust ruling eliminated the discount system. The new pricing structure not only enabled secondary competitors, such as Crown Cork and Seal and National Can, to gain market share, it also encouraged many large customers to start making their own cans. As competitive pressures pushed prices down, the can manufacturers also had to cope with mounting materials and labor costs as steel suppliers and the United Steelworkers took advantage of Korean War-related shortages. At the same time, new materials were beginning to make inroads. Between 1950 and 1960 packagers of motor oil and citrus concentrates switched their requirements of 4 billion cans per year from steel ("tin") cans to aluminum and then to fiber-foil containers. For the traditional can industry, the 1950s was a period of narrowing margins and falling profits.

The response of American and Continental, the only companies in the industry with substantial financial reserves, was to diversify. While Continental invested in plastics, insurance, and energy exploration. American diversified into chemicals (M&T Chemicals, Inc.) and paper products. (Dixie-Northern and Marathon, producers of paper cups, tissues, towels, and folding cartons).

In an April 1961 *Fortune* article, Lucias Clay, then president of Continental Can, stated, "The tin can is a fundamental part of the U.S. economy and will never grow less than the economy grows." In the same article, another industry statesman concluded, "The one certainty in the business is that the can will be around for as long as people like food and hate work." Such statements rang hollow as margins continued to be squeezed under the dual onslaught of new packaging materials and self-manufacturing. There were, to be sure, encouraging signs as well. Consumption of beer and soft drinks began to increase rapidly during the 1960s, and other signs pointed to an industry recovery in the 1970s.

American Can decided to move on two fronts. Diversification continued as the company invested in timberlands and sawmills for its paper-products business, in the promising resource recovery and recycling field, and in several shortlived ventures involving glass and plastic containers and printing. At the same time, it (along with others in the industry) invested heavily in can plant modernization to be in position for the "fat" 1970s.

The 1970s came, but prosperity for the canning industry did not. The tepid 5% growth of the 1960s dwindled to a meager 3%. Moreover, the new and lighter two-piece can was rapidly displacing the traditional three-piece can in the growing beverage sector. American Can, among others, was saddled with a great deal of excess, obsolete, three-piece can manufacturing capacity.

Cutting Back Can Manufacturing

In 1972 management in American Can dropped the second shoe: The company would not only seek growth in other businesses, it would scale back its metal-can operations. This decision launched an effort that would result by 1980 in the closing of fifty plants and a reduction of the metal-can work force from 18,000 to fewer than 10,000. The company was committed to remaining an active competitor in the can business, however, partly because of the significant pension and health-care costs employee contracts would trigger if it exited. Thus, American Can continued to invest to improve productivity and product quality.

To remain competitive in the beverage industry the company invested in facilities to manufacture the new two-piece can. Eight plants were built by 1980 at a cost of $200 million. This new beverage can capacity was about half of the old three-piece capacity, so that American Can deliberately lowered its market share from 20 percent to 10 percent. This was considered to be the minimum required to meet the needs of major customers.

In its food-can business, the company embarked on a costly recapitalization program to convert its three-piece soldered technology to newer, leadfree types of food cans. The conversion program cost American Can more than $100 million and was deemed necessary to remain competitive in an industry with very poor growth prospects. The company also expanded its position in nonmetal packaging, particularly in high-technology plastics, where it saw profitable growth opportunities.

Specialty Retailing

With heavy stakes in can and paper manufacturing, management set out to invest in businesses requiring relatively little fixed capital. In time, influenced by the company's success in the consumer towel and tissue business, the search led to consumer distribution businesses. The reasoning was straightforward: With increasing diversity of consumer needs and rapid improvements in information technology, there had to be better ways of transferring merchandise from producer to consumer than the archaic system of wholesalers, retailers, and other middlemen. American Can entered this field in 1977 with the purchase of Pickwick, the world's largest distributor of music records, for $103 million. This move was followed in 1978 by the acquisition of Sam Goody, a chain of record stores, for $5.3 million. (Both companies performed well until the end of 1979, when the record industry went into a slump, and profits dropped off sharply.)

In line with its diversification strategy, American Can plunged ahead in 1978 with a major acquisition of Fingerhut for $137 million. Fingerhut, one of the largest U.S. direct-mail marketers, concentrated on blue-collar consumers. The firm's marketing strategy stressed building its list of active mail-order purchasers, targeting its various offers and catalogues to the most responsive segments of its customer list, and extending credit as a principal marketing tool. Fingerhut did no manufacturing, so as to retain maximum flexibility in its product offerings.

The targeting of product offerings was the most unusual element of Fingerhut's marketing strategy. It began with a customer's first order, which was shipped with an accompanying questionnaire seeking information about his or her family and lifestyle. Customer responses and a record of purchases enabled Fingerhut to develop a profile of each customer. The more products purchased, the more elaborate the profile. This information was then used to select product offerings for each individual customer. As an example of the individual attention Fingerhut provided, parents received advertisements for suitable gifts several weeks before a child's birthday.

A Change in Leadership

In 1980 Woodside assumed the chairmanship of American Can. One of his first actions was to organize some of his top people into a so-called strategic-analysis committee responsible for developing recommendations on corporate direction and asset redeployment.

This committee soon came to several conclusions. First, the large fixed-asset investments required for paper and can manufacturing, coupled with volatile inflation and high interest rates, limited American Can's growth. Second, distribution and specialty retailing was an attractive field for the future, as demonstrated by Fingerhut's rapid and profitable growth. Third, the generally high multiples commanded by good distribution and specialty retailing firms limited American Can's opportunities for acquisitions in this field as long as its own share price was depressed. On the basis of these findings, the committee recommended a further withdrawal from the capital-intensive industries and identification of another business area for growth to complement American Can's commitment to specialty retailing.

The committee went on to identify criteria for the kind of business American Can should select. In a presentation two years later to the board, it reported that "Best businesses for the 1980s will have: strong competitive positions; focused or specialized market positions; positions where distribution is critical; low fixed-capital intensity; and liquid assets." The report went on to explain the reasoning behind the selection of these criteria:

> To have a strong competitive position, a business must have identifiable advantages over its competition. We believe certain industries offer more opportunities to develop these advantages than others. These "attractive" industries offer opportunities to find niches and thereby develop specialized market positions. Usually niche opportunities are plentiful in industries which have fragmented customers, suppliers, and competitors.
>
> Businesses where distribution is critical and where value is added at the distribution level should also perform well through the 1980s. Use of information-based marketing and target marketing provide comparative advantages to companies skilled in their use. They also provide a means for better satisfying the increasing diversity of consumer needs.

The data in Table A on American Can's business portfolio were also presented to accentuate the severity of the company's problems as of 1979. The data show the extent to which American Can conformed to the criteria for growth and profitability in the 1980s.

With board approval, management began to carry out the committee's recommendations. The search for a new growth area initially identified eleven areas for further analysis. At the same time, American continued in 1981 to expand its retailing operations by acquiring Figi's, a catalogue retailer of food, for $23.5 million. It also invested in a computerized home-banking service,

Table A   American Can's business portfolio, 1979.

Relative Attractiveness of Business	Distribution of Assets	Distribution of Net Income
High	10%	7%
Medium	27%	12%
Low	63%	81%

HomServ, and developed a home-shopping service, ViewMart. These were later discontinued on the grounds that computerized shopping would require too much capital and would involve excessive technological risk, given its early stage of development.

By 1981 financial services began to emerge as the most attractive area for American Can's growth drive. This was a fragmented business with many marketing niche opportunities. It was a business in which distribution and information-based marketing (some of AmCan's strengths) were critical. And it was a business in a state of upheaval, with many opportunities for entry.

According to plan, the resources for growth would come from the reallocation of assets tied up in American Can's capital-intensive businesses: metal cans and paper products. The Dixie-Northern paper-based operations supplied 25 percent of the company's revenues and were far more profitable than the metal-can business. They were also more salable and would bring in the money needed. On March 31, 1981, the American Can board of directors approved a plan to sell the paper business as a whole, rather than piecemeal, to preserve as many jobs as possible. On July 2, 1982, the assets of Dixie-Northern—most of the U.S. pulp mills, timberland cutting rights, and paper converting plants— were sold to James River Corporation for $334 million in cash and $89 million in James River preferred and common stock. By 1984 the market value of American Can's James River stock was close to $150 million.

In the meantime, American Can had begun exploratory acquisition discussions with several financial services companies.

Enter Gerald Tsai, Jr.

Soon after American Can announced the proposed sale of its paper business, Woodside received a letter from Gerald Tsai, Jr., owner of Associated Madison Companies, Inc., a life insurance holding company, congratulating him on the move and inquiring about the possibility of a joint venture that would use Fingerhut's mailing system to sell insurance. Tsai, born in Shanghai, had acquired a national reputation in the early 1960s with the Fidelity mutual fund group as an astute stock-picker and a master of market timing and then as founder of the ill-fated Manhattan Fund. The letter led to discussions off and on for almost a year.

As Woodside and Tsai became better acquainted, they developed the idea

Table B Financial Services acquisitions and investments.

Date	Company	Amount Invested ($ millions)
April 1982	Associated Madison Companies, Inc., including: National Benefit Life (life, health, and disability insurance) Triad Life (mortgage protection life insurance) Mass Marketing Systems International	$127
Sept. 1982	Transport Life Insurance Company (credit plus other types of insurance)	$152
Jan. 1983	PennCorp Financial, Inc. (replacement term insurance, plus other types)	$295
Sept. 1983	American Capital Corporation (mutual fund manager and investment advisor)	$38
Oct. 1983	Voyager Group, Inc. (credit insurance)	$45
Jan. 1984	G. Tsai & Company (institutional brokerage)	$3.75
Feb. 1984	Ticor (title and mortgage insurance)	$50

of using Tsai's expertise in the insurance business and his company, Associated Madison, as a possible vehicle for American Can's entry into financial services. In April 1982, a deal was struck in which American Can acquired Madison for $127 million in stock and cash and Tsai, who became American Can's largest individual shareholder as a result, was named executive vice-president in charge of the financial services sector.

After acquiring Associated Madison, American Can embarked on an acquisition strategy to develop its financial services business. By early 1984, Associated Madison had acquired three additional insurance firms, a large money management company, and an institutional brokerage firm. (See Table B for a list of the acquisitions.) In addition, the firm invested $50 million in a leveraged buyout for Ticor, the largest title insurance company and one of the largest mortgage insurance companies in the United States. As part of this arrangement, Associated Madison received warrants to obtain two-thirds of the common stock and 80 percent of the votes for $2 million, plus an option to acquire the rest of Ticor's stock at a future date.

In a speech to analysts, Tsai explained the thinking behind these moves:

> Our *strategy* in moving into the financial services industry was to exploit certain selected segments of the market, *to develop specialty niches*. The basic strategy of our financial services sector *is not to compete with the likes of Sears or Merrill Lynch*. We have specific groups of customers and their particular financial needs in mind in designing products or organizing our distribution network. . . . We sell products that fill *specific needs of readily definable groups*.[1]

1. G. Tsai, Jr., "American Can's Strategy for Competing in the Evolving Financial Services Industry," presented to the Financial Analysts' Federal Atlanta Conference, February 24, 1984.

The acquisitions provided numerous examples of this niche strategy. National Benefit Life (acquired with Associated Madison) sold term insurance to the upscale market for estate-building purposes. Penncorp Financial also sold term insurance, but it focused on upper-middle-income individuals. Its insurance was sold under a long-term contract by the A. L. Williams Agency, a firm of some 60,000 part-time agents. A second focus at Penncorp was the sale of accident and health insurance to small-town business owners and managers through a captive sales force of 3,500.

American Can officials were also strong proponents of low-cost mass marketing and third-party endorsed sales. (These sales occurred, for example, when a bank sold credit life insurance as part of an automobile loan.) Mass Marketing Systems International was used to market insurance products to Master Card and Visa customers of major banks. Several of the acquired companies were active in third-party endorsed sales:

- Transport Life had marketing relationships with banks, farm credit bureaus, and the motor carrier industry.
- Triad Life sold mortgage-redemption insurance through 800 cooperating savings and loan institutions.
- Voyager used auto dealers, small loan companies, and banks as outlets for its credit and property life insurance.

Although there had not been much time to develop synergies among the various subsidiaries, officials at American Can believed such benefits could be important. As one opportunity, Tsai noted the potential for a sizable influx of mutual fund business through the sales efforts of the A. L. Williams agents who were selling term insurance for Penncorp. Their slogan was, "Buy term and invest the difference."

Reorganization

On June 28, 1983, Chairman Woodside announced the creation of a three-member office of the chairman to replace the eight-member operating committee. The reason for this executive restructuring was to "develop a very flexible organization where the decisions are made pretty far down in the corporation." The members of the office of the chairman included Woodside, Gerry Tsai (now vice-chairman), and President Frank Connor, a twenty-seven-year American Can veteran experienced in a number of its businesses. (Chief Financial Officer Ken Yarnell was added in February, 1984.

At the same time, Woodside created four new corporate committees. The executive committee, chaired by Woodside, was given responsibility for developing corporate strategy and the overall direction of the company. The acquisition/divestment committee, chaired by Connor, was responsible "for determining that the corporation and its units were effectively pursuing acquisition/divestment programs consistent with strategic priorities and financial capabilities." The investment committee, chaired by Tsai, was "responsible

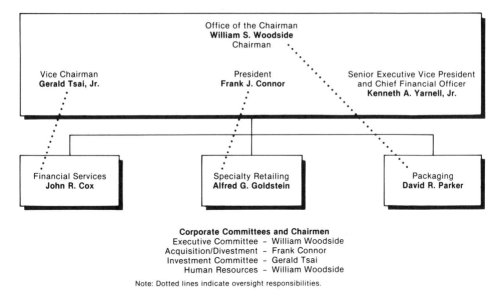

Corporate Committees and Chairmen
Executive Committee – William Woodside
Acquisition/Divestment – Frank Connor
Investment Committee – Gerald Tsai
Human Resources – William Woodside

Note: Dotted lines indicate oversight responsibilities.

Figure A Organization chart, 1984.

for all business investments above a certain dollar value, for fixed assets, working capital and cash infusions." The human resources committee, chaired by Woodside, was "responsible for developing human resource policies and programs needed to attain strategic business objectives."

In November 1983, *Inside Management,* an American Can house publication, reported Chairman Woodside's view of how the decentralization would work:

> We're not going to be a holding company. I see a holding company as exerting financial and only financial controls. Perhaps our approach can best be described as a management company, one that provides a correct balance of decentralization of operations with corporate policy and oversight responsibility.
>
> Generally speaking, the sector executives are being held accountable for profitability of their sector. They have to have a strong feel for their business and how they're going to run things. They will now have total control of costs, and as a result, they have to look quite differently at the decision-making process.
>
> Each sector executive will establish a sector board that will function as an internal board of directors. The sector board will consist of officers of the business units in the sector as well as a representative from the other sectors to allow cross-fertilization. A member of the office of the chairman will also be on each board so that one of us is involved in every key issue in the corporation.

Connor was to have oversight responsibility for the specialty retailing sector, Tsai for the financial services sector, and Woodside for the packaging sector. (See Figure A for a chart of the executive organization.)

Table C Distribution of net assets ($ billions).

Growth/Profit	1979		1983		1988 (projected)	
High	$0.17	10%	$0.68	37%	$1.65	54%
Medium	0.45	27%	0.59	32%	0.91	30%
Low	1.05	63%	0.57	31%	0.52	17%
Total	$1.67	100%	$1.85	100%	$3.05	100%

The Situation in Early 1984

As of early 1984, American Can could boast of considerable progress in its efforts to redeploy assets from its earlier investments in capital-intensive slow-growth businesses. As shown in Table C, the assets deployed in high-growth businesses increased fourfold from 1979 to 1983.

As indicated by the projection for 1988, the asset turnaround was still very much under way. The real measure of success, of course, would not be asset redeployment, but profitability. Management had set as corporate objectives for 1988 earnings per share to exceed $10 and ROE to exceed 15 percent.

To fuel the growth of high-profit businesses, management planned to invest another $500 million over the next two years, with $400 million going for acquisitions and $100 million for internal development. Potentially these funds could come from the sale of the following properties: over half a million acres of timberlands in the Southeast and Great Lakes regions, appraised at approximately $200 million; the attractive home-office building of 600,000 square feet situated on 186 acres in Greenwich, Connecticut, being offered for $195 million; and its Canadian and U.K. packaging operations for approximately $200 million. Whether the company could dispose of these assets at favorable prices would depend on whether it could find interested buyers. In this connection, the proposed sale of the Canadian and U.K. packaging operations to First City Financial of Vancouver fell through in April, 1984.

Management had to devise strategies for the three sectors with these corporate objectives and resources in mind. Exhibit 1 provides financial data for each business sector.

Packaging

The packaging sector, with nearly $2 billion in worldwide sales for 1983, had four principal operations: steel food cans; aluminum beverage cans; flexible plastic packaging films; and squeezable plastic tubes and bottles. The packaging sector executive vice-president was David Parker, who had been hired from The Boston Consulting Group in 1976 to direct American Can's strategic planning.

Each of the sector's businesses offered different opportunities and limitations. For example, growing Food and Drug Administration concern with the

Exhibit 1   American Can business sector information, 1981–83 ($ millions).

	1981	1982	1983
Revenues			
Packaging			
Domestic metal cans	$1,286.9	$1,177.1	$1,147.2
Performance plastics	221.0	251.4	317.6
International	571.7	581.3	477.4
Total packaging	$2,079.6	$2,009.8	$1,942.2
Specialty retailing	696.3	753.9	847.8
Other businesses	2,060.5	1,299.7	556.4
Consolidated revenues	$4,836.4	$4,063.4	$3,346.4
Financial services	—	103.8	730.8
Total revenues	$4,836.4	$4,167.2	$4,077.2
Business Operating Income			
Packaging			
Domestic	$ 67.1	$ 20.6	$ 42.0
International	68.6	48.8	30.5
Total packaging	$ 135.7	$ 69.4	$ 72.5
Specialty retailing	5.8	30.1	47.8
Other businesses	81.5	13.9	3.3
Financial services[a]	—	15.3	125.2
Total	$ 223.0	$ 128.7	$ 248.8
Asset Composition			
Packaging			
Domestic	$ 641.7	$ 633.3	$ 636.2
International	334.2	338.6	288.2
Total packaging	$ 975.9	$ 971.9	$ 924.4
Specialty retailing	500.3	465.5	536.4
Financial services	—	332.7	758.9
Other businesses	1,092.2	555.5	317.3
Corporate	267.4	321.6	293.5
Total	$2,835.8	$2,647.3	$2,830.5

Source: Annual report
a. Equity in pretax earnings of financial services subsidiaries.

possibility of lead ingestion from the soldered seam in the traditional three-piece steel food can had led American Can in 1982 to invest in new technology for manufacturing welded and two-piece (seamless) lead-free cans. This investment, which was part of a $350 million five-year capitalization program to lower costs and improve quality, was viewed by management as both defensive and offensive. On the one hand, the change to lead-free cans was necessary to remain in the food-can business. On the other hand, it offered an opportunity to recapture some or much of the self-manufactured business as food companies faced the large conversion costs.

At risk was the possibility that food manufacturers might try to bypass the lead-free can with a self-produced "plastic can." This interest in substitute material was reported in the *Wall Street Journal* on March 28, 1984:

> Campbell has decided to phase out the tin soup can. The famous can, with its red-and-white label and gold medallion, has been a cherished corporate symbol since 1897. The company's annual canned-soup sales top two billion units, and Campbell is the nation's third-largest can manufacturer, behind American Can Co. and Continental Group.
>
> Other soup companies say they are experimenting with can alternatives. But Campbell's testing is widely considered the most advanced. And the stakes are particularly high for Campbell. Just revamping production facilities could cost $100 million or more.
>
> The company expects to introduce new soup packages regionally as early as this fall but the infiltration will be gradual. "The can is going to be around for a long time," says Herbert Baum, vice-president. So far, the company hasn't settled on a specific alternative to the tin can.

Frank Connor believed that American Can had invested more in plastics technology than other packaging companies and was well positioned to serve this demand should it materialize. The company considered itself the leader in high-barrier multilayered packaging produced either by laminating several materials together, such as plastics, paper, and foil, or by coextruding plastics with different properties as one substance.

The pride of the packaging sector was the tube and bottle division. The division's plastic laminate tube, Glaminate®, first introduced commercially in the late 1960s, held nearly 100 percent of the U.S. dentifrice market. In 1983, the division introduced the plastic Gamma® bottle for oxygen-sensitive foods that previously could be packaged only in glass or metal containers. Named "package of the year" by the Packaging Institute of America, the squeezable Gamma® bottle was being phased in by Heinz for its ketchup and by Lipton for its Wishbone brand barbecue sauce.

Specialty Retailing

The specialty retailing sector, with 1983 sales of nearly $850 million, had two principal operations: catalogue sales through Fingerhut, Figi's, and Michigan Bulb (a catalogue distributor of garden and nursery products acquired on January 31, 1984, for $22 million in cash and notes); and retailing through Musicland, the world's largest retailer of prerecorded music products, with over 410 specialty stores. The sector executive vice president was Alfred Goldstein, who had worked twenty-three years for Sears, Roebuck & Co. in consumer retailing before joining American Can in 1979 as senior vice president, consumer business.

Exhibit 2 Selected data for Fingerhut Companies, 1979–83 ($ millions, except per share data).

	Fiscal Years Ending Late December				
	1979	*1980*	*1981*	*1982*	*1983*
Income Statement Data					
Revenues	$242.6	$286.5	$363.9	$417.5	$513.5
Net income	11.6	11.9	16.2	22.6	31.8
Pro forma adjustments					
Michigan Bulb net income					1.3
Interest expense (after tax)					(4.7)
Net income					$ 28.4
Earnings per share					$ 1.28
Balance Sheet Data					
Actual					
Working capital	$ 80.3	$ 95.2	$101.6	$128.5	$161.5
Total assets	214.7	233.5	291.2	299.2	351.1
Long-term debt	2.1	1.9	10.0	9.7	5.4
Shareholders' equity	151.8	163.7	180.0	189.2	221.0
After pro forma adjustments					
Working capital					$163.2
Total assets					383.3
Long-term debt					95.5
Shareholders' equity					154.0

Source: Fingerhut Companies, Inc., Preliminary Prospectus, February 1, 1984.

Note: The pro forma adjustments reflected the anticipated sale of 3,700,000 shares of Fingerhut stock to the public at a price of $22.00 per share ($20.54 net). In addition, they incorporated the following activities that took place in January 1984:
1. Borrowing of $143 million to finance a dividend payment of that amount to American Can.
2. Borrowing of $22 million to acquire Michigan Bulb.
3. Acquisition of Michigan Bulb.
The adjustments assumed that the $76 million in stock proceeds were used to reduce the above debt.

On February 1, 1984, Fingerhut Companies, Inc., issued a preliminary prospectus announcing an initial public offering of 20 percent of the company's shares. As shown in Exhibit 2, sales of $512 million and earnings of $31.8 million were reported in 1983, up from sales of $287 million and earnings of $11.9 million in 1980. (Pro forma 1983 sales were 87 percent from Fingerhut, 7 percent from Figi's and 6 percent from Michigan Bulb, using the latter's full-year revenue figure.)

The Fingerhut public offering served several purposes. Possibly the most important was to provide the specialty retailing sector with its own vehicle for making acquisitions. As explained in the prospectus, "establishing a public market for the [Fingerhut] common stock could enable it to issue equity securities in connection with possible future acquisitions." Fingerhut shares were expected to command a higher multiple than those of the parent company, making them more powerful for acquisition purposes. The prospectus also mentioned the possible positive effect the Fingerhut valuation would have on the price of American Can's shares in recognition of its 80 percent ownership of this valuable property. In addition, with a public market valuation, Fingerhut would be able to offer management incentives, including stock options, directly related to the company's performance.

Financial Services

The financial services sector accounted for $731 million in revenue and $125 million in pretax earnings in 1983. Net after-tax earnings were approximately $85 million, which provided a 12 percent average return on average capital employed. The face amount of new insurance sold in 1983 was $41 billion, up 65 percent from 1982. This amount placed American Can among the top ten insurance companies. Gerry Tsai described the businesses in the financial services sector as of February 1984:

> Today, Associated Madison owns sixteen insurance companies, the American Capital Corporation, a mutual fund management firm in Houston with $5 billion in assets under management, and a major investment with ultimate ownership in Ticor of Los Angeles. Ticor represents the nation's largest commercial and residential title insurance operation and probably the second-largest residential mortgage insurance company. American Can also owns a securities brokerage firm.

Tsai went on to point to the sector's future direction:

> As to the future direction of American Can Company, we intend to aggressively expand our financial services sector both by internal growth and by selective acquisitions.
> American Can has publicly stated its commitment to the services business and particularly to the financial services area of the economy. AC intends to invest up to $1 billion in the financial services business. To date AC has already committed over $750 million to the sector.
> The reason for our commitment is clear: the financial services business has real opportunity. We view the industry as fragmented and trending toward deregulation. . . .
> Much of our future sales growth will occur from two sources: first, cross-marketing or so-called add-on sales, such as selected insurance coverages being marketed to eighteen million customer names through our Fingerhut subsidiary, the largest direct mail merchandising company in the United States; second, through our growing staff of sales representatives and marketing outlets.

Some managers wondered about American Can's ability to continue an aggressive acquisition program and at the same time build competitive advantage by developing marketing synergies among the financial services subsidiaries

Exhibit 3 Selected financial data for American Can, 1979–83 ($ millions, except per share data).

	1979	*1980*	*1981*	*1982*	*1983*
Working capital	$ 639.1	$ 660.7	$ 634.3	$ 326.5	$ 282.8
Current assets to current liabilities	1.8	1.8	1.8	1.4	1.4
Net property, plant and equipment	$1,063.7	$1,177.1	$1,167.1	$ 879.6	$ 784.6
Total assets	2,682.4	2,822.0	2,835.8	2,647.3	2,830.5
Long-term debt	493.4	573.8	562.6	622.1	700.4
Preferred stock	41.4	28.6	28.6	28.6	201.4
Common shareholders' equity	$1,016.8	$1,048.4	$1,041.7	$ 804.1	$ 914.0
Total debt to total capitalization[a]	34.8%	38.0%	37.6%	46.0%	39.6%
Interest coverage (estimated)	5.3	2.7	2.1	—	2.3
Return on average equity	12.7%	8.0%	7.0%	—	8.7%
Earnings per share (fully diluted)	$ 6.44	$ 4.26	$ 3.77	$ (7.31)	$ 3.60
Dividends per share	2.83	2.90	2.90	2.90	2.90
Average number of common shares	19,321	19,328	19,353	18,700	20,016
Fully diluted shares	19,864	19,864	19,954	18,700	23,002
Common share prices					
High	41⅛	36½	45¼	35¾	49½
Low	33¾	27	28⅜	25¾	30⅛
Average	37⅜	31¾	36¾	30¾	39¾
Price/Earnings Ratio (P/E)	6–5	9–6	12–8	nm[b]	14–9
Average number of employees	55,000	51,000	46,800	36,800	29,800

Source: Annual report and Standard & Poor's NYSE stock reports.

a. Debt and total capitalization include short-term debt and current maturities of long-term debt.

b. Not meaningful.

and between the financial services sector and Fingerhut. As one executive put it, "We will probably have to make a choice between adding more pearls and stringing a necklace."

John Cox might have been one reason that Woodside and Tsai were comfortable moving on both fronts. He had been recruited in September 1983 to head the financial services sector. Before joining American Can, Cox had been executive vice-president of CIGNA Corporation, in charge of all property/casualty group operations and all international life insurance operations. Before that, he had been president and chief operating officer of INA Corporation, a $5 billion company, when it merged with Connecticut General Life Insurance Company to form CIGNA in March 1982.

Exhibit 4   Income statements, 1981–83 ($ millions).

Years ended December 31	1981	1982	1983
Revenues (exclusive of financial services)	$4,836.4	$4,063.4	$3,346.4
Costs and expenses			
Product cost	3,886.8	3,297.1	2,721.0
Administrative and selling	726.6	652.9	501.8
	$4,613.4	$3,950.0	$3,222.8
Equity in pretax earnings of financial services			
subsidiaries	—	15.3	125.2
Business operating income	$ 223.0	$ 128.7	$ 248.8
Other income and deductions			
Interest expense and other, net	(41.5)	(51.7)	(59.2)
Corporate expenses	(55.2)	(56.9)	(59.9)
	$ 126.3	$ 20.1	$ 129.7
Unusual items			
Provision for Latin American investments			(24.0)
Gains on James River common stock issuances			10.4
Provision for business restructure	(29.1)	(247.9)	
Gain on sale of Dixie-Northern operations		51.6	
Other	10.1	(5.5)	9.4
	$ (19.0)	$ (201.8)	$ (4.2)
Income (loss) before income taxes and			
extraordinary gain	107.3	(181.7)	125.5
Provision (benefit) for income taxes	30.6	(48.8)	31.0
Income (loss) before extraordinary gain	$ 76.7	$ (132.9)	$ 94.5
Extraordinary gain			5.6
Net income (loss)	$ 76.7	$ (132.9)	$ 100.1
Dividends on preferred stock	3.7	3.7	25.0
Income (loss) applicable to common stock	73.0	136.6	75.1

Source: Annual report

Cash Flow and Leadership

"It's amazing that we have done so much so quickly without a major hitch or setback," reflected Ken Yarnell, chief financial officer, "but the ultimate success of American Can's tranformation is really dependent on what we do from here on." Yarnell saw cash flow as a key problem for the company. Financial services had improved its earnings markedly, but was still a net user of cash, with breakeven prospects at best for its future period of growth. Specialty retailing, in Yarnell's view, had done well just to finance its own rapid growth; it had not generated any excess cash. Only the packaging sector had generated cash, and this sum was modest.

The firm's capital structure was also an important issue. The acquisition

Exhibit 5   Financial position statements, 1982–83 ($ millions).

December 31	*1982*	*1983*
Assets		
Current assets		
Cash and short-term investments	$ 103.7	$ 61.2
Receivables, net	582.9	533.8
Inventories	391.9	327.9
Other	87.3	91.1
Total current assets	$1,165.8	$1,014.0
Investment in and advances to financial services		
subsidiaries	332.7	758.9
Investment in James River Corporation	93.8	106.5
Property, plant and equipment, net	879.6	784.6
Cost of acquired businesses in excess of net assets	56.6	53.4
Other assets	118.8	113.1
	$2,647.3	$2,830.5
Liabilities		
Current liabilities		
Short-term debt and current portion of long-term debt	$ 86.7	$ 31.0
Accounts payable, trade	332.9	302.9
Accrued and other liabilities	344.7	364.5
Reserve for business restructure	75.0	32.8
Total current liabilities	$ 839.3	$ 731.2
Long-term debt	622.1	700.4
Employee benefits related to plant closings	132.7	131.5
Reserve for business restructure, noncurrent	58.5	40.0
Other liabilities	49.6	13.3
Deferred income taxes	112.4	98.7
Redeemable preferred stock	28.6	201.4
Common shareholders' equity		
Common stock (issued: 1983, 22,771,762 shares; 1982,		
20,002,049 shares)	250.0	284.5
Capital in excess of par value	13.0	86.5
Cumulative translation adjustments	(28.1)	(41.2)
Earnings reinvested	618.4	633.4
	$ 853.3	$ 963.2
Treasury stock	(49.2)	(49.2)
	804.1	914.0
	$2,647.3	$2,830.5

Source: Annual report

Exhibit 6 Statement of changes in financial position, 1981–83 ($ millions).

Years ended December 31	*1981*	*1982*	*1983*
Operations			
Income (loss) before extraordinary gain	$ 76.7	$(132.9)	$ 94.5
Charges and credits to income not affecting funds			
Unremitted pretax earnings of financial			
services subsidiaries		(15.3)	(125.2)
Income taxes of financial services subsidiaries		2.2	39.4
Provisions for Latin American investments			24.0
Provisions for business restructure	29.1	247.9	
Gain on sale of Dixie-Northern operations		(51.6)	
Depreciation and cost allocated to cut timber	113.4	107.1	83.3
Other	46.2	(65.3)	(37.9)
	$ 265.4	$ 92.1	$ 78.1
Working capital			
Receivables	(47.3)	(31.8)	(34.9)
Inventories	20.1	63.6	(22.2)
Accounts payable and accrued liabilities	33.5	23.8	42.9
Other	(30.0)	(26.1)	7.4
Additions to property, plant and equipment	(162.3)	(148.8)	(113.5)
Advances from (to) financial services subsidiaries		(43.1)	26.3
Other	1.7	(35.5)	(28.4)
Funds provided (used) by operations	$ 81.1	$(105.8)	$ (44.3)
Financing and investment activities			
Acquisition of financial services subsidiaries		(271.5)	(357.9)
Issuance of redeemable preferred stock			173.0
Business divestments		423.0	45.6
Investment in James River Corporation		(88.8)	(8.0)
Sale of James River Corporation stock			26.7
Issuances of common stock		9.1	95.7
Common and preferred dividends paid	(59.8)	(59.4)	(77.9)
Increase in treasury stock, net		(39.6)	
Debt transactions			
Proceeds from long-term debt	14.6	107.9	122.5
Reductions of long-term debt	(27.1)	(35.2)	(29.0)
Increase (decrease) in short-term debt	(3.6)	.7	5.2
Other	8.5	(9.5)	5.9
Funds provided (used) by financing and			
investment activities	(67.4)	36.7	1.8
Change in cash and short-term investments	$ 13.7	$ (69.1)	$ (42.5)

Source: Annual report

program had required substantial borrowing, so that American Can's debt as a percentage of total capital reached 46 percent at year-end 1982, well above the mid-30 percent range maintained in prior years (see Exhibit 3). A two-million-share equity issue in 1983 reduced debt capitalization to 39.6 percent of total. However, Yarnell and other senior managers believed it was important to continue to work toward a mid-30 percent target and to improve the coverage ratio. (Financial statements are provided in Exhibits 4 to 6.)

One possible solution to the cash-flow problem would be to acquire a cash-generating business. Management's thinking on this issue was still sketchy, but Woodside had begun to discuss the idea of a fourth sector.

Future leadership was also a concern. Woodside's ability to think strategically was generally acknowledged as a key element shaping the company's redirection efforts. No one else in the office of the chairman could claim his breadth of experience with each of the company's major business areas. To prepare for his departure, Woodside had used committee and sector oversight assignments to expose Connor and Tsai to those parts of the corporate operations with which they were less familiar.

In commenting about the future, Woodside said, "I don't want us to be a holding company. I want things to mesh and be cohesive."

Bard MedSystems Division

Intrapreneurial Showcase

At an annual meeting of C.R. Bard's top management in May 1986, Robert McCaffrey, chief executive officer, announced a special award to the Med-Systems Division in recognition of its accomplishments. In his remarks, McCaffrey praised the division for the exemplary manner in which it had adhered to and successfully carried out the corporation's basic strategy of "decentralization, concentration, and innovation." The division's return from red ink to black and, more important, its strong prospects for future profitability were offered as evidence of the merits of providing distinctive products to a specific market segment where Bard could develop a competitive advantage.

In deciding to make a special award to this division, McCaffrey had not only wanted to give this struggling unit the recognition it deserved for its impressive accomplishments to date, but also to have it serve as a showcase, setting an example for other young managers to emulate and a standard to achieve. McCaffrey was clearly pleased with MedSystems' accomplishments, but even more delighted with the spirit and ingenuity which had led to these results.

This event came as a sweet moment of vindication for the division, which until recently had been viewed by many as the "corporate garbage dump," and especially for its general manager, Richard Klein, who was to have been fired two years earlier. Klein found the pleasure of this moment of glory somewhat attenuated by the daunting task his division still faced of transforming the recent turnaround they had accomplished into a truly successful Bard business operation.

C.R. Bard was a rapidly growing health care products company with emphasis on cardiovascular, urological, surgical, and general health applications. According to its 1985 annual report, hospitals, physicians and nursing homes purchased approximately 90 percent of its products, most of which were used once and discarded. The company, employing approximately 7,200 people worldwide, reported for 1986 revenues of $548 million and net income of $51.2 million. The appendix describes C.R. Bard. The body of this case focuses on the history and operations of the Bard MedSystems division.

An Inauspicious Start

In September 1978, Klein, then a 34-year-old plant manager in charge of producing plastic catheters and guidewires for Bard's USCI Division, was asked to meet with George Maloney, president of the corporation. At that meeting, Maloney, who saw Klein as "a young, eager-beaver manufacturing engineer", unexpectedly offered him an opportunity to head up the troubled MacBick Division, explaining that new product development was likely to be the unit's key challenge. Klein readily accepted.

While Klein did not hesitate in his decision, there was abundant reason to do so. A forward to the 1977–79 three-year plan (prepared in 1976) had read:

> During the past five years, the MacBick Sales Division has been operated as a separate entity and as a consolidated, integrated part of Medical Products Division. MacBick has not operated as a profitable division of the company during this time period.
>
> MacBick product lines are sold direct to hospitals. They can generally be characterized as being low gross profit, mature, commodity in nature and fragmented as to in-use areas in the hospital. MacBick Sales Division has no strong customer identification.

Klein received other warning evidence as well. As he remembered the occasion, "When I told my friends about the new job, their reaction was 'You've got to be out of your mind. MacBick is Bard's garbage dump. Why would you want to go there?' " Indeed, MacBick had already run through two general managers since it had been spun out from the Medical Products Division only one year earlier to market steel hospital carts, pharmacy cabinetry, sterile packaging, non-woven products (masks, gowns), arterial blood gas kits, and other miscellaneous items.

This diverse line of unassociated products was a "collection of leftovers and discards", according to Dan Doyle, MedSystem's vice president of marketing, who had started as a MacBick sales representative in 1973. He explained:

> MacBick had been acquired by Bard in the late 1960's for its urological products. These were stripped out and joined to the company's core business, leaving the small and shrinking hospital cart business and an odd assortment of other items. Since MacBick was one of the few Bard units with a direct sales force, it became a dumping ground for other divisional losers on the grounds that direct selling might possibly be what was needed to increase sales. What we ended up with was a collection of dated commodity products in small, declining markets.

Klein's reasoning and response to Maloney's offer was characteristic of the man. He described his thinking at the time:

> MacBick really appealed to me because it was in such bad straits. The only direction it could go was up. Moreover, the president of the company asked me to do it. I'm a loyal employee, and when the president asks you to do something, you do it. I didn't even ask him what the new salary

would be. It was only later, when I was to relocate and needed to make out a mortgage application requiring such information, that I asked.

George Maloney described MacBick as an eclectic group of product lines and a good group of people. He said that he would like to see what I could do with them. Based on my earlier problem-solving successes with Raytheon and then with Bard, I considered myself a good technical generalist rather than an engineer. I guess I took on the job with a great deal of self confidence.

See Exhibit 1 for biographical information about Richard Klein.

Klein's self-confidence was soon to be put to the test. MacBick's sales manager had been reassigned to another division the Friday before he was to take over. Klein's recollection of the subsequent events was vivid even eight years later:

I had heard from several people that there was really only one person in Bard who could step in and take over as sales manager, but that he had already declined the job offer from the group vice president responsible for MacBick. I wanted to try again and called my new boss to tell him of my intention. I guess he didn't like the implication that I thought that I could succeed where he had failed. In any case, he blew his stack and bawled me out so loudly that I had to hold the phone a foot away from my ear. Maloney, who just happened to be walking past the group VP's office at that moment, witnessed this event. The next thing I knew, I got a new boss as of the second day in the job. I was to report to Maloney.

The first day was to reveal another surprise. As Klein sorted through the division general manager's in-basket, he uncovered a set of instructions for requesting corporate R&D funds. Intrigued by this unfamiliar item, he soon discovered that every Bard division contributed one percent of its sales each year to an R&D kitty which was then reallocated to divisions, upon request, for specific projects. He also learned that MacBick had never made a request for funds.

Klein's immediate reaction was to try to get some money for the division. He and his top managers spent the next two weeks trying to identify some project for which they could ask money. This effort resulted in a proposal to conduct market research on medical packaging (one of the division's product lines) and an award of $49,000. Klein later observed, "From then on, we had never not asked for money."

One of Klein's first hires during his first week as divisional president was a commercial artist. He explained why he had accorded such high priority to this particular talent:

Some people questioned this hire. They thought it was an odd place for a troubled division to be spending money. My view was that the division desperately needed to sell itself to insiders as well as to outsiders and that professional quality presentations were needed. We really had to make the best of what we had, which wasn't much. When we made presentations to the management committee, we injected humor and cartoons trying to get the people in a good frame of mind. I suppose we were trying to distract

Exhibit 1   Klein's intrapreneurial record.

Richard Klein, born June 10, 1944, the eldest of four children, grew up in Queens, New York. Following studies at Northeastern University, where he received a Bachelor of Science in Industrial Engineering degree in 1967, Klein went to work for Raytheon in Waltham, Massachusetts.

Klein remembered two "intrapreneurial successes" while at Raytheon. The first occurred shortly after he joined the company. At the time, the Raytheon name and other identifying information were epoxy-spray-painted on each electronic module. With a major increase in volume anticipated, Klein was asked to assess the paint booth requirements. His study showed the need to expand from two booths to thirty-two, a number which far exceeded available space.

Klein volunteered to solve the problem. After several months he devised a machine which could stamp the information on modules with fast-drying epoxy paint, something more senior engineers had said could not work. The process was so rapid that one machine would more than equal the capacity of the needed thirty-two paint booths. This accomplishment so impressed management that Klein was selected to participate in a special two-year manufacturing management training program just six months after joining the company.

Several years later, as manager of new business planning, Klein achieved his second enterprising success, creating an entire department which utilized time-sharing computing for sophisticated manufacturing planning and forecasting (years before the availability of minicomputers).

In 1974, faced with a divorce, Klein considered leaving Raytheon to become a consultant specializing in time-sharing computing techniques. Instead, faced with a severe economic downturn resulting from the first oil crisis, he joined C.R. Bard as a materials manager and was assigned to a division suffering from a one million dollar back order and from excessive inventories. In his first month he recognized the cause of the problem to be the lack of a good manufacturing planning system. In ten months, Klein was able to solve the problem by developing special software programs, (the algorithms were still in use in 1987). The back order was subsequently reduced to an acceptable $100,000 level and inventories also reached acceptable levels. This success, in his view, led to his promotion to plant manager in 1976. Two years later, Maloney asked him to head MacBick. By then, Klein had earned an MS in Engineering Management from Northeastern University and an MBA degree from Babson College. He had also remarried and started a family.

them from noticing that we had so little to offer in the way of real business prospects.

In Search of a Mission

Klein quickly assigned top priority to finding products which could provide the division with growth in sales and profits. He described the initial efforts:

> I first concentrated our attention on the products we had in hand to see if there might not be a diamond in the rough among them. I was convinced that we could come up with some winners if we tried hard enough. During the next six months, we must have considered every conceivable odd-ball way to breathe life into our tired product lines.

Klein went on to describe one of the more successful outcomes, a promotional campaign for MacBick's sterile packaging:

> One day between flights while prowling around the airport—I can't ever keep still. I'm the kind of guy who has to read while he eats or be doing something while he waits—anyway, I saw a cute little furry white seal in a gift shop and suddenly had an idea. So I bought one and wrote the manufacturer for a quote to make a batch of seals with blue fur. Our plastic sterile bags and pouches turn blue when they are sealed by heat and pressure, and the blue seal stuffed animal seemed a good fit with our Blue Seal trade mark.
>
> We distributed blue seals at the trade shows and gave them to nurses. They were a great hit. We created a blue seal cartoon character for our advertising and promotional materials. In time, we gained a disproportionate share of market awareness, when compared to our giant competitors, and sales increased nicely.

The blue seal also became an important device for improving divisional morale. Klein described this aspect of the Blue Seal campaign:

> At one of MacBick's national sales meetings, Dan [Doyle] dressed up as a blue seal and brought the house down. We then featured a photo of him clowning with Maloney on the front page of the division's house organ to create some excitement and a sense of corporate recognition of our efforts.

Notwithstanding the popularity of the Blue Seal campaign, MacBick's successes during the first year turned out to be modest and few. Most of MacBick's product development efforts were characterized by Klein as false starts and outright failures. He described some of these disappointments:

> Flushed with the success of Blue Seal, we went on to create 'The Wizard' to promote unit dose packages and 'The Three Bears' for our hospital carts. Neither campaign ever took hold. The three bears idea, for which I have to take full credit, was the biggest disaster of them all. Luckily, these undertakings didn't cost us too much. Still, we were stymied. The sterile packaging was a small market, and nothing else seemed to work.

In 1980, Klein and his management team decided to propose *Medication Management* as the division's charter. The idea was to develop a cohesive group of "products for the formulation, preparation, storage, distribution, dispensing, and control of medication". At the time, only the steel carts, pharmacy cabinetry, and unit dose packaging, accounting for less than 40 percent of the division's sales, fit the target. Intentionally broad in scope, the charter aimed for new products which "were more sophisticated, had elements of disposability, and involved the pharmacy call point."

As soon as the management executive committee had approved this charter, MacBick began to introduce product line extensions to fill in the missing pieces of a yet-to-be defined total system. At the same time, it began divesting or discontinuing those product lines which did not fit the Medication Management concept.

Some product introductions, such as the new pharmaceutical carts, met with limited success. This product was a standard hospital linen cart with a closed container affixed so that drugs and medication could be kept under lock and key during a nurse's rounds. Most of the new product introductions—such as oral syringes and a computer system for preparing medication labels—turned out to be, in Klein's words, "fiascoes." Sales and profits lumbered on unimpressively through 1979 and 1980.

In June 1981, MacBick's long and increasingly desperate search for a winning product was to be rewarded. The breakthrough took place at a hospital pharmacist's convention where the division had assembled a panel of eight pharmacists to help MacBick's management assess eight new product proposals then under consideration. Klein described the event:

> When we finished our presentation, and it had become obvious that the proposed products were all pretty crummy, I turned to the panel and asked them for some ideas. There was no response. I should have thanked them for their efforts, paid them their honorarium, and called an end to the session. Instead, I became insistent and kept pushing them until one of them mumbled, 'Well, this probably is of no interest, but . . .' and went on to describe an experimental project in analgesia-on-demand being done at the University of Kentucky. That comment got a second pharmacist to tell of some development work a company called Auto-Syringe was doing with syringe pumps for infusing medication at his Rockville Center, New York hospital.
>
> That was it! I felt that we might be on to something big. So, shortly after the meeting ended, I sent one of my top managers straight to Kentucky, and I went to New York to look into what was going on.

As a result of this investigation, Klein was convinced that a syringe pump for infusing medications would be a great improvement over the common gravity feed, plastic mini-bag intravenous (IV) system. A small pump infuser could be more cost effective, more precise in the dosage given, less wasteful of medicine, and in certain circumstances more convenient for the patient. Klein was particularly mindful of this last point when he remembered the frustration he had experienced the year before in trying to conduct management meetings while tied down to his hospital bed by the conventional IV apparatus used in the treatment of an infection.

The concept of "patient controlled" analgesia was equally exciting since patients were anxious about pain throughout their hospital stay. Moreover, reasoned Klein, since pain was a subjective phenomenon, who could better control it than the patient.

Klein's enthusiasm for the new products was not universally shared at Bard. He recalled some of the initial reactions:

> When I began to talk about the possible products with people back at Bard, the response was very negative. "It's crazy. You can never succeed in that area. The major companies have a stranglehold on the infusion pump and mini-bag businesses," were the discouraging words of one corporate officer. Another thought that we could never get the idea of patients dispensing morphine analgesics through a machine accepted by the doctors. They would see it as an infringement on their work and possibly unsafe.
>
> Whatever merit these arguments of discouragement might have had, as I saw it, we had no choice. Our backs were up agains the wall. When I went to the management committee I had a cartoon which showed a tall evergreen with all the branches cut off with the exception of a small sprout at the top which was labeled "infusion pumping and control." Also in this cartoon was a lumberjack identified as George Maloney with an ax ready to cut down the tree and a lumber truck ready to cart it off. [See Exhibit 2.] I pleaded that the infusion pump was our last chance. If it didn't succeed, George would and probably should cut us down.

A number of people involved with the decision questioned the proposal, wondering if this was not just another false trail leading to another dead end. In the end, possibly swayed by Klein's enthusiasm and the recognition that this was MacBick's last chance, the management executive committee voted in favor. Maloney gave some insight into how the decision was made: "When the committee is faced with difficult investment or allocation situations, McCaffrey will often end the debate with the comment, 'Let them play another nine'. Over the years, MacBick had gotten to play the extra nine time and again, and this was one such occasion." McCaffrey later recalled being favorably impressed by the "sheer persistence of the man."

Birth of Bard MedSystems

Klein set out to acquire Auto-Syringe. Bard bid up to $12 million but eventually lost to Baxter Travenol, which purportedly paid $17 million for the company. By then, Klein had identified two other potential acquisitions for entering the infusion pump business. One of these, Harvard Apparatus, a small company in Eastern Massachusetts producing old-style syringe pumps, became Bard's next target. The company had sales of about $2 milliion, split evenly between syringe pumps for medical and bioscience applications. After some difficult negotiations, Klein and Maloney were able to settle on an acquisition price of $2½ million plus a conditional payment of $1½ million, which subsequently failed to materialize. Klein remarked, "What we got was an established name in the business, a safe—albeit somewhat antiquated—product, and some good technical people. A year later we sold the bioscience portion of the company back

Exhibit 2 A typical MedSystems' presentation slide.

to the original owners for over $1 million, so that our total cost for Harvard Infusion Pumps roughly totalled a little over one million dollars.

With the acquisition completed, Klein had the division's name changed to Bard MedSystems, retaining MacBick as a product brand name for hospital carts and cabinetry and Harvard for infusion pumps. Fifteen months of intensive product development resulted in a new generation syringe pump called a Mini-Infuser. Exhibit 3A is an advertisement for this product.

The Mini-Infuser posed a much more complex sales challenge than anything the division had ever faced. The point of sales for its traditional products typically had been in only one or two hospital departments. Since Mini-Infusers would be used throughout the hospital and would infringe on the practices of physicians, nurses and pharmacists, the decision to change IV systems would involve many people and departments. Doyle and Klein knew that it would be necessary to start with a prestigious hospital as a showcase.

The first successful sale was to Beth Israel Hospital in Boston. According to Klein, this hospital had 400 beds and a need for 100 to 150 pumps. He calculated that the hospital could save from $100,000 to $150,000 a year by replacing the mini-bags holding intravenous solutions with the new infusion pump. Each bag cost $1.25, and a patient requried four per day. By using the intravenous pump, the hospital only paid 10 cents per application. These savings would enable the hospital to recuperate its investment in pumps in four to five months. The prospects of improved accuracy of drug delivery and increased convenience for the patients and nurses had also been important considerations in Beth Israel's decision to try the Mini-Infuser.

According to Doyle, the big companies supplying solution bags soon acted to thwart MedSystems' sales campaign. Their price for a bag was eventually reduced to 85 cents, and their large field sales forces made a concerted effort to convince hospitals not to switch. Doyle remarked, "We were threatening a very profitable product for companies like Abbott and Baxter Travenol. They were not about to lie down and roll over for us."

Building a Management Team

Closely related to Klein's concerns over the years with discovering and developing new products was that of building a strong management team. When he took over MacBick, he got a small sales force with the department manager's position recently vacated and an even smaller marketing group headed by his unsuccessful predecessor. A sister division manufactured its products and handled its financial accounting.

After six months, Klein succeeded in having the plant that manufactured hospital carts reassigned to his unit. A few months later top management approved his request to add a controller to his management team.

One of Klein's major concerns was upgrading his key department heads. In 1980, he replaced the plant manager with Don Martin, a plant engineer who showed broad talents. The following year he promoted his strongest product

Exhibit 3A Advertisement for the Mini-Infuser.

123

manager, Dan Doyle, to head marketing. And when he got another good plant manager, Don Johanson, with the Harvard Apparatus acquisition, he convinced him to take charge of engineering and product development. Klein saw these moves as crucial to the division's success:

> I believe that if you get the right team, you can do anything. So right from the beginning I spent a lot of time building my own management team. By the end of the first year I had the nucleus of a staff. When Johanson agreed to take over engineering, that put the last key piece in place.
>
> While I am pretty outspoken as a person, my style is really participative. I see myself as coaching a team on which there are good players.

Don Martin described one assignment which was a revealing example of Klein's interest in developing people:

> In 1980 and 1981, Dick insisted that everyone on his staff go out with the sales force and make sales calls for five days each year. It was an eye opener for me. I could see that this was where the action was and the experience broadened my interests beyond manufacturing. I also got a better idea about what manufacturing meant in this division.

The PCA: A Second Major Product

As efforts to market the Mini-Infuser mounted, the division continued to work on the development of the second infusion pumping and control (IPAC) product idea, patient controlled analgesia (PCA). The device would alllow a patient to self-administer morphine or other narcotic drugs within permissible dosage levels. As a result, a patient could counter pain with timely small dosages, reducing both discomfort and drug usage.

Because of the stringent requirements for safeguards and controls on drug dispensing, it took two years to develop the first PCA device. In April 1984, the morning Klein was to present to the management executive committee MedSystems' plan for launching this new product, it was featured on *Good Morning America*. Klein had the televised discussion videotaped and, 45 minutes later, opened the presentation with it. He later remarked, "It was lucky timing and great showmanship."

The MedSystems managers were elated with their situation and prospects. The division had launched a distinctive product—the Mini-Infuser—which had a market potential greater than that of all of its then existing products together. It now had a second product coming on stream with equal if not greater potential. See Exhibit 3B. As one Bard executive remarked, "MedSystems was the ugly duckling turning into a beautiful swan."

A Rocky Road

The division's success had not come easily. Its relations with corporate staff had been a major source of friction over the years. Klein described the problem:

Exhibit 3B Advertisement for the patient controlled analgesia device.

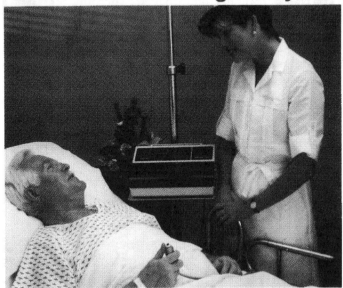
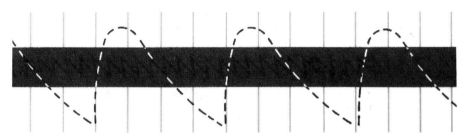
125

> It was really frustrating trying to work with the corporate staff. Part of
> the problem was that we were too small and too unimportant for them to
> bother much with us. On top of that, they were forever seeing why some-
> thing or other couldn't or shouldn't be done. It was difficult to get any real
> support from them.

A senior staff executive described the source of the problem differently:
"Klein was always very intense and dogged. The only time you heard from
him was when he wanted something. Whatever it was, he would want it right
away and just his way. He would never stop pestering you to the point that
his behavior became irritating and counterproductive. To put it simply, he was
generally regarded as a real pain in the ass." Klein knew of his reputation,
explaining, "I can be outspoken, persistent, and even pushy when necessary.
The staff's obvious disdain for our ragtag operation probably brought out the
worst in me. My aggressiveness and MacBick's unimportance within Bard
combined to increase their enmity and resistance."

Klein's relationships with his direct line superiors had also posed difficulties. After a year with Maloney, he was assigned to a group vice president
who more or less ignored him. In 1981, MacBick was reassigned to a group
vice president who was later characterized by a senior Bard executive as a
manager who just could not fit into the Bard culture.

In 1983, Bill Little, a New Zealander who had started as a sales trainee in
Johnson & Johnson and joined Bard ten years later to head its U.K. operations,
was given group responsibility for MedSystems. Little, who was also responsible for two other larger divisions, described his early relationship with Klein:

> Klein and I just didn't get along. Part of it might have been that we had
> been peers as divisional presidents and the new relationship was awkward.
> The biggest problem though was his unpredictability. One day we would
> agree on a strategy. The next day Klein would spark other ideas and be off
> on another tack. This would drive me crazy. When somebody promises to
> do something, I expect it to get done. This was not always the way Klein
> operated. Moreover, he was often bucking the system. He was not a cor-
> porate player. He always knew best. Often it was true, but not always. He
> would fight the way things were done even if such a fight were counter-
> productive. In short, Klein was a nonconformist.

In Bard, each division had to pay its own way. In 1984, MedSystems was
experiencing a significant net loss. According to Little, "Klein's biggest single
mistake was to let his enthusiasm run away with him. He was always out too
far ahead of himself." Little's philosophy was characterized by a wall plaque,
which read, "Yesterday is cancelled. Tomorrow is a promissory note. Today is
cash in hand."

By early 1984, Little, frustrated by his inability to work with Klein, went to
Maloney and said that the MedSystems general manager had to go. Faced with
the many complaints senior staff executives had voiced about Klein, Maloney
finally concluded, albeit reluctantly, to acquiesce to Little's request.

McCaffrey, who had the final say, quashed the decision with the comment, "Bull ____! I don't know Klein from Adam, but he is the only guy around here trying to build a new product area. There's no way we are going to fire him just because people find him hard to work with." McCaffrey was later to remark, "I have always understood that thoroughbreds are hard to ride. Klein, in his own way, was a thoroughbred."

Loss of the PCA

The sense of recovery and even jubilation that Klein had experienced in connection with the coming launch of MedSystems' second major new product was to be short lived. At the April 1984 Three-Year Plan presentation, MedSystems' management announced that the PCA System would be released nationally later that year. However, the division, at the same time, expressed concern over its limited number of experienced sales representatives.

Later, when reviewing this presentation, the management executive committee concluded that a simultaneous launching of two new product concepts through MedSystems would be a mistake. The decision was then made to transfer the PCA line to the Electro Medical Division (Bard EMS) to insure that the product would receive adequate support.

When Klein was informed of this action at the May 1984 annual Bard Management meeting, he was devastated. He recalled:

> The decision to take PCA away hit me like a bolt of lightning. It was my pet project—something we had been working toward for four years. And then to have it taken away like that—oh, they gave me reasons like the PCA requiring surgeons calls and MedSystems' lack of selling resources. But having a product that would allow us to call on doctors was exactly what we were trying to do.

Klein thought seriously of offering his resignation and expressed this intention to management. He was told that he was reacting to his feelings and not thinking rationally about the situation. He was advised to take a week to think the matter through.

Within 24 hours, he told corporate management that he would stay and began to prepare a resume. He later added, "In 1984, if the right opportunity had come along, I would have left Bard."

Klein described his subsequent actions:

> We were now a one-product company again and desperately needed critical mass. We had to find an area where no other division had a charter. So with the management executive committee's concurrence, we picked "anesthesia." We tried to go for an acquisition, but management said no to the deal we came up with. We proposed that MedSystems merge with Bard's small Critical Care Division which had some products positioned in anesthesia. Senior management again vetoed the idea. I began to feel like I was walking through a gauntlet. At the same time, I never stopped trying to get back PCA.

Recovery in 1986

Early in 1985, George Maloney met with the senior management of American Hospital Supply Corporation, and a discussion ensued about the prospect of one of their divisions, American McGaw, selling Mini-Infusers. Maloney discussed this idea with other Bard corporate personnel, and it was agreed that Klein should endeavor to negotiate an agreement with McGaw, which had a sales force of 130 specializing in selling intravenous therapy products. An agreement resulted which specified that McGaw would purchase 15,000 units per year for two years.

The agreement went into effect in September 1985.

At the same time, Klein and his management team developed a rationale and strategy for returning the PCA to their division. In effect, MedSystems argued that the PCA was central to its long-term development of specialty drug delivery pumps. With McGaw assuming the responsibility for selling Mini-Infusers, Little and Maloney were convinced that this was a good strategy, and the concept was endorsed by the management executive committee during the budget review for 1986.

On January 1, 1986, the responsibility for the Harvard PCA system was transferred back to Bard MedSystems, along with an ambitious $10.5 million sales goal that Bard EMS had set for 1986. PCA pump sales for the last six months of 1985 had totalled $2.75 million.

In early 1986, MedSystems proposed to Janssen Pharmaceuticals, a major Johnson & Johnson company, the development of a specialty pump to use with its promising new narcotic anesthesia, Alfenta. According to Doyle, Janssen was attracted to the proposition because of the need for a simple and safe method of administering the drug in the operating room. Subsequent discussions led to the concept of the Alfenta pump, which, according to Doyle, was to be "tremendously user-friendly and indestructible" and the first hospital pump to be designed for one specific drug.

In December 1986 Janssen received FDA approval for Alfenta. Under the marketing arrangement, the new pump would be jointly sold by the 120-person Janssen and 23-person MedSystems sales forces. MedSystems was responsible for producing the units and for providing sales support to assist Janssen's drug salespeople handle this unfamiliar device. Doyle estimated that up to 10,000 of the approximately 35,000 operating rooms in the United States were potential customers for at least one pump each. The overseas market would require a reconfigured pump deisgn because different protocols were followed in administering drugs for anesthesia.

During 1986, Klein also began a campaign to broaden MedSystems' presence in the drug delivery field. The 1987–89 Three-Year Strategic Plan, submitted in May 1986, identified Cormed, Inc. as an acquisition candidate for MedSystems' entry into the rapidly growing outpatient/home drug infusion market.

While Cormed enjoyed the position of number one market share for ambulatory pumps and number two for associated implantable access ports, the company was widely regarded as being troubled with old technology products and inadequate R&D. When questioned about these deficiencies, Klein responded that Bard was buying an established name, a market position, and a flow of sales, much as it had done with Harvard Apparatus four years earlier. Klein also decided to go after Cormed because of his conviction that it was easier in Bard to get approval for an acquisition than for internal development when entering a new field, since management could see an operating cash inflow as of the time the investment was made. In September 1986, Bard acquired Cormed for $9½ million.

One of Klein's first actions was to instruct Cormed's management to develop in 1987 a new pump incorporating the latest microprocessor technology. MedSystems' technology group would provide support in the development of the product concept and engineering to the extent possible. While the technology from the motor to the control system was familiar ground to MedSystems' engineers, the pump itself employed peristaltic action (contractions that force the fluid along, like squeezing a tube), which involved different technology than that of driving syringes. The advantages of peristaltic technology for ambulatory care were that the pump could be made smaller and could deal with larger applications (up to 200 milliliters of drug versus a maximum of 60 milliliters for syringes), permitting more time between refillings. (The syringe pump could administer small doses more accurately, an important advantage for many hospital applications.) By January 1987, Klein had also reached an agreement with a Swiss firm to supply Cormed with the world's smallest ambulatory pump, the size of a credit card.

Success and Respectability

As 1986 progressed, it became increasingly apparent that MedSystems would make its first profit in years. The division's financial results are shown below in Table A. The most pleasing element in the 1986 results for MedSystems management was PCA's $11.7 million new sales for the year, exceeding what was thought to be the ambitious target of $10.5 million.

Klein's relationships with corporate headquarters also improved markedly in 1986. Group vice president Little, who seemed at ease in discussing the subject, said, "I get along fine with Klein now. We've worked out a comfort-

Table A MedSystems' sales and net income,[a] 1977–86.

	1977	1978	1979	1980	1981	1982	1983	1984	1985	1986
Sales ($ millions)	22.4	21.4	21.4	23.5	26.1	30.1	26.8	22.1	22.2	39.6
Net Income ($000)	356	916	442	578	632	(296)	416	(1854)	(1622)	1608

a. Financial figures disguised to protect confidentiality of the data.

able relationship." Klein, in turn remarked, "I have developed a good relationship with Bill. As it works, 75 percent of the time we agree, 20 percent of the time I convince him to go my way, and 5 percent of the time he insists I go his way." And Maloney later observed, "Little now knows how to tell Klein in no uncertain terms when to stop."

The increasingly constructive nature of the relationship between the two men was indicated in a controversial divisional appointment. In December 1986, Klein put Doyle in charge of sales and marketing to give Doyle broader management responsibilities and to free himself to devote more attention to the recent Cormed acquisition. He had previously cleared this move with Gene Schultz, the corporate vice president for personnel, with his group vice president Little, and with Maloney. Doyle's new title was vice president and business manager. When McCaffrey later discovered the intention of the title change, he rescinded the promotion in no uncertain terms. In his view, the sales function was too important in Bard to report to anyone other than the divisional general manager. Klein recalled Little's role in the incident: "One thing I'll have to say for Bill, he stood up on my behalf and made clear that I had gone through all the right channels on this one. I appreciated that."

Klein's relationships with corporate staff had also improved considerably in 1986. Klein remarked on this change, "In part, I've toned down and learned to live more with the system. In part, it's just easier to have a good relationship when you're respected and have credibility. The growing recognition top management has given our division has certainly helped create a more favorable climate."

Divisional Challenges

The management award announced by McCaffrey was in recognition of outstanding performance; it did not mark the successful completion of Klein's mission. Indeed, Klein felt that the pressures and risks were mounting as the stakes grew larger and expectations grew higher. He remarked, "Before we were a penny-ante operation with little in the way of risk, accomplishment, or promise. To exaggerate a bit, we could get by with wild promises, frenetic action, and funny presentations. That is no longer the case."

The senior MedSystems managers identified several issues which they considered as major challenges before them.

A Secure Business Base

In 1986, the MedSystems division had made its first profit in years. Klein felt a need to prove that it had not been the result of accident or luck. What worried him most was the division's heavy dependence on one product, the PCA pump. (Mini-Infuser sales growth had stalled under the McGaw arrangement.) The division risked a major setback should any serious problem arise with PCA's performance. To illustrate this risk, Klein mentioned that one patient had died while connected to a Harvard PCA pump. Fortunately for Med-Systems, the cause of death was not clear and could not be attributed to the pump. He went on to assess the division's vulnerability within Bard: "Should we be required to recall our devices, divisional gains to date could be wiped out overnight. However, I think that we have gained enough credibility in Bard to weather the storm."

Klein saw the Alfenta pump as broadening the division's product base and reducing this risk. The new Cormed pump would provide additional security, and Klein was eager to introduce even more products to reduce the risk of failure as well as to fuel the rapid growth he was planning.

The risk of product failure or misuse was not the only threat to the security of MedSystems' performance. Competitive pressures were also increasing rapidly. Klein noted:

> When we started pushing the Mini-Infuser, we were the only one trying to do something in the field. We created a new exciting business out of what was a backwater. Now, industry giants like Becton-Dickenson, Abbott Laboratories, and Baxter Travenol have all become very interested. To give you an example, one of these firms recently introduced a new infuser pump that is a direct copy of our Mini-Infuser. We are suing them for patent infringement, and while we will probably win this skirmish, the future challenges are not likely to be so easy to defend.
>
> Not only do these firms have more resources than Bard, they are more committed. They have been long involved in this business with their profitable IV feeding systems and are 100 percent committed. Bard is new to the field and is still not sure what investment to make. The problem for us is to remain number one. I see our situation as somewhat analogous to that experienced by Apple Computers. They created the personal computer field only to be out-muscled by IBM when the prize became attractive enough.

Managing Technology

Distinctive high quality infusion pumps and controls had been at the heart of MedSystems' remarkable recovery. As the division broadened its scope and as competitive products proliferated, the challenge MedSystems faced in managing new product development grew with the increasing number of products under consideration, level of sophistication, range of technologies, and time pressures.

Investments in new product development had increased each year, reaching a planned level in excess of $4.5 million in 1987. Highest priority was given to a family of "smart pumps." The Medsystems 1987–89 Three-Year Strategic Plan described these products as follows:

> . . . Computer-based delivery systems with microprocessors capable of interpreting complex pharmacokinetic algorithms which will automatically adjust the drug dosage over time.
> The Harvard Chronofusor System will be the first self-contained pump with the capability to deliver drugs pharmacokinetically. Algorithms devel-

oped by drug companies for their specific products or by researchers at major medical institutions can be input to the device manually or through preprogrammed, Bard-supplied cartridges.

Anesthesia Drug Intravenous Administration System (ADIAS), available in late 1987, will semiautomate the delivery of anesthesia narcotics and vasoactive drugs in the operating room. Pump modules will permit uninterrupted drug therapy as they can be moved, with the patient, through the postoperative recovery room and intensive care.

Closed loop systems, the "ultimate" in drug delivery, is a 1987/88 project currently in the earliest, definition phase and, therefore, not budgeted. Consisting of a "smart pump," like the Chronofusor, a catheter(s), and a sensor(s), this system will measure a patient's specific physiological feedback (e.g., blood pressure) for the real time control of medication delivery. IVAC, a division of Lilly, recently introduced such a system.

New and possibly competing technologies were also under scrutiny. Transdermal infusion, which supplied medication directly through the skin, was one example. According to the division's plan, "potential applications included therapies for many chronic illnesses, such as pain management, alcoholism, drug addiction, hypertension."

The pressures for new product development posed a management problem for the division. Doyle was concerned that these pressures might divert the division from maintaining product leadership in its established lines. As he explained the situation, MedSystems had one engineering group responsible for the maintenance of existing product lines, for line extensions, and for the development of new products. The product managers generally put pressure on this group to improve existing products and, to some extent, to develop product line extensions. R&D management was inclined to favor new product development. Doyle commented on the problem of maintaining a proper balance between these competing demands:

> These days we have more good ideas than we can handle. A big challenge is to get the right priorities. What really concerns me is that the division will worry too much about tomorrow's products and not enough about today's. The PCA, for example, has tremendous opportunities. Its market saturation is less than 10 percent. Since it is doing so well in the marketplace there are some who believe that our development work should focus elsewhere. That's wrong. In my view, the division needs to devote a major part of its engineering resources to this product.

The Mini-Infuser Arrangement

The Kendall-McGaw arrangement also posed some difficult problems for MedSystems' management. The 1987–89 Strategic Plan described the situation as follows:

> When MedSystems signed the Supply and Distribution Agreement with McGaw, effective October 1, 1985, little did we know how agonizingly slow they would be to capitalize on the Mini-Infuser opportunity.
> Our analysis of McGaw activity indicated a multiplicity of problems:

- Upper management's preoccupation with their acquisition by Kendall [from American Hospital Supply Corporation] during the fourth quarter, 1985.
- A good marketing strategy but weak sales action plan, i. .., the inability of management to communicate an effective "how to" strategy to the field.
- Competing field priorities, i.e., some major, high gross profit McGaw products compete directly with the Mini-Infuser so their representatives are prohibited from selling to current McGaw accounts.
- Novice product managers assigned to Mini-Infuser System. Three turned over in six months.
- For the first six months, McGaw did not advertise or develop new support literature.
- Underestimation of the effort and follow-up needed to sell this "concept."

To support McGaw, we have introduced additional sales incentives to the MedSystems sales force to help convert trials, loaned them additional trial pumps to lift the ban on new trials, and forced a closer relationship between our Mini-Infuser product manager and his new McGaw counterpart(s).

With second-year contract negotiations to take place in August/September, Bard has several viable alternatives:

1. Stay with McGaw but reduce future annual purchase commitments; for example, 15,000 pumps to 6,000 pumps. They would demand that we give them the right to manufacture disposables, but then we would demand a sizeable, fixed-percentage royalty.
2. Terminate contract with McGaw and distribute Harvard Mini-Infuser System through our Harvard PCA dealer network. Compete against McGaw as it unloads excess pump/set inventory on marketplace. Take back all disposables contracts as provided for in the current agreement.
3. Same as (2) . . . but assumes that Bard and McGaw agree on equitable penalty for cancellation of current 15,000 pump purchase commitment. McGaw, therefore, would have no products to unload on market. Harvard PCA dealer network could sell more pumps and sets. Reasonable sales volume is based on 8,000 pumps.
4. Transition year. Terminate contract with McGaw. McGaw unloads excess inventory of pumps/sets on market. MedSystems sells existing microbore tubing sets direct, and looks to Harvard PCA dealer network to increase sales volume of Harvard Mini-Infuser System incrementally. Assume no new pump sales.

Alternative	Pumps (Units)	Total Sales ($)	Gross Profit* ($)
1	6,000	5,200K	2,100K
2	2,500	3,800K	2,000K
3	8,000	7,400K	4,000K
4	0	3,500K	2,200K

*Disguised

The McGaw contact also complicated the situation for Klein in developing an idea he had for supplying prefilled syringes for Mini-Infuser applications. He explained:

> Pharmacists don't like to fill syringes if they don't have to. We consequently saw an opportunity for supplying prefilled syringes, for use with the Mini-Infuser.
>
> When we first proposed this idea to McGaw, they disagreed and would not support such a program. That stymied us for a year. When we threatened to go forward ourselves, McGaw finally came around. Now we are trying to work out an arrangement in which a drug company prefills syringes to be sold by the McGaw sales force in connection with Mini-Infusers. What complicates the negotiations is to find a way for Bard to get a piece of the payoff as a non-operating partner in a three-way agreement.

Divisional Charter

As MedSystems grew in size and scope, conflicts between its business interests and those of other Bard divisions were likely to increase. According to Klein, the distinctive nature of his division's charter exacerbated the problem. While the other divisions tended to focus on particular hospital departments (such as urology, cardiology, and surgery), the customer base for MedSystems' products cut across hospital organizational lines. The competition for PCA within Bard had reflected in part this problem of overlapping interests.

With the acquisition of Cormed, MedSystems obtained a line of indwelling catheters and ports (implantable devices to provide long-term drug delivery into the body). This put it in direct competition with Bard's Davol division, which also produced and sold these items as part of its newly developed mission aimed at the oncology (relating to cancer) market.

Klein believed that MedSystems was justified in laying claim to these products, explaining,

> After Davol was acquired in 1980, its charter became "wound management." It was a good organization, but in need of new products. So when Evermed (market leader for indwelling catheters) was acquired in 1983, the group vice president, who had come from Davol, came up with the idea of adding oncology to Davol's charter and gave the new unit to it instead of to us. This was a mistake, in my opinion, because these products fit so closely with our pumps.

From that time on, Klein began a campaign to communicate within Bard that MedSystems was more than "a pump company." The 1987–89 Three-Year Strategic Plan stressed this point, illustrating it on page one:

> Harvard's product line consisted entirely of syringe pumps which, at that time, represented only the tiny "small-volume" niche of the infusion pumping and control (IPAC) market, an arena dominated by several large competitors, e.g., IMED, IVAC, Abbott, Travenol. To the uninitiated, IPAC means intravenous (IV) therapy; but the development and proliferation of new drug delivery products for hospital, outpatient, and home infusion validate the concept of IPAC as a MULTI-MODALITY, TOTAL SYSTEM . . .

IT IS SHORTSIGHTED TO THINK OF MEDSYSTEMS AS JUST A "PUMP COMPANY."

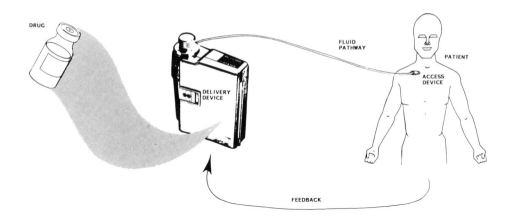

Martin gave some idea of MedSystems' competitive drive in speaking about the product overlap with Davol:

> To have two divisions in Bard manufacture and sell the same products could be questioned. Internal competition, however, also has motivational benefits. We are all psyched up to clean out Davol's clock. Of course, they probably would like to do the same to us. But we have the advantage of supplying an integrated system. In time these operations might be consolidated, but for now, its up to both divisions to show their stuff.

Klein as Manager and Intrapreneur

In assessing Klein as a general manager, his direct reports made the following list of strengths and weaknesses:

- He sets high standards. You will either gear up or gear out. If you don't meet his expectations, he drives you crazy.
- He is very optimistic, with a tendency to see opportunities instead of problems.
- He works closely with his people and gives them opportunities to grow.
- He is very creative, often coming up with unusual solutions.
- He sometimes runs too fast for the group with a flood of ideas.
- He comes up with a lot of bad ideas—as well as good ideas. Since he is so persistent, blunt, and even domineering by nature, it takes a lot of skill and patience to turn him around without having a knock-down, drag-out battle.

In connection with this last point, one of MedSystems' executives described the key role he and his colleagues had to play:

> We have to serve as a foil for Klein, trying to keep him on the right path. He is good at talking to people and generating ideas. Our job is to evaluate these ideas without slowing down his aggressive and inquisitive nature. Even if there is only one good idea in a hundred, it is important to uncover it. I just hope that we don't begin to lose this ability as the division gets bigger.

Klein was described as hard to work for, but those who had learned how indicated a great deal of respect for him. Klein in turn described himself as changing over time:

> I used to go after everything with no give. But I've learned that I cannot fight every battle. Now I'm more selective. Sometimes I'll even give up on an issue to gain position for another.

He went on to describe some of the lessons he had learned as a general manager:

> One thing I've learned is that one person cannot accomplish all that much by himself. You need good people to make a division succeed. A corollary lesson is that you have to help other people to succeed for them to help you to succeed. The third lesson is that you have to be able to deal with setbacks and failures. I've certainly experienced lots of failures along the way.

In the May 1986 corporate top management meeting, Klein gave a presentation about intrapreneuring. He might have had himself in mind when he opened with the following definition for intrapreneur from Gifford Pinchot's book *Intrapreneuring*:

> Any of the "dreamers who do". Those who take hands-on responsibility for creating innovation of any kind within an organization. The intrapreneur may be the creator or inventor but is always the dreamer who figures out how to turn an idea into a profitable reality.

In a series of statements accompanied by cartoons, he identified some of the key attributes of such a person:

- Intrapreneurs *are* different. (See Exhibit 4.)
- Intrapreneurs have dogged determination, intensity, and a sense of urgency.
- "Popularity" is often a casualty of intrapreneuring.
- Intrapreneurs *are* highly visible.

On another occasion, he described the importance of an organization being able to deal with deviant behavior:

> I kept running into the reaction, "Why can't you do things like everyone else?" What an organization has to be able to do is to put a leash on its people and then to allow them to do their own things. In my opinion, nothing overwhelms creativity more completely than excessive structure.
>
> George Maloney has been great in this respect. He gives me advice and then lets me learn from experience.

Exhibit 4 Cartoon used in defining intrapreneurs.

"Why can't you just shit in the woods like every other bear?"

When asked about his future career plans, Klein responded:

I receive calls every few months from people who are checking on my availability. The money offered almost always exceeds what I am currently receiving, sometimes by a factor of two. But I am not a job jumper, moving from one company to another. I like Bard, and I feel it takes time in one place to accomplish something worthwhile.

On the other hand, I've been at this job for eight years, and I'm ready to do something else. I realized recently that I am one of the senior division general managers in terms of years in office. I'm also older than most. Their average age is forty; I'm forty-two.

I've been a good general manager. McCaffrey once said, "You're nobody until you know how to make money." Now I've made money. I'm becoming less interested in the nitty gritty details. My value to the company is in coming up with strategies, building management teams, and motivating people. The company really needs me beyond this particular division.

I would like to take on the broader responsibilities of a group vice presidency. I am trying to show my ability and maturity. I am trying to prove that I can operate in a corporate environment.

I've been with the company thirteen years; there is a risk of becoming stereotyped and pigeonholed if you stay in a job too long. I think it's important for me to move on pretty soon, or my opportunities are going to dry up.

Klein spoke about his career ambitions with a touch of the same dogged determination and optimistic expectation that had marked his behavior in managing the Bard MedSystems division over the past eight years.

The Importance of Corporate Context

In reviewing the events of MedSystems' impressive performance, McCaffrey observed:

Klein deserves a lot of credit for MedSystems' turnaround, but it is important to recognize the other important contributors to this outcome. As he himself pointed out, his key people also deserve much credit. It was, and continues to be, a team effort.

Perhaps less obvious, but no less vital to MedSystems' results, was Bard's deep commitment to decentralized management, to a market focus, and to providing distinctive products of value to the customer. This core concept served to guide Klein and his team in their decisions and to aid corporate management in assessing their proposals. Everyone involved had a common framework which gave direction and which allowed for experimentation and failures along the way.

McCaffrey continued:

Klein seemed to think that his showmanship presentations were a decisive factor in winning top management support. Actually, the cartoons and hype had the effect of putting me off more than winning me over. What really gained top management's attention and support was the division's dedication to finding and building a business that would focus on specific markets and supply differentiated, quality products. As a result, we were willing to make exceptions for MedSystems. For example, the corporate management would probably have said no to another division had it requested R&D funding for the kind of market research project proposed by Klein in 1978. We let MedSystems go with other questionable proposals when it seemed important to divisional morale to do so. Everyone involved—MedSystems' management and senior management—had to take some risks and had to have a measured faith in our abilities to learn from our mistakes and to capitalize on our breaks. That, it seems to me, is an important part of what management is really about.

Appendix: C.R. Bard, Inc.

C.R. Bard founded his company in 1907 to sell catheters for the emerging medical specialty of urology. Catheters were devices for draining a person's bladder when an obstruction of the urinary tract prevented its normal functioning. The introduction in the 1930's of a catheter with a balloon on the end to hold it in place greatly expanded the use of these devices, and Bard's sales multiplied from $150,000 in 1929 to over $45 million in 1968 under the able leadership of Harris Willits. With reference to the balloon (Foley) catheter, which, in 1987, continued to be the most widely used bladder drainage device, Willits remarked, "That product made this company, and we had the best one made!"

Under Wendell Crain, who succeeded Willits as Bard's president and CEO in 1968, the company introduced many new medical equipment and supply products and expanded international operations. Crain also set out to reduce costs by expanding the company's manufacturing operations and by instituting asset and expense control programs. Over the next seven years, sales rose to $131 million and profits from $3.5 million to $9.7 million.

In 1975, Bard's board of directors became concerned that excessive attention to manufacturing and control had seriously weakened Bard's traditional strength in marketing. As a result, the board decided to change the leadership of C.R. Bard.

New Leadership

On February 9, 1976, Bob McCaffrey was appointed Bard's president and CEO. An outside member of the board explained his selection: "He's a salesman. He is intelligent, widely read, has a good feel for managing people, and has some experience in manufacturing . . . [but] the key factor in his selection was that he was a marketing man."

McCaffrey had started as a salesman for Johnson & Johnson, rising to become president of one of its small companies. In 1966 he left Johnson & Johnson to join Howmedica, a company making orthopedic cement and implants, rising to the positions of executive vice president and chief operating officer in 1974. Commenting on his decision to leave that company for Bard, McCaffrey said, "You can't tell yourself you're a professional manager and turn down a crack at being the CEO of a publicly held company."

During McCaffrey's first year, marketing and product development expenditures were increased. To strengthen management's marketing perspective, he promoted George Maloney, a divisional president who had joined Bard in 1959 as a sales representative, to group vice president.

In June 1977, McCaffrey presented his written analysis of the situation to the board, excerpts of which follow:

> Bard began strictly as a marketing company and started, about a decade ago, to enter manufacturing. As so often happens, in the intervening ten years, the manufacturing influence at Bard has become the dominant one

with a waning influence on the part of marketing. As a result, there is a conglomeration of product in a couple of divisions which makes for very ineffective sales concentration.

The ideal organization for Bard should be properly decentralized. Product lines should give a good opportunity for salesman concentration. The marketing and manufacturing of a product [should] be in a single division to avoid intercompany pricing problems.

The story (in the field) is that Bard is a monolith which isn't going anywhere . . . It is our plan to develop divisional alignments in Bard adhering to very clearly defined product areas. We expect to staff each division with the best possible people, to be selected either inside the company or out. We expect division's management to develop a thoroughly thought-out and lucid charter. This will enable them to focus on building share of market on existing products and strengthen their franchise by developing other products within the dictates of their charter.[1]

McCaffrey lost no time in implementing the proposed reorganization. Operations were restructured to achieve specialization by markets. To reassert Bard's traditional marketing strength, salespeople focused on these markets, each of which was defined by a particular medical specialty.

To spearhead the reorganization, Maloney was promoted to executive vice president in charge of operations and was also elected to the board of directors. By the end of 1977, Bard had been reorganized into ten domestic and five international divisions. This structure, with minor modifications, continued to be employed in 1987. Exhibit 5 contains a company organization chart. Exhibits 6 and 7 show C.R. Bard's financial results for selected years.

Decentralization, Concentration, Innovation

Over the years, McCaffrey continued to emphasize the need for divisions to focus on attractive markets and to provide distinctive products of value to the customer. This general strategic idea gradually was refined into a core concept of "decentralization, concentration, and innovation."

In McCaffrey's opinion, the effective decentralization of operating authority had to be coupled with strong corporate oversight and control. Accordingly, Bard had developed strong financial controls and an active management executive committee. This committee of eight people—comprising the CEO, COO, CFO, controller, vice chairman, and three group vice presidents—reviewed all major operating issues. Each division general manager would come before the committee to present the division's three-year plan, to initiate discussion of the divisional budget, to review management resources, and to discuss major actions and problems. Corporate staff units were purposely kept small to prevent them from getting overly involved in divisional affairs. As Gene Schultz, vice

---

1. Source: Harvard University case, *C.R. Bard, Inc.*, 381-180

Exhibit 5 C.R. Bard, Inc., company organization chart, 1986.

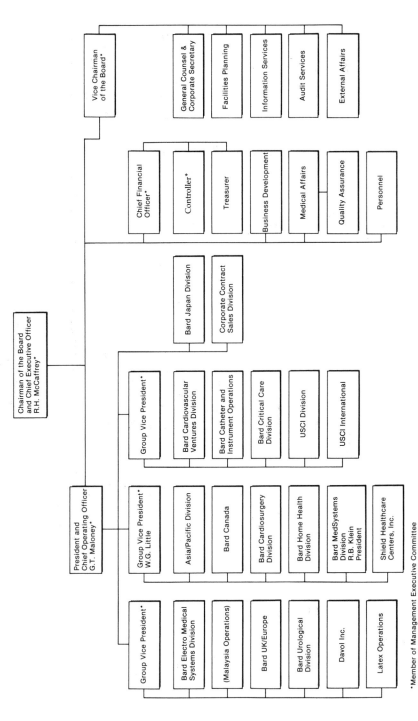

Chairman of the Board
and Chief Executive Officer
R.H. McCaffrey*

Vice Chairman
of the Board*

General Counsel &
Corporate Secretary

Facilities Planning

Information Services

Audit Services

External Affairs

Chief Financial
Officer*

Controller*

Treasurer

Business Development

Medical Affairs

Quality Assurance

Personnel

President and
Chief Operating Officer
G.T. Maloney*

Group Vice President*

Bard Japan Division

Corporate Contract
Sales Division

Bard Cardiovascular
Ventures Division

Bard Catheter and
Instrument Operations

Bard Critical Care
Division

USCI Division

USCI International

Group Vice President*
W.G. Little

Asia/Pacific Division

Bard Canada

Bard Cardiosurgery
Division

Bard Home Health
Division

Bard MedSystems
Division
R.B. Klein
President

Shield Healthcare
Centers, Inc.

Group Vice President*

Bard Electro Medical
Systems Division

(Malaysia Operations)

Bard UK/Europe

Bard Urological
Division

Davol Inc.

Latex Operations

*Member of Management Executive Committee

Source: company document

Exhibit 6 C.R. Bard, selected financial results 1979–86 ($ million, except per share amounts).

	1979	1980	1981	1982	1983	1984	1985	1986
Net sales	160	219	295	343	397	417	465	548
Net operating income	22	34	46	56	64	64	74	89
Net income	14	15	23	27	33	35	42	51
Total assets	141	204	223	256	287	329	385	423
Working capital	73	83	94	110	129	149	173	153[a]
Net property, plant, equipment	38	53	60	70	75	83	92	90
Long-term debt	2	34	33	38	37	41	39	36
Shareholders' equity	113	125	144	168	194	222	257	266[b]
Return on average share-holder's equity (%)	12.5	12.6	16.7	17.4	18.3	16.9	17.5	19.6[b]
Debt/equity ratio (%)	—	—	22.9	22.6	19.3	18.3	15.3	13.6
Share price high	5¼	8⅛	11	17½	23⅜	18⅞	22	40⅜
Share price low (adjusted for splits)	3⅝	3½	6⅝	9⅛	13⅝	9½	10⅞	18¾
Number of employees	3,900	5,500	6,135	6,360	6,200	6,000	6,350	7,200

Source: C.R. Bard Annual Reports.
a. Excludes $25 million short-term investments placed in 1986.
b. A significant number of shares were repurchased by the company in 1986.

Exhibit 7   Bard sales by medical specialty ($ million).

	1980	1981	1982	1983	1984	1985	1986	Six-Year Growth
Cardiovascular	45	64	83	107	129	153	190	4.2x
Urological	74	88	103	106	90	100	109	1.5x
Surgical	23	51	60	68	70	80	94	4.1x
General Health (includes MedSystems division)	32	36	36	44	57	58	60	0.9x
Foreign and Export	46	57	61	72	71	76	94	2.0x

Sources: 1985 annual report and 1986 fourth quarter report.

president of personnel, noted, "That way we can't get in peoples' way. There is no time to make work for others."

Bard had a policy of promoting from within whenever possible. Top management spent one week each year assessing strengths and weaknesses of each manager. As Schultz noted, "We are small enough to know the people in the trenches."

Salaries were generally above average for the industry. Bard also had a widespread stock incentive scheme which for operating managers was based on a discretionary assessment of corporate earnings, divisional profits, and an individual manager's performance. Turnover among salaried personnel was low.

In a presentation to security analysts in Europe during October 1986, McCaffrey summed up his views of the importance of Bard's management approach with the following comment:

> I truly believe that Bard's management ability and style are most important in differentiating us from our competitors.
>
> An important element of Bard management is the exceptionally strong spirit of teamwork—within Bard divisions, and between Bard divisions and the corporate staff.
>
> The word teamwork is used frequently—by perhaps every corporation or group—but teamwork really means something at Bard because Bard's people really make it happen. This has a lot to do with our continuing success. It also makes Bard an enjoyable place to work, and we have fun to boot.

Bowater Computer Forms, Inc.

> When we decided to go into the computer forms business, I looked at a lot
> of companies with the thought of buying our way in. After a careful search
> I decided that given our strategy we had best go from the ground up. So
> then we decided to find the best person in the field to run the operation,
> and we did—we found Bill Detwiler, who had had a similar idea while he
> was working at Willamette, a major forms supplier.

Ron Toelle, the vice president of corporate development for Bowater Inc.,
leaned forward in his chair to describe the situation at Bowater's subsidiary,
Bowater Computer Forms, Inc. (BCFI).

> Bill has done a superb job of creating this organization. He's a real en-
> trepreneur. The question we now have is whether the skills that are needed
> for running a start-up can be carried into the new, large organization, and
> whether the centralized decision making that characterized the start-up can
> be decentralized. Bill is Swiss by background and is a very autocratic guy.
> He's been trying valiantly to change his attitudes and behavior and get his
> hands off the machines. However, even though he professes great democ-
> racy, he still tends to have all the answers himself.

The Parent

Bowater, Inc., was the largest domestic producer of newsprint in the United
States, and a major producer of coated publication paper. Through most of its
history it had been the American subsidiary of the British corporation Bowater,
Ltd. In 1984, a decision was reached that it would be in the shareholders' best
interest to separate the North American and British operations. At the time the
company was earning a net income of $72 million on sales of $887 million from
two large paper mills in Tennessee and South Carolina and two medium-sized
mills in Canada.

Management attributed Bowater's success in the United States over the years
to its strategy. The company had focused on the highly efficient manufacture
of a limited number of commoditylike products (see Table A). Scale economies
and a favorable location in the Southeast (which had low raw material costs
and a growing market) resulted in some of the best operating margins in the
industry.

Table A Bowater financial results by sector, 1984.

	Sales	*Profits*
Newsprint	66%	72%
Pulp	11	5
Coated paper	10	23
Other	13	small loss

Source: Merrill Lynch.

Concerned with the possible negative impact that television and other forms of electronic communication might have on the volume of newspapers, periodicals, and other printed materials that used Bowater's products, U.S. management began in the late 1970s to consider a strategy of diversification. The ten-year plan in 1979 described management's views on diversification in the context of the company's overall objectives:

Bowater North America seeks to accomplish the following objectives:

1. Generate increased profits and cash flows
2. Continue to develop U.S. pulp and paper operations
3. Diversify into a limited number of new businesses
4. Achieve superior performance

The company's first move was to enter the rapidly growing computer forms business, concentrating on the large-volume, commoditylike stock continuous forms (the blue- or green-barred paper to record output from computers). A year later, in 1981, Bowater's managers selected the expanding home-center retail business as the second diversification target. One of its appeals was the opportunity to integrate backwards into the manufacture of building products.

In 1984, A. P. Gammie, chairman, president, and CEO of Bowater Inc., reaffirmed the company's diversification strategy in a memorandum to the board of directors:

As indicated in our Business Plan, the strategic direction for Bowater favored by the Executive Committee comprises two principal elements. One is to realize the growth potential in the pulp and paper business without increasing our dependence on newsprint. The other is to diversify into related businesses which require less capital than pulp and paper operations. In this way, Bowater would reduce its exposure to any future setback which newsprint might encounter and, at the same time, broaden its opportunities for maintaining the high returns on assets and equity that it has generated in the past.

It is useful to consider, in a conceptual sense, the sort of company we want Bowater to be ten years from now. Ideally, we would like to have a third or more of the company's profits to be generated from activities outside pulp and paper within ten years.

Exhibit 1 Total forms industry, 1985 estimate ($6.0 billion).

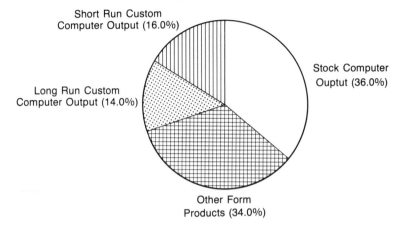

The Computer Forms Industry and BCFI Strategy

The business forms industry, estimated to have an annual domestic market of $6 billion in 1985, produced a wide variety of business paper products including register forms, carbonless forms, custom and stock unit forms, sales books, stock computer output paper, and long-run and short-run custom output paper. (See Exhibit 1 for a breakdown of major product sales.)

The appeal of the business forms industry to Bowater management rested on several industry factors. First, the business forms market was growing at a higher rate than any other segment of the printing industry and at a much higher rate than the GNP. Second, long-run continuous computer output paper accounted for the bulk of that growth as a result of the huge data-processing demands of large firms such as banks, airlines, and oil companies. (See Exhibit 2.)

Though forms-industry analysts fretted in the 1970s over claims that America was moving toward a paperless society, in which data would be processed purely on video displays, by 1986 this outcome appeared increasingly unlikely. Bowater management believed that the computer forms market would enjoy healthy growth well into the 1990s, because IBM and other computer manufacturers had made a major and enduring commitment to line-hole continuous-output paper.

Due to the high shipping costs of paper and the degree of required customization, the forms industry had been characterized for many years by a fragmented structure with as many as 600 small regional "converters." Most of these firms, attempting to sell a very broad line of products, ran their factories as job shops. Approximately seventy-five firms competed in the computer-output paper segment and, according to BCFI's management, only one national and four regional firms had sought to specialize to any degree within that segment. See Table B for the sales figures of the major forms suppliers.

Exhibit 2 Business forms industry, sales (1970–85).

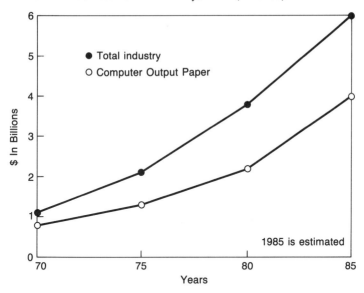

Table B Total 1984 estimated sales for major U.S. forms suppliers (in millions of dollars).

Company	Stock Computer Output Paper	Long-Run Computer Output Paper[a]	Total U.S. Forms[a]
Moore	300	450	1,200
Willamette	105	155	155
Standard Register	65	100	340
Uarco	60	95	325
Duplex Products	60	60	342
Chicago Stock Tab	60	60	60
SCM Allied Egry	50	70	150
Data Documents	45	70	150
Star Business Forms	45	45	60
Wallace Comp. Serv.	40	80	170
Total	830	1,185	2,952
Total Industry	2,000	3,700	5,600
BCFI	44	56	56

a. Stock computer output paper is included in the long-run computer output paper figure, which in turn is included in the Total U.S. Forms column.

Source: BCFI 1985 Strategic Plan.

The Entrepreneurial Phase

When Detwiler was hired in January 1980 he had a strategic concept, a corporate name, a bank account—and that was all. Within three months he hired a team of people he had known over the years. He first took on Marty Allan to assist him in administration, then Larry Hatfield to head sales, and Norm Pellegrine to run manufacturing. The only member of the initial team to come from Bowater, Inc., was the controller, Denis Tontodonato.

Toelle had told Detwiler that he could put the corporate headquarters "anywhere East of the Rockies," so Detwiler selected a site in Plano, Texas, a sprawling northern suburb of Dallas dotted with industrial plants and crisscrossed with expressways. This location was desirable, because land was inexpensive, unions were rare, persons with manufacturing experience were readily available, and it was in a region of the sunbelt that was both centrally located and economically booming.

Detwiler immediately began construction of the first plant and brought it on line in December 1980. A second plant in Scottsburg, Indiana, began production in December 1982. The third plant, in Sparks, Nevada (a suburb of Reno), was nearing completion for start-up in July 1986, and two more were planned before the end of the decade.

Manufacturing

The manufacturing strategy of BCFI was to bring economies of scale to the converter industry by minimizing short- and customized-production runs. As Toelle described it, "We get the best equipment possible, and we run the blazes out of it, 24 hours a day, 349 days a years." The employees in BCFI's plants worked twelve-hour shifts—four days on, then four off, three on, then three off.

The actual production process was simple. Large rolls of paper weighing from 1,000 to 2,500 pounds were brought by rail from paper mills to the BCFI plants. The rolls were fed into machines that cut the paper to the proper width, printed lines (if necessary), punched holes in the sides, and folded it—all at a speed of almost fifty miles an hour. Indeed, the process was so elementary that the cost of the raw material—the paper rolls—accounted for approximately 60 percent of total costs, as shown in Table C.

Plant personnel paid close attention to quality. Samples of the paper shipped from the mills were tested for moisture content and other key variables; rolls that did not meet the standard were returned. This attention to quality extended throughout the manufacturing process. As Detwiler described it:

> We are working to have the reputation as a top-quality house. Every box that goes out of the plant has the initials of the operator who produced it. We can tell when it was made, and on what machine, and by whom. We can even identify the roll it came from and go back to the paper mill if a problem arises which is tied to raw material.

Table C Percentage of total cost of delivered product.

	12" x 8½" IBM 3800	14⅞" Two-part stock
Paper	66	56
Labor	8	10
Carbon paper	—	12
Other manufacturing	5	4
Distribution	6	5
Sales	8	7
General and administrative	7	6
	100	100

Source: BCFI 1985 Strategic Plan.

Because of the importance of the quality and cost of paper to producers of converted goods, some firms, such as Willamette, were vertically integrated. Detwiler explained why Bowater favored purchasing paper supplies on the open market:

> Though on the surface it might seem advantageous to have a secure, in-house supply of paper, in practice the benefits are illusory. For one thing, paper is normally transferred at market prices, so that the paper mills can show a normal profit. Moreover, when the paper mills have old plants, the costs can be higher than is available on the open market. But the biggest problem is that the mill tends to focus attention on outside customers rather than on internal transfers, which are taken for granted. So we can get better treatment from paper companies in an arm's-length transaction than if we had to rely on a sister operation.

Detwiler personally conducted many of the purchasing negotiations with BCFI's large paper suppliers.

> I get heavily involved with the paper because it represents such a large part of our total costs that any price changes affect us directly on the bottom line. I also do it, because having the president of the company involved gives us more clout with the paper companies. We enter into long-term contracts; we sit down with suppliers and show them the three-year demand growth curve. These contracts protect our supply requirements for our rapid growth. We are already an important customer for paper suppliers.

Sales

With its strategy of focusing on large-volume orders of stock forms, BCFI management regarded national accounts as a prime target that would eventually account for over 50 percent of its total sales. By 1986, national accounts represented about 35 percent of total sales. National accounts differed greatly in their practices: about 10 percent were fully centralized, controlling orders and inventories for all their operating units; about 60 percent centralized the purchase order and allowed required units to order their supplies as needed; and 30 percent only approved suppliers, permitting individual units to purchase supplies from a selected list of suppliers. The sales force worked out of twenty-three district offices, each of which had its own warehouse and distribution center.

In contrast to the rest of the industry, salespersons were paid on salary (combined with annual bonus incentives based on contribution) rather than on commission. Hatfield attributed much of the firm's success to this compensation policy, since it encouraged cooperation rather than competition within the sales force and enabled the company to provide coordinated service to a firm with facilities and offices throughout the country.

> The commission system is designed to get people to take lots of little, bad orders rather than to look for good ones, ones which enable us to have long production runs. It also creates a lot of fighting over territory. We don't have that. We have a team and the people we hire have to be willing to be team players. But it's hard to teach new people that they don't have to take every order that comes their way!

Although Bowater had had no difficulty recruiting experienced salespeople from other companies, the time required to educate and transform new recruits into "team players" was seen by management as a significant constraint on the rapid growth of the company. Experience had shown that salespeople who refused to learn eventually clashed with the others and usually chose to leave.

There were fifty-four salespeople in all, fifty-one men and three women, and Detwiler and Hatfield expected to recruit ten salespeople with industry experience each year for the next five years. Each salesperson was expected to generate $3.5 million in sales per year.

To land a national account with a major firm took patience, experience, and much direct personal contact. As David McBride, vice president of sales, described it, "Some people just think that all you have to do to make a sale in this industry is to hire a gorilla, burn a price on his chest, and send him out to take orders. But price is not the most important thing—it's service to the customer."

Detwiler concurred:

> We are a supply item for most companies, and though in some ways we are a commodity, we represent a critical link in their entire system. Their computers can't print output without our paper and so they want no stock-outs. So we have to maintain quality, make deliveries on time, and respond quickly to problems 100 percent of the time.

The salespeople were encouraged to make cold-call sales visits to firms to try to identify key decision makers and major competitors. Sometimes the key person would be a manager of the company's computer data-processing division. These people tended to be concerned about quality and availability. Other times the key person was the purchasing agent, who, as long as he or she received no complaints about a product, focused on price. When a "sponsor"—someone within the firm who would like to see the business go to BCFI—was located, that person was carefully nurtured and provided with samples to test. BCFI salespersons also had entertainment allowances, in contrast to competitors, whose salespeople had to pay for entertainment out of their commissions. When an account was finally landed, the salesperson was responsible for maintaining close contact—usually weekly—to monitor any quality problems and to prevent stock-outs.

Hatfield said:

> When I was in the field I used to have coffee with the purchasing guys from my major accounts every Monday morning. After they trusted me, I was often able to do the inventory and ordering for them, and I would make sure that they never ran out. It really got so that I knew their needs better than they did.

Such personal contacts also helped the sales force cope with a recurring problem in the industry: the great volatility in paper prices that had to be passed immediately along to customers in order to maintain desired profitability levels. Although some customers negotiated fixed annual prices or capped increases, most continued to follow the traditional industry practice of purchasing at market price. Maintaining good relations with these latter customers could be a problem at times when prices increased. BCFI salespersons worked hard to educate them about raw material price trends and to build trust.

As BCFI expanded its operations, it encountered increasingly severe competitive resistance. As a result, establishing a position on the West Coast proved to be more difficult than originally forecasted. In Detwiler's view, the competitors had come to recognize BCFI as a committed contender who had to be taken seriously and whose progress must be impeded as much as possible.

Prices were kept in line through national pricing guidelines. The "A" price was the lowest a salesperson could go without approval of the district manager; "B" was the lowest a district manager could go without consulting the regional manager; and "C" was the lowest a regional manager could go without talking to the vice president. District and regional sales managers were also responsible in their areas for expense control, account and market sales strategies, sales forecasting, hiring and firing, and training.

BCFI had also initiated a small reseller program in 1985 to promote Bowater products with retail stores for personal computer users. The program was handled through manufacturers' representatives and guided by the vice president of retail sales, Marty Allan.

Production Scheduling and Inventory Control

To minimize delivery time, BCFI tried to supply customers from inventory in the distribution center. Production scheduling was largely dedicated to replenishing and adding to inventory in accordance with forecasted needs. According to Detwiler:

BCFI currently handles better than 98 percent of its business from inventory, including contract jobs. We find this approach works very well in our established markets. The new market regions pose some problems because of the rapid change in the volume and mix of orders.

The complex task of coordinating the needs of the sales force with the constraints of manufacturing and of balancing inventory levels in distribution centers fell to several staff persons, most notably Ray McDowell, the vice president for technical services, who was responsible for production scheduling. Virtually all of the firm's production reporting, inventory systems, accounting records, sales data, and other data-processing needs were handled centrally by a single IBM 38 computer in Plano, under the supervision of MIS manager Patty Dockery.

Under McDowell's guidance, BCFI maintained a close watch on stock inventory levels and used these to prepare production orders. The central computer would keep a record of the approximately 125 items sold to some 2,000 customers over the previous sixteen weeks and would identify both the peak and trend in sales. Since demand was expected to continue to grow at a rapid rate, the peak sale of the earlier period was selected as the "safety stock" level for the next, so that an order of the same size could automatically be filled from inventory. Salespersons also filed Volume Change Notices to signal significant changes in sales; these were entered from terminals in the sales regional offices directly into the computer in Plano.

The desired safety stock levels were then compared to current inventory levels and the difference was categorized as "commit jobs" within a certain week—that is, an order for a production run in a plant. These orders were compiled and assigned to presses in the plants by McDowell's office. The plant managers in Plano and Scottsburg had the option of rearranging the order of runs or the use of the machines, as long as by the end of each week all of the assigned orders had been produced.

McDowell's job was not always smooth, because the sales and production function had different objectives when it came to scheduling. People in sales wanted to make sure that their delivery dates were met, while the plant managers wanted the longest possible runs in order to maximize efficiency and tons per hour. As a result, the size and location of finished-goods inventories were critical issues. Some persons in production, including vice president for manufacturing Norm Pellegrine, believed that production scheduling should be handled by the manufacturing function. McDowell, an engineer and M.B.A., did not seem to mind. As he put it, smiling, "I work on the principle that if you have everybody—sales, manufacturing, and finance—equally angry with you, then you are probably doing a good job."

Challenges of the Professional Phase

In the first six years of its existence, Bowater Computer Forms had grown from a tiny start-up to a firm of 350 employees and $76 million in sales (see Exhibit 3

Exhibit 3   Financial data, 1985 ($ millions).

Sales	$77	Cash	a
Cost of sales	59	Inventories	$17
Depreciation	2	Accounts receivable	8
Gross margin	16	Fixed assets, net	18
Distribution	5	Total assets	$44
GS&A	8	Accounts payable	4
Operating income	3	Deferred tax	3
		Bowater ownership	37
		Total liabilities	$44

Selected financial ratios

Gross fixed assets per sales dollars	8.2%
Inventory turnover	5.4X
Days sales outstanding	40
Operating profit as percentage of sales	4.3%

a. Less than $500,000.

for financial data). Everyone expected the growth to continue, and probably to accelerate, as the applications for computer technology expanded not only within large firms but within small companies and individual homes. The 1985 Bowater Strategic Plan projected that by 1993, when the market was expected to begin showing the first signs of maturation, the firm would have expanded to five plants and forty-five district offices around the country.

To make the heady transition from a relatively small firm to one that would break into the ranks of the *Fortune* 500 with hundreds of millions in sales by 1990 required the adept handling of several delicate management problems— the degree of centralization to maintain, the development and professionalization of managers, and the selection of proper distribution methods to reach the dynamic and diversifying market.

Centralization versus Decentralization

From the beginning Detwiler's strategy called for a tightly coordinated interplay between production and sales so that a local salesperson would have the authority and ability to commit the company to produce and deliver large orders to a national account at multiple delivery points within price guidelines. Under his strategy, the centralized authority over sales guidelines, production schedules, and inventories was the key to BCFI's competitive edge. In his view, to decentralize would be to create confusion. Said Detwiler:

> The only time I ever hear about decentralization is from Connecticut. They keep talking about it, but I don't know what they mean. At first I thought they meant having functions represented at each regional plant—

but that had been tried at other forms companies and I know it has not been successful. For example, I know of one company that has multiple plants and each one was a different division and had its own sales force. The division was a god unto itself! If there was a transfer, there was a $7\frac{1}{2}$ percent margin for each plant. Each plant had different equipment, and a different cost system. This structure was a deterrent to trying to sell national accounts.

While most of Detwiler's senior managers seemed to agree with him, there were some feelings in Scottsburg and at headquarters in Darien that Detwiler was holding the reins too tightly. Jim Ginter, the new plant manager in Scottsburg, described the situation from his point of view:

> We are committed to centralization. I see both sides of the issue. From one standpoint, it's great; I only have to worry about inventories in and manufacturing out. On the other hand, we are a thousand miles from Texas. We could react quicker to some situations—for example, problems in transportation—if we didn't have to find the person responsible in Plano before we could act.
>
> I don't know that some person punching buttons on a computer in Plano is really sensitive to production issues. I am not sure he or she knows the business well enough. We see green paper already running on this machine, and they are telling us also to run it on that machine. We could make the shift, but that would foul up the computer.
>
> And what if the rolls of paper don't come in on time? Then what? The schedule goes out the window. We get all our shipping orders from Plano; if the computer doesn't spit out shipping orders for a couple of hundred pallets before 5 P.M., the stuff just piles up. The scheduler is a thousand miles away, and stuff is coming off the line, and the shippers are standing around with nothing to do. And if the computer line goes down, then what do I do? It happens all the time.
>
> I don't know the answers. We just have to make things work. Bill Detwiler believes in this system, and so I have to believe in it too! He has built sales from nothing to $100 million so he must know what he is doing. I'm not really a proponent of decentralization, but I guess in some ways I am, because I know that we could control some areas more efficiently since we could react quicker when changes or unpredictable situations occur.

Pellegrine agreed:

> I am not a great believer in centralized management. This is the third company I have been with, and I have had good and bad experiences with it. I'd like to see the plant managers and regional vice president of sales work together to solve problems in inventory, particularly in finished goods inventory, rather than funnel all this through headquarters. I think centralization in certain areas—accounting, finance, purchasing—is good. Bill, on the other hand, has had bad experiences with decentralization. If left to him, Bill would make every decision; he would schedule every press. He's very good. He knows the manufacturing side and the marketing side and he's got that entrepreneurial spirit.

Said Toelle:

Bill is a very centralized kind of guy. He likes to make decisions himself and to control things from the top. He was so used to going into the plant and checking things that he and I finally decided that we had to move him and the other senior people out of the front office at the plant and into a corporate office in the RepublicBank building. And at first, he didn't want to go. So the degree of centralization is still an open question. That's a decision to be made down the pike.

Managerial Development and Promotion

The senior managers of BCFI also cited the challenge of developing managers fast enough to meet the demands of the rapidly expanding firm as a pressing problem. Three aspects of the company's approach aggravated the situation. First, the preoccupation with the day-to-day crises of a new company had blunted the managers' ability to take time to develop their subordinates. Second, in striving to achieve break-even performance as rapidly as possible, BCFI managers had deliberately held down administrative costs. Third, the centralized structure and strategy meant that the plants were judged on production costs and the sales offices on revenues and profit contribution, leaving the total profit responsibility—and the broad outlook of a general manager—to Detwiler alone.

By the spring of 1986 the senior managers had taken several steps to address the need: They had moved the corporate offices away from the plant, hired a human resources director, and brought up a new layer of managers to handle operating issues.

The Move to the New Office. In February 1986 the senior managers moved out of their offices in the front of the Plano plant and into a large suite occupying the entire eleventh floor of the modern RepublicBank office building several miles away. In conversations with the casewriter, several of the senior managers jovially suggested that they had made the move with relative ease compared to their colleagues. Sitting in his new, spacious, blue corner office Detwiler said:

> I have a great team, very fired up, very hands-on. But they didn't want to move over here to the new office. I had to drag them kicking! My Finance VP said to me, "But who's going to close the books at the end of the month?" and I told him, "You're going to have to train someone else! What if you were sick?"

In a later conversation, Finance Vice President Denis Tontodonato said:

> The four of us who started the business—Bill, Norm, Larry, and I—are really cut from the same mold. The move here and the transition to a professional mode was not as difficult for me, because I was the corporate controller for the Bowater parent before I came down here and I'm glad to roll my sleeves back down and do the work I used to do. But Bill by his nature just loves to get involved, and it was tough for him. We even kid him about it.

The Human Resources Manager. During the first five years, BCFI had employed an outside consultant to develop a detailed performance appraisal system for all employees based on weighted combinations of productivity, achievement of goals, and absenteeism. In January 1986, Bill Detwiler hired Michael Anders, formerly a human resources manager for the Harris Corporation, as the new director of human resources and charged him with the task of improving the managerial development within the firm.

Said Anders:

> It's going to be painful to move the company from one stage to the next; it's going to require a lot of detail management. In the entrepreneurial stage, if the senior managers needed a price quote, they would just decide it themselves. Now they can't do that because they have set up price guidelines.
>
> Bill tended to be involved in every aspect of the business and had the reputation of being pretty domineering. He's working hard to make the transition to a new style. If he's able to pull it off, he will be one of the few who has. But he is making a great effort. He is allowing people to make more decisions.
>
> One good thing about Bill is that he will not tolerate "yes" people. He'll play devil's advocate just to make sure you can support your opinion. He tests people. He'll pick a fight to see if you are strong in your resolution. So people tend to speak their minds in meetings.

In February 1986, six weeks after he had joined the firm, Anders was in the process of assessing BCFI's needs and planning his first steps.

Establishing a New Mid-Management Layer. To strengthen the operating management ranks and to free up the senior managers to deal with broader issues, Detwiler had authorized establishing a secondary level of managers, including a set of regional sales vice presidents and a new inventory manager. (See Exhibit 4 for an organizational chart.) This move, however, had created some tension within the company, because despite management's stated policy of promoting from within, Detwiler had felt obliged to hire some of these people from outside the firm to acquire the necessary expertise.

As McDowell described it:

> A lot of people joined the firm with high expectations. They were told that this was a growth company with a bright future and real potential for advancement. But the future has arrived, and it doesn't look so bright. There's only one president and the slots below him are filled by relatively young managers. The pyramid has gotten tight.

McDowell was particularly aware of the problem, since he had recently had to confront the disappointment of one of his employees in inventory control. This employee was upset that despite her five-year tenure as an inventory and production scheduler at the company, she had been passed over for promotion in favor of an outsider. This employee commented:

> From the moment you get hired here they dangle the policy of promotion from within like a carrot before your face, but then they don't take the

Exhibit 4 Organizational chart.

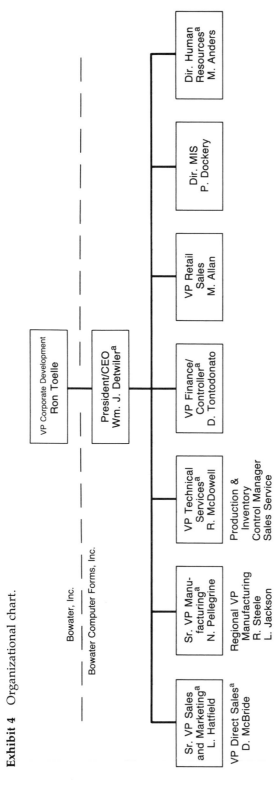

Bowater, Inc.
- - - - - - - -
Bowater Computer Forms, Inc.

VP Corporate Development
Ron Toelle

President/CEO
Wm. J. Detwiler[a]

Sr. VP Sales
and Marketing[a]
L. Hatfield

VP Direct Sales[a]
D. McBride

4 Regional VPs
District Managers

Sr. VP Manu-
facturing[a]
N. Pellegrine

Regional VP
Manufacturing
R. Steele
L. Jackson

Plant Managers

VP Technical
Services[a]
R. McDowell

Production &
Inventory
Control Manager
Sales Service

VP Finance/
Controller[a]
D. Tontodonato

VP Retail
Sales
M. Allan

Dir. MIS
P. Dockery

Dir. Human
Resources[a]
M. Anders

[a]Office in new building.

157

time to develop people within the company and they go to the outside. So a lot of people are discouraged.

Now Ray has said he will help me with career planning and I am hopeful that it will help. There are other people who are unhappy here; they feel the company did me wrong. They ask me, "Why are you staying?" I tell them, "I still believe that if I pay my dues I will get what's coming to me."

Dissatisfaction with the promotion policy was also expressed in the plant. Said one operator:

The policy of promotion from within is a bunch of BS. I had a lot of hope when I came here. They told me it's a growth company with a lot of potential. I even took a few management courses. But they won't develop you, and they won't promote you. There's people out there who have been stuffing boxes for five long years!

Maybe if you scratch their backs, you'll do all right. But in a pinch Detwiler is going to go hire his buddies from the outside. And you know something? Ninety percent of the workers agree with me.

Said another, a lead man who had been promoted:

There is opportunity here, if you work. But they don't give you a lot of training; they just pop you in the new job and then it's sink or swim. I was lucky because I had a good manager.

According to Anders, the percentage of employees promoted to their current position from within the company, as of January 30, 1986, was as follows: executive staff, 80 percent; mid-management (administration), 67 percent; mid-management (sales), 53 percent; regional management, 100 percent; and supervisors, 86 percent. The over-all average for these categories was 74 percent. The company's total workforce comprised 81 percent male/19 percent female and 73 percent non-exempt hourly/27 percent salaried employees.

Dispute over the Reseller Program

An additional problem for BCFI was the simmering debate over policy between Hatfield, senior vice president of sales and marketing in charge of the national account direct-sales force, and Allan, vice president of retail sales in charge of the reseller program. The reseller program had been started in November 1984, after a market research study had projected that individual and small business owners of personal computers would account for over 45 percent of the market for continuous computer paper by the mid-1990s.

Allan had served for several years as the vice president of administration, coordinating production scheduling, purchasing, and inventories. In 1984 Allan switched full time to the reseller program, and tasks formerly under his control were divided between Hatfield's and McDowell's departments.

Allan had begun in 1982 by attempting to sell directly to personal computer owners through direct mail. The sales pitch included lower prices, because the product would be purchased "direct from the factory," innovative packaging (in the form of a container that turned into a sturdy "dead files" storage box), and promotional add-ons such as a free diskette with every box of paper.

The direct-mail campaign turned out to be less successful than anticipated, because the lists of computer owners were chronically out of date. Allan then persuaded Detwiler to move to a full-fledged reseller program that would seek to place BCFI's products with wholesalers and retailers. Sales would be directed to large accounts such as discount mass merchandisers, computer store chains, department stores, book store chains, and the like. Detwiler agreed on the condition that the program would be profitable by the end of the first year.

Sales in the reseller program were made through eighteen manufacturer's representative firms and had totaled $1.7 million in 1985, the program's first year. Allan projected that sales from this program would be significant to BCFI within five years.

Hatfield was opposed to the reseller program on the grounds that it undermined and confused BCFI's principal marketing thrust. He noted:

> You can't control the reps; in fact, they control you, because they tinker with price and demand. It's against what we set out to do—go for long runs and big accounts. Instead they shoot for small numbers and volumes.
>
> Moreover, they aren't Bowater employees, and yet they make themselves out to be. They have Bowater cards and Bowater stationery. But they aren't really loyal; in fact, they are following the historic route of trying to break down the sales force.

Allan saw it differently:

> The charge that the reps aren't loyal isn't fair. They have given up other lines to handle ours exclusively. And they aren't selling at low prices and volumes—since they are on commission, the higher the volume and price, the higher the amount of money they make.
>
> We have two different marketing problems and two different solutions. We have a direct sales force to focus on the *Fortune* 2000, and we have a group of reps to sell to retailers such as Computerland, Target stores, or IBM product centers.

The two men were particularly disturbed at reports from the West Coast about a large retail chain that had been approached by both the direct sales force and the reps. The reps were trying to place BCFI paper in the stores, while the direct salespeople were trying to sell for the company's own data-processing needs. A vice-president of the chain had called BCFI headquarters to inquire why the reps were quoting a much higher price than the direct sales force.

To Allan, this problem was one that could be solved through more effective management of the boundaries; to Hatfield, it was a sign that, the larger the reseller program became, the more it would undermine the BCFI direct-sales strategy. Said Hatfield:

> I don't think the reseller program is a good idea because it is not sanctioned by sales. It's really one of Bill's special projects. History has shown that you cannot split your organization like this.

Detwiler had sided squarely with Allan. As he told a casewriter:

> The small-user segment of the market is going to be big, and we need to
> be in there. Hatfield is just going to have to get religion on this one. We are
> going to have to persuade him.
> *Casewriter:* And if he genuinely believes it's a bad idea and won't be
> persuaded?
> *Detwiler:* It could affect my opinion about his qualifications to be con-
> sidered as one of my potential successors.

Pressures and Problems of Rapid Growth

The final challenge of the new phase was deciding how to respond to pressure
on BCFI to accelerate its expansion. The industry was expanding at such a rate
that most of BCFI's growth was coming from the increase in demand rather
than from taking sales away from competitors. The relatively small capital investment required by each plant (only $12–15 million per plant, compared to
$250 million or more for a paper machine) combined with the robust profit
projections were prompting members of the parent company's board to encourage Detwiler to consider expanding into new product lines and to accelerate the schedule for bringing the new plants on-line.

As one board member put it:

> The growth is there, the business is there, the money is there—why not
> move faster? The slower we move, the more time we give competitors to
> copy our approach or to find ways of stopping or outflanking us.

Detwiler was reluctant to have BCFI move any faster than it was already
doing. He vividly recalled how, in the face of a forecast upturn in industry
demand, it had been decided to open the Scottsburg plant several years ahead
of schedule, to his eventual dismay. The accelerated expansion had caught
BCFI short of qualified staff, and the necessary transfers of people to Scottsburg disrupted the Plano operation. By the time the Scottsburg plant had come
on stream, demand had subsided, and BCFI losses had increased. This deterioration of performance occurred before the BCFI strategy had proven itself
and, consequently, Bowater senior managers' confidence in the subsidiary was
shaken.

In the second quarter of 1984, as monthly losses were mounting, Toelle
began to pressure Detwiler to pursue margins rather than volume. This shift,
under the black cloud of headquarters' dissatisfaction, caused considerable
consternation in BCFI's ranks, especially among the sales personnel. Many
salespeople felt that the new objectives were premature and unrealistic, and
that the rug had been pulled out from under them. Toelle argued, and Detwiler concurred, that proving the viability of BCFI's strategy was of paramount importance.

Detwiler launched an all-out drive to achieve break-even results in 1984. As
shown in Table D, BCFI achieved that goal, and recaptured the parent company's confidence and enthusiasm.

Table D   BCFI actual operating profit (000s of dollars).

	Actual
1982	(2,820)
1983	(3,465)
1984	925
1985	3,061

Apart from the caution induced by his earlier experiences, Detwiler was reluctant to overtax BCFI's human resources capabilities. In his view the company was limited in the number of experienced managers who could supervise the start-up and operation of new plants, and it took time to develop and promote supervisors and plant managers to take on tasks as the plants came on-line. Moreover, as Bill pointed out, a strategy of accelerating the rate of growth contained some hidden dangers.

> We keep getting pressure from Connecticut to bring the plants on fast and to look at cut sheets [8½″ – 11″ individual pages], labels, and other products. We hear them, and then we sit in our strategic planning meetings and ask ourselves: Should we do this? Do we want to risk spreading ourselves so thin? Do we really want a guy who is taking $10,000 orders for stock to stop and spend the extra time taking a $500 order for labels? And how fast can we push the growth of our manufacturing capacity before quality begins to suffer? Success in this industry depends on maintaining a tight strategic focus and a reputation for quality and service. How far and how fast can we go before these things suffer?
>
> For my part, I would like to see BCFI increase its sales over the next five years at an average 21 percent annual rate—which is just half of what we averaged these past three years—and to earn by the end of this period 15 to 17 percent operating profit and 30 percent return on investment. Based on the information flowing down to me, those targets might not be ambitious enough for some people.

British Petroleum Company p.l.c.

The first five months of 1984 witnessed a major restructuring of the U.S. petroleum industry. The stage had been set by T. Boone Pickens' attempt to take control of Gulf Oil. Against this backdrop, Texaco announced on January 6 that it had agreed to acquire Getty Oil for $10.1 billion. Then on January 24, Royal Dutch Shell announced a $55-per-share bid for the 30.5 percent minority holdings of its U.S. subsidiary, Shell Oil Company, for a total outlay of $5.2 billion. Gulf's struggle to fend off Pickens led on March 5 to an agreement whereby Standard Oil of California (SOCAL) would acquire Gulf's shares for $13.2 billion in cash. And on May 16, Mobil Oil received FTC clearance to acquire Superior Oil for $5.7 billion (see Exhibit 1). Even Exxon, barred by antitrust considerations from making any significant U.S. oil company acquisitions, was reported to have purchased nearly 1.6 percent of its own shares and to have put the market on notice that more purchases were to come.

It was little wonder that amid this flurry of activity, speculation should arise about possible changes in British Petroleum's (BP's) hands-off treatment of its U.S. subsidiary, Sohio, which accounted for about 40 percent of BP's total assets. This speculation was the subject of an article in the *International Herald Tribune*, March 16, 1984:

> LONDON—British Petroleum Co. appears to be seriously considering a move to tighten its grip on Standard Oil Co. of Ohio.
>
> Though BP owns 53 percent of the Cleveland-based company, it hitherto has always allowed Sohio's managers a free hand to run the company. Only two directors on Sohio's fifteen-member board are from BP, and the question of control is sensitive.
>
> Many analysts say BP eventually may have to follow the current fashion among oil majors and buy up oil reserves. First, however, the company would be likely to "tidy up" the Sohio situation.
>
> An outright purchase of the minority shares seems unlikely. At Sohio's current share price, that would cost well over $5 billion, and BP says it wants to reduce its debt further. But the company has other options.

As if in response, the *Guardian* reported on the same day the following denial by BP's chairman:

Exhibit 1   Major oil company mergers, 1984.

Company Acquired	Getty	Gulf	Superior	Shell
Acquirer	Texaco	Socal	Mobil	Royal Dutch Shell
Date announced	1/6/84	3/5/84	3/11/84	1/24/84
Acquisition price per share	$128	$80	$45	$58
Percent purchased	100	100	100	30.6
Total price ($ billions)	10.1	13.3	5.7	5.5
Oil reserves (billion barrels)	1.24	1.6	1.0	1.4
Total shares outstanding (end of 1983, in millions)	79.1	165.3	127	309
1983 equity book value ($ billions)	5.46	10.1	2.5	11.4[a]
1983 share price				
High	100½	48	41¾	51
Low	48¼	29¼	26¾	34⅝

a. $3.5 billion for the 30.6% minority interest tendered.

Sir Peter Walters was vehement in denying that BP will now look for acquisitions, or that it will increase its 53 percent shareholding in Sohio in the U.S. BP was doing nothing about changing its stake, he said, and such a move would not fit corporate strategy: the group was keener on getting high quality acreage developed. BP's main objective continues to be the reduction of its debts.

And on March 23, Walters was quoted in the *Investors Chronicle* as saying, "A Sohio buyout is not in our current horizons."

Despite these categorical denials, speculation concerning BP's intentions continued, as indicated in this report by the executive editor of the Finance and Industry column in the *Times* of April 11, 1984:

The big shake out in the American oil business has not gone unnoticed at Britannic House, BP's headquarters in London. The company, it seems, is thinking long and hard how best to improve its relationship with Sohio, BP's 53 percent owned United States subsidiary. A number of options for giving BP management tighter and more effective control over the running of its cash rich U.S. offspring are being studied as part of a general, and overdue, review.

. . . and in this conclusion to an article on British Petroleum in *The Economist* of April 21:

The poor performance of Sohio's nonpetroleum business has not gone unnoticed at BP (whose own minerals diversification remains a loss-maker). In particular, BP has never been happy with Sohio's $1.8 billion purchase in 1981 of Kennecott, the copper mining and metals company, whose losses since then have totalled $354m. Some observers reckon that BP will eventually follow Royal Dutch/Shell and bid for the minority shareholding in its American subsidiary.

The actions of other oil companies could at most serve only as an indicator for BP. Whatever decision BP might make about its relationship with Sohio would have to take into account the corporation's other activities and management's conclusions about its strategy. British Petroleum clearly had other possible uses for its funds. Exploration for new sources of oil and gas was an especially important investment alternative. On numerous occasions, Sir Peter had stated his preference for finding new oil over buying someone else's oil in the ground. BP's activities in gas, chemicals, minerals, coal, and other businesses also presented opportunities for major investments. In 1984, on its seventy-fifth anniversary, British Petroleum was the largest industrial concern in the U.K. and the fifth largest in the free world.

Company History

The Early Years

Started as the Anglo-Persian Oil Company in 1909, the firm was soon to become one of the largest producers of oil in the Middle East. In 1914 the British government—at the urging of Winston Churchill, then First Lord of the Admiralty—invested £2 million in Anglo-Persian to help finance the development of its Iranian oil concessions. The goal was to ensure a stable source of fuel for the Royal Navy as signs of war began to mount.

In return for its investment, the government received a 51 percent share of the company. With the protection afforded by the British government and the cheap source of supply in Iran, Anglo-Persian was able to make a reasonable return for its stockholders as a seller of Iranian crude oil and bunker fuel without having to invest large sums in refining or marketing. Despite this favorable situation in Iran, however, over time the firm began to extend its oil operations geographically and into downstream facilities. It first established oil operations in Iraq, where major quantities of oil were discovered in 1927, and then in 1934 entered Kuwait on a fifty-fifty basis with Gulf Oil Corporation.

The company changed its name in 1935 from Anglo-Persian Oil Company to Anglo-Iranian Oil Company and in 1954 to British Petroleum Company. The BP name had been originally connected with Anglo-Persian's U.K. marketing organization.

Setbacks and Advances in the 1950s and 1960s

"It's an awful blow to wake up one morning and find you have lost most of your oil." This comment by Lord Strathalmond, chairman of the British Petroleum board, referred to the nationalization in 1951 of BP's Iranian oil concessions and assets valued at up to £500 million. In one stroke, BP's world production of oil plummeted from 42 million tons to under 10 million, and its refining capacity from 32 million tons to about 8 million.

In 1954, following the fall of Dr. Mosaddeq as prime minister, a new government in Iran invited BP to return. Iran was no longer to be BP's exclusive preserve, however, according to an April 1, 1969, *Forbes* article. "BP got back into Iran, but not without the assistance of the world oil industry and a tightly enforced embargo, which finally toppled Mosaddeq. As was to be expected, BP had to pay a price. What had once been its own was reduced to a 40 percent share in an international consortium."

BP was to receive £204 million from its new partners in return for their 60 percent interest. By 1955, BP was once again enjoying a high rate of return on equity from its Middle East crude oil production.

Then a series of events began in 1958 that was to have major repercussions for the oil industry. A sharp recession in the United States late that year pushed down the market price of crude oil. In February 1959, Shell Oil lowered the posted prices on its Venezuelan production to counteract the falling market prices. A week later, BP lowered the posted prices on its Kuwait, Iran, and Qatar production in an attempt to capture some share in the U.S. market as an outlet for its excess Middle East production. An early reaction to these price cuts was the imposition of import restrictions for U.S. markets. The firms that had developed production in Venezuela and elsewhere to supplement U.S. domestic sources for the U.S. market began looking for other outlets in competition with existing supplies from the Middle East, thereby further depressing world crude prices.

These moves reduced profits for all the major international oil companies. They also reduced payments to producing nations. Provoked by what some government officials considered arbitrary moves by the major oil companies, representatives of several oil-producing nations met to discuss their response. These meetings led in 1960 to the formation of the Organization of Petroleum Exporting Countries (OPEC).

Foreseeing OPEC as a potential threat to the traditional oil company control of pricing and volume, BP actively sought to diversify its sources of crude oil. As a result of these efforts, it developed important fields in Libya, Abu Dhabi, and Nigeria. While BP succeeded in reducing its dependency on Iranian oil from 76 percent in 1950 to 34 percent in 1968, the expanding membership in OPEC effectively prevented it from lessening its exposure to this body. By 1968, 97 percent of BP's crude oil production still originated in OPEC countries.

With the increasing uncertainty of the terms under which OPEC oil would be obtained, BP's interest in its Alaskan exploration intensified. Although it had long been established as one of the seven major international oil companies, BP did virtually no producing, refining, or marketing in the United States, the world's largest consumer of oil products.

Expansion and Diversification

The Alaskan Discovery and Sohio

In March 1969, word arrived at Britannic House, London, that BP had struck oil on Alaska's North Slope. Several aspects of the Alaskan find made it immensely interesting to BP management. First there was the sheer size of the discovery. An early engineering report indicated recoverable reserves of as much as 4.8 billion barrels. Then there was the security of this supply in comparison with Middle Eastern sources.

The relative profitability of Alaskan crude oil was also an important feature. Estimates of profit after tax for Alaskan crude ranged from $0.65 to $1.15 per barrel, compared with about $0.26 per barrel for Middle Eastern crude. This difference resulted in large part from the lower royalty and income tax on U.S crude oil production.

Perhaps the most attractive feature of the Alaskan oil discovery was the opportunity it gave BP to enter the U.S. market. As Sir Eric Drake remarked at the time in a *Forbes*, April, 1966, article:

> The Americans have a wonderful fenced-in park from which they draw their profits. If you happen to have oil in it, quite naturally you can make a bigger profit. We had really given up hope a few years ago, but now we have some prospects with Alaska. . . . Frankly, the margin on American oil is higher than anywhere else in the world and you certainly can't expect to match it with Middle Eastern oil.

With this level of profitability, BP could ultimately afford to enter the U.S. retail gasoline market aggressively, and greatly improve the company's overall balance in the production, refining, and marketing chain. While this strategy might assure BP's long-run position in the U.S. market, the financing needed to develop immediately and simultaneously the Alaskan field and a U.S. distribution system to market its output would have strained the company's resources. The capital BP would require for drilling and pipeline construction in Alaska was estimated at $1.2 billion over a five-year period.

In anticipation of finding oil in its Prudhoe Bay concession, based on nearby discoveries in early 1968 by other oil companies, BP embarked on a two-stage effort to bridge the gap between its goals and its resources. Later that year, the company purchased two large refineries and 9,700 retail outlets in the eastern United States formerly owned by Sinclair Oil and Atlantic-Richfield. The acquisition of these properties gave BP refinery and end-user market outlets for about 200,000 barrels per day of crude oil production. It also added $400 million to BP's debt. Although this obligation would be repaid rather quickly once North Slope oil began to flow, the self-liquidating feature of the debt would be lost if completion of the project were delayed.

Following its own discovery of oil in 1969, BP proposed to swap its Alaskan properties and the refining and distribution facilities acquired from Sinclair and Atlantic-Richfield for an equity interest in Standard Oil Company of Ohio (Sohio). This action promised to give BP a U.S. management team for its U.S. operations, a factor of vital importance to the company. In addition the swap would transfer the burden of financing the Alaskan interest to Sohio. At the same time this move would convert Sohio from its historical crude short position to being a major potential supplier of crude oil to the U.S. market. Before the BP swap proposal, Sohio had sold about 180,000 barrels of petroleum products per day to end users, against crude production of only 30,000 barrels per day. Sohio was well known for its strengths in marketing, achieving market penetration of nearly 30 percent in gasoline sales in Ohio.

BP's ultimate ownership interest in Sohio was to vary between 25 percent and 54 percent, depending on the sustainable crude oil production reached on the Alaskan North Slope properties by January 1, 1978. If sustainable production was below 200,000 barrels per day, BP would own 25 percent of Sohio. Once daily production reached 200,000 barrels, BP's ownership would rise on a sliding scale from 34 percent to a maximum of 54 percent. The higher figure would obtain if production reached or exceeded 600,000 barrels per day by the end of 1977. On any production between 600,000 barrels per day and 1.2 million barrels per day (or the highest level of production reached before January, 1978), BP would retain a 75 percent direct interest in the profits generated. Sohio would receive the remaining 25 percent. Sohio would receive 100 percent of any profits on production in excess of 1.2 million barrels per day.

North Sea Oil—The Forties Field Discovery

A significant dimension was added to BP's corporate future with what appeared to be a major discovery of BP acreage in the North Sea in October 1970. A year later, the drilling of four appraisal wells had established the existence of a major new oil field—the Forties field—with total reserves of some 4.4 billion barrels. The recoverable reserves were projected at approximately 1.7 billion barrels of a desirable high-gravity and low-sulfur-content oil.

North Sea oil, in addition to representing a politically stable source of supply, promised to show a higher profit per barrel than oil obtained from the Middle East or North Africa. Since oil from the North Sea would meet only a small fraction of Europe's total needs, its delivered market price would be largely a function of Middle East crude prices.

Because the Forties field was so far offshore, in deep water, and subject to severe weather conditions, the capital investment associated with developing it was high. BP estimated that the cost of development would run between £300 million and £400 million spread over a four-year period, an amount then equal to a full year of BP's capital expenditures. While BP presumably could have financed the project as part of its normal capital expenditures, this would have required sharp reductions in the spending plans for other areas of its business. To avoid this alternative and to escape giving away a portion of the equity in the field as it had done with the Alaskan discovery (via the Sohio merger), BP decided to face the full brunt of the financing challenge.

BP's relatively heavy debt burden, combined with its reluctance to sell additional equity, made negotiating a loan of £300 to £400 million difficult. The difficulty was compounded by the fact that environmental concerns were delaying approval of the trans-Alaskan pipeline. Even if construction were to begin in 1972 or 1973, oil deliveries from Prudhoe Bay would not begin before 1976 or 1977.

Because the Forties field was in a secure area, however, and because it appeared to contain enough oil to generate revenues equal to five times its development cost, BP considered the possibility of attempting to finance it on the credit strength of the project alone rather than on the credit strength of the company overall.

Project financing was arranged by creating a nonprofit company (to be known as Norex) that was controlled by the managers of a bank consortium. Norex would buy the rights to a portion of the Forties field oil production from BP Development on a forward basis (prior to actual production) and simultaneously contract to sell the oil as it was produced at a fixed price to BP Trading under a long-term sales agreement. The banking consortium would loan money to Norex, which, in turn, would remit these funds to BP Development to develop the field, as prepayments for the oil. Once the oil began to flow, the cash generated by its sale to BP Trading would be used by Norex to service its loans from the banks.

A major goal of the proposed financing from BP's standpoint was to shield the company from the large initial cash drain the Forties field development implied. Another goal (equally important, given the vagaries of weather and the difficulties that might be expected in deep-water ocean engineering), was to insulate BP from loan repayment terms that were unrelated to actual cash returns from the project.

The First Oil Shock, 1973–1974

The oil price shock in late 1973 and early 1974 marked an end to cheap oil. The price per barrel increased from $3 on October 1 to $10.95 by January 1, 1974, as a direct result of an Arab oil minister's agreement to cut exports of oil by 5 percent and to impose an embargo against nations that were identified as pro-Israel in the Yom Kippur war of October 1973.

The effect of this action was dramatic. The cut in supplies coupled with the large price increase triggered a global recession. Overall crude oil trade decreased by about 11 percent over the next two years. On the bright side for oil companies was a threefold appreciation of oil inventory value, making possible large "inventory stock profits." On the dark side was OPEC's escalation of demands. Emboldened by their easy success in increasing royalties and taxes, the OPEC nations next began to demand an increase in their share of ownership. In time, this move led to outright nationalization. For example, Saudi Arabia took 60 percent ownership of Aramco, by far the world's largest producer of oil in 1974, and 100 percent ownership in 1980. Kuwait moved even faster, nationalizing the Kuwait Oil Company in 1975.

BP's oil interests in Alaska and the North Sea took on added importance with these events. In the United States, passage of the Federal Lands Right-of-Way Act of 1973 removed the legal obstacles to the construction of the trans-Alaska pipeline. Oil was expected to flow from Alaska in 1977. With most of the submarine pipeline installed and the first of two platforms well under construction, production of North Sea oil was expected to begin in 1975.

The Oil Industry Diversifies

With oil prices up, demand down, and oil-producing properties being nationalized in an increasing number of countries, the prospects for the oil industry were bleak, and many of the major oil companies began to look elsewhere to maintain a satisfactory return on investment. A bulge of inventory stock profits was available to these companies for making acquisitions.

Mobil Oil made the most dramatic move when it acquired 54 percent of Marcor for $840 million in 1974. Marcor was the parent company of Montgomery Ward & Co., a retail and catalog sales outlet, and Container Corporation of America, a manufacturer of paperboard packaging. Changing its name to reflect its broadened business interests, Mobil declared in its 1976 annual report, "Mobil Corporation is more than an oil company. . . . [It has] realized its major diversification objective."

Gulf's initial interests were directed toward real estate development, coal, and minerals. (It had the largest privately owned deposit of uranium ore in the world.) In 1975, it made an abortive attempt to acquire Rockwell International, a manufacturer of defense and industrial equipment. Exxon, in contrast, moved into electronic office equipment, investing close to $1 billion between 1973 and 1981. In addition, Exxon acquired Reliance Electric Company, a manufacturer of electric motors and other electrical equipment, for $1.2 billion in 1979. And Standard Oil of California (Socal) moved to minerals in 1975 with the 20 percent acquisition of AMAX, a major producer of various metals and minerals, for $350 million.

The idea of diversifying into nonoil businesses appealed to BP management also. Its interest became focused on businesses closely related to oil or to the firm's extractive skills. Earlier moves into petrochemicals and animal feed were expanded, and major entries were made into coal and minerals.

Petrochemicals. BP first became involved in petrochemicals in 1947, when it established with Distillers Corporation a joint company to manufacture basic materials derived from naphtha. In 1967, BP became the second largest chemical manufacturer in the United Kingdom when it acquired Distillers' chemical interests. These interests were substantially augmented at the end of 1978 when, at a cost of $400 million, BP acquired Union Carbide's chemicals and plastics interests in Europe (low-density polyethylene, ethylene oxide, and other derivatives) and Monsanto's polystyrene business in the EEC.

Animal Feed. By 1970, BP's researchers had become intrigued by certain biological "bugs" capable of transforming the waxy content of crude oil into pure protein. Interest soon developed in the idea of using biomass technology to produce protein for commercial sale while improving crude composition by reducing undesirable wax. Animal feed was seen as the best market for such protein.

To enter this business, BP acquired several animal feed firms. These firms provided people experienced in the feed business and ready distribution for the expected new biomass output. While the technology worked as expected, it proved not to be competitive with soya as a source of protein and was abandoned in 1973. By then, the animal feed firms had shown themselves to be quite profitable in their own right, and BP continued to expand this business, adding breeding and meat processing. By the 1980s, BP was second only to Ralston Purina in the size of its animal-feed operations.

Coal. Starting in the mid-1970s, BP built its coal business gradually on the grounds that this business offered prospects for growth and that it complemented the company's other energy interests. By 1978, BP had become the eighth largest private-sector coal producer in the world, with major interests in Australia, South Africa, Canada, and the United States (under Sohio).

Minerals. BP first entered minerals in the mid-1970s, creating an in-house department to develop its interests. Subsequently, in 1980, in what was then the London Stock Exchange's largest-ever takeover bid ($970 million), it acquired Selection Trust, the London-based international mining house. The following year, Sohio acquired Kennecott, the largest producer of copper in the United States. These two acquisitions placed the BP group among the world's largest mineral companies.

Other. By the close of the 1970s, BP had entered a number of other businesses as an outgrowth of its technical interests and discoveries. These ventures included a joint company with Lucas (a large manufacturer of auto parts) to develop and market photovoltaic solar power systems, a major U.K.-based computer services and consultancy company, a joint venture to manufacture insulation materials, and an acquired company manufacturing reinforced plastic materials and carbon fiber.

The Second Oil Shock, 1978–79

The prolonged containment of petroleum demand resulting from conservation and sluggish economic recovery held the barrel price of crude oil at the $12 level during the mid-1970s. With inflation, the value of the crude oil barrel had actually decreased to less than $9 in constant 1973 dollars. Mounting dissatisfaction in OPEC with perceived depressed oil prices erupted when revolution struck Iran in late 1978. The sudden reduction in that country's crude output from 5.2 million barrels per day (bpd) to 3.1 million bpd produced chaos in the world economy. The price of oil jumped to $20 per barrel and continued to rise until it reached the $32–$40 range in 1981.

As the largest participant in the Iranian Oil Consortium, with a 40 percent share, BP was severely hit by the effects of the revolution. It suffered further blows in 1979 from the nationalization of its assets in Nigeria and a cutback in supplies from Kuwait. As shown in Table A, these losses were tempered somewhat by the increased flows from Alaskan and North Sea sources.

BP management's growing discomfort with oil prospects was chronicled by the chairman's statements in the annual reports for that period:

The end of the year was overshadowed by events in Iran that started a chain of reactions the final outcome of which it is not yet possible to see. . . . It would be prudent to accelerate the search for new oil and the development of alternative energy. . . . (1978)

For the world at large, I believe that the principal lesson of 1979 is that it would not be prudent for the oil-importing countries to count on receiving in the future larger supplies from OPEC than they are receiving today. (1979)

. . . although oil and gas will remain our main businesses for many years, we have moved decisively to supplement these with sources of future growth. Our direct interests in coal production have been steadily expanded, and with the recent acquisition of Selection Trust, we now have an integrated worldwide minerals company. . . . (1980)

Organizational Restructuring and New Strategic Directions

In December 1980 Chairman David Steel announced a major restructuring of the British Petroleum organization, explaining, "The main feature of this group reorganization is to segregate our different international businesses, whilst retaining a managerial structure and control system which ensures cohesion on a national level both at home and abroad." The following reasoning was given at a management conference: "Almost all of us, the bosses, and almost all our staffs have been trained as oil men. If these new businesses are to succeed, their executives must perform and be judged by their own industries' standards and expertise, and not by the oil industry's. . . . [E]ach business must follow its own strategy taking account of the conditions and opportunities found in its own industry."

The new organization comprised three principal groupings: group head office (GHO), the businesses, and supporting services. (Exhibit 2 depicts a 1984 modification of this structure.)

GHO was responsible for working out the objectives and strategy for BP as

Table A BP's crude oil statistics.

	1976	1978	1980	1976–1980
(A) Crude Oil Sources				
Alaska	–	600	710	+710
North Sea	180	470	510	+330
Iran	1,760	1,020	40	−1,720
Nigeria	420	360	–	−420
Others	1,180	1,270	1,130	−50
Total	3,540	3,720	2,390	−1,150
(B) Refinery Throughputs	1,900	2,000	1,920	+20
Crude oil balance (A − B)	1,640	1,720	470	−1,170

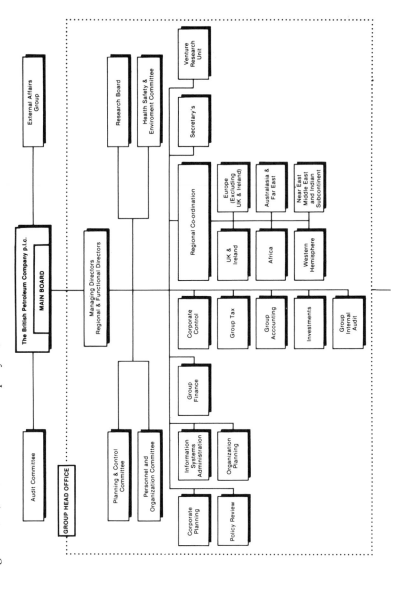

Exhibit 2 BP group, central organization, 1984. *Source:* BP company chart.

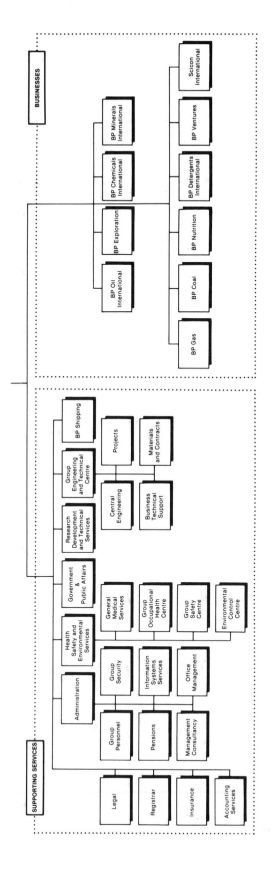

a whole and for allocating resources to the different businesses. National organizations reported to regional directors who were part of GHO.

Nine businesses were established:

1. BP Oil International (including the acquisition, refining, and marketing of oil)
2. BP Exploration (including the exploration and development of both petroleum and gas)
3. BP Chemicals International
4. BP Minerals International
5. BP Gas (including the acquisition and marketing of gas)
6. BP Coal
7. BP Nutrition
8. BP Detergents International
9. BP Ventures

A tenth business, SCICON International, was added in May 1982 to develop BP's interests in information technology. These businesses and the national organizations were to relate to each other in a matrix structure.

A New Chairman and Retrenchment

On November 28, 1981, Peter Walters succeeded Sir David Steel as chairman of BP.[1] The company Walters was to lead was well into its second year of falling profits and still heading downhill as the oil industry continued to experience surplus supplies and an acute price weakness. In his first chairman's letter to shareholders (1981), Walters noted his concern with "how BP would operate in a more slowly growing world economy. . . ."

The *Daily Telegraph* gave the following account of Walters' intentions on his first working day as chairman:

> Peter Walters has set a five-year target to knock British Petroleum into a more profitable shape. . . . Oil marketing and refineries along with chemicals are in the middle of a traumatic and costly overhaul but the "haemorrhaging" has stopped; gas is important but still small in the total reckoning; and it will be five years before Walters reckons the investment in minerals and coal starts to pay off.

And in a related article, the *Telegraph* commented, "The financial challenge is already clearly visible—a target of a 10 percent real return on capital invested, after tax, for new expenditures. . . . [I]t is a measure of the Main Board's commitment to make all the group's assets work for their living."

1. *Business Week,* May 7, 1984, made the following comment about the change in leadership: "Over the years, BP chairmen almost invariably came from the same old-boy network that staffed the foreign service. But Walters is different. The son of a policeman and graduate of Britain's state-run secondary school system and Birmingham University, he rose through BP's downstream and North American operations rather than along the Middle Eastern and African path followed by his Oxford-educated predecessor, David Steel."

And work for their living they did. Walters put pressure on the oil marketing and chemical businesses to shift emphasis from volume and market share to profitability. He later noted: "Our traditional businesses were in a mess. I tried to make clear to all the managers that there would be no sacred cows. My loyalty was to the company's future, not to its historical past. As to the oil business, I no longer believe in the advantages of vertical integration. Each step in the chain has to stand on its own feet."

The changes in BP Oil International were notable for their scope and for the extent to which they represented a break from tradition. In contrast to its traditional role of marketing about half of BP's annual 240 million tons of heavy Middle East crude, the refining and marketing business was now supposed to run a profitable operation quite independently of the greatly cut back production arm (to about 40 million tons annually). To do this, the new unit began to focus on selected markets (such as transportation fuel instead of industrial heating) and to shift its marketing emphasis from Europe to the rapidly growing Pacific Basin region. Refining capacity in Europe accordingly was reduced by about 30 percent.

These actions, however, were not unusual for the industry at this time. In discussing the oil industry as a whole, *The Economist* (October 15, 1983) noted:

> The companies' strategies for becoming competitive are similar. First, close redundant old plants. In 1980–82, BP reduced its European refining capacity by about 30 percent, Shell by 19 percent, Mobil by 16 percent, Exxon by 11 percent and the rest of the industry by 9 percent.
>
> The second step is to improve remaining refineries by investing in one of the several technologies which can squeeze more light products, like petrol, out of a barrel of even gunky crude. At many companies, downstream capital expenditure is reaching record levels—even though capacity is being reduced.
>
> The third part of most strategies is to redeploy assets to concentrate a company's strength on profitable markets.

Inherent in the efforts to redirect the various businesses was Walters' concern with getting BP's financial house in order. The 1980 acquisition of Selection Trust had placed a heavy financial drain on BP, and, coupled with reduced oil profits, had pushed up BP's debt-equity ratio to 37.3 percent. Even more worrisome, more than half of the company's debt financing was short term. As one of the directors remarked, "I share the chairman's commitment to get the financial ratios right. I do not like the slender debt coverage that we have. The company needs financial headroom capable of seizing opportunities and withstanding recession and unforeseen misfortune."

In his drive for financial headroom, Walters insisted on cost cutting and on a more selective investment program. As one senior executive noted, "The chairman focused on getting the present operations under control for the medium term. He did this in two ways: by austerity measures and by major cutbacks in the underperforming business areas such as downstream oil [refining and marketing] and chemicals."

An equity-rights issue also figured in management's plans for generating financial headroom. This move was blocked, however, when Her Majesty's government decided to divest itself of a major portion of its BP holdings, reducing its ownership from 38.85 percent to 31.73 percent. The tender sale on September 23, 1983, of 130 million common shares was oversubscribed and raised about £526m ($789m). The government pledged not to sell any more BP shares for two years.

As the government was preparing its tender offer, BP surprised everyone with an announcement that it was selling 12 percent of its valuable North Sea holdings. Saddled with a marginal tax rate of more than 90 percent on the Forties income stream, BP figured the properties would be worth more to companies with North Sea capital expenditures to offset profits. As noted in the *Financial Times*, September 12, "each 1 percent of the Forties Field is worth £95m in present-day value untaxed, only £6m to BP at full tax, and is being offered by BP at £22m."

Despite the government's quick elimination of the most appealing potential tax allowances, BP completed the sale of shares to 21 companies, raising £293 million ($390m) in exchange for an 11.65 percent share of ownership (reducing BP's share from 95 percent to 83 percent). In reporting this move, *Business Week*, October 3, 1984, was prompted to conclude, "It was at this point that observers realized how far the company was prepared to carry the portfolio-management approach. BP's new style of buying and selling properties may be teaching the rest of the oil industry a lesson in flexible management."

1983 Results

The difficult and sometimes painful efforts in 1981 and 1982 to improve BP's performance began to pay off handsomely in 1983. Typical of the general acclaim for BP in the business press was the *Times'* announcement on March 16, 1984:

Profits Pour in for Shell and BP

> Shell and BP yesterday both announced large increases in their profits—BP by 55 percent, Shell by 38 percent—as well as increased confidence for stable world oil prices and supplies in the coming year. Both increased their dividends by 20 percent.

The profit turnaround was perhaps most vividly portrayed in *Business Week*, May 7, 1984, in the bar chart shown as Figure A.

Table B breaks down 1983 financial data by business segment.

Walters' letter to the shareholders opened, "Taken as a whole, 1983 was a good year for the BP Group." The reservation implicit in this otherwise positive announcement reflected some major disappointments on the company's exploration front.

On September 14, 1983, Prime Minister Margaret Thatcher officially opened BP's Magnus field in the North Sea (first discovered in 1973). With reserves of 565 million barrels (about one-fourth the size of the Forties field), Magnus was a welcome addition to the company's oil holdings, although its location in waters

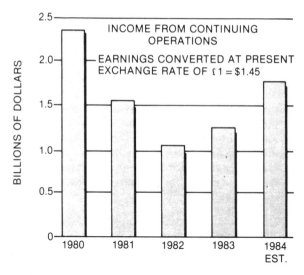

Figure A BP's earnings recovery. *Source:* British Petroleum Co., BW estimate.

over 600 feet deep and its complex geological structure resulted in oil-lifting costs of around $9 per barrel, compared with $2 for the Forties field.

But the big gambles were taking place in other parts of the world. As reported in *Barron's,* August 8, 1983:

> The "Mukluk Prospect" isn't the title of the latest Robert Ludlum thriller, though it packs all the excitement and danger of the best-selling author's typical cliffhanger. Rather, Mukluk is one of this year's hottest oil exploration sites, about 20 miles off Alaska's frigid and forbidding north coast, and the leading prospector there is Standard Oil Co. of Ohio.

On November 13, 1983, Sohio announced its best estimate of petroleum reserves at the Mukluk field to be 1.5 billion barrels, although the reserves could go as high as 4 to 5 billion barrels.

Table B 1983 Segment operating results (£ millions).

	Exploration	Oil Int'l[a]	Gas	Chemicals	Minerals	Coal	Nutri- tion	Deter- gents
Operating profit	1,096	205	80	(81)	(26)	0	27	3
Turnover	4,862	20,067	542	1,715	251	419	723	169
Capital employed	3,066	4,037	494	982	434	420	198	61
Capital expenditure	879	239	82	49	78	78	17	6

Source: 1983 annual report
Note: Exchange rate: $1.45 = £

a. BP Oil International was responsible for trading, refining, and marketing oil worldwide.

Then, on December 6, the *Wall Street Journal* reported the daunting news that the "Mukluk field offshore Alaska—considered the U.S.'s brightest oil prospect in 15 years—is starting to look to some of its partners like one of the biggest busts in the industry's history."

And on January 23, 1984, it reported:

> Standard Oil Co. (Ohio) confirmed that its Mukluk well offshore Alaska is a dry hole and took a $310 million pre-tax write-off of much of its investment there. . . .
>
> In a related move, British Petroleum Co., which owns 53 percent of Sohio and has its own interest of 7 percent in Mukluk, said it will take a net write-off of about $140 million to cover most, but not all, of its investment. BP said that $56 million of its write-off stems from its direct interest in the Mukluk drilling block, and the rest from its interest in Sohio.

BP geologists later surmised that they had been probably 40 million years too late—when, somehow, Mukluk had been breached and leaked.

With the demise of Mukluk, China was seen by industry observers as "BP's best hope for topping up the group's oil reserves." On May 10, 1983, the China National Offshore Oil Corporation signed contracts with an international consortium headed by BP, which had a 45 percent share, to launch a major offshore exploration and development effort in the South China and Yellow Seas. The Chinese estimated potential offshore reserves at around 70–100 billion barrels of oil. Although these figures were thought to overstate the resources, even the more conservative oil company estimates (from 20 to 40 billion barrels), would allow production eventually to match or even exceed North Sea output.

Then in early 1984, the first results were announced: four dry wells. Atlantic-Richfield decided to discontinue exploration.

In reviewing these events, the chairman's letter in BP's 1983 annual report had the following to say about the nature of oil exploration:

> In Alaska our hopes of a major hydrocarbon discovery at Mukluk unfortunately came to naught, despite the area's high geological promise. In the South China Sea, the first wells drilled in a programme to explore an area fifty-five times the size of a North Sea block have now proved to contain only very limited hydrocarbon deposits.
>
> I mention these disappointments rather than our many successes, because they highlight a factor often overlooked by the casual observer of the oil industry—namely risk. Public attention is directed, understandably, towards our successes—fields such as Forties, Prudhoe Bay and Magnus—and towards the rewards accruing from them. Yet outside the Middle East, only one well in fifteen to twenty results in a commercially exploitable find.

The continuous decline in BP's net proven reserves from 1979 through 1983 is illustrated in Figure B.

Accent on the positive was given by Basil Butler, business chief executive for BP Exploration, "Despite Mukluk and China, 1983 was actually one of BP's

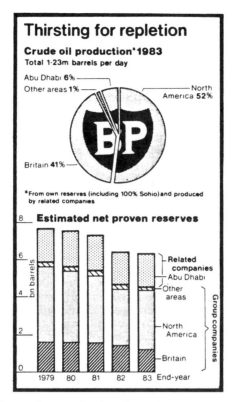

Figure B Thirsting for repletion: Crude oil production, 1983. *Source: The Economist,* October 15, 1983, p. 84.

more successful exploration years in recent times." A discovery of four major gas fields in the North Sea announced in March 1984 provided added solace to BP explorers. The fields held 2.5 trillion cubic feet of estimated recoverable reserves, equivalent to 450 million barrels of oil, or the size of the Magnus oil field. BP announced its intention to invest £1.3 billion to develop the fields as a source of supply for the government-owned British Gas Corporation.

The Oil Industry Returns to Oil

The changing tone of the chairman's letters to shareholders gave some evidence that Peter Walters seemed to be backing off from his predecessor's conviction that BP would have to rely increasingly on its diversified businesses for further growth. In the 1982 annual report Walters followed a lengthy discussion about oil exploration with the comment, "I do not wish to imply any diminished attention or dedication to our diversified nonoil businesses." By 1983, his focus on oil was even more apparent:

Today our interests extend into a wide range of business areas, from chemicals to telecommunications and from mining to nutrition. But, as the cover of this report symbolically denotes, oil has always been the core of our business and is likely to remain so for the foreseeable future.

This apparent return to oil as the business for growth reflected an industry-wide phenomenon, as indicated in the following account from *The Economist*, October 15, 1983:

Five years ago, even the most conservative of the seven sisters was diversifying into coal and synfuels. The more ambitious took on a hodge-podge of minerals, paper-making, electronics and other non-oil businesses. Now the emphasis is back on oil (preferably in North America).

Their experience so far confirms the judgment of Texaco's chairman, Mr. John McKinley. He says: "We've looked at all the alternatives and we just don't see any businesses where our expertise can make us as much money as oil."

The change in emphasis is not complete though. Some are still putting money into coal. And with only a couple of exceptions . . . companies are hanging on to their 1970s energy acquisitions.

The relative reduction of total capital expenditures for nonoil activities by the big oil companies since 1977 (shown in Figure C) was accompanied by a marked increase in exploration and production expenditures. Although the noncommunist world's proven oil reserves were rising, the amount of oil production controlled by the oil companies was declining (see Figure D).

In a speech on February 15, 1984, Sir Peter Walters (who had been knighted in the 1984 New Year's Honours List) spoke about investment trends in the oil industry and in BP:

Investment—upstream and downstream—rose from some $20 billion per annum in 1970 to $140 billion by 1981, equivalent to an annual rate growth of 19 percent. Of course inflation had an impact, but even so, in real terms

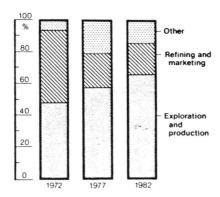

Figure C Percentage of total capital expenditure (seven sisters). *Source: The Economist,* October 15, 1983, p. 85.

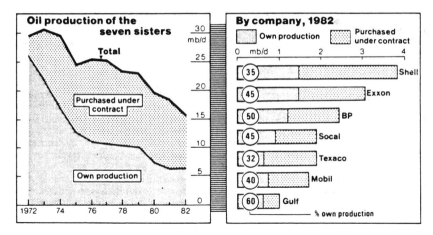

Figure D Oil production of the seven sisters. *Source: The Economist*, October 15, 1983, p. 86.

the annual growth rate was still about 10 percent, reflecting the stimulus given by an oil price that climbed dramatically from about $2/bbl at the beginning of that period. Within the totals, the major growth area by far was upstream, which in 1971 accounted for only a third of investment, and as much as two-thirds of the much higher amounts spent 10 years later.

Looking to the future, I see investment picking up—in particular because demand should increase, and because of the higher costs of the fields and technologies. Even a relatively small increase in the real price of oil over the rest of the decade (which, as I have said, is what I expect) would, according to Chase Manhattan's figures, makes investment grow to possibly $200–250 billion (in money-of-the-day terms) by 1990.

From all this, it should be clear that the oil industry is committed to substantial investment "upstream." My own company, for example, is currently exploring in 24 countries. In 1982–83 our exploration budget was twice as high in real terms as in 1979; and it is being maintained at that level (about £400 million p.a. in real terms) over the next five years.

Increasing investments in exploration was one response to the quest for additional oil sources. Buying established reserves in the ground was another. As noted in *Business Week*, March 26, 1984.

It may be sheer coincidence that Mobil, Texaco, and Standard Oil of California—three of the four partners in the Arabian American Oil Co.—have decided in quick succession to pump $29 billion into oil mergers. But more likely, a common reason lies behind the trio's rush to buy oil reserves in the U.S. and other high-profit areas: They want to be in command of their destinies again. That means concentrating on areas where they still control the flow of oil from wellhead to gasoline pump.

While the takeover fever among U.S. oil companies might have seemed far removed from BP's world, Royal Dutch/Shell's tender offer to buy up the approximately 30 percent of its U.S. subsidiary, Shell Oil Co., that was publicly owned could not be so easily dismissed. The following account in *Business Week,* February 6, 1984, seemed relevant to BP's situation as well as to Shell's:

> To Sir Peter Baxendell, Chairman of Royal Dutch/Shell's committee of managing directors, the U.S. is "a major and, in all probability, increasingly important area." Analysts and industry executives say that the Reagan Administration's unwillingness to challenge oil-industry takeovers—including Texaco Inc.'s record-shattering $10 billion attempt to buy Getty Oil Co.—sent out a signal: Even foreign companies should have no problems on the merger trail.
>
> "Royal Dutch would have done this years ago, except for its fear of antitrust problems," says E.V. Newland, Royal Dutch/Shell's former strategic-analysis chief. And, adds David L. Johnson, an analyst, the Royal Dutch/Shell move "makes it easier for the group to make acquisitions in the U.S. in the future."

It was this context that had set oil analysts and investors to wondering what changes, if any, Sir Peter Walters might make in BP's arm's-length relationship with Sohio. Characteristic of the resulting speculation was the following account in the *Times,* April 11, 1984:

> The one option so far ruled out is the simplest: buying out the minority Sohio shareholders, as Shell is doing with Shell Oil. This would allow BP to get its hands on Sohio's cash flow and use it however it wished. It would however be expensive—at least $6 billion—and also something of an admission of defeat.
>
> However, there is no shortage of other options. Among those that BP is studying are: selling off part of Sohio to the minority shareholders in return for greater BP control of the rump; reorganizing the capital structure of the BP/Sohio group to give BP a greater interest in Sohio's operations; gradually reducing BP's shareholding as the production and cash flow from Alaska starts to decline; and siphoning off the Prudhoe Bay cash flow in the form of royalty trusts.[2]

Exhibit 3 contains a history of BP's financial performance from 1974 through 1983.

Sohio

When Standard Oil Company, the giant oil trust founded in 1870 by John D. Rockefeller, was broken up into thirty-four regional companies, the piece left in Cleveland was given the original refinery, some storage tanks, and the state

---

2. Most royalty trusts involve overriding royalty or net-profit interests carved out of a company's working interests in specific producing properties. The interests are transferred to an independently administered trust, "units" of which are distributed to company shareholders. The units can be traded like shares of stock. Ownership of the properties remains with the corporation.
The royalty income is not subject to U.S. corporate taxes. Moreover, the corporation generally pays no tax on the appreciation in the royalty—that is, the difference between the value of the royalty when distributed and its original cost.

Exhibit 3 BP group financial highlights, 1974–83 ($ millions except per share data).

	1974	1975	1976	1977	1978	1979	1980	1981	1982	1983
Balance Sheet (December 31)										
Cash	$ 2,225	$ 1,635	$ 1,174	$ 1,422	$ 2,408	$ 3,188	$ 6,006	$ 3,917	$ 2,560	$ 1,329
Current assets	9,019	7,908	7,839	8,897	11,454	17,807	22,033	19,862	17,438	14,565
Total assets	15,108	14,590	14,917	17,281	26,513	34,716	42,396	44,316	42,548	39,457
Current liabilities	6,725	5,437	5,672	6,007	8,642	12,311	15,590	15,443	14,214	10,597
Finance debt due within one year	- - - - - - - - data not available - - - - - - - - -					1,977	3,791	5,353	4,715	1,801
Long-term debt	1,115	2,174	2,570	2,882	6,637	6,108	5,838	6,314	6,224	6,219
Common equity	6,109	5,379	4,837	6,232	7,639	11,059	14,133	14,732	13,988	13,977
Percent long-term debt/ capitalization	14.9	27.1	32.3	30.6	41.7	30.3	24.4	24.7	24.7	24.2
Return on assets (%)	8.8	2.0	2.1	4.3	4.1	11.8	8.8	4.4	2.7	3.1
Return on equity (%)	19.9	5.1	6.0	12.4	13.1	38.5	26.9	13.2	8.1	9.0
Income Statement (Year ended December 31)										
Revenues	$18,354	$15,718	$17,988	$23,035	$29,127	$40,501	$49,368	$49,192	$47,524	$47,122
Operating income	5,502	3,316	3,458	4,653	6,222	11,676	13,427	6,696	6,236	6,845
Capital expenditures	1,157	1,351	1,373	1,222	1,897	2,508	4,087	5,627	6,247	4,420
Depreciation and other noncash items[a]	- - - - - - - data not available - - - - - - -			473	973	2,010	1,852	2,118	2,909	3,519
Interest expense	186	302	396	473	973	903	1,054	1,295	1,216	913
Net before taxes[b]	5,339	3,077	3,032	4,198	4,539	9,686	11,618	4,645	3,734	3,765
Net income	1,118	293	306	688	907	3,598	3,430	2,047	1,160	1,257
Dividends	133	142	131	177	198	727	770	737	648	666
Share Information										
Share prices ($) High	14.1	12.4	14.0	16.8	18.9	35.3	48.0	39.6	23.8	27.3
Low	4.5	4.5	9.5	13.4	13.8	17.5	26.1	17.9	17.5	18.0
Number of shares (millions) (adjusted for 4:1 split in 1979)	1,534	1,534	1,534	1,536	1,538	1,546	1,563	1,676	1,817	1,823
	$2.34	$2.22	$1.81	$1.75	$1.92	$2.12	$2.33	$2.03	$1.75	$1.52

Source: *Standard & Poor's, Value Line,* and *Annual International Financial Statistics.*
U.S. $/£ Sterling (yearly average)
a. Items not involving the movement of funds comprised principally depreciation and exploration expenditures written off.
b. Included equity in earnings of nonconsolidated subsidiaries.

183

of Ohio as the marketing base where it could use the Standard Oil name. Under this arrangement, The Standard Oil Company (an Ohio Corporation) commonly known as Sohio, became successful as Ohio's dominant supplier of gasoline and other petroleum products. Without any significant petroleum reserves of its own, it depended on other oil companies for its crude oil.

Sohio's position was suddenly transformed in 1969 when it agreed to trade up to 54 percent of its shares in exchange for a major portion of an oil field with potential for producing 1.5 million barrels per day. Sohio would become one of the major producers of crude oil in the United States.

Instead of a bonanza, however, the first several years brought Sohio a great deal of grief. Environmental battles and technical problems pushed the cost of the trans-Alaskan pipeline from an originally estimated $900 million all the way to $9.3 billion—and Sohio to the brink of financial embarrassment. To complete the project, the company had to borrow about $4.6 billion in 1977.

The bold gamble paid off. The North Slope field in Prudhoe Bay started flowing in 1977 just as oil prices soared, tripling in just nineteen months. Sohio's sales and profits ballooned to $14 billion and $1.95 billion in 1981, more than ten times and forty-six times those of a decade earlier. Its 15.9 percent return on sales was by far the highest in the industry.

As sales and profits went up, so did the concern of Sohio's chairman, Alton Whitehouse, Jr., about how to convert the temporary growth from a finite oil field to a sustainable level of operations. As reported in a *Business Week* feature story on Sohio on August 25, 1980:

> It either must undergo what will probably amount to the biggest redeployment of assets in the annals of U.S. business, or it will end up producing what Whitehouse calls "the biggest burp in corporate earnings history." With utter irony, Whitehouse and his staff say they have concluded that the company has too much money and must spend it too quickly, when so few U.S. plays are available, to stay in the major leagues in oil. Within 20 years, they say, Sohio will be forced to obtain most of its profits from business other than conventional oil and gas.
>
> Sohio, which has not previously disclosed these plans, has thus become the first major oil company to make plain that it views diversification out of conventional energy not merely as a hedge against declining oil supplies but as the main path to its livelihood within the next two decades.

In June, 1981, Sohio made its move—the acquisition of Kennecott, the largest U.S. producer of copper, for $1.77 billion. The rationale for this move was given in *Business Week*, April 26, 1982:

> This cyclical industry expected a copper shortage and higher prices in the 1980s, and Kennecott's chairman, Thomas D. Barrow, concluded that Kennecott's best hope was to find an ultra-rich acquirer who could fund these coming opportunities. Sohio had its own motivations. The reserves in its rich oil field would be half gone by 1987, and Sohio wanted to build long-lived assets that would survive Alaskan oil.
>
> Now Barrow is racing to use Sohio's cash to take advantage of the expected upturn in copper. One industry consultant is "looking for a price

explosion toward the end of next year." World copper inventories are lean, and the financial and political problems in many developing countries could keep supplies tight and prices high until the late 1980s.

Unfortunately for Sohio, these expectations of a copper boom were not fulfilled, and the financial results were disappointing. Successive Sohio annual reports noted this profit deterioration:

> Kennecott Minerals Company operated at a loss in 1981 compared with a profitable operation in 1980. The principal cause of this reversal in profitability was low metals prices throughout the year. (1981)

> Copper prices on the Commodity Exchange (Comex), New York, fell to an average 66 cents a pound in 1982 from 79 cents a pound in 1981. Copper prices, adjusted for inflation, fell to the lowest levels since 1935. As a result, Kennecott Minerals Company had an operating loss of $189 million in 1982. Sales of $595 million in 1982 were 40 percent lower than in 1981. (1982)

1983 was another poor year for the beleaguered copper unit, which experienced a pretax loss of $91 million. According to the *Wall Street Journal*, April 19, 1984, while Whitehouse still expected Kennecott's extensive copper reserves to be beneficial in the long run, his view for the present was, "It's a very sick industry."

Whitehouse's disappointments were not confined to copper. Early on December 4, 1983, the head of Sohio's exploration received a brief, disastrous phone call, "We just got a log. It's water." The log was a reading taken at the much-heralded Mukluk, the most expensive well in history and the site widely considered to be the best U.S. prospect for a big oil strike—an "elephant" in trade jargon. The Mukluk failure had cost Sohio $310 million, but even more important was the company's loss of its leading candidate to replace the North Slope field in the late 1980s, when its output was expected to start declining.

The significance of finding a replacement for Sohio's North Slope oil was apparent from the company's crude position in 1982, shown in Table C. The small amount of non-Alaskan crude oil produced in 1982 incurred a $361 million net loss before taxes because of its high production cost.

Although none of Sohio's other exploration sites compared with Mukluk in size and potential, the company did have some promising leases in the Gulf of Mexico and acreage in the oil-active Rocky Mountain Overthrust Belt and the gas-rich Anadarko Basin in Oklahoma. For the near term, Sohio could expect

Table C Sohio's crude position.

	Alaska	Lower 48 States	Total
Crude oil reserve (million bbls)	2,773	46	2,818
Crude oil production (thousand bpd)	595	17	612
Average crude oil wellhead price ($/b)	$18.26	$29.06	—

Exhibit 4 Sohio financial highlights, 1974–83 ($ millions).

	1974	1975	1976	1977	1978	1979	1980	1981	1982	1983
Balance Sheet (December 31)										
Cash	$ 118	$ 84	$ 165	$ 188	$ 417	$1,283	$ 1,998	$ 475	$ 163	$ 91
Current assets	642	656	841	1,558	1,883	2,855	3,646	3,317	2,430	2,486
Total assets	2,621	4,220	6,260	7,778	8,326	9,209	12,080	15,743	16,016	16,362
Current liabilities	341	450	540	997	1,346	1,447	3,077	4,438	2,977	2,509
Long-term debt	805	1,949	3,627	4,688	4,398	3,822	3,529	3,878	4,185	3,843
Common equity	1,232	1,450	1,539	1,670	2,032	3,086	4,562	5,963	7,221	8,094
Percent long-term debt/ capitalization	38.4	56.0	68.6	71.9	65.4	50.3	39.8	36.1	33.8	29.2
Return on assets (%)	5.5	3.6	2.6	2.3	5.0	13.4	17.0	14.0	11.8	9.3
Return on equity (%)	10.7	9.1	9.1	10.1	21.8	45.9	47.3	37.0	28.5	19.7
Income Statement (Year ended December 31)										
Revenues	$2,166	$2,484	$2,912	$3,511	$5,192	$7,916	$11,023	$13,457	$13,529	$12,067
Operating income	207	252	302	606	1,517	2,900	4,542	4,853	4,602	4,200
Capital expenditures	700	1,642	1,699	1,104	762	515	1,007	2,592	2,708	2,298
Depreciation	68	82	82	169	405	486	695	825	905	1,291
Interest expense	62	122	258	436	487	439	357	573	613	402
Net before taxes[a]	186	187	193	247	672	2,077	3,846	4,022	3,397	2,655
Net income	126	127	137	181	450	1,186	1,811	1,947	1,879	1,512
Share Information										
Earnings per share	0.86	0.86	0.89	1.09	2.00	4.92	7.37	7.92	7.63	6.36
Dividends per share	0.34	0.34	0.34	0.34	0.42	0.61	1.40	2.25	2.55	2.60
Number of shares (millions)	144.9	153.7	154.2	190.5	240.0	245.4	245.6	245.9	246.0	246.0
Share price High	21.5	21.3	20.2	22.8	21.8	46.5	91.5	72.8	42.3	58.9
Low	9.4	11.1	15.4	17.3	14.4	20.0	39.6	36.1	26.3	35.0

Source: *Standard & Poor's* and *Value Line*.
a. Included equity in earnings of nonconsolidated subsidiaries.

a sharp rise in oil from Alaska, since its agreement to take less oil from Prudhoe Bay for two years as a means of readjusting its ownership expired in September, 1984. As a result, Sohio's earnings were expected to rebound in 1984.

Downstream business always had been, and continued to be, Sohio's strong area. Compared with disappointments in exploration and copper, profits from refining and marketing increased from $266 million in 1981 to $390 million in 1982, and then to $453 million in 1983. Sohio's small refining capacity compared with its sizable crude oil supply allowed the company to provide its refineries with the right quantities of the most profitable kinds of crude oil at the right time. (Exhibit 4 contains a history of Sohio's financial performance.)

The Unpredictable Future

In a lead article entitled, "Trying to Stave Off a New Oil Shock," *Business Week* on June 4, 1984, reported:

> The conflict between Iran and Iraq, limited to the northern end of the Persian Gulf for so long that it became known as the "forgotten war," has spread to oil-producing states 200 miles to the south, raising the risk of the third oil shock in a little more than a decade.
>
> Despite attempts by the United States and the Saudis to come up with a solution to the crisis, no one is sure whether any plan to keep the gulf open to oil shipping will work. "It is an illogical war," Prince Bandar bin Sultan, the Saudi ambassador to Washington, said recently. "It's the unpredictability that worries us."

Whatever the outcome of the "forgotten war," the threat was a grim reminder of the fragility of world oil supplies and of the benefits in controlling ample oil reserves in politically safe regions.

Cray Research, Inc.

> The purpose of my new company is to design and build a larger, more
> powerful computer than anyone now has.
>> Seymour Cray, *Chippewa Falls Herald Telegram*, May 1972

Cray Research was dedicated to making the fastest computer in the world. In
1976, four years after its founding, the company installed its first system, the
Cray-1 Serial One. Within a few years, Cray Research dominated the world of
supercomputers, so called because of the speed at which they operated. Sixty-
five of its systems had been installed worldwide by January 1, 1984, and annual revenues were $170 million.

Cray Research had clearly achieved the objective of its founder, Seymour
Cray, and had done so with entrepreneurial flair. Seed money had been raised
on the strength of Seymour Cray's reputation as the world's leading designer
of supercomputers. The first Cray employees were expatriates from other computer companies who had followed Seymour in pursuit of his goal. The first
machine was assembled in a rented storefront in Chippewa Falls, Wisconsin.

The company's very success, however, created pressures that ran counter
to Seymour Cray's desire to have a few engineers sitting in a clean, quiet room
thinking up ways to make computers run faster. Success challenged Cray Research's strategy, management, and culture.

Public ownership, which had been necessary to finance the fledgling enterprise, brought pressure for growth in earnings. Continued growth could be
achieved only by serving a broader market than the limited number of high-
powered scientific laboratories that valued Cray's raw computer power. Hardware design was the vital consideration for these classic supercomputer customers. Other users were somewhat more concerned with software, service,
and price, and these requirements called for a different way of doing business.

With growth had come administrative complexity. Faced with this personal
bête noire, Seymour Cray resigned from Cray Research in 1981, bringing to the
fore an issue that had haunted the firm over the years: "Is there life after
Seymour Cray?" On resigning, he agreed to serve as an independent contractor to his own company. Cray Research had the right of first refusal on his
designs until 1985.

Another problem taking up a good deal of management's attention was
how to preserve the entrepreneurial spirit that had been key to Cray's success.

The organizational philosophy had been to work in small groups, but by 1984 Cray had more than 1,500 employees and was still growing.

As if the problems of success were not sufficient to try Cray Research's young management team, the company also faced worldwide competition dedicated to toppling the Cray supercomputer from its throne. This threat was summed up in a *Newsweek* article in July 1983:

> The Japanese have announced a two-pronged plan to build advanced computer technologies. One project is the $100 million eight-year National Superspeed Computer project, which aims at producing machines 1,000 times faster than the existing Cray-1 built by Cray Research of Minneapolis. The other, the $500 million, 10-year Fifth Generation Computer project, is focusing on artificial intelligence. Both are now being countered by American efforts, including a Pentagon request for up to $1 billion over the next five years for superspeed and artificial intelligence technologies. Although behind, Great Britain and France have also launched national supercomputer projects.

With such interest in advanced computer technology mounting, Cray management could not afford to take its leadership in the industry for granted.

Cray: The Man and the Company

Seymour Cray had one professional goal: to design and build the fastest, most powerful computer in the world. Several times in his thirty-year career, he traded his position as a company's key computer designer for the freedom to sit in his cottage on Lake Wissota in Wisconsin with pencil and graph paper, writing the Boolean algebraic equations that would be translated into one of his phenomenal machines. The founding of Cray Research was one such move for freedom.

Seymour, as he was called by the press and by his employees, already had established a reputation as a computer genius and as the "father of the supercomputer" when he struck out on his own. *Forbes* magazine described him as "not just another scientist, but a national resource."

The First Supercomputer

It was at Control Data Corporation (CDC) in Minneapolis that Seymour was credited with the birth of the supercomputer and earned his reputation. The evolution toward speed began with the replacement of vacuum tubes by germanium transistors in the CDC 1604. In the 6600, Seymour pioneered the use of silicon transistors to increase the speed over that possible with germanium. But it was the 7600 that qualified as a supercomputer and was responsible for CDC's dominant share of this market from its introduction in 1969 until its eclipse by the Cray-1 in the mid-1970s.

To earn the title of supercomputer by 1980, a system had to perform more than 20 million computations per second and be capable of vector as well as scalar processing. Vector processing involved simultaneous performance of many calculations; scalar processing performed one calculation at a time.

Cray Research, Inc.

The early 1970s brought a change in CDC's business strategy that ran counter to Seymour's philosophy. The company merged with Commercial Credit Co. and began to shift its emphasis and resources away from scientific toward commercial applications.

CDC's refusal to fund Seymour's proposal to develop a machine faster than the 7600, coupled with the seemingly inevitable increase in corporate duties, made Seymour decide to move on. He left CDC with the company's blessing and with four of his colleagues to start his own company.

Cray Research was funded with $500,000 of Seymour's own money, $500,000 from CDC's Commercial Credit Co., and $1.5 million from fourteen other investors. Seymour was president and chief executive officer, and as founder, he made the rules. His company would build and sell one machine at a time and each machine would be a supercomputer. All models would be compatible with each other. The sale price of each machine would include a margin to cover ongoing research and development. Most important, the organization would leave him free to devote his entire time and energy to the design of the next Cray supercomputer.

An additional $6.1 million in private financing was raised during the next three years. The financing depended wholly on Seymour's reputation, since the company had no product on the market. By the time the Cray-1 was ready to be introduced in 1976, however, all the seed money had been used up. Help came in the form of John Rollwagen, who had joined Cray the preceding year. Rollwagen had an engineering degree from MIT and a Harvard MBA, was a native Minnesotan, and had worked at CDC. At Cray he was first hired in the marketing area, but his real role soon became apparent. Seymour wanted him to raise more money.

In March 1976, Rollwagen arranged a public stock offering. Cray had no sales, no earnings, a $2.4 million deficit, and was faced with further losses. The market for supercomputers was projected at eighty users worldwide. Nevertheless, the financial community reaffirmed its faith in Seymour Cray: The offering raised $10 million. Later that month, the first Cray-1, five times faster than the CDC 7600, was installed at the Los Alamos National Laboratory, in New Mexico, on a trial basis.

When the third machine was sold for $8.8 million in December, 1977 (Seymour had dismantled the second because of a design problem that slowed the machine down), the company made good on its seed money and showed its first profit. From that moment, Cray was in a surge of rapid growth, selling five machines in 1978, five in 1979, and nine in 1980. (See Figure A for the growth of customer installations and Exhibit 1 for the resulting financial performance.)

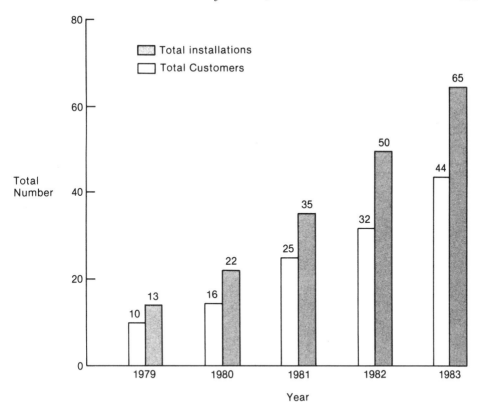

Figure A Growth of customer installations, 1979–83. *Source:* Cray Research, Inc.

Success

The year 1981 was pivotal. Cray had passed several milestones: revenues of $100 million, earnings of more than $1 per share, and employment of more than 1,000 people. Thirty-five Cray systems had been installed.

At the end of the year, Seymour announced his plans for developing the Cray-2. His new machine, performing 500 million to one billion calculations per second, would be six to ten times more powerful than the Cray-1 and its follow-on model, the Cray-1/S. The speed would be increased by shortening the wires through which the electronic signals traveled from four feet to sixteen inches. The central processing unit (CPU) would measure twenty-six inches high by thirty-eight inches long, compared with the Cray-1 CPU's dimensions of six by nine feet.

The miniaturization produced significant increases in heat as well as in speed. Most experts agreed that a rise of 18°C in junction temperatures halved the life of integrated circuits. The Cray-1 had been cooled by circulating freon, the refrigeration coolant, through channels surrounding the integrated circuit boards, but that method could not be applied to the smaller, more densely packed

Exhibit 1 Financial summary, 1972–83 ($ thousands).

	1972[a]	1973	1974	1975	1976	1977	1978	1979	1980	1981	1982	1983
Revenue:												
Sales	—	—	—	—	—	$ 8,816	$ 8,357	$26,496	$37,645	$ 65,207	$ 91,535	$125,008
Leased systems	—	—	—	—	450	2,261	7,349	12,545	17,558	27,604	35,623	26,151
Service fees	—	—	—	—	59	317	1,471	3,674	5,545	8,831	13,991	18,531
Total revenue	$	$	$	$	$ 509	$11,394	$17,177	$42,715	$60,748	$101,642	$141,149	$169,690
Net income (loss)	$ (72)	$ (527)	$ (944)	$ (887)	$(1,551)	$ 2,027	$ 3,501	$ 7,819	$10,900	$ 18,170	$ 19,000	$ 26,071
U.S. regions												
Revenue	—	—	—	—	—	—	$14,646	$14,293	$43,784	$ 90,852	$110,486	$ 87,443
Operating profit	—	—	—	—	—	—	7,448	3,259	20,225	49,926	51,191	37,772
International subsidiaries												
Revenue	—	—	—	—	—	—	2,531	28,422	16,964	10,790	30,663	82,247
Operating profit	—	—	—	—	—	—	1,042	19,817	10,280	2,482	15,531	39,383
Working capital	$2,375	$1,783	$3,314	$5,756	$10,786	$ 9,083	$ 7,498	$13,949	$53,543	$ 61,927	$98,600	$129,436
Long-term debt	—	—	—	2,720	2,720	3,321	4,670	3,029	7,876	12,360	33,741	37,612
Stockholders' equity	2,478	1,961	3,664	3,434	12,054	14,636	20,638	28,623	75,803	94,951	144,561	172,385
Operating and financial ratios:												
Return on stockholders' average equity	—	—	—	—	—	15.2%	19.9%	31.7%	25.6%	22.0%	18.6%	17.0%
Net income as % of revenue	—	—	—	—	—	17.8%	20.4%	18.3%	17.9%	17.9%	13.5%	15.4%
Current ratio	—	21.3:1	19.8:1	65.7:1	18.3:1	16.1:1	3.6:1	2.6:1	4.3:1	3.8:1	4.6:1	3.7:1
General data												
Cumulative systems installed	—	—	—	—	1	3	8	13	22	35	50	65
Number of employees at year end	12	21	30	45	124	199	321	524	761	1,079	1,352	1,551
Earnings (loss) per share	$(.04)	$(.18)	$(.20)	$(.18)	$(.17)	$.19	$.29	$.63	$.85	$1.32	$1.38	$1.77
Stock price												
High	—	—	—	—	2⅞	4⅛	11	16⅞	48½	48⅜	45¾	57⅛
Low	—	—	—	—	1⅞	2	3½	7¾	12¾	28	20	36⅜
Price/Earnings Ratio	—	—	—	—	NM[b]	43-21	51-16	27-12	57-15	37-21	33-14	32-21

a. April 6 (date of organization) to December 31.
b. Not meaningful.

Cray-2. Seymour solved the problem by immersing the entire computer in fluorocarbon, an inert liquid used for, among other things, artificial blood replacement in transfusions.

The Cray-2 would be priced over the Cray-1 and would require new software. The date of the first delivery was set for 1984.

Seymour had designed the Cray machines to be aesthetically appealing as well as functional. The Cray-1, pictured in Figure B, was shaped into an arc of columns containing modules and wiring surrounded by a knee-high padded bench housing the power supply. This configuration prompted the press to call this machine the "world's most expensive loveseat." When the Cray-2's liquid-immersion system was introduced, the machine was nicknamed the "world's most expensive aquarium."

Seymour's Independence

The year of accomplishment, 1981, was also the year Seymour moved to greater independence in his relationship with Cray Research. Aware of Seymour's

Figure B   The Cray-1 Computer.

aversion to administrative problems, John Rollwagen sensed a need to face the implications of the company's rapid growth and increased complexity. As a result he initiated discussion with Seymour to see how the latter could avoid the kind of distractions that had caused him to sever his company connections in the past. Andrew Scott, one of Cray's founders and its legal counsel, soon joined the deliberations. Rollwagen explained, "There were no boundaries to our discussions. We explored all kinds of possibilities, such as Seymour quitting the company, stopping further growth, selling the company, and the like."

These discussions extending over several months finally led to an open-ended agreement, set forth in a two-page document that gave Cray Research the commercial rights to Seymour's designs through 1985 (later extended to 1987) in return for development funding. Andrew Scott, who had crafted the document, noted, "The agreement was intentionally brief and ambiguous. The relationship between Seymour and the company would have to flow from mutual decisions made in the light of changing conditions." John Rollwagen, who

Exhibit 2 Corporate organization chart, 1984.

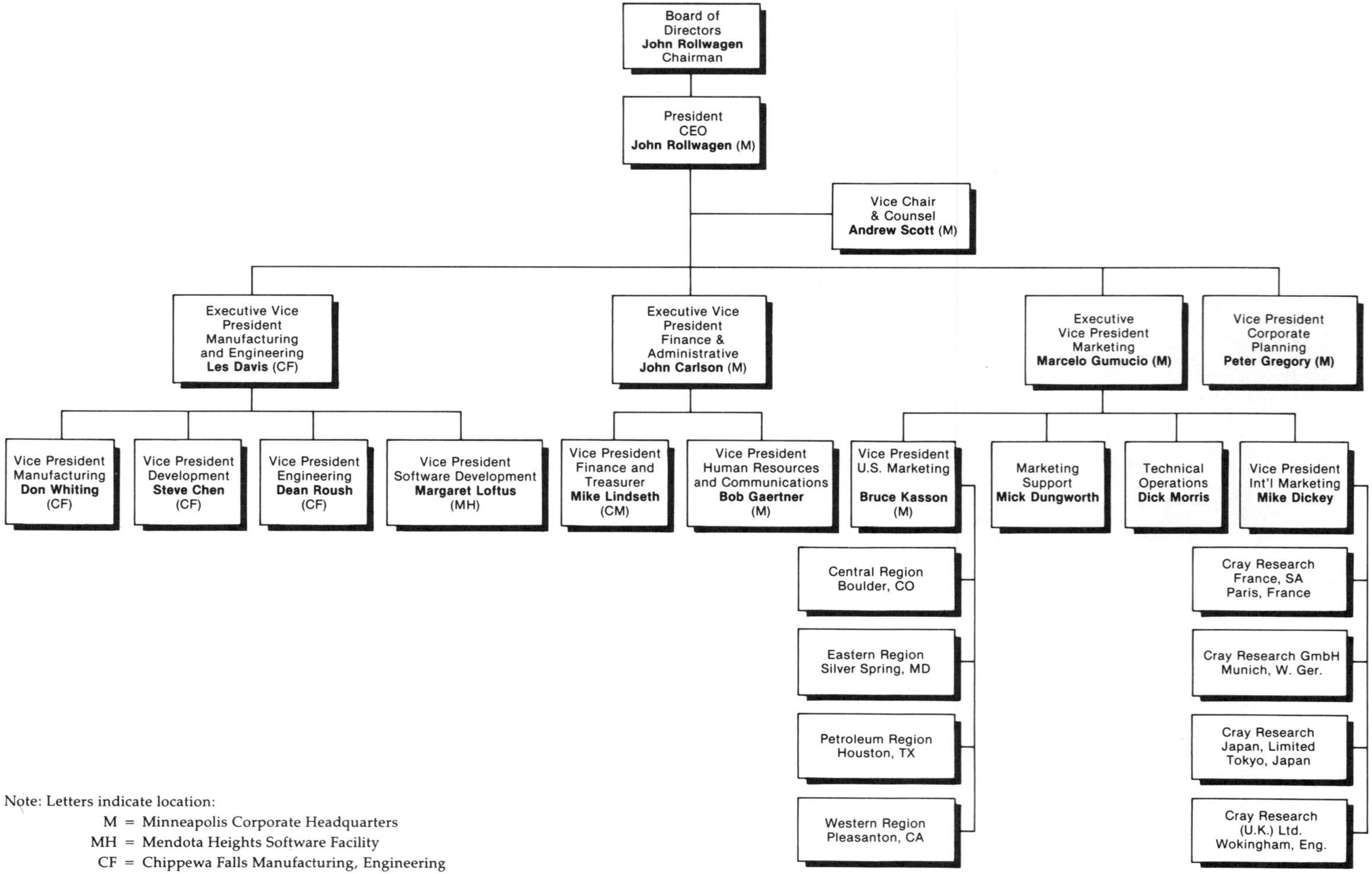

Board of Directors
John Rollwagen
Chairman

President CEO
John Rollwagen (M)

Vice Chair & Counsel
Andrew Scott (M)

Executive Vice President Manufacturing and Engineering
Les Davis (CF)

- **Vice President Manufacturing**
  Don Whiting (CF)
- **Vice President Development**
  Steve Chen (CF)
- **Vice President Engineering**
  Dean Roush (CF)
- **Vice President Software Development**
  Margaret Loftus (MH)

Executive Vice President Finance & Administrative
John Carlson (M)

- **Vice President Finance and Treasurer**
  Mike Lindseth (CM)
- **Vice President Human Resources and Communications**
  Bob Gaertner (M)

Executive Vice President Marketing
Marcelo Gumucio (M)

- **Vice President U.S. Marketing**
  Bruce Kasson (M)
  - Central Region Boulder, CO
  - Eastern Region Silver Spring, MD
  - Petroleum Region Houston, TX
  - Western Region Pleasanton, CA
- **Marketing Support**
  Mick Dungworth
- **Technical Operations**
  Dick Morris
- **Vice President Int'l Marketing**
  Mike Dickey
  - Cray Research France, SA Paris, France
  - Cray Research GmbH Munich, W. Ger.
  - Cray Research Japan, Limited Tokyo, Japan
  - Cray Research (U.K.) Ltd. Wokingham, Eng.

Vice President Corporate Planning
Peter Gregory (M)

Note: Letters indicate location:

M = Minneapolis Corporate Headquarters
MH = Mendota Heights Software Facility
CF = Chippewa Falls Manufacturing, Engineering

194

had already succeeded Seymour as president and CEO in 1977, would also assume the duties of chairman (Exhibit 2 shows Cray's organization chart). Seymour was free to spend his time finishing the Cray-2 and thinking about the next-generation supercomputer, the Cray-3.

The X-MP

In 1983, Cray Research introduced the X-MP a supercomputer that could operate at three to five times the speed of existing Cray models. The product was noteworthy in another regard: For the first time in more than two decades, the world's fastest computer was credited to someone other than Seymour Cray. Steve Chen, a computer designer who had joined Cray Research in 1980 and later became vice president of product development, had succeeded in multiplying the Cray-1's performance.

While Seymour had been increasing computer speed through miniaturization, Steve Chen took the alternative design route of parallel processing, or multiprocessing (the "MP" in the new machine's name). The method involved using a number of CPUs in a parallel configuration to solve different parts of a problem simultaneously. The X-MP's two Cray-1 processors were synchronized through clusters of shared registers in the CPU intercommunication section and through central memory. The X-MP also had as standard equipment a solid-state storage device with additional storage capacity that would allow more rapid access to large data files.

Unlike the revolutionary Cray-2, the X-MP had been designed to use software compatible with Cray's existing machines. In comparing his efforts with Seymour's, Chen said, "There is a different philosophy behind the X-MP. I deliberately settled between the Cray-1 and Cray-2. The reference point was to redesign everything by taking advantage of the existing software and the current technology."

The success of the X-MP came as a surprise to most people at Cray Research, including Seymour, who was reported to have said, "Well, you guys have *finally* learned how to do this," before returning to redesign the Cray-2 to operate at even faster speeds than originally planned. By early 1983, one X-MP had been installed, orders for several others had been booked, and Chen was working on the next model, which would have four processors.

Cray's rapid growth promised to accelerate with the successive phasing in of the X-MP, the Cray-2, and their even more powerful descendants.

The Growth Challenge

With the introduction of its first machine, Cray Research quickly dominated the narrow supercomputer market niche. The Cray-1 essentially knocked CDC out of its dominant position. According to a former CDC salesman, few, if any, CDC 7600s were sold after the Cray-1's introduction. CDC introduced its more powerful CYBER 205 in 1981, but by that time 35 Cray-1 systems had been installed. This rapid growth posed two quite different kinds of issues for management—one philosophical and the other strategic.

The philosophical issue had to do with how far the company would deviate from Seymour Cray's original concept of focusing on state-of-the-art applications. Over the years, Cray had broadened both its customer base and its product offering. The decision to expand had gained support from the professional managers hired the run the increasingly complex organization and was in effect ratified with Seymour's departure. John Carlson, Cray's chief financial officer, explained, "This company is driven by profitability. It's important to our investors to show a continued increase in earnings per share." Still, some senior managers had reservations and even misgivings. Top management continued to face the question of just how far to change the basic character of the business.

The strategic issues associated with rapid growth had to do with deciding where and how Cray Research should compete and with finding ways to preserve the entrepreneurial spirit that had contributed so vitally to the firm's success. To evaluate how to grow, top management continually assessed the markets, Cray's offerings, and the competition.

Markets

The 1976 projected total market of 80 supercomputer users soon expanded with a spreading awareness of the benefits to be gained from increased speed and power. By 1983 *Forbes* magazine estimated the worldwide market to be close to 400 potential customers, many of which might use more than one unit. Peter Gregory, Cray's director of corporate planning, set the long-term potential market at closer to 600 users, with about half designated as "probables." The growing demand for supercomputers was highlighted in the following *Fortune* account:

> A wave of technological change is poised to sweep over the computer industry. Faster and cheaper computers will allow users to do things they can't today. . . .
>
> The demand for faster but cheaper computers grows continuously. Sales of "supercomputers"—fast, specialized, hand-built, and expensive number-crunchers—have been taking off. Cray Research, Inc., a Minneapolis company (1983 sales: $170 million), got orders for 25 supercomputers last year vs. 16 in 1982. The burst of sales was ignited by technological advances that made possible deep price cuts—as much as $5 million on a $10-million Cray—and put the machines within reach of more users.
>
> Today's supercomputers are too slow for many potential tasks. Some jobs now take weeks or months—for example, simulating the airflow around an entire airplane in flight. Users have identified additional applications that would take hundreds or thousands of times longer; one would create a minutely detailed three-dimensional model of a fusion reactor's interior at work.[1]

Bob Walan, hired as Cray's first salesman in 1976 and manager of the central region since 1981, noted that buyers had changed over the years from the

---

1. "Reinventing the Computer," *Fortune*, March 5, 1984, p. 86.

"classic Cray customers" to a broader industrial market. The original classic customers were sophisticated, state-of-the-art scientific users who bought the basic hardware and developed their own software programs to take advantage of the machines' capabilities for their specific purposes.

Industrial customers included two groups distinguished by their software requirements. The petroleum industry, which Walan called "neoclassic," was similar to the classic customer in that it called for the most powerful Cray units to do scientific work. Petroleum industry users looked to Cray for assistance in developing support software to make their programs run faster and more easily on a Cray.

The other industrial customers typically added a Cray to an existing computer network and expected all the software to be supplied. Walan estimated that, in 1984, Cray's sales breakdown for the classic, neoclassic, and general industrial customer groups respectively would be 25 percent, 25 percent, and 50 percent in units and 40 percent, 30 percent, and 30 percent in dollars. Looking ahead, Peter Gregroy estimated that the long-term revenue potential for Cray supercomputers to these three markets might be something like 25 percent, 40 percent, and 35 percent, respectively.

Supercomputer users shared several common characteristics. First were their complex computational needs for large-scale research and development projects, which exceeded the power and speed supplied by conventional systems. An example was the nuclear research carried out by Cray's first customer, the Los Alamos Scientific Laboratory. Research included weapons design, laser fusion and isotope separation, magnetic fusion energy research, and nuclear reactor safety.

A second shared characteristic was the need to simulate a physical phenomenon. A supercomputer could be used to develop models of weather conditions, to simulate an event such as a space flight or a nuclear explosion, or to trace seismic activity connected with the underground flow of gas, water, and oil. John Rollwagen described the resulting advantage:

> Before, when an aeronautical engineer designed a wing, he or she had to slice it up in cross sections because the computers could only do a two-dimensional analysis of the wing. This meant the engineer had to be a very good mathematician, because dividing a wing into cross sections is not intuitive; it's fairly abstract. Now, with supercomputers, it's possible to do a three-dimensional analysis which means you can fly the whole wing in the computer mathematically and obtain three-dimensional graphics. This output conforms to concepts that the engineer is comfortable with and permits a greater play of creative intuition.

A worldwide effort to research weather and climatic conditions, the Global Atmospheric Research Program, resulted in a highly visible application of supercomputers. Massive amounts of data were transmitted from observation stations around the world to the European Center for Medium-Range Weather Forecasts (ECMWF) in Reading, England, which used a Cray-1. The Cray allowed ECMWF to produce ten-day forecasts within a few hours, based on the assimilation of millions of data elements gathered worldwide. The constantly updated forecasts extended the usual five- to six-day predictions on which industries such as agriculture, air service, shipping, construction, and energy relied.

A third customer characteristic was the ability to afford a large outlay for computer services. A single Cray machine was priced from $4 million to $17 million and required annual operating expenditures of close to half a million dollars.

Selling a Cray computer to a new customer in an established market took about two years. The first year included initial customer contact; benchmarking, which involved stringent performance capability tests; customer visits to see the manufacturing process in Chippewa Falls; working out the method of financing; and the signing of a letter of intent. Installation and acceptance of the system occurred during the second year. The customer had to accept or reject the system within thirty days of delivery. Revenue was recognized on acceptance.

Opening a new market was a slow process. The first calls to the petroleum and automotive industries were made in 1976. The initial contracts were not signed until 1981 for petroleum and 1983 for automotive.

Cray had eight regional offices to sell and service its products worldwide: four in the United States and four overseas. A typical U.S. sales office employed thirty-five site engineers, fifteen site analysts, seven sales analysts, three salespeople, four administrators, and five regional managers, for a total of around seventy people. This team was responsible for selling and servicing the product within its designated region and was expected to show a profit after installing two systems. Marketing fees, paid by headquarters, and service fees from customers provided revenues for each office.

Product Offerings: Hardware

In early 1984, Cray Research offered two basic computer models (Cray 1/M and X-MP) and two new peripheral machines (a solid-state storage device and an input-output subsystem). For most applications, the Cray computers were basically add-on rather than stand-alone products. Cray could interface with a wide variety of computer systems, including IBM, Honeywell, DEC, Date General, CDC, and Univac. (A CDC supercomputer, in contrast, could interface only with a CDC system.) (See Exhibit 3 for a description of the Cray system configuration.)

The S series had been introduced in 1979 as an improvement to the Cray-1. The 1/S had a larger memory and greater input/output capabilities. Late in 1982, this model was supplanted by an M series, which was equal to the S units in speed and power but used metal oxide semiconductor technology in the circuit design, allowing significant cost reductions. The M was offered in late 1982 at prices ranging from $4 to $7 million, compared with the $8–$13 million range for the S.

In addition to introducing the lower-priced M model, Cray had lowered 1983 prices on the X-MP from $11–$14 million to $9–$11 million. These pricing

Exhibit 3 Cray system configuration and glossary of terms. *Source:* Casewriter's interviews.

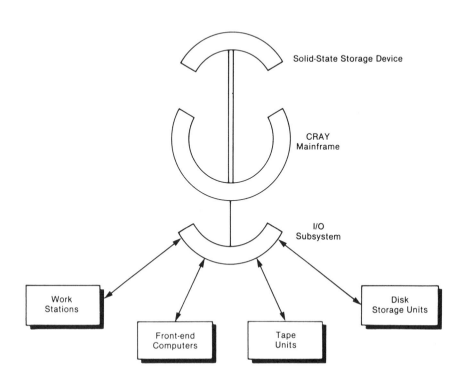

Solid-State Storage Device: Provides additional high-speed storage capacity like a disk file, but with performance improved by factors up to 100. Reduces input-output (I/O) time.

Mainframe: Contains the central processing unit (CPU), a core memory, and peripheral interfaces. The Cray-1 contained a single CPU; the X-MP had two in parallel.

I/O Subsystem: Acts as data concentrator for input to CPU and distributes output from CPU. Handles I/O for front-end computer systems and peripheral devices, such as disk and tape units. Contains multiple I/O processors and can contain additional buffer memory (secondary storage).

I/O Processors: Two required and two optional processors in the I/O subsystem designed to assist the CPU's I/O operations by "predigesting" data.

Work Stations: Locations of users' consoles which can be connected directly with the I/O subsystem or with the front-end computers.

Front-end Computers: Interface between mainframe and user. A Cray could interface with IBM, Honeywell, DEC, Data General, CDC, Systems Engineering Laboratories, and UNIVAC computers.

Tape Units: Mass storage device using magnetic tapes and requiring sequential access.

Disk Storage Units: Mass storage device using flexible (floppy) mylar disks to record information.

moves, which were attempts to broaden the market, initially disrupted sales by confusing customers. It took about eight months to reestablish orderly marketing. A year later, the *Wall Street Journal* reported that the strategy had successfully expanded Cray's market beyond its traditional base.

Each Cray computer was built to order, with a choice of memory sizes and number of input-output processors. It took two to three months to define the specific details of a system and to order and test the parts. Most components were designed specifically for Cray and were purchased from several outside sources. All hardware was then built, assembled, and tested in Chippewa Falls. Wiring and building modules took four months, and an additional four months were spent testing a machine on the floor.

About 80 percent of the manufacturing costs were for material and 20 percent for labor and overhead. Each machine was delivered with $250,000 worth of spare parts belonging to Cray. Maintenance was done on-site by Cray employees assigned to the unit on a full-time basis.

The Cray-2 and the next-generation X-MP were both scheduled for introduction in 1985. The new X-MP, using four CPUs in parallel, would be twice as powerful as the X-MP; the Cray-2 would, in turn, be four times as fast as the original X-MP, but would require new software. Because of these characteristics, the Cray-2 was expected to appeal to the classic customers (for whom raw power was critical), the next X-MP to the industrial customers (for whom proven software was important).

The X-MP and the Cray-2 were both breakthroughs in supercomputer technology. The X-MP was the first supercomputer capable of doing parallel processing. This design configuration represented a major achievement in supercomputer architecture. In contrast, the Cray-2 achieved increased speed through a new packaging of existing chip technology and the miniaturization of integrated circuit boards.

Seymour also had a project under way to increase the speed factor by using a new chip technology to replace silicon. His research team was experimenting with gallium arsenide, a substance whose electron mobility was four to five times that of silicon. He planned to use the new technology in the Cray-3.

Chen's and Seymour's differing approaches, parallelism and chip technology, were mirrored in industry research. There were close to fifty projects on parallelism in the United States in 1984, while chip technology was the prime focus of Japanese engineers.

Business Week reported that for 1982 Cray had been number one out of 776 companies in research and development (R&D) dollars per employee ($20,958) and number four in R&D as a percentage of sales (20.1 percent). The company's total R&D outlay for 1983 was more than $25 million.

Product Offerings: Software

Cray Research offered basic operating software with the hardware. This software included a Fortran compiler to gain access to the Cray internal logic and basic operating instructions for the Cray machines.

The proper amount of software programs and support had long been a point of contention in the Cray organization. Margaret Loftus, vice president in charge of software operations, explained her view of the problem: "This company was founded by hardware engineers whose main interest is in designing more powerful hardware. Software is a bother for them. What's changing, however, is the customer mix, with more and more users who need software to run their Crays. Before, we had difficulty selling software to the sophisticated scientific labs. Now, we have difficulty selling a Cray without software."

Loftus stayed in close touch with the regional and country managers to determine customer software needs. Major software requirements were the responsibility of the 260-person Mendota Heights, Minnesota, staff. On-site problems were handled by software field-support groups in each of the regional offices.

As the result of much lobbying, Loftus had succeeded in obtaining an increase in the software budget. The traditional 5 percent of operating profit would be expanded in 1984 to 7.5 percent, or about $15 million, for all software activities around the world. Loftus believed that software was, and would continue to be, the biggest constraint to the company's growth.

Financial Arrangements

With sales prices for Cray supercomputers in the millions, financing arrangements became an important element in the company's product offerings. Cray systems could be purchased or leased. Citicorp and U.S. Leasing handled all full-payout leases. These leases, amounting to $150 million in 1984, were not included in Cray's balance sheet. Cray financed directly all one-and three-year operating leases. Once installed, each system required a service contract amounting to about $25,000 to $50,000 per month.

John Carlson, Cray's chief financial officer, portrayed the company as having two businesses: manufacturing and financing. He ran the latter from Minneapolis, being involved in the financial arrangements for each machine.

Financing terms were arranged to result in a revenue breakdown of about 50 percent from sales, 40 percent from leases, and 10 percent from service fees. Carlson's aim was to have the cash flow from sales be used for production and that from leasing and service be sufficient to cover overhead costs, which comprised research and development, marketing, general and administrative, and customer engineering.

Research and development was the starting point for the budget, with first claim on 15 percent of total revenues. This amount was evenly divided, with the first 5 percent going to Seymour Cray, the second 5 percent going to other hardware development, and the third 5 percent going to software development. Expenditures for engineering and development and for marketing and administration in dollars and as a percentage of total revenues had been those figures shown in Table A.

For plant expansion and special projects, the company turned to external

Table A Expenditures in dollars and as a percentage of total revenues ($ thousands).

	1983		1982		1981		1980	
Engineering and development	$25,540	15.1%	$29,513	20.1%	$17,037	16.8%	$ 9,552	15.7%
Marketing and administration	$30,975	18.3%	$23,880	16.9%	$17,709	17.4%	$10,438	17.2%

financing. Because of Cray's needs for additional equity and debt financing, Carlson and Rollwagen devoted considerable attention to establishing and maintaining good relationships with the financial and investing communities. Assessing Cray's financial situation in 1984, Rollwagen concluded: "While raising money to finance growth is of essential importance to us, I do not see it as a constraint at this time. We believe that our debt/equity ratio could go as high as 50 percent. And our ability to raise equity funds is currently limited only by our own attitudes toward growth."

The Cultural Challenge

While rapid growth may have eased the financial officer's job, it resulted in serious problems for John Rollwagen and the other senior officers who were concerned with preserving the entrepreneurial spirit and small-company atmosphere they so valued. From the company's inception, management looked to the individual for accomplishing what had to be accomplished. Each person was allowed to define his or her own goals within the corporate mission. The growth in employee numbers and the geographic dispersion of activities, however, worked to undermine the Cray style of management.

In an attempt to capture the essence of what the Cray culture was all about, executives met in 1982 to write a one-page document called "The Cray Style" (see Exhibit 4). The in-house publication, *Interface*, introduced the statement as "an essay about our employees, our work relationships, our work environments, our attitude toward work and our belief in Cray products." It was described as an "attitude" to guide employees in everyday decisions and as a "style" that would evolve with the company.

Emphasizing Individual Initiative and Action

An organization could hardly have had a better role model for individual initiative and action than Seymour Cray. Seymour was his own man, whether designing new supercomputers or perfecting his skills as an accomplished windsurfer. This spirit was prized and practiced in management's ranks. Steve Chen's leadership in developing the X-MP and Margaret Loftus's efforts to multiply Cray's software capabilities were notable examples of individual

Exhibit 4 The Cray style. *Source:* 1982 annual report.

At Cray Research, we take what we do very seriously, but don't take ourselves very seriously.

We have a strong sense of quality—quality in our products and services, of course; but also quality in our working environment, in the people we work with, in the tools that we use to do our work, and in the components we choose to make what we make. Economy comes from high value, not from low cost. Aesthetics are part of quality. The effort to create quality extends to the communities in which we work and live as well.

The Cray approach is informal and nonbureaucratic. Verbal communication is key, not memos. "Call, don't write" is the watchword.

People are accessible at all levels.

People also have fun working at Cray Research. There is laughing in the halls, as well as serious discussion. More than anything else, the organization is personable and approachable, but still dedicated to getting the job done.

With informality, however, there is also a sense of confidence. Cray people feel like they are on the winning side. They feel successful, and they are. It is this sense of confidence that generates the attitude of "go ahead and try it, we'll make it work."

Also, there is a sense of pride at Cray. Professionalism is important. People are treated like and act like professionals. Cray people trust each other to do their jobs well and with the highest ethical standards. They take what they **do** very seriously. But Cray people are professional without being stuffy. They take a straightforward, even simple, approach. They don't take **themselves** too seriously.

Because the individual is key at Cray, there is a real diversity in the view of what Cray Research really is. In fact, Cray Research is many things to many people. The consistency comes in providing those diverse people with the opportunity to fulfill themselves and experience achievement. The creativity, then, that emerges from the company comes from the many ideas of the individuals who are here. And that is the real strength of Cray Research.

---

achievement, as was the company's reliance on one person to open its first commercial market. As President Rollwagen described it: "When we started to sell to the petroleum companies, just one man, George Stevenson, took on the industry. This idea of one man taking on a new industry is an attitude that goes through the company."

Management's preference for working in small groups where a personal touch could be maintained was borne out in the choice of locations for its principal organizational units. Headquarters was moved twenty miles from Mendota Heights to downtown Minneapolis in 1982, leaving the suburban facility to concentrate on software engineering and sales. In Chippewa Falls, Wisconsin, 120 miles from Minneapolis, research was carried out by several teams, and the manufacturing and engineering staffs worked in discrete groups.

A decision in 1982 to make profit centers of the four domestic regional sales offices represented another attempt to keep decision units small. This change moved operating responsibility from headquarters to the field sites, as had been done years earlier for the overseas offices.

A decision to create a new subsidiary was seen by John Rollwagen as another important way for Cray Research to encourage and reward individual initiative and action.

Circuit Tools, Inc.

In October 1983 Cray's board of directors voted to spin off a new, majority-owned subsidiary in a related field. The new venture was a vehicle for the firm to achieve growth while maintaining its focus on supercomputer hardware.

The new company, Circuit Tools, Inc. (CTI), was the result of a project conceived by John May, who had worked in the software-applications group at Mendota Heights. In an effort to tap the market potential in the semiconductor manufacturing industry, he set out to adapt for use on the Cray-1 a widely employed program called SPICE, which had been developed at the University of California, Berkeley, to verify the operational effectiveness of newly designed integrated circuits. A year's effort in rewriting the software resulted in a new program, C-SPICE (the "C" referring to Cray), which could take advantage of the supercomputer's speed.

Since none of the integrated circuit manufacturers owned Cray hardware, May came up with the idea of offering his applications software on a commercial time-sharing basis. He took his idea to Cray's development committee, which decided that C-SPICE fell outside the company's principal direction for software business.

May then considered marketing the product on his own and wrote a business plan. Subsequently, the development committee suggested that he submit a proposal. After several discussions, May's plans were approved. According to the final arrangements, Cray would invest about $1.5 million for 80 percent of the new company's shares. May was to receive 10 percent of the shares, and the remaining 10 percent would be available for distribution to his managers. "I had originally envisaged my own company to be much smaller than CTI is turning out to be," May said, "but Cray kept pushing me to think it out. In time I began to see more possibilities."

CTI was considered a prototype for other spin-off ventures that would motivate entrepreneurial efforts in Cray. If CTI succeeded, John May, who was in his mid-30s, could earn a great deal of money. If not, he could return to Cray.

Personal Incentives

Although the CTI arrangement might serve as a powerful incentive in special cases, it could not substitute for—nor was it designed to compete with—the more traditional incentives for Cray personnel. Financial compensation, exciting assignments, and an attractive work environment were seen by management as key considerations in attracting and keeping the talented people on whom Cray Research so depended.

According to John Rollwagen, the appeal of Cray's compensation scheme rested on two features. First, the company paid well by industry standards. In addition to high base-compensation levels, it offered a generous profit-sharing plan. Ten percent of pretax profits were distributed to all Cray employees, allocated in proportion to salary. In 1983, this bonus amounted to about 10 percent of an individual's base salary. As a special incentive, 8 to 10 percent of all Cray personnel were included in a leadership category of profit-sharing. This group was awarded two and one half times the general profit-sharing bonus. Company officers were eligible for a cash bonus of 40 percent of base salary, executive officers 55 percent, and the CEO 65 percent. These higher awards, however, were part of the target total-compensation package for managers, whereas the bonus awards for lower-level employees were incremental to their target salaries. For example, John Rollwagen's total compensation was decided by the board through the common practice of using as a reference the compensation received by CEOs of comparable companies. The bonus (at-risk) compensation was a component of this figure. Stock options were also employed, but had become an increasingly less important incentive over time.

The second important feature of Cray's compensation system was the "dual ladder" concept. Under this policy, a person devoted to technology could receive compensation comparable to someone in management. For example, Steve Chen's compensation in 1984 was close to the level for an executive vice-president.

Although management recognized compensation as an important motivational device, it considered other elements as even more powerful inducements to personal commitment. John Rollwagen explained:

> Association with Seymour Cray and with the world's most powerful computer provides a great deal of inspiration in our ranks. Maybe 90 percent of our employees have never met Seymour, but everyone knows Seymour stories. There's the one about Seymour building a new sailboat each spring, sailing it over the summer, and then burning it at the end of the season so that he wouldn't be bound by that year's mistakes when he sets about designing a more perfect craft for the following year. That's also the way Seymour approaches computer design. It says a great deal about innovation. Some of the Seymour stories probably aren't exactly true, but I wouldn't deny them for the world.
>
> In my judgment, the most powerful incentive we provide our people is recognition. Individuals are given responsibility, and they are given credit. We talk more about people than we do about functions. Individual people are the key to our success, and we try to make that clear.

The Technological Challenge

During the early years of the emerging supercomputer industry, Cray had little competition in the narrowly focused market. CDC had turned its attention elsewhere, and no one else had more than a passing interest in this esoteric extreme of the computer business. By the 1980s, however, commercial interest in supercomputers had begun to pick up. Technological advances in hardware and componentry had spurred industry growth. As of early 1984, Cray had supplied sixty supercomputers, Control Data, twenty-one, and Denelcor (largely U.S. government funded), four. So far, Cray had led the race, but competitors were beginning to snap at its heels.

The Race for Technological Supremacy

The race for technological supremacy implied more than commercial competition. As noted in *Fortune*, March 5, 1984, "With the fortunes of entire nations, not just companies, at risk, the race to dominate these 'information technologies' has become an international competition in which governments encourage and subsidize the participants." Salient among the national efforts were the $100 million supercomputer and $500 million artificial-intelligence projects in Japan and the Pentagon's corresponding request for $1 billion to counter the Japanese on both fronts.

The stakes and status of the contest were spelled out by a panel of fifteen U.S. scientists who returned from a trip to the Far East with the conclusion that "U.S. leadership in supercomputing is crucial for the advancement of science and technology and, therefore, for economic and national security. . . . [U]nder current conditions there is little likelihood that the United States will lead in the development and application of this new generation of machines."[2]

One unprecedented move in the U.S. private-sector technology race was the consolidation of research and development talent into the nonprofit Microelectronic and Computer Technology Corporation (MCC), organized in 1982 by CDC Chairman William Norris to develop state-of-the-art computer technology. MCC, which was based in Austin, Texas, had a staff drawn from eleven companies in 1983, with an annual budget of $75 million. Any company that wished to join this consortium would donate scientists and researchers for a period of up to four years and would fund research. In return, member companies would have the right to use the results. The consortium itself would not put out a product, but would own licenses and patents exclusively for three years. Individual member companies would manufacture and market the technological advances.

Newsweek called MCC a "bold departure from the way research is usually done" and brought up the issue of antitrust laws. The possibility of antitrust action had deterred IBM from joining. Cray, Texas Instruments, Intel, and several other companies also decided not to join. Cray's President Rollwagen said, "It really could be a yeasty place to work, but how the technology gets transferred back to the member companies is a mystery to me. There'll be a technological exchange—it may be positive for the country, but it probably won't be for the individual companies. Our system is based on individuality, not a sense of community as in Japan."

Norris's renewed interest in supercomputing was possibly the spur for CDC to spin off its supercomputer operations into a separate, publicly held subsidiary, ETA Systems, Inc. CDC would attempt to rise $100 million through public

2. *Science Digest*, September 1983, p. 49.

or private stock offerings, reducing its ownership to no more than 40 percent. The new firm would develop a 10-billion-calculations-per-second (10 gigaflop) computer for delivery by the end of 1986. "Control Data made the move because small, entrepreneurial companies can design, manufacture, and market such computers better than large companies," stated a company spokesman.

In response to CDC's announced plans, a manager at NEC, a Japanese computer company, was quoted in the October 17, 1983, issue of *Business Week* as saying, "We have the semiconductor technology to compete. We don't think Cray and Control Data have the capability to keep up. That's what success depends on and all the Japanese companies have it." A U.S. supercomputer authority in turn remarked, "The Japanese emphasis appears to be on device technology rather than on improved computer architectures. While faster components and innovative ways of arranging them are both necessary to push supercomputers to greater speeds, new architectures will likely be more important than faster devices. If the Japanese Superspeed Project doesn't exploit new architectures, it may not be much of a competitive factor."

Recent and impending Japanese supercomputer offerings were described in *High Technology* in May 1984:

> While Japan pursues its long-term development projects, three Japanese companies are making waves with several existing or soon-to-exist supercomputers. Hitachi has already delivered its 630 megaflop (million-floating-point-operations-per-second) computer. . . . The forthcoming Fujitsu VP-200 will operate at 500 megaflops. Finally, NEC plans 1985 shipments of its SX-1, rated at 570 megaflops and its SX-2, rated at a staggering 1.3 gigaflops (billion floating-point operations per second).

Figure C shows the projected progress of supercomputer peak performance through 1992. The above article included the following caution about comparing supercomputer speeds:

> "The greatest threat is to our brochuremanship," says ETA's Lincoln, referring to the high peak performances claimed for the Japanese machines. . . . Thus, until the Japanese computers are tested with some real applications, it's difficult to evaluate their relative power.[3]

The competition that worried Cray corporate planner Peter Gregory was not the Japanese, MCC, or CDC; it was IBM. Gregory predicted IBM would introduce a machine in 1984 that would not only compute on the basis of perfor-

---

3. The variation between peak rating and actual performance resulted from a crucial division of labor between scalar and vector processing. A supercomputer with a fast vector mode but slow scalar mode would process some programs more slowly than a supercomputer having a lower peak (vector) rating but a fast scalar capability. It was for this reason that a Cray-1 offering a 250-megaflop peak rating and scaler processing at 80 MIPS, could outperform for many applications a Cyber 205 with a 400-megaflop peak rating and scalar processing at 50 MIPS. Other parameters determining a particular machine's ability to execute a particular program rapidly included component switching speeds, machine cycle times, memory size, compiler efficiency, pipelining capability (having repetitive sequential steps performed simultaneously), and peripheral-device capabilities. In effect, maximum machine speeds could be compared only for specific applications, and even then often only on the basis of actual trial runs.

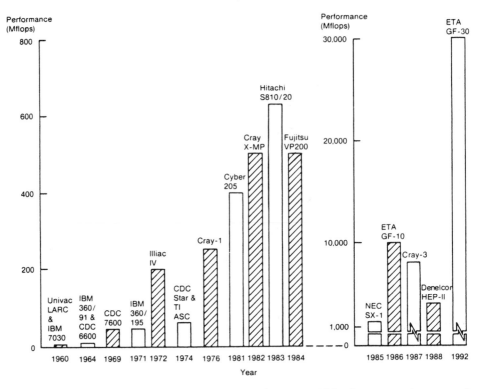

Figure C Competing supercomputers' peak performance. This chart approximates each machine's theoretical peak mega-flop (million floating-point operations per second) rating, which is rarely attained in actual operations. For example, the 64-processor Illiac IV never came close to its theoretical peak performance. *Source: High Technology,* May 1984.

mance, but would appeal to organizations already committed to IBM systems.

Even Seymour voiced concern over the possibility that Cray might lose its lead in the supercomputer industry. In looking back at the company's impressive success record, he reflected: "We were fortunate in not having had any major things go wrong. I don't think we've been tried yet." To which John Rollwagen responded: "It is my job to make sure that nothing goes wrong."

A Strategic and Organizational Challenge

On May 14, 1984, members of Cray's top management attended a presentation on the company's performance in the petroleum industry that underscored an issue of great concern to them: Should the company change its strategic direction and emphasis?[4] If so, how far, how fast, and in what way? The report

4. The presentation concluded a field study by the following second-year Harvard MBA students: G. Eastman, D. Harding, K. Hollen, S. Mickel, M. Newlin, and S. Nyquist. Quoted material in this section was taken from an accompanying written report.

focused on actions Cray might have to take to protect and improve its enviable market position in light of some customer dissatisfaction and growing competitive threats.

As the report acknowledged, Cray had been remarkably successful in developing the petroleum market, selling ten machines to eight oil companies in just three years. This success was attributed to the company's ability to offer an "excellent product to an industry thirsty for computational power," essentially unencumbered by any competition.

The report went on to characterize the petroleum market by first comparing it with Cray's original customers:

> Cray has traditionally sold to government users who have purchased primarily on performance. They have demanded very little in the way of software support, IBM compatibility or hardware peripherals. They buy on the basis of speed.
>
> The petroleum companies, on the other hand, have huge existing investments in software and in IBM hardware. While they are interested in speed, they do not want speed at the expense of incompatibility. Petroleum companies are looking for trouble-free solutions to complex scientific problems.
>
> In the early 1980s, oil companies were swimming in cash and searching for attractive investments. Exploration production costs had been increasing rapidly, and reservoirs of new oil discoveries were declining in size compared to previous years. As a result, geologists, geophysicists, and reservoir engineers were encouraged to develop more sophisticated analytical techniques to evaluate oil investment projects. These techniques demand significant computational power to obtain reasonable accuracy. As a result, technically advanced reservoir engineers and state of the art geophysicists turned to the supercomputer industry to find the needed computational power. Although Cray's software support was limited, oil companies were able to solve significant engineering problems with the Cray. Oil companies regarded the Cray as a small exploration expense that paid off handsomely.
>
> Reservoir engineering demand is increasing 20–30 percent per year and seismic processing demand is increasing 30–50 percent per year by one customer's conservative estimates. Thus, the oil industry's thirst for computational power is large and growing.

Customer interviews led to the following findings on Cray's hardware, software, and responsiveness:

> We have found that Cray has generally met customers' price and performance expectations for hardware. However, customers believe Cray should expand memory capacity and improve networking capability to satisfy users in the petroleum industry. Finally, the Cray hardware is considered reliable, but not as good as IBM, which sets the standard for most users in petroleum industry data processing shops.
>
> Most Cray customers feel "software" was the weakest aspect of an otherwise highly attractive product. They are dissatisfied with the current software offerings as well as associated support.

Specifically, the software was criticized as not user-friendly, not well documented, and not designed for petroleum applications. The basis of comparison was IBM, since it set the standard for most users in the petroleum industry. According to several customers, the Cray software people were "too theoretical as a result of their experience with government labs and would have to become more practical if they are to meet petroleum customer needs."

This last remark touched on a broader concern about the extent to which Cray was really committed to serving the petroleum industry. The following customers' comments on this issue were reported:

- Cray is not as devoted as IBM to understanding the petroleum industry.
- There is no strategic commitment to the exploration industry from the top of Cray.
- We are looking for a supercomputer manufacturer to *serve* the oil industry.

The report went on to describe Cray's vulnerability and the dilemma management faced:

> Although switching costs are high (perhaps over $2 million to redevelop software for a new system), they do not represent an insurmountable barrier to entry given machine costs of $10 million or more. Thus, we see an opportunity for a competitive entry due to customer ambivalence or even dissatisfaction with Cray's software offerings. At the same time, there is an opportunity for Cray to respond to its customers' needs more aggressively and to build these entry barriers for itself.
>
> The nature of Cray's clientele is changing. More of Cray's sales will be to repeat customers and the management organization needed to maintain the petroleum region is growing. Furthermore, competitors are about to enter the market. This totals to a big demand for marketing dollars for the petroleum region.
>
> At the same time the company is facing the prospect of serious technological challenge to its position as maker of the world's fastest computers. The decision thus becomes how Cray will divide its resources (money, management, software, peripherals, manufacturing, etc.) in this new environment. If Cray continues to be a technology company, a maker of high speed boxes, that's fine, but the company may have to accept a slow-down in exploiting the commercial sector. If Cray wants to be more marketing driven, that's fine, too, but there probably will be technological sacrifices or delays that must be dealt with. Additionally, there will be an element of culture shock as the company moves away from being technology driven and toward being marketing driven.
>
> Can Cray be both technologically driven and marketing driven? Maybe, but management is going to have to clearly think through how it will balance the competing demands for resources.

Although the specific recommendations of the study dealt with changes within the existing Cray structure, the idea of creating an organizational unit with business reponsibility for the petroleum industry was raised for consideration. The students recognized that such a move was likely to exacerbate the problems management was facing in trying to maintain a cohesive, entrepreneurial company ambience. Although some differences might arise over future hardware requirements, the major potential source of conflict would be software development.

Competition for resources would arise between the applications-oriented software needs of the petroleum industry and the operating system-oriented software needs for Cray's new machines. This competition, in turn, would further complicate the existing software-hardware battle for funds.

DAAG Europe

Dr. Robert Pelz, managing director of Deutsche Aufzugs A.G. European regional headquarters (DAAG Europe), faced a dilemma as he reviewed the 1969 preliminary financial statements, for they showed a continuing deterioration of the company's current accounts. During 1969 accounts receivable and inventories had increased by 42 percent and 48 percent, respectively, while sales increased only slightly more than 10 percent for the same period. Moreover, the company had failed to show profits on contracted sales of new elevators for the fourth consecutive year. Some action would have to be taken to improve DAAG's financial performance in Europe.

Yet, Pelz fully realized that these financial results were a direct consequence of the company's long-term strategy to develop low-cost operations through a European-wide rationalized manufacturing operation. This strategy brought related changes to every aspect of doing business. Pelz did not wish to jeopardize the major transformation still under way, therefore, by any action he might take to remedy the immediate financial problems.

The following introduction provides a brief description of the elevator business in Western Europe as viewed by executives of the Deutsche Aufzugs A.G. European regional headquarters (DAAG Europe) located in Frankfurt, Germany. It pertains primarily to passenger elevators and covers events only up to 1969.

The Passenger Elevator

With the arrival of the high-rise building, the passenger elevator passed from being a convenience to becoming a necessity. While usually an unobtrusive element of large buildings, elevators often occupy over 5 percent of the available volume in a building and account for about 3 percent to 7 percent of the total building cost.

The elevator system is made up of three major subsystems: (1) the electromechanical system, which guides and propels the elevator; (2) the electrical/electronic system, which controls the elevator movement in terms of acceleration, deceleration, and direction; and (3) the elevator cab itself, with its moving doors. There are two basic lifting systems—the hydraulic type for low and slow applications, and the electric, cable-driven type for any application—with many technical variations, a dozen or so basic circuits for the command controls, and countless configurations for the cab.

While the technology associated with each of these systems has remained fundamentally the same over the past thirty years, the product nonetheless calls for relatively demanding technical content and expertise. First, since elevators transport people vertically and are exposed to the possibility of falling, they have to be absolutely safe and reliable. As one observer noted, "If your elevator should ever fall, it could ruin your whole day." Second, an elevator is a means of public transportation. As such, it is essential that it be "idiot proof" (that is, the mechanism should not be damaged or cause injury because of an error by the operator), and that it also be vandal resistant. Third, for reasons of safety as well as of comfort, the elevator shaft and guide rails have to be straight within reasonably small tolerances and have to remain so. The difficulties here are that the dimensions of buildings are far from exact, and large buildings often sag or are otherwise distorted over time. One of the most skillful jobs in the elevator business is trueing up the system when it has been installed. Fourth, accelerating and decelerating an elevator for comfortable riding poses difficult propulsion and braking problems for the larger and faster units. In a high-rise office building, for example, an elevator might travel at speeds as high as thirty feet per second (the equivalent of about three stories). The system has to be capable of decelerating the cab (weighing anywhere from one ton empty to almost three tons fully loaded) from that speed to a dead stop within one-quarter inch of a given point, and it has to do all this in a way that maintains passenger comfort.

Passenger elevators are generally classified as Class A or Class B units. Class A elevators are defined within the industry as the large and high-speed units (over 300 feet per minute) with relatively sophisticated electronic controls. These elevators are typically employed in large office buildings, large hotels, and other high-rise buildings where pedestrian traffic is heavy. Class B elevators are defined as the small, slow-speed units (around 200 feet per minute) with manually operated swing doors found in small office buildings and apartments. In most cases, Class B units do not have complex memory systems.

The Western European Customers

Up to 1969, the markets for Class A and Class B elevators were distinct and had to be approached differently. In most cases, the customer for Class B elevators was the general contractor. The contractor in smaller building projects in Europe was often responsible for the design, costs, and overall management of the building, including the elevator.

Government agencies were also major customers for Class B elevators, especially for apartment buildings. In dealing with this market, a DAAG elevator salesman would call on the local housing authority, the project coordinator, and the general contractor. The general contractor was again considered to be the most important link in this highly price-oriented market.

In contrast to the Class B market, several people were usually involved in the purchase decision for Class A elevators—typically, the architect, the general contractor, and high-ranking managers of the company owning or planning to use the building. In the opinion of DAAG management, the architect was the person most influential in selecting an elevator.

Dr. Robert Pelz, managing director of DAAG Europe, described DAAG's approach to this market:

> Our salesmen learn about possible contracts in several different ways. For example, our marketing department monitors the future building activity in a given region and alerts the appropriate salesmen to upcoming projects. However, there are not many potential contracts which the salesmen learn about for the first time in this manner. Most of our contracts are brought to the salesmen's attention by the architects themselves. DAAG, after all, is well-known throughout Europe.
>
> It is our policy to have the DAAG salesman contact the architects in his region on a regular basis, whether or not he knows of a definite contract possibility at the time of calling. After all, there are not all that many people who deal with larger building projects. The nature of the salesman's work brings him into contact with architects on a regular basis anyway, as most of our salesmen already have contracts in progress. We estimate 80 percent of our sales in Europe are made to about 2,500 individual customers who are constantly involved in the design of major buildings.

Architects calling on the company to provide elevator engineering consulting for their building projects were another important source of information for DAAG salesmen. To encourage this practice, it was company policy for salesmen to urge the architect to call for competitive bids. "In this way," noted the DAAG executive, "he can see for himself that DAAG can best supply his needs."

DAAG generally commanded a 10 percent premium in price over local competitors, as did the other major elevator manufacturers (Otis, Schindler, and Westinghouse). In selling elevators, DAAG salesmen stressed quality and service and played down price considerations. Although price was discussed in broad terms early in the contract negotiations, the actual price was not set until all specifications had been described. This delay of three to six months was enough time, according to DAAG management, to show why the extra cost was justified. Pelz described the advantages DAAG offered:

> You see, an elevator can cause an architect more trouble than most anything else in his building. If the president of a company who is housed in a particular building has trouble with an elevator—for example, if a door doesn't work properly—he will probably complain directly to the owner. The owner will, in turn, blame the architect. The architect not only wants to avoid such nuisances, he also has to guard his reputation for quality work.
>
> DAAG elevators can also save the architect and the building owner money in the long run. The installation of elevators is one of the last steps in the construction of a building. Any delays in installing elevators will therefore cause a similar delay in making the building serviceable and this could be extremely costly. For example, we have a fifteen-million-mark contract to

install twenty elevators in the Lorelei Tower in Frankfurt. This is a forty-six-story-high office building costing over 300 million German marks. Now, if the elevators were to cause a month's delay in opening the building, the additional cost just in terms of one month's extra interest charges on the full investment would run about three million marks. Even more impressive would be the rental income lost for that month which would come to about five million marks. These figures give you some idea of how valuable our rapid and dependable installation can be for the architect and building owner.

Finally, DAAG offers one of the finest maintenance services in the trade. Even though the price of our service contracts runs about ten percent above our competitors' in many European countries, we service virtually all the installed DAAG Class A elevators and about eighty percent of the Class B units. In many respects, we consider ourselves primarily a service company. And while we sell our service contracts quite separately from elevators, the architect has this in mind when he selects an elevator.

Overall, I would say that an architect will usually make his decision on a DAAG elevator on the basis of past experience with the product and his relationship with a particular DAAG salesman.

With the exception of the largest high-rise buildings, the typical time period for DAAG's involvement with a given Class A elevator installation in Europe was about three years. A year would usually elapse between the initial proposal and the signing of the contract, the materials would be shipped from the factories roughly a year later, and final installation would be completed after another year.

Because elevator sales often involved large sums of money and tended to be made at irregular intervals, DAAG salesmen were paid straight salaries. A well-qualified salesman for Class A equipment earned about $14,000 per year in 1969. Salesmen for Class B equipment and for maintenance service received about $7,000 to $8,000 per year.[1] Salesman were also reimbursed for all out-of-pocket expenses. By way of comparison, the average DAAG factory worker earned about $3,000 per year.

Manufacturing Operations

An elevator system is made up of many individual parts, such as mechanical relays, motors, ropes (suspension cables), sheet metal, steel railing, and electronic circuitry. Most smaller firms purchase these parts for assembly and even subcontract certain subassembly work. In contrast, the largest elevator firms traditionally manufacture almost all of the required parts. According to one DAAG executive, this extensive backward integration is almost a matter of pride for these companies.

The variety of parts to be produced and handled is many times greater than that needed for current operations because of maintenance service require-

---

1. In Germany, DAAG employed five Class A salesmen, about forty Class B salesmen, and twenty-five service salesmen. Total annual sales cost in 1969 amounted to almost 2 million German marks for sales of 130 million German marks.

ments. DAAG, for example, serviced units that had been produced as long as forty years ago. In addition to its own units, DAAG typically provided parts for elevators that had been produced by the many companies it had acquired over the years. The resulting high number of different components required DAAG and the other major elevator manufacturers to carry large parts inventories.

Field operations is another salient characteristic of the elevator manufacturing business. The extent of field operations in 1969 was indicated by the composition of DAAG employment in Europe. Out of a total force of 13,000 employees, 6,000 were manual workers in the field compared to about 3,700 factory workers. About half of the field workers were responsible for elevator erection and the other half for maintenance service. Because of their deep involvement with building construction, elevator manufacturers shared the building industry's special problems with respect to weather conditions, scattered sites, and sensitivity to economic conditions.

The Elevator Market and Industry Structure in Europe

The elevator business in Europe tended to be subdivided into national markets because of different building codes and in some cases because of tariff barriers. The codes generally defined the nature of the safety features that had to be employed. For example, car doors were not required for certain Class B elevators in France; however, such an elevator, called a flush hoistway, was prohibited in Germany.

The suppliers of these markets differed between Class A and B elevators. The Class B sector was largely served by many small firms that competed in a local or national area. The Class A sector in Europe was dominated by the multinational firms: Otis, Schindler, DAAG, and to some extent Westinghouse. A number of strong local competitors also existed in many European countries. The size of each national market for all elevators in 1969 and DAAG's principal competitors for Class A elevators are given in Exhibit 1. European expenditures for construction and for elevators during 1970–1974 are forecasted by country in Exhibit 2.

The Otis Elevator Company was the world's largest manufacturer of elevators. In addition to passenger and freight elevators, the company also produced escalators worldwide and a line of material-handling equipment, automobile hydraulic lifts, and golf carts in the United States. Founded as a U.S. company in 1853, the company began a rapid expansion of operations overseas at the turn of the century. By 1969, affiliated companies in forty-six countries and sales representatives in sixty-nine other countries generated almost half of the company's total sales of $536 million.

Schindler A.G. was a family-owned and operated Swiss elevator firm with sales of approximately $170 million in 1969. It produced a line of high-quality products and was represented in all the European markets. Schindler held a ninety percent share of the Swiss elevator market (both Class A and Class B), and it also held important market positions in Germany and France. Most of

Exhibit 1 Estimated European elevator sales in 1969 and DAAG's major competitors for class A equipment.

| Country | Sales (Class A & B) | | | DAAG's Major Competitors |
	Units (thousands)	Value ($ millions)	Average Value ($ thousands)	
Austria	2.0	23	11.5	Wertheim, Sovitch, Otis
Belgium	1.4	21	14.9	Westinghouse, Schindler, Otis
Denmark	0.3	6	18.4	(data not available)
France	11.4	102	9.0	Otis, Westinghouse, Schindler, Soretex
West Germany	11.0	165	15.0	R. Stahl, Schindler, Otis, Haushahn, Manessman
Italy	11.1	57	5.2	FIAM, Schindler, SABIEM, Otis
The Netherlands	1.7	20	11.8	Schindler, Otis
Norway	0.4	5	13.2	Kone
Portugal	2.1	10	4.6	Comportel, Esacec, Otis
Spain	10.1	52	5.1	Schindler, Zardoya
Sweden	1.2	14	12.1	Kone
Switzerland	3.4	38	11.2	Schindler, Schlieren
United Kingdom	5.2	87	16.8	General Electric (U.K.)
Total	61.3	600	9.8	

Source: Official statistics and company data

Exhibit 2 Average annual European building construction and elevator sales forecast, 1970–1974.

	Construction ($ billions)			Elevator Sales ($ millions)			Ratios (%)		
	(A) Total	(B) Res.	(C) Non-res.	(D) Total	(E) Res.	(F) Non-res.	D/A	E/B	F/C
Austria	2.1	0.9	1.2	28	11	17	1.33	1.24	1.40
Belgium	4.1	1.3	2.8	27	11	16	0.11	0.83	0.58
Denmark	2.2	1.0	1.2	8	3	5	0.36	0.32	0.40
France	25.6	9.6	16.0	141	56	85	0.55	0.59	0.53
West Germany	29.4	10.4	19.0	194	78	116	0.66	0.74	0.61
Italy	14.8	6.5	8.3	69	28	41	0.46	0.42	0.50
The Netherlands	5.8	2.5	3.3	24	10	14	0.41	0.38	0.44
Norway	1.9	0.7	1.2	7	3	4	0.37	0.40	0.35
Portugal	1.5	0.7	0.8	13	5	8	0.87	0.74	0.98
Spain	4.5	2.3	2.2	67	27	40	1.49	1.17	1.91
Sweden	4.6	1.5	3.1	18	7	11	0.39	0.48	0.35
Switzerland	1.5	0.6	0.9	48	19	29	3.20	3.20	3.20
United Kingdom	12.6	4.3	8.3	113	45	68	0.89	1.05	0.82
Total	111.6	42.6	69.0	758 (100%)	303 (40%)	455 (60%)	0.68	0.71	0.66

Source: Official statistics, except for Switzerland and Portugal, where company estimates were used

Schindler's manufacturing facilities were in Switzerland, although it did have plants in several other European countries.

DAAG Europe was a subsidiary of the Pace Garner Corporation (usually referred to simply as Pace), a large diversified U.S. firm with a major division that manufactured elevators, escalators, and conveyor equipment for the U.S. Canadian, and Latin American markets. Pace was represented in almost all major European countries by independent subsidiaries, which for management purposes reported to DAAG Europe. With few exceptions, all of these European subsidiaries, with combined sales in 1969 of about $160 million, produced Class A and B elevator equipment under the DAAG name.

Westinghouse Elevator (a subsidiary of the Westinghouse Company) had estimated worldwide elevator sales of about $150 million in 1969; 70 percent of these sales were made in the United States. DAAG management did not consider Westinghouse as strong a competitor in Europe as Otis or Schindler.

While competition among the big four in Europe was keen, each knew the strengths and the limits of the others. Looming as unknown adversaries were the large Japanese companies, such as Mitsubishi, that had developed excellent Class A elevator equipment and were beginning to compete for contracts abroad. As of 1969, the Japanese had not bid for elevator contracts in Europe, but European elevator manufacturers considered the Japanese's first attempt as imminent.

The potential severity of the Japanese threat was yet to be gauged. Some European elevator people believed that the structural requirements of the business (namely, the close relationships between salesmen and architects and the need to provide extensive maintenance service) would block or at least greatly curtail Japanese entry. Others disagreed, arguing that the Japanese had learned to provide quality service from their experience in selling automobiles and various industrial equipment in the United States and Europe. According to the latter, the Japanese could develop a strong position in the European elevator market in four or five years.

Origins of the DAAG Europe Strategy

DAAG Europe's situation in 1969 regarding organization, marketing, and manufacturing could be traced back to a series of moves initiated in the early 1960s by Pelz, then managing director of the German operating company, DAAG. One of the early moves occurred in 1964 when he proposed to the U.S. corporate management (Pace Garner Corporation, located in Chicago, Illinois) that the company acquire the rival German firm, Rechtbau A.G. The most compelling reason for this acquisition was that it would boost DAAG's share of the German market from 20 percent to a commanding 35 percent.

Rechtbau itself had been formed in 1960 through a merger of three German elevator companies. Dr. Wagner, managing director of Rechtbau, had engineered this merger in an effort to create a company that could compete with Otis, Westinghouse, DAAG, and Schindler. When Rechtbau was still unable to support the costly engineering and development work necessary to extend its operations from supplying elevators for small apartment and office buildings to the more profitable market for high-rise buildings, Wagner next attempted to form a multinational coalition with some of the larger independent elevator firms in other major European countries. Failing to interest these firms in joining forces with Rechtbau, Wagner decided to sell the company to one of the four dominant firms. Thus, if DAAG did not merge with Rechtbau, presumably one of its key competitors would pick up the German firm's 15 percent market share.

Pelz, who had been a member of the German diplomatic corps prior to joining DAAG, won his case. M. B. Bentley, president of Pace Garner, approved the acquisition on Pelz's terms. Wagner was appointed president of the new firm and Pelz vice president. The two men were given three years to make the merger work without interference from Chicago. Aside from the requirement to reconcile its accounting system with that of Pace, the new German company was on its own. As a DAAG executive later remarked, "Pelz had put his neck on the line. He had to make the merger work."

In taking over Rechtbau A.G., DAAG acquired the largest manufacturer of Class B elevators in Germany. While each of DAAG's major European affiliates manufactured and sold Class B elevators, these efforts (almost always representing a continuation of business carried out by firms acquired in earlier years) were generally played down and assumed only secondary importance among DAAG's activities. This policy could be attributed to the generally low profitability associated with the Class B elevator, as well as to the fragmented nature of the market. DAAG was organized to deal with the limited number of large and relatively sophisticated architectural and construction firms in Europe. The Class B market—requiring contact with many small, local building contractors—had traditionally been served by similarly small, local elevator manufacturers. The distinctly different requirements for selling and servicing Class B elevators had long dissuaded DAAG from emphasizing this market. Moreover, many DAAG executives were of the opinion that DAAG's image as a manufacturer of high-quality and highly sophisticated elevators might be tarnished if DAAG attacked the Class B market in a major way.

Pelz believed that DAAG was wrong in neglecting this market segment, especially in Europe, where it accounted for about 50 percent of the industry's total elevator sales.[1] He argued that DAAG could not afford to ignore one-half of its potential market in Europe. He thus set out to launch an attack on this sector of the market from the enlarged base of Rechtbau's Class B business, and he did so with some ideas on how a large, multinational firm might compete for these sales.

The Move to Standard Models

Elevators had always been custom designed for each building project. The elevator had to fit the space allotted—or left over—for this purpose. Elevator

---

1. Pace headquarters management estimated Class B elevators to represent less than 30 percent of total U.S. elevator sales. This estimate was only approximate because of the limited availability of market data.

companies competed on the basis of their ability to meet these architectural specifications.

Around 1961, Pelz became attracted to the possibility of manufacturing and selling standardized elevator models. He knew as did others in the industry that elevators, although designed and manufactured to customers' individual specifications, were basically similar in design, engineering, and construction. This similarity was especially true for Class B elevators. Pelz reasoned that if a line of elevator models similar to a line of automobile models could be developed, major savings would result from reduction in design costs and from economies associated with multiple production. Important savings would also accrue from the opportunity to standardize the technical and administrative processing of contracts. For example, the extensive engineering documentation officially required for an elevator system and its working parts had to be prepared for each custom unit, while the original documentation could serve for repeat sales of a standard model.

The idea of standard models was not entirely novel to the elevator industry. One of DAAG's German competitors had attempted to introduce standard models in 1952. This effort met with little success and was abandoned. Pelz was convinced of the need to move in this direction, nonetheless, and he consequently initiated the design of the first standard elevator model for the German apartment-building market in 1962. This model, the MOD-S, was introduced in early 1963.

The new model met with some resistance from customers; it met with much more resistance from the DAAG organization and its sales force. Despite this lack of enthusiasm, the company managed to sell about 230 units the first year, and Pelz planned to build a factory at Mainz to produce the MOD-S. The acquisition of Rechtbau provided DAAG with a new factory at Köln that was well suited for producing the standard elevator model and also with a large clientele for Class B elevators. Access to an operating factory represented a gain of two years for DAAG, and the Mainz project was consequently abandoned.

While the acquisition of Rechtbau admittedly gave impetus to DAAG's concept of standard models, Pelz firmly believed that the move to standard models was the only way DAAG could make the Rechtbau acquisition successful. He agreed with the general sentiment that a company like DAAG could not compete effectively against the small firm for Class B elevator business under the present way of doing business. It would be necessary to change the nature of the Class B elevator business to suit DAAG's strengths. In Pelz's opinion, the standard elevator model was the way to effect such a change.

His experience with the MOD-S convinced Pelz that standard Class B elevator models would be successful only when manufacturing and installation costs could be reduced sufficiently to permit prices to be some 10–15 percent lower than current levels, while still enabling the company to make a profit. Some of these cost savings would come from a reduction in parts inventories, special jigs and tools, and from a simplification of fabrication procedures. Important additional savings could be gained, however, only with an appreciably increased production volume compared to the volume handled by the individual DAAG companies in 1964.

The needed volume could be generated reasonably quickly, Pelz reasoned, if the other DAAG European subsidiaries were to join Germany in developing standards models for their own markets as well. Eventually, if the standard elevator concept proved out, maximum advantage would be gained as models were extended to the Class A part of the business, and as both Class A and B models were standardized for all of Europe.

The Beginnings of a European Concept

Pelz had already begun to lay the groundwork for his idea of a European regional organization during his discussion in Chicago concerning the Rechtbau acquisition. Theretofore, each of Pace's foreign subsidiaries had reported directly to Pace Elevator divisional headquarters in Chicago. The large headquarters staff customarily become deeply involved with operations in each of the subsidiaries. Functional staff members at Chicago tended to work directly and closely with their functional counterparts in the field.

Pelz had found these relationships cumbersome and frustrating as he tried to manage the company in Germany. This U.S.-based, centralized organizational arrangement would be even more dysfunctional if the European subsidiaries tried to coordinate their actions. Thus, Pelz argued for a European regional management on two grounds. First, the move to standard elevator models in Europe would require a great deal of coordinated effort best supervised on the spot. A related point was the rapid integration taking place in the European Common Market, which would undoubtedly call for other forms of coordinated action on the European continent. Second, an increasingly important part of DAAG's business in Europe would come from Class B elevators, and the Chicago staff was not particularly competent in advising the Europeans on this type of business.[2]

Although the newly formed German DAAG had yet to prove itself, Pelz had once again been sufficiently persuasive to gain his point. In late 1965, the general managers of Pace's European elevator companies were to report to Pelz as managing director of DAAG European regional headquarters. The subsidiaries remained legally independent entities owned by Pace.[3]

Shaping the New Relationship

Pelz saw his first task as managing director to be that of convincing each subsidiary to offer a line of standard elevator models for the Class B market seg-

2. Class A business accounted for almost 90 percent in value of all new elevator installations by Pace Elevator Division in the United States.
3. With few exceptions, all of these European subsidiaries, with combined sales in 1969 of about $160 million, produced Class A and B elevator equipment under the DAAG name.

ment. By 1966, the German DAAG had developed a product line of eight models for the German apartment-building market. He acknowledged, however, that it might not be feasible to market German elevators in other European countries where tastes, building codes, and market conditions were different. Moreover, while the subsidiaries had for years done little more than adapt the company's U.S. elevator designs to meet local needs, Pelz anticipated that country managers might tend to resist if he tried to relieve them of this engineering and design function. In order to lessen such resistance, as well as to give the national companies an opportunity to gain experience with standard models, he consequently decided to permit each subsidiary to develop its own national line of standard Class B elevator models as the first step.

Pelz's persuasive powers were put to the test as he tried to sell the standard model concept to the national companies reporting to him. The general managers voiced doubt as to the applicability of German experience with elevator models to their national markets. Moreover, even in Germany the results were only preliminary and certainly not clear cut.

The resistance voiced by each country manager no doubt reflected an opposition also expressed by his sales force. The salesmen were proud of the DAAG reputation for being able to produce the highest quality equipment for whichever design the architect specified. The idea of selling standard, off-the-shelf elevators, even if only for Class B business, was somewhat repugnant to them. Furthermore, most salesmen doubted that standard models would catch on—at least not rapidly enough to maintain sales performance.

These attitudes were too deeply ingrained, these men too important to his purpose, and their arguments too valid for Pelz to turn them aside. He knew that he had to sell not only the customer on the idea of standard models, but more importantly, he also had to sell each member of the DAAG sales forces.

Lowering Price

In 1965, Pelz moved to induce the DAAG salesmen in Germany to sell the MOD-S line of standard models by lowering prices by about 9 percent from an already artificially low base. (The price in 1963 had been set to reflect prospective cost savings.) He made this reduction to create the widest possible price spread between the standard and traditional elevator models. As a result of this move, annual MOD-S sales in Germany almost trebled in 1965 to a volume of 1,321 units.

Shortly after the price cut for MOD-S elevators, DAAG began to lower its prices on Class A elevators as well. While Pelz wanted his salesmen to switch from selling traditional Class B elevators to standard models, he did not want to divert their energies from selling Class A elevators. The MOD-S price cut had had that effect to some extent, and he believed it necessary to make a comparable price reduction for the Class A equipment, if a proper balance of sales effort was to be maintained between the two. Quite apart from this reasoning, as a DAAG executive later explained, the company's prices for Class

A elevators were lowered throughout Europe almost unconsciously at this time, because of the general enthusiasm in DAAG for expansion and growth. By bringing its prices down, DAAG once again increased unit sales.

Competitors in both markets soon countered with price cuts of their own. Pelz knew the lower DAAG prices could be justified and maintained only when manufacturing costs had been fully driven down by means of large economies of scale.

The European Models

In Pelz's view, these economies of scale could be achieved by moving to the next major phase of his plan—standard European models. By 1968, the development of Class B models had been successfully completed on a national basis. Germany, France, Italy, and the U.K. each had a line of between ten and fifteen models. The smaller DAAG companies—such as Austria, Belgium, and Holland—adopted variations of the models designed in larger neighboring companies. As a result, eighty standard models accounted for 90 percent of the the DAAG total Class B elevator sales on the European continent.[4]

The transition to standard models had been helped, as a DAAG executive pointed out, by increasing the company's Class B elevator business through acquisitions. From 1965 through 1969, Pace had expanded the European elevator operations by establishing five additional subsidiaries in Sweden, Denmark, Switzerland, Portugal, and Austria. During this same period, the DAAG European region had also acquired (through its existing subsidiary companies) some thirty small, local elevator firms that manufactured or serviced Class B elevators. Exhibit 3 shows the expansion of the DAAG European region from 1965 through 1968.

In 1968, DAAG management began working on the development of European models to replace the Class B national models and the Class A customized units. One of its major tasks was to build up an engineering group in Europe that would be capable of developing these new designs. Because of the need to satisfy the half-dozen different (and sometimes even conflicting) construction codes to be found on the European continent, the technical demands for designing a compatible model would exceed anything the DAAG engineers in Europe had formerly been called upon to do.

Early on, management decided to give the Class A development program a higher priority for several reasons. Class B national models were already beginning to produce some economies of scale. The incremental savings to be gained from further standardization of these elevators would therefore be much less than would be the case of Class A elevators. Moreover, the managers and salesmen for each subsidiary would probably object to any change from their

---

4. While the differences in national building codes at the time limited the standardization of design in several important respects, management estimated that a line of twenty to twenty-five standard European-oriented models would have been sufficient to deal with most of the conflicting requirements.

Exhibit 3 Creation and expansion of the DAAG European region, 1965–68.

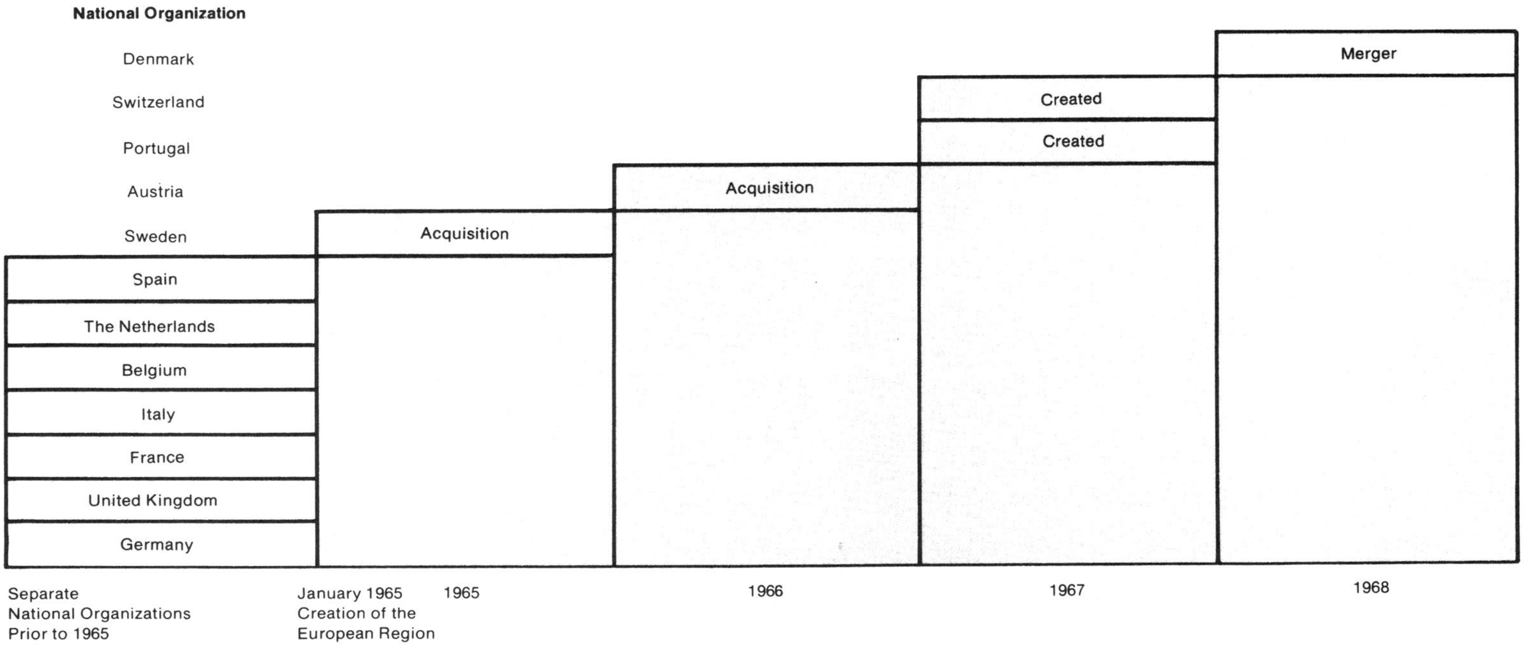

National Organization

National Organization				
Denmark				Merger
Switzerland			Created	
Portugal			Created	
Austria		Acquisition		
Sweden	Acquisition			
Spain				
The Netherlands				
Belgium				
Italy				
France				
United Kingdom				
Germany				

| Separate National Organizations Prior to 1965 | January 1965 Creation of the European Region 1965 | 1966 | 1967 | 1968 |

Source: Company document

national models so soon after bringing them to market. Finally, the tangle of local building regulations for apartment buildings was proving to be much more difficult to deal with than was true for major high-rise building projects.

The DAAG line of Euopean Class A elevator models, the Europa, was scheduled to be introduced in 1970. This product line was to include fifteen models. The different models would carry between eight and twenty-four passengers and have several configurations with respect to such features as speed, door widths, and maximum number of floor stops.

The introduction of a DAAG line of European Class B models, to be known as the Continental, was projected for 1973. The development of this line was to take place in three stages. In the first stage, the ninety or so national models, including those in the U.K., would be replaced with thirty European models. The second stage would witness a reduction of European models to twenty, while the ultimate objective was to have ten European models. This final objective was based on the fact that five to seven models accounted for about 80 percent of Class B sales in each major market. The actual timing for the second and third stages would depend in large measure on the rate at which building codes in the EEC could be harmonized.

Production Rationalization and DAAG Europe

The major payoff in a move to standard elevator models would come from the economies of scale associated with a rationalized production arrangement. As a DAAG executive noted: "We do not know exactly what the increased savings through greater mass production will be, but common sense tells us it will be a lot. The largest selling German model has sales of about 1,500 units per year. We estimate the largest European model will have sales of between 3,000 and 4,000 per year."

Pelz's objective was to have each factory specialize in the production of standardized components that could then be sold to DAAG assembly plants within each market. Prior to 1965, each plant manufactured or purchased locally all the components it needed to manufacture all the elevators sold in its market area. By 1969, DAAG had begun to implement the first phase of its plan to rationalize production, whereby the company's EEC factories (two in Germany, one in France, and one in Italy) were to specialize in producing and exchanging a number of basic components. These components were priced at full cost plus a 25 percent charge for intercompany transfers.

The second phase, to be completed around 1974, would also bring the factories in the U.K., Spain, and Austria into this arrangement. At that time, each factory would produce certain major elevator subunits (such as the motor, relays, and the control mechanism) to supply other plants. To ensure a safe supply, critical components would be made in two plants.

A Deteriorating Financial Position

As Pelz reviewed the situation in 1969, he was impressed with the progress that DAAG had shown in four short years in its attempt to move toward stan-

Exhibit 4 DAAG European region elevator unit sales and average price per unit.

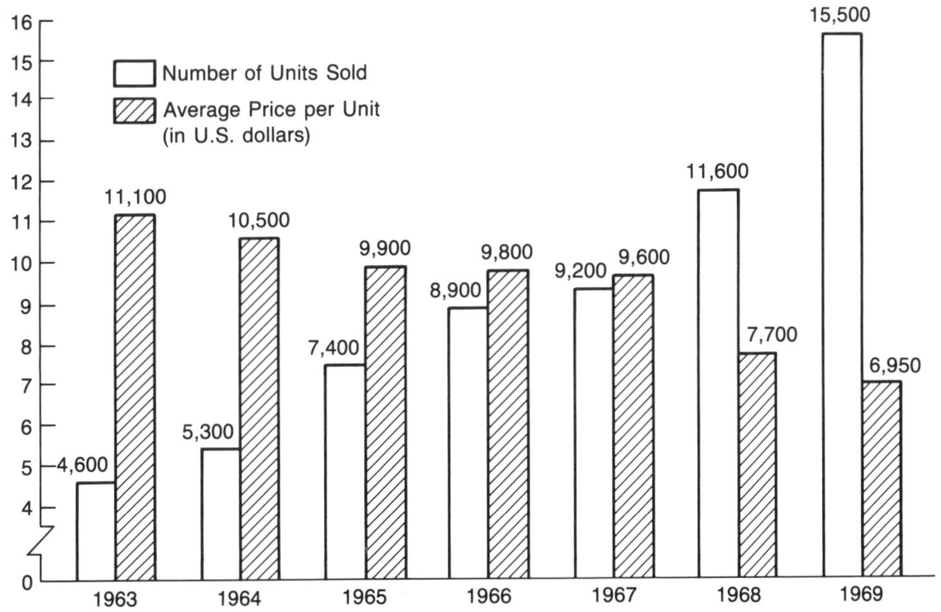

Source: Company document

dard models and rationalized production facilities. Moreover, the company's strategy had led to a better than threefold increase in unit sales and to a more than doubling of DAAG's share of the European elevator market since its inception in 1963. Exhibit 4 graphically shows the decline of the average unit price during the period 1965 to 1969 and the corresponding increase in unit sales. Since the price decline in Exhibit 4 resulted from a combination of actual price cuts and an increasing proportion of less costly Class B business, price changes for a single unit (the MOD-S) are shown in Exhibit 5. The price changes for the MOD-S were said to be representative of most DAAG elevator units during this period.

Profits, however, had suffered as a consequence of the failure to achieve cost savings sufficiently high to cover the decline in prices during this time. An even more pressing financial problem in Pelz's opinion was the rapidly deteriorating working capital position for DAAG Europe. Exhibits 6 and 7 contain the financial results for DAAG Europe during the period 1965 to 1969.

New equity and additional debt were generally ruled out by Pelz as viable financial moves at that time. DAAG Europe had just assumed additional long-term debt of $3 million in 1969. Moreover, this financing had been arranged contrary to the advice of corporate headquarters in Chicago, which had a long-standing policy of keeping the firm's capital structure as debt free as possible. Pace's policy to hold 100 percent ownership of its overseas subsidiaries wherever possible precluded selling equity on the market.

Exhibit 5   Index of average price and manufacturing cost of the MOD-S German model.

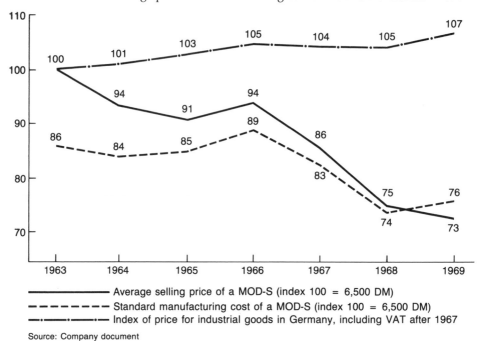

Average selling price of a MOD-S (index 100 = 6,500 DM)
Standard manufacturing cost of a MOD-S (index 100 = 6,500 DM)
Index of price for industrial goods in Germany, including VAT after 1967

Source: Company document

One possible response to the financial problem was for DAAG simply to raise the prices of elevators. DAAG management felt certain that the competitors were experiencing similar financial pressures, since they had also dropped their prices. The principal question in Pelz's mind was how quickly and how far the competition would follow DAAG in raising prices. A unilateral price increase by DAAG could give the competitors an opportunity to make inroads in important markets at a time when DAAG was attempting to effect economies of scale through volume production.

A tightening of credit terms had been considered by DAAG management as another possible avenue for relieving the current financial burden on the company. Payments were usually stretched out over two to three years with a major portion due after the completion of the job. Pelz had a proposal before him recommending that DAAG adhere to the industry's pro forma payment schedules, which for Germany involved collecting a down payment of 30 percent at the time the contract was signed, an additional 30 percent when the elevator was delivered, 30 percent at the completion of the job, and the final 10 percent when the building received official approval (see Exhibit 8). Actual payment schedules, however, had long been more liberal than the announced formula. Moreover, as Pelz knew, his competitors employed increasingly generous payment schedules to counter DAAG's aggressive pricing. On certain occasions, for example, Westinghouse reportedly required only a 10 percent

Exhibit 6 DAAG Europe balance sheets, 1966–69 ($ millions).

Years Ended December 31	1966	1967	1968	1969
Assets				
Cash and marketable securities	1.1	1.9	1.4	.8
Net notes & accounts receivable	36.0	36.9	39.4	56.5
Associated companies receivables	6.1	7.1	11.3	15.0
Total receivables	42.1	44.0	50.7	71.5
Inventories	31.5	25.0	27.2	40.1
Cost of contracts in progress	64.2	65.8	74.1	88.1
Total inventories	95.7	90.8	101.3	128.2
Prepayments	.7	.6	.5	.8
Less billings on contracts in progress	(71.5)	(73.0)	(75.5)	(86.2)
Total current assets	68.2	64.4	78.4	115.2
Property, plant, equipment	38.8	40.7	41.3	50.7
Depreciation	(14.7)	(17.0)	(18.4)	(21.1)
Net plant, equipment	24.1	23.7	22.8	29.6
Deferred charges	3.0	2.7	2.8	3.6
Total assets	95.3	90.9	104.2	148.5
Liabilities and Capital				
Short-term loans	23.2	17.0	23.0	41.2
Notes & accounts payable	12.5	10.3	12.3	21.9
Associated company payables	4.7	5.6	7.6	7.7
Accrued liabilities	4.5	6.5	9.3	14.6
Income tax	2.5	2.5	2.1	2.5
Total current liabilities	46.7	42.2	54.4	88.1
Long-term notes & accounts payable	9.5	8.8	6.9	12.9
Total liabilities	57.1	51.1	61.5	100.9
Reserves for pensions & severance indemnities	—	4.2	4.2	4.6
All other reserves	7.3	3.5	9.4	11.0
Capital stock	17.0	17.0	17.2	19.3
Surplus	13.8	14.9	11.7	12.4
Net worth	38.1	39.8	42.6	47.5
Net worth exclusive of reserves for pensions	38.1	35.5	38.4	42.9
Total liabilities & capital	95.3	90.9	104.2	148.5

Source: The figures represent a consolidation of individual company accounts taken from company records.

down payment and no further payment until completion of the project. In other instances, Westinghouse did not even require the customer to make a down payment.

Another possible step for DAAG was to reinstate a price-escalation clause

Exhibit 7 DAAG Europe profits and bookings, 1965–69, and a financial analysis of the statements ($ millions).

	1965	1966	1967	1968	1969
Profits and Bookings					
Net profit before tax[a]	3.6	3.3	3.7	3.9	4.0
New sales bookings	73	87	88	89	108
Service bookings	33	38	43	46	51
Total bookings	106	125	131	135	159
Analysis of the Financial Statements					
Current assets ÷ Current liabilities		1.46	1.53	1.44	1.31
Cash plus receivables ÷ Current liabilities		0.93	1.09	0.96	0.82
Collection period in days		121	121	135	162
Inventory/Sales (excluding cost of contracts in progress)		0.25	0.19	0.20	0.25
Debt/Net worth		0.25	0.22	0.16	0.27

Source: The figures represent a consolidation of individual company accounts taken from company records.

a. Net profit reflected the results of elevator contracts completed and service contracts performed during the year, as well as manufacturing variances for the year.

Exhibit 8 Pro forma payment schedules on class A contracts in Germany, France, and Switzerland, 1969.

Germany	
Signing of contract	30%
Delivery to job site[a]	30%
Completion[b]	30%
Final acceptance[c]	10%
Switzerland	
Signing of contract	30%
Three months prior to delivery	30%
During the course of erection	10%
Completion	30%
France	
Signing of contract	30%
Delivery to job site	30%
Completion	40%

Source: Company document

a. DAAG management estimated that the time between booking a contract and delivery of the elevator to the job site ran an average of one year. The actual order usually did not arrive until six months after the closing of the contract. This one-year figure did not include the three to six months that normally elapsed between the time a bid was submitted and a contract was closed.

b. Erection time (from delivery to completion) for Class A elevator projects ranged between two months and two years, with an average of one year.

c. Final acceptance occurred when both the owner and the building authorities approved the building. Final acceptance normally followed the completion of construction by one to four months.

in new elevator sales contracts to protect against inflation. Customer pressure during the competitive battle of the mid-1960s had led DAAG and the other elevator manufacturers to accept fixed price contracts. Increasing inflation rates during the late 1960s led to losses for major projects that had been negotiated anywhere between two to five years earlier. For DAAG to tighten credit terms or to press for escalation clauses, in Pelz's opinion, would have it run risks similar to those it would run in raising prices.

Daewoo Group

"If we work hard, there is no limit to what we can achieve. Hard work was a key to making our company as it is today. Hard work . . . and a sensitivity to the currents of business change. This sensitivity enabled us to position ourselves in line with the flow of opportunities in Korea and around the world." Kim Woo-Choong was explaining how in just sixteen years he had built one of the largest business empires in Korea.[1] In June 1984 Sweden's King Carl Gustaf XVI conferred on Kim, chairman of Daewoo Group, the International Business Award, a token of recognition awarded every three years by the International Chamber of Commerce to honor an "entrepreneur who has contributed to the idea of free enterprise by either creating or developing his own company."

Founded in 1967 by Kim with an initial investment of $18,000, Daewoo grew to become one of the four largest privately held group companies in Korea. In 1983 the group, with 77,240 employees, recorded $4.3 billion sales (of which exports accounted for $2.5 billion), $44.8 million profits, and $2.3 billion in total assets. (Exhibit 1 contains a record of financial performance.) Initially a textile and garment exporter, Daewoo's business activities had grown to include shipbuilding, construction, financial services, and the manufacture of machinery, automobiles, home appliances, and telecommunications devices.

That Daewoo had navigated a remarkable course of change and growth in its short life was evident. Less evident, perhaps, were the troubled waters that lay ahead. Growing worldwide trade protectionism had begun to impair the company's export opportunities. At the same time, rising wage rates in Korea were eroding a key competitive advantage that Daewoo and other Korean firms had held in the international arena. And the firm's very growth had brought with it problems of how to manage the increasingly complex organization. Among the important challenges were the need to find ways of preserving the employees' dedication to hard work and the managers' spirit of risk taking that had been so central to Daewoo's past success. Chairman Kim acknowledged these problems and challenges, while expressing confidence that Daewoo had strategies and resources to cope with them and to continue its remarkable record of growth.

1. In keeping with Korean custom, the surname is given first. After the first full use of names in this case, only surnames will be used.

Exhibit 1 Consolidated operating and financial statistics ($ millions).

	1983	1982	1981	1979	1978
Summary of operations and earnings					
Sales	$4,251	$3,346	$2,938	$1,871	$1,188
Operating income	142	174	223	136	101
Interest expense	76	77	115	76	47
Earnings before income taxes					
and minority interests	65	63	94	73	51
Income taxes	23	23	32	30	22
Net earnings	45	38	60	27	18
Summary of balance sheets					
Current assets	1,425	1,081	1,308	1,005	727
Investments and advances	242	189	147	178	101
Property, plant and equipment					
and other assets	622	588	433	692	426
Total assets	2,289	1,858	1,888	1,875	1,254
Current liabilities	1,327	1,078	1,290	1,105	726
Long-term debts and other accounts	697	586	461	658	424
Stockholders' equity	265	194	137	112	104
Key financial ratios					
Return on sales (%)	1.1	1.1	2.0	1.4	1.5
Return on equity (%)	17.0	19.6	43.8	24.1	17.3
Current ratio (%)	107.4	100.3	101.6	90.9	100.1
Debt/equity ratio (%)	762.6	857.7	1,278.1	1,574.1	1,105.7
Exchange rate (won/U.S. dollar)	795.5	748.8	700.0	485.0	485.0
Number consolidated companies	7	7	9	10	8

Note: The consolidated figures were for Daewoo Corporation and its subsidiaries in which it held 50% or more share ownership. In 1983, these subsidiaries comprised Koryo Leather, KOSCO, Daewoo Electronics Company, Korea Capital Corporation, Daewoo Development and Daewoo International (America) Corporation. Daewoo Motor, as a joint venture, was not included.

Daewoo Group did not publish its consolidated annual report in 1980.

Figures in U.S. dollars converted only for convenience.

Daewoo and Korean Industrial Policy

Daewoo's history reflected that of the Korean economy. As government policy in the late 1960s and early 1970s promoted the export of light goods, Daewoo became one of the nation's front-running exporters. When Korea began in the mid-1970s to shift its focus from light to heavy industries, Daewoo extended its domain from exporting textiles and other light goods to manufacturing heavy industrial goods. In the early 1980s, in line with the government's economic plan to emphasize electronics, Daewoo extended its business activities to home appliances, telecommunications, and other electronic equipment. In effect, Daewoo was at one and the same time a major beneficiary of and an important contributor to Korea's economic growth.

Light Industry Exports

With the successful completion of its first five-year economic plan (1962–66) emphasizing the development of import substitution industries such as oil refining, fertilizers, fibers and textiles, the Korean government was ready to move ahead with a new industrial policy of export-led economic growth. Korea's new commitment was set into motion in 1967 with the second five-year economic plan. The year 1967 also marked the birth of Daewoo.

At age 30, Kim, with the assistance of three business associates and a typist, founded Daewoo Industrial Company, Ltd., to export textiles. He came to this new venture with seven years' experience with a medium-sized garment manufacturing exporter and with half of the initial capital funds, which he had had to borrow from his partner. Although the title of president was conferred on one of his associates, who was several years his senior, Kim's leadership was obvious from the start. In Korean, the characters for *dae* and *woo* mean "great universe." But *woo* is also part of Kim's given name, Woo-Choong, pointing to the close identity of man and company.

Daewoo's first business was in exporting tricot fabrics to Singapore, where they were reexported to Indonesia and Africa. In 1968, as diplomatic relations between Indonesia and Singapore deteriorated, Kim promptly redirected Daewoo's exports directly to Indonesia. With this move, Daewoo soon gained a leading position as a textile exporter to Southeast Asia and Africa with export sales growing from $580,000 in 1967 to almost $4 million in 1969.

During this period, Daewoo made the decision to expand its manufacturing and marketing activities. In the 1960s, the Korean textile industry supplied cheap, unskilled labor based on CMT (cutting, making, and trimming). The Japanese trading houses supplied raw and submaterials and also sold the products to the overseas retail trade. As a result, Korean manufacturers had recourse only to a small part of the potential profits. Moreover, the scale of Korean operations was too small to supply large customers' requirements. Chairman Kim decided to go after the more profitable parts of the business through a number of what were then pioneering and bold moves for a Korean company. Central to his plan was the construction of a new textile factory with twenty lines of sewing capacity at a time when a factory with four to six lines was considered a large operation. To provide this factory with the needed raw materials, the company established a branch on Osaka, a center for supplies. Then in 1969, branch sales offices were opened in Singapore, New York, and London to market the output. Recognizing the importance of quality, Kim installed quality-control equipment identical to that used by Sears, Roebuck. Impressed with the new facilities and favorable prices, Sears became Daewoo's first major client to be followed by J.C. Penney, Montgomery Ward, and others.

Yoo Ki-Bum, an executive managing director who had begun his career at this time, described this important transformation of the young company: "I am still excited by what we were able to accomplish in those early years. We really worked very hard to make a success of our new business. Most employees worked from early in the morning until midnight to get the product out. It was during this period the Daewoo spirit of challenge, creativity, and sacrifice first blossomed."

The resulting clothing products were enthusiastically received by American consumers, and Daewoo's exports more than doubled in 1970 as a result. About this time, Kim became convinced that the U.S. government would sooner or later impose an import quota on textile products. He therefore set out to gain a favorable position for Daewoo by pushing its textile products into the United States with less regard to profitability. As a result of this action, Daewoo succeeded in increasing fivefold its exports into the United States, establishing itself as the leading supplier of textile products from Asia.

In 1972 the U.S. government imposed an import quota on textile products from Hong Kong, Taiwan, and Korea. Since the allocation of quota in Korea was in turn based on recent past exporting performance, Daewoo was awarded about 30 percent of the total. As a result, by the mid-1970s, Daewoo had become one of Korea's most profitable firms.

Public Ownership and Diversification

Based on its success in exporting textiles to the United States, Daewoo expanded its sales to Europe. Following this expansion, Daewoo management saw an opportunity to export other light-industry products to its markets, relying on its established reputation as a competitive supplier of quality products. At the time, a number of Korean manufacturing companies were in trouble due to a lack of expertise in overseas marketing. This situation enabled Daewoo to begin a round of acquisitions for expansion into other consumer products.

To support this expansion program, in 1973 Daewoo issued new common shares, amounting to 25 percent of the corporation's total issued shares, for sale on the Korean securities exchange. The issue sold at a premium of 330 percent over par value. One year later, the Korean government set in motion a new policy to encourage large Korean companies to go public in their ownership.

With funds secured from the sale of stock, with bank loans, and with cash flow from its flourishing textile exports to the United States, Daewoo acquired fourteen companies and took major positions in two other firms. By 1975 Daewoo had transformed itself from a solitary textile firm into a group of companies engaged in manufacturing and trading textiles, leather goods, and other light-industry products. Expansion was not limited to the manufacturing sector. During this phase of growth, Daewoo also began its diversification into banking and financing businesses.

In 1975 Daewoo Industrial Company was officially designated a general trading company. This designation, which had been initiated by the Korean government as a means of increasing and diversifying exports, gave the recipient special access to certain export financing and increased credibility in foreign markets.

Transition to Heavy Industry Manufacturing

By 1976, optimistic about the future world economy as well as the competitive potential of Korean companies, the Korean government began to promote the development of heavy industry sectors, such as machinery and shipbuilding. Generous bank financing was made available for investments in these sectors. In line with this objective, the government singled out a few of the most capable companies to develop heavy industry in Korea.

When Kim was asked in 1976 by the Korea Development Bank to take over the ailing Hankook Machinery, Ltd., one of Korea's largest producers of diesel engines, rolling stock, and industrial machinery, his executives opposed the move. The firm had not once shown a profit in thirty-eight years of operations under Japanese and then Korean ownership. Debts of the troubled firm exceeded Daewoo's total equity by twofold.

Chairman Kim nonetheless accepted the government bank's invitation. He changed the name of Hankook Machinery to Daewoo Heavy Industries, Ltd., made himself president, and took personal charge of turning around this new acquisition. He remarked on this experience: "I needed to get directly involved to make the right decisions. I often slept at the factory. One of the things I learned was that the workers were working overtime for the pay without adding much value. The machinery was turning, but it wasn't producing anything."

Instead of cutting back the workers' hours, Kim's response was to generate more business through aggressive marketing coupled with improved product quality. In this way, workers could be ensured of legitimate overtime work and job security. Production cost was lowered through the direct purchase of parts and components, and the company's original capital of $25 million was increased to $52 million. In the first year, Daewoo Heavy Industries achieved break-even operations. Small profits were made and dividends paid in the second year. This success enhanced Kim's reputation as a manager in the eyes of government officials and the public.

His reputation as a competent manager, coupled with his access to substantial funds through the financial institutions under his control, enabled Kim to acquire Korea Steel Chemical Company in 1977 and the Saehan Motor Company (a 50–50 joint venture with General Motors) and Okpo Shipbuilding Company in 1978. Daewoo's decision to take over the Okpo shipyard, a near-bankrupt enterprise, was prompted by the government's strong urging. The shipyard was to feature the largest dry dock in the world with a capacity to hold a one-million deadweight ton tanker. It was only 25 percent completed when Daewoo took it over, but the dry dock and yard were completed in 1981, and profits were recorded in 1983.

Chairman Kim

To understand Daewoo, one must first understand Kim Woo-Choong, its founder and chairman. Born in 1936, he experienced a youth of Japanese rule and war, followed by economic deprivation and then another war. His father, a professor, had been one of the few Koreans to receive a diploma from a Japanese national university, and his mother was one of the rare women of her day to obtain a university degree. "It was my mother, a devoted Christian, who encouraged all of us to stand on our own feet and to go our own independent ways," explained Dr. Kim Duk-Choong, one of Kim's brothers and a professor of economics.

The Korean War, 1950–53, forced Kim's mother to play the dominant role in the upbringing of the family. His father and an elder brother, a physician, were abducted by North Korean soldiers in July 1950 when Seoul was overrun. "I saw my father taken away with my own eyes. I was thirteen at the time," Kim said. He never saw or heard from his father and brother again.

Chairman Kim remembered the days when he had to support his mother, three brothers, and a sister on his earnings as a newspaper delivery boy. He recalled: "One evening I returned home exhausted and hungry. There was only a single bowl of rice available for the five of us. I fibbed that I had already eaten. My mother told the young ones to eat the rice, also claiming to have already eaten. Then each in turn urged the other to eat the rice. Of a sudden, we all looked at each other, hugged and burst into tears. That was the happiest moment in my life."

Following the Korean War, Kim attended Yonsei University with a scholarship covering tuition and a small stipend for books. Income from odd jobs covered most of his living expenses.

At age forty-six, Chairman Kim projected an air of authority and boundless drive. His belief in the virtue of hard work served to unify his actions and thoughts. "Other than hard work," he once said, "I have no hobby." For him, that meant a sixteen-hour workday, 365 days a year. Christmas and New Year's would find him in the Middle East where business was unaffected by these holidays.

This devotion to work was connected to Kim's pride in his heritage. In his mind, Korea and its pride had almost fifty years of catching up to compensate for the Japanese occupation from 1910 through 1945 and for another ten years of turmoil during the Korean War as a battlefront in the East-West global struggle. Kim was not alone in this view. From times of antiquity, the people of the Korean Peninsula have had to struggle to preserve their identity and cherished culture from recurrent invasions by the Chinese, Mongols, and Japanese. Chairman Kim conveyed this sense of mission in his thoughts about Daewoo:

> I am concerned about our standing as a country and as a society. Our culture used to be the source of Japanese learning. Under the Japanese rule during 1910 to 1945, however, Koreans were deprived of opportunities to obtain higher education. Nowadays, more than 300,000 college graduates enter the society every year. With 40 million people, 59 million if united, Korea can become as advanced as any country in the world. But to catch up with the rich countries, we must work as hard as the Americans and Japanese did when they built up their countries. One of my cherished dreams has been to show people around the world that Korea can produce the highest quality products at the lowest prices.

In 1983 Daewoo management launched a program for revitalizing the managerial spirit, stressing the need for creativity, challenge, and sacrifice as key elements for continued success. Chairman Kim's reflections on these desired managerial attributes helped to define the kind of company he wanted Daewoo to be:

> Creativity comes from hard work. To become wise, it's not how many books you read but how much you concentrate in your reading that is important. Business is the same. Traveling around the world, I can see money everywhere. It is in the street and in the houses. It is in America and in Africa. It is everywhere, but you have to work hard to see it and to get it. If you try hard enough, you will see more money than you could possibly collect in the time you have.
>
> Ten years ago we were a small company, but even then we felt a sense of challenge to become an important factor in our national scene. Since we had little money, the only way for us to grow was to rescue seriously troubled companies. And this we did by showing the workers what it meant to work hard.
>
> Many people point to the Japanese management systems as the reason for their success. But what can a system do without good people? You need people who are dedicated *and* experienced. The only advantage the Japanese firm has over a Korean firm is the experience of its people. You take shipbuilding, for example. The Japanese welder has 20 years' experience and our Korean welder about two years' experience. But that advantage will lessen over time.
>
> The American company is not what it used to be. In the old days, Americans worked hard to challenge new frontiers. But as their economy got mature, they became more interested in nice houses, jogging, and having a good time than in doing business. How can you compete without dedication? It is not the management system that is not working in American companies, it is the people not working hard.
>
> Korea is no exception to this cycle of hard work. As the standard of living improves in Korea, we shall eventually lose the spirit of working hard. Until we get to that stage, we have to keep growing our economy.

In October 1980, Kim announced his decision to donate all of his personal holdings in Daewoo Corporation, worth over $40 million, to a foundation dedicated to the Korean people. He explained that in a capitalistic society such as Korea, businessmen had a responsibility to become national leaders, and that only those who were willing to sacrifice their personal interests could truly take on such leadership roles. "When a businessman starts to count his own wealth, his life as a businessman comes to an end. After all, profits are for reinvestment, not for enjoyment." At the same time he declared his intention to dedicate himself to professional management. This move alone set him apart from other Korean business leaders.

Senior Management

Unlike other group companies, where members of the owner's family would typically fill key managerial positions, none of Daewoo's senior managers were related to Kim. As to the managers' abilities, he once said, "I always thought that I could achieve whatever I had set out to do on the strength of my own efforts. But Daewoo grew more rapidly than I expected, and this was possible only as a result of the efforts of the capable and dedicated managers within the group."

The senior management team shared two characteristics: their young age and their educational background. These commonalities served to create a tightly knit management group with strongly shared values. With the exception of Cho Dong-Jae, president of Daewoo's Pusan factory, and one of the founding members of Daewoo, all of the senior managers including Kim were born in the late 1930s. This age distribution reflected a result of historical events. Hong Soung-Bu, president and director of the group planning department explained:

> Men in their early forties are in some ways a special group in Korea. They are the people who had experienced the harsh years of the Korean War during their adolescence, and more important, are the first generation in many years to have received a regular education at the university level. As a result, they take nothing for granted and know how to get things right. Since many of their seniors were killed or injured in the war and few had the benefit of a proper education, the generation of the late thirties has had to step into important positions at a relatively young age.

The binding ties of school camaraderie were also readily apparent. Kim and six of the other ten senior executives in Daewoo had attended the prestigious Kyunggi High School. Since admission was based on the results of a rigorous entrance examination, preparation began early in life, even to the extent of taking special training before kindergarten so as to gain admission into the best school at each rung of the educational ladder. The students of Kyunggi High School could boast an average IQ somewhere between 130 and 140. The graduates were not only gifted individuals, but generally possessed self-confidence and an ability to persevere as a result of the gruelling preparatory training they had experienced. Similarly, eight of the eleven top Daewoo executives were graduates of the prestigious Seoul National University.

Although Daewoo considered itself to have gone much further than any other large Korean firm in developing professional management, Kim continued to dominate decision making on important issues. In recognition of his experience and personal dedication to Daewoo, managers would invariably turn to him for direction on all significant matters. When asked if his practice of centralized decision making might become unwieldy as Daewoo grew in size and complexity, Lee Kyung-Hoon, president of Daewoo Corporation's trading division, answered: "Strong leadership—even dictatorship, although one doesn't use this word in a corporate setting—is sometimes essential in the growth phase of any corporation."

Not everyone agreed. Another manager saw problems with the chairman's involvement in operations: "Although Chairman Kim has delegated considerable authority to the presidents of several group companies, he still gets involved with the operating decisions in many Daewoo units, causing some confusion among subordinates, and inhibiting the development of those presidents as field commanders."

In Kim's mind, the issue of leadership was tied in with that of succession:

> I know my strength as an entrepreneur; I also know my weakness as an organization builder. I can be an asset for Daewoo so long as it grows rapidly and a liability when it needs to be stabilized. When that time comes, I shall resign as chairman and hand over the job to a manager capable of structuring managerial systems in the group. Once my successor accomplishes stabilization, it will be time for him to turn over the chairmanship to someone else with entrepreneurial skills. This time, the entrepreneurial leadership would operate through a coordinated system.

Although not publicly announced, Kim had selected his successor and his successor's successor and was grooming them for the job. He had not set a specific date for stepping down.

Group Structure and Business Strategies

As of March, 1984, Daewoo Group comprised twenty-five companies in twelve industrial sectors as shown in Exhibit 2. Daewoo Corporation, which included the trading, textile, and construction activities as three divisions, performed the role of holding company for the group. Its shares were publicly traded, as were shares of Daewoo Heavy Industries and a few Daewoo financial companies. The complex ownership network is described in Exhibit 3.

The president for each of Daewoo's business units was responsible for its strategy and for its results. The appendix describes the major business units and their strategies. Although each business plan was tailored to the opportunities and challenges facing the particular business unit, there were several underlying strategies that characterized the overall direction of the group.

Higher Technology

A move to higher technology was perhaps the most pervasive change taking place in Daewoo. According to Lee Hun-Jae, an executive director in charge of strategic planning: "We started with the textile business, and gradually moved into more complex technology in shipbuilding, machinery and automobiles. In my opinion, the future of Daewoo, and of Korea, lies in high technology."

This move to higher technology was being implemented in two ways. First, there was a change in the mix of businesses. The transformation, which had begun with the diversification from textiles and light industries to shipbuilding and heavy industries, was now aimed at entering and building a capability in high-technology electronics. This latest phase was positioning Daewoo to compete in telecommunications, computers, robotics and the underlying electronics componentry, such as integrated circuits, digital switching, and optical fiber transmission. To gain these capabilities, Daewoo had entered into technology licensing agreements with firms such as Northern Telecommunications and Siemens.

Exhibit 2 Affiliated companies within Daewoo group, 1984.

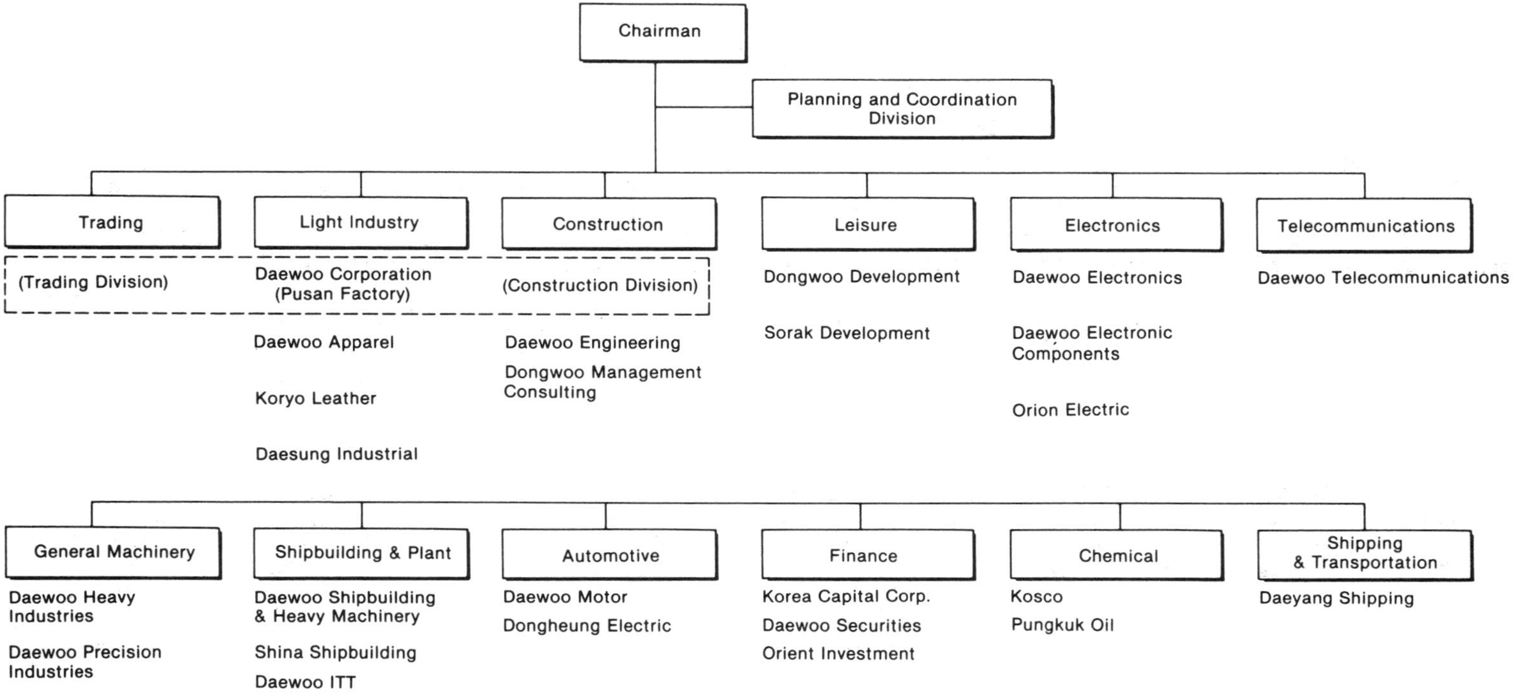

Chairman

Planning and Coordination Division

Trading

(Trading Division)

Daewoo Corporation (Pusan Factory)

Light Industry

Daewoo Apparel

Koryo Leather

Daesung Industrial

Construction

(Construction Division)

Daewoo Engineering

Dongwoo Management Consulting

Leisure

Dongwoo Development

Sorak Development

Electronics

Daewoo Electronics

Daewoo Electronic Components

Orion Electric

Telecommunications

Daewoo Telecommunications

General Machinery

Daewoo Heavy Industries

Daewoo Precision Industries

Shipbuilding & Plant

Daewoo Shipbuilding & Heavy Machinery

Shina Shipbuilding

Daewoo ITT

Automotive

Daewoo Motor

Dongheung Electric

Finance

Korea Capital Corp.

Daewoo Securities

Orient Investment

Chemical

Kosco

Pungkuk Oil

Shipping & Transportation

Daeyang Shipping

Note: Associated companies and overseas subsidiaries were not included.

Exhibit 3 Daewoo group companies' ownership structure (in %).

Shareholder	Daewoo Corporation	Daewoo Apparel	Orion Electric	Daewoo Heavy Industries	Daewoo Securities	Orient Investment
Affiliated Companies						
Daewoo Corporation			9.99	31.86	9.15	10.14
Daewoo Apparel	0.58					
Daesung Industrial	0.38					
Daewoo Engineering				0.14		
Dongwoo Management Consulting	0.06					
Dongwoo Development	0.14					
Daewoo Electronics			6.68			
Daewoo Heavy Industries			17.05		3.48	2.80
Korea Capital Corp.	12.89					23.47
Orient Investment	0.60				1.47	
KOSCO					0.80	0.77
Pungkuk Oil				2.75		
Total Affiliated Companies	14.65		33.72	34.75	14.90	37.18
Associated Companies						
Shinsung Tongsang	0.71					
Foundations						
Daewoo Educational Foundation	3.26				4.17	
Daewoo Foundation	19.15	9.99		4.66	2.59	6.51
Seoul Press Foundation	0.37			0.35		
Total Foundations	22.78	9.99		5.01	6.76	6.51
Total Daewoo-related Companies	38.14	9.99	33.72	39.76	21.66	43.69
Non-Daewoo Owners	61.86	90.01	66.28	60.24	78.34	56.31
Total	100.0%	100.0%	100.0%	100.0%	100.0%	100.0%

Note: The exhibit shows ownership structures of publicly held companies only. Among the nonpublic companies, Daewoo Motor is 50% owned by Daewoo Corporation (50% by GMC). Daewoo Shipbuilding is 47.36% by Daewoo Corporation and 16.8% by other Daewoo related companies (35.84% by Korea Development Bank). Daewoo Electronics is 23.67% by Daewoo Corporation and 26.33% by other Daewoo related companies.

Second, technology in existing business operations was to be upgraded. The automation of textile manufacturing and computer-aided design and manufacturing (CAD/CAM) in the manufacture of heavy equipment were two examples of this change. An electronics planning committee had been set up to coordinate the efforts taking place within the various business units.

OEM Supply

A second common characteristic of the various business strategies was the emphasis placed on the OEM (original equipment manufacturers) supply business. Although Daewoo actively developed its own branded products, a large and growing proportion of its output was directed to supplying other firms with manufactured products bearing their names. Textile goods had always been manufactured to supply distributors such as Sears, Roebuck and branded lines such as Oleg Cassini, Christian Dior, London Fog, and Calvin Klein. In heavy machinery, much of the future growth would come from supplying firms such as Caterpillar with specific products for worldwide sales. For example, in April 1983 Daewoo signed a ten-year contract to manufacture fork-lift trucks in the 4,000–6,000-pound capability class for worldwide sales. Dale Turnbull, president of Towmotor, a wholly owned subsidiary of Caterpillar, said, "These all-new lift trucks will maintain Caterpillar quality standards in products offering high value at very competitive prices." Negotiations were under way in 1984 to extend this arrangement to include earth-moving equipment.

In automobiles, while Daewoo continued to compete in the Korean market with its own branded vehicles, management saw the company's major growth opportunity to be in supplying General Motors with parts and with a small, inexpensive automobile for worldwide distribution. Finally, Daewoo Electronics favored expanding its U.S. business by supplying leading U.S. distributors with television sets, microwave ovens, and other appliances rather than promoting its own branded items.

Yoon Young-Suk, president of Daewoo Heavy Industries, explained management's reasoning for this approach:

> Korea may not have new product development capability, but it does have a good manufacturing capability. I don't think this has really been understood in the international market. U.S. companies are now fighting against Japanese manufacturers worldwide. Korean companies can be used as an important building block in their global strategy.
>
> We can produce the same product at a price 25 percent lower than Americans and 10 percent lower than Japanese. They say it is because our labor is cheap. There is a certain truth in that. But it is not the whole story. We are achieving cost reduction not only in labor-intensive industries, but also in technology- and capital-intensive industries as well. One of the most important reasons is our relations with vendors. First of all, we can purchase parts locally at a very low price, because we pay them in cash instead of three-month promissory notes. Second, we lower their price by providing various services to them, such as providing them with quality control systems and free service in checking their measuring instruments. Then, we regularly invite our vendors to our factory and show them why precision is so important. As a result, defect rates of the parts supplied from outside went down from 25 percent to 3 percent this year, which allowed vendors to lower prices on parts by 17 percent. Right there, we were able to save $25 million. Another factor in our low price is overhead. We do not spend as much as our competitors in general and administrative expenses, and we do not add as high margins.

Daewoo management, however, saw limitations in the long run to its role as a contract supplier of parts and products. This strategy would be viable only so long as Daewoo could maintain a competitive advantage in manufacturing. Moreover, it placed Daewoo in a disadvantageous position in negotiating margins with the contracting company that held the trademark and the market franchise. As a result, management was exploring ways to control its own marketing networks and brands.

An Emphasis on People

Lee Woo-Bock, founding member and vice chairman of Daewoo Group, noted the manner in which Daewoo developed its human resources:

> Daewoo's commitment to its people is an important plus for morale. We believe every person has potential. If a person is doing poorly, we start with the assumption that the company is not employing that person in accordance with his or her talents. In line with this belief, we have never fired anyone from an acquired company. We work hard to motivate these people.
>
> We are also actively building the depth and quality of our managerial and technical capabilities. We began in 1976 to recruit many well-educated people from Europe and the United States. And about 5 years ago we began a program of sending 20 to 30 engineers and managers for study abroad.

When Yoo Ho-Min, a managing director of Daewoo Corporation, was asked what he considered to be the most important factor in Daewoo's success, he responded:

> The spirit of being in a family has made this company what it is. Every Daewoo Corporation employee receives a present on his or her birthday. If employees are sick at home or at the hospital, their boss and fellow workers will visit them just like relatives. You will see Chairman Kim staying overnight at the home of a Daewoo executive on the eve of a parent's funeral [a Korean custom for one's relatives and close friends]. When one of our general managers was killed in the tragic downing of a Korean airliner by the Soviet military near Murmansk in 1978, he was promoted posthumously to the rank of director, his wife was awarded 70 percent of his salary for the rest of her life, and his children received scholarships for college. We think of ourselves more as the Daewoo family than as the Daewoo Group.

Extensive Financial Sources

In view of their ambitious growth goals, Chairman Kim and Vice Chairman Lee had devoted considerable attention over the years to the task of expanding the firm's outside financing. As a result of their efforts, Daewoo was generally recognized as being the most sophisticated Korean firm in financial expertise and sourcing.

Suh Hyung-Suk, executive vice president of Daewoo Corporation, remarked on the company's financial structure:

> Daewoo Corporation has actively increased its equity base through the open market. Its debt-equity ratio of 7.6 would seem very high compared to an average American company, but such a comparison can be deceptive. For one thing, a general trading company requires substantial short-term

export financing. Also, the lack of consumer financing in Korea and Korean ExIm Bank's requirement for suppliers to carry consumer credit makes our obligation higher. In any event, we have a far more favorable financial structure compared to the typical Japanese trading company with its debt-equity ratio of between 20 and 30.

As of 1983, Daewoo's portfolio of financial companies included three companies, as shown in Exhibit 2, but the group indirectly exerted influence on a number of other financial companies through stock ownership and personal relationships with their management. This latter group included the First Bank of Korea, Korea Merchant Banking Corporation, and more recently, KorAm Bank.

KorAm Bank was opened in March 1983 as Korea's first joint-venture commercial bank. The Bank of America held 49.9 percent of the ownership; the remaining 50.1 percent was owned by eleven Korean companies, with Daewoo holding the largest share with 9 percent. This position reflected Daewoo's role in conceiving the idea and initiating discussions with the American partner.

Daewoo's involvement in off-shore financing was also expanding in the early 1980s. In the early 1970s, the group pioneered in establishing foreign subsidiaries to help gain access to local bank credit. Until 1981, the external financing of Daewoo Corporation and its foreign subsidiaries consisted exclusively of bank loans. Since 1982, Daewoo, assisted by Chemical Bank and Goldman Sachs, issued commercial paper on two occasions in the U.S. money market for a total of $100 million. The company also planned to tap the Eurobond market and then eventually to issue debentures and stocks in the U.S. capital market.

Having foreseen the necessity of diversifying its capital sources, Daewoo hired Peat, Marwick, Mitchell & Co. in 1976 to start producing consolidated financial statements by U.S. accounting rules. To a question of why Daewoo was not listed in *Fortune's* 500 largest companies outside the U.S. in which nine other Korean companies had appeared, Suh Hyung-Suk replied, "We didn't want to [be], because the figures of all the other Korean companies are combined, and ours are consolidated. It's like comparing the size of balloons and pebbles." Were Daewoo to report its financial results on a combined basis instead of consolidated basis, its 1982 sales of $6.1 billion would have placed it sixty-fifth on the *Fortune* list, behind Hyundai (forty-first) with $8 billion and the Sunkyong group (sixty-second) with $6.3 billion.

In contrast to most Korean companies, which sought little publicity, Daewoo was very active in promoting its image through advertising and press releases. A representative of Hill and Knowlton, a well-known U.S. public relations firm, served full time as an on-site consultant to help the company become better known to the financial community, especially in the United States. Excerpts from a six-page advertisement published widely in the U.S. business press in mid-1983 are shown in Exhibit 4.

Daewoo's financial constraints were undoubtedly connected with two other corporate strategies: growth by acquisitions and joint ventures; and limited risk exposure.

Exhibit 4 Company advertisement. *Source:* Daewoo International (America) Corporation.

What makes your employees exceptional is what makes our employees exceptional.

They begin with the best education.

Take Chung-Hyun Nam, Vice President of Daewoo Engineering. He has a Ph.D. in Civil Engineering from the University of Wisconsin.

And Young-Kook Kang, Managing Director of Daewoo Heavy Industries. He has a Ph.D. in Electrical Engineering from Columbia University.

And Keh-Sik Min, Managing Director of Daewoo Shipbuilding, earned a Ph.D. in Naval Architecture and Marine Engineering at MIT.

The list continues. It's one reason Daewoo continues to grow. There are 70,000 good people at Daewoo. Get to know a few, and you could discover what a lot of American companies have already.

DAEWOO

BECAUSE GOOD PEOPLE MAKE GOOD PARTNERS.

C.P.O. Box 2810, 8269 Seoul, Korea
Tlx.: DAEWOO K23341—4

안녕하십니까.

대우는 16년이라는 짧은 역사에도 불구하고 연 매출액 33억 5천만불을 자랑하는 국제적인 대기업으로 성장했습니다. 이처럼 놀라운 성장의 원동력은 인재양성을 위한 대우의 꾸준한 노력에서 비롯하고 있읍니다. 대우는 초창기부터 인재를 아끼고 키우는데 정성을 다해 왔으며 그 결과 오늘과 같은 단단한 저력을 갖추기에 이른 것입니다.

대우의 인재들은 오대양 육대주에서 일하고 있읍니다. 그들은 언어의 벽을 모릅니다. 영어, 불어, 독어, 중국어 등 다양한 언어를 사용하는 세계곳곳의 고객들에게 대우는 한결같이 깊은 신뢰를 얻고 있읍니다. 다음 페이지를 계속 읽어 보십시요. 그러면 대우가 얼마나 커다란 능력을 지니고 있으며 얼마나 깊은 신뢰감을 주는 기업인지를 알게 될 것입니다. 대우는 성실하고 유능한 인재들이 이끌어가는 기업입니다. 대우를 귀하의 파트너로 불러 주십시오.

감사합니다.

Language has never been a barrier to Daewoo.

In just 16 years, we've become a leading multinational company with $3.35 billion in sales. Because from the beginning, we've dedicated ourselves to developing the talent, ideas and energy of our people. So now, when a company needs the help of experts, we're able to offer them what they're looking for.

I'm proud to be Chairman of a company with that kind of reputation. If the contributions we've been making to industry haven't already come to your attention, read the following pages. They'll tell you more about our recent ventures.

You'll see how Daewoo people have earned the confidence of a wide range of companies around the world. Because whether you speak Korean, English or any other language, one fact is understood. Good people make good partners.

김 우 중

대표이사 회장

Woo-Choong Kim
Chairman

Growth by Acquisition and Collaborative Arrangements

Every major new business entry for Daewoo had involved the takeover of an existing troubled company. Daewoo acquired Hankook Machinery Company to form Daewoo Heavy Industries, Okpo Shipbuilding Company to form Daewoo Shipbuilding, Saehan Motor Company to form Daewoo Motors, and Taihan Electric Wire Company's Home Electronics Division to form Daewoo Electronics. This approach enabled the young firm to take a major position in each of these new business sectors with little or no call on its limited financial reserves, since the purchase price was low and in several cases the arrangements included the transfer of bank loans.

As a result of these experiences, Daewoo management had gained considerable confidence in its ability to turn around troubled companies. Chairman Kim also saw a social benefit from this approach: "Which is a better arrangement for the nation, to rescue failing companies and to put their facilities and people to work, or to let them collapse while starting brand-new ventures?"

Daewoo was also eager to participate in collaborative arrangements with foreign firms for the same financial reasons as well as for acquiring needed technology or distribution. These collaborative arrangements ranged from joint ventures (General Motors, Bank of America and ITT) to long-term production contracts (Caterpillar).

Limited Risk Exposure

Contrary to his reputation as a business leader willing to take big risks for the sake of growth, Kim believed he was cautious in his commitments:

> I always prepare a second and third alternative in case the preferred course of action fails to materialize. A number of companies have tried to emulate our growth pattern by taking big risks. They failed because they did not recognize our policy of never positioning ourselves in a live-or-die, bet-your-company situation.

Share of Market

Although not a deliberate strategic choice, Daewoo found itself in second or third position among Korean firms in many of its business fields, including overall exports. This result reflected Kim's decision to enter new fields with Daewoo's limited resources rather than to specialize in just one or two businesses. It also reflected, according to some managers, that most of the companies had had low market shares when acquired and were still in the process of moving to high market shares. Others argued that being No. 1 among Korean companies was irrelevant, at least for the important world markets, because Daewoo was really competing against larger Japanese and other foreign firms as well as its compatriots. Still, the market share ranking did raise the question in management's mind as to whether Daewoo should continue to

Exhibit 5 Major investment plans, 1984.

Company	Investment	1984 Capital Requirements ($ millions)
Daewoo Corporation	• resources project	6
	• plant project	9
	• computerized cutting and raw material handling system	10
		(Total Project)
Daewoo Heavy Industries	• Caterpillar project	12 (45–50)
	• defense industry project	20 (40)
	• technical center and aircraft project	26
Daewoo Shipbuilding and Heavy Machinery	• construction of a yard for steel structure manufacturing	39
	• expanding and improving manufacturing capability	30
Daewoo Motor	• manufacture of world car	86 (125)
	• parts manufacture	14
Daewood Electronics	• expanding and improving manufacturing capability	43
	• operating funds to produce microwave ovens and other new items	44
Others		227
Affiliated companies total[a]		566

a. Total capital requirement during 1984–1986 was approximately $1.2–1.3 billion dollars (based on fixed projects as of January 1984).

press ahead on all fronts or should focus its efforts so as to gain national or even world leadership in selected areas.

Resource Limitations

Whatever preferences Daewoo management might have as to which businesses to emphasize, it would have to take into account the resources available to it, both in financial and human terms. As shown in Exhibit 5 and in the appendix, the funds required to carry out the plans put forward by the group companies would amount to $1.2–$1.3 billion. Although creative and aggressive financing could be counted on to cover some of the shortfall between this figure and the funds available, Daewoo management would have to make some choices among the proposed investments.

The limits on human resources had to do with the need to bring on board the professional talent needed to compete in high-technology businesses. Chairman Kim had stated publicly that Daewoo would have over 1,000 scientific and engineering PhDs by 1990. Finding these people and learning how to manage them was recognized as a major challenge for Daewoo management.

Opportunity Knocks?

On February 15, 1984, Daewoo received an official invitation from the Korean Ministry of Commerce and Industries to participate in a competitive bid procedure for the sale of a government-owned, large-scale integrated circuit (LSI) plant. This opportunity brought into sharp focus the difficult strategic choices management faced as to the direction, emphasis, and timing of the company's commitments.

The Korean government had set up the plant in 1980 to develop national expertise in LSI technology. The subsequent entry by the Samsung and the Lucky-Goldstar groups into LSI operations removed the need for the government's continuing involvement. Although dedicated to research and development activities, the plant was capable of producing annually 150,000 four-inch diameter wafer starts, which could yield over 20 million integrated circuit chips. These chips were used for television sets, telecommunication equipment, and other industrial applications.

Daewoo management had reason to believe that it could win the award with a bid of $40 million. An additional $40 to $45 million would have to be invested in equipment to make the plant economic for mass production. This sum compared favorably with the $100+ million requirement Daewoo had been confronting in considering the possibility of leapfrogging the current LSI technology by moving directly to the newly emerging VLSI (very-large-scale integrated circuits) technology. Either move would require an additional annual investment in R&D of $10 to $15 million.

For Daewoo, the plant acquisition offered both advantages and disadvantages. The most important advantage was in getting some 200 workers and engineers with three to five years' experience. This acquisition of trained people coupled with existing operating equipment would help to speed up Daewoo's entry into high-technology electronics by two years.

Less favorable was the age of the equipment. In this rapidly changing field, three-year-old equipment was dated. The greatest disadvantage, however, was one of timing. Daewoo and General Motors were just bringing to a close lengthy negotiations that would require each partner to invest $125 million in new Korean facilities to build small cars for sale in the United States. This arrangement would place heavy demands on Daewoo's financial and managerial resources.

Daewoo management had two days to respond to the government concerning its intentions to bid or not.

Appendix: Major Affiliated Companies of the Daewoo Group

Among the twenty-five affiliated companies, five stood out in their importance to the Daewoo Group: Daewoo Corporation; Daewoo Heavy Industries, Ltd.; Daewoo Shipbuilding and Heavy Machinery, Ltd.; Daewoo Motor Company; and Daewoo Electronics Company. Each of the "Big Five," as they were commonly called, is described briefly below.

Daewoo Corporation

Daewoo Corporation was the senior unit in the group, given its history and role as the holding company for the other affiliated companies. It was formed in 1981 as a result of a merger of the Daewoo Industrial Company (trading and textiles) and Daewoo Development Company (construction). Its total sales of $4 billion and net income of $44 million in 1983 both ranked first among the 274 firms listed on the Korean securities exchange. Daewoo Corporation comprised three major divisions: trading, Pusan factory, and construction.

Trading division. Daewoo Industrial Company, which in 1981 became the trading division of the newly formed Daewoo Corporation, had been one of the ten Korean firms officially designated as a general trading company in 1975. Daewoo's trading business was concentrated on exports of textiles and garments (31 percent), ships and off-shore structures (28 percent), steel and metals (15 percent), machinery (6 percent), home appliances (5 percent), footwear (3 percent) and other products (12 percent).

The trading division's overseas network included fourteen subsidiaries and sixty-four offices engaged in selling, financing, and information gathering. In January, 1983, Daewoo was the first Korean company to open an office in Washington, D.C.

Although Daewoo's trading emphasis was expected to remain on exports, the company was seeking to expand with importing and overseas resource development. In 1983 the trading division imported $272 million of raw materials and merchandise, and was engaged in eight resource development projects. In May, 1983, Daewoo announced an agreement with a German firm for a joint uranium exploration and development project in Canada expected to produce annually 2,000 metric tons of yellow cake.

This move to imports and to overseas development reflected the increasingly gloomy outlook that Daewoo management saw for international trade because of growing protectionism. Lee Kyung-Hoon, president of Daewoo Corporation's Trading Division, expressed his concern: "In every single country of the world, scholars preach free trade, businessmen argue for free trade, and policy makers advocate free trade. But talking and doing are two different things. Despite the rhetoric, what we see is increasing protectionism in various forms. As it is, Korea's export volume amounts to only 1.3 percent of the world's total, and I am confident that it will continue to grow through counter-trade and other innovative means."

Pusan factory. Daewoo's Pusan factory was the world's largest textile plant. In 1982 it employed 8,600 workers and produced 72 million pieces of men's, women's, and children's clothing worth $203 million, representing 10.1 percent of Daewoo's total exports. Over the years, its customer emphasis had shifted from chain stores to brand manufacturers. In management's view, brand-name products not only increased the factory's value added, they also were less vulnerable to demand fluctuations.

Lee Yon-Ki, vice president in charge of the Pusan factory, was proud of the excellent labor relations the plant had enjoyed, pointing to the recent workers' vote against unionizing. However, he was concerned about Daewoo's weakening competitiveness against smaller firms with lower wages.

In light of the reduced growth opportunities in textiles, Daewoo management was seriously considering the possibility of setting up the Pusan factory as a separate concern with its own name.

Construction division. Daewoo's diversification into construction was as much by chance as by plan. In 1973, Daewoo purchased a half-constructed building in front of Seoul Railway Station to locate its headquarters. To complete the building, Daewoo acquired a small construction firm in order to obtain the necessary construction license. By 1983, the firm had advanced in its ranking among the Korean construction firms from 600th to second, next only to Hyundai.

In 1976 the company began overseas construction. At that time, the center of activity for the Korean construction industry was in the Middle Eastern countries of Saudi Arabia, Kuwait, Iran, and Iraq, where as many as ninety-seven Korean companies were competing. Instead of moving into this already congested arena, Daewoo focused on smaller but less competitive markets. Its first overseas business was initiated in Sudan when Daewoo was invited to build the National Guest House for $20 million. Daewoo was subsequently awarded an $88 million turnkey project to build a tire manufacturing plant. Daewoo soon expanded its operations into Sudan's neighboring countries—Libya, Morocco, and Tunisia.

In early 1983 the prospect of overseas construction business showed signs of waning. As OPEC's official oil price went down by $5 per barrel in March, so did construction activities in these countries. Chairman Kim, however, was undaunted by this trend:

> We can use such a slowdown in construction activities as an opportunity to increase market share. In a soft market, cost becomes a very important factor. With our dedicated people and efficient management system, we can outbid companies from advanced countries. It also gives us an opportunity to trim our overhead further, thereby increasing our international competitiveness. Our construction works used to aim at simple civil works. Now we are making every effort to raise value added by moving into sophisticated construction. We have formed a number of consortia with construction companies in advanced countries to get involved in such projects.

In 1983 Daewoo increased its construction orders by 50 percent over the previous year, with $2.3 billion worth of works to complete.

Along with other construction companies from Korea, Daewoo was actively looking for market diversification. In contrast to its competitors, which had moved to friendly countries such as Malaysia, Indonesia and Thailand, Daewoo was attempting to enter the markets traditionally less hospitable to Korea. Chairman Kim's target markets were Nigeria and Iran, both of which had big populations, large territories, and substantial oil money, but which were difficult to deal with because of the political situations. Kim explained the reason for his strategy:

> While the challenge is greater, so are the rewards. When you finally gain business in such difficult environments, you gain a protected market. We are willing to invest money on a long-term basis in order to enter such a market, and to lose money in one business if we can make it up in another. We have a concept of a total market approach in which all of our businesses get involved in a coordinated way.

Daewoo Heavy Industries, Ltd.

Daewoo Heavy Industries, Ltd., was created when Daewoo acquired deficit-ridden Hankook Machinery, Ltd., in 1976 and merged it with its previously acquired Dongkook Precision Machinery Company. The company produced diesel engines, rolling stocks, industrial machinery, earth-moving equipment, machine tools, and defense products.

In April 1983, the company signed a ten-year contract with Caterpillar Tractor Company to manufacture fork-lift trucks with a 4,000–6,000 pound capability for worldwide sale. The company was planning to invest $45–50 million for this project. Daewoo was also committed to a $25 million investment for defense products and another $25 million for strengthening the technology center, which was responsible for developing products such as robotics, laser-cutting machines, and automation systems. To provide the funds required, Daewoo Heavy Industries increased equity by $20 million in 1983, and it was planning an additional $25 million increase in equity and a bond issue of $20 million with a four-year maturity.

The company's main lines of business comprised machine tools, rolling stock, heavy machinery, and diesel engines for automotive uses. President Yoon Young-Suk was confident about his company's international competitiveness in the machine tool business with existing technologies. In three to five years, however, advanced countries were expected to bring out new technologies, such as intelligent machinery, which could make the existing technologies economically obsolete. Rolling stocks were big in volume and profitability, but future demand was difficult to project because of its dependence on government purchases. Heavy machinery promised the best potential in terms of growth and stability of demand, but the market was fragmented.

Daewoo Shipbuilding and Heavy Machinery, Ltd.

In its first year of operation, Daewoo received orders for and built a number of ships, including a 128,000 dwt shuttle tanker ($52 million) and four 22,500 dwt chemical tankers ($31 million each), simultaneously with construction of a one-million dwt dock. Since then, Daewoo completed construction of seven semi-submersible offshore rigs (worth $539 million), a 140,000 dwt bulk carrier ($38 million), a barge-mounted seawater treatment plant to be used in the Prudhoe Bay oilfields off Alaska for secondary recoveries by ARCO Alaska Inc. ($226 million), and a low-density polyethylene plant for Al-Jubail Petrochemical Company in Saudi Arabia ($120 million). In 1983, the company received the largest shipbuilding contract ever awarded, worth about $600 million, to build twelve container vessels for the U.S. Lines. It also completed construction of a second dry dock with a capacity to build 350,000 dwt vessels to accommodate the increased demand.

In spite of such brisk activities, in 1982, the first full year of operation, the company suffered a loss of $9 million on sales of $485 million. In 1983, the company made a net profit of $7.5 million on $517 million sales. Prospects for 1984 were much brighter, and the company expected to earn sizable returns from its operation. Explaining the reasons for the expected successful operation of the company, Managing Director Kim Tae-Koo singled out the existence of a vast pool of young people who worked twelve hours a day with a motivation to increase productivity to the level of Japanese workers.

Kaifu Hachiro, a leading authority in the shipbuilding industry and former vice president of Nissho-Iwai, one of the Japanese general trading companies with a strong position in the shipbuilding business, projected that worldwide market in the next fifteen years would belong to Korean shipbuilders. According to him, Korea would soon replace Japan as the leader in the industry. Such a remark would have been considered far-fetched in 1982 when Japanese shipbuilders took the lion's share with 48.5 percent of the world's total orders, while Korean shipbuilders were at a distant second with 9.3 percent. In 1983, however, the competition between the two became closer. Korean shipbuilders' share increased to 19 percent, while the Japanese share went to 57 percent.

Hong In-Kie, president of Daewoo Shipbuilding, shared Kaifu's views: "In Korea we expect to assume a leadership role in the world's shipbuilding industry. However, we are realistic enough to know that no one lasts at the top forever. Some developing countries such as China will become competitive sooner or later, and will eventually supplant Korea. In the meantime, we must work hard to realize our potential."

Although aggressively seeking shipbuilding contracts, Daewoo Shipbuilding had also expanded its offshore structures and plant equipment business. Chairman Kim related the two:

> In the long run shipbuilding is a better business for us than is offshore structures, such as oil rigs. Oil production is a relatively lucrative business, and the oil companies can afford to pay reasonable prices for oil rigs. But shipping companies have to complete on a global scale, and cost effective-

ness is the name of the game. So far as shipping companies are cost conscious, Korean shipbuilders have a definite advantage.

Today, however, the shipping business is slack and so is the shipbuilding business. Compared to 40 million dwt worth of orders per year in the past, there is only 15 million dwt worth of orders nowadays, 40 percent of which will be nationalized. So we are competing in a market with only 9 to 10 million dwt worth of orders. At best, Korea can capture 40 percent of the market, or about 4 million dwt. With our capacity and that of Hyundai's, that is not enough, so we have to move to other businesses to stay alive. The shipbuilding business is cyclical and will improve some day. When an upturn arrives, whether it is caused by a major international war or an economic boom, we can easily make money.

By the end of 1983, the company was in the process of constructing a skidway to accommodate construction of super-sized steel structures as big as 250 meters wide and 250 meters long. Daewoo's top management was also considering adding another dock with a capacity for building or repairing vessels up to 350,000 dwt in size. The required investment for the two projects was estimated at around $50–60 million.

Daewoo Motor Company

Shinjin Motor Company, the predecessor of Daewoo Motor Company, had been the industry front runner in Korea with over 50 percent of the domestic market in the 1960s. In 1972, the company entered into a 50–50 joint venture with General Motors, and changed its name to General Motors Korea (GMK). Beginning in 1975, its competitor Hyundai Motor Company captured the market with a subcompact called "Pony," which was domestically designed and produced. According to Choi Myung-Kul, president of Daewoo Motor Company, GMK was in a difficult position, since its engine facilities, constructed before the first energy shock of 1973, were geared primarily to making engines with a displacement suited for intermediate size cars. With the introduction of the fuel-efficient Pony by Hyundai, GMK's market position in the passenger car segment was eroded.

In 1976, the Shinjin group experienced financial difficulties and its shares in GMK were sold to the government-owned Korea Development Bank. The name of the company was subsequently changed to Saehan Motor. In 1978, the government requested Daewoo to acquire the Korean interests in the company. Mr. Choi said that Daewoo had wanted to acquire the company anyway, because of its strategic fit with the diesel-engine manufacturing capability of Daewoo Heavy Industries Ltd.

The motor industry, however, was heavily controlled by the government in Korea, whose policy was geared toward discouraging car ownership, because cars were seen as luxury items. The result of high taxes on ownership and gasoline was evident in the car-ownership figures: 7 units per 1,000 people in Korea, compared to 32 per 1,000 in Taiwan, 65 in Brazil, 70 in Mexico, and 115 in Argentina.

In August 1980, the government decided to restructure the industry. Daewoo was required to give up ownership of Saehan Motor Company only to have the edict nullified three months later. During this period, most of Daewoo Motor's inventories had been liquidated and many of the dealerships discontinued. At the same time, one of the worst recessionary periods hit the market during 1980 to 1982. Daewoo management, however, was constrained from action because investment decisions were in the hands of GMC expatriates.

In 1982, Daewoo negotiated with GMC for the latter to relinquish the right to manage the company. Under Daewoo direction the company changed its name to Daewoo Motor and launched a new small car that gained a 40 percent market share in 1983 in the small-car segment (which in turn represented roughly one-half of the total passenger-car market).

Although the domestic market remained small with 76,000 passenger vehicles until 1982, it was beginning to expand and was projected at 120,000 in 1983. Industry observers projected 20 percent plus growth rates over the next few years. Among the three automakers in Korea, Daewoo Motor's capacity of 90,000 units per year was the second (Hyundai's capacity was 175,000, and Kia's 75,000).

On March 7, 1984, the *Wall Street Journal* reported that General Motors and Daewoo had signed a "memorandum of understanding" to produce cars in Korea for export to the United States. The partners were said to be planning a $500 million expansion project to be financed by investments of $125 million by each partner and $250 million in loans. The resulting facilities would be capable in 1986 of producing 167,000 small, front-wheel-drive passenger cars that GM would design. GM would sell about 80,000 of these vehicles in the U.S. along with its lineup of small Japanese cars from Suzuki, Isuzu, and its proposed joint venture with Toyota.

An earlier report noted that Hyundai was constructing a factory capable of producing 300,000 front-wheel-drive passenger cars annually when completed in 1985. Like Daewoo, Hyundai planned to export half of its added capacity.

Daewoo Electronics Company

Daewoo acquired the troubled electronics division of Taihan Electric Wire Company early in 1983 and merged it with Daewoo Electronics Company, a small audio instrument maker. The new company manufactured most major home appliances—such as TVs, refrigerators, air conditioners, washers, and dryers—with a share of roughly 15 percent to 30 percent of the domestic market in each category.

Later in the year, the Ministry of Commerce and Industry (MCI) promulgated guidelines for electrical equipment manufacturers that would have them move into higher technology. According to these guidelines, these companies were to limit manufacture of home appliances and other consumer electronic products to 40 percent of their total output. The share of computers, electronic switching systems, and semiconductor memory chips was to be raised from the current 13 percent to 24 percent, while that of components and parts manufacturing would shrink from 45 percent to 36 percent by 1986.

Electronics manufacturers had anticipated the need for such a change. Daewoo Electronics, along with Samsung Electronics and Gold Star Electronics (a Lucky-Goldstar affiliate) had already begun to place more emphasis on the development of new products. In 1983 Hyundai Group joined the industry with a plan to invest $500 million in electronics over the following four years. This plan included setting up a subsidiary R&D firm in California's Silicon Valley.

Daewoo Group's future plans for expanding its high-technology electronics also involved its telecommunications unit. Daewoo Telecommunications was to look into the possibility of manufacturing semiconductors as well as computers and telecommunications. The initial stress with computers would be on the development of technology to manufacture and supply hardware to domestic and overseas mass markets. In the field of telecommunications, efforts would be made to develop such technologies as digital switching, pulse code modulation, optical communication, and bipolar metal-oxide silicon semiconductors. For this, Daewoo would need to invest substantially in R&D.

General Electric's Strategic Planning: 1981

On December 21, 1980, the General Electric Company announced that John F. Welch, Jr., would become chairman and chief executive officer effective April 1, 1981. Welch had spent twenty years in GE's operating organization—first in the plastics business, later in consumer products, and then as vice chairman. At forty-five he would be replacing the retiring Reginald H. Jones, a man described by some as a "legend." Indeed, the *Wall Street Journal* reported that GE had "decided to replace a legend with a live wire."

The company that Jack Welch would be leading was the tenth largest industrial corporation in the United States and the only firm among *Fortune's* ten largest that could be characterized as diversified. Its financial performance was solid—AAA bond rating, 19.5 percent return on equity, and $2.2 billion in cash and marketable securities. In addition GE's management systems and in particular its strategic planning system were most highly regarded; the following comments were typical:

> Probably no single company has made such a singular contribution to the arts and wiles, the viewpoints and the techniques of large-scale corporate management as GE. . . . Today the technique uppermost in the minds of GE top management is planning—a preoccupation in which GE is again an acknowledged master and innovator among corporate giants.
>
> *Management Today*, August 1978

> Shortly after I took this job, I visited some people at the Defense Department because I had heard that they had just finished an exhaustive survey of industrial planning systems. They told me I was probably inheriting the world's most effective strategic planning system and that Number Two was pretty far behind.
>
> Daniel J. Fink, Senior V.P., Corporate Planning and Development, General Electric

> When Japanese managers come to visit us, they don't ask to see our research centers or manufacturing facilities. All they want to know about is our management system.
>
> A General Electric executive

GE's excellent performance and reputation were no guarantee of future success. Jack Welch would be challenged to meet the company's long-term objective of increasing earnings per share 25 percent faster than the growth in GNP in the face of tougher foreign competition and a continued slowdown in the growth of GE's traditional businesses. To meet this challenge, he would have to decide how to stimulate and promote growth and what role GE's famed planning system would play in the years ahead.

Origins of Strategic Planning

As the decade of the 1960s was nearing a close, a number of circumstances came together that led to a major reexamination of the way General Electric was being managed. One of the more salient of these was the company's profitless growth (see Exhibit 1 for financial information). While sales in 1968 of $8.4 billion were 91 percent higher than in 1960, net income had increased only 63 percent and return on total assets had fallen from 7.4 percent to 6.2 percent. This lackluster profit performance came at the same time that three major ventures—commercial jet engines, mainframe computers, and nuclear power systems—were demanding more and more of the company's financial resources. Pressure on corporate management was mounting: GE's "sacred Triple A bond rating" was in jeopardy.

Improving this financial situation was no easy task. In 1968 GE was widely diversified, competing in twenty-three of the twenty-six two-digit SIC industry categories, and was decentralized into ten groups, forty-six divisions, and over 190 departments. Indeed, diversification and decentralization had been the major strategic and organizational thrusts of GE's two prior CEOs—Ralph Cordiner, 1950 to 1963, and Fred Borch, 1963 to 1972. Under decentralization, GE's departments became organizational building blocks, each with its own product-market scope and its own marketing, finance, engineering, manufacturing, and employee-relations functions. One GE executive noted:

> In the 1950s, Cordiner led a massive decentralization of the company. This was absolutely necessary. GE had been highly centralized in the 1930s and 1940s. Cordiner broke the company down into departments that, as he used to say, "were a size that a man could get his arms around." And what the company would say after giving a man his department was, "Here, take this $50 million department and grow it into $125 million." Then the department would be split into two departments, like an amoeba.

In addition to decentralization, Cordiner pushed for expansion of GE's businesses and product lines. With growth and diversity, however, came problems of control:

> The case for Cordiner lies in his improvement of GE's numerators and in his creation of a truly remarkable "can-do," organization. He was the champion of volume and diversity and of make rather than buy. He built a company unmatched in American business history in the capacity to pursue

Exhibit 1 Ten-year statistical summary, 1961–70 ($ millions, except per share amounts).

	1970	*1969*	*1968*	*1967*	*1966*	*1965*	*1964*	*1963*	*1962*	*1961*
Sales of products and services	$8,726.7	$8,448.0	$8,381.6	$7,741.2	$7,177.3	$6,213.6	$5,319.2	$5,177.0	$4,986.1	$4,666.6
Net earnings	328.5	278.0	357.1	361.4	338.9	355.1	219.6	272.2	256.5	238.4
Earnings per common share	3.63	3.07	3.95	4.01	3.75	3.93	2.44	3.05	2.89	2.70
Earnings as a percentage of sales	3.8%	3.3%	4.3%	4.7%	4.7%	5.7%	4.1%	5.3%	5.1%	5.1%
Earned on share owners' equity	12.6%	11.0%	14.8%	15.9%	15.7%	17.5%	11.5%	14.9%	15.0%	14.8%
Cash dividends declared	$235.4	$235.2	$234.8	$234.2	$234.6	$216.7	$197.7	$183.1	$177.5	$176.4
Dividends declared per common share	2.60	2.60	2.60	2.60	2.60	2.40	2.20	2.05	2.00	2.00
Market price range per share	94½–60¼	98¼–74⅛	100⅜–80¼	115⅞–82½	120–80	120¼–91	93⅝–78¾	87½–71¾	78½–54¼	80¾–60½
Current assets	$3,334.8	$3,287.8	$3,311.1	$3,207.6	$3,013.0	$2,842.4	$2,543.8	$2,321.0	$2,024.6	$1,859.7
Current liabilities	2,650.3	2,366.7	2,104.3	1,977.4	1,883.2	1,566.8	1,338.9	1,181.9	1,168.7	1,086.6
Total assets	6,309.9	6,007.5	5,743.8	5,347.2	4,851.7	4,300.4	3,856.0	3,502.5	3,349.9	3,143.4
Total share owners' equity	2,665.1	2,540.0	2,493.4	2,342.2	2,211.7	2,107.0	1,944.2	1,889.2	1,764.3	1,654.6
Plant and equipment additions	581.4	530.6	514.7	561.7	484.9	332.9	237.7	149.2	173.2	179.7
Depreciation	334.7	351.3	300.1	280.4	233.6	188.4	170.3	149.4	146.0	131.6
Total taxes and renegotiation	309.4	313.2	390.5	390.1	409.1	403.8	277.3	331.4	298.7	289.9
Provision for income taxes	220.6	231.5	312.3	320.5	347.4	352.2	233.8	286.7	254.0	248.9
Employees—average worldwide	396,583	410,126	395,691	384,864	375,852	332,991	308,233	297,726	290,682	279,547
Gross national product (current $ billions)	982	936	869	796	753	688	636	595	564	523

Source: General Electric annual reports; *Business Statistics,* U.S. Department of Commerce, p. 245, for GNP.

those objectives. In the sense of home-grown know-how, GE *could* do almost anything; and, in the sense of in-house capacity, GE could do a lot of things simultaneously.

But the very expansiveness and evangelism that were Cordiner's strengths were flawed by permissiveness and lack of proportion. "We can do it" too often became "we should do it." For example, massive investments with long payback periods were undertaken simultaneously in nuclear power, aerospace, and computers, with a blithe self-confidence in GE's ability to "do-it-ourselves." A sort of "marketing macropia" persisted in which previously constrained market segmentations and product definitions were escalated beyond experience or prudence.[1]

As Fred Borch faced the challenges of leading General Electric in the mid-1960s, internal studies of the company's problems began to proliferate. One such study set out to give management a tool for evaluating business plans by delineating the key factors associated with profitable results.[2] Another study undertaken by GE's Growth Council tried to determine how the company would properly position itself to meet its long-term goal of growing faster than the GNP. Despite these and other staff studies, however, profitless growth continued.

Reg Jones assessed the company's situation at the time:

> Our performance reflected poor planning and a poor understanding of the businesses. A major reason for this weakness was the way we were organized. Under the existing structure with functional staff units at the corporate level, business plans only received funcational reviews. They were not given a *business* evaluation.
>
> True, we had a corporate planning department, but they were more concerned with econometric models and environmental forecasting than with hard-headed business plan evaluation. Fortunately, Fred Borch was able to recognize the problem.

In 1969 Borch commissioned McKinsey & Co. to study the effectiveness of GE's corporate staff and of the planning done at the operating level. He commented on McKinsey's study:

> They were totally amazed at how the company ran as well as it did with the planning that was being done or not being done at various operating levels. But they saw some tremendous opportunities for moving the company ahead if we devoted the necessary competence and time to facing up to these, as they saw it, very critical problems.
>
> In their report, they made two specific recommendations. One was that we recognize that our departments were not really businesses. We had been saying that they were the basic building blocks of the company for many years, but they weren't. They were fractionated and they were parts of larger

1. James P. Baughman, "Problems and Performance of the Role of Chief Executive in the General Electric Company, 1892–1974," mimeographed discussion paper, July 15, 1974.
2. This approach eventually led to the PIMS model that has been made available to industry at large by the Strategic Planning Institute.

businesses. The thrust of the recommendation was that we reorganize the company from an operations standpoint and create what they call Strategic Business Units—the terminology stolen from a study we made back in 1957. They gave certain criteria for these and in brief what this amounted to were reasonably self-sufficient businesses that did not meet head-on with other strategic business units in making the major management decisions necessary.[3] They also recommended as part of this that the 33 or 35 or 40 strategic business units report directly to the CEO regardless of the size of the business or the present level in the organization.

Their second recommendation was that we face up to the fact that we were never going to get the longer-range work done necessary to progress the company through the '70s, unless we made a radical change in our staff components. The thrust of their recommendation was to separate out the ongoing work necessary to keep General Electric going from the work required to posture the company for the future.

Introduction of Strategic Planning

In reporting the results of the McKinsey study to GE's management in May, 1970, Fred Borch noted: "We decided that their recommendations on both the operating front and the staff front conceptually were very sound. They hit right at the nut of the problem, but the implementation that they recommended just wouldn't fly as far as General Electric was concerned. We accepted about 100 percent of their conceptual contribution and virtually none of their implementation recommendations."

To develop an approach for implementing the McKinsey recommendations in a way suitable for GE, Borch had set up a task force headed by Group Vice President W. D. Dance. This group spent two intensive months preparing alternatives and recommendations for consideration by the corporate executive office.

As a result of these efforts, a decision was made to restructure GE's corporate staff into two parts. The existing staff units, which provided ongoing services to the CEO[4] and to the operating units, were grouped as the corporate administrative staff reporting to a senior vice president. The administrative staff would deal with functional, operational matters. As a counterpart, a corporate executive staff was created to help the CEO plan the future of the company. It comprised four staff components—finance, strategic planning, technology, legal and governance—each headed by a senior vice president.

---

3. The general characteristics of an SBU were defined as follows: a unique set of competitors, a unique business mission, a competitor in external markets (as opposed to internal supplier), the ability to accomplish integrated strategic planning, and the ability to "call the shots" on the variables crucial to the success of the business.

4. The CEO here refers to the corporate executive office, which included the chairman and chief executive officer and the vice chairmen. GE usually had two or three vice chairmen.

Establishing Strategic Business Units

The task force anticipated several problems in implementing McKinsey's recommendation to create strategic business units reporting directly to the CEO. One problem had to do with GE's existing line-reporting structure of groups, divisions, and departments. McKinsey's proposal had been to abandon GE's current organizational structure and to reorganize on the basis of SBUs. The task force was concerned that such a change might seriously jeopardize the successful functioning of GE's operational control system. To avoid this risk, management decided to superimpose the SBU structure on the existing line-reporting structure. For ongoing operations, managers would report according to the group-division-department structure. However, only units designated SBUs would prepare strategic plans.

As shown in Figure A, a group, division, or department could be designated an SBU. This overlay of a strategic planning structure on the operating structure resulted in a variety of reporting relationships. When a department was named an SBU, for example, the department manager would report directly to the CEO for planning purposes, but to a division manager for operating purposes. GE managers expressed the opinion that this approach provided the company with the best of both worlds—tight operational control on a comprehensive basis and planning at the relevant levels. One manager commented:

> In theory, the intervening layers of management were supposed to be transparent for planning purposes and opaque for control purposes. In

Figure A SBU overlay on existing organization.

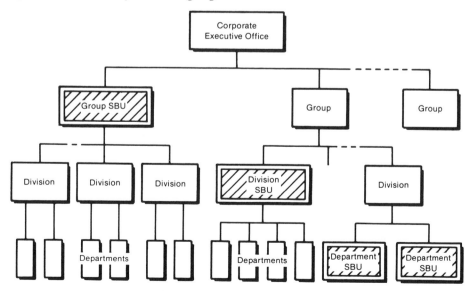

practice, they were translucent for both. Even though the department or division SBU managers were to report directly to the CEO for planning, they would normally review their plans with the group executive. In a sense, we loosened the SBU structure to allow personal influence and power to shape the important strategic decisions.

The designation of SBUs posed a second problem for the task force. According to GE executives, about 80 percent of the SBU designations could be readily agreed upon. The designation of group, division, or department, as the appropriate SBU level, became controversial for some of the business operations. In these cases Fred Borch would make the final judgment, often based on his "comfort index" with the business and with the manager running the business. Not until the end of 1972 were all of the SBU designations completed. Of the forty-three SBUs, four were groups, twenty-one were divisions, and eighteen were departments. Two other problems on the task force's agenda concerned the kind of information to be contained in an SBU plan and the numbers and kinds of people to staff the planning effort.

Defining a Business Plan

Even with the reduction in the number of business plans from 190 departments to forty-three SBUs, the CEO faced a formidable task of review. One GE manager noted that "Borch had a sense that he wasn't looking for lots of data on each business unit, but really wanted fifteen terribly important and significant pages of data and analysis."

To deal with this problem, three of the group vice presidents were asked to work with three different consulting companies (Arthur D. Little, Boston Consulting Group, and McKinsey & Co.) to find a way to compress all of the strategic planning data into as effective a presentation as possible. For example, GE's collaborative effort with McKinsey led to the development of the nine-block summary of business and investment strategy shown in Figure B.[5] One GE executive commented that "the nine-block summary had tremendous appeal to us not only because it compressed a lot of data, but also because it contained enough subjective evaluation to appeal to the thinking of GE management."

The only instructions for the SBU manager on the content of a business plan was a listing of the topics to be covered. Over time, new topics were added and some were deleted. But the corporate office never specified how each topic should be treated. The following list contains the topics specified for the 1973 SBU plans:

1. Identification and formulation of environmental assumptions of strategic importance.

---

5. See Exhibit 2 for a description of GE's 1980 criteria for assessing industry attractiveness and business position.

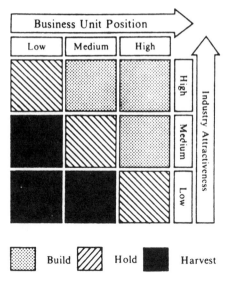

Figure B Investment priority screen.

2. Identification and in-depth analysis of competitors, including assumptions about their probable strategies.
3. Analysis of the SBU's own resources.
4. Development and evaluation of strategy alternatives.
5. Preparation of the SBU strategic plan, including estimates of capital spending for the next five years.
6. Preparation of the SBU operating plan, which detailed the next year of the SBU strategic plan.

Reg Jones, who became GE's chairman and chief executive officer in December 1972, added a proviso on how the plans were to be presented:

> At our general management conference in January 1973, I stirred up quite a few members of that audience when I said that I expected every SBU manager to be able to stand before a peer group and, without benefit of visual aids, give a clear and concise statement of his strategic plan. And that every manager reporting to him should fully understand that statement and be able to explain it to his troops. I meant it. When that happens, then you can say that planning has become a way of life.

Staffing the Planning Effort

With the new SBU planning approach in place, the question remained of how to staff the effort. Here, two important actions were taken. First, each SBU manager was required to hire an SBU strategic planner. Because of the limited number of experienced strategic planners in the company at that time, many

Exhibit 2 GE's 1980 criteria for investment priority screen.

Criterion	Measure
Industry Attractiveness	
1. Market size	• 3-year average served industry market dollars
2. Market growth	• 10-year constant dollar average annual market growth rate
3. Industry profitability	3-year average ROS, SBU, and "Big Three" competitors • Nominal • Inflation adjusted
4. Cyclicality	• Average annual percent variation of sales from trend
5. Inflation recovery	• 5-year average ratio of combined selling price and productivity change to change in cost due to inflation
6. Importance of non-U.S. markets	• 10-year average ratio of international to total market

Criterion	Measure
Business Position	
1. Market position	• 3-year average market share (total market) • 3-year average international market share • 2-year average relative market share (SBU/"Big Three" competitors)
2. Competitive position	Superior, equal, or inferior to competition in 1980: • Product quality • Technological leadership • Manufacturing/cost leadership • Distribution/marketing leadership
3. Relative profitability	3-year average SBU's ROS, less average ROS, "Big Three" competitors • Nominal • Inflation adjusted

Note: Shading indicates measure used for the first time in 1980.

266

of the people filling these posts were hired from outside the company, an unusual practice for GE.[6]

Second, both the SBU general managers and strategic planners were required to attend special strategic planning seminars set up at GE's Management Development Center in Crotonville, New York. Each department and division general manager (over 240 in number) was also given a metal suitcase with a slide and tape show to present to subordinates after taking the course.

Acceptance of Planning: 1972–77

In the 1950s and 1960s, a characteristic of GE was the belief that the company could succeed in all of the businesses in which it competed. A frequently voiced reaction to strategic planning and particularly to the nine-block analysis was that it legitimized exiting from certain businesses. According to *Fortune*, "GE stopped making vacuum cleaners, fans, phonographs, heart pacemakers, an industrial X-ray system, and numerous other products that failed to deliver the returns Jones demanded." During Jones's entire tenure as CEO, a total of seventy-three product lines were exited.

GE's successful exit from the mainframe computer business in May, 1970, also played a pivotal role in legitimizing divestitures; as one manager commented:

> While the sale of GE's computer business actually preceded the adoption of strategic planning, somehow people began to connect the two. From then on it became fashionable to prune businesses. And Jones's subsequent promotion gave even more credibility to those managers who were willing to face up to the fact that certain businesses had to be exited.
>
> The planning system was just another tool which enabled a manager to face up to certain inevitabilities. Prior to this, we had really operated with a "floating J curve." In other words, businesses would forecast two or three years of flat or declining profitability, but then all of the numbers would point upward. What Jones was able to do with the computer business and what strategic planning revealed was that the floating J curve was a fantasy.

Impact on the Business Mix

As shown in Table A, one impact of strategic planning was a shift in GE's mix of businesses. Reg Jones commented:

> Another source of confidence for us is the continued development of a strategic planning system that provides a strong discipline for differentiating the allocation of resources—that is, investing most heavily in areas of business that we identify as offering the greatest leverage for earnings growth,

---

6. Over time, many of the SBUs developed planning staffs and the planning positions were filled internally. By 1980 there were approximately 200 senior level planners in GE. About half of these were career planners, while the others rotated through the position as part of their career development.

Table A   GE's business mix (%).

	Sales		Earnings	
	1970	*1977*	*1970*	*1977*
Consumer products and services	22.8	23.5	29.6	29.6
Power systems	21.5	18.0	26.5	6.9
Industrial components and systems	23.1	20.6	28.4	17.6
Technical systems and materials	28.5	23.1	9.1	22.7
Natural resources	0.0	5.4	0.0	18.0
International	15.9	14.3	20.1	6.5
Corporate eliminations	(11.8)	(4.9)	(13.7)	(1.3)

Source: General Electric 10–K reports for 1970 (recast for organizational changes) and 1977.

while minimizing our investments in sectors we see as growing more slowly or remaining static. [1973 annual report]

Comparing the company today with the General Electric of only a few years ago shows that, in selectively allocating our resources to the growth opportunities identified through strategic planning, we have developed decidedly different sources of earnings and a different mix of businesses, whose potentials for profitable growth exceed those of our historic product lines. [1976 annual report]

As Table A illustrates, a major contributor to the shift in GE's business mix was the acquisition in 1976 of Utah International, a billion dollar mining company with substantial holdings of metallurgical coal.[7] Many saw in Utah a potential hedge against inflation and numerous opportunities for synergy with GE's other businesses. While not denying these benefits, *Fortune* reported:

Jones wanted to make a lasting imprint on his corporation by providing a new source of earnings growth and creating what he likes to call "the new GE." Utah provided him with a means to make that concept credible. When the opportunity arose, he relied not on his hallowed planning staff, but rather seized the chance to personally lead his company into its biggest

7. General Electric's 1976 annual report related a pooling-of-interest exchange of 41 million shares of GE common stock for all outstanding shares of Utah International, effective December 20, 1976. Utah International's 1976 earnings were $181 million and sales were $1,001 million. The company's principal operations included the mining of coking coal, steam coal, uranium, iron ore, and copper. By far the most important contribution to 1976 earnings came from Australian coking coal supplied under long-term contracts to Japanese and European steel producers.

move in many years. As Jones himself now acknowledges: "Nothing in our strategic planning said that we should acquire Utah International."[8]

Internal developments also contributed to the shift in business mix, as described by one of GE's senior executives: "Much of the recent growth has come from the internal development of businesses brand new to GE. For example, engineered materials didn't even exist as a business in 1960. It was just a bunch of research projects. Now, it will have sales of $2 billion, it will make $200 million net, with an ROI of 18 percent, and it will have plants all over the world. The company's experiences with aircraft engines, information services, and several other businesses have been much the same."

Impact on Management Systems

By 1977 the impact of strategic planning was being felt by GE's other management systems. For example, manpower evaluation and selection had been keyed to the strategic plans. A manager in the executive manpower department noted: "The strategic plans gave us, for the first time, a means by which we could evaluate if a manager really delivered on what he said he would do. All we have to do is check the previous plans. This also helps when there are job changes. We can now determine what current problems are caused by earlier mistakes, so the wrong person doesn't get blamed."

In the area of incentive compensation, performance screens were developed that separated financial and nonfinancial objectives for the business. This was intended to provide greater emphasis on longer-term considerations, and it did to some extent, but as one manager noted, "It's a great theory, but in a crunch it's the financial results that matter."

In terms of GE's organization structure, only one major change was apparent. This was the dissolution of the corporate executive staff and the return to a number of separate functional staff components. Reg Jones explained: "The corporate executive staff was originally set up with two major objectives: to straighten out the venture messes and to devise a planning system to prevent those troubles in the future. By 1974 the venture problems were solved, and we had a planning staff that was managing the new strategic planning process. By 1975 we dissolved the [corporate executive] staff."

Assessment of Strategic Planning

By 1977 strategic planning had won widespread management support for a variety of reasons. GE executives commented as follows:

> "In the views of some managers, there was more planning being done in the mid-1960s than today. There was lots of futurism, scenario writing, contingency planning, and model building. But those efforts were not related to the problems of our ongoing businesses as is the SBU analysis."

8. "General Electric's Very Personal Merger," *Fortune,* August 1977.

"Not specifying the precise format of a strategic plan turned out to be very useful. For one thing, it enabled the SBUs to avoid spending time on issues that weren't important to them. More important, it provided room for some creativity and originality in the writing of the plans."

"Since strategic planning was implemented, our real growth businesses have been funded, even when we were cash short in 1974 and 1975. The key is for the guy who is running a growth business that requires resources to gain the confidence of the people at the top of the organization. Strategic planning can help to get that confidence."

An internal audit of strategic planning, completed in December 1974, reported that "the overwhelming feeling is that strategic planning has become ingrained in General Electric: 80 percent felt there would be no slippage and 16 percent only minor slippage if corporate requirements for SP [strategic planning] were removed."

Not surprisingly, complaints of shortcomings in GE's strategic planning were also voiced. Some of the complaints reported in the audit had to do with the excessive effort devoted to cosmetics and upward merchandising of strategic plans. Another set of complaints had to do with a perceived ineffective review of SBU plans. The audit reported, "One issue is clear: the operations managers feel that corporate-level reviewers do not understand their businesses well enough to be competent reviewers."

The earlier review of strategic plans at the division and group levels was also considered by many managers as ineffective. The reason for this failing was attributed to the fact that managers at these levels typically "were really participants in generating the plans and thus were not objective reviewers." At the CEO level, on the other hand, the review of all forty-three SBU strategic plans was requiring an inordinate amount of time and effort.

Pressures for current earnings were also cited as undermining the strategic planning process. One executive, quoted in the audit, commented: "Strategic planning process won't work in General Electric, at least not in the context in which we are trying to make it work. The company needs to project an attractive financial and cash-flow image. The pressure to provide a steady profit growth and a sustained P/E ratio results in short-term demands on operations which disrupt long-term programs."

A Single General Electric and Value Added

The problem corporate management had in evaluating forty-three SBU strategic plans was coupled with a growing concern about a lack of integration and cohesiveness among the many business initiatives under way. By the mid-1970s, SBU planning, while helping to strengthen GE's competitive positions and to improve profits, was also leading to a balkanization of the company. GE appeared to be moving in the direction of becoming a holding company.

This development ran directly counter to a basic GE management tenet. As early as 1973 Jones addressed management about the need to work "with the grain" rather than against it in reshaping the company. Prominent among the "abiding characteristics of General Electric," according to Jones, was "a strong preference for a single General Electric identity, despite our broad diversification." The world-famous GE monogram symbolized this core identity.

Coupled with the concept of a single GE identity was the notion of "value added." The recurrent attacks on big business, aimed at dismantling U.S. industry giants in the interest of increased competition, posed a serious potential threat to GE. As one senior GE executive explained: "The whole has got to be significantly greater than the sum of its parts. We have nothing to defend (against increasing external pressures to break up or, at a minimum, harass very large companies) unless we have a very effective, productive corporate level." Given top management's strong preference for a cohesive General Electric, SBU strategic planning, good as it was, was not adequate for GE's needs. Something more was needed.

Integrating Strategic Planning: 1977–80

At the general management conference in January 1977, Reg Jones announced his intention to "revise GE's strategic planning system and to establish a 'sector' organization structure as the pivotal concept for the redesign effort." The proposed changes aimed to improve the strategic planning review process and to develop a cohesive plan for GE as a single, integrated entity.

Improving the Strategic Planning Review Process

In Jones's mind, corporate review of SBU plans suffered from overload. He explained:

> Right from the start of SBU planning in 1972, the vice chairman and I tried to review each plan in great detail. This effort took untold hours and placed a tremendous burden on the corporate executive office. After awhile I began to realize that no matter how hard we would work, we could not achieve the necessary in-depth understanding of the forty-odd SBU plans. Somehow, the review burden had to be carried on more shoulders.

Creating the sector structure was Jones's way of spreading the review load. The sector was defined as a new level of management that represented a macrobusiness or industry area.[9] The sector executive would serve as the GE spokesperson for that industry and would be responsible for providing management direction to the member SBUs and for integrating the SBU strategies into a sector-strategic plan. The sector-strategic plan would focus heavily on development opportunities transcending SBU lines but still within the scope of the

9. Robert Frederick, the executive who had been assigned the tasks of introducing the sector structure and making it work, explained the new nomenclature: "We picked the word *sector* because no one knew what it meant. In that way there would be no preconceived notions of what the sectors would do."

sector. The corporate executive office would thereafter focus its review on the strategic plans of the six sectors.

Below the sector, the SBU continued to be the basic business entity. To permit greater competitiveness (and visibility) for important strategic businesses within certain SBUs, however, GE introduced the concept of business segments. For example, the Audio Department became a business segment within the Housewares and Audio SBU, because it was a unique business that could operate more effectively within the SBU than on its own.

Figure C   Sector-SBU structure.

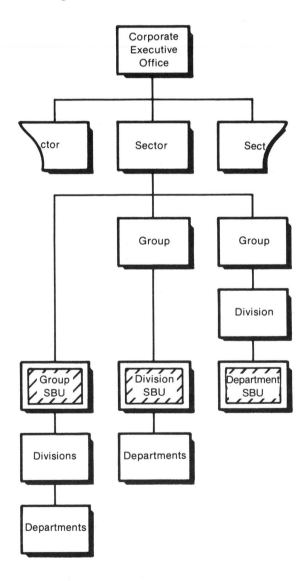

The new organizational line structure is depicted in Figure C. The dual organization in use since 1971—SBUs for planning; group, divisions, and departments for operations—was supplemented by the sector-SBU structure. The earlier designations of group, division, and department were retained to indicate the relative size of an SBU.

Along with improved review, the new sector structure was also seen as clarifying the responsibilities for business development in GE. According to a senior corporate strategic-planning staff executive: "Conceptually, SBUs are expected to develop new business opportunities by extending into contiguous product-market areas. Sectors are expected to develop new SBUs by diversifying within their macroindustry scopes. And corporate is expected to develop new sectors by diversifying into unserved macroindustries."

Improving strategy review and business development were two visible reasons for the new sector structure. (The organization chart on page 274 shows the new sector structure and management assignments.) Jones also had a private reason for this organizational change:

> I had a personal road map of the future and knew when I wanted to retire. Time was moving on, and I could see a need to put the key candidates for my job under a spotlight for the board to view. The sector executive positions would provide the visibility.
>
> The men were assigned to sectors with businesses different from their past experience. I did this not only to broaden these individuals but also to leaven the businesses by introducing new bosses who had different perspectives. For example, major appliances had long been run by managers who had grown up in the business. I put Welch, whose previous experience had been with high-technology plastics, in charge to see if he could introduce new approaches.

Strategic Integration and Corporate Challenges

Along with improving strategic review, Jones saw a need to develop a cohesive plan for GE as a single integrated entity. His concern reflected two problems that appeared to be growing in parallel with SBU planning itself:

> Over the years, we were discovering serious discontinuities among the SBU plans. At the operating level, we were suffering unnecessary costs from duplication and from uncoordinated actions.
>
> At the strategic level, we seemed to be moving in all directions with no sense of focus on what I saw as major opportunities and threats for the 1980s. For example, I saw a need to push forward on the international front, a need to move from our electromechanical technology to electronics, and a need to respond to the problems of productivity. We need a way to challenge our managers to respond to these pressing issues in an integrated fashion.

To provide corporate direction and impetus on such issues, GE introduced the concept of corporate planning challenges. As shown in Figure D, the planning challenges set the stage for the annual strategic-planning cycle. Each year

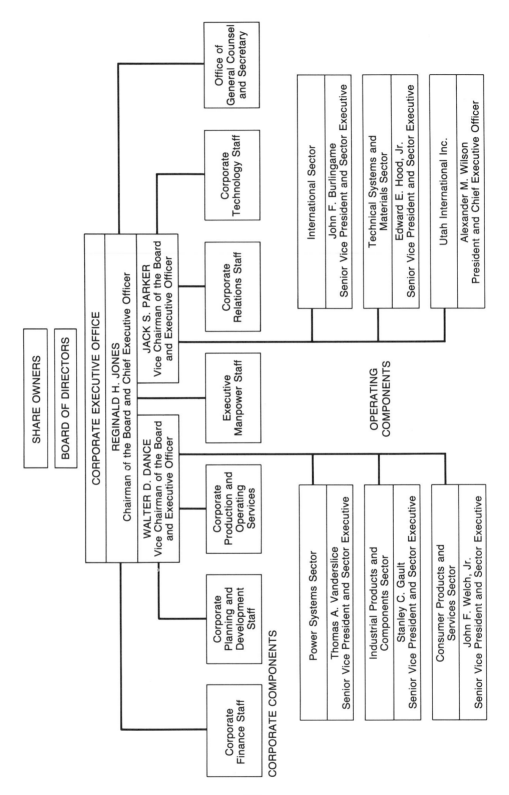

SHARE OWNERS

BOARD OF DIRECTORS

CORPORATE EXECUTIVE OFFICE

REGINALD H. JONES
Chairman of the Board and Chief Executive Officer

JACK S. PARKER
Vice Chairman of the Board
and Executive Officer

WALTER D. DANCE
Vice Chairman of the Board
and Executive Officer

Office of
General Counsel
and Secretary

Corporate
Technology Staff

Corporate
Relations Staff

Executive
Manpower Staff

Corporate
Production and
Operating
Services

Corporate
Planning and
Development
Staff

Corporate
Finance Staff

CORPORATE COMPONENTS

OPERATING
COMPONENTS

International Sector

John F. Burlingame
Senior Vice President and Sector Executive

Technical Systems and
Materials Sector

Edward E. Hood, Jr.
Senior Vice President and Sector Executive

Utah International Inc.

Alexander M. Wilson
President and Chief Executive Officer

Power Systems Sector

Thomas A. Vanderslice
Senior Vice President and Sector Executive

Industrial Products and
Components Sector

Stanley C. Gault
Senior Vice President and Sector Executive

Consumer Products and
Services Sector

John F. Welch, Jr.
Senior Vice President and Sector Executive

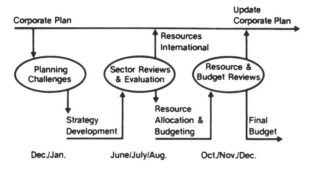

Figure D Annual planning cycle.

the CEO would issue a number of specific challenges that had to be addressed in the strategic plans of the SBUs and the sectors. For example, a 1980 corporate challenge called for SBUs and sectors to plan for a productivity improvement appropriate for their industry to counter worldwide competitive threats. The productivity target for GE as a whole was set for 6 percent.

The selection of challenges was seen by Jones as a vital function of the chief executive officer:

> It's the job of the CEO to look ahead. Planning can be helpful, but it is really our job to look at the decade ahead. You look at the environment and couple that with your knowledge of the operations. You begin to see gaps that are beyond the plans. You have studies made to examine the possible shortcomings.
>
> For example, as a defrocked bookkeeper, I have always had a concern about technology. In 1976, I commissioned a companywide study of our strengths, weaknesses, and needs in technology. The findings—sixteen volumes of them—triggered a technological renaissance in GE. We stepped up our R&D budgets, built up our electronic capabilities, and reoriented our recruiting and training activities. Now every SBU has a firm technological strategy integrated with its business strategy.

In addition to the CEO as a source of challenges, the restructured management system included two new approaches for generating planning challenges. One element aimed at fostering GE's international activities, the other at integrating GE's planning for critical resources.

International sector. To increase the importance and the visibility of international operations in GE, Jones set it up as a sector. It was, however, to play a special role among sectors. In addition to preparing a sector plan for GE's overseas affiliates, the international sector was also given responsibility for fostering and integrating international business for General Electric as a whole.

A subsequent effort to integrate electric-iron manufacturing on a worldwide basis illustrates one of the roles that the international sector was intended to play. The SBU responsible for irons had developed a newly designed iron that it planned for production in a single small country. At international sector urging, the SBU reconsidered and ultimately decided on rationalized multicountry production in three countries, including two larger countries with international sector affiliates. This approach improved cost and market-share potentials in affiliate countries, as well as cost effectiveness on a total GE system basis. This intervention led to an internal joint venture for irons between the international sector and the SBU to share risks and rewards on a worldwide basis.

Resource planning. Corporate management's concerns with GE's handling of critical resources were to be dealt with through another companywide integrating mechanism. For this purpose, senior corporate staff executives were given responsibility "for an objective assessment of key resources and the identification of issues impacting the company's strategic strengths." These assessments of financial resources, human resources, technology resources, and production resources would lead to planning challenges to the sectors and SBUs wherever practices needed to be improved.

Planning for human resources illustrated how this approach was to work. The vice president in charge of this planning described two of the issues he had subsequently raised for management consideration:

> One of the major human resources issues GE has had to face had to do with the potential impact of transferring work and jobs to overseas locations. This practice has important implications for the company, for the employees, and for the communities involved which had to be thought through beforehand. Another important issue had to do with GE's image as it relates to recruiting college graduates. In the next few years GE has to hire some 2,800 scientists and engineers, competing with some glamorous firms for the good people.

Implementing the New Structure

In characteristic fashion, GE management recognized the need to allow time for the new structure to take root. As the initiating report stated: "The objective of integrated levels of planning is just that—an objective. It may take two or three cycles to accomplish."

True to this schedule, Jones made the following assessment three years later: "The sector approach has turned out to be very successful. It even exceeded my expectations. Now I can look at six planning books and understand them well enough to ask the right questions. I could not do that before. The sectors also gave the board and me an excellent means of deciding on my successor. By 1979 the competition had been narrowed down to Burlingame, Hood, and Welch, and these men were moved up to vice chairman positions." (Exhibit 3 contains biographical data on Jones, Welch, Burlingame, and Hood.)

Jones was also pleased with the progress GE had made in responding to a number of corporate challenges. He pointed with particular pride to the "technological renaissance" that had been launched at GE:

Exhibit 3   Biographical data.

Reginald Harold Jones: born Stoke-on-Trent, Staffordshire, England, 1917. B.S. in Economics, University of Pennsylvania, 1939. Joined the General Electric Company in 1939 as a business trainee and traveling auditor, 1939–1950; assistant to controller, Apparatus Department, 1950–1956; general manager, Air Conditioning Division, 1956–1958; general manager, Supply Company Division, 1958–1961; vice president, General Electric, 1961; general manager, Construction Industries Division, 1964–1967; group executive, 1967–1968; vice president finance, 1968–1970; senior vice president, 1970–1972; vice chairman, 1972; president, 1972–1973; chairman of the board and chief executive officer, 1973–1981.

John F. Welch, Jr.: born Massachusetts, 1935. BSCHE, University of Massachusetts, 1957; MSCHE, University of Illinois, 1958; Ph.D., 1960. Joined the General Electric Company in 1960 as a process development specialist for chemical development operations; process development group leader, 1962; manager–manufacturing polymer products and chemical development operations, 1963; general manager, Plastics Department, 1968; general manager, Chemical Division, then Chemical and Metallurgical Division, 1971; vice president and general manager, Chemical and Metallurgical Division, 1972; vice president and group executive, Components and Materials Group, 1973; senior vice president and executive, Consumer Products and Services Sector, 1977; vice chairman and executive officer, 1979; chairman of the board and chief executive officer, 1981.

John Francis Burlingame: born Massachusetts, 1922. B.S., Tufts University, 1942. Joined GE in 1946; vice president and general manager, Computer Systems Division, 1969–1971; vice president–employee relations, 1971–1973; vice president and group executive, International, 1973–1977; senior vice president, International sector, 1977–1979; vice chairman, 1979–.

Edward Exum Hood, Jr.: born North Carolina, 1930. M.S., Nuclear Engineering, North Carolina State University, 1953. Joined GE in 1957 as a powerplant design engineer; vice president and general manager, Commercial Engine Division, 1968–1972; vice president and group executive, International, 1972–1973; vice president and group executive, Power Generation, 1973–1977; senior vice president and sector executive, Technical System and Materials, 1977–1979; vice chairman, 1979–.

These past few years, we have pressed hard the challenge to change the company's basic technology from electromechanical to electronics. Today we have a true companywide effort to apply the new microelectronics and the related information-based technologies to every possible product, service, and process in GE.

The proposed purchase of Calma, a leading producer of interactive graphics equipment, and the acquisition of Intersil, a maker of advanced microelectronic chips, give evidence to this commitment.[10] Perhaps our

10. According to GE's 1980 annual report, Intersil was acquired for $235 million. The Calma acquisition was cleared by the Federal Trade Commission in early 1981. The purchase agreement called for an initial payment of $100 million, and additional payments of up to $70 million with the exact amount determined by Calma's sales over the next four years.

commitment to broad-based innovation is best expressed by our rising investment in research and development. Since 1977, we have increased GE-
funded R&D expenditures 85 percent to $760 million. Total R&D, including
external funding, reached $1.6 billion in 1980.

GE in 1980: A Call for Growth

In a presentation to the financial community at the Hotel Pierre in New York
City on December 11, 1979, Jones pointed to how GE was "positioned to achieve
the objective of sustained earnings growth, faster than the growth of the U.S.
economy, in the 1980s." He added: "General Electric is embarked on a course
of large-scale innovation, productivity improvement, and business development for the 1980s, and we have built up the financial resources to bring that
bold and entrepreneurial strategy to a successful conclusion."

Challenging Static Forecasts

This public promise of rapid growth carried major implications for strategic
planning. At the annual general management conference at Belleair held a month
later, Daniel Fink, the newly appointed senior vice president for corporate
planning and development (development had been added to stress the growth
objective), questioned the adequacy of the existing strategic plans to meet Jones's growth challenge. He began by reviewing the recent and projected changes
in business mix. The relative earnings figures are summarized in Table B. (See
Exhibits 4 and 5 for more detailed financial statements.) Armed with these
figures, Fink then argued:

> Our implied strategy seems to be one of slowing, or even halting, the
> aggressive and successful diversification of the past decade. The vision of
> GE in 1984 that we get from the long-range forecasts is very much like GE
> in 1979—same product mix, same international mix, same strategy of lever-
> aging earnings over sales growth.
> How can that be? And—more important—do you believe it? Do you be-

Table B GE's business mix (%).

	1968	1979	1984	Projected Change
Electrical equipment	80	47	44	−3
Materials	6	27	27	0
Services	10	16	19	+3
Transportation	4	10	10	0
International	16	40	43	+3

Exhibit 4 Ten-year statistical summary, 1971–80 ($ millions, except per share amounts).

	1980	*1979*	*1978*	*1977*	*1976*	*1975*	*1974*	*1973*	*1972*	*1971 (2-for-1 stock split)*
Summary of operations										
Sales of products and services to customers	$24,959	$22,461	$19,654	$17,519	$15,697	$14,105	$13,918	$11,945	$10,474	$9,557
Operating margin	2,243	2,130	1,958	1,698	1,528	1,187	1,171	1,070	877	772
Earnings before income taxes and minority interest	$2,493	$2,391	$2,153	$1,889	$1,627	$1,174	$1,181	$1,130	$963	$847
Taxes	958	953	894	773	668	460	458	457	385	333
Net earnings	$1,514	$1,409	$1,230	$1,088	$931	$688	$705	$661	$573	$510
Earnings per common share	$6.65	$6.20	$5.39	$4.79	$4.12	$3.07	$3.16	$2.97	$2.57	$2.30
Dividends declared per common share	$2.95	$2.75	$2.50	$2.10	$1.70	$1.60	$1.60	$1.50	$1.40	$1.38
Earnings as a percentage of sales	6.1%	6.3%	6.3%	6.2%	5.9%	4.9%	5.1%	5.5%	5.5%	5.3%
Earned on average share owners' equity	19.5%	20.2%	19.6%	19.4%	18.9%	15.7%	17.8%	18.4%	17.5%	17.2%
Dividends	$670	$624	$570	$477	$333	$293	$291	$273	$255	$250
Market price range per share	63–44	55⅛–45	57⅝–43⅝	57¼–47⅜	59¼–46	52⅞–32⅜	65–30	75⅞–55	73–58¼	66½–46½
Price/earnings ratio range	9–7	9–7	11–8	12–10	14–11	17–10	19–9	24–17	25–20	26–18
Current assets	$9,883	$9,384	$8,755	$7,865	$6,685	$5,750	$5,334	$4,597	$4,057	$3,700
Current liabilities	7,592	6,872	6,175	5,417	4,605	4,163	4,032	3,588	2,921	2,894
Share owners' equity	8,200	7,362	6,587	5,943	5,253	4,617	4,172	3,774	3,420	3,106
Total capital invested	10,447	9,332	8,692	8,131	7,305	6,628	6,317	5,679	5,118	4,754
Earned on average total capital invested	17.3%	17.6%	16.3%	15.8%	15.1%	12.5%	13.4%	13.7%	12.7%	12.3%
Total assets	$18,511	$16,644	$15,036	$13,697	$12,050	$10,741	$10,220	$9,089	$8,051	$7,472
Property, plant and equipment additions	$1,948	$1,262	$1,055	$823	$740	$588	$813	$735	$501	$711
Employees—average worldwide	402,000	405,000	401,000	384,000	380,000	380,000	409,000	392,000	373,000	366,000
Gross national product (current $ billions)	2,626	2,414	2,128	1,900	1,702	1,529	1,413	1,307	1,171	1,063
Common stock performance	$44–63			General Electric common share price						$47–67
	759–1000			Dow Jones Industrial Index						798–950
	111–161			Standard & Poor's Industrial Index						99–116

Source: General Electric annual report, 1980; U.S. Department of Commerce for GNP; Moody's.

Exhibit 5 Financial statements, 1979 and 1980 ($ millions).

Balance Sheets	1980	1979
Assets		
Cash	$1,601	$1,904
Marketable securities	600	672
Current receivables	4,339	3,647
Inventories	3,343	3,161
Current assets	9,883	9,384
Property, plant, and equipment	5,780	4,613
Investments	1,820	1,691
Other assets	1,028	956
Total assets	$18,511	$16,644
Liabilities and Equity		
Short-term borrowings	$1,093	$871
Accounts payable	1,671	1,477
Progress collections and price adjustments accrued	2,084	1,957
Dividends payable	170	159
Taxes accrued	628	655
Other costs and expenses accrued	1,946	1,753
Current liabilities	7,592	6,872
Long-term borrowings	1,000	947
Other liabilities	1,565	1,311
Total liabilities	$10,157	$9,130
Minority interest in equity of consolidated affiliates	154	152
Common stock	579	579
Amounts received for stock in excess of par value	659	656
Retained earnings	7,151	6,307
	$8,389	$7,542
Deduct common stock held in treasury	(189)	(190)
Total share owners' equity	8,200	7,362
Total liabilities and equity	$18,511	$16,644

Income Statements	1980	1979
Sales		
Sales of products and services to customers	$24,959	$22,461
Operating costs		
Cost of goods sold	17,751	15,991
Selling, general and administrative expense	4,258	3,716
Depreciation, depletion and amortization	707	624
Operating costs	$22,716	$20,331
Operating margin	2,243	2,130
Other income	564	519
Interest and other financial charges	(314)	(258)
Earnings		
Earnings before income taxes and minority interest	2,493	2,391
Provision for income taxes	(958)	(953)
Minority interest in earnings of consolidated affiliates	(21)	(29)
Net earnings applicable to common stock	$1,514	$1,409
Earnings per common share (in dollars)	$6.65	$6.20
Dividends declared per common share (in dollars)	$2.95	$2.75
Operating margin as a percentage of sales	9.0%	9.5%
Net earnings as a percentage of sales	6.1%	6.3%

lieve we'll really have the same product mix in view of even the most obvious technological changes we can see ahead? Do you really think that international mix will hold, despite the faster growth of many world markets? And that we can have the same strategy of leveraging earnings over sales, just as if that last tenth of a point was as easy to achieve as the first?

It's that contradiction of a steady-state GE and a rapidly changing world that gives us, I think, the key strategic issue as we enter the '80s. How do we attain the vision now to reject that static forecast and then take the strategic actions that will move us forward in the '80s, just as we did in the '70s?

Fink next disputed the basis on which the existing strategic plans had projected growth:

Back in '68 we earned 4½ percent on sales, by '74 it was 5 percent, 6 percent in '78, and the LRFs [long-range forecasts] say 7 percent in 1984, but it doesn't follow that just because the company went from 5 percent to 6 percent in the '70s, it will easily move up to 7 percent in the '80s.

There are several reasons for caution. First, most of our SBUs, urged on by last year's business development challenge, carry the expense burden of major investment plans. And finally, we'll be twice as dependent on productivity, rather than price, for inflation recovery. So, under these circumstances, we certainly must consider the 7 percent at risk.

Just suppose we hold our ROS at the current 6 percent level. The difference in '84 would be almost $400 million of net income and widening each year. To compensate for that shortfall, we would have to add something like $6–$7 billion of sales. That's another sector.

These are big increments. They aren't going to be achieved by simple extensions of our current businesses. They do demand a period of unprecedented business development in the '80s. Unprecedented business development. Consider what that has to mean to a company that has already made the largest acquisition in U.S. business history; that has produced more patentable inventions than any other company in the world; and that already is the largest diversified corporation on *Fortune* 500 list.

Realigning GE's Resources

The first step to generating unprecedented business growth in the 1980s was to select the target areas with the greatest potential for GE. In-depth corporate-planning staff analysis led to the definition of six broad business areas. These areas, called *arenas*, were identified as follows:

- Energy
- Communication, information, and sensing
- Energy applications-productivity
- Materials and resources
- Transportation and propulsion
- Pervasive services (nonproduct-related services such a financial, distribution, and construction)

A common characteristic of the arenas was that they cut across sector organizational lines. Fink described the dilemma and indicated a need for new approaches:

> How are we going to tackle these new opportunities which cut across organization lines? Sometimes the solution is to reorganize and collect those synergistic businesses under single management. But there are too many opportunities out there. We'd have to reorganize every three days just to keep up with them.
>
> How many times have you heard customers, or even competitors, say, "If you guys could only get your act together!" Well, we're going to have to get our act together if we're to tackle some of these new opportunities. We're going to have to develop coventuring techniques, motivation and measurement techniques that have thus far eluded us. It won't come easy; it's nontraditional. It's not traditional for those of us who learned to manage at the John Wayne school of rugged individualism.

To get GE's "act together," the CEO issued explicit arena-related challenges to launch the 1981 planning cycle. Each challenge listed the specific sectors and corporate staff units to be involved and designated the sector responsible to lead the effort. One of the specific challenges related to the energy applications-productivity arena, for example, was to develop a strategic business plan to exploit the growing opportunities associated with factory automation and robotics. The industrial products and components sector, which was already heavily involved with factory automation, was given lead responsibility for this factory of the future challenge. Support roles were assigned to the information and communications systems group (a unit in the technical systems and materials sector) because of its experience with mobile communications, and to the corporate production and operating services staff unit, because of its responsibility for improving productivity within GE itself.

Just how this cross-organizational business development would function still had to be worked out. Jones clearly viewed this approach as preliminary and evolving: "I don't want operating managers worrying about arenas for a while. At this point in time, arenas are for our use at the corporate level. They help to give us another view of the company." The provisional nature of the arena approach was also indicated in the following comment by a senior executive: "The success or failure of the arena concept will depend to a great extent on how hard corporate management pushes it."

The Next Steps

The General Electric Jack Welch was preparing to lead in 1981 was in the midst of actively probing a panoply of new technology businesses. Lively discussions were being held in offices throughout the company on what GE should do about the factory of the future, the office of the future, the house of the future, the electric car, synthetic fuel, and the like. The list of opportunities seemed endless. Clearly, GE would have to make some hard choices. In this connection, Welch was reported to have said: "My biggest challenge will be to put enough money on the right gambles and to put no money on the wrong ones. But I don't want to sprinkle money over everything."[11]

What kind of management system would he need to meet this challenge? Jack Welch had used SBU and sector planning to build businesses and later had a hand in shaping GE's approach to strategic management. He laid to rest any idea of dismantling the apparatus in place: "GE was a well-run company before anyone ever heard of John Welch. Most of the corporate revolutions you hear about are when a guy moves from company X to company Y and tips it upside down. Sometimes it works and sometimes it doesn't. That won't happen here."

Despite this commitment, Welch was inheriting a management system undergoing major changes. Crossroad choices would have to be made here as well. The 1981 management audit indicated numerous important management system issues for attention:

- Can the sectors as presently defined accommodate the size and diversity of company operations in 1985? In 1990? Alternatives?
- The 1981 corporate strategy was developed through an arena segmentation that is deliberately different from the GE sector segmentation. Is this useful to the CEO in developing a vision for the company? Will it be a workable approach that leads to truly integrated strategies?
- Is there a better way than our international integration process to determine and pursue company international objectives?

How these management system issues were handled would be influenced by the broad substantive issues GE faced. While opinions differed as to priorities, senior managers agreed on several key challenges. Reg Jones put dealing with inflation at the top of his list. Increasing productivity and increasing international business were also high on his and everyone else's list of major issues. For many senior executives, increasing entrepreneurship and new ventures in GE were also a major challenge in view of the company's ambitious growth goals.

The list of issues—both those having to do with substance and those having to do with management systems—was long, far too long for all to be dealt with in depth. Management would have to be selective in choosing areas for attention. One executive neatly summed up his views of the situation with the comment: "GE is going to be a very exciting company these next few years. You can just feel the electricity in the air."

---

11. *Business Week*, March 16, 1981.

General Electric: 1984

When Jack Welch took office in April 1981 as the new chairman and chief executive officer of General Electric, he described his vision for the company he was going to lead:

> A decade from now I would like General Electric to be perceived as a unique, high-spirited, entrepreneurial enterprise . . . a company known around the world for its unmatched level of excellence. I want General Electric to be the most profitable highly diversified company on earth, with world-quality leadership in every one of its product lines.

By 1984, Welch had regrouped sectors, invested heavily in both new and core businesses, divested from other GE businesses, changed the company's approach to planning, and cut back staff. According to the 1984 annual report:

> Across your company, a strategy has been formulated, with clear focus on our key businesses and where they're going. The resources are in place to get them there. And most important, an atmosphere, a culture, is being created where concepts like agility, excellence, and entrepreneurship—the real stuff of world competitiveness—are coming to life.

The results were impressive. Profits rose from $1.5 billion in 1980, the year before Welch became CEO, to $2.3 billion in 1984. The increase in earnings, credited to improve operating margins, had occurred despite only slight increases in sales over the same period. Increased profits also had gone hand-in-hand with increased investment in future growth. Funds for research and development programs in 1984 were at a record $2.3 billion, over 8 percent of sales. (Exhibit 1 contains a financial summary.)

GE was often in the news, and a favorite pastime of the business press was to evaluate Welch's actions and plans. One of these articles (*Forbes*, March 26, 1984) concluded with an admission by Welch that he was "only at the 15 percent mark of what he intends to do." He did not elaborate on the specifics of the 85 percent that remained to be accomplished. Regardless of the direction he would take in the future, virtually everyone agreed that GE had changed during Welch's first four years.

Exhibit 1A Five-year statistical summary, 1980–84 ($ millions, except per share amounts).

	1984	1983	1982	1981	1980
Sales of products and services to customers	$ 27,947	$ 26,797	$ 26,500	$ 27,240	$ 24,959
Operating margin	2,845	2,549	2,405	2,447	2,243
Operating margin as a percentage of sales	10.2%	9.5%	9.1%	9.0%	9.0%
Earnings before business restructurings, income taxes, and minority interest	3,501	3,063	2,753	2,660	2,493
Net earnings	2,280	2,024	1,817	1,652	1,514
Net earnings as a percentage of sales	8.2%	7.6%	6.9%	6.1%	6.1%
Net earnings on average share owners' equity	19.1%	18.9%	18.8%	19.1%	19.5%
Net earnings per share	$ 5.03	$ 4.45	$ 4.00	$ 3.63	$ 3.33
Dividends declared per share	$ 2.05	$ 1.875	$ 1.675	$ 1.575	$ 1.475
Total assets	$ 24,730	$ 23,288	$ 21,615	$ 20,942	$ 18,511
Property, plant, and equipment additions	2,488	1,721	1,608	2,025	1,948
Average employment—worldwide	330,000	340,000	367,000	404,000	402,000
—United States	241,000	245,000	261,000	289,000	285,000
Gross national product (current $ billions)	$ 3,661	$ 3,305	$ 3,073	$ 2,938	$ 2,626
Common Stock Performance					
GE common share price	$59⅜–48¼	$58⅞–45⅜	$ 50–27½	$35–25⅝	$ 31½–22
Dow Jones Industrial Average	1287–1087	1287–1027	1070–777	1024–824	1000–759
Standard & Poor's Industrial Index	170–147	173–138	143–102	138–113	140–98

Source: General Electric annual report, 1984; U.S. Department of Commerce for GNP; Moody's.

Exhibit 1B   Industry and geographic segment information ($ millions).

	Total revenues					Net Earnings	
	1984	1983	1982	1981	1980	1984	1983
Consumer products	$ 3,858	$ 3,741	$ 3,943	$ 4,202	$ 3,998	$ 228	$ 163
Major appliances	3,650	3,078	2,751	3,132	3,012	223	156
Industrial systems	4,274	4,228	4,705	5,364	4,907	73	84
Power systems	6,010	5,878	6,093	6,015	5,703	486	439
Aircraft engines	3,835	3,495	3,140	2,950	2,660	251	196
Materials	2,241	2,060	1,791	2,050	1,877	262	182
Technical products and services	4,803	3,825	3,546	3,005	2,424	232	210
Financial services[a]	448	397	286	239	193	336	285
Natural resources	609	1,579	1,575	1,722	1,374	117	301
Corporate items and eliminations	(792)	(598)	(638)	(825)	(625)	72	8
Total	$28,936	$27,681	$27,192	$27,854	$25,523	$2,280	$2,024
Outside the United States	$ 7,703	$ 9,148	$ 9,412	$10,190	$ 9,597	$ 419	$ 668

a. Note 4 of 1984 and 1982 annual reports explains GE's income from financial services and other sources as follows:

Other Income ($ millions)	1984	1983	1982	1981	1980
GECC	$329	$271	$205	$129	$115
Marketable securities and bank deposits	323	239	239	230	229
Royalty and technical assets	83	58	60	59	52
Customer financing	75	69	58	80	72
Other items	179	247	130	116	95
Total	$989	$884	$692	$614	$564

The Early Months

When Jack Welch took over the reins of office, he made it clear that anything and everything was open to question. For example, what would the role of sectors be? How would strategic planning change? Would acquisitions play a greater or lesser role than in the past compared to internal development? Would the corporate staff play a greater or lesser role in transforming GE? Different answers to these questions would vie for attention and support, with Welch as the final arbiter.

His first move was to travel throughout the $28 billion GE territory, meeting people, looking at operations and asking questions. When he returned to corporate headquarters in Fairfield, Connecticut, it was with a firmer idea of how he would proceed on his course.

Several months later, in early August, Welch announced a major restructuring of GE's organization, which had been in place since 1977. Two new sectors were created to implement the firm's commitment to grow its microe-

Net Earnings			Assets			Plant, property, and equipment additions			Depreciation, depletion, and amortization		
1982	1981	1980	1984	1983	1982	1984	1983	1982	1984	1983	1982
$ 146	$ 225	$ 241	$ 2,382	$ 2,297	$ 1,997	$ 283	$ 235	$ 180	$ 143	$ 120	$124
79	82	104	1,370	1,030	1,101	111	80	78	75	68	73
148	212	218	2,670	2,569	2,478	264	228	251	151	158	139
384	242	223	3,689	3,242	3,574	243	252	228	179	173	185
161	149	141	3,317	2,523	2,174	356	218	140	136	129	93
148	189	170	2,362	2,030	1,682	425	231	243	149	147	120
218	144	99	2,778	2,052	1,698	340	216	198	166	124	106
203	145	126	2,312	1,929	1,634	—	—	—	—	—	—
218	284	224	946	2,558	2,565	347	162	237	67	122	114
12	(20)	(32)	2,904	3,058	2,712	119	99	53	34	43	30
$1,817	$1,652	$1,514	$24,730	$23,288	$21,615	$2,488	$1,721	$1,608	$1,100	$1,084	$984
$ 680	$ 574	$ 639									

lectronics and other technology-related businesses and to develop opportunities in its financial and information-service businesses. The two sectors were called "Technical Systems" and "Services and Materials." (See Exhibit 2A on page 298 for the new organizational structure.)

The Technical Systems Sector combined all of GE's business units that made intensive use of microelectronics, such as industrial electronics, advanced microelectronics, medical systems, mobile communications, and aerospace. As such, the sector contained nearly all activities that were critically involved in GE's "Factory of the Future" strategy.

Services and Materials combined some of GE's fastest growing businesses, including: GE Credit Corp. (GECC), whose recent earnings had been growing 18 percent annually; GE Information Services Co. (GEISCO), whose sales had been increasing 24 percent annually over the past ten years; and the Engineering Materials Group, which had been growing at 20 percent annually. In addition to pursuing growth, the sector was to seek opportunities for integrating GE's credit and information services offerings and operations.

This change in the sector structure was coupled with a new approach to planning. Strategic-planning reviews under Welch marked a major departure from earlier practice in two respects. First, top management dealt directly with the strategic business units (SBUs) and not with the sectors. In place of the larger meetings held in the past, Welch involved only the SBU manager and the responsible vice chairman in the review. Second, he directed the review around key issues for each business and not around comprehensive strategic documentation or planning concepts. For example, one issue that was raised

Exhibit 1C   Financial condition ($ millions).

	As of December 31	
	1984	1983
Assets		
Cash	$ 1,859	$ 1,828
Marketable securities	514	677
Current receivables	5,509	5,249
Inventories	3,670	3,158
Current assets	$11,552	$10,912
Property, plant and equipment—net	7,690	7,697
Investments	3,717	2,945
Other assets	1,771	1,734
Total assets	$24,730	$23,288
Liabilities and equity		
Short-term borrowings	$ 1,047	$ 1,016
Accounts payable	1,931	1,993
Progress collections and price adjustments accrued	2,403	2,551
Dividends payable	250	228
Taxes accrued	673	685
Other costs and expenses accrued	2,303	2,215
Current liabilities	$ 8,607	$ 8,688
Long-term borrowings	753	915
Other liabilities	2,668	2,247
Total liabilities	$12,028	$11,850
Minority interest in equity of consolidated affiliates	$ 129	$ 168
Common stock	$ 579	$ 579
Other capital	640	657
Retained earnings	11,667	10,317
Less common stock held in treasury	(313)	(283)
Total share owners' equity	$12,573	$11,270
Total liabilities and equity	$24,730	$23,288

repeatedly in these early reviews was what each SBU would be doing to benefit GE in 1990.

    Some of Welch's reasoning for these changes was disclosed in a classroom discussion at the Harvard Business School on April 27, 1981:[1]

1. General Electric, Jack Welch, 1–182–024.

One of the things that's happened is with our planning system. It was dynamite when we first put it in. The thinking was fresh; the form was little—the format got no points—it was idea-oriented. Then we hired a head of planning, and he hired two vice presidents and then he hired a planner, and then the books got thicker, and the printing got more sophisticated and the covers got harder and the drawings got better. The meetings kept getting larger with as many as sixteen to eighteen people involved. Nobody can say anything with that many people around.

So one of the things that we have put into place is a way to achieve more candor, more constructive conflict. So we've gone to what we're going to call CEO[2] meetings, where the three of us will have meetings with SBU managers, one on three, two on three, in a small room.

Welch did not believe at the time that one could describe an overall strategy for a company like GE. He said:

Everyone likes to ask me what's the strategy for General Electric. Well, how can you have a strategy for a company that in the last five months has committed a billion and a half dollars in Montgomery, Alabama, for plastics plants, has made five acquisitions of software companies, has put $300 million into Erie, Pennsylvania, to expand a locomotive operation, has built a microelectronics center in North Carolina, has opened a new copper-exploration venture in Chile with Getty. There is no neat bow one can put on this.

But one can set an objective, one central theme to run through every bone of that company, every corner of it, every person in it, and that is: look at where you are in '82, where you'll be in '85, and probably, more importantly, where you'll be in '90. The issue facing every one of the people that manage our business is: can you be number one or number two in the game you're going to play, in the war you're going to wage, in the skirmish you're going to be in? Can you clearly go to war, go to the skirmish, with good equipment, good arms, good troops, with anything else you want to use as a metaphor? Can you play in that arena as a number one or number two player?[3]

For Welch, being number one or number two called for a stress on quality and excellence. He made the following comments to GE managers early in his tenure:

To me quality and excellence mean being better than the best. This achievement requires an introspective assessment of everything we are, do, say or make, and an honest inquiry, "Are we better than the best?" If we aren't, we should ask ourselves, "What will it take?," then quantify the energy and resources required to get there. If the economics, the environment or our abilities determine that we can't get there, we must take the same spirited action to disengage ourselves from that which we can't make better than the best.

2. Corporate Executive Office: Chairman Welch, Vice Chairman J. Burlingame, and Vice Chairman E. Hood.
3. Transcript #5–383–022, comments to a class of Harvard Business School students, December 4, 1981.

Becoming Number One or Number Two

During his first four years, Welch pursued his plan for being "better than the best" by building businesses through acquisition and internal development and by exiting businesses that could not meet the test of being number one or number two. Within this broad spectrum of efforts to reallocate GE's resources, his primary concern was in building those areas designated for growth: microelectronics and financial/information services. These would be the businesses that would most change GE from its current configuration.

Building Growth Businesses

One growth area which was targeted for development was factory automation. Estimating the world market for automation at $30 billion by the early 1990s, GE announced in 1981 that it would spend $500 million to become a "world supermarket of automation."

James A. Baker, the Sector Executive of Technical Systems who became the oft-quoted spokesman for the company's move toward automation, referred to the concept as the "Factory of the Future." Baker warned industry leaders that they would have to "automate, emigrate or evaporate." He spoke of the need for automation and the part GE would play:

> Automation is the last best hope for American industry and must be pursued no matter what the cost. The choice is biting the bullet or biting the dust. . . . [T]here are few options left. And what we're telling you is that we can do it better than anyone else.[4]

The Calma and Intersil acquisitions, made several months before Welch took office, were purchased to fill in some of the gaps in GE's high-technology capabilities. Calma was the world's fourth largest manufacturer of CAD (computer-aided design) systems and produced CAM (computer-aided manufacturing) systems as well. CAD/CAM systems, with the capability for cutting production time in half, would provide the operating mechanisms for the Factory of the Future. Calma, growing at a rate of 40 percent annually, was purchased for $100 million down and $70 million to be paid later from earnings.

Intersil, one of the major manufacturers of integrated circuits in the world, was purchased for $235 million. The acquisition was GE's second entry into the integrated-circuit industry. It had been one of the first manufacturers of integrated circuits nearly twenty years before, but had exited the business when it sold its mainframe computer business in 1970. Intersil provided state-of-the-art semiconductor technologies for GE and non-GE products and systems.

The highly touted success of Japanese manufacturing seemed to assure major growth for factory automation in the Western world. Notwithstanding this favorable outlook, GE was still looking for a breakthrough in the field. Its 1983 annual report stated that the large development expenses associated with its

---

4. *Stock Market Magazine*, April–May 1982.

drive for world leadership in automation, coupled with flat sales in industrial electronics because of the slow economic recovery, had caused losses of nearly $40 million during the year. In 1984, a similar loss was reported on "modestly improved revenues."

Another area that GE had targeted for high-technology growth was medical systems. GE was the number one manufacturer of diagnostic-imaging equipment worldwide. In the early 1970s, GE had turned its lackluster X-ray business around by putting an advanced CAT (computer-assisted tomography) scanner on the market, which soon had worldwide market share approaching 70 percent. In the early 1980s, GE developed a Nuclear Magnetic Resonance (NMR or MR) imaging device that used a powerful magnet to produce cross-section photos of the body's tissue, painlessly, without X-rays or surgery. An MR machine was able to pinpoint areas missed by a CAT scan, since it could "see" through solid mass.

An indication of GE's competitive strength in the field was given in the following account about Johnson & Johnson's Technicare Corp. (*Business Week*, May 14, 1984): "In MR scanners, for instance, GE's Welch makes no bones about his willingness to spend whatever it takes to be the leader. Technicare President Joseph G. Teague, however, says: 'We don't have it as a realistic strategy to be No. 1,' in the U.S. in several years. Matching GE's expenditures dollar for dollar, he adds, could be 'frivolous and very expensive'."

In addition to the MR scanner, the medical-systems division was developing a lower-cost, simpler version of its CAT scanner. Total funds invested in both projects were over $100 million.

GE carried the "supermarket" concept over to its information services, with the goal of becoming a "supermarket of software services." GEISCO (General Electric Information Services Company) had launched a program to acquire computer software companies to strengthen its business portfolio in five target areas: banking, manufacturing, financial services, management reporting, and energy. Total funds for acquisitions and investments in key service businesses amounted to $650 million in 1983.

Building Core Businesses

Despite all the investments in the more glamorous growth businesses, GE did not ignore its older, core businesses where special opportunities could be found. In practice, many of these opportunities were connected to GE's high-technology thrust into the Factory of the Future. As one sector executive noted: "We never appreciated just how profitable a 2 percent growth business could be when automated."

In a speech in 1982 to the Association of Iron and Steel Engineers on the topic of revamping basic industry, James Baker advised his audience: "Go back to your mills. Look at the operation as if you were preparing to serve a growth market and ask yourself if its yield . . . and particularly its quality . . . is what it should be."

GE itself took Baker's advice, automating many of its older plants to keep them number one or number two. A $300 million project to automate the firm's seventy-year-old locomotive facilities in Erie, Pennsylvania, was the largest such investment in GE's history.

Between 1980 and 1983, the company spent close to $500 million modernizing its major appliance group. A $38.6 million investment set up a CIM (computer-integrated manufacturing) system in the dishwasher plant, automating production from order to delivery. The showcase factory was to be a model for other appliance operations, like the refrigerator plant, which was scheduled to be gutted and refitted for robot assembly at a cost of $100 million. Another $135 million was slated to expand and automate the production of a new rotary compressor for use in GE refrigerators and small air conditioners. Additional investments of a similar nature were planned for the next four years in the amount of $800 million.

The locomotive and dishwasher units were named by *Fortune* (May 28, 1984) as being among America's ten best-managed, most efficient factories. The article said about the automation of the locomotive plant: "The payoff has already been impressive: Automation has saved the huge Erie works from extinction and propelled GE into the front ranks of the world's locomotive manufacturers."

In some cases, business development was more than investments in plant and equipment; it was a shift in the manufacturing base. For example, the decision to consolidate GE's lamp operations and invest $250 million to modernize production resulted in the closing of ten plants in five states and a reduction of 1,400 employees in the work force.

Exiting Businesses

While GE was involved in building businesses, it was also taking a hard look at those businesses that could not meet the challenge of being number one or number two. If the analysis showed top management that additional investments could not promote a good return and competitive success, the decision was made to divest. As a result, GE sold off 118 businesses from 1981 through 1983, for more than $3.5 billion.

One of the most newsworthy divestitures was the sale of Utah International, an Australian coal property that had been a sector by itself, for $2.4 billion. The sale was announced in October 1983, and was finalized in April, 1984. *Forbes* (March 26, 1984) commented on the sale: "Utah International was a highly profitable property producing coking coal, but GE saw no future in it. Vice Chairman John Burlingame, one of Welch's former rivals for the top job, handled the negotiations with the Australians and says, "There are better places that we would rather put our money and effort. The more so since Utah's main market, coking coal for steel, is depressed and in surplus capacity." GE kept just one part of Utah, Ladd Petroleum, as insurance for GE's plastics needs.

Another move that caused a stir in the press at the end of 1983 was the sale of GE's housewares division to Black & Decker for $300 million in cash and notes. The division, which produced small appliances such as irons and toaster ovens, had been part of GE since the early 1900s. GE explained that the divestiture was made to allow the consumer sector to concentrate its resources in the major appliance line. Even though GE had had the dominant market share in small appliances, its profits were still below company averages.

In 1982, GE also began exiting from one of its more recent business entries: nuclear-plant construction. The company accepted no new plant orders, agreeing to fulfill a backlog of orders stretching into the 1990s. Because of earlier commitments, it would remain in the nuclear-fuel business and the nuclear-plant servicing business after the backlog was fulfilled.

Other divestitures included the sale of all but one of GE's broadcasting outfits, spurred by the success of competitors. Vulnerability to housing cycles was the factor in the sale of the residential central air-conditioning business to the Trane Company for $150 million in cash and 15 percent of Trane stock. GE decided to remain in the small air-conditioner business (units for windows and walls) because of its strong competitive position.

The Three-Circle Concept

As GE built and exited businesses, Jack Welch grappled with the problem of finding a concise way to talk about GE to managers and outsiders. He wanted a concept that would have strategic meaning for GE as well as provide a simple way to describe what the company *was* as well as what it *was not.*

As Welch and corporate management looked at potential acquisitions and divestitures in 1983, a notion of major business configuration began to emerge. The result was a conceptualization of the company as competing in three areas.

In the three-circle concept, as it came to be called, all businesses were divided into (1) core, (2) high-technology, or (3) services areas. *Only* businesses that dominated their markets would be placed in one circle or another. Fifteen businesses qualified (see Figure A). Those outside these circles—the businesses that did not meet the criteria of being number one or number two—either had to come up with a strategy to get in a circle or be divested.

Investment planning became aligned to the three-circle concept. Welch announced the strategies in the 1983 annual report. The focus for the six core businesses was "reinvestment in productivity and quality." For the five high-tech businesses, it was to "make certain these businesses stay on the leading edge through a combination of synergistic acquisitions and substantial investments in R&D." In the key-service businesses, the strategy was to "grow these opportunities by adding outstanding people, who often can create new ventures all by themselves, and by making contiguous acquisitions."

Welch said of the three-circle concept:

> We have our hands on a simple, understandable strategy for where we are, where we are not, where we can't find a solution and where we have to disengage. We have to get used to the idea that disengaging does not mean bad people or bad management—it's a bad situation, and we can't tie up good resources, good dollars, chasing it.

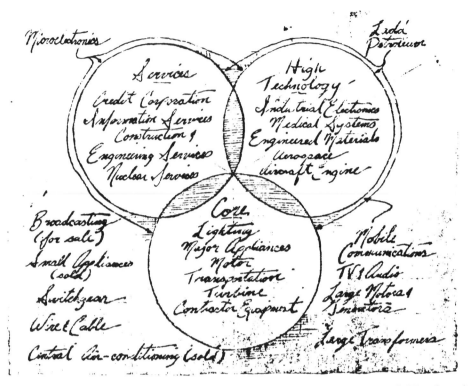

Figure A The shape of the new GE. Jack Welch's shorthand rundown of GE is based on three circles, covering the traditional "core" businesses (around 33% of profits), the high-technology businesses (30% but rising) and the services (29%). Around these main groupings lie the remainder of the businesses. Some are profitable, some lose money. Among them, they account for around 18% of sales. *Source: Forbes,* March 25, 1984. (Reprinted by permission of *Forbes* Magazine, © 1984 Forbes, Inc.)

In GE's thinking, the three circles were interrelated. The core businesses needed advanced process technology and strong service offerings to improve their competitiveness. High-tech companies served customers who were looking for solutions to problems as well as products, so that a linkage with services was important for maintaining a competitive edge in the industry. And service businesses, in turn, could not remain competitive without the benefits of the latest technology.

The Changing GE Organization

In addition to the evolution of GE's strategy, structural and administrative changes had taken place under Welch's chairmanship. One area that had received a good deal of press coverage was destaffing. Other important areas of change were planning, organization structure, and incentives.

Destaffing

When Jack Welch took office, the U.S. economy was in its deepest decline since the Great Depression. In addition to this external pressure, Welch came to the chairman's office with the sense that GE's bureaucracy and the levels of organization and staff had grown too large. As a result, he placed a great deal of emphasis on what became known as destaffing. From 1980 to 1984, the total work force was reduced from 402,000 to 330,000. Of this total, about 37 percent could be attributed to divestitures of businesses. The remaining reductions represented a conscious effort to reduce staff and levels of organization.

These efforts had earned Welch the nickname of "Neutron Jack" in the press, an allusion to the neutron bomb, which wiped out people while leaving the buildings intact. Although Welch believed the label to be exaggerated, he was convinced that a company the size of GE needed to stay "lean and agile" to be competitive. Welch acknowledged that becoming "lean" went hand-in-hand with destaffing, but went on to state that GE had no intention of becoming "mean" in the process. He felt GE had a responsibility to people who were not needed, and that any action should "pass the fairness test that we'd like to be treated with ourselves." In this connection, *Crain's Cleveland Business* (July 11, 1983), conceded that GE had used a "humane ax," in laying off 1,500 Ohio workers. The article pointed to the firm's offers of job counseling and placement alternatives and its efforts to explain the "inescapable necessity of it all."

Planning

As noted above, two changes Welch had made in the planning process were to reinstate direct SBU reviews and to focus the reviews around key issues. Welch also advocated less reliance on staff. The planning staff of 200 in 1980 had been cut in half by 1984. The purpose was to have "general managers talking to general managers about strategy, rather than planners talking to planners."

In line with this, Welch had dropped the requirement that every business have a strategy approved each year. A business in stable condition with an approved strategy in place would only have to be reviewed every two to three years. A business in a dynamic environment with changing strategies would be under continuous review.

These changes were explained by Mike Carpenter, GE's recently hired vice president of corporate planning. Carpenter, who had spent the previous decade as a vice president of the Boston Consulting Group, said:

> I've tried to separate strategy and planning. Strategy is thinking through the basics of a business; planning is developing programs to support these strategies. I've been trying to put more emphasis on strategies and less on

formal planning. Most of my staff is spending its time looking for acquisitions. When we do get involved in SBU strategies, it's as a member of the team working to develop viable, competitive strategies for the business. We spend little staff time consolidating or comparing plan books.

Many of the changes in planning were begun before I joined the company. The objectives of the changes are to debureaucratize the process, focus the process on strategy, make it an ongoing process responsive to the time-frame needs of the business, make it the general manager's process, not the planner's process, and make it selective. This has implied some significant changes for the role of my organization. The most important being that we are no longer the corporate policeman, and our relationship with the SBUs is cooperative, not adversarial.

Organization Structure

When Jack Welch became chairman in 1981, General Electric was administered by six sector organizations reporting to the Corporate Executive Office. By 1984, the number of sectors had been reduced to four and several major businesses reported directly to the CEO. As shown in Exhibit 2B, medical systems, financial services, and plastics were among the businesses reporting to the CEO. A senior executive commented: "No one is quite sure what the role of the sectors will be in the future. My hunch is that they will slowly disappear and eventually the fifteen major businesses that fall within the three circles will all report directly to the Corporate Executive Office."

In mid-1984, John Burlingame, one of the vice chairmen, announced his planned retirement at the end of the year. Larry Bossidy, formerly Sector Executive for Services and Materials and the individual most often associated with the growth and success of the General Electric Credit Corporation, was promoted to the position of Vice Chairman and a member of the CEO.

Welch considered choosing good people to be his most important job. Accordingly, he extended and increased his role in both the selection and review of key managers.

Incentives

In the area of incentives, Welch sought to institute new ways of recognizing employees for their individual contributions. For example, Corporate Executive Office (CEO) Awards were given to individuals who made special one-time contributions to a business venture, project, disposition, acquisition, etc.

Special Stock Option Awards were developed to help build long-term identification with the company for new people, to retain key individuals in an acquired company, to reward a long-term contribution to individuals not eligible for regular stock-option grants, and to induce individuals to either take or stay in an usually difficult or high-risk position.

Other incentives for key positions included restricted stock and special bonuses for meeting sales and income objectives in critical new businesses.

Welch's Philosophy

As the strategic moves and changes to organization and management processes took place during the four years of his chairmanship, Welch was forming a management philosophy. Over time, Welch had coalesced his thinking around ten key company values, which he described at a corporate officers meeting in the fall of 1983. Being number one or number two headed the list, followed by becoming and staying lean and agile. The remaining eight fell into three categories: how to get to the top, how to behave as a company to stay there, and how to fund the process.

Getting to the Top: Ownership, Stewardship, and Entrepreneurship

Welch believed that one of the keys to GE's success was a sense of pride in the company, such as that exhibited at several plants where employees wore tee-shirts reading "GE is ME." He called this ownership.

Ownership was a method of behavior that he tried to encourage by giving greater powers of delegation, by raising capital appropriations levels, and by holding fewer and faster reviews. His aim was to drive the ability to act further down in the organization.

> If we can think of ownership as just saying more "Grab it! Run with it! Take responsibility! Make the decision. Give the management awards. Make the sales plans. Do the things you want to do to run your business faster every day," we've got something.

Stewardship, which had been a popular word at GE for twenty years, was the responsibility that accompanied ownership. It was not only an obligation toward GE's assets, i.e., people, buildings, balance sheets, etc., but it was working at capacity to further the competitive success of the company. Welch said:

> Stewardship is an obligation. It's not some noblesse oblige attitude where people can work at 45–50 percent of capacity or believe they have lifetime employment. Stewardship is working at 100 percent to 150 percent. Stewardship in the end is what your jobs are all about. It's your challenge: to take the assets you have, drive them to newer and better heights through excellence, through taking charge, and make this enterprise better in 1990 than it is today.

Entrepreneurship was the kindling with which Welch wanted to start the fires of the other values leading to competitive success. To attain ownership and stewardship, he advocated that managers create and maintain an entrepreneurial environment and a sense of entrepreneurial responsibility.

Because the risks and rewards were not the same for entrepreneurship in a $30 billion enterprise as they were in a small company, he conceded that the term might be a misnomer. The concept, nonetheless, was essential to allow new ideas to surface and to create new ventures for the company.

Exhibit 2A Organization chart, 1981.

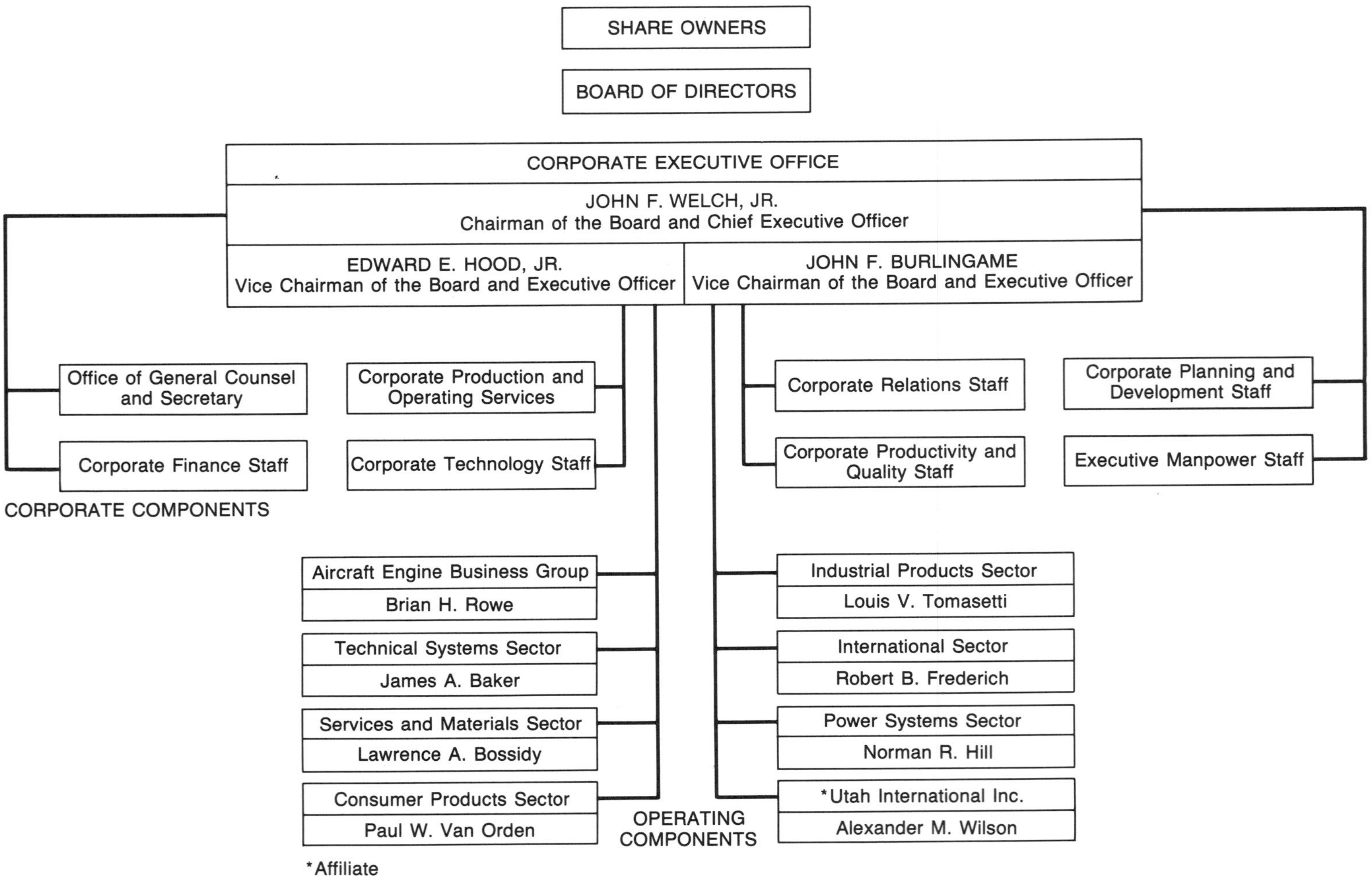

SHARE OWNERS

BOARD OF DIRECTORS

CORPORATE EXECUTIVE OFFICE

JOHN F. WELCH, JR.
Chairman of the Board and Chief Executive Officer

EDWARD E. HOOD, JR.
Vice Chairman of the Board and Executive Officer

JOHN F. BURLINGAME
Vice Chairman of the Board and Executive Officer

Corporate Planning and Development Staff

Executive Manpower Staff

Corporate Relations Staff

Corporate Productivity and Quality Staff

Office of General Counsel and Secretary

Corporate Finance Staff

Corporate Production and Operating Services

Corporate Technology Staff

CORPORATE COMPONENTS

Industrial Products Sector
Louis V. Tomasetti

International Sector
Robert B. Frederich

Power Systems Sector
Norman R. Hill

*Utah International Inc.
Alexander M. Wilson

Aircraft Engine Business Group
Brian H. Rowe

Technical Systems Sector
James A. Baker

Services and Materials Sector
Lawrence A. Bossidy

Consumer Products Sector
Paul W. Van Orden

OPERATING COMPONENTS

*Affiliate

298

Exhibit 2B Organization chart, 1984.

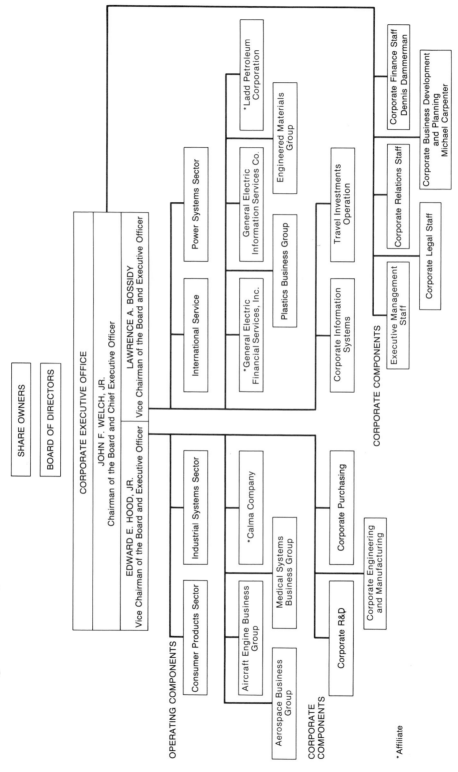

How to Behave:
Excellence, Quality, Reality and Candor, and Communications

Having a company ethic dedicated to ownership, stewardship, and entrepreneurship could get GE to the first spot in a tough, competitive world, according to Welch, but other values would keep it there.

Excellence, like ownership, was a method of behavior at the individual level. Welch suggested the best way to measure excellence was the "mirror test":

> This is the one, whether you're putting on make-up or shaving, where only you know whether or not the excellence is there—is absolutely at the heart of your everyday activity. You can't be at this level at all times, but you've got to keep driving yourself. Are you setting the standards of excellence? Are you demanding the very best of yourself?

Quality was accomplished by individual excellence on the part of every GE employee. The concept of product quality had always been central to GE's policy, but Welch wanted to push that value beyond the product to instill a commitment to quality as a pervasive way of life, to have an all-embracing concept that included products, services, fulfillment of citizen responsibilities, and communication to the outside world.

Excellence and quality could not be realized if there was no atmosphere allowing reality and candor. The early move to have one or two SBU managers meet with the CEO was made to foster a willingness to share problems and bring around a sense of trust in the corporate hierarchy. Welch believed that, at every level, each employee should have enough trust in his or her boss to seek a joint solution to a problem and should have enough self-confidence and belief in the company to approach that process with reality and candor. The trust element was critical to the concepts of quality and excellence.

In addition to the internal dialogue necessary for successful operations, Welch felt the communication of GE's strengths and values to the outside world was central to implementing the philosophy of GE. Understanding, embracing and being able to articulate to the financial and shareholder communities what GE was doing was essential to the success of the goal of remaining number one or number two. To understand and communicate GE's philosophy, Welch said: "You've got to embrace it, feel it, believe it. If you don't, you come back and recheck it and understand what we're doing. Without that group in Louisville or that group in Cleveland, everybody embracing what we're going to do, we haven't got a prayer."

Funding: The Investment Philosophy

The values that focused on getting to the top and staying there were necessary but insufficient without the financial support to bring them to fruition. The tenth value of Welch's management philosophy dealt with how to pay for competitive success.

Welch believed that all investments should be directed only to the markets that GE *could* dominate. Those markets that did not fit the long-term growth strategy would be abandoned. He set 15 percent as the overall annual growth rate, with the admonition that short-term investment decisions should not be made simply to meet the growth rate at the expense of long-term issues.

Reactions

In a company as large and diverse as General Electric, reactions to Jack Welch's first four years as CEO were bound to be varied. The following sample of comments from GE managers give some idea of the range of impressions and judgments to be found in the GE organization:

> "There was a lot of resentment to the destaffing in my department and Welch was feared. But personally, I welcomed it. I knew we had deadwood and I was happy that we were being forced to face up to it."

> "All the words sound great—entrepreneurship, ownership, risk taking— but at my level [subsection manager], it's making budget that still counts."

> "During the first two years, I didn't see much change. But then we got a new general manager who is right out of Welch's mold. Our business is now a different place—much more spirited, self-critical, and energetic."

> "I don't see much change. My business has been in the fast-moving part of the company, and we've been managed this way for years. I think that some of the older parts of the company may be feeling some change, but for me it's been a continuation of the way things have always been and the way they should be."

> "Welch has succeeded in keeping us from becoming complacent and is focusing our attention on worldwide competitors. That's an important accomplishment in a big company where we tend to become complacement and focus on our own organizations and promotions."

> "Many of the changes [in planning] have been excellent. But we are relying almost totally on people. That's fine until some of those people make big mistakes. Then we may miss not having those systematic plans."

> "The key issue for me is—what happens if you take a risk and fail. Welch is trying hard to convince us that it's OK, as at Halarc.[5] But I wonder. The people who get rewarded in a failure are those who recommend getting out, not those who recommended getting in."

Issues

Among the many issues faced by GE management since Jack Welch had become CEO in 1981, two had garnered a great deal of publicity. One had to do with the huge funds GE had accumulated for investment. The other concerned

---

5. See Appendix A for a description of the Halarc venture.

Welch's desire to increase the level of risk taking and entrepreneurship within the company.

The $5 Billion War Chest

At the end of 1983, GE had $2.5 billion in cash and securities. With the sale of Utah International, that amount surged to over $5 billion prompting questions about whether or not GE would join the current trend toward major acquisitions. Welch responded in the 1983 annual report: "The question has been raised: What will we do with the money? The short answer is: It's not going to burn a hole in our pocket."

In 1983, GE had used a database of 6,000 potential candidates to identify potential acquisition candidates. The business development staff conducted an in-depth analysis of more than 100 large candidates within this group, identifying only four as strategically and financially attractive.

Guidelines for analysis had been laid out by corporate planner Mike Carpenter. The most important criteria was that ownership by GE should increase shareholder value by causing the acquired company's growth rate or profitability (or both) to increase over what it otherwise would have been. He pointed out that the acquisition would have to create enough value to pay the acquisition premium, noting that premiums had increased to 50 percent from 20 percent in 1970. "Acquisitions take place in a marketplace like any other [business deal]," he said. "It's tough making good acquisitions when you have to pay a 50 percent premium."

To emphasize this point, Carpenter described how he and his staff had ruled out several large ($1 to $8 billion) high-technology candidates as overpriced. According to their analyses, the share-price premiums needed to complete these acquisitions placed in doubt GE's ability to earn an attractive return on its investment.

While Carpenter stressed that the highest return would come from those acquisitions that built from the strategic strengths of GE's existing businesses, he advised against limiting thinking to a certain size of possible acquisitions and whether or not they would fit neatly into the current GE boundary lines. "We can acquire businesses bigger than our existing ones," he said. "We can acquire businesses that cut across group or sector boundaries. We can acquire particular businesses from large companies. We can acquire companies where only specific pieces are of interest to us."

In the spring of 1984, GE Credit Corp. announced the purchase of Employers Reinsurance Corp. for $1.08 billion, expanding GE's financial-services activities. Mike Carpenter explained the thinking behind the acquisition and how the opportunity had become available:

> We have analyzed many financial services businesses in the last year or so, and reinsurance has consistently come near the top of the list in terms of growth, return on investment and competitive defensibility. It's a business GE knows through its Puritan Insurance Company [a subsidiary of GECC], although we have been a small player in the past. In looking at the

largest 250 financial services companies and screening them for business attractiveness and company performance (in terms of return on investment and growth), ERC was identified as a member of an elite group of top-performing financial-services companies. ERC is the number two or three reinsurer in the U.S. and has grown more rapidly and earned higher returns—a 24 percent return on equity in reinsurance—than the leader, General Re. Nevertheless, we're buying the company at the same multiple (1.9 times book value) that General Re shares sell for in the stock market at what we believe is at or close to the bottom of the reinsurance cycle.

Interestingly, the original idea for the ERC acquisition came from Puritan Insurance. At an early stage in the game, my organization got involved, tried to help them evaluate the acquisition and frame the issues that needed to be addressed before raising it with the CEO. But I think it is important to note that one of our smaller, farther-flung entities was the prime mover in the largest acquisition General Electric has made in recent years.

ERC became available when its parent, Getty Oil, was acquired by Texaco, which wanted to concentrate on historic businesses in the oil and gas industry. We negotiated with Texaco to buy ERC at a price we thought was fair.

Despite the ERC acquisition and numerous smaller acquisitions (GE had acquired over fifty businesses since 1981), it was still unclear how General Electric would spend its considerable cash reserves.

Internal Growth

Closely related to the problem of investing GE's cash reserves was the issue of encouraging internal growth, new business development, and entrepreneurship within the company. Jack Welch placed importance on these developments and attempted to foster them in several ways. One was to encourage investments in growth businesses. Another was to reinforce the organizational values of entrepreneurship, ownership, and stewardship. While still another was to change compensation practices.

In addition to these efforts, Welch had placed greater emphasis on new business ventures within the corporation. Although these ventures were not funded at the corporate level, the ventures served to focus attention on between sixty to eighty new business development efforts and their managers. Indeed Jack Welch often commented on the importance of ventures in developing managers:

> The ventures are far less important than the product of the processes, which are the people. By having high visibility on these people—each having their own P&L statement, their own game, competing against the world— we get a chance to look at how they perform. They can blow it and they lose a little money, it doesn't matter. We get a feel for who they are and what they can manage. We get far more out of the people end of ventures than we do out of the earnings end.

GE made a point of publicizing venture activities as one way of encouraging managers to propose their own ventures. For example, a recent issue of the

GE Monogram, the company magazine, highlighted three particular ventures (see Appendix A). Nevertheless, Jack Welch was probably correct that GE got less out of the earnings end of ventures than the people end. For on the earnings side, ventures not only faced the problems inherent in any start-up business, but had the added problems of being part of a big company and dealing with existing organizational boundaries. For example, the company's cogeneration venture had dealings with five GE businesses and nine departments. Finally, even if a venture were successful, there were problems of sufficient size. As one executive noted: "We have a problem with ventures because of our need to think big. At GE unless you can create a $150 million business, it's not going to affect things much. We can create lots of small businesses. The problem is in creating the $150 million departments, and even more important, in creating the groups and sectors of the future."

Financial Systems

While some of the problems in creating internal business development only pertained to ventures, many managers indicated that GE's financial systems had a more pervasive negative effect on entrepreneurship. As one manager noted, "More than ever before, we are being told to innovate and invest for the long haul. But our financial system tells us to make our quarterly and annual projections. At times, the profit pressure is intense."

Traditionally, GE's financial systems had centered around the annual budget for each operating unit. The preparation of these budgets, leading to a set of figures by December, began in July and involved extensive negotiation between the operating units, the intervening layers of management, and the corporate office. An operating unit's budgeted net income, the bottom line, had generally come to be regarded as a commitment that each general manager would meet "at all costs." Dennis Dammerman, GE's chief financial officer, described some of the problems that the company experienced with this approach to budgeting:

> The stress on making your numbers had some unfortunate consequences for us. First, because it was so important to meet your budgeted commitments, there was a lot of gaming going on on the part of the operating managers to get a low enough target. Then, once the budgets were set, some operating managers would resort to dysfunctional actions when necessary to meet their targets. For example, if a business experienced a downturn in demand, important development programs might be halted. This behavior obviously flies in the face of our efforts to make this a more entrepreneurial company.
>
> Jack Welch was also dissatisfied with a budgeting system that locked us into a set of figures prepared eighteen months in advance of their use. This practice didn't enable us to respond to new opportunities that arose in the interim.

To address these problems, two changes were introduced to GE's budgeting process. First, the controller's office prepared a set of financial objectives for each operating unit. These targets were based on an analysis of economic forecasts and of ongoing programs and commitments at each of the operating units. Although the operating units were free to suggest revisions to the proposed target, the intent was to reduce the amount of game playing and bargaining over targets and to establish targets that more realistically reflected each unit's prospects.

A second change in 1984 contributed further to realistic target setting. Relabeling budgets as operating plans, operating managers would now be free to propose a revision of the figures at any time that business conditions of the competitive situation changed significantly from the original assumptions. The intent of this change was to provide operating management with a more flexible structure under which he or she could respond to new opportunities or unexpected setbacks. Performance evaluation was made against the revised targets. The new approach also served to bring new developments to top management's attention.

Dennis Dammerman commented on these changes:

> The changes we have made in our financial system reflect Jack Welch's desires to have General Electric responsive to changes in the environment and to new opportunities, and to have important resource allocation trade-offs surface to the top of the organization.
>
> Overall, I would rate the underlying concepts of our new approach to be quite good. Our execution to date, however, has left a lot to be desired. One undesirable result has been the inclination of our operating units to call in changes without adequate documentation. And, as you might expect, we are more likely to receive calls from businesses in trouble than from those experiencing better-than-planned-for results. When the troubled businesses submit new operating plans, they often call for lower revenues, unchanged expense levels, and lower net income. Under the old system there was no question that people would respond to the lower sales forecast by cutting costs in order to meet net income. We seem to have lost some of the commitments to fixing problems that we used to have from our general managers.
>
> Despite these problems we are committed to making the concept of operating plans work, because we are convinced that it is consistent with developing a more responsive and entrepreneurial climate within the company.

Appendix A

Taking a Swing

Aaron. Ruth. Mays. Robinson. Killebrew. Mantle. The top six home-run hitters in baseball history. Hall of Famers all.

But fame comes in many guises. For these baseball immortals, it comes not only in slugging records, but also from being among the leaders in career strikeouts.

One reason, of course, is that the fiercer the swing a batter takes, the higher the risk of walking back to the dugout with his head down than circling the bases, doffing his cap, and collecting applause. The cautious hitters, the bunters, may not strike out as often, but their names and faces don't shown up on bronze plaques with the same frequency as those who take the big swing.

What follows are stories about three big swings taken by GE entrepreneurs.[1] One missed. The others connected—and it looks like they have a good chance of clearing the fences. Their technologies and markets are totally unrelated, yet they share one thing: an almost counter-cultural view of the risk/reward equation.

If GE is to continue to put distance between itself and the bunters of the business world, it *must* take the big swing with increasing frequency. That may mean some strikeouts along the way. But the prospects of hitting a home run make the risks worthwhile.

Halarc

In 1979, General Electric decided to reinvent the light bulb.

A small team of engineers and planners assembled in the back shops of GE's Lamp Products Division to bring life to a bold decision—skip the traditional low-volume commercial market, and take a $10 light bulb directly to price-sensitive consumers.

The design was complex, the risks clear.

If it worked, it could revolutionize a market that had hardly budged in a century. But it didn't. In the end, the venture failed, but the team won.

The halide arc lamp—or Halarc as it was called—was one of the hottest ideas on the board of GE's venture game since . . . well, since Edison first flipped the switch. Everyone knew that the odds on losing were high.

"This wasn't a case where everyone thought we had a sure thing," recalls Dr. Richard Kashnow, then product general manager for the Halarc Product Section. "The risk/reward equation all along was very clear. But we believed in Halarc and the value it offered consumers. We took a lot of pains to get across that careers wouldn't be on the line if it didn't work out."

The Halarc idea was to miniaturize a version of a highly sophisticated light source that offered three hard-to-get advantages: good color, high efficiency, compact size.

It could shine like a regular 150-watt bulb, last five times longer, and use only one-third the electricity. For consumers, the savings over the lifetime of the bulb were attractive—about $40 in typical markets, up to $75 in areas like New York City, where electricity costs were high.

---

1. Only one of the stories is reproduced here. The other two dealt with cogeneration and programmable controllers.
Source: Reproduced with permission from the *General Electric Monogram*, Spring 1984.

Back in 1979, it seemed the timing couldn't be better—smack in the middle of the decade's second energy crisis, with consumers clamoring for energy-saving devices.

As in most ventures, the team struggled through months of design failures and breakthroughs. A miniature electronic power supply had to be designed, so that the whole unit could be screwed into a regular incandescent socket.

The technology of the lamp design only permitted it to operate in base-down positions, such as in table lamps. A more versatile design, planned for the second phase of development, proved to be more difficult than anticipated. So the marketing plan was altered.

Finally, after two years of technical and market-niche modifications, Halarc went into a ten-month marketing test study in two cities—Des Moines, where it sold for roughly $10, and Salt Lake City, where it carried an eye-popping price tag of about $15.

Consumers balked. While they liked the product, they didn't like the price tag.

Part of the problem was that the one-time frantic interest in energy efficiency and long-term value had dimmed. By 1981, in the heat of recession, consumers had shifted away from energy savings and demanded bargains. it was lights out for Halarc.

But that's only half the story. Halarc is now a living legend for GE's risk-takers. Because looking over the shoulder of the Halarc team was every other ventures group throughout the company, watching to see if General Electric was willing to make good on its promise to reward those who try as well as those who win.

"We wanted to make sure that all the people involved in Halarc—who had really done a good job and made a lot of progress—didn't get their careers disrupted because of the way it worked out in the marketplace," says Kashnow, now general manager of the Quartz and Chemical Products Department. "We took a lot of care not only to communicate that, but to make sure that they had appropriate career opportunities when it was over."

The bargain held up. When the decision was made in the summer of 1983 to put Halarc on the back burner, the section held award parties, dinners, and ceremonies for the group.

Top management—from the CEO to the sector executive, group executive, and division manager—got the message through to those who devoted years of their careers to Halarc that their work was appreciated.

Additional attention was given to team members to make sure that appropriate job assignments were waiting for them. It wasn't hard. Since the team had attracted a lot of the best in the business, they were in demand.

"Only certain people are attracted to risk-taking," Kashnow explains. "We've got to preserve the kind of culture that allows people to take those risks."

Far from collecting dust on museum shelves, Halarc opened new frontiers in state-of-the-art technology for the industrial market where buyers are more accustomed to high initial costs and life-cycle paybacks. And, as the technology matures, Halarc may find its way back into the consumer market at a lower price.

For risk managers and players, Halarc offered another reminder—to recognize risk up front, manage it properly, and not get caught off guard when the project doesn't work out.

Even though the big swing never connected, it left its mark.

It got the message through to people about the company's concern for individuals, about a culture that encourages people to try again, and about the commitment of management to share the risks.

Gold Star Co., Ltd.

On April 6, 1984, Chung Jang-Ho, the recently appointed executive managing director of exports for Gold Star, was informed of the U.S. International Trade Commission's determination that an "industry in the United States is materially injured by reason of imports of color television receivers from the Republic of Korea which are sold at less than fair value." The resulting antidumping penalty added another obstacle to an already difficult course for establishing Gold Star as a major premium brand name in the United States for home electronic products. Apart from a climate of growing protectionism in Europe and the United States, Chung had to resolve the somewhat conflicting pressures from two even more pressing developments. One was an apparent effort by U.S. and Japanese electronics firms to dislodge Gold Star from its U.S. beachhead. The other, which had direct repercussions on export strategy, was a major challenge in Korea to Gold Star's domestic leadership position in home electronics products.

Chung had returned from the Harvard Business School's Advanced Management Program in late December 1983 to assume his new position. An accountant by training, his previous position had been executive managing director of the corporate planning department for the Lucky-Goldstar group to which the Gold Star company belonged. In his new job, he reported to Huh Shin-Koo, the hard-driving and successful president of Gold Star, who was counting on exports to contribute significantly to the company's growth.

Lucky-Goldstar Group

The group's history dated back to 1931, when Koo In-Hwoi opened a dry-goods store in Chinju. In 1945, when Korea regained its independence, Koo moved from retailing to trade and subsequently, in 1947, into the manufacture of cosmetics and toiletries. His early success came with Lucky toothpaste, which enjoyed a virtual monopoly in the Korean market until the importation of consumer goods was liberalized in 1982. In the meantime, profits gained from this product were invested in the manufacture of chemical products, home electronics products (1958), a newspaper (1964), and oil refining (1967). Koo Cha-Kyung, the eldest son of the founder, succeeded to the chairmanship on his father's death in 1969.

In the 1970s, the Lucky group, as it was then called, concentrated on consolidating and strengthening its position in its key businesses, growing through capacity expansion and the development of related products. Exhibit 1 identifies the resulting portfolio of seven business areas and twenty-three principal companies for the group. In chemicals, oil refining, and electronic products, Lucky was the pioneer and undisputed industry leader in Korea.

Under Chairman Koo's direction, the group's sales and profits had grown from $164 million and $500,000 in 1970 to $7.2 billion and $71 million respectively in 1983. These results placed the Lucky-Goldstar group (renamed in September 1984 to reflect the increased importance of its Gold Star electronics business) in fiftieth position among the *Fortune* 500 largest industrial corporations outside the U.S. in 1983. Table A contains highlights of the group's recent financial results.

Group Management Philosophy

This growth reflected certain general values that had shaped management's approach to business. Any actions Chung might wish to take with respect to Gold Star's exports would need to conform to these values.

An Emphasis on Harmony. From the company's inception, its leaders cultivated *Inwha*, literally meaning harmony in human relations, as a guiding doctrine of management. In line with this principle, management sought harmony in making decisions and in formulating strategies. A senior executive described this credo:

> Having its roots in Confucian doctrine, *Inwha* is commonly understood as an important ethical order ruling interpersonal relationships. It was, however, Lucky-Goldstar's founder, Koo In-Hwoi, who first extended the application of this humanistic order to business and management. He perceived that unity, creativity, and excellence could be achieved through *Inwha*. The present chairman, Koo Cha-Kyung, has continued to regard the spirit of *Inwha* as essential to business management, recognizing that it is subject to reinterpretation as times change. His belief is based on a simple premise that business is carried out by people, is managed by people, and aims to serve the well-being of its people.

Even though many Korean companies were known to have adopted employee-oriented policies, the Lucky-Goldstar group was widely recognized as foremost in this regard. Group policies stated explicitly that no abrupt personnel changes were to be made that would cause employees unnecessary hardship. It was also well known that college graduates wishing to continue their MBA studies would choose Lucky-Goldstar group companies, because of their liberal and supportive policies regarding education for employees. Although some of the top executive spots were filled by members of the owners' families, all of these employees had risen to the top from entry levels, and only able family members survived.

Table A Major statistics of the Lucky-Goldstar group ($ million).

	1979	1980	1981	1982	1983
Sales	3,378	4,522	5,287	5,447	7,193
Exports	659	765	1,073	1,056	2,085
Net income	70	25	45	74	71
Total assets	2,601	2,994	3,198	3,745	4,266
Employees (000)	53	43	46	42	50
Overseas offices	37	43	52	58	62

Diversification Based on Related Products. Ever since the founding of Lucky Chemical Co. in 1947, the group had followed a course of safe, gradual diversification. Chairman Koo Cha-Kyung explained the group's successive moves into new business fields in the following way:

> My father and I started a cosmetic cream factory in the late 1940s. At the time, no company could supply us with plastic caps of adequate quality for cream jars, so we had to start a plastics business. Plastic caps alone were not sufficient to run the plastic molding plant, so we added combs, toothbrushes, and soap boxes. This plastics business also led us to manufacture electric fan blades and telephone cases, which in turn led us to manufacture electrical and electronic products and telecommunication equipment. The plastics business also took us into oil refining, which needed a tanker shipping company. The oil-refining company alone was paying an insurance premium amounting to more than half the total revenue of the then largest insurance company in Korea. Thus, an insurance company was started. This natural step-by-step evolution through related businesses resulted in the Lucky-Goldstar group as we see it today. For the future, we will base our growth primarily on chemicals, energy, and electronics. Our chemical business will continue to expand toward fine chemicals and genetic engineering, while the electronics business will grow in the direction of semiconductor manufacturing, fiber-optic telecommunications, and, eventually, satellite telecommunications.

Market Leadership Based on Technological Leadership. The Lucky-Goldstar management prided itself on the technological leadership it had maintained among Korean companies in each of its major businesses. This leadership had enabled the group to enjoy monopoly positions in new products over extended periods. In 1983, the government revealed a list of monopoly products in the Korean market, with Lucky-Goldstar accounting for twenty-one, the largest number held by any Korean company. Chairman Koo Cha-Kyung emphasized the role of technology development in the following way: "Outsiders may judge our group as ultraconservative because of our financial policies which emphasize stability over growth. Nevertheless, we have never neglected investing in technological development. On average, we have spent 6 percent of the group's

Exhibit 1 Lucky-Goldstar group's principal companies (1983).

Field	Company	Main Products or Activities	Established	Sales ($000)	Employees	Joint-Venture Partner
Chemicals	Lucky, Ltd.	Chemical products	1947	$ 473,341	5,600	
	Lucky Continental Carbon	Carbon black	1968	30,597	230	Continental Carbon Co., U.S.
Electricity, Electronics, and Communications	Gold Star Co. Ltd.	Electric and electronic products, minicomputers, mainframes	1958	967,312	14,200	
	Gold Star Cable	Electric wire and communication cable, heavy machinery	1969	228,838	4,030	Hitachi Cable, Ltd., Japan
	Gold Star Tele-Electric	Telecommunication equipment, computer peripherals, automatic-control systems, medical equipment	1969	76,307	2,650	Siemens A.G., West Germany
	Gold Star Electric	Telecommunication products	1970	67,717	2,600	Nippon Electric Co., Japan
	Gold Star Instrument & Electric	Electric and electronic equipment for industrial process-control systems	1974	62,344	1,700	Fuji Electric Co., Japan
	Gold Star Precision	Precision electronic equipment	1976	28,324	930	
	Shinyeong Electric	Electrical equipment	1971 (1978)[b]	47,429	1,450	Mitsubishi Electric Corp., Japan
	Gold Star Semiconductor	Transistors, ICs, LSIs, ESSs, computers, CAD/CAM	1976 (1979)	62,161	1,530	Western Electric Co., U.S.

Category	Company	Business	Year			Foreign partner
	Gold Star-Alps Electronics	Electronic equipment	1970	62,417	3,250	Alps Electric Co., Japan
Energy and Resources	Honam Oil Refinery	Refined petroleum products	1967	2,883,237	1,560	Caltex Petroleum, U.S.
	Korea Mining & Smelting	Nonferrous metal smelting	1936 (1971)	285,399	1,500	
Construction and Engineering	Lucky Development	General construction	1969	302,964	1,150	
	Lucky Engineering	Technical services	1978	6,999	220	
Securities, Insurance, and Finance	Lucky Securities	Brokerage, dealing, underwriting	1973	14,459	590	
	Pan Korea Insurance	insurance	1959 (1970)	46,986	680	
	Pusan Investment & Finance	Short-term finance	1973 (1980)	16,128	120	
	Gold Star Investment & Finance	Short-term finance	1982	16,942	90	
Trade and Distribution	Lucky-Goldstar International Corp.	Exporting, importing, manufacturing	1953	1,134,365	3,160	
	Hee Sung Co., Ltd.	Advertising and supermarket retailing	1971	48,226	510	
Public Services	Yonam Foundation [a]	Scholarships	1969	—	10	
	Yonam Educational Institute [a]	Education	1973	—	160	

a. Nonprofit entities.
b. Years in parentheses indicate when acquired by Lucky-Goldstar Group.

turnover in research and development. We will continue to spend a substantial amount of money in R&D in order to keep up with the rapidly changing nature of the business."

Joint Ventures. One way the group had developed its technology effectively over the years was by entering into joint ventures with foreign firms possessing advanced technologies. These arrangements gave Lucky-Goldstar an edge over rival companies at home and provided a channel for entry into new overseas markets. Six of the eight major joint ventures were in electronics and are described in Exhibit 1. In addition, Lucky Continental Carbon had been set up with Continental Carbon Company (a subsidiary of Conoco) in 1968 to produce carbon black (1983 sales: $30 million), and the Honam Oil Refinery was a 50–50 joint venture with Caltex Petroleum to produce petroleum products (1983 sales: $2.9 billion). Honam could process 380,000 barrels per day, accounting for 48 percent of Korea's total refining capacity in 1983. Chairman Koo explained how he had come to view joint ventures:

> Joint-venture partners typically want to make profits as quickly as possible, even at the expense of long-term growth potential. We as a Korean company, however, want to grow our business on a long-term basis. We recognize this difference in orientation, and therefore will form a joint venture where we do not have necessary technologies, and where we can make money quickly. On the other hand, we will form a wholly owned company where we expect long-term growth but not a quick profit.
>
> Based on our experience, I am generally disappointed with the way certain large companies behave as joint-venture partners. They are very slow to act, typically taking at least two years from the idea to the decision. Also, local managers have very little influence on the decisions made at headquarters. Smaller companies, on the other hand, are quick to act, and also very attentive to the local conditions here in Korea. Now we are more inclined to do business with smaller, tightly managed companies than with giant multinationals.

Gold Star Co., Ltd.

The Lucky-Goldstar group's electronics business started in 1958, when Gold Star Co., Ltd. began producing vacuum-tube radios, something no Korean company had done before. Thereafter, the company successively introduced electric fans (1960), refrigerators (1964), black-and-white TVs (1966), elevators and escalators (1968), room air conditioners (1968), washing machines (1969), package air-conditioning equipment (1975), cash registers (1977), color TVs (1977), electric typewriters (1980), microcomputers (1982), microwave ovens (1982), and compact disc players (1983), each a first for Korea. Gold Star was also the first in Korea to conduct electronics business abroad, with the export of radios to America (1962), licensing of color TV manufacturing technologies (1980), and foreign direct investment in the United States to establish manufacturing plants (1981).

Table B   Major statistics of the Gold Star Co. Ltd. ($ million).

	1979	1980	1981	1982	1983
Sales	541	419	578	620	967
Exports	161	192	247	217	380
Net income	12	−15	15	13	34
Total assets	508	427	469	484	613
Employees (000)	16	11	10	9	12
Overseas offices	8	10	14	17	18

Starting in 1969, eight electronics-related firms were spun off from Gold Star to produce such products as wire and cable, industrial electronic equipment, and telecommunication equipment. In 1984, Gold Star Company continued to be the largest and most profitable firm in the Korean electronics industry. Table B shows the company's recent financial performance.

As can be seen in the financial figures, Gold Star's growth was not without interruption. 1980 was a particularly bad year in which the company experienced a cash drain serious enough to drive it to the brink of insolvency. This financial setback was attributed largely to two unforeseen disruptive events. First, in 1979, the second oil shock resulted in a sharp decrease in overseas and domestic demand, as well as an increase in manufacturing costs. Then, in October of that same year, Korean president Park Chung-Hee was assassinated. Political chaos ensued, leading to a severe depression in the domestic economy. A further disruption was the death of the company's president as a result of an automobile accident.

Recognizing the serious nature of Gold Star's financial position in the midst of the recession, Chairman Koo brought in Huh Shin-Koo to turn the electronics company around. Huh, a senior member of the owner family, was widely respected within the group as a tough and skillful marketer.

President Huh quickly took major steps to revive morale within Gold Star and to turn its finances around. His first move was to streamline manufacturing facilities by closing down inefficient plants and rationalizing manufacturing operations. The existing manufacturing facilities reflected the accumulation of piece-meal expansion moves that had been made over the years. As a result of the changes, each of the surviving plants specialized in a limited number of products, so as to benefit from scale economies.

Overhead costs were also drastically cut. At the same time, President Huh made major investments to strengthen the company's competitive position, including a decision to establish a sizable TV manufacturing plant in the United States. President Huh also sought to improve sales operations by cutting unnecessary expenses and improving after-sales services. Finally, he took measures to improve employee morale by eliminating internal bureaucratic red tape and improving intracompany communications.

In August 1981, the Korean government's decision to allow public broadcasting of color TV programs came as a welcome opportunity. (Color TV had been banned by the Park administration on the grounds that it would encourage conspicuous consumption and thus widen the disparity in consumption patterns between rich and poor.) Largely as a result of the new policy, Gold Star's 1981 domestic sales increased by 46 percent and the preceding year's loss figure of $15 million became a profit of $15 million. In 1982 domestic sales grew 22 percent and in 1983 another 46 percent.

Organization. Exhibit 2 shows Goldstar Co.'s organization in June 1984. Under President Huh Shin-Koo, two executive vice presidents were responsible for management and production, and two executive managing directors were responsible for domestic and export marketing of all the electronic products except computers, elevators, and package air-conditioning equipment.

Products and Production Facilities. Goldstar produced five major categories of products: video, audio, kitchen appliances, computers, and others. Video products included color TVs, black-and-white TVs, monitors, and VCRs. Audio products included audiocassette recorders and stereo components. Kitchen appliances included refrigerators, washing machines, and microwave ovens. Computers included personal computers (called FAMICOM), microcomputers (MIGHTY), minicomputers (DPS6), and mainframes (DPS8). Other products included room air conditioners, elevators, escalators, motors and industrial machinery. As shown in Exhibit 3, color TV was by far Gold Star's most important product in 1983.

Product development was prominent in Gold Star management's plans. The company's R&D facilities, located in Seoul, Pyungtaek, Gumi, and Changwon, employed about 330 engineers and supporting staff. In 1983, R&D expenses amounted to $47.8 million, which represented 4.9 percent of Gold Star's total sales. Regarding the role of R&D, President Huh explained:

> For the next ten years, it is obvious that we should move into computer-based intelligence equipment, laser-telecommunications, and semiconductors. All of these new businesses, however, require advanced technologies. Unlike the United States and Japan, in which private firms can easily tap well-educated human resources, we have an extra burden of educating our own people within the company in order to develop technologies. Each year we select 70–80 undergraduates, 40–50 graduates, and several postgraduate students and provide them with full scholarships. Upon graduation, they will come to work for us. Some of these talented people will be sent abroad for further advanced studies.

Gold Star's production facilities were scattered around Korea. The major plant manufacturing TVs was located in Gumi, a city (located about 170 miles from Seoul) which had been designated by the government in 1972 to become an electronics center. Computers, office equipment, VCRs, and audio equipment were manufactured in Seoul, while the Changwon plant (250 miles from Seoul) manufactured electrical appliances. In 1981, Gold Star established its

Exhibit 2 Gold Star Co.'s organization.

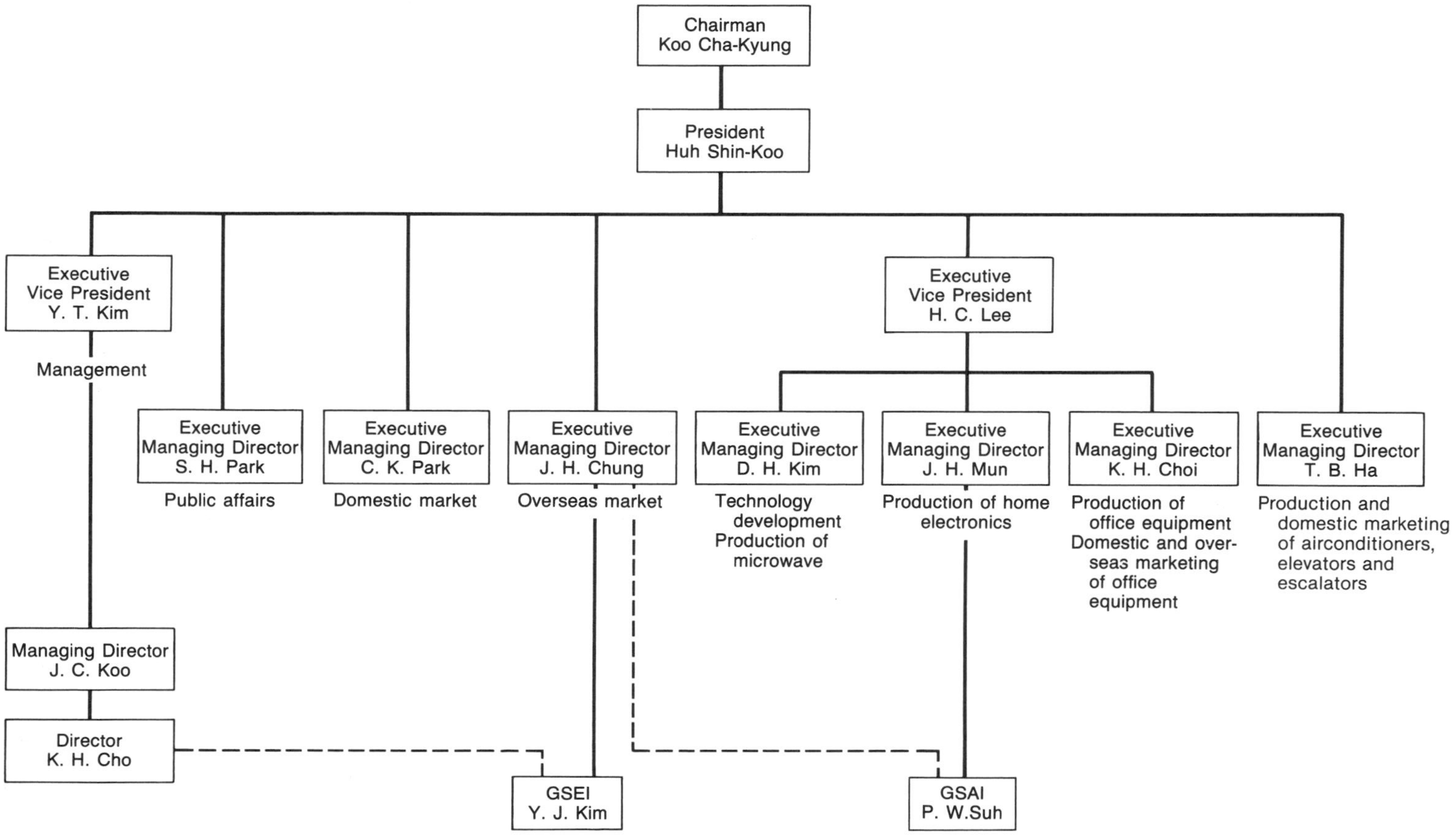

Exhibit 3   Gold Star Co.'s sales breakdown by product ($ million).

Product	1979	1980	1981	1982	1983	1983 (%)
Color TV	33	83	230	216	307	31.8
B&W TV	104	60	91	71	60	6.2
VTR	—	—	—	15	38	3.9
Audiocassette recorder	38	27	35	43	54	5.6
Stereo	16	38	26	11	10	1.0
Refrigerator	143	48	69	89	123	12.7
Washing machine	19	13	20	21	32	3.3
Microwave oven	—	—	—	6	30	3.1
Elevator/escalator	3	16	12	14	20	2.1
Others	186	144	95	134	293	30.3
Total	542	419	578	620	967	100.0%

first overseas assembly plant, in Huntsville, Alabama. Named Gold Star America Inc. (GSAI), this wholly-owned subsidiary had an initial capacity of 150,000 color TVs a year. In 1983, it was expanded to 300,000 units and then in May, 1984, to 450,000 units. In 1984, the manufacture of office equipment and VCRs was also initiated in the newly constructed Pyungtaek factory.

Markets. In 1983, over 60 percent of Gold Star's sales were to the domestic market. With a population of some nine million families and an average GNP per family of $8,700, markets for home appliances in Korea were quickly being saturated. The company estimated the following 1984 saturation levels for its most important products: color TV, 65 percent; B&W TV, over 90 percent; refrigerators, 80 percent; and audiocassette recorders, 88 percent. With respect to its new growth products, VCRs were expected to reach at least 50 percent of the Korean market by 1990. Microwave ovens, however, were not expected to become a major kitchen appliance, because they were not well suited for Korean cooking.

As shown in Exhibit 4, the U.S. market dominated Gold Star's overseas sales, accounting for 68 percent in 1983.

Gold Star's Operations in the United States

Gold Star first entered the U.S. market in 1961. However, it was not until 1978, when the company set up a U.S. marketing subsidiary, Gold Star Electronics International Inc. (GSEI), that sales became significant. Under GSEI, the number of local distributors increased from fifty-seven to 2,500 in 1982 and the number of service centers from twenty to 1,540 during the same period. Sales volume rose from $13 million in 1978 to $151 million in 1983 and net profits from $16,000 to $4.1 million. To accommodate the rapid growth, in 1981 GSEI moved from its original location in New York to larger facilities in New Jersey

Exhibit 4 Gold Star Co.'s sales breakdown by region (1983) ($ million).

Product	Total	Domestic (Korea)	USA	Canada	Latin and South America	Europe	Asia	Middle East	Africa	Others
Color TV	306.5	164.4	108.2	10.0	6.5	4.8	6.1	5.0	1.3	0.2
B&W TV	60.1	—	39.4	3.5	2.1	9.2	1.7	1.9	2.3	—
Combi TV	15.3	—	14.4	0.7	0.1	—	0.1	—	—	—
Audiocassette recorder	54.2	30.9	3.0	1.0	1.0	11.1	1.9	1.8	3.5	—
Refrigerator	122.8	109.3	9.1	0.7	—	—	1.8	1.9	—	—
Washing machine	31.9	30.9	0.4	—	0.3	—	0.3	—	—	—
Microwave oven	30.0	11.6	17.8	0.6	—	—	0.6	—	—	—
Fan	7.4	6.2	0.3	—	—	—	0.2	—	0.1	—
Others	338.8	233.7	65.5	5.5	3.7	13.3	9.4	4.6	3.1	—
Total	967.0	587.0	258.1	22.0	13.7	38.4	22.1	15.2	10.3	0.2
Percent	100.0	60.7	26.7	2.3	1.4	4.0	2.3	1.6	1.0	—

and opened local offices in Los Angeles, Chicago, and Dallas. The major products GSEI handled were color TVs, black-and-white TVs, microwave ovens, and audiocassette recorders. Color TVs were by far the most important item, accounting for 51 percent of sales in 1983. Headquarters in Korea continued to deal directly with major OEMs, (such as Zenith and GE), large retailing chains (such as Sears Roebuck), and large importers (such as Emerson).

One of the primary reasons for creating GSEI was to establish the Gold Star trademark in the United States. As a result, it was decided to sell only products carrying the Gold Star label through GSEI. While sales volume increased over time, this increase was less than hoped for. In the meantime, Gold Star's archrival, Samsung Electronics, chose the private-brand policy for its entire product line, and passed Gold Star in export volume. This setback caused Gold Star's top management to reconsider the GSEI's brand policy. Kang Kil-Won, a Gold Star executive vice president taking a sabbatical leave as a visiting professor of marketing at the University of Illinois, recalled this change of policy:

> We discussed at great length the merits and demerits of a private-brand policy. Some argued that the private-brand business would kill our hungry spirit and jeopardize our attentiveness to promoting the Gold Star brand. But others argued that the private-brand business would help us to increase sales volume quickly, without the burden of accounts receivables and after-sale services. They also pointed out that our corporate philosophy of *Inwha* would best be promoted by an international division of labor: manufacturing by us, marketing by them. The latter argument prevailed, and in 1980 we decided to seek private-label business through GSEI.

The flow of Gold Star's color TV sets to the U.S. market is shown in Figure A below. The OEM sets typically involved some particular design requirements by the purchaser; the private label sets were basic Gold Star units with another nameplate.

Figure A   Gold Star Co.'s flow of color TVs to the U.S. market.

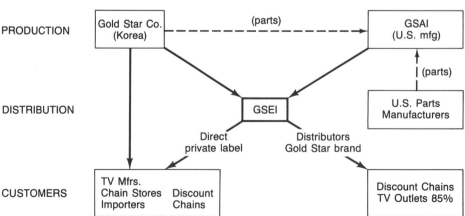

About 85 percent of GSEI's sales were to discount chains. To prevent destructive price cutting on Gold Star products, GSEI attempted to offer some exclusivity to its distributors. Gold Star labeled sets were sold only to noncompeting chains; private-label sets were not restricted in this way. For example, since Zayre carried Gold Star models, such sets were not made available to Caldor, a direct competitor. K-Mart, another competitor, carried Gold Star sets with a KMC label.

In 1984, GSEI had eleven salesmen (six Korean and five American) operating out of the New Jersey headquarters and branch offices in Chicago, Dallas, and Los Angeles.

U.S. Manufacturing. After two years of importing Korean products through GSEI, Gold Star management began to consider the possibility of manufacturing in the United States, for two reasons. The first was mounting trade barriers. U.S. restrictions on color TV imports from Korea started in late 1978 with the resolution of an Orderly Marketing Agreement (OMA) between the U.S. International Trade Commission (ITC) and the Korean government. Lee Hee-Chong, executive vice president, recalled the situation at the time. "The OMA agreement was originally planned for one year. But in 1979 the ITC extended it for another two years, and we recognized that some form of protectionism would continue. We then began to devise ways to cope with it." The second reason was that Gold Star could not easily respond to the rapid technological innovation in the U.S. and to the increasing design awareness of American consumers with the practice of manufacturing exclusively in Korea.

By 1980, seven Japanese TV manufacturers and one Taiwanese had located plants in the United States. Gold Star management began to consider a similar course of action. According to President Huh Shin-Koo:

> We were sharply divided concerning the pros and cons of setting up a manufacturing plant in the U.S. Some argued that such a move would be a big mistake, because we would have to deal with American workers without knowing how. Moreover, they questioned our ability to achieve costs and quality comparable to our Korean plant. Others stressed the need to have operations inside the trade barriers.

After considerable debate, President Huh decided in favor of investing in the United States. Lee Hun-Jo, president of the group's general trading company, Lucky-Goldstar International Corporation, and at that time president of the Chairman's Office, explained how top management thought about this investment:

> Korea was rapidly transformed from an agrarian to an industrial society in the 1960s. Because our domestic economy was still weak, we had to sell products overseas. With little experience in exporting, we relied on Japanese traders, who kept most of the profits and left us with almost nothing. This experience taught us that we should know foreign markets before we develop substantial business there. When the occasion arose for us to invest in the U.S., we considered it as an opportunity to learn about the U.S.

market. In that sense, our attitude concerning U.S. entry was a very humble one.

A careful site search led Gold Star to Huntsville, Alabama, where Dr. Werner Von Braun and some 200 other German scientists had helped to launch the NASA space exploration project in the 1950s. Alabama had initiated a program to develop Huntsville into an electronics center patterned after California's Silicon Valley and Boston's Route 128. The state supplied $10 million worth of industrial revenue bonds for GSAI, at about 8 percent annual interest. It also provided job training for new employees of the company.

President Huh explained how the plant capacity of 150,000 units a year had been decided:

> At the time, we had been exporting 400,000 units of color TVs to the U.S. market, 300,000 in the Gold Star brand, and the rest in private brands. We figured that at least half of the Gold Star branded TVs would find a market, even under depressed market conditions. In other words, 150,000 was an amount we could be sure of selling in the U.S. market.

Successful Operation

The Huntsville plant began operations in July 1982 and in 1983 produced 143,000 standard nineteen-inch manual rotary selector color TV sets. As shown in Table C, the net cost for the U.S. sets was comparable to that for sets imported from Korea. Some of the parts and materials used for U.S. production were shipped from Korea. Overall quality levels for the U.S.- and Korean-manufactured products were considered comparable.

Management had anticipated a loss for the first three years of operations. Unexpectedly, GSAI showed a profit of $1.1 million on sales of $24.5 million in 1983, and GSAI President Suh Pyung-Won saw even brighter prospects for 1984. He attributed this happy turn of events to a recovery of the U.S. TV market, close collaboration with the Korean operations reflecting Gold Star's *Inwha* philosophy, and the positive support provided by Alabama State.

Encouraged by the early results, Gold Star management authorized GSAI to expand its facilities. A second assembly line was completed in July, 1983, and construction of a second plant began a month later. President Huh Shin-Koo explained this expansion program as follows:

> Our business style is not to start with a giant plant and then get into trouble selling products, but to start with a small plant and develop manufacturing and marketing capabilities simultaneously on a step-by-step basis. Then, as our volume increases to about 250–300,000 units, we will split the existing workers into two groups and use the existing facility on a double-shift basis. When the volume exceeds 300,000 units, we will build the second 150,000-unit facility, and move the second-shift workers to that facility. As a result, the second facility would be run by a group of workers with the same expertise and dedication to the company as the first one. We do not believe in the merit of instant scale economies so much as in a slow and steady approach to a new business environment. We will learn American

Table C Comparison of U.S. costs for color TVs originating from Gold Star in Korea versus GSAI in the United States (based on 19" rotary model in 1983).

	Korean Sets	*U.S. Sets*	*Difference*
Material	$133.86	$150.91	$17.05
Labor	3.39	6.18	2.79
Other	5.43	7.71	2.28
Manufacturing total	142.68	164.80	22.12
Transportation	7.69	—	− 7.69
Damage en route	varies	—	?
Duty	7.13	—	− 7.13
Total landed cost	$157.50+	$164.80	< $ 7.30

business through trial and error, but we will also make certain that we limit the business risk under our control.

A third assembly line, raising the first plant's capacity to 450,000 TV sets, was completed and staffed in April, 1984, and site preparation for a third plant began in June, 1984. The third plant would produce microwave ovens starting in 1985, and a projected fourth plant was scheduled for 1986 to produce "high tech" products such as VCRs and personal computers. Exhibit 5 shows a bird's-eye view of how the completed complex would look.

As of June 1984, GSAI employed about 200 workers. Employee morale was considered to be high. Several union attempts to organize the plant had failed to gain workers' support.

Color TV in the United States

The unions were not the only ones to notice Gold Star's presence in the U.S. According to Nam Yong, who had been associated with GSEI since its inception and now served as GSEI marketing vice president, "A number of established competitors—such as RCA, Zenith, Sanyo, and Sharp—are now attacking us with predatory prices for their basic TV models in an attempt to cut our market out from under us. They can afford to do this with the support of profits from their higher tech products. While we can make such products, we do not have the right distribution for them. Our problem is that our brand name is still weak in terms of awareness and that makes it difficult for us to get department stores and specialty shops to introduce our line."

Demand. In 1983, the U.S. demand for color TV sets increased to over 15.2 million sets, from the 11–12 million level in the previous three years. This market expansion took place in spite of the fact that over 99 percent of all U.S. households had at least one TV set. According to a report by the U.S. International Trade Commission, "Innovation in styling and technology, such as

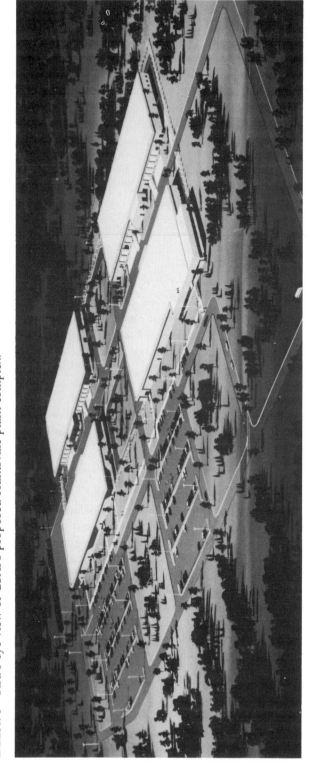

Exhibit 5 Bird's-eye view of GSAI's proposed Huntsville plant complex.

324

wireless remote control and random-access channel selection, stimulated demand. In addition, the growing popularity of electronic games, videotape recorders, and videotape cassettes, which can be attached to television receivers, was having a positive influence on the demand for television receivers."

Consumption of color TVs in the U.S. market was concentrated in the nineteen-inch screen category, which accounted for 52 percent of the total sales in 1983. It was followed by 13-inch models with 19 percent of total demand, and large-sized models (20 inches and over) with 22 percent.

Channels of Distribution. Color TVs sold in the U.S. reached the ultimate consumer in two ways. In the two-step system, the producer or importer sold the merchandise to a wholesale/distributor, which then sold it to retail outlets. In the one-step system, the producer or importer sold directly to a retail outlet. Generally, only large accounts were involved in one-step distribution.

A substantial number of color TVs were sold under private-brand labels (i.e., the brand name of the retailer, not that of the producer). Private-label retailers such as Sears, Roebuck, J. C. Penny and K-Mart supplied prospective producers with specifications for a particular model television receiver or surveyed the specifications of sets currently being produced and picked the models that best suited their needs. Such private-label merchandisers would then solicit bids from producers and negotiate contracts for particular receivers for a model year. Such retailers typically purchased receivers from several producers, foreign and/or domestic. The percentage distribution of U.S.-produced and imported sets in 1983, as reported by the ITC, is shown in Table D.

Suppliers. Exhibit 6 lists the major brands in the U.S. color TV market. In 1983, 70.3 percent of the demand for color TV sets was supplied by seventeen domestic producers, and the remaining 29.7 percent by several hundred importers. As shown in Exhibit 7, domestic production increased 13.0 percent in 1983 to 10.7 million units, while imports more than doubled to 4.5 million units. As a result, the increased demand in 1983 (3.6 million sets) was largely

Table D Distribution pattern of U.S. color TVs, 1983.

Market	U.S. produced	Imported
Private label	14.6%	10.8%
Discount	3.5	20.0
Department stores	4.7	6.8
Catalog	.7	.4
Full-service dealer	12.3	22.4
Buying groups	5.9	11.5
Wholesale distributor	44.7	12.7
Other	13.6	11.3
	100.0%	100.0%

Exhibit 6 Major color TV brands in the U.S. (%).

Rank	Brand	Estimated 1984	1983	1982	1981	1980	1979
1	RCA	19.0	20.0	20.0	20.0	21.0	21.0
2	Zenith	17.5	18.5	19.4	20.5	20.5	20.5
3	GE	7.6	8.1	8.0	7.7	7.5	6.9
4	Sears	7.1	7.1	7.25	7.2	7.5	7.9
5	Sony	6.5	7.0	7.0	7.0	6.5	6.5
6	Magnavox	5.7	6.0	6.5	6.9	7.0	7.2
7	Sylvania	4.2	4.5	4.0	4.0	4.0	3.9
8	Quasar	4.0	4.5	5.0	4.9	5.0	5.0
9	Panasonic	4.0	3.56	2.5	2.1	2.0	2.2
10	Hitachi	2.7	2.5	2.25	2.0	1.7	1.85
11	Sharp	2.5	2.0	1.5	1.5	1.5	1.5
12	Montgomery Ward	2.45	2.25	2.5	2.7	2.25	2.1
13	Mitsubishi	2.0	1.7	1.5	1.2	1.0	1.0
14	Sanyo	1.55	1.5	1.5	2.0	2.0	2.0
15	J. C. Penney	1.5	1.5	1.5	1.5	1.5	1.5
16	Toshiba	1.4	1.3	1.4	1.1	1.0	1.0
17	Samsung	1.2	0.6	0.45	0.4	—	—
18	Curtis Mathes	1.2	1.2	1.2	1.0	1.0	1.0
19	Philco	1.0	1.0	1.0	1.2	1.2	1.2
20	*Gold Star*	1.0	0.8	0.75	0.8	—	—
21	Emerson	1.0	—	—	—	—	—
22	Sampo	0.6	0.55	0.5	0.5	—	—
23	Capehart (NATM)	0.6	—	—	—	—	—
24	Portland	0.5	0.38	0.35	—	—	—
25	NEC	0.5	—	—	—	—	—
26	Teknika	0.4	0.5	0.5	—	—	—
27	AOC brand	0.4	—	—	—	—	—
28	Tatung	0.3	0.3	0.3	—	—	—
29	JVC	0.3	—	—	—	—	—
30	Fisher	0.25	—	—	—	—	—

Source: Company document.

met by imports. Although Japan increased its shipment by 67.5 percent to 1.4 million sets, it was displaced as the number one importer by Korea, with its shipment of 1.6 million sets.

Statistics of domestic shipments by company were not available, but Exhibit 8 shows that four U.S.-owned companies had a manufacturing capacity that stood at 9.5 million in 1983. Six Japanese-owned companies had 29.4 percent with 2.8 million units. The share of capacity, however, was not an appropriate indicator of each company's production, as some Japanese-owned firms operated more than one shift, according to the ITC report.

Exhibit 7 U.S. consumption of color TVs by sources of supply.

Item	1980	1981	1982	1983	Rate of growth 1982–83 (%)
		Quantity (1,000 units)			
Domestic shipments	9,731	10,085	9,482	10,718	13.0
Imports from					
Japan	435	734	813	1,362	67.5
Korea	293	391	621	1,573	153.3
Taiwan	303	457	446	1,056	136.8
All other	256	312	305	539	76.7
Total	1,288	1,895	2,184	4,530	107.4
Apparent U.S. consumption	11,019	11,980	11,666	15,248	30.7
		Relative Size (%)			
Domestic shipments	88.3	84.2	81.3	70.3	
Imports from					
Japan	3.9	6.1	7.0	9.0	
Korea	2.7	3.3	5.3	10.3	
Taiwan	2.7	3.8	3.8	6.9	
All others	2.3	2.6	2.6	3.5	
Total	11.7	15.8	18.7	29.7	

Source: USITC Publication 1514, "Color Television Receivers from the Republic of Korea and Taiwan," April 1984, p. A–37.

In recent years, two major developments had taken place in the domestic manufacturing sector of color TVs. First was a fundamental relocation of certain production operations, resulting in a new international division of labor. U.S. producers had either closed their plants entirely or had transferred an increasingly large portion of their production of labor-intensive components to other countries in an effort to cut labor costs. For example, RCA imported color chassis from its facilities in Taiwan and Mexico, Zenith imported color modules from Mexico and Taiwan, and GE produced color chassis and parts in Singapore. In addition, all black-and-white sets were obtained from their offshore plants. One source estimated that RCA, GE, and Zenith had an average of 50 percent of their value added from abroad. In contrast, Japanese and other foreign firms had started manufacturing operations in the U.S. to avoid import restrictions. The result was a reduction of the number of U.S.-owned firms from nine in 1976 to five in 1983, and an increase in the number of foreign-owned firms from four to twelve.

The second development was the adoption of technological improvements to reduce total labor content of TV manufacturing. Value added by direct labor

Exhibit 8 U.S. producers of color TVs.

Ownership and Firm	1976	1977	1978	1979	1980	1981	1982	1983	1983 U.S. Capacity (1,000)	Plant Location	Labor Unionized	Brand Names
U.S.-owned:												
Curtis-Mathes Manufacturing Co.	X	X	X	X	X	X	X	X	50	Athens, TX	?	Curtis Mathes
General Electric Co.	X	X	X	X	X	X	X	X	700	Portsmouth, VA	No	GE
RCA Corp.	X	X	X	X	X	X	X	X	2,000	Bloomington, IN and 2 others	Yes	RCA
Wells-Gardner Electronics Corp.	X	X	X	X	X	X	X	X	?	Chicago, IL	?	Teknika
Zenith Radio Corp.	X	X	X	X	X	X	X	X	2,000	Springfield, MO and 5 others	Yes	Zenith
GTE Sylvania, Inc.[a]	X	X	X	X	X							
Admiral Group	X	X	X									
Andrea Radio Corp.	X											
Warwick Electronics, Inc.[b]	X											
Dutch-owned:												
North American Philips Corp.	X	X	X	X	X	X	X	X	1,000	Greenville, TN Jefferson City, TN	Yes	Philips

328

Japanese-owned:

Company									Capacity (000)	Location	U.S. picture tube	Brand(s)
Sony Corp. of America	X	X	X	X	X	X	X	X	650	San Diego, CA and & other	No	Sony
Matsushita Industrial Co.	X	X	X	X	X	X	X	X	600	Chicago, IL	No	MIC, Panasonic, Quasar
Sanyo Manufacturing Corp.	X	X	X	X	X	X	X		800	Forrest City, AR	Yes	Sanyo
Mitsubishi Electric Sales	X	X	X	X	X	X			?	Santa Ana, CA	?	Mitsubishi
Toshiba America, Inc.	X	X	X	X	X				300	Lebanon, TN	Yes	Toshiba
Sharp Electronics Corp.	X	X	X	X					300	Memphis, TN	Yes	Sharp
Hitachi Consumer Products America, Inc.	X	X	X						150	Anaheim, CA	No	Hitachi
U.S. JCV Corp.	X	X							?	Elmwood Park, NJ	Yes	JVC

Taiwan-owned:

Company									Capacity (000)	Location	U.S. picture tube	Brand(s)
Tatung Co. of America, Inc.	X	X	X						?	Long Beach, CA	Yes	Tatung
Sampo Corp. of America	X	X							240	Atlanta, GA	No	Sharp

Korean-owned:

Company									Capacity (000)	Location	U.S. picture tube	Brand(s)
Gold Star of America, Inc.	X								300	Huntsville, AL	No	Gold Star

a. GTE Sylvania was purchased by North American Philips Corp. in January, 1981.

b. The television-manufacturing facilities of Warwick Electronics, Inc., were purchased by Sanyo Electric, Inc. (Japan), effective December 31, 1976.

Source: USITC Publication 1514, "Color Television Receivers from the Republic of Korea and Taiwan," April 1984, pp. A-8, A-9.

in the U.S., expressed as a share of the total value of domestically assembled color TV sets, decreased from 8.6 percent in 1980 to 7.4 percent in 1983.

Among the several hundred importers of TV apparatus in the United States, thirty to thirty-five firms were reported by ITC to account for over 80 percent of all imports. They were either producers of TVs themselves or private-label retailers.

GSEI's Strategy. From the beginning, Gold Star management had had in mind positioning the company's brand name in the U.S. as one of high quality and good value. But the need to build volume quickly so as to obtain economies of scale for exporting and later for the new U.S. plant required an early emphasis on selling low-cost standard models through discount chains. GSEI management was convinced, however, that for the long run, Gold Star would have to sell higher margin products through department stores and specialty shops. As price competition for the basic color TV models intensified, management felt the need to act on its strategy to move upscale. Kim Young-Joon, GSEI president, described his plan of action:

> To upgrade our position in the U.S. market, we have to do three things more or less at the same time. These are to increase brand awareness through advertising, to introduce higher margin products, and to sell through outlets where higher margins can be sustained. Here, for example, is an ad we are using to support our upscale move [see Exhibit 9]. In line with this plan, we have raised our advertising expenditures from less than $1 million to $8 million [amounts disguised] for 1983. This amount is still small compared to our competitors—RCA, Panasonic, and Sanyo probably spend over $30 million each—but it's all we can really handle to start with.
>
> As for products, we are looking to introduce twenty-five-inch color TV consoles and monitors in 1984 and VCRs the following year. These higher margin items are necessary to interest higher margin outlets to carry us. We shall also put a few more features on the basic models for these stores to distinguish the products they receive from the ones now carried by discount chains. Finally, we are busy trying to line up department stores like Macy's and Federated in L.A. and specialty stores like Lechmere's in Boston to handle our line of products. We have already gained entry into Fredder's Department Store in Chicago where Gold Star will serve as a step-up model from a competitor's discounted TV.

Confident that this strategy made sense and would work, GSEI management found itself beset on another front. Pressures for a major increase in volume were mounting from Gold Star in Korea as the parent company faced increasing competitive pressures from other Korean firms. The only way for GSEI to increase sales volume quickly would be through discount chains where it was currently geared to operate. GSEI management was reluctant to do so. In its opinion, such a move would interfere with its program to upgrade Gold Star's position in the U.S. market. Even more seriously, such a move would force GSEI to abandon its policy of selective distribution, with an effect of further weakening margins and ultimately Gold Star's image as a quality product.

Exhibit 9 A 1984 advertisement.

The rising star in electronics is not from the land of the rising sun.

It's not Sony. Or Panasonic. Or Toshiba. Or Sanyo. Or Mitsubishi. Or Hitachi. Or Sharp. Or Sansui. Or TEAC. Or NEC.

It's not one of them, even though those well known Japanese electronics companies have earned a well deserved reputation for excellence.

But, in all fairness, they've had their day in the sun.

And it's time for the rising sun to make way for the rising star.

Goldstar Electronics.

We're part of a 7.5 billion dollar Korean company.

And we manufacture a line of TV's, VCR's, microwave ovens, radio cassette players, computer monitors, and other electronic products

that are giving our competitors fits.

For they can't figure out how we can offer such state-of-the-art quality at such reasonable and affordable prices.

The fact is, we don't do it with mirrors. Or magic.

We do it with young, aggressive and creative management.

We do it with inspired engineering.

And we do it with the very latest production techniques.

Then we pull all these elements together at our plant in Huntsville, Alabama, where we produce hundreds of thousands of quality color TV's and microwave ovens annually.

You can see the end result of all this talent and effort in our sales. For it seems that consumers just can't get

enough of Goldstar products.

Last year, our TV sales alone were up 50%. We sold 2.5 million radio cassette players. And we sold over 1 million microwave ovens.

We're going to continue this success in the years ahead by introducing some of the most innovative products you could imagine.

And we're confident we'll succeed because we've got the products, the leadership and, perhaps, most importantly, a commitment to settle for nothing less than success.

So, if in the very near future, the rising sun doesn't seem as bright as it once was, you'll know why.

It's been eclipsed by the rising star. Goldstar.

GoldStar

Expensive electronics. Without the expense.

331

Korean Consumer Electronics Industry

For ten years, Gold Star had the Korean electronics field largely to itself. In 1968, Samsung (one of the four largest diversified group companies in Korea, along with Gold Star, Hyundai, and Daewoo) entered this attractive business. As a latecomer to the Korean market where the Gold Star name was almost synonymous with consumer electronic products, Samsung emphasized exports as its avenue for growth. The competitive battle between these Korean giants would play itself out years later in the lucrative color TV arena.

The Korean color TV industry which was launched in 1973 grew rapidly in its pioneer days. A 17 percent revaluation of the yen against the U.S. dollar in the mid-1970s and U.S. restrictions on Japanese imports of color TVs through an orderly marketing agreement (OMA) led to a rapid expansion of exports from Korea. The opportunity presented by the Japanese OMA spurred a major color TV capacity expansion among Korea manufacturers.

Then, with total color TV unit capacity approaching nearly 2 million, Korea came under U.S. restrictions to limit its 1979 imports to 298,000 sets. Political disruptions (President Park's assassination) depressed the Korean home market at the same time. The resulting shock to the Korean consumer electronics industry eventually led to the entry of another powerful group company, Daewoo, as it acquired these insolvent business interests from Taihan Electric Wire. Finally, in 1982, Hyundai, the largest and most profitable Korean group company, announced its intention to enter the electronics field with an investment of $500 million and the establishment of an advanced technology unit in Silicon Valley, California.

While Daewoo and Hyundai potentially posed formidable competitive threats for the future, it was Samsung that drew Gold Star management's immediate attention. As U.S. trade restrictions eased, Korean color TV imports increased from 293,000 to 1979 to 621,000 in 1982 and then jumped to 1.6 million sets in 1983. Samsung, which had adopted an aggressive pricing policy, led Gold Star by a small margin in the battle for U.S. market share. As shown in Table E, Gold Star held the leadership share position in the most important Korean consumer electronic product markets.

Gold Star's brand awareness in Korea was even stronger than its volume share. A recent consumer survey had indicated that over 80 percent of the respondents had selected Gold Star as the best Korean color TV set available.

The ITC Ruling

On May 2, 1983, the U.S. International Trade Commission received a petition alleging dumping by Korean and Taiwanese color TV suppliers. The U.S. Department of Commerce instituted its investigations of the alleged dumping of color TVs in the U.S. by Korean and Taiwanese suppliers on October 27, 1983, following a preliminary determination by the International Trade Commission that such sets were being sold at less than fair value. The following excerpt

Table E Market shares of major consumer electronic products in Korea (1983).

	Gold Star	*Samsung*	*Daewoo*	*Others*
Color TV	45.0	36.8	12.5	5.7
Refrigerator	48.9	41.9	9.2	—
Washing machine	50.7	35.9	13.4	—
Microwave oven	45.7	54.3	—	—

from the *Federal Register* (March 1, 1984) gives some indication of the complexity of the issues involved:

> Gold Star argues that its trademark creates a significant commercial difference between merchandise sold in Korea and to the U.S. Purchasers [in Korea] are willing to pay a higher price because of the presence of a trademark. . . . Without an adjustment for the effect of a trademark on market value, the Department cannot ensure an "apples to apples" fair-value comparison.
>
> Zenith argues that a trademark's value is a function of the success of the seller's advertising, sales promotion, and after-sale servicing in convincing customers of the quality of the trademarked merchandise. Commerce should not adjust twice for the effect on value of those efforts.
>
> DOC Response: To the extent there was a value of the trademark, over and above the cost of creating the trademark recognition, it is an intangible. A company would have to show us how it took that intangible into account in setting its prices . . . before we would grant such an adjustment.

On April 5, 1984, the ITC issued its report finding the largest Korean and Taiwanese color TV suppliers guilty of dumping. The following report appeared in the *Asian Wall Street Journal* on April 6:

> The International Trade Commission rules Thursday that imports of color television receivers from South Korea and Taiwan are injuring domestic producers. Earlier, the U.S. Commerce Department determined that nearly all color TVs made in Korea and Taiwan have been exported to the U.S. at unfairly low prices, generally below the "home-market" prices for the same products.
>
> According to the ITC, the penalty duties to be assessed by the Commerce Department against the Korea sets will average about 14.64 percent of the import price, while the antidumping duties on the sets from Taiwan will average 5.56 percent.[1] The duties will vary widely from company to company, however.

Korean manufacturers generally were astonished by the size of the penalty. The earlier DOC determination had recommended 3–4 percent. The ITC penalty essentially removed Korea's cost advantage with respect to the Japanese.

---

1. The average penalty imposed on Gold Star's imports was 14.77 percent.

In *News Review* (April 7, 1984), a columnist noted how the Japanese would most benefit from the ITC ruling and speculated as to Japan's possible role in instigating the ITC petition. During the following period of crises among Korean suppliers, it was reported that Japanese manufacturers dramatically increased the exports of complete TV sets to the U.S. market by 169 percent.

Gold Star's response to the DOC ruling was one of the issues Chung was still trying to hammer out in late December 1984. Gold Star had already raised its minimum price for U.S. TV imports by 5 percent, and an expansion of GSAI's manufacturing plant that would double capacity was under way.

Chung's Dilemma

The contradiction of pressures in the U.S. were multiplied for Chung Jang-Ho when he considered the Gold Star export strategy as a whole. The interests of his subordinates, superiors, and peers all seemed to be at odds.

GSEI's managers were most concerned about the attack by American and Japanese suppliers that threatened to undermine Gold Star's still somewhat precarious position in the United States. Consequently, they assigned a high priority to implementing the program of upgrading Gold Star's market segment with higher margin products and distributors. As an indication of this priority, Chung had learned informally that GSEI marketing favored raising the 1985 advertising budget to $20 million instead of the originally planned $12 million [figures disguised]. He also knew that, in GSEI's judgment, to abandon its policy of selective distribution for discount chains would undermine its upscaling strategy.

Product supplies for the U.S. posed another problem for Chung. GSEI president Kim was known to favor shifting his source of supply from Korea to GSAI (the U.S. manufacturing plant in Alabama) as soon as possible. For obvious reasons, Chung's Gold Star colleagues in manufacturing wanted to retain in Korea as much of this volume as possible. Kim's position was that U.S. sourcing would eliminate the trade-protection problems that consumed so much management time and constrained GSEI's options. Moreover, the lead time necessary to change products in the Korean facilities had averaged 90 to 120 days, whereas GSAI claimed the Huntsville complex capable of making such conversions in half that time. The shorter lead time was seen as an increasingly important capability for GSEI as it moved to higher margin products where the novelty of design features became a key competitive weapon. Although he was not directly responsible for manufacturing decisions, Chung was nonetheless involved by virtue of his active role in coordinating all the U.S. field operations.

Gurney Seed & Nursery Corp.

"Cash flow is our number one concern today!" With these words, John Kemp, chief financial officer of Gurney Seed & Nursery Corp., sought to indicate management's priorities for its first budget since having acquired ownership of the venerable mail-order company seven months earlier through a leveraged buy-out arrangement. With him were Major General Harry W. Brooks (ret.), chairman and CEO, and Keith Price, president and COO. The company's vice president of finance, who reported to Kemp, also attended. The November 8, 1984, meeting was the final step in a four-month-long effort to establish a budget for the new corporation. Working from recommendations put forward by Gurney's staff, the four corporate officers were preparing a final operational plan for submission to the Bank of New York, the firm's major lending institution.

The basic issue underlying all other considerations concerned how the company should go about paying off the large debt that had been incurred to buy Gurney from Amfac, a *Fortune* 500 conglomerate located in San Francisco. Within this broad context, two questions received considerable attention. Would the forecast for 1985 bear out and provide the company with the cash needed to pay the interest on the debt? What could be done to reassure employees who had seen three different managements in five years, and who, because of management's decision to scale down operations, faced a lay-off of forty-two workers?

Gurney's History

Gurney Seed and Nursery Company was founded in 1866 by Colonel C. W. Gurney in Monticello, Iowa, as a retail and mail-order establishment specializing in seeds and plants. In 1897, headquarters were moved to Yankton, South Dakota. While the colonel and his son proved to be astute businessmen, successive generations did not, and the company went bankrupt in 1940. Revived and sold in 1942, Gurney became profitable again until 1969, when it was sold to a speculator named Jack Hesse.

Hesse was the first owner of Gurney to have no interest in running the operation. Instead, his focus was on building a business empire, and to that end he diverted Gurney's cash flow, leveraging the company to fund new acquisitions. In 1980, with Gurney deep in debt, Hesse sold out to Amfac, a company engaged in wholesale distribution, food processing, retailing, hotels and resorts, Hawaiian sugar, and land operations. A year later, Amfac also acquired Henry Field, one of Gurney's closest rivals, and created two new support companies, Dakota Advertising and Dakota Data Resources to form a Mail Order Division. This division in turn was then joined with several large nurseries and some other related businesses to make up the Horticulture Group with 1981 sales of about $85 million. See Exhibit 1 for an organization chart of the Mail Order Division within the group and corporate structure.

Amfac viewed the horticultural business as a vehicle for rapid growth. Sales of the Mail Order Division alone were projected to increase from $36.6 million in 1981 to more than $300 million by the end of the decade. Contrary to such optimistic projections, however, the group soon experienced rapid sales and profit declines in its nursery business. In 1982, the recession began to affect its mail-order business as well. Exhibit 2 shows selected financial data for Gurney from 1977 to 1980, and for Gurney with Henry Field from 1981 to 1982.

In May 1982, General Harry W. Brooks (then age fifty-three), a thirty-year veteran of the U.S. Army who had been a senior vice president and director of public relations with Amfac for four years, was put in charge of straightening out the ailing Horticulture Group. Later that year, Brooks hired John Kemp (then age forty), a Harvard MBA with seventeen years of prior management experience with Xerox, General Foods, and Chrysler, as vice president of strategic planning for the Horticulture Group. Kemp remarked on this decision, "As a black, the chance to work with Harry Brooks in the Horticulture Group personally appealed to me. Brooks was one of the few blacks I knew who really had senior-level line-management responsibility in a large corporation."

When the full impact of the recession hit in 1983, revenues from the Mail Order Division dropped to $33.1 million, and the Horticulture Group as a whole experienced a $55.3 million loss, primarily due to the write-offs of excessive crops planted prior to 1982. With the need to improve overall corporate financial performance (Amfac experienced a net loss of $68 million on sales of $2.3 billion in 1983), corporate management decided to divest the entire Horticulture Group in line with its new strategy (as stated in the 1983 annual report) "to focus on core businesses that show the greatest promise for future growth."

Brooks, Price, and Kemp were convinced that the mail-order business was an inherently attractive one that had suffered in a corporate environment geared to manage big-business operations. As Amfac entered negotiations with several potential buyers, these three men, and Donald Miller, a friend of General Brooks and a graduate of the Harvard Advanced Management Program, who was not associated with the business, teamed up to propose a leveraged buyout of Gurney, Field, and the Dakota subunits. With some reluctance, Amfac management was finally persuaded to sell the Mail Order Division to this group for $16.5 million. The four men put up $250,000 of their own money and borrowed the rest to make the purchase.

Exhibit 1 1983 AMFAC organizational chart.

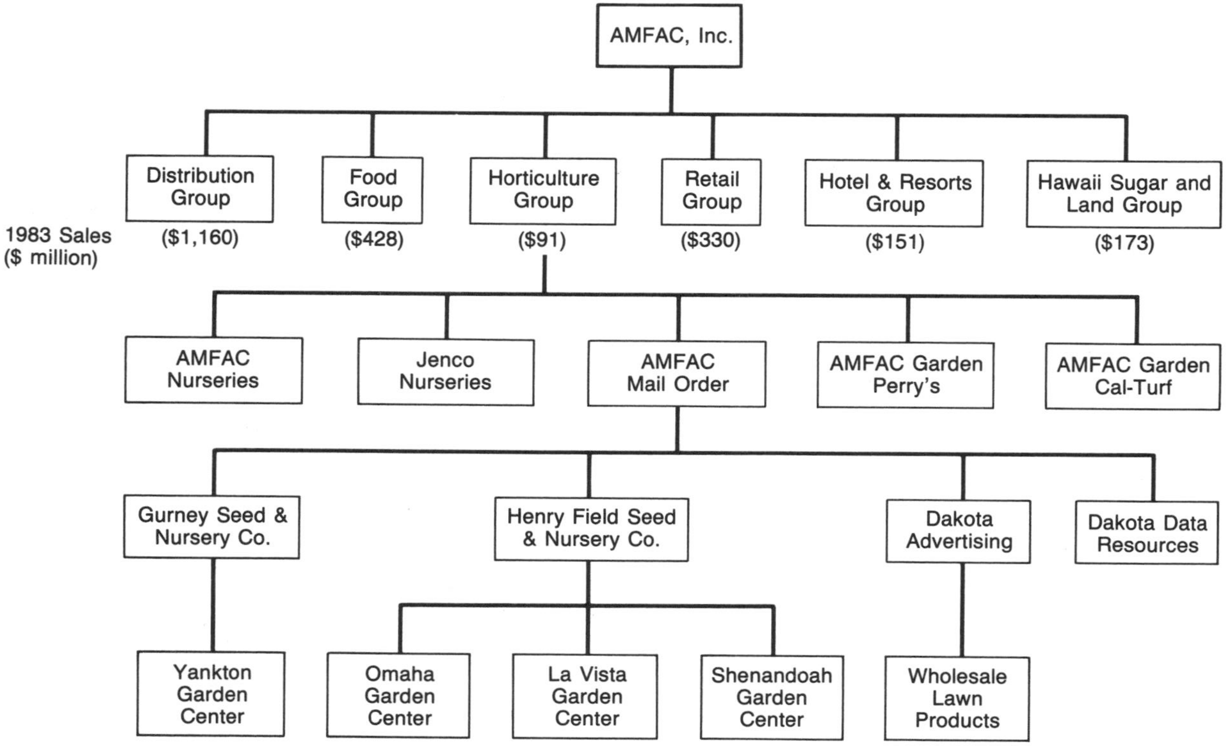

AMFAC, Inc.

1983 Sales
($ million)

| Distribution Group ($1,160) | Food Group ($428) | Horticulture Group ($91) | Retail Group ($330) | Hotel & Resorts Group ($151) | Hawaii Sugar and Land Group ($173) |

AMFAC Nurseries — Jenco Nurseries — AMFAC Mail Order — AMFAC Garden Perry's — AMFAC Garden Cal-Turf

Gurney Seed & Nursery Co. — Henry Field Seed & Nursery Co. — Dakota Advertising — Dakota Data Resources

Yankton Garden Center — Omaha Garden Center — La Vista Garden Center — Shenandoah Garden Center — Wholesale Lawn Products

Exhibit 2 Selected Gurney and Henry Field financial data (1977–82) ($ thousands).

	Gurney only								Gurney and Henry Field			
	1977	(%)	1978	(%)	1979	(%)	1980	(%)	1981	(%)	1982	(%)
Revenues	13,950	100.0	14,687	100.0	17,954	100.0	21,415	100.0	36,578	100.0	34,892	100.0
% Base mail order	93.4%		94.1%		93.9%		95.3%		87.7%		88.4%	
% Other	6.6%		5.9%		6.1%		4.7%		12.3%		11.6%	
Cost of sales	5,090	36.5	4,980	33.9	5,503	30.7	6,502	30.4	12,112	33.1	10,981	31.5
Gross margin	8,860	63.5	9,707	66.1	12,451	69.3	14,913	69.6	24,466	66.9	23,911	68.5
Distribution	2,106	15.1	2,138	14.5	2,471	13.7	3,207	15.0	5,006	13.7	4,782	13.7
Selling	4,273	30.6	4,613	31.4	4,989	27.8	6,683	31.2	12,017	32.9	13,397	38.4
G&A	1,628	11.7	1,669	11.4	2,114	11.8	1,627	7.6	2,906	7.9	3,019	8.6
Group allocation	—	—	—	—	—	—	174	0.8	350	1.0	496	1.4
Contribution	853	6.1	1,287	8.8	2,877	16.0	3,222	15.0	4,187	11.4	2,217	6.4
Gurney	853		1,287		2,877		3,222		3,747		2,438	
Henry Field	—		—		—		—		440		(221)	
Allocated charges	107	0.8	630	4.3	(23)	(0.1)	205	0.9	350	0.9	472	1.4
Income tax provision	299	2.1	290	2.0	1,043	5.8	1,497	7.0	1,858	5.1	801	2.3
Net income	447	3.2	367	2.5	1,857	10.3	1,520	7.1	1,979	5.4	944	2.7
Average total capital	2,539		2,251		2,401		2,881		6,171		6,744	
ROTC	12.5%		24.3%		53.3%		55.6%		34.4%		16.9%	
Gurney	12.5%		24.3%		53.3%		55.6%		60.1%		33.9%	
Henry Field	—		—		—		—		7.5%		(3.0%)	
Cash generated	28		1,589		1,088		(1,044)		677		(58)	
Gurney	28		1,589		1,088		(1,044)[a]		1,762		208	
Henry Field	—		—		—		—		(1,085)		(266)	
Simple Cash Generation (before corporate charges)	434		2,509		2,108		832		4,320		1,711	

a. Caused by fiscal year change at time of acquisition.

The Mail-Order Business

The first mail-order customers in the U.S. were farmers and trappers who were unable to travel long distances to retail outlets, but their selection of goods was limited to a narrow range of products at premium prices. Capitalizing on the improvement of rail transportation, Aaron Montgomery Ward set up a business in 1872 to bypass retail middlemen, cut prices, and offer a wide range of durable goods by mail, for cash. Montgomery Ward was followed into the general merchandise mail order business by Sears, Roebuck & Co. in 1886. By the early twentieth century, Sears, Roebuck proclaimed itself as "the Cheapest Supply House on Earth," and its catalog was known to farm families as the "wish book."

Changing population patterns in the United States in the mid-1920s prompted the largest two catalog companies, Sears and Montgomery Ward, to open hundreds of retail stores. Those outlets began to generate more profits than their mail-order operations, as automobile travel to stores became easier and faster than shopping by mail. As a result, mail-order shopping began to wane.

The spiraling price of gasoline, the rapid increase in the number of households with two working spouses, and the mounting traffic congestion in urban and suburban centers all worked to reverse this downward trend during the 1970s. As noted in *Forbes* (May 7, 1984):

> Sears was offering a variety of goods, mostly to people who lived a half day away from the nearest big store. Now, of course, it's just the opposite: The shelves are only minutes away. But high labor costs, . . . parking, traffic and crime are obstacles. So the ordeal of shopping takes half a day.

Technology in the 1980s played an increasingly important role in reducing the time required to process and distribute orders. Powerful computers that recorded inventory and electronically routed orders through automated warehouses were employed by major catalogers to speed products to customers. The use of toll-free telephone numbers and around-the-clock staffs to operate the electronic information systems further improved customer service.

This growth in technology in time increased both the business potential and the capital costs associated with efficient mail-order operations. By 1984, the mail-order industry, with total sales of $150 billion and growing at a rate of 15 percent annually, had become dominated by big players. The largest U.S. catalog companies included Sears with 1983 sales in excess of $2 billion, J. C. Penney ($1.7 billion), Montgomery Ward ($1.2 billion), and Fingerhut (over $500 million).

The mail-order seed and nursery business in 1985 was a highly competitive market, characterized by dozens of small regional catalogers and three national companies. Geography played an important role in segmenting the business. The seed and plant requirements were distinctive for different areas of the country, because of temperature, rainfall, and customer preferences. Furthermore, each company tried to project a distinctive image that would appeal to special mail-order audiences. As reported in *The Boston Globe* (February 8, 1985):

Rob Johnston, President of Johnny's Selected Seed, notes, "Every seed company has its own personality and it comes across in the catalog." The Johnny's catalog, filled with graphs and information geared toward organic horticultural methods, is earnest and educational. On the other hand, Gurney's looks and reads like a colorful Sunday comic strip with photos of 307-pound giant squash with captions such as "this balloon won't fly."

Gurney's management competed most directly on the national level with the Burpee and Park Seed companies. A June 1983 strategic analysis sized up the competition this way:

Burpee [a subsidiary of ITT]—Even though their primary appeal is to a slightly different market segment [more emphasis on flower seeds as compared to Gurney's emphasis on vegetable seeds], Burpee is our major competitor. Over the last several years they have appeared indecisive as to business direction and are certainly several years behind the industry in mail-order techniques. However, they will remain stiff competition on the east coast and throughout the northeast for the next several years just on the strength of their name.

Park Seed Company—Like Burpee, their appeal is to a slightly different market segment. However, with their base in the South and Southeast, they overlap our market and represent the second strongest competitor. Under family ownership, they tend to be conservative and behind the industry in many areas.

We strongly believe neither of these companies has grown as rapidly nor been as profitable as Gurney in the last five years, including 1983. We further believe that with the exception of the southern U.S., we have captured the biggest share of the market.

In 1985, ITT was reported to have included Burpee among the businesses that were being considered for divestment as part of a major move to generate funds.

Gurney's Products and Market

Gurney and Field both offered a full range of over 4,000 garden-related items in their catalogs. These items fell into three broad categories: garden seed, nursery goods, and merchandise (garden-related equipment and supplies). Table A shows the relative importance of each of these categories.

Customers. Gurney had an active customer list (i.e., persons who had made a purchase within three years) of approximately 2.7 million names and Field of 1.3 million names. Since management considered customer loyalty a potent force in buying behavior, the two lists were not commingled. Kemp noted, "Gardening involves a big investment in time and effort before you see the results. Therefore, people tend to stick with a company which has provided consistent satisfaction over the years." He estimated a 25 percent overlap in customers in 1984.

Demographically, Gurney and Field customers were about the same. Their

Table A   Gurney's 1984 sales and margin statistics.

	Sales ($)	% of Sales	Gross Margin (%)
Garden Seed	9,900,000	33	81.5
Nursery	15,900,000	53	67.4
Other (catalog merchandise, retail & wholesale sales, and list rental)	4,200,000	14	50.0
Total	30,000,000	100	

median age was fifty years, and median family income was $21,000. Some 94 percent were homeowners, with an average garden size of 2,500 square feet. Geographically, customers lived in midwest and western states, with the heaviest concentration in Illinois, Minnesota, and Wisconsin. They tended to stay put: 90 percent lived in the same town they had lived in ten years earlier. Although most of the customers were not farmers, they were predominately rural, and were dependent upon farm income. Any drop in retail food prices or increase in the price of seed or nursery products also had a significant negative impact on the quantities ordered.

Catalogs

The principal means by which Gurney reached its customers was through catalogs sent out several times a year. The critical success factor in getting a good response from a catalog mailing was in having the catalogs in the customers' hands well before the start of the growing season.

Active customers were mailed a sixty-four-page spring catalog in December. If this catalog failed to elicit a response by late February, another copy was mailed to serve as a reminder. A smaller version (forty-four pages) was sent to prospective customers. In late March, another sixty-four-page special sale catalog featuring new products and sell-out prices was mailed to active customers. In August, a smaller fall planting catalog was mailed.

Management regarded Gurney's catalogs as more "folksy" than those offered by competing firms. In physical make-up the company's catalog had always been *Life* magazine size (11" x 16"), printed on stock paper, in contrast to the 8 ½" x 11" glossy paper catalogs generally used in the industry. Exhibit 3 displays a typical page from a Gurney catalog.

Gurney's Business Cycle

Production of the spring catalog, which began on August 1, marked the start of Gurney's business cycle. Sizable outlays of cash were required for layout, printing, artwork, and photography from August through November. In fall, production costs also began to increase as seasonal workers were hired to pre-

Exhibit 3 Page from 1985 Gurney catalog.

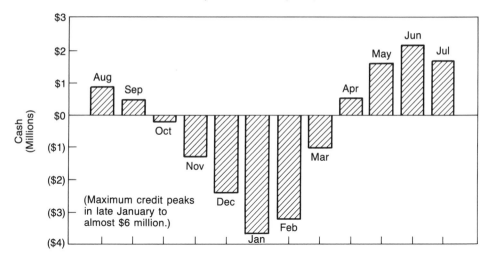

Figure A Typical cash position cycle for Gurney operations (monthly average).

pare and package seeds and other nursery items. Postage alone for mailing spring catalogs amounted to over $1 million. As a result of these activities, working capital requirements usually peaked in January.

As orders with cash payments began to arrive in mid-January, the company began to reduce its short-term debt. Cash inflows were typically great enough to retire all of Gurney's short-term debt by April 1.

As a general rule, about 85 percent of the entire year's cash inflows were received from February through July (50 percent in March and April). The remaining 15 percent were received in late summer in connection with the fall catalog. (Sales were recognized when the product was shipped; cash receipts when received with the order.) Figure A shows the seasonal impact on Gurney's cash position.

Operations

The company's principal operations included the preparation of catalogs, the production (farming) and purchasing of products, packaging, order taking, shipping, and customer service. Apart from catalog production and data processing, Gurney and Field were independently run.

Located near the banks of the Missouri River in Yankton, South Dakota, Gurney's farming facilities consisted of 525 acres of owned, and 67 acres of leased land. Twenty percent of its catalog products were produced on its own farm, including small flowering plants and vegetable seeds. Outside wholesale vendors provided the remaining 80 percent of catalog items, including all merchandise and such exotic nursery items as bulbs imported from Holland.

During the planting and harvesting seasons, the base crew of 220 farm workers ballooned to about 650 workers. During spring, several hundred seasonal workers were added to handle order taking, packaging, and shipping. All seasonal and full-time employees were nonunion and, except for those doing manual labor, most were women who had been with Gurney for many years.

Dakota Data Resources (DDR), a wholly owned subsidiary of Gurney, maintained the mailing lists, processed orders, tracked sales of catalog items, and collected financial data for both Gurney and Field. The company, located in its own building in downtown Yankton, used IBM 4300 series hardware and 150 IBM 3277-2 display terminals that were operated by part-time seasonal workers. During the peak season, DDR was capable of processing 30,000 mail orders daily.

Also located in downtown Yankton was Dakota Advertising, Gurney's in-house agency. This unit, employing a full-time staff of writers, artists, copy editors, and printers, did lay-out, design, graphic production, printing, and mailing of all Gurney's and Field's catalogs. Like DDR, Dakota Advertising hired additional workers during the peak season.

Henry Field's operating facility in Shenandoah, Iowa, performed many of the same functions as Gurney's facility, such as planting, harvesting, and shipping orders to customers. The company owned 135 acres, and leased 400 acres in the immediate area on which 25 percent of its products were grown. In addition to its mail-order operations, Field owned three retail garden centers (two in Omaha, Nebraska, and one in Shenandoah) that provided 15 percent of its annual revenue.

Keith Price, in charge of operations, had his office in Yankton. Harvesting, packaging, and shipping operations in South Dakota and Iowa were controlled by nursery managers who were responsible for meeting production schedules, stocking adequate inventory, and shipping orders in a timely fashion.

Harry W. Brooks, John Kemp, and two staff assistants occupied Gurney's corporate headquarters in San Bruno, California. By establishing headquarters near San Francisco, Brooks believed that the corporation would make itself more accessible to financial resources, as well as give top management a broader perspective on the marketplace. Another reason for putting headquarters in San Francisco was Brooks's confidence in Keith Price as the chief operating officer. Price had been Gurney's executive vice president in charge of marketing, and he was selected by Brooks in 1983 to assume the presidency of Amfac Mail Order Division.

By separating headquarters from operations, Brooks believed it would facilitate entering new businesses over time. Plans were under way to create, as of December 1, 1984, a new holding company, Advanced Consumer Marketing Corporation, to provide an organizational structure for such expansion in the future. See Exhibit 4 for the new organization chart.

The Leveraged Buy-out

Following lengthy negotiations, the four owners reached an agreement with Amfac management to purchase the seed and nursery mail-order business for $16.5 million through a leveraged buy-out arrangement. The exchange of own-

Exhibit 4 Gurney's revised organizational chart (December 1984).

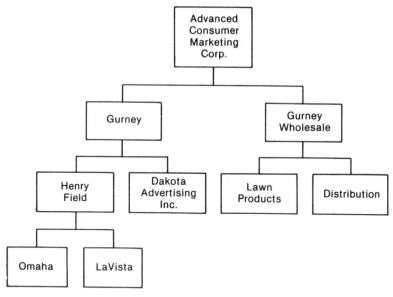

ership took place on Monday, April 30, 1984, and involved the following financial transactions (in $ million):

Amfac's Considerations		*New Owner's Financing*	
free cash flow from		free cash flow	$5.2
operations, Jan. 1–Apr. 30	$5.2	long-term debt	8.0
cash	10.1	short-term debt	1.85
note	0.5	note to Amfac	0.5
transfer of debt		other debt	0.7
to new owners	0.7	equity	0.25
Total	$16.5		$16.5

The short-term debt was further reduced on that day by $700,000 from orders received over the weekend. A summary of the new company's debt is shown in Exhibit 5.

The 1985 Budget

John Kemp saw the main objective for Gurney's 1985 budget to be the reduction of short- and long-term debt. The firm's short-term debt position was of particular concern to him, standing at a million dollars at a time when the company should have had substantial cash on hand. Complicating the situation was the need Kemp saw to change the loan's restrictive covenants and the difficulty management had in forecasting 1985 conditions for the seed and nursery

Exhibit 5 Summary of debt and interest expense.

Payee	Description of debt	Principal Amount (as of 10/1/84)	Interest Rate and Payment Schedule	Estimated Total Interest to be Paid 10/84 to 10/85[a]
Amfac	Five-year subordinated note	$500,000	12%; yearly payments	$60,000
American State Bank	Existing loan on fixed assets due in 1988	663,943	9.75%; semi-annual payments	65,092
Bank of New York	Principal term loan to buy the company	8,000,000	Prime rate to 6/30/87; .25% + prime to 6/30/90; .50% + prime to 6/30/94 Thirty-two consecutive quarterly installments of principal beginning 9/86	960,000 (assuming 12% interest rate for 1985)
Bank of New York	Facility fee (an additional compensation to the bank for entering into the loan agreement)	1,999,998	Twelve consecutive quarterly installments of $166,667 beginning 3/31/89	—
Bank of New York	Short-term debt	up to 8,000,000	Variable	—
Other	Loan from Harry Brooks, due in 12/85 (for sub-chapter S purposes)	233,000	12% (three payments in 1985 with principal due 12/85)	20,970
	Lucille Foster Trust, due 1992	71,793	8%; monthly payments	4,946
				Total $1,449,508

a. No repayment of principal was scheduled for this reporting period (10/84 to 10/85).

mail order business. (A restrictive covenant imposes specific constraints upon the borrower to protect the lender's interests.)

Kemp explained his reasons for wanting to change the loan covenants: "At the time of the closing, many facts regarding the ultimate balance sheet, the accounting policies, and the size of inventory were unknown to the Bank of New York and to Gurney. Since then, we have had unexpected tax write-offs for inventory and catalogs. We have also decided to remove from the balance sheet about $3.4 million in prepaid expenses for catalogs and to recognize marketing expenses as period costs. The major thrust of our proposed changes is to emphasize cash flow over profits so as to minimize our tax exposure. As a result, the original covenants no longer make any sense."

Kemp sought to make the following specific changes in the bank loan agreement terms:

1. Minimum net worth covenant:

	as agreed	proposed
October 31, 1985	$ 750,000	$(3,600,000)
October 31, 1986	2,250,000	(2,800,000)
October 31, 1987	4,250,000	(1,700,000)
October 31, 1988	7,050,000	300,000

2. Short-term line of credit:

Elimination of the requirement that short-term credit be limited to the sum of 90 percent of accounts receivable plus 80 percent of inventory plus 50 percent of net prepaid expenses. With management's decision to reduce inventories and to eliminate most prepaid expenses, the short-term funds available under this formula fell well below the $8 million ceiling. The bank was also to remove a stipulation requiring Gurney to have ninety consecutive debt-free days in its short-term line of credit account.

In preparing an economic overview for the business, Kemp had found 1984 to be a confusing year from which to project. Some of the sources of confusion included the following considerations: The U.S. was experiencing a high growth in GNP, but farm income had sagged; interest rates had declined during the first quarter, risen during the second and third quarters, and were again declining at year end; and unemployment had decreased but was still above the 1981 level of 7.5 percent. Moreover, according to Kemp, the industry's overall catalog sales had been dropping 10 percent per annum over the depressed 1981–84 period. His report to management concluded, "All of these factors make predicting 1985 all but impossible."

Notwithstanding these difficulties, Kemp had had to make several major assumptions in order to prepare pro forma financial projections. First, a prime rate of 11.25 percent was assumed for 1985, 12.75 percent for 1986, and 12 percent thereafter. A shift of 100 basis points (1 percent) in the prime rate would change Gurney's annual interest burden by $120,000.

The projections also assumed a low and stable general inflation rate of 4 percent for 1985. Because food prices were a major component in the inflation rate, a high inflation rate generally meant rising food prices. For Gurney's, higher inflation meant that more people would want to grow their own food, hence increasing demand. A second bonus from inflation was that it reduced the real interest rate that the company had to pay. The projections for inflation and interest rates were thought to be on the conservative side. Finally, Kemp assumed that the recession had bottomed out for the segment of the population served by the mail-order horticultural industry. Although the reelection of President Reagan and the likely resulting cutback on farm-support programs had been anticipated, the full impact of such changes on future farm income was difficult to predict.

As Kemp worked on the 1985 economic overview, operating managers were busy preparing operational plans. Kemp describes how management had set them to work on this assignment:

> No longer do we have a parent company around to bail us out at the end of the year. That means that we have to get our people to think in new ways. For example, we told our marketing people to put together a marketing plan with reduced costs. But we didn't tell them how to reduce those costs, nor did we tell them how much to reduce them. Even though we have a figure in mind of what those costs should be, we want them to propose cost reductions and to show what happens as those cuts are made. Then we'll sit down and talk.

When the various projections and proposals had been reviewed and adjusted, Kemp then began to prepare a variety of detailed financial projections. Monthly financial data for the 1985 base case are contained in Exhibits 6 and 7. This model was based on the following assumptions: a 25 percent reduction in catalog mailings for 1985; effective price increases of 4.5 percent for Gurney's products and 2.5 percent for Field's; no change in response rate or average order size when compared to 1984; labor and benefits cost reductions totaling $757,000; and an inventory reduction of $1.7 million. A sensitivity analysis with respect to response rate is given in Exhibit 8. Base case projections through 1988 are included in Exhibits 9 and 10.

The budget document concluded that (1) the company could withstand another year of lower than anticipated results, and (2) the upside potential was great. However, the financial projections incorporated policies concerning price increases and cost reductions that still had to be examined and decided in the budget meeting under way.

Price Increases

Product price increases were up for final approval in the November budget meeting. Gurney's prices were to rise by 4.5 percent and Henry Field's prices by 2.5 percent. Field's increase was less, because its prices were already comparatively higher than Gurney's. The net effect of those increases was an expected increase in average order revenues of 2 percent for Gurney and 1 percent for Field.

Part of the price increase would have to cover an anticipated 10 percent increase in postal and United Parcel Service shipping charges. In 1984, Gurney's postage expenses were about $1.5 million and UPS shipping about $1.7 million. Commenting on the price hike as a whole, Kemp noted, "We sell value. We're not the cheapest, but we're also not the most expensive. Our customers know that."

In addition to raising prices, management was thinking of increasing the average order size as a way of increasing revenues. Adding new products to the present catalogs was one approach under active consideration.

Cost Reductions

Kemp saw a major job for the new owners to be one of making the organization more cost and cash conscious. He remarked:

> Amfac had programmed people to think about rapid growth. Investments in staffing and facilities were made in anticipation of much larger and more complex operations. The pockets were deep and not too much attention was paid to cash. But when you are dealing with a small, privately owned company, P&L is meaningless. Cash is king.
>
> In a large organization, sometimes you would have to put a sunroof, automatic windows, and tinted glass on a proposal to get it through. You knew that they were going to strip off those layers, and you hoped that enough of your proposal would remain to recognize it when they got through. If the boss didn't like the numbers you brought him, you went away and brought him back some new numbers that he would like.
>
> That kind of game playing just doesn't make any sense for us. Our job now is to peel down the onion to its essence and to make people very concerned with cash flow. For example, under Amfac, Gurney always paid vendors within thirty days. Now, we slow down such payments. Labor and benefits were two other areas where we saw a need to reduce expenditures.

The seed and nursery business was highly labor intensive. Gurney and Field had spent nearly $4 million on wages and salaries in 1983, exclusive of advertising and data-processing labor costs. In October, 1984, management decided to cut the line work force by forty-two workers, based on a careful analysis of the expected business outlook for 1985. The resulting annual savings were projected to be $453,000.

The health plan was also targeted for savings. Kemp wanted to introduce a new plan that would provide a more comprehensive health coverage and would also include seasonal workers. At the same time, he proposed that employees pay a monthly fee and be liable for a $200 deductible. The net effect would be to save the company $206,000 annually.

In line with these moves, Amfac's practice of supplying many executives with a company car was discontinued, resulting in an expected savings of $39,000 for 1985.

Management's efforts to improve the economics of the company was strongly influenced by its concern that value be given for dollars spent and that muscle

Exhibit 6 1985 end of month pro forma balance sheets for base case (11.25% interest rate).

	Beginning Balance	Nov.	Dec.	Jan.	Feb.	Mar.	Apr.	May	Jun.	Jul.	Aug.	Sept.	Oct.
Current Assets													
Cash	$100	$100	$100	$100	$100	$100	$100	$613	$688	$100	$100	$100	$100
Accounts receivable	563	509	399	442	678	839	1,052	944	407	318	298	291	356
Inventory	3,986	4,250	5,298	6,263	5,774	4,423	3,211	2,717	2,640	2,874	3,011	3,286	3,523
Net prepaid expenses	184	141	145	180	245	219	178	141	129	132	143	158	193
Total current assets	4,833	5,000	5,942	6,985	6,797	5,581	4,541	4,415	3,864	3,424	3,552	3,835	4,172
Fixed Assets													
Property & equipment (at cost)	7,833	7,849	7,853	7,863	7,933	7,950	7,958	7,958	8,023	8,109	8,111	8,111	8,119
Less accum. depreciation	(344)	(405)	(466)	(527)	(588)	(649)	(710)	(771)	(832)	(893)	(954)	(1,015)	(1,076)
Net property & equipment	7,489	7,444	7,387	7,336	7,345	7,301	7,248	7,187	7,191	7,216	7,157	7,096	7,043
Other Assets													
Noncurrent receivables*	34	34	34	34	34	34	34	34	34	34	34	34	34
Other assets	61	61	61	61	61	61	61	61	61	61	61	61	61
Prepaid interest	935	924	913	902	891	880	869	858	847	836	825	814	803
Total other assets	1,030	1,019	1,008	997	986	975	964	953	942	931	920	909	898
TOTAL ASSETS	13,352	13,463	14,337	15,318	15,128	13,857	12,753	12,555	11,997	11,571	11,629	11,840	12,113

Current Liabilities

Short-term debt (Bank of N.Y.)	$2,667	$3,445	$4,530	$5,994	$3,579	$1,549	$515	$0	$0	$348	$1,012	$1,205	$2,228
Current interest due	150	274	403	185	323	438	156	185	273	98	190	288	129
AP & accrued expenses	886	1,788	4,141	4,172	3,878	2,392	1,043	890	912	1,182	691	837	952
Current portion of long-term debt	38	38	38	39	39	39	39	40	40	40	41	41	41
Income taxes payable (receivable)	0	0	0	0	0	0	0	0	0	0	0	0	0
Unfilled orders	734	447	535	1,465	3,062	2,375	1,218	569	427	482	912	1,187	679
Total current liabilities	4,475	5,992	9,647	11,855	10,882	6,793	2,971	1,684	1,652	2,150	2,846	3,558	4,028
	500	500	500	500	500	500	500	500	500	500	500	500	500

Long-Term Liabilities

Deferred interest (Bank of N.Y.)	1,057	1,067	1,076	1,086	1,096	1,106	1,116	1,127	1,137	1,147	1,158	1,169	1,179
Long-term debt (Bank of N.Y.)	8,000	8,000	8,000	8,000	8,000	8,000	8,000	8,000	8,000	8,000	8,000	8,000	8,000
Other long-term debt	1,439	1,439	1,439	1,438	1,438	1,438	1,402	1,401	1,168	1,168	1,167	1,167	1,131
Total long-term liabilities	10,496	10,506	10,515	10,524	10,534	10,544	10,518	10,528	10,305	10,315	10,325	10,336	10,310
TOTAL LIABILITIES	15,471	16,998	20,663	22,880	21,917	17,837	13,990	12,712	12,457	12,965	13,671	14,393	14,839

Stockholder's Equity

Common stock	250	250	250	250	250	250	250	250	250	250	250	250	250
BEGINNING retained earnings	n/a	(2,369)	(3,784)	(6,575)	(7,811)	(7,038)	(4,230)	(1,486)	(407)	(709)	(1,644)	(2,292)	(2,803)
Net income for the period	n/a	(1,415)	(2,791)	(1,236)	773	2,808	2,744	1,080	(303)	(935)	(648)	(511)	(173)
ENDING retained earnings	(2,369)	(3,784)	(6,575)	(7,811)	(7,038)	(4,230)	(1,486)	(407)	(709)	(1,644)	(2,292)	(2,803)	(2,976)
Total stockholder's equity	(2,119)	(3,534)	(6,325)	(7,561)	(6,788)	(3,980)	(1,236)	(157)	(459)	(1,394)	(2,042)	(2,553)	(2,726)
TOTAL EQUITY & LIABILITY	13,352	13,464	14,338	15,318	15,128	13,857	12,753	12,555	11,997	11,571	11,629	11,840	12,113

*Long-Term Deferred Tax

Exhibit 7 1985 monthly pro forma profit and loss statements for base case (11.25% interest rate).

	Nov.	Dec.	Jan.	Feb.	Mar.
Sales					
Mail order	497	141	800	2,872	6,043
Wholesale products	36	8	71	362	184
Retail stores	65	171	25	43	120
Other	100	44	144	57	144
Total sales	708	364	1,040	3,334	6,491
Cost of Goods Sold					
Mail order	138	39	222	796	1,674
Whole products	18	4	36	181	92
Retail stores	42	111	16	28	78
Other	55	22	72	29	72
Total COGS	253	176	345	1,033	1,916
Gross Margin					
($)	455	188	695	2,301	4,575
(%)	64.28%	51.57%	66.79%	69.02%	70.48%
Expenses					
Selling	1,274	2,464	1,320	662	499
Shipping & distribution	89	44	127	387	786
General & administrative	222	222	222	222	222
S.F.H.Q. expense	38	38	38	38	38
Prepaid expense amort.	43	0	0	0	26
Depreciation	61	61	61	61	61
Total expenses	1,727	2,829	1,768	1,370	1,632
Income before Interest					
and Taxes	(1,272)	(2,641)	(1,073)	931	2,943
Deferred interest	21	21	21	21	21
Interest expense	123	130	143	138	115
Interest income	1	1	1	1	1
Income before Taxes	(1,415)	(2,791)	(1,236)	773	2,808
0% Effective tax rate	0	0	0	0	0
Net Income					
Period	(1,416)	(2,791)	(1,236)	773	2,808
Cumulative	($1,415)	($4,206)	($5,442)	($4,669)	($1,861)

Apr.	May	Jun.	Jul.	Aug.	Sept.	Oct.	Total
5,593	2,684	714	183	187	359	880	20,952
286	28	11	0	1	2	1	990
490	867	418	169	129	211	146	2,854
138	119	99	65	38	65	165	1,188
6,507	3,698	1,242	417	355	637	1,192	25,984
1,549	743	198	51	52	99	244	5,804
143	14	6	0	1	1	1	495
319	564	272	110	84	137	95	1,855
69	60	50	33	19	33	83	593
2,080	1,380	524	193	155	270	422	8,748
4,427	2,317	717	224	200	367	770	17,236
68.04%	62.67%	57.77%	53.69%	56.30%	57.60%	64.63%	66.33%
473	405	465	685	365	366	358	9,337
729	364	116	49	50	73	140	2,954
222	222	222	222	222	222	222	2,668
38	38	38	38	38	38	38	450
41	37	12	0	0	0	0	159
61	61	61	61	61	61	61	732
1,564	1,127	914	1,055	737	759	819	16,299
2,863	1,191	(196)	(831)	(537)	(393)	(49)	937
21	21	21	21	22	22	22	254
99	91	88	88	93	97	104	1,309
1	1	3	5	3	1	1	19
2,744	1,080	(303)	(935)	(648)	(511)	(173)	(607)
0	0	0	0	0	0	0	0
2,744	1,080	(303)	(935)	(648)	(511)	(173)	(607)
$883	$1,962	$1,660	$725	$77	($434)	($607)	

Exhibit 8   1985 sensitivity analysis (Nov. 1, 1984 to Oct. 31, 1985) ($ thousands).

	90% Resp. CASE	95% Resp. CASE	BASE CASE	105% Resp. CASE	110% Resp. CASE
Total sales	23,895	24,940	25,984	27,029	28,074
Net income	(1,885)	(1,245)	(607)	31	666
Stockholder's equity					
Common stock	250	250	250	250	250
Ending retained earnings	(4,254)	(3,614)	(2,976)	(2,338)	(1,703)
Total stockholder's equity	(4,004)	(3,364)	(2,726)	(2,088)	(1,453)
Net increase in funds	(835)	(197)	439	1,075	1,708

not be cut with fat. This led it to investigate the areas of catalog production and customer service.

One of the largest expenses in Gurney's annual budget was the cost of putting together catalogs. Dakota Advertising, the in-house agency, had a $10 million ($1 million in overhead) operating budget. Although John Kemp considered these expenses to be high, he and his partners had not resolved whether they could or should be cut. Kemp described the dilemma they faced:

> Our catalogs don't really change much. The prices are changed, the pages are moved around a little, but it's pretty much the same from year to year. Right now I'm asking myself this: If we reduce staff at Dakota and just use pages from last year's catalog, change prices, and move things around, would we generate the same revenue? Will our customers notice or care? Dakota needs to justify that $1 million in labor and overhead as we go forward.

With respect to customer service, each year the company received some 60,000 letters of complaint (in connection with 1.4 million orders). While many complaints were due to incorrect addresses or quantities, others were due to orders that were delayed until a customer's full order could be filled, or because substitutions were made for out-of-stock goods. Keith Price favored a policy of filling orders as soon as merchandise became available, instead of waiting for a shipment to become complete. He estimated that such a policy might incur additional postal expenses of about $10,000, but he noted, "In the past we have made poor decisions on substitutions, deliveries, processing and right down the line. Customer dissatisfaction leaves us open to the competition. Therefore, we're doing all we can to improve in this area."

Strengthening the Company

In Kemp's view, one major reason for management's difficulties in putting together a tight budget was an inadequate management-accounting system. He remarked:

Exhibit 9 Base case balance sheet projections (Oct. 31, 1985 to 1988).

	Beginning Balance	Ending 1985	Ending 1986	Ending 1987	Ending 1988
Current Assets					
Cash	$100	$100	$100	$943	$3,553
Accounts receivable	563	356	404	414	432
Inventory	3,986	3,523	3,523	3,523	3,523
Net prepaid expenses	184	193	193	193	193
Total current assets	4,833	4,172	4,220	5,073	7,702
Fixed Assets					
Property & equipment (at cost)	7,833	8,119	8,405	8,691	8,977
Less: accum. depreciation	(344)	(1,076)	(1,808)	(2,540)	(3,272)
Net property & equipment	7,489	7,043	6,597	6,151	5,705
Other Assets					
Noncurrent receivables*	34	34	34	34	34
Other assets*	61	61	61	61	61
Prepaid interest	935	803	690	592	509
Total other assets	1,030	898	785	687	604
TOTAL ASSETS	13,352	12,113	11,602	11,911	14,010
Current Liabilities					
Short-term debt (Bank of N.Y.)	$2,667	$2,228	$794	$0	$0
Current interest due	150	129	124	115	114
AP & accrued expenses	886	952	1,091	1,125	1,149
Current portion of long-term debt	38	41	41	41	41
Income taxes payable (receivable)	0	0	0	0	0
Unfilled orders	734	679	699	713	713
Total current liabilities	4,475	4,028	2,750	1,994	2,017
Long-term Liabilities					
Deferred interest (Bank of N.Y.)	1,057	1,179	1,316	1,468	1,638
Long-term debt (Bank of N.Y.)	8,000	8,000	8,000	8,000	8,000
Other long-term debt	1,439	1,131	1,059	987	915
Total long-term liabilities	10,496	10,310	10,375	10,455	10,553
TOTAL LIABILITIES	15,471	14,839	13,625	12,949	13,070
Stockholder's Equity					
Common stock	250	250	250	250	250
Retained earnings	(2,369)	(2,976)	(2,272)	(1,287)	691
Total stockholder's equity	(2,119)	(2,726)	(2,022)	(1,037)	941
TOTAL EQUITY & LIABILITY	13,352	12,113	11,602	11,912	14,010

*Long-term deferred tax

Exhibit 10   Base case funds flow projections (1985 to 1988) (fiscal year Nov. 1 to Oct. 31).

	1985	1986	1987	1988
Funds Provided				
Net income	(607)	703	985	1,978
Depreciation	732	732	732	732
Deferred taxes	0	0	0	0
Prepaid interest	132	113	97	84
Deferred interest	122	136	152	170
Subtotal	379	1,685	1,967	2,963
Funds Applied				
Increase (decrease) working capital	(654)	(106)	(29)	(5)
Increase (decrease) fixed assets	286	286	286	286
Decrease (increase) long-term debt	308	72	72	72
Subtotal	(60)	252	329	353
Net increase in funds	439	1,434	1,637	2,610

Amfac's reporting system was near worthless for management purposes. It was based on a return-on-total capital concept, and it lacked the analytical tools for a manager to make any reasonable decisions.

We want to watch every penny going out and every purchase coming in. One of my high-priority efforts is to introduce a management-information system which will help management and employees to know exactly what is going on in the company. We're in a situation now where strategy is mixed up with day-to-day operations. We have to solve our internal reporting problems first, and then we can work on strategic planning.

Improving employee relations was also high on Harry Brooks' list of priority objectives. Kemp described the initial efforts:

At a series of meetings, Harry Brooks sat down with all of Gurney and Henry Field employees. The question he asked was, "If you had the power to change anything in the company, what would you change?" Out of this came employee-action groups to research particular problems. Some of the complaints were easily correctable. For example, one complaint heard repeatedly was about the conditions of the ladies' rooms of our hourly employees. We fixed that and generated some goodwill. We have a very low turnover rate among our employees and that says a lot. We have an obligation to them not to mess things up.

Bonuses were given to hourly employees. Incentives for managers and other wage earners, however, were considered inadequate. As a result, Kemp was developing with outside assistance a pension and profit-sharing plan for these individuals. Management decided, however, that it would be a bad move to introduce such a plan at a time when employees were being dismissed. Brooks observed, "What we need first is an upsurge in orders. When we beat plan, then we can talk about profit sharing. We'll delay the pension plan until the business gets turned around."

Management was also considering reintroducing credit cards as a way of increasing order size. An earlier attempt to use credit cards had to be discontinued when the customer-service department was flooded with calls and letters of complaint. Gurney's customers objected on the grounds that prices would have to be increased to cover the cost of credit.

Since Gurney was the only major mail-order seed company that did not offer credit, Brooks planned to test the idea again in 1985. He felt that a careful low-key introduction of the credit card would be necessary for its acceptance. Brooks was willing to risk alienating some customers to gain the advantages of a credit card. Not only would credit enable some customers to increase their order size, the cards would also permit the company to take telephone orders. Up to this point, all orders had to be accompanied by cash, check, or money order.

New Businesses

Improving Gurney's present operations dominated management's thinking in 1984, but preliminary discussions were also under way on how to offset the strong seasonality of the business. The initial focus of these deliberations was on expanding the current customer base through extending geographic coverage, and by introducing new product lines. Consideration was being given to the possibility of putting out a Christmas catalog that might include such items as mail-order needlepoint kits, horticultural products for urban dwellers, high-quality gardening tools, and popcorn makers or other types of home gadgets. A second possibility under consideration was a joint venture with another mail-order house, such as L. L. Bean, to sell its clothing in Gurney's catalogs. Management's enthusiasm for these avenues of diversification was somewhat tempered by the poor outcome associated with an earlier attempt to sell vitamins by mail.

For 1985, the company had budgeted $200,000 for developing new mail-order products. For Gurney, development meant finding and testing available products. This policy applied to horticultural items as well. According to Price, "We can go to any good agricultural college, say the University of Nebraska or Iowa, and buy new seed varieties for less than Burpee spends on developing their own seed strains."

An example of a related venture was expansion of the company's wholesale lawn program. It involved the sale of lawn fertilizer and garden products through 580 Gurney authorized distributors. Kemp estimated the annual sales potential for the business at between $1 and $2 million.

Further out in management's thinking was to enter entirely new businesses that could temper Gurney's seasonal cycle. Examples of possible businesses included radio stations, TV stations, and other kinds of mail order. Redefining

Dakota Advertising's role as a stand-alone business serving other clients as well as Gurney presented another possibility. The new organizational structure (Exhibit 4) had been put in place to permit adding such new businesses as separate divisions.

The Bottom Line

For Brooks, Price, and Kemp, Gurney was an adventure, a challenge, and even a "chance of a lifetime." Whether their efforts would ultimately lead to success or failure, in November, 1984, these three men were all "having fun" and were excited about future prospects. John Kemp summed up his feelings:

> We have a chance to do something really meaningful with the business. Look, all of us potentially are going to be rich. All we have to do is pay off the bills, and we can sit back and watch the money roll in. We'd like to do something with that money like set up a scholarship program for disadvantaged kids in South Dakota, and give more to our employees.
>
> We can control our destiny. We have a free rein to exercise creativity and imagination. But, this first year we have to think about survival. I believe that if we are patient and get our act together first, we will be successful in this venture.
>
> Success to me is enjoying what you do and being good at it. It has nothing to do with money or title. People who feel successful . . . are!

Johnson & Johnson (A)

> We believe the consistency of our overall performance as a corporation is due to our unique form of decentralized management, our adherence to the ethical principles embodied in our Credo, and our emphasis on managing the business for the long term.
>
> Statement of Strategic Direction

> Our culture is really it. That's what brought us together when the Tylenol tragedies hit. Without it, we would not have been able to manage the crisis as effectively as we did.
>
> James E. Burke, Chairman & CEO

In 1983, Johnson & Johnson (J&J) was widely regarded as one of the world's most successful health care companies. Over a twenty-year period, sales had grown at a compound annual rate of 14 percent, and earnings per share (EPS) at 17 percent. (During the 1970s, J&J's EPS growth rate was approximately double the average for the *Fortune* 100 largest industrial companies.) By 1982, J&J's worldwide revenues exceeded $5.7 billion and net income $473 million, placing it 55th in sales and 28th in net income on the *Fortune* 500 list of industrial companies. The underlying operations employed over 77,000 people based in fifty countries and sold products in 149 nations (see Exhibit 1 for financial data).

The company had also acquired a reputation for management excellence. A *Fortune* survey of industry executives to rank the management excellence of the 200 largest U.S. corporations placed J&J third overall and first among health care companies. This case describes the distinctive philosophy J&J espoused and the managerial systems and practices employed to put it into operation.

Company Background

J&J began with Robert Wood Johnson, an apothecary by training. At age thirty-one Johnson attended a seminar offered by Sir Joseph Lister, a noted English surgeon, who propounded the theory of "antisepsis." The year was 1876 and postoperative mortality rates were as high as 90 percent. The following account typified accepted surgical procedures at that time: "Unclean cotton, collected

Exhibit 1 Financial information, 1972–82, selected years ($ millions except per share figures).

	1972	1977	1980	1981	1982
Operating Statement					
Sales Revenues					
Domestic	880	1,714	2,634	3,026	3,304
Foreign	438	1,200	2,204	2,373	2,457
Total	1,318	2,914	4,838	5,399	5,761
Net earnings (after taxes)	121	247	401	468	523[b]
Percentage of sales revenues	9.2	8.5	8.3	8.7	9.1[b]
Per shara data[a]					
Earnings	0.72	1.41	2.17	2.51	2.79[b]
Dividends	0.15	0.47	0.74	0.85	0.97
Balance Sheet					
Cash and marketable securities	83	368	359	427	365
Other current assets	564	912	1,612	1,775	1,888
Fixed and other assets	334	740	1,372	1,618	1,956
Total	981	2,020	3,342	3,820	4,209
Current liabilities	179	383	774	881	900
Certificates of extra compensation	23	30	33	38	43
Long-term Debt	31	37	70	92	142
Deferred credits and others	15	91	197	281	325
Stockholders' equity	733	1,479	2,269	2,528	2,799
Total	981	2,020	3,342	3,820	4,209
Ratios and Other Information					
Return on equity	17.8%	17.8%	18.8%	19.5%	19.6%[b]
Number of employees (000's)	43.3	60.5	74.3	77.1	79.7
Number of stockholders (000's)	28.6	31.2	35.6	38.2	43
Average shares outstanding (millions)[a]	168.6	175.2	184.8	186.4	188.0

a. Per share data adjusted to reflect three-for-one common stock split in 1981.
b. Excluded, in 1982, an extraordinary charge of $100 million ($50 million after taxes or $0.27 per share) associated with the withdrawal of Tylenol capsules.

from sweepings on the floors of textile mills, was used for surgical dressings; surgeons operated in street clothes and wore a blood-spattered frock coat like a badge of honor."

Robert Johnson, then a partner in a small firm manufacturing pharmaceutical preparations, was impressed with Lister's theories and nurtured the idea of applying them. For this purpose, he joined with his two brothers, James and Edward, in establishing Johnson & Johnson to "manufacture and sell medical, pharmaceutical, surgical and antiseptic specialties and analgesic goods."

Table A Sales and operating profits (in %).

	Consumer	Professional	Pharmaceutical	Industrial
Sales	43.0	33.5	19.4	4.1
Operating profits	42.4	17.9	36.9	2.8

The firm was incorporated in 1887 with $100,000 of capital and began operations with fourteen employees on the fourth floor of what had been a wallpaper factory.

When the founder and first president died in 1910, J&J was already firmly established as a leader in the health care field. During Robert Johnson's tenure, the company had introduced revolutionary surgical dressings, established a bacteriological laboratory, and, in 1888, even published a book, *Modern Methods of Antiseptic Wound Treatment*, which for many years remained the standard text on antiseptic practices.

The company grew rapidly over the years as the result of new-product introductions and international expansion. New health care products were added through internal development and through the acquisition of established companies. One measure of the firm's recent performance in this regard was given by an independent nationwide survey in 1982 comparing the ten-year record of successful new-product launchings for eighteen major health and beauty aid manufacturers, including Bristol-Meyers, Procter & Gamble, and Kimberly-Clark. J&J was at the top of the list.

In 1982, J&J's products spanned four major groupings: consumer (baby care, surgical dressings, first aid, nonprescription drugs); professional (surgical dressings, sutures, diagnostic products); ethical (prescription) pharmaceutical; and industrial (nonwoven fabrics, edible sausage casings). The percentage sales and operating profits for these product groups in 1982 are shown in Table A.

International expansion began with the establishment of an affiliate in Canada in 1919 and one in Great Britain in 1924. By 1982, almost half of J&J's revenues and earnings were produced overseas.

The challenge of managing rapid growth in J&J was to do it in a way that would preserve the familylike atmosphere so valued in the company. When asked what it was like to work in J&J, a senior executive described it as follows:

> The prime motivator in J&J is the opportunity to grow with more responsibility. It runs through the entire organization. When we look at people in comparable jobs in other high-quality companies, we find that they are typically three to five years older than our managers.
>
> Another motivator is the climate. There is both respect for the individual and concern for the team. This is evident in our decision making. Everyone is free to argue his or her point of view. But once a decision is made, everyone is expected to do his or her best to make it work. In that way, even if a plan isn't exactly optimal, we make it succeed. In short, it's a nice company. People are nice to each other . . . and it's a nice place to work.

J&J's Philosophy and Culture

Robert Wood Johnson, the "General," son of the founder, and chairman of J&J from 1938 to 1963, was generally credited as the individual most responsible for shaping the company's philosophy and culture. Widely exposed as a young man to business around the world, he developed strong convictions about the merits of free enterprise and the ineffectiveness of large, ponderous organizations. Jim Burke, chairman and CEO since 1976, recounted: "He was convinced that if you have sensible people who know each other, in a small enough group, somehow or other problems would get worked out."

The General also held strong convictions about the public and social responsibilities that any business firm must assume. In 1947 he expressed his thoughts in a book, *Or Forfeit Freedom:*

> The evidence on this point is clear. . . . Institutions, both public and private, exist because the people want them, believe in them, or at least are willing to tolerate them. The day has passed when business is a private matter—if it ever really was. In a business society, every act of business has social consequences and may arouse public interest. Every time business hires, builds, sells, or buys, it is acting for the . . . people as well as for itself, and it must be prepared to accept full responsibility for its acts.

These convictions about enterprise and social responsibility were reflected in J&J's decentralization and in its enduring statement of beliefs, the Credo.

Decentralization

General Johnson's firm belief about the inherent superiority of small, autonomous units led J&J on a consistent path toward decentralization. Autonomy was preserved for new acquisitions, and new independent units were spun off from existing organizations whenever they appeared ready to respond to new market opportunities on their own. This process continued over the years, leading to an assemblage of some 150 companies.

The nature and purpose of J&J's decentralization were described in the 1981 annual report:

> Johnson & Johnson is not one company but many. . . . The largest has 6,300 employees; the smallest, at year-end had six. . . .
>
> Whatever their size or location, they share a commitment to meeting the special needs of a well-defined customer. In doing so, they create a wide variety of innovative ways to successfully run their businesses.
>
> We feel that the secret to liberating that productivity is decentralization—granting each company sufficient autonomy to conduct its business without unnecessary constraints. In short, we believe decentralization = creativity = productivity.

Jim Burke elaborated on the concept:

> The basic concept behind the decentralization philosophy is to try to organize each business around a given market need and a given set of cus-

tomers. It's easier said than done but that's really it. . . . Ethicon is an example of a business that's built around the needs of the surgeon sewing people together . . . and their success is based upon their understanding that what they are is an extension of the skills in the hands of the surgeon. With this approach they built this business out of nothing.

The Credo

General Johnson's views on public and social responsibility were formalized in the 1940s as the company's Credo. This statement underscored the company's responsibilities to its customers, to its employees, to the communities in which it operated, and finally to its stockholders. Described by J&J managers as the underlying and unifying philosophy guiding all important decisions, the Credo was prominently displayed in every manager's office (see Figure A).

Burke described the influence of the Credo on J&J managers as follows:

> All of our management is geared to profit on a day-by-day basis. That's part of the business of being in business. But too often, in this and other businesses, people are inclined to think, "We'd better do this because if we don't, it's going to show up on the figures over the the short term." This document allows them to say, "Wait a minute. I don't *have* to do that. The management has told me that they're really interested in the long term, and they're interested in me operating under this set of principles. So I won't."

One expression of the Credo was "Live for Life," a positive health program for J&J employees. In 1976, Burke asked a senior line-operating manager to figure out how the company could mount a program to make J&J employees the healthiest in the world. The findings of an exhaustive two-year study led to the introduction of a program focusing on four principal areas: exercise, nutrition, stress control, and the cessation of smoking. "Live for Life" was designed to encourage employees "to create their own programs for improving their life styles and getting rid of bad health practices that lead to illness and disability." In support of this plan, flextime arrangements permitted employees to use new in-house health fitness facilities daily, and a variety of programs— such as "kick the smoking habit" group sessions, classes on weight control and nutrition, and yoga—were offered. As one senior executive noted, "It's a great program for the participants. The company also benefits from the feeling it engenders among our people that J&J really cares for its employees."

Notwithstanding the universal acknowledgement accorded the Credo within J&J, Jim Burke perceived some degree of tokenism and a need to inculcate in the managers the values underlying this statement. He described his actions in 1979:

> People like my predecessor believed the Credo with a passion, but the operating unit managers were not universally committed to it. There seemed to be a growing attitude that it was there but that nobody had to do any-thing about it. So I called a meeting of some 20 key executives and chal-lenged them. I said, "Here's the Credo. If we're not going to live by it, let's

Our Credo

We believe our first responsibility is to the doctors, nurses and patients,
to mothers and all others who use our products and services.
In meeting their needs everything we do must be of high quality.
We must constantly strive to reduce our costs
in order to maintain reasonable prices.
Customers' orders must be serviced promptly and accurately.
Our suppliers and distributors must have an opportunity
to make a fair profit.

We are responsible to our employees,
the men and women who work with us throughout the world.
Everyone must be considered as an individual.
We must respect their dignity and recognize their merit.
They must have a sense of security in their jobs.
Compensation must be fair and adequate,
and working conditions clean, orderly and safe.
Employees must feel free to make suggestions and complaints.
There must be equal opportunity for employment, development
and advancement for those qualified.
We must provide competent management,
and their actions must be just and ethical.

We are responsible to the communities in which we live and work
and to the world community as well.
We must be good citizens — support good works and charities
and bear our fair share of taxes.
We must encourage civic improvements and better health and education.
We must maintain in good order
the property we are privileged to use,
protecting the environment and natural resources.

Our final responsibility is to our stockholders.
Business must make a sound profit.
We must experiment with new ideas.
Research must be carried on, innovative programs developed
and mistakes paid for.
New equipment must be purchased, new facilities provided
and new products launched.
Reserves must be created to provide for adverse times.
When we operate according to these principles,
the stockholders should realize a fair return.

Johnson & Johnson

Figure A   The Johnson & Johnson credo.

tear it off the wall. If you want to change it, tell us how to change it. We either ought to commit to it or get rid of it."

The meeting was a turn-on, because we were challenging people's own personal values. By the end of the session, the managers had gained a great deal of understanding about and enthusiasm for the beliefs in the Credo. Subsequently, Dave Clare and I have met with small groups of J&J managers all over the world to challenge the Credo.

Now, I don't really think that you can impose convictions or beliefs on someone else. However, I do believe that if I really understand what makes the business work, then I can prompt you to think through the facts and come to see just how pragmatic the philosophy is when it comes to running a business successfully. . . . And I think that's what happened here.

For some J&J managers, the strongest evidence of the Credo's power was in the company's response to the Tylenol crisis. In 1982, seven people died after ingesting Tylenol capsules that had been laced with cyanide. Even though the poisoning had occurred outside J&J premises and was limited to the Chicago area, J&J withdrew all Tylenol capsules from the U.S. market at an estimated cost of $100 million. At the same time, the company initiated with the medical and pharmaceutical communities a comprehensive communication effort involving 2,500 employees throughout the J&J organization. This response prompted the *Washington Post* to write that "Johnson & Johnson has succeeded in portraying itself to the public as a company willing to do what's right, regardless of cost."

Putting the J&J Philosophy into Operation

The key organizational units for J&J were the operating company at the business level and the executive committee at the corporate level. The relationship between these two units was carefully managed to produce the cohesive independence that had become a cultural hallmark of J&J's operating structure. Strategic planning, compensation systems, and human resource management were among the major support systems to this relationship.

The Operating Companies

J&J's 150 operating units were for the most part integral, autonomous, and wholly owned subsidiaries. Each company had a well-defined mission (or "franchise") and submitted monthly, quarterly, and annual financial reports, as well as dividends. The importance of the company mission was described by the Codman & Shurtleff Company president:

> We spend a lot of time talking about mission, not from the point of view of protecting our turf but to ensure that the mission of the business is defined well enough so that we can see that we're not going at it helter-skelter. Our mission is to develop, on a worldwide basis, electromechanical and electro-optical equipment and devices to aid the physician in performing least-invasive surgery.

What this mission statement does is to make it very clear to us what fits into our business and what would merely diffuse our resources. We think of our franchise as one that is snug enough and neat enough in terms of technological requirements to be managed on a worldwide basis and not implicate other J&J companies, beyond the fact that what we're doing here may speed up the use of their products or, for that matter, the demise of their products.

To keep established missions reasonably focused, a new company was created when any new or peripheral product or market handled by an operating company was deemed important enough to warrant a separate dedicated effort. For example, McNeil Consumer Products Company was created in 1976 to focus exclusively on the consumer product opportunity for Tylenol. It did so with great success, guiding the brand to a preeminent position in the over-the-counter analgesic business. McNeil Pharmaceutical was left free to concentrate on prescription products, including Tylenol with codeine, which became the industry leader in number of new prescriptions in the United States.

In similar fashion, Ortho Diagnostic Systems, Inc., became a separate company in the 1970s to focus on products for blood banks and clinical laboratories, while Ortho Pharmaceutical concentrated on its products for family planning, dermatology, and other fields. In 1982 Technicare Ultrasound was split off from Technicare Corporation to concentrate on ultrasound medical diagnostics. Technicare Corporation continued its activities in CT scanning, nuclear medicine, and the newest modality, nuclear magnetic resonance. One senior executive described his personal experience with this process of setting apart new businesses:

> I started with what was then called the Hospital and Professional Division. Over the years, that unit was a source for some eight or nine spinoffs. Every time we identified a new major market opportunity, we would test it and then split it off as a new company. Our handling of disposable surgical soft goods, including gowns, linen, and face masks is a good case in point. Originally, these products were included in our broad product line. Along the way, we began to see a huge potential for these disposable items. So we developed a dedicated business approach within our unit, tested it and then spun it off, creating Surgikos, with its own mission. That's a good example of what has happened eight other times in just this one company, and the same thing is happening throughout J&J.
>
> In each of these cases, growth opportunity was the driving force for creating a separate organization. In effect, two companies were able to develop greater sales volume and opportunities than a single company could have done by itself.

Among the 150 J&J companies, some 20 to 25 were referred to as source companies. These companies were leaders in developing products and markets that were the basis for new-company formation. Table B lists the principal J&J companies and their major products.

As the number of companies continued to grow, senior management began

Table B Principal domestic operations, 1982.

Company	Major Products
Chicopee	Fabrics for commercial and industrial customers.
Codman & Shurtleff, Inc.	Surgical supplies including instruments, equipment and disposables.
Critikon, Inc.	Products for hospital critical care units, such as oxygen monitoring systems, and cardiovascular catheters.
Devro	Edible natural protein sausage casings and other collagen-based products used by food processors.
Ethicon	Products for precise wound closure, including sutures, ligatures and mechanical wound closure instruments.
Extracorporeal, Inc.	Dialysis fitters and machines for endstage renal disease; oxygenators for open heart surgery, and heart valves.
Iolab Corporation	Intraocular lenses for cataract surgery.
Janssen Pharmaceutica, Inc.	Pharmaceutical products used for anesthesiology and systemic fungal pathogens.
Johnson & Johnson Baby Products Company	Consumer baby products including powder, shampoo, oil, cream and lotion.
Johnson & Johnson Dental Products Company	Serves dentists and dental laboratories with a broad range of restorative products (e.g., porcelain for crowns and bridges) and preventive products (e.g.: Prophylaxis paste).
Johnson & Johnson Products, Inc.	The Health Care Division provides consumers with wound and oral care products; the Patient Care Division offers wound care products to hospitals; the Orthopaedic Division markets surgical implants and fracture immobilization products.
McNeil Consumer Products Company	Line of acetaminophen-related products, including Tylenol, CoTylenol Cold Formula, and Sine-Aid.
McNeil Pharmaceutical	Prescription drugs for the medical profession including analgesics, major tranquilizers, anti-inflammatory agents and muscle relaxants.
Ortho Diagnostic Systems	Products for blood analysis in blood banks and clinical laboratories.
Ortho Pharmaceutical	Prescription and nonprescription contraception products and dermatological products for professional skin treatment.
Personal Products	Products for female hygiene.
Pitman-Moore	Products for animal health.
Surgikos	Disposable packs, crowns, and surgical specialty products for use in major operative procedures.
Technicare	Products in diagnostic imaging—computer tomography (CT) scanning, ultrasonic images, nuclear medicine systems and digital X-ray.
Xanar	CO_2 surgical laser systems.

to look for ways to bring some order to what otherwise might become an un-manageable hodgepodge. Jim Burke described his thinking on this issue:

> What we want to do is to look at each of those businesses that appear to have a worldwide franchise opportunity and to run them as world businesses. The ideal arrangement would be, for example, to have a world Ethicon business [surgical sutures]. Ethicon would have independent, product-related companies in 30 or 40 countries. Where the business in a particular country wasn't large enough to justify a separate company, the products would be sold by a so-called umbrella company in that country.
>
> So, 10 or 15 years from now, we would like to have a collection of global J&Js. It won't be easy to do because a number of our businesses are not so simple to segregate as is Ethicon.

Each operating company was headed by a president, general manager, or managing director, who reported directly or through a company group chairman to a member of the executive committee. J&J had fourteen company group chairmen. The J&J organization structure is shown in Figure B.

Dave Clare, J&J president and chairman of the executive committee, described how this management structure had evolved:

> Years ago, each operating company reported directly to one of the executive committee members. As the number of individual units multiplied around the world, we were faced with the dilemma of how to maintain a line organization relationship between each of the managements and the executive committee members. We had two choices. We could expand the executive committee, or we could transfer to another group of individuals much of the operating responsibilities which had historically been handled by the executive committee. We chose the latter approach.

Each company group chairman reported to a member of the executive committee and was responsible for an assigned group of operating units. Where the assigned group included a number of smaller overseas units, the latter reported to a vice president under the company group chairman. Some managers were concerned that this layering of management responsibilities might slow company reaction time or reduce the autonomy traditionally accorded each operating company. Burke acknowledged this concern:

> Some of the operating managers do make the argument that there are too many layers of decision making within the company. In some cases a company reports to a vice president, a company group chairman, and the executive committee.
>
> The real key is what these layers do. If they become operationally oriented—and there are instances where they do—then we have a real problem. But there are plenty of other instances where that's not the case at all.

Dave Clare was on record as stating:

> We don't want the managing director of any unit, any place in the world, to feel that he hasn't the right, the responsibility, or the ability to go direct to his executive committee member with his problems and his challenges.

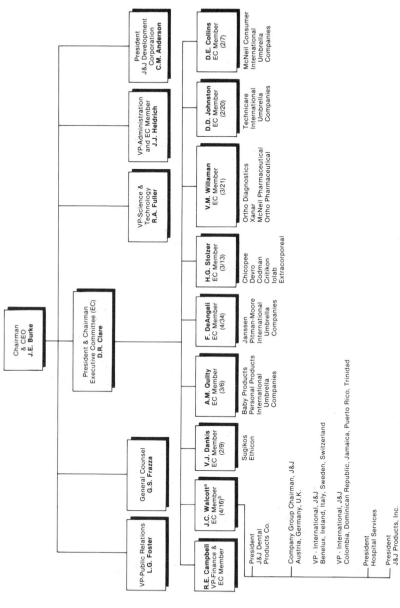

Figure B Organizational structure, 1983.

a. Responsibilities are listed in detail for J.C. Walcott for illustrative purposes. For all other EC members, only major company responsibilities are listed.

b. Figures indicate the numbers of direct reporting relationships versus the total number of independent units under that particular EC member. Thus, J.C. Walcott has 4 executives reporting directly to him, but is responsible for 16 operating units.

369

. . . We don't want to lose touch with the operating managers of the businesses. And we don't want to have them feel that they've lost touch with their executive committee or company group chairman member.[1]

Executive Committee

The eleven-member executive committee (EC) was the principal management group responsible for the company's policies and operations. Four of these members (the CEO, the president, and the vice presidents for finance and administration) had corporate general management responsibilities; the other seven were contact executives for specific operating segments.

The EC met almost daily for lunch, usually with a flexible agenda. Quarterly, it would meet for two or three days to discuss major issues. Burke described the role he saw for the EC:

> In my judgment, the executive committee should spend most of its time on two issues: one is resolving conflicts among operating units; and two is selecting the right opportunities to pursue. In this business, there's no longer any problem in finding opportunities. The problem is in sorting them out and taking the ones you can do the best job with.
>
> We don't really want operating companies to worry about these issues. Their primary job is running their businesses. Of course, they are in a good position to identify opportunities or to sense conflicts with other units. When they do, they should bring these issues to the executive committee.
>
> I feel good about the way the executive committee has evolved in recent years. Seven or eight years ago, it was 95 percent involved in operational matters. Today at least 60 percent of its time is devoted to policy issues. It ought to stay that way or even shift further towards policy.

To illustrate the kind of policy issues addressed by the EC, Clare noted: "The major part of an upcoming quarterly meeting will be to review the strategic plans that have been submitted by all our units. Our emphasis is on the five- and ten-year planning horizon and major problems and programs that we see presented by the companies."

Strategic Planning

In the 1970s, J&J institutionalized a bottom-up strategic planning process. Burke described the reasoning behind this action:

> We were growing very fast, but the key decisions were often being made at the operating companies in an opportunistic, ad hoc manner. The operating managers were growing the businesses, but the overall change wasn't planned.
>
> I decided we had to get into strategic planning. But we wanted the planning to come from the bottom. We wanted the managers to understand that every company had the responsibility for its long-term business.

---

1. "World Wide" (J&J company publication), October 1980, p. 6.

The strategic planning approach that was implemented worked on a ten-year cycle. To avoid recasting long-term forecasts each year, the ten-year projections were revised every five years. The emphasis was on qualitative forecasts rather than numbers, as was indicated in Burke's admonition to the company managers.

> If you want numbers, keep them to yourself. We don't want them. What I want as chairman of the operation is a two-page summary for every J&J company in the world. It should be a statement of your strategic mission and should explain the convictions you have about the future of the business and a little bit of how you're going to get there. I'm going to read it, and everybody between you and me is going to read it. I really only want four numbers—sales and profits for the current year, and sales and profits for five years out. Those numbers in aggregate will help us to see whether or not there is enough growth inherent in our current businesses to maintain our historical growth rate. We want you to understand that we're not going to hold you accountable for those numbers. We *are* going to hold you accountable for the strategic mission statement.

In keeping with its decentralization philosophy, senior management eschewed the idea of developing an explicit corporate strategy. In 1980, however, Burke did write "A Statement of Strategic Direction" to serve as a guideline for strategic planning (Figure C).

Operating Plans

In addition to the strategic plan, the operating companies prepared two-year operating plans, which included narrative concerning specific policies, programs, and actions as well as the financial budget for the following year. Financial controls in J&J were characterized by managers as direct and tight.

Operating plans were initiated in the fall as each company president reached agreement on his proposal with an EC member or with his group chairman. Approval had to await an EC meeting in November, where the performance of J&J as a whole was assessed and individual plans adjusted accordingly. In May each budget was subjected to a detailed review, and in August to a less stringent up-date review. Dave Clare pointed out the executive committee's limited role in this process: "As a committee we don't examine in detail the specific short-term plans of an individual company. We rely on the individual executive committee member with his line organization to address these things."

Each operating company was expected to finance its own investments to the extent possible. Investment decisions were based on detailed cash-flow analysis and were normally implemented by granting reductions in a unit's profit-after-tax targets to allow it to retain the needed funds.

Executive Compensation

Historically, senior executives in J&J were well compensated. General Johnson had often said, "Make your top managers rich, and they will make you richer."

We believe the consistency of our overall performance as a corporation is due to our unique form of decentralized management, our adherence to the ethical principles embodied in our Credo, and our emphasis on managing the business for the long term.

There are certain basic principles that we are committed to in this regard:

- The responsibility for our success as a corporation rests in the hands of the presidents and managing directors of our companies. Each must assume leadership in every facet of the business, including the definition of strategic plans and providing for management succession.
- We will attempt to organize our businesses based on the clearly focused needs of the end users of our products and services. In many instances business units will be structured around the worldwide franchise philosophy. We will continue, however, to rely on "umbrella" companies to develop local markets for any of our franchises where this appears to be the best way to initiate cost-effective, long-term growth.
- We will seek, where possible, to achieve or maintain a leadership position in our markets of interest. It is recognized that this can only be accomplished through maintaining, over the long term, end benefits superior to our competition. In this regard, we are committed to improving our internal research and development capability, and to utilizing external sources that provide access to new science and technology.

- We are dedicated to exceptionally high growth. To achieve this we must be well-positioned in growth markets, and each management must be aggressively innovative and strive to grow faster than the markets in which it competes.
- Each management must know how to invest effectively in future earning power while recognizing that it is easier to reduce profits short term than to increase them long term. We further believe that growth should be financed primarily from earnings. This means our companies must generally make above-average profits to support higher rates of growth.
- Acquisitions are viewed as an appropriate way to achieve the strategic goals of a given company or as a way for the corporation to expand the scope of its current business. Such acquisitions - of products, technologies, or businesses - will be evaluated for growth potential, fit with current or future businesses, management capacity, and economic feasibility. There are no other restrictions on the identification of acquisition candidates.

Corporate management is responsible for providing resources, guidance, leadership, and control of the various business entities within the framework of these principles. Management's most important responsibility is the one it shares with presidents and managing directors in attracting the kind of people who can manage our businesses in the future, providing them with the kind of environment that maximizes their potential and with a system that rewards them appropriately for their accomplishments.

Figure C   Statement of strategic direction.

In 1973, J&J's chairman was the highest paid executive in the United States and one of the first to earn more than $1 million a year.

The compensation package for senior executives included a base salary, bonus, stock grants (over a period of three years), stock options, and phantom stock called Certificate of Extra Compensation. These components are shown in Table C.

In an average year, counting only the cash bonus and the current value of the stock grant contract along with its dividend yield, the current incentive compensation typically totaled about 30 percent to 35 percent of base salary. Longer-term compensation, while not readily calculable, added appreciably to that amount.

The compensation awards were the responsibility of the management com-

Table C   Compensation package.

> *Base Salary*—company commitment
> *Bonus*—guidelines as a percentage of base salary
> *Stock Grants*—there were no guidelines for annual awards. An executive received the grant over three equal yearly installments. Since there were no restrictions on the sale of these shares, this grant was considered current compensation.
> *Stock Options*—there were guidelines on the maximum awards for different salary categories (e.g., 2× salary for salaries between \$50,000 and \$70,000). Options were awarded deeper in the organization than for most other companies. Options were not vested for a period of seven years.
> *Certificate of Extra Compensation* (CEC)—no guidelines. CEC was reserved for the top 1% of executives and was not paid out until the executive retired, died, or otherwise left the company. The value of the "units" was determined by a complex formula depending on the overall corporate performance. (A typical operating company president retired with a CEC value in excess of \$1 million.)

pensation committee, comprising Jim Burke, Dave Clare, and Bob Campbell (vice president for finance). Its duties were to decide how much in aggregate to award in a given year and how the rewards should be distributed. Its functioning was described as follows by an operating company president: "It's an extremely subjective evaluation but very serious. Burke and Clarke spend two weeks every year on nothing but performance evaluation."

Central Staff Support Functions

J&J had corporate staff groups in human resources and personnel, legal, finance, science and technology, and management information services. Considerable attention was given to defining their roles, so as not to undermine the philosophy of decentralized operations.

Human Resources and Personnel. While the individual operating companies were responsible for all the traditional personnel functions, the corporate staff served to ensure uniformity in such areas as compensation and personnel policies. For this purpose, the corporate HR&P staff conducted yearly organizational planning audits. These audits required each company president to present to top corporate management an overview of the company's human resource situation. This overview was to include projected personnel needs, five-year succession plans, identification of people with advancement potential, and any anticipated changes in organizational structure.

To manage staffing requirements and executive career development, J&J maintained a computerized managerial skills inventory form for each manager. When an open position could not be filled from within an individual company, a comprehensive corporatewide search was conducted for suitable candidates. Conversely, J&J also had a search program to identify opportunities for managers desiring a change in position or in need of developing specific skills.

Legal. Legal support for domestic operating companies was provided through the general counsel's office at headquarters.

Finance. Each operating company had its own chief financial officer reporting to the company president. The corporate financial staff provided budgeting and reporting guidelines and was responsible for overall financial policy. The implementation of financial policies throughout J&J was coordinated by a council of chief financial officers that met quarterly.

Science and Technology. An office of science and technology was created in 1979 to formalize the function of scanning the environment for technological developments. Burke described this new unit as "our radar for new and emerging technology which might have applications to our current businesses or which might suggest a whole new business for J&J."

Management Information Services. This function revealed most clearly the underlying tensions between central staff and the autonomous operating units. When started in 1970, the management information center (MIC) was set up to provide large-scale, efficient computer information handling for J&J as a whole. With advances in computer technology, each company wanted to manage its own information system. An executive described what happened:

> The computer information services was an interesting experience in centralization versus decentralization. And it was not without its conflicts and controversies. During the ten-year period from 1970 to 1980, there was an incredible amount of infighting between the corporate management information center people and the management boards of the individual operating companies. All kinds of white papers were being written about why an operating company should do its own thing, with MIC countering why it would cost more money. Finally, Jim Burke stepped in and said, "Look, if the operating companies can afford to decentralize it, why shouldn't they?"

By 1983 each major operating company had its own computer information system. The corporate MIC primarily served headquarter's needs.

The Challenge to Decentralization

Reflecting on the pressures and changes he saw in J&J, Burke commented:

> There's an increasing merging and interaction between the different segments of our business that runs counter to our decentralized approach. The pharmaceutical business, the hospital and professional business, and the consumer business are merging at a lot of levels that nobody even understands. The public is getting intimately involved in health care. There has been a 1,000 percent increase in health information going to the public through TV in the last seven years. There's a revolution in terms of consumer information and there's a revolution in terms of technology that cuts across our ability to market health care in any of its dimensions.
>
> We've got 150 business units now. We could easily grow to 300 companies over the next 10 to 15 years. If you look at the corporation's central problem, it's how to manage an increasingly larger organization to obtain the same kind of energy that is released from smaller units.

Johnson & Johnson (B):
Hospital Services

Decentralization = Creativity = Productivity

J&J's 1981 annual report cover

Immediately after he attended the fall 1982 session of the Harvard Business School Advanced Management Program, Pete Ventrella, vice president corporate staff and general manager of the Hospital Services Group for Johnson & Johnson (J&J), was told of an important change in his responsibilities. The Hospital Services Group, a transitional corporate unit set up to explore a new approach to serving the hospital market, was to become a full-fledged J&J operating company, and Pete was to be its president. Under the new arrangement, J&J's Hospital Services would be responsible for consolidating all order taking, customer invoicing, and distribution of products supplied to hospitals by thirteen other J&J companies that had hitherto performed these functions.

In his new assignment, Ventrella not only faced the normal administrative problems of start-up, he would also have to centralize major operating functions in a company that had made decentralization and managerial autonomy keystones in its corporate philosophy. Describing his new responsibilities, Ventrella said:

> Our customers are changing; the hospital marketplace is changing! We've been asked to develop a corporate capability in the automated order-entry and distribution areas which will lead to the servicing of our customers in a better way than affiliate companies could do on their own. Ultimately the supply companies have the ability to limit where this thing goes. A year from now when Jim Burke and Dave Clare [J&J president] ask the companies "What do you think about Hospital Services?" I want them to say, "It's serving us and the customers better. . . ." Somehow, that has to be the final response.
>
> Each of our companies has a very well-defined mission statement which gives it its own product franchise. The question is, "How can Hospital Services be complementary to this approach without disrupting all the good things you get from decentralization?"

J&J and the Hospital Supplies Business

In 1982, thirteen J&J companies and divisions sold close to $2 billion worth of supplies and equipment to the medical professional markets. Two-thirds of this volume was sold in the United States, and the major part of these sales was to hospitals. As shown in Figure A, these units collectively served all of the twenty-three medical specialties certified by the American Board of Medical Specialties. Each unit operated independently, with its own manufacturing, sales and distribution network, service capability, and research and development.

U.S. health care costs in 1982 were estimated at over $320 billion.[1] Hospital care accounted for almost 40% of this total.[2] The U.S. professional purchases of supplies, pharmaceuticals, and equipment were thought to be around $15 billion in total and around $9 billion for the segments served by J&J.

The hospital system had begun to change dramatically during the 1970s. Rapidly escalating costs, growing government involvement in medical payments (in 1980, about 55 percent of every dollar that went to hospitals was paid by the government), rising consumerism, new and expensive equipment, and increasing competition for the health care dollar were forcing hospitals to seek new ways to provide health care at lower costs. As an indication of these pressures, after 1974 hospitals experienced cost increases at twice the rate of inflation and were able to recover only about 85 percent of these increases.

In response to these pressures, hospitals were adopting strategies to contain costs and to generate revenues. These new efforts in turn were bringing about substantial administrative changes in the industry. While medical professionals continued to have a strong voice in recommending products and services, purchasing decisions were increasingly being shifted from the doctor or nurse to administrators, business managers, and material managers. These business-oriented managers sought cost reductions through more efficient and stringent purchasing practices.

The cost pressures on hospitals also fostered explosive growth of multihospital systems that sought to contain costs through standardization, consolidation of health services, management information services, and group purchasing. As one measure of the change occurring on this front, for-profit hospital chains were reported to have grown even faster than the computer and drug industries in the 1970s, with revenues in excess of $12 billion in 1980.[3] By 1982, multihospital systems represented 30 percent of the total hospital facilities in the United States and were projected to represent 70 percent of all hospital beds by 1990.

The multihospital system had changed the hospital business from a cottage industry to big-league corporate operations. Further, the changes were likely to continue, with an industry forecast indicating that by 1990 as few as 600

---

1. "Businesses are Forming Coalitions to Curb Rise in Health-Care Costs," *Wall Street Journal,* June 17, 1982, p. 31.
2. *Health Care Financing Review,* Summer 1979, cited in "Health Maintenance Organization Medical Products and Services Markets," Frost & Sullivan, 1980.
3. G. Kinkead, "Humana's Hard-Sell Hospitals," *Fortune,* November 17, 1980, p. 68.

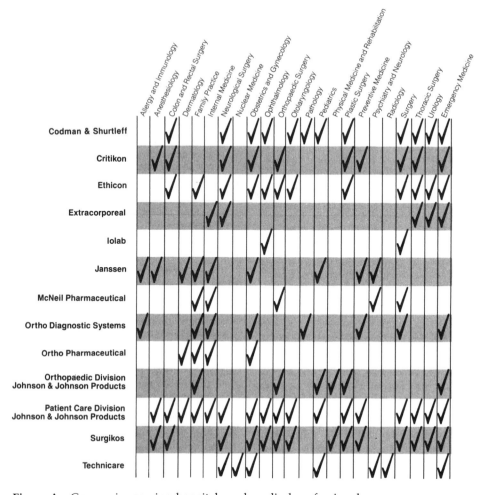

Figure A   Companies serving hospitals and medical professionals.

purchasing groups would be making the majority of U.S. hospital purchases. As a result of this trend toward fewer and larger purchasing units, hospitals were gaining leverage vis-à-vis their suppliers.

A firm that had capitalized on these trends was the American Hospital Supply Corporation (AHS). Described as the success story of the 1970s, it had grown from a small distributor to the largest hospital supply manufacturer and distributor in the United States, with $2.5 billion in revenues and 27 percent of the market, by tailoring its strategy to the changes in the hospital industry. This strategy targeted hospital administrators and purchasing managers, rather than medical practitioners, offering volume discounts, guaranteed three-day delivery, and improved information handling. A newspaper article described AHS's success as follows: "American Hospital Supply turned this trend [the emergence of large investor-owned hospital groups] to its advantage by developing computerized inventory control, ordering and distribution systems that could speed its wide range of products across the country more efficiently than its competitors, while cutting hospitals' costs and freeing its salesmen to respond to individual customer needs."[4] The article went on to describe how AHS would do a study of the hospital's paper-flow process before installing, free of charge, a computerized automated ordering system that linked the purchaser with its central computer.

Pete Ventrella commented on how the industry changes evolved:

> It was our distributors which, by the very nature of their business, were adjusting to certain business-oriented changes at the hospitals much more rapidly than were the product-oriented manufacturing concerns. Distributors such as American Hospital Supply began investing heavily in business systems for the marketplace. This approach was in marked contrast to J&J's, which invested primarily in product R&D through its individual companies.
>
> What became increasingly clear over time was that for every dollar hospitals spend on a product, they spend a dollar on administration and logistical support. As manufacturers, we had naturally focused attention on product costs and product value added. We began to appreciate that the opportunity for J&J to add value for the customers was twice as large when distribution logistics were included.

J&J viewed its primary competition as those firms that manufactured goods and equipment for the health care field—corporations such as Baxter Travenol, Procter & Gamble, Bristol-Myers, Warner Lambert, 3M, and Kendall Corporation. Ventrella saw this focus as one reason for J&J's delayed response to the changing environment: "Since we primarily see competitors as manufacturers, we had not thoroughly examined how the distribution companies were responding to new opportunities that resulted from business-centered changes occurring among our hospital customers. And this development is really what triggered our decision to investigate how we could capitalize on these trends."

Hospital Services Group

Genesis

J&J management had been neither unaware of nor unconcerned about the changing nature of the hospital supply and equipment business. Jim Burke explained why the firm had not responded sooner:

> We have looked at this problem of distribution in the hospitals area off and on for fifteen years. Each time we did, we came up against the J&J culture. We would say, "Even though there's a lot of money involved here, the fact is that we seem to be functioning well, and our survival is not at stake. So, let's back off."

4. N. Peagam, "American Hospital's Bays Gets Credit for Turning Distribution into Service," *Wall Street Journal*, September 1, 1981, p. 12.

Dave Clare, who in 1967 had headed up a major study of the hospital supply business, explained how the J&J culture had influenced his committee's thinking:

> We could see opportunities for economies through centralizing our marketing services. But we started with a belief that bigness can be bureaucratic and ineffective. When we add to that orientation the strong opposition to centralized marketing and distribution voiced by a number of company presidents, we concluded that the potential benefits were not sufficient at the time to make the changes required. We also recommended that the situation be reexamined every five years.

The recommendation for a reexamination every five years was not implemented for two reasons. First, Dave Clare, a leading proponent of the change, had by then been promoted to the executive committee, with responsibility for companies serving other markets. Second, until 1979 the situation had not been perceived by top management to have changed sufficiently to trigger any further action. Other problems were seen to have higher priority. For example, in 1976, when Jim Burke was promoted to chief executive officer and Dave Clare to president, the decision was made to deal with a major reorganization of the pharmaceutical business before tackling the hospital services problem.

In mid-1979, attention was again turned to the hospital supply question. It was now apparent that with government action intensifying the cost-containment pressures on hospitals, change in the medical field would be rapid. J&J was no longer able to adjust gradually to the shifts occurring with its hospital customers. Toward the end of 1979, Jim Burke and Dave Clare called a meeting of the hospital and professional company presidents. Top management put the following challenge to the group: "This is a big part of our corporation's business. Let's talk about how we can grow faster and serve the customer better in the decade of the 80s!"

Project Chatham

At a meeting in New Brunswick, N.J., home of J&J's corporate headquarters, a special committee of J&J hospital company presidents was established to examine several marketing strategies and determine how the corporation could best meet the challenges of the hospital market in the 1980s. The committee was chaired by Jack Walcott, a member of the executive committee and chairman of J&J Products Inc. Pete Ventrella was one of the members. Thinking back, Walcott recalled:

> I was well aware of how our strong belief in decentralized operations had led us in 1967 to decide against a joint distribution system for hospitals. But since then, there were important changes and trends in the hospital industry that we could not ignore. Moreover our stake in that business had increased through the addition of a broader base of products, including our expanded offerings in pharmaceuticals and diagnostic instruments.
>
> Clearly, there was a strong impetus from the top for reexamining our

position. Dave Clare, who has considerable experience in operations, was concerned that we were not getting enough leverage out of a billion-dollar business. Jim Burke has a marketing perspective and was concerned about our competitive posture in the field.

The study, code named Project Chatham, gathered momentum over the 1980–81 period. The committee met once or twice a month and added a full-time coordinator. A major consulting firm was commissioned to analyze the hospital business, including regulatory developments. The committee members also sought information directly from medical professionals and hospital administrators.

The committee's deliberations were complicated in two ways. With respect to problem definition, the consultant's market research findings were susceptible to different interpretations about the extent to which buying behavior had really changed or was going to change in the future. This ambiguity left open to debate just when to institute organizational changes.

With respect to possible organizational and procedural changes, the committee had to contend with the problem of finding an approach that was suitable to the different practices and commitments among the participating companies. For example, distribution practices ranged from 100 percent direct sales to 100 percent independent distributor sales among the thirteen companies. Delivery, service, and credit policies also varied widely. Even the importance of the hospital business in comparison with other markets varied from company to company.

Affiliate Company Resistance

During the Project Chatham deliberations, some J&J affiliate companies refuted the suitability of a centralized hospital services concept that would consolidate certain marketing and distribution functions. A senior J&J executive who had been involved with Project Chatham described his impression of the concerns voiced by these companies:

> It came down to some companies not wanting any change that had the potential of usurping the autonomy and control they had in running their respective businesses. Because of our decentralized philosophy that had been ingrained in companies over time, affiliates had the tendency to look parochially rather than broadly at the changes that were taking place in the hospital market. This colored their understanding of how these changes in hospitals could have an effect on the future of their own businesses in the long term.
>
> Ethicon had the strongest reasons for maintaining the status quo. This company held a leading market position in supplying sutures for precise wound closure and had been termed one of the most successful franchises J&J ever had.
>
> On the other side, it was important for HSG to include Ethicon because of the important leverage this well-known company would provide for the whole group. Moreover, Ethicon had become something of a weathervane on the participation issue.

Continuing strong support of the Hospital Services concept by top corporate officers kept a reluctant Ethicon in the project. Burke gave his view of the situation: "Ethicon would say, 'We agree that eventually we're going to have to do this. We also agree that you have to do this now for the other companies, but not for us.' From their point of view they were absolutely correct. They didn't need it now. But they're going to need it someday."

Formation of Hospital Services Group

In April, 1981, the Project Chatham committee recommended that J&J create a unit that would provide a consolidated distribution network, including a common customer-service group and an electronic order entry/customer information system, for those hospitals and hospital distributors ordering from any and all J&J companies. The recommendation included provisions for the development of a corporate (1) purchase agreement program; (2) capital equipment financing program; (3) equipment services program; and (4) identity program.

In making its recommendations, the Project Chatham committee stressed that the plan would allow J&J to position itself better to talk to the hospital as a corporate customer. The committee sought to capitalize more effectively on J&J's highly regarded name and to begin to speak with one voice to the hospital field on a number of business issues.

These recommendations were approved by the executive committee. The Hospital Services Group (HSG) was formed to develop action plans and to implement the approved programs. Ed Hartnett, a former executive vice president of Ethicon and then a group vice president of J&J Products Inc., was appointed general manager of HSG. His support staff soon included one of the company's top distribution experts and a computer specialist.

In March 1982, Hartnett presented to the executive committee a report on HSG that defined its mission and goals and described the status of its programs.

Mission:
   Develop and implement programs for J&J as a corporation, on behalf of the professional companies, that respond to the needs of hospitals and distributor customers.

Goals:
1. Improve the corporation's competitive position in the hospital industry through common strategies that can be utilized by its professional companies.
2. Build, with the business leaders in the hospital marketplace, the recognition that Johnson & Johnson as a corporation is responsive to their needs.
3. Develop programs that complement and strengthen the decentralized product franchises each of the companies has established among the medical and nursing professionals.

4. Seek internal economies of scale and productivity gains that result in increased profitability longer term.

The major programs under development were described in detail; these programs included:

1. *Incentive purchase plan (IPP).* A corporate umbrella volume-incentive agreement under which each company would continue to set its individual marketing, pricing, and selling practices.
2. *On-line order entry/customer information system.* A computer system tying all J&J companies into one data base, so as to provide automated order entry, consolidated customer order service, and support for a physical distribution network.
3. *Consolidated physical distribution network.* A network of eleven warehouses for supply items that would provide three-day service for 90 percent of J&J's hospital and distributor customers.
4. *Corporate identity program.* To explain J&J's total role in the hospital supply and equipment business.
5. *Sales cross-training program.* To familiarize J&J sales representatives with the total scope of J&J's hospital business.
6. *Capital equipment leasing program.* To finance the leasing or purchasing of all J&J medical equipment products.
7. *Combined equipment service program.* An intracompany, shared equipment service program to improve overall service capabilities.
8. *Hospital business understanding plan.* Although each J&J company would continue to monitor change in its specific target audience, HSG would be responsible for understanding the administrative and business side of hospital operations and for supplying this information to the appropriate company. Issues would include competition, cost containment, federal and state reimbursement, revenue planning, capital funding, and inventory management.

The committee recommended a three-phase roll-out for involving the J&J companies in the HSG marketing services, starting with supplies, then moving to pharmaceuticals and finally equipment. Table A shows the sequence in which the individual J&J companies would be phased into the program.

Distribution Policies

Under the proposed approach to hospital sales, each J&J product company would continue to be responsible for promoting its products to the appropriate doctors and nurses in the hospitals. HSG would be responsible for distribution. It would play a somewhat different role, however, for direct sales and for sales through distributors (see Figure B).

For direct sales to hospitals, HSG would serve as a direct link between the

Table A   Hospital Services roll-out sequence, 1984–86.

	Supplies	Pharma- ceuticals	Equipment, Instruments, and Other
J&J Products, patient care	√		
J&J Products, orthopaedic	√		√
Surgikos	√		
Codman	√		√
Critikon	√		√
Extracorporeal	√		√
Ortho Diagnostic Systems	√		√
Ethicon	√		
McNeil Pharmaceutical		√	
Ortho Pharmaceutical		√	
Janssen		√	
Iolab			√
Technicare			√
Overall Sales			
Dealer	59%	26%	4%
Direct	41%	74%	96%

supplying company and the customer. Its principal activities would include holding inventories at regional warehouses, processing hospital orders, making deliveries, invoicing hospitals, and handling credit and accounts receivable.

For sales through distributors, HSG would serve as a link between the supplying company and its distributors, performing the same functions for the distributors that it performed for hospitals in direct sales. Should a hospital order distributor-handled goods directly from HSG, the order would be referred to and billed through a distributor, whether the goods were delivered from the J&J warehouses or from the distributor's stock. In such cases, the distributor was urged to service the account directly to earn the 6 percent to 10 percent commission it received.

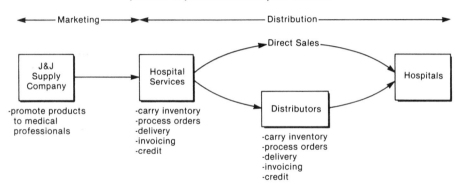

Figure B   Marketing and distribution flows.

Johnson & Johnson Hospital Services

In September 1982, Ed Hartnett was promoted to the position of company group chairman, with responsibility for Ethicon and its related overseas companies. (See the Johnson & Johnson (A) case for a description of the company group chairman's job.) Pete Ventrella took charge of HSG. As 1982 drew to a close, the decision was made to establish HSG as an independent company and to appoint Ventrella as its president.[5] He described some of his concerns as he first took over the new Hospital Services Company:

> There were numerous specific issues to be settled, most of which were important to the companies involved. For example, decisions had to be made as to who should own the inventory in the warehouses, what the credit and payment terms would be, and even whether the supply company field salesmen or Hospital Services people should introduce these programs to the customers. While in no way meaning to lessen the importance of these specific issues, I did come to recognize two broad concerns. One was how to build a company in the J&J environment. The other was how to get this new company accepted inside as well as outside the corporation.
>
> Legal and tax considerations certainly influenced the decision to set up HSG as a separate company. But organizational considerations might have been even more important. We needed experienced people to launch and to run this somewhat delicate operation, and setting it up as a line company made it easier to attract good people in J&J. To give you some idea of the problem, we will soon have over 100 people on board and that number will grow to over 500 in three years' time.
>
> Having a company status helps, but we're not totally out of the woods on how to make Hospital Services an attractive assignment for J&J people. People will want to be able to say, "Look what we've contributed to the corporation." But how do you measure the contribution which results from

5. Ventrella had joined J&J in 1959 after graduating from Colgate University and completing a stint with the Air Force. He had started as a sales representative with the Hospital & Professional Division and rose to vice president and general manager of the Patient Care division by 1979.

our services and distinguish it from the impact which results from the product development and selling efforts performed by the supplying companies?

This difficulty in measuring contribution also affects how we get accepted by the other companies in J&J. It's easy when you have a clear-cut profit to show. And that brings me back to one of the specific issues on my mind. Should Hospital Services charge the companies just for costs or should the charges include a profit margin and return on investment? The participating companies will certainly want to keep their expenses down, and those companies who see this operation as increasing their costs will object strenuously to any increase for the purpose of our showing a profit. But, then again, charging only costs obscures the fact that we might be adding a significant value through our services and trade relationships. Being a break-even cost center in some ways undermines the company concept and deprives me of an important tool for motivating my staff.

In 1983, two new small J&J supply companies were added to the Hospital Services' roster. Xanar, which had been organized in October 1981 to design and manufacture carbon dioxide surgical laser systems, began product sales in January 1983. Irex, acquired in February, 1983, manufactured and distributed ultrasound equipment (nuclear magnetic resonance modality) for cardiovascular applications.

1983 Executive Committee Plan Review

Pete Ventrella was scheduled to report to the executive committee on March 23, 1983, on Hospital Services' status and plans. This would be his first update on the company's activities since becoming president.

The report revealed that the overall net annual operating costs for the Hospital Services activities (total Hospital Services costs less related savings in the supply companies) would be about $26 million (cost and sales figures have been disguised). It went on to point out that this added cost could be covered by an incremental sales increase of roughly 3 percent. The difficulty in making a precise cost-benefit analysis was in ascertaining what the sales performance might have been without the new distribution services.

Among other information, the report delineated the responsibilities to be carried out by Hospital Services and those remaining to the companies (see Table B).

The introduction of a corporate tag-line policy illustrated the kind of details in which Hospital Services was engaged. The following excerpt from a letter Dave Clare wrote to the company presidents emphasized the importance of promoting J&J's corporate identity with the professional market:

> The name Johnson & Johnson is a trademark synonymous with high standards of product performance, bringing instant recognition to the products and companies that carry the name.
>
> In the past we have not used the Johnson & Johnson name with many of our hospital companies. However, the changing nature of the profes-

Table B Division of responsibilities.

Hospital Services Responsibilities	Responsibilities Remaining with Companies
Customer services	Marketing
Order processing	Pricing
Credit	Inventory
Distribution	Recalls
Invoicing	Product
Accounts receivable	performance
Corporate identity	Inquiry
IPP	Nonhospital
Hospital business	business
understanding	Specials
Reimbursement	International
	Internal reporting

sional business has made it important for us to enhance recognition of our corporation as a broad scale supplier of products and services to the professional market. Accordingly, we plan to integrate the corporate tag line, "a Johnson & Johnson company," into our hospital company logotypes as a major step in fostering the recognition.

As a result, ten of the professional companies were to include an identification with J&J as shown below:

ETHICON
a *Johnson-Johnson* company

On March 21, two days before the executive committee review, Pete Ventrella was scheduled to meet with the president and the chairman of Ethicon to try to settle a difference of opinion on inventory placements. Ventrella described the issue for discussion:

Ethicon is willing to stock its most popular items (25 percent of its codes) in all eleven warehouses, but would like to stock its complete line in only three or four locations. Why? Because this step would reduce Ethicon's inventory costs by about $3 million by their estimate. We feel that in order to preserve the original concept of a hospital or distributor customer being able to make one phone call to order any J&J product—and then to have such products shipped on one truck with one bill of lading, one invoice, and one monthly bill to the customer—we cannot make an exception to our plan, at least not initially, until we see what value the customer puts on this capability.

Monsanto Company:
The Queeny Division

"Well, all hell broke loose this morning. What do I have to do this afternoon to pull my group together and get some agreement?" Chris Hubbard asked himself. As General Manager of Monsanto's "Queeny Division" [a fictitious designation], Hubbard had spent the best part of the last day and a half with his immediate subordinates trying to get consensus on next year's operating budget. After a rough morning, he had used lunch as an opportunity to get away and plan how he could resolve the issues that were blocking progress.

In the past, budgeting had been straightforward: The previous year's budget was adjusted according to the changes that Hubbard and his department managers agreed would be necessary. This year, however, the Queeny Division had been asked to employ a new budgeting process, Priority Resources Budgeting (PRB), as part of Monsanto's effort to improve the management of overhead costs. The new process had proved to be far more time-consuming and complicated than the old.

During the past several months, Hubbard's department managers had worked with their subordinates to identify explicitly the tasks for which they were responsible and to attach specific estimates of benefits and costs to each task or activity. Each manager had then met with his key subordinates to rank the tasks ("increments," in PRB terms) from highest priority to lowest. The primary goal of this effort was to give priority to overhead activities that supported the unit's tactical and strategic business plans. A second important goal was to control the level of overhead expenditures.

Based on meetings with each of his department managers to discuss their rankings, Hubbard believed that the process was achieving these two goals. PRB had required reams of paper and a substantial commitment of time, but until today, notwithstanding a certain amount of grumbling and confusion, the effort appeared to have gone smoothly.

Hubbard was now in the middle of his divisional ranking meeting. The goals of the meeting were the same as at the department level, but the task was more complex. While ranking increments within departments had often required that difficult decisions be made, the commonalities among the functional activities facilitated choices and trade-offs. Trying to decide whether the next $300,000 should be spent on sales or R&D was altogether different. This interfunctional ranking seemed to Hubbard to produce an atmosphere of competition. Managers behaved as if they were in a zero-sum game, and Hubbard was worried that the conflict would undermine his efforts over the past two years to develop a spirit of teamwork in his group.

"I've never seen John Coulson so angry," he reflected, "and his commodities group produced three-quarters of last year's cash flow. And sales really has me stumped. What is the right level of support for that function? I guess we are wrestling with some issues we should have confronted before, so things aren't all bad. But I'm sure of one thing—if we can't pull together on this budget, it's going to be a tough year."

Monsanto Company

Monsanto's headquarters were located in a campuslike setting on the outskirts of St. Louis, Missouri, not far from where John F. Queeny founded the company in 1901 to manufacture saccharin. In 1978, Monsanto's sales of $5 billion were fourth largest in the U.S. chemical industry. Net income before taxes was $576 million. Over 62,000 employees staffed its 175 plants and 135 offices around the world. Exhibit 1 shows recent financial results.

Monsanto's widely diversified line of chemical products included agricultural chemicals (herbicides, pesticides, etc.); chemical intermediates (petrochemicals, process chemicals, etc.); industrial chemicals (detergents and phosphates, rubber chemicals, plasticizers, etc.); plastics and resins; textiles (man-made fibers); and industrial process controls. To a large extent, Monsanto sold its products to other industries rather than to end users. A major exception was agricultural chemicals.

Exhibit 1 Financial results ($ million).

	1978	1977	1976	1975	1974	1972	1969
Sales	5,019	4,595	4,270	3,625	3,498	2,225	1,939
Operating income	632	610	668	547	550	216	191
Net income	303	276	366	306	323	122	116
Total assets	5,036	4,350	3,959	3,451	2,938	2,237	2,012
Long-term debt	1,224	1,031	915	845	587	576	454
Shareowners' equity	2,579	2,401	2,253	1,977	1,755	1,294	1,205
Net income as a percentage of							
Net sales	6.0%	6.0%	8.6%	8.4%	9.2%	5.5%	6.0%
Average shareowners' equity	12.2%	11.9%	17.3%	16.4%	20.0%	9.7%	9.8%
Average total assets	6.4%	6.6%	9.9%	9.6%	11.8%	5.6%	5.0%

Sources: Monsanto Company 1978 annual report; and Monsanto Company 1978 corporate data book.

The Management Style

In 1972 John M. Hanley joined Monsanto as president. Aged fifty, Hanley had spent his entire career at Procter and Gamble, and his arrival from the outside broke with a long-standing Monsanto tradition to grow its own leaders. His arrival signaled a new approach to management and, especially, an increased emphasis on marketing.

From the start, Hanley saw a need to develop a new administrative structure with which to formulate and implement changes. By 1974, such a structure began to emerge, and with it a distinctive management style. Later Hanley was to write: "The Monsanto Management Style is the process by which we define what we want to accomplish and the framework in which we pursue our Corporate Objectives."

The process by which the Management Style was implemented is shown in Exhibit 2. Top management set corporate objectives and policies. Given these statements, Monsanto's senior operating managers produced explicit statements of strategy ("Direction Papers"). Operating companies and similar units then produced "Summary Long-Range Plans," followed by more detailed statements of strategies and tactics, called "Operational Plans." Next, individual managers identified the results they must achieve (the "Management by Results" program) to support the Operational Plans. The budgeting process was then supposed to develop explicit statements of organizational goals and resource commitments for a one-year period.

In the late 1970s, Hanley and other senior managers became increasingly concerned with the weakness of the link between business strategies and the budgets for Marketing, Administration, and Technology (MAT) expenses and for Factory Indirect Expense (FIE). Specifically, Hanley said:

> As we continue to extend the entire planning process, it is important for Monsanto to ensure that its total MAT expenses are both optimally allocated to support the various business strategies of the company and held to a level consistent with the planned overall financial results of the corporation.[1]

After investigating a variety of budgeting systems, it was decided that zero-based budgeting (ZBB) offered the most potential. In 1978, Priority Resource Budgeting (PRB),[2] a form of ZBB modified to fit Monsanto's particular needs, was tested in several Monsanto units. PRB was introduced throughout two Monsanto Companies in 1979, including the Monsanto Commodity Chemicals Company.[3]

---

1. In 1978, MAT expenses for Monsanto totaled $643 million. This amount represented almost 14.7 percent of total operating costs for the year.
2. See the Appendix for a description of the Priority Resource Budgeting (PRB) system.
3. The Monsanto Company was organized into major business units, each of which was also called a company. Exhibit 3 shows the corporate organizational structure. The Monsanto Commodity Chemical Company is a fictitious unit.

Exhibit 2   Schematic of Monsanto's management style.

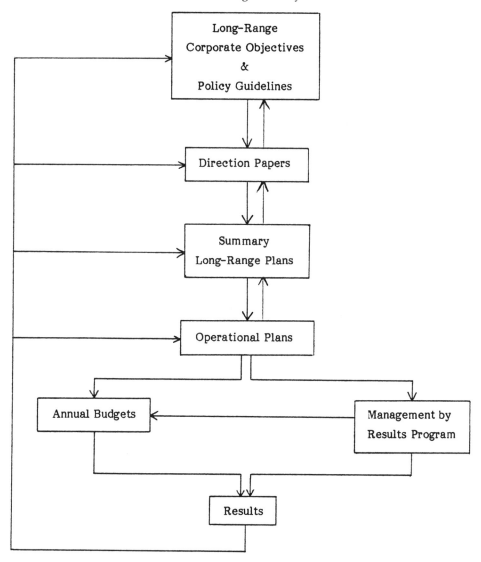

The Queeny Division

The Queeny Division was one of three operating divisions that made up the Monsanto Commodity Chemicals Company. (See Exhibit 4 for an organization chart). For most of its history, the Queeny Division's product line had been dominated by six successful commodity chemicals for the food-processing and related industries. Management of these products had been divided between two departments, each of which had responsibility for three of the major com-

Exhibit 3 Corporate organization structure, 1978.

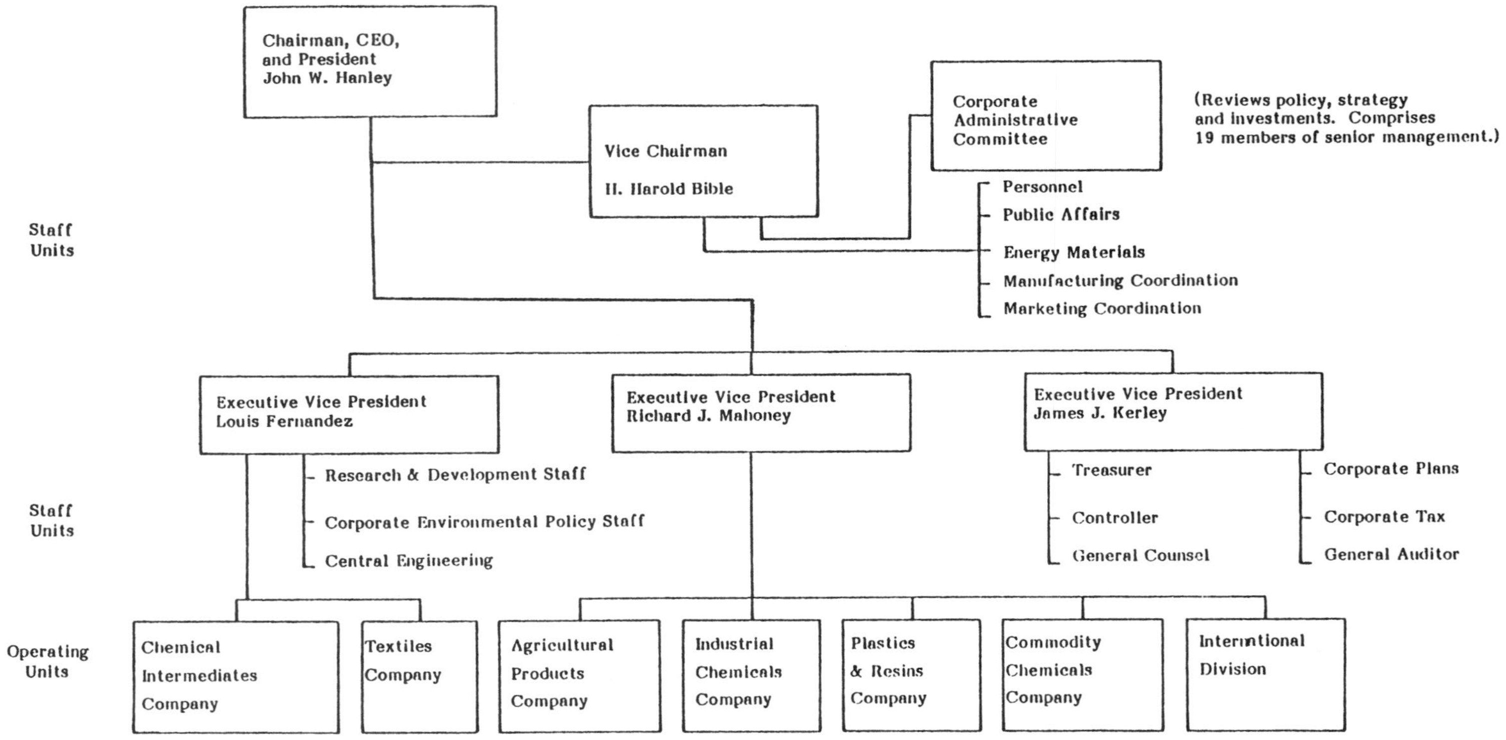

Chairman, CEO, and President
John W. Hanley

Corporate Administrative Committee

(Reviews policy, strategy and investments. Comprises 19 members of senior management.)

Vice Chairman
H. Harold Bible

- Personnel
- Public Affairs
- Energy Materials
- Manufacturing Coordination
- Marketing Coordination

Executive Vice President
Louis Fernandez

- Research & Development Staff
- Corporate Environmental Policy Staff
- Central Engineering

Executive Vice President
Richard J. Mahoney

Executive Vice President
James J. Kerley

- Treasurer
- Controller
- General Counsel

- Corporate Plans
- Corporate Tax
- General Auditor

Staff Units

Staff Units

Operating Units

Chemical Intermediates Company

Textiles Company

Agricultural Products Company

Industrial Chemicals Company

Plastics & Resins Company

Commodity Chemicals Company

International Division

392

Exhibit 4 Monsanto Commodity Chemical Company organization structure.

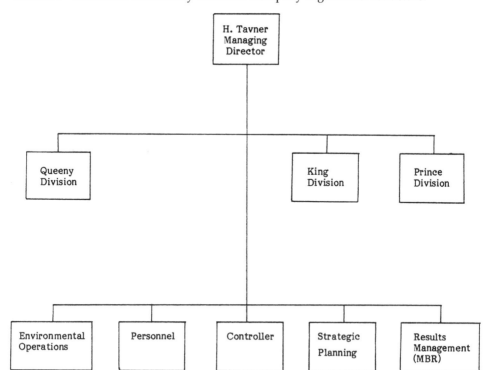

modity items as well as a number of minor related commodity and consumer products. In 1970, Chris Hubbard and Norm Brewster were the department heads of these units.

Market analysis during the early 1970s had shown that four of the six commodity products were in the "mature" stage of their product life cycle and the other two were in "late growth." While the 1972 profit picture was quite good, Queeny management confronted the prospect of little, if any, further growth from its major products.

George Rinder, then the General Manager of Queeny, had responded by increasing the division's support of several of its newer products and by stepping up new product-development efforts. One of his first moves was to place the promising oil additive chemical products into a newly created department. Norm Brewster, who had championed this relatively new line, left his department to head up the new unit. In 1975, Rinder decided to separate the faster growing consumer chemicals from the slower growing commodity chemicals. As a result of the reorganization, Chris Hubbard's department was given responsibility for all commodity chemicals, and Fred Ellis (who stepped in when Brewster moved to oil additives) was given responsibility for all consumer chemicals.

In May 1977, Rinder was promoted to Managing Director of the Commodity Chemicals Company.[4] In turn, Hubbard became General Manager of Queeny, and Coulson took charge of the Commodity Chemicals Department.

In 1979 Queeny's performance was projected to be as follows (dollars in millions):

Department	Sales	Net pretax income	Growth rate
Commodity Chemicals	$600	$90	Slow
Consumer Chemicals	$ 80	$ 9	Rapid
Oil Additive Chemicals	$220	$60	Medium

The structure of the organization managed by Hubbard in 1979 was essentially identical to that which he took over in 1977. (Exhibit 5 contains an organization chart for the Queeny Division.)

The Queeny Division Ranking

"In an hour we begin again," thought Hubbard. "I'd better figure out how to make sense from the confusion we generated this morning. When this is all over, I'm going to have to spend a quiet weekend sorting out all I've seen of PRB."

"The seeds for what has been happening in this ranking meeting were planted in the one-on-one review sessions I held with each of my manager's over a week ago," Hubbard reflected.[5] "Joe Roboh's was the easiest and most informative session. As soon as he knew I was committed to doing some basic research, he loosened up. I like the result of his R&D ranking meeting in that they fit our strategy. But I could see some potential problems coming from the big shift in research effort from Commodity Chemicals to Consumer Chemicals. I expected a backlash on that from John Coulson, and we sure got it."

"John is doing a good job with Commodity Chemicals, and his PRB analysis showed it. Still, I don't think he's fully taken to heart that he is in a mature market. He thinks he can grow and resents all the attention Fred Ellis is getting with Consumer. Competent but defensive is the way I'd characterize his behavior in our one-on-one meeting. He knew he wasn't going to get as much R&D as he wanted."

"Leo Nicholson was disappointing. His analysis was not so hot. He said his salesmen were all busy selling, and there was no time to fill out the forms.

4. Rinder was seriously injured several months later as a result of an accident and elected to retire early from Monsanto. He was replaced by Henry Tavner, General Manager of the King Division.
5. The "one-on-one" review meetings were held between a ranking manager and each of his decision unit managers prior to the ranking meeting. According to the Monsanto Company Priority Resource Budgeting Manual (1978): "This meeting is *not* a decision-making meeting but rather an informational meeting." Exhibit 6 contains background information on each of the key managers in the Queeny Division.

Exhibit 5   Queeny division organization structure.

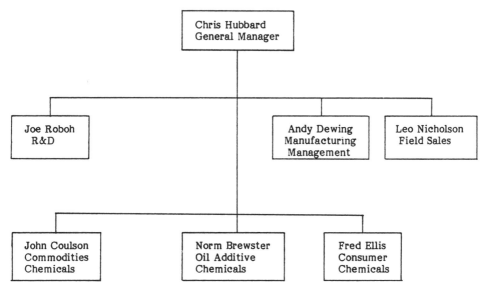

I must admit, though, I have a tough time defining a sales increment myself."

"The other men were about as I expected. Fred Ellis was well prepared and aggressive. He intends to grow, and he can make a good case for it with Consumer. Norm Brewster was confident and protective. Too confident, maybe; Oil Additives has been so successful that they may only have looked at where they needed *more* resources. I'm not sure they checked to see which areas are fat, and some are, for sure. Andy Dewing, on the other hand, was a little discouraged. He didn't see that PRB made any sense for manufacturing, and I think he still feels that way.

"When I think back on it, every one of those guys gave me signals about what was likely to happen during this Division ranking meeting. At least next year I'll try to make better use of that information."

The Division Ranking Meeting: First Day

Hubbard's thoughts turned to the ranking meeting. Yesterday morning the ranking had seemed mechanical, easy—almost trivial. The thresholds reviewed in the one-on-one meetings were accepted without debate, except that Nicholson hadn't studied all the other guys' work and that slowed things down a bit. Andy got a laugh when he said, "Hell, Leo, you're in the big leagues now. You've got to read this stuff *before* you come to meetings."

Ranking the items just after the threshold was no real problem, although during the later afternoon there were a few disagreements. As could be antic-

Exhibit 6   Biographies of participants at Queeny's PRB ranking meeting.

Chris Hubbard,	age 41, had worked at Monsanto for 18 years. His first job had been as field salesman, but he was soon transferred into a product department where he worked for George Rinder. He became a department head when Rinder moved up to the Division General Manager's post. In 1977 he replaced Rinder as General Manager of Queeny. Hubbard was an intelligent, reasonable man with a low key management style. He had worked hard to build team spirit among his managers.
Joe Roboh,	age 45, had been at Monsanto for over 20 years, the entire time in R&D. His staff now numbered over 60 and along with most of them he shared an enthusiasm for basic research. He believed that most of Monsanto's R&D dollars had to be spent on immediately commercializable research, but as he told his people: "We do the commercial stuff because it pays the bills, but it's basic research that keeps us intellectually alive and secures the future of this company!"
Andy Dewing,	age 57, had spent his career in manufacturing at Monsanto. Seven plant managers, and through them several thousand people, reported to him. Only his divisional headquarters staff was being ranked at this meeting; all the others would be ranked within their own plants. Dewing was widely respected as a hard-nosed guy who got things done.
Fred Ellis,	age 35, had joined Monsanto in manufacturing in 1967. Four years later he moved to field sales, then to the marketing staff. He became a product department head in 1973. Ellis believed strongly that Queeny's growth would have to come from Consumer Products.
Norm Brewster,	age 39, had joined Monsanto in the early sixties as an engineer. After three years in a plant, he had taken a leave of absence to go to a well-known midwestern business school. On his return he had progressed rapidly and was one of the two product department heads when Rinder became Queeny's General Manager. When Rinder created the Oil Additive Chemicals Department, he put Brewster in charge of it.
John Coulson,	age 37, had been at Monsanto for thirteen years. When Hubbard was promoted to General Manager, Coulson took over the Commodity Chemicals Department. He was ambitious for his area and hoped that he could appeal for support to Hubbard. He had a somewhat excitable personality but was well liked and respected by his subordinates.

Leo Nicholson,	age 35, was new to his job as Manager of Queeny's field sales. Only two months before he had headed up the Central Region Sales Office, where he had worked for almost thirteen years. He had made his reputation as a salesman, and his skills as an administrator were not yet fully tested.
Jack Eckert,	age 29, was a first-level manager in Monsanto Chemical Commodities Company's Controllers Department. This was his first time as a PRB analyst, and he was unsure what to think of it. On the one hand he wanted the exposure; on the other hand he was frightened of making mistakes or antagonizing anyone.

ipated, most differences of opinion centered on the question of relative priorities of untried growth products versus proven and profitable mature products. Agreement was reached amicably in each case. Exhibit 7 contains the final page of the Queeny Division's PRB ranking table as it appeared at the end of the first day. It shows that eighty-two increments had been ranked with cumulative expenses at 88 percent of the current level and headcount at 85 percent of the current level.

When the meeting broke up at around four in the afternoon, Hubbard was confident that, while the next day would bring some difficult issues, the group would continue to work well together to resolve them. "In retrospect," he mused, "I can see why those disagreements yesterday afternoon were so easily resolved. We were still well below what everyone figured to be the minimum funding level."

The Division Ranking Meeting: Second Day

Trouble had started early in the morning. Hubbard remembered one exchange almost word for word. John Coulson, defending his interest, had thrown up his hand like a traffic cop to confront Joe Roboh on the ranking of the R&D increments.

"Wait a minute Joe, your next four increments all involve basic research aimed at Consumer products."[6]

"Well, that's where the future is, John."

"But we're in the present and won't ever reach the future unless we pay our bills," Coulson said adamantly. "There's no support for my stuff!"

"Calm down. If we want to get to the future, we have to start now. Besides,

6. Exhibit 8 shows the R&D ranking table.

Exhibit 7 Queeny division ranking table after the first day of the ranking meeting.

PRIORITY RESOURCE BUDGETING RANKING TABLE

Ranking level: Queeny Division

Rank	Increment Number	Decision Unit Name	Incremental Expense ($K)	Incremental Headcount	Cumulative Expense ($K)	Cumulative Headcount	1979 Expense ($K)	1979 Headcount	% of 1979 Expense	% of 1979 Headcount	Notes
77	2 of 4	Manufacturing mngt	98	2	9,793	95			82	77	Better liaison with plants. Faster A.R. analysis.
78	1 of 1	AZ-42 Cost reduction (R&D)	305	3.5	10,178	98.5			82	80	Attempt 2¢/lb cost reduction
79	5 of 10	East region (field sales)	85	1.5	10,263	100			86	81	Open office in No. Carolina (includes p/t secy.)
80	2 of 5	R&D mngt	49	1	10,312	101			86	82	Assistant to the Director
81	2 of 4	Consumer products	150	2	10,462	103			87	84	Develop new markets for A2 products
82	3 of 4	Consumer products	112	1	10,574	104			88	85	Full development of all identified market areas. Advertising research.

(Current commitments to decision increments were to be indicated in these columns. Since decision increments were being used for the first time, these data were not available for inclusion).

Exhibit 8   R & D ranking table showing increments at point of debate between Coulson and Ellis.

PRIORITY RESOURCE BUDGETING RANKING TABLE

Ranking level: R&D Director

Rank	Increment Number	Decision Unit Name	Incremental		Cumulative		1979		% of 1979		Notes
			Expense ($K)	Headcount	Expense ($K)	Headcount	Expense ($K)	Headcount	Expense	Headcount	
54	3 of 5	R&D mngt	22	1	4,162	52			78	75	Statistical typist
55	2 of 5	AZ-42 liquid (Chemical Commodities)	115	2.5	4,277	54.5			80	79	Liquid applications research (high temperature)
56	3 of 4	S.P.P.-29 (Consumer)	195	1.5	4,472	56			84	81	Process development
57	4 of 4	S.P.P.-29 (Consumer)	85	.5	4,557	56.5			85	82	Process development
58	3 of 5	Food Products Preservatives (Consumer)	115	2	4,672	58.5			87	85	New process research
59	1 of 3	NH-42 High Density (Consumer)	120	1.5	4,792	60			90	87	Manufacturing yield improvement
60	1 of 2	ALPHA-12 (Commodities)	180	2	4,972	62			93	90	Basic research on use as paint base

(See explanation on Exhibit 7.)

we have applications research and production service for Commodity Chemicals in the threshold."

"But that's just a tiny bit. Hell, my products pay the salaries around here, and we deserve a fair shake. I want those increments that have my stuff in them ranked now, before we spend all we've got on a future we're not sure exists."

At that point, Fred Ellis broke in. "John, demand in your markets isn't growing, and competition may soon start to drive your margins down. I know you're producing most of the cash generated by Queeny, but we ought to use that cash to support the best opportunities we've got, and right now those opportunities are in Consumer. Besides, when you consider . . ."

Coulson interrupted, "That's bull! Our demand continues to grow and our competition won't change all that much. The fact of the matter is, Commodity Chemicals continues to be the mainstay of this division, and we would be crazy to weaken it. Process improvements, and that means R&D, and hard-driving marketing are what it will take to keep this cash cow producing."

Hubbard recalled that he had interrupted at that point to get the facts straight. He had asked Joe Roboh exactly how much applications research and production support for Commodities was in the budget so far. Joe confirmed that production support was equal to 100 percent of the level expended during the past year. "I don't think we can change that, since all our production is sold in advance and we have to be able to deliver," he said. But applications research had been cut to 30 percent of the current level for Commodities. For Oil Additive Chemicals, production support was at 120 percent and applications research at 140 percent. Consumer was at 140 percent and 100 percent, respectively for the two same areas. Roboh thought that more should be spent for Consumer applications research.

Hubbard wondered whether getting the facts helped, though. Coulson had just sat there without saying a word. Looking for a way to calm the situation down, Hubbard had turned—mistakenly as it turned out—to Andy Dewing.

"Tell me, Andy, what about you? What kind of manufacturing support do you have in the budget for John? Is it enough to see that all of his stuff is out the door on time?"

"Sure, just as long as I have my eight people.[7] Frankly, Chris, I think this whole thing is dumb. We know how to run our business. I sure as hell know how I run my end of it. This is just another system trying to tell us what to do, and you know, I told that guy, that PRB, ABC, alphabet-soup guy that was supposed to help me with this, 'I only have one increment, eight people, and ten years on the job has taught me that eight is the right number.' But no, he made me play games, and now I have four levels or increments[8] or whatever they're called, and who knows or cares what's in them? You want the plants to produce on time and at spec? I need eight guys, no more, no less. And no

7. Dewing's staff at headquarters consisted of eight people. The manufacturing line personnel in the plants were not included in these deliberations.
8. Exhibit 9 shows Dewing's PRB analysis.

matter how many increments or whatever you cut that into, it adds up the same. I can't guarantee anything until I get *all* my men."

Hubbard was flustered a bit by that, he remembered. "You mean you can't operate with less than eight?"

"I mean I can't say what will happen with less than eight. It all depends on the risk you want to take. Four may be enough, or two, or none if you're lucky."

That was the first time I got angry, Hubbard reflected. "Well, why *isn't* your threshold eight people? What are we fooling around with less for?"

"Don't ask me. I tried to do the right thing and make it eight. Ask him," Andy said, and pointed at Jack Eckert, the PRB coordinator. "It was my PRB analyst who said I couldn't have eight in my threshold."

"Wait a minute, Andy," replied a very much on-the-spot Eckert. "I wasn't at your sessions when you did your original analysis, but I suspect that the guy who worked with you said that the threshold could not be *equal* to the current level. That's a basic assumption in PRB. You have just told us how to view your department: The major issue is *risk*. How willing is Queeny to risk a production delay or quality-control problem? For which products? Which customers? What are the costs of a delay?"

"We can't take those risks and keep our customers. How much risk do you say we should take, Jack?" countered Andy.

"You have to make that decision," Jack replied. "My job here is to facilitate the process, not to make operating or budgeting decisions. You have to make that decision, and you have made it, year after year. All the system does is help you attach different prices to different levels of risk. The choice is yours."

Andy smiled ironically. "You say that like it's easy."

"I don't mean it to sound easy," Eckert said, looking around the room.

Coulson spoke up, "I think we should give Andy all of his men right now. All these management systems sound fine, but we know what's going to happen if the plants back up. We need the same amount of production as last year, and his staff worked full time then."

Nodding his head, Brewster called out, "I agree with John; let Andy have his people next."

Hubbard moved to get closure. "I think that's right. Anyone disagree? . . . No? Then Andy, we'll accept all your other increments now."

Relaxing, Andy responded, "Good! That finishes my part. Can I get back to work now, Chris?"

"No, I want you involved in the rest of the ranking. A lot of the decisions we still have to make could indirectly affect your department."

Hubbard wondered whether he had moved for closure too soon. Andy's impassioned complaint had interrupted the flow of the meeting, and Hubbard had wanted to return to the question of how much research support to devote to Commodity Chemicals.

Coulson raised the point immediately. "We still haven't answered the question we began with. I still think I should get more support from R&D."

Exhibit 9 Summary of Dewings's analysis.

PRIORITY RESOURCE BUDGETING DECISION UNIT SUMMARY

1) Decision Unit Name: Cost Cent. # Manufacturing Management #0100	2) Division/Department Queen/MCCC	3) Decision Unit Mgr. Andy Dewing	4) Date 8/1/79	7) Decision Unit Results to be Worked Towards in 1979

5) Purpose of Decision Unit

Manage the utility and service functions of the Queeny Division plants and manage the manufacture of Queeny's commodities, oil additive, and consumer products to meet the agreed to unit costs and volumes.

A. Improve production yields 10% in S.P.P. –29.

B. Improve COGS in ALPHA-12 by 5%.

C. Implement $1.5 million of cost reduction programs.

D. Implement rehabilitation of existing facilities to meet safety and environmental needs.

6) What Does Your Unit Do and What Resources Are Used to Do It?

8 people. *Director of Manufacturing* is department manager. He supervises those below him and is responsible for overall planning; 4 *Managers, Manufacturing* each assigned to one or more products, follows up on all manufacturing problems, coordinates capital appropriation requests, provides technical assistance and expertise when required and coordinates with division R&D. 2 *Manufacturing Services Managers* for Utilities and Service at plant locations and coordination of Division function; and one *secretary.*

	Incremental			
	People	% 1979	Expense	% 1979
Unit Res. Sup.	3	38%	225	50

8) What Will Be Done at the Threshold Level?

Maintain major administrative activities for plants.

– Manage only most profitable products in division
– Minimal planning and control of all other products
– Generally treat plants as a "wasting asset"

Requires:
    1 Director Manufacturing,
    1 Manager Manufacturing,
    1 Secretary

9) Why Are These Activities Essential

• Need to keep plants operating at economic production levels.

• This level of effort would result in problems in production scheduling, lower yields, and higher COGS.

12) Incr. No.	13) What will be done at this Increment and what Resources are needed?	14) Why should this increment be funded?	15) Unit Res. Sup.	16) What Incremental Resources are needed?		17) What Cumulative Resources are needed?			
				People	Expense	People	% 1978	Expense	% 1978
2 of 4	Reallocation plant management to pick up limited planning and control for all products. Begin low level of cost reduction programs (.5 million) Requires: 2 Managers	Ensure that all product areas are "covered" from manufacturing planning/control. Bring yield and COGS down to planned levels.		2	98	5	63	323	72
3 of 4	Cover all plants and product areas. Allow for coordination of capital projects, full cost reduction program, and limited implementation of rehabilitation program. Requires: 2 Managers	Achieve planned increases in yield, improvements in COGS, and cost reduction programs.	A B C	2	108	7	88	431	96
4 of 4	Full implementation of rehabilitation program. Additional cost reduction opportunities (.5 million) Requires: 1 Manager	Meet government imposed deadlines on plant rehabilitation.	D	1	49	8	100	480	106
			ESTIMATED EXPENSE 1979 (Basis: Six-month Act.)			8	100	450	100

403

Hubbard nodded, he recalled. "Joe, where is the rest of John's support?"

"Spread across my last eight increments, numbers 67 to 74."[9]

"OK, John," Hubbard said as he turned to examine the display that explained what was in each of those increments, "if you could have two of those, which would they be?"

"I'll need three. Number 67 is the area where we have the best opportunity, but 67 alone doesn't do much for us. Increments 68 and 71 will give that project the punch it needs to produce some applications we can take to the market."

Brewster broke in, "Remember, Chris, we haven't yet funded any of those new Oil Additives projects I spoke to you about, and . . ."

Coulson interrupted. "We have already ranked three of your exploratory research projects, Norm. The increments you have left look like long shots to me, and my projects have pretty clear near-term benefits."

"These new projects have a lot of potential," Brewster countered, "and I think the results we've gotten in my group over the last five years show that investments in R&D for our business pay off."

Dewing spoke up, "Look, why don't we give John one of his increments, then Norm one of his, then John, and so on?"

Coulson responded before anyone could reply. "But aren't we supposed to rank each increment with the idea that it really is the most important thing available, and not simply trade around? My projects are critical and should go in the budget now!"

Everyone started speaking at once. After some fifteen minutes of spirited argument, Hubbard intervened. "Look, we're getting nowhere on this one. Let's move on to something else for awhile and come back to this later."

The group made good progress on several items until Norm Brewster got upset. At the time, the group was discussing advertising, and the debate was whether Oil Additive Chemicals' increment should come before Consumer Chemicals.

"Right now I've got 90 percent of current advertising expense in the budget," Brewster said. "Rates will go up at least 15 percent, and if we take my next increment I'll be just short of my current level in advertising purchase power. If we take Consumer's increment, Fred will be at 160 percent of current. I don't even understand why we're wasting time talking about it."

"Maybe it's time to start cutting your advertising," Chris explained. "You've been spending at high levels, but you dominate the market now, and you keep telling me you get terrific word-of-mouth. You haven't convinced me that this advertising increment will have much effect on either your share or profitability."

"I'm the one who needs the advertising," Fred Ellis interrupted. "Consumer is right where you were a few years ago. We are at 'take-off.' We have terrific products in a growth market, and we have to get out there and establish a dominant position. Right now, getting more awareness and supporting our distributors is critical."

---

9. Exhibit 10 shows the R&D ranking.

Exhibit 10   Last page of Joe Roboh's R & D ranking table, expressing the priorities of Queeny's R & D department.

PRIORITY RESOURCE BUDGETING RANKING TABLE

Ranking level: R&D director

Rank	Increment Number	Decision Unit Name	Incremental		Cumulative		1979		% of 1979		Notes
			Expense($K)	Headcount	Expense($K)	Headcount	Expense($K)	Headcount	Expense	Headcount	
65	4 of 5	R&D mngt	39	1	5,325	67.5			99	98	Budgeting and financial assistant
66	5 of 5	R&D mngt	22	1	5,347	68.5			100	99	Second statistical typist
67	3 of 5	AZ-42 liquid	115	2.5	5,462	71	(See explanation on Exhibit 7.)		102	103	Liquid applications research
68	4 of 5	AZ-42 liquid	230	2.5	5,692	73.5			105	107	High altitude applications
69	3 of 3	SUR food preservative	85	1	5,777	74.5			108	108	New freezing applications
70	1 of 2	SUR cost reduction	185	1.5	5,962	76			111	110	Achieve 1¢/100 lb by 1982
71	5 of 5	AZ-42 liquid	98	1.5	6,060	77.5			113	112	Low temperature applications
72	2 of 2	SUR cost reduction	75	.5	6,135	78			114	113	Achieve 1¢/100 lb by 1981
73	5 of 5	PV-12	105	1	6,240	79			116	114	Continue environmental hazard tests to fail safe level
74	3 of 3	IAPA	300	2	6,540	81			122	117	New fertilizer applications

405

Brewster looked straight at Chris. "If our ad budget gets cut, I can't promise the profits we've delivered in the past. We've been damn successful, and our advertising has been an important part of our marketing program. It doesn't make sense to change a successful strategy."

Hubbard wasn't sure whether he was grateful that Nicholson interrupted at this point, or whether it would have been better if they had resolved the ad question.

"Here we are talking about advertising, and we don't even have enough people in the field to take orders. Right now the budget only gives me skeleton crews in three sales offices. We don't have anyone out traveling around."

"You mean we haven't ranked your whole staff yet?" Coulson asked in amazement.

"No."

Coulson sat up straight, exasperated. "That means the whole ranking is screwed up! What are we supposed to do now?"

Hubbard broke in, "Leo, if you were going to add one person to those ranked so far, what office would you do it in?"

"There's no way to answer that Chris, We may sell in the East, but then again the East could be slow and all our sales come from the West or Central. There's no way to tell."

Coulson chimed in, "We've just never gotten a handle on how to judge the marginal utility of a salesperson. There's no useful information."

"What you mean," said Ellis, "is that we don't know what information is useful."

Leo replied, with a look that said he had been through all this before, "Whichever, we don't have it. We know we need to add salespeople, and that means we need to add them everywhere."

That comment led to an extended discussion about how many salespersons were needed. The discussion produced lots of ideas but no resolution. Eventually everyone agreed that the Queeny sales force could not be cut, and that probably Nicholson should be given budget for two new people to be added where necessary.

Then came the issue of where the sales force should fit in the ranking. Should it simply be added now, or should it be inserted among increments ranked earlier in the meeting? The group decided to put it in earlier, but after twenty minutes of discussion still had not decided where.

"This is a mess," Coulson protested. "There's no way to compare Leo's need for salesmen with my need for more R&D and for more guys on my commercial staff. How are we supposed to compare one against the other? They're apples and oranges."

"I don't think there's an easy way," Hubbard replied.

"I don't want an easy way . . . just a way!" Coulson was pushing.

"But you know, John," said Ellis, "this is the first time we've sat down together and really talked about all our departments in this much detail."

"How is the talk helping?" asked Coulson.

"That's a good question, John," Chris said. "Why don't you guys try to answer it over lunch, and let's meet again at 1:30."

As Hubbard finished his own lunch he began to formulate a plan for resolving the issues that remained open.

Appendix: The Priority Resource Budgeting (PRB) Concept*

How do you plan your vacation? Do you say: "Last year, we went to Florida and spent $1,000. Let's add 10 percent for inflation, and go!" Or do you think: "Should we go on vacation, or use the money and time for something else? What other expenditures do we have coming up? How much money do we have to spend for a vacation? Where should we go? Should we fly or drive? Should we camp or stay at a motel?"

The second approach, of course, makes more sense. Priority Resource Budgeting (PRB) encourages the same kind of approach. PRB asks us to question the costs themselves. Why are we spending the money? What are we getting in return? How can we better spend the money? PRB involves cost/benefit trade-offs throughout the organization.

How PRB Works

1. Identify "Decision Units." A Decision Unit is the smallest meaningful group of people and/or other resource devoted to achieving a common significant business purpose. It can be a traditional cost center, a program, or a group of activities. Typical Decision Units include between five and fifteen people and a dollar budget of about $150,000 to $400,000.
2. Analyze each Decision Unit. Each manager is asked to analyze the Decision Unit(s) for which he or she is responsible. Answers to the following seven specific questions guide this analysis.
   - What is the purpose (goal) of the Decision Unit?
   - What Decision Unit results (special accomplishments) are to be worked toward next year?
   - What does the Unit do (activities), and what resources are used to do it?
   - What alternative methods for achieving the purpose are feasible?
   - What is the minimal level of service the Unit could provide and still remain viable? Why are those services essential? In PRB language, this is defined as the "threshold level."
   - What additional increments of service can be provided?[1]
   - Why should these additional increments be funded?

1. Think of increments as the building blocks of resources (either money or people) that are added to achieve more completely the Unit's purpose and results. Each increment you add should be able to stand alone. Increment Two (for example) could be the addition of two people. The activities and services they provide will be above and beyond the first threshold limit. And if the two people were not added, the services and activities of the threshold limit would still be performed. Continue the same logic with Increment Three, Four, etc.

*Source: Monsanto Company PRB Manual.

Exhibit 11   Decision unit analysis.

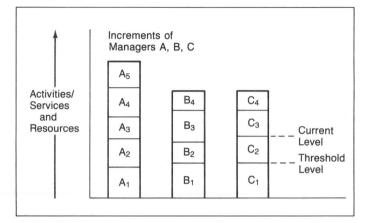

3. Rank in order of priority the Decision Unit increments obtained from
   the analysis in Step 2. The first ranking actually occurs at the Decision
   Unit level when the manager arranges his or her increments in order
   of their importance (Exhibit 11). The next ranking occurs at the organizational level immediately above. The ranking involves the manager,
   peers, and their immediate supervisor. Together, these people rank all
   their increments—based on the objectives of the group and the organization (Exhibit 12). That ranking is based on the written analyses and

Exhibit 12   Decision unit ranking.

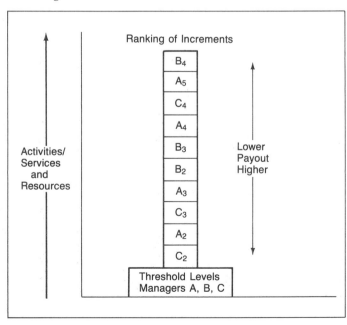

Exhibit 13   Ranking process summary.

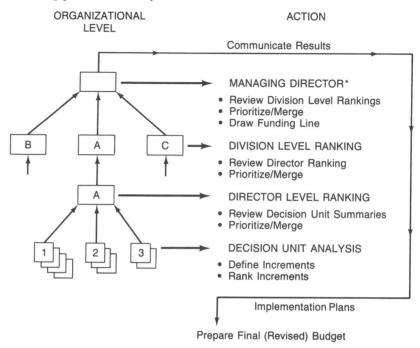

ORGANIZATIONAL LEVEL — ACTION

Communicate Results

MANAGING DIRECTOR*
- Review Division Level Rankings
- Prioritize/Merge
- Draw Funding Line

DIVISION LEVEL RANKING
- Review Director Ranking
- Prioritize/Merge

DIRECTOR LEVEL RANKING
- Review Decision Unit Summaries
- Prioritize/Merge

DECISION UNIT ANALYSIS
- Define Increments
- Rank Increments

Implementation Plans

Prepare Final (Revised) Budget

* Corporate management reviews the budget.

discussions between the Decision Unit managers and the ranking manager. The give and take of those meetings is vital in determining the priorities that are ultimately published. Exhibit 13 portrays an overview of the ranking process.

4. Prepare the organization's formal budget, based on the decisions made in Step 3. The final product of the preceding meetings and analyses is a ranking table for the entire organization. Subsequent to the final ranking meeting, that ranking manager studies the resulting ranking table, makes any required adjustments, decides which increments should and which should not be funded, and draws a "funding line" on the table that indicates the increments that have been approved, those that have not, and costs of each.[2] The ranking table thus is a record of all the decisions that have been made in the Priority Resource Budgeting process (Exhibit 14). Not only does it show what will and will not be funded in the upcoming year, it also ranks activities in priority so that adjustments during the year can be made more easily.

2. While the funding was "drawn" or set by the Managing Director of each Monsanto Company, each divisional general manager would indicate a recommended funding level for his unit at the conclusion of the divisional ranking.

Exhibit 14   Funding the increments.

As the supervisor looks at the ranking of increments, the "normal" breakout would look something like the diagram. Beyond the threshold limits, there are some areas where the payout is high. At the top of the tower there might be some increments which are not likely to merit serious consideration. In between, lies the "grey area" where the desirability of the increment is arguable. The funding line typically falls somewhere in the grey area.

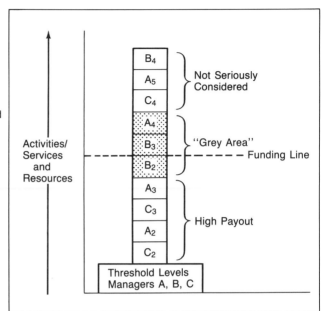

5. The final budget, although prepared in a vastly different fashion from traditional budgets, is similar in format to the end product of the traditional approach. The cost breakdowns (e.g., salaries, bonuses, travel) feed directly into the company's existing budgeting and control system.

National Medical Enterprises

This company will be fulfilled when we encompass all aspects of health care in a totally coordinated system. We are in the total health care market; an individual product is irrelevant. Right now the situation is like a jigsaw puzzle: We have 1,000 pieces and no picture to go by.

Richard K. Eamer (age fifty-six), chairman and chief executive officer of National Medical Enterprises (NME), was discussing his vision for the company he had founded with two colleagues in 1969, fifteen years earlier. In 1984, the company reported sales in excess of $2.5 billion and a net income of $121 million. (Both sales and net income had experienced an annual growth rate of more than 40 percent over the preceding ten-year period.) Among proprietary (for-profit) hospital management companies, NME had singled itself out with respect to its diversification, participating in nearly all major areas of health care including acute, long-term psychiatric and home care, as well as the supply of health products. "We could be as big as GE by the turn of the century . . . or bigger," continued Eamer, leaning forward to emphasize his point. "We're not limited."

Chairman Eamer's optimism about the business prospects in health care was not shared by everyone in the industry. Articles expressing doubts and warnings about the future health of the industry appeared in the national press. According to *Forbes* (June 4, 1984); "American hospitals are in more trouble than even pessimists may suspect. . . . Depending on whose estimates you use, hundreds of the nation's 7,088 hospitals may become insolvent over the next four years."

In another article on June 18, *Forbes* commented, "Anyone who thought the health care business could only go in one direction—up—is now in for . . . disillusionment."

Certainly, the 1980s marked a time of discontinuity for the U.S. health care industry as pressure mounted to contain ballooning costs. A major change to the basis for Medicare payments, the rapid growth of health maintenance organizations (HMOs),[1] and the introduction of other payment schemes had encouraged the emergence of new approaches to health care delivery. The industry was in visible ferment, and the general or acute care hospitals—which were

---

1. See glossary at the end of the case.

the traditional providers of surgical, diagnostic, therapeutic, and related ancillary (clinical laboratory testing, ambulance, emergency) services—were the most seriously threatened by the new competition for each health care dollar.

To deal with these pressures, NME reorganized its core acute-care hospital service to encourage experimentation and adaptation. In 1984, a new division, the Health Care Systems and Services Group, was created to develop new approaches for feeding patients to NME's hospital facilities. As part of this move, two experienced young men, Scott Gross and Bill Piche, both age thirty-eight, were put in charge of the Hospital Group (acute care hospitals) and the newly created Health Care Systems and Services Group respectively. It would be their task to work out new health care approaches and the relationships of their units with each other as well as with the other units in the new organizational structure. The outcome of their efforts would undoubtedly affect the future of NME.

As noted by John C. Bedrosian (age 49), senior executive vice president and one of the three NME founders:

> It is hard to predict where the health care industry is going. Up to now, a company should have done well competitively with any sense at all. Now there will be winners and losers for the first time in the industry. The question is: who wins? who loses? who suffers? in the coming shake-out.

The U.S. Health Care Industry

Health care had come under public and legislative scrutiny in the 1980s as a result of skyrocketing costs. By 1984, various proposals to limit health care spending coupled with new approaches for delivering health care promised to increase competitive pressures and to disrupt further what had been a safe and profitable business.

The traditional health care field had been modest in size and fairly simple in structure. In 1950, total national health care expenditures were $12.7 billion, or 4.9 percent of the gross national product (GNP). In 1960, these figures were $26.9 billion and 5.3 percent. The industry was made up primarily of nonprofit general-purpose facilities and private physicians who provided services paid for by private insurance programs such as Blue Cross/Blue Shield or by the patient directly. By 1983, total expenditures had risen to $355 billion, or 10.8 percent of the GNP, making health care the second largest industry in the U.S., following food and agriculture.

The health care industry had become a complex structure of nonprofit and for-profit business facilities offering many products and services paid for by a multitude of public and private programs. The impetus for this change had its roots in one piece of legislation under the Johnson administration: the federally funded Medicare and Medicaid national health care insurance programs that assured treatment for the elderly and the poor. With the availability of public money, the health care industry entered a phase of explosive growth.

Table A Selected health care cost increases, 1980–82.

	Inflation Rate (CPI)	*Medical Care*	*Hospital Room*	*Physicians' Services*
1980	13.5%	10.9%	13.1%	10.6%
1981	10.4%	10.8%	14.9%	11.0%
1982	6.1%	11.6%	15.7%	9.4%

Source: U.S. Bureau of Labor Statistics, Consumer Price Indexes, Annual Averages.

The reimbursement scheme allowed hospitals to charge whatever they needed to cover their costs. These guaranteed payments prompted established hospitals to initiate programs of capital expansion. The legislation also included provisions allowing investor-owned hospitals a reasonable return on equity (about 11 percent pretax at that time) on government reimbursed services. This lured new for-profit organizations into the field. Expenditures for hospital services soared from $9 billion per year in the early 1950s to close to $150 billion in 1983, representing 41.4 percent of total health-care spending for that year.

Accompanying the national debate that had led to the federal health programs was a growing public expectation of entitlement with respect to health care. Pressure mounted for more company-sponsored group employee health care plans. The resulting shift from individual to company-supported payments in turn encouraged further expansion and upgrading of medical facilities, since many of the programs followed the government's lead in calculating reimbursements based on a hospital's most recent entitled costs.

By the 1980s, spokesmen for both public and private insurers were becoming increasingly vociferous in their criticism of health care costs as out of control. They pointed to data, such as shown in Table A, to make their case.

The culprit was clearly identified. As reported in *Business Week* (October 15, 1984), "There were no real controls within the system," says Donald R. Melville, President and Chief Executive of Norton Co. in Worcester, Mass. "We wrote a ticket to provide free health care without limits."

Added J. Alexander McMahon, president of the American Hospital Association, "The whole message was to expand." And *Forbes* (September 10, 1984), described how the "message to expand" worked:

> Third party insurance is perfectly engineered to remove incentives to keep costs down. Businesses pay premiums for employees, and insurance companies pay the bills. Employees have no reason to shop for cheaper care; so providers have no reason to be cost-effective.
>
> A system of blank checks is bad. Worse, since doctors charge on a fee-for-service basis, they have strong incentives to sell as much as they can. Because the doctors dominate the demand for services, they have the power to do so.
>
> Doctors decide whether hospitalization is necessary (and for how long),

what tests to perform and what medicine to give. Doctors' fees might be a small portion of the bill, but "they control 80 percent to 85 percent of costs," says Glenn Witt of the Iowa Health Policy Group. "We found that doctors put patients in hospitals too often, asked for too many tests and kept them there too long."

The bubble of expanding costs was burst by Congress in 1983 when it changed the basis for hospital reimbursement. Under the new law, Medicare set flat-fee rates for 467 categories of treatment, called "diagnostic-related groups" (DRGs). These payments were to cover all hospital costs except those for physician services, the cost of capital, outpatient services, and services associated with psychiatric or rehabilitation units.

While the full force of the new law was not expected to take effect until 1987, there was an immediate twofold response to DRG legislation by the health care industry: hospitals reduced patients' average stay to reduce costs; and specialized health care facilities, not covered by DRG fee limitations, sprouted to siphon off patients requiring minor treatment. The net impact of these two developments was to reduce markedly hospital utilization (census).

New DRG legislation was not the only threat to hospital revenues. Hospital utilization was further reduced by a rapid growth of hospital maintenance organizations. HMOs were organized health clinics operated to provide comprehensive treatment for a flat fee. Kaiser-Permanente, the first HMO, was set up in the 1940s, but the concept did not flourish until 1973, when Congress passed the Health Maintenance Act providing federal funds to aid in the establishment of such preventative health units. By 1984, approximately 15 million Americans (6 percent of the population) belonged to some 300 HMOs in the United States, making it a $7.5 billion industry growing at a 20–25 percent annual rate.

Much of the impetus for the expansion of HMO membership came from U.S. corporations and insurance companies as a way to contain health costs. Industrial companies like Ford, GM, and IBM initiated HMO programs for their employees. (Ford reported a savings of $12 million over two years as a result of its employee-based HMO.) Prudential, Blue Cross/Blue Shield, and CIGNA were among the insurance companies operating HMOs with large enrollments.

To protect their position, hospitals too began to adopt more aggressive approaches. Their response to HMOs was the preferred provider organization (PPO), a hybrid between HMOs and the traditional fee-for-service. Under this arrangement, treatment continued to be offered on the basis of fee-for-service. The fee schedule, however, was reduced when member physicians and hospitals were used. An important distinction between HMOs and PPOs was the party at risk. With PPOs, the losses and gains associated with heavier and lighter than normal health care usage were borne by the paying party (i.e., insurance company, corporation, or individual). With HMOs they were born by the health care provider.

Notwithstanding these attempts by hospitals to stem the tide of change, industry observers were predicting a further erosion of their heretofore preeminent position in the health care field. According to *Forbes* (June 4, 1984):

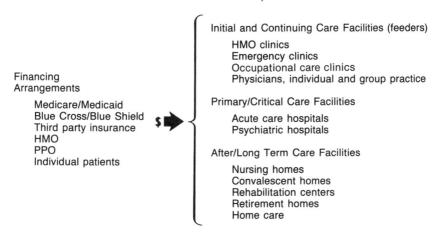

Figure A   Overview of the U.S. health care system.

Even such for-profit hospital operations as Humana and Hospital Corporation of America are not immune to the onslaught of HMOs and other new competition. According to a study by the California Hospital Association, 64 percent of the for-profit hospitals will experience revenue shortfalls in the first year that DRG-based Medicare payments go into effect.

Emerging Industry Structure. A net effect of the changes to health care was to lessen the overwhelmingly dominant role that hospitals and private practice physicians once played. Figure A depicts a simplified view of the health care industry in 1984. The typical interrelationships between patients, the financing arrangements, and the health care delivery systems are described in Exhibit 1.

As indicated in Exhibit 1, for-profit organizations had become a major force in the various health care delivery systems. Ownership of clinics and nursing homes was highly fragmented in 1984, but five companies dominated the acute-care segment, owning over 40 percent of the approximately 1,100 for-profit hospitals in the U.S. Exhibit 2 provides comparative information on the size and activities of these five companies.

The Growth of NME

National Medical Enterprises could trace its roots to Richard Eamer's professional background. On graduating from law school in 1960, he began specializing in health care and hospital law. His earlier training as a CPA gave him a special interest in the economics of hospital operations. During the next eight years his clients included over eighty hospitals, both voluntary nonprofit and proprietary, and hundreds of physicians.

By 1968, a number of his clients were urging him to form a proprietary company in order to facilitate the raising of capital and to assure more effective organizational growth for their hospitals. Joined by colleagues Leonard Cohen,

Exhibit 1 Typical health care provider and financing relationships.

	Acute-Care Hospitals	HMO Centers	Emergency Care (Free standing)	Nursing Homes/Rehab. Centers	Psychiatric Hospitals
Purpose	Emergency and general patient care; Surgery; Medicine; Out-patient services	Preventative, on-going health care	Emergency care for minor injuries and major problems	Long-term and on-going convalescent and rehabilitative care	Care for acute and chronic psychiatric patients
Primary Source of Funds	Blue Cross/Blue Shield; Medicare/Medicaid; Private insurers	Employees; Individuals	Privately insured individuals	Medicare/Medicaid; Private Insurance	Medicare; Private Insurance; Blue Cross (extended benefits only)
For-Profit Share of Total Market, (1983)	12% of beds; 17% of hospitals (Source: Federation of American Hospitals)	28% of all plans (Source: Interstudy, Inc. HMO Status Report, 6/83)	98% (30% chain owned) (Source: SMG Marketing Group)	Nursing homes only: 81% (15% chain owned) (Source: American Healthcare Association)	17% of hospitals (Source: National Assn. of Private Psychiatric Hospitals)

Health Care Reimbursement and Insurance Organizations

	Medicare/Medicaid	Third Party	HMO	PPO
Health Care Delivery				
Physicians	Selected by patient	Selected by patient	Contracted by HMO	Selected by patient from employer approved list
Hospitals	Selected by physician or patient	Selected by physician or patient	Owned or on contract; Emphasis on out-patient clinics or doctors' offices	Selected by physician or patient
Reimbursement				
Physicians	Payment on rigid schedule	Paid based on standard fees; Fee-for-service; Rigid schedule for Blue Shield	Standard rate schedule for salaried basis	On contract: Fee-for-service; Not on contract: Based on standard rates, but patient pays larger amt.
Hospitals	Standard rate schedule; DRGs	Reimbursed for standard charges; Fee-for-service	Standard rate schedule	Fee-for-service

Exhibit 2 Comparative data for the five largest hospital management companies (1984).

| | Total acute and psychiatric hospitals (owned, managed and under construction) | | Gross Revenues ($ million) | Percentage of revenue by sector | | | |
	Beds	Facilities		Hospitals	Psychiatric and Substance Abuse	Nursing	Other
Hospital Corporation of America	59,946	417	4,178.2	89.6	5.5	—	4.9
American Medical International	19,673	142	2,422.7	92.0	8.0	—	—
Humana	18,311	92	2,606.4	100.0	—	—	—
National Medical Enterprises	16,311	142	2,524.0	53.8	8.1	25.8	12.3
Charter Medical Corporation	5,798	56	493.3	49.3	41.7	—	9.0

Sources: 1985 Directory of Investor-Owned Hospitals; and company annual reports.

417

also an attorney and CPA, and John Bedrosian, an attorney, Eamer launched NME in 1969 with an initial public offering. With the proceeds of $23 million, the new company purchased four general (acute-care) hospitals, three convalescent (nursing) homes, and two office buildings. By the end of its first year, NME had acquired an additional general hospital, an additional convalescent home, and three building sites for new acute-care hospitals. At the same time, it had entered the health care equipment and supply business with the acquisition of one company and the start-up of a second.

Eamer had a definite vision for NME, which he articulated in the company's first report:

> We think it important that you who share in the ownership of NME have some insight into the motivation of its management as well as our views on the problems that confront the industry, because these views—which we hold very strongly—will have a continuing effect on our policies and operations.
>
> The health care field has become the sick man of the American economy, and no token action is going to make it well. Nothing less than a massive coordinated effort by the government, the existing voluntary hospital system, the medical and the paramedical profession and private enterprise can solve the problem.
>
> [The traditional] hospital typically lacks any of the basic advantages enjoyed by any modern, sophisticated business organization—mass purchasing, statistical comparisons and evaluation, competent business development and financial management.
>
> The hospital industry is essentially where the grocery industry was at the advent of the supermarket chain. Although it deals with life and death and not food supply, our industry can still learn the lessons that other industries have already absorbed.

While NME's initial principal focus had been on expanding its acute-care hospital network, it also made major inroads in the convalescent home field with the purchase of an 84.5 percent stake in Hillhaven Nursing Homes in 1979 for $38.7 million and in the psychiatric care field with the acquisition of Psychiatric Institute of America (PIA) in July 1982 for $150 million. Hillhaven was second in the industry in the number of nursing home beds; PIA was the largest in its field. By 1984, NME owned, operated or managed a total of 553 health care facilities in the U.S. and abroad. The geographical location of these facilities is shown in Exhibit 3.

By design, acquisitions had accounted for the preponderance of NME's growth. Leonard Cohen, president and chief operating officer, explained the company's policy, "Time and experience were the reasons for our emphasis on acquisitions. The field was fast moving, and we wanted to strike while the iron was hot. We were able to get an established position and experienced managers. And by keeping the acquired management on board, we also got new blood in the company."

To support the rapid pace of expansion and the many acquisitions, NME was involved in a continuous stream of financing. Over the 1975–84 ten-year

Exhibit 3 Facilities owned, operated or managed by National Medical Enterprises in 1984. *Source:* 1984 Annual Report.

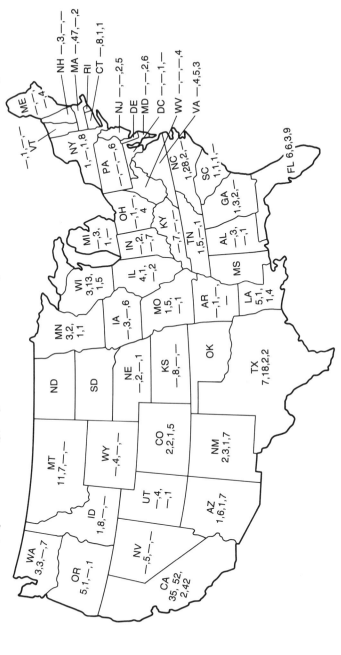

Key: Acute and Primary Care, Long Term Care, Psychiatric and Substance Abuse, Home Care

	Acute and Primary Care	Long Term Care	Psychiatric and Substance Abuse	Home Care
Total facilities	98*	271	31	153
Total beds	12,595	34,980	2,220	N.A.

*Includes 1 in Puerto Rico and 3 in Saudi Arabia

419

Exhibit 4   National Medical Enterprises' financial data. *Source: Value Line.*

1986 | 1987 | 1988 | 1989   Value Line

October 5, 1984

TIMELINESS 2 (Relative Price Performance Next 12 Mos.) Above Average

SAFETY 3 (Scale: 1 Highest to 5 Lowest) Average

BETA 1.40 (1.00 = Market)

	Target Price Range
High —	3.2 2.9 2.6 3.2 2.2 1.0 1.6 1.1 2.7 5.6 6.6 15.2 23.0 23.8 32.4 25.6
Low —	1.6 1.0 1.8 1.7 0.6 0.3 0.8 0.4 1.5 2.7 3.3 6.5 12.5 9.8 20.1 17.6

Insider Decisions 1983

	M	J	J	A	S	O	N	D	J	F	M	A	M	J	J
to Buy	2	0	0	0	0	2	0	4	0	1	0	1	3	1	0
to Sell	6	0	0	0	0	2	1	2	1	1	1	1	2	0	0

Institutional Decisions

	2Q'83	3Q'83	4Q'83	1Q'84	2Q'84
to Buy	65	63	54	64	53
to Sell	48	51	53	44	46
Hldg's(000)	25308	24883	22298	25350	25640

(Continued from Capital Structure)
shares at $27.72. Includes $197.0 mill. 8% sub. debs. ('08), each convertible into 29.59 shares at $33.80.

10.0 x "Cash Flow" p sh

Options Trade On ASE

5-for-4 split 3-for-2 split 10% div'd 10% div'd

Relative Price Strength

	Percent 12.0
	shares 8.0
	traded 4.0

	1968	1969	1970	1971	1972	1973	1974	1975	1976	1977	1978	1979	1980	1981	1982	1983	1984	1985	87-89E
Revenues per sh	--	.76	.99	1.22	1.50	2.64	3.69	4.69	5.26	7.11	8.23	7.80	13.37	15.93	19.89	27.11	29.73	33.50	50.00
"Cash Flow" per sh	--	.06	.10	.12	.15	.23	.30	.37	.42	.54	.68	.60	.97	1.36	1.92	2.45	2.94	3.55	6.00
Earnings per sh	--	.06	.09	.10	.11	.16	.17	.20	.25	.30	.40	.47	.73	.99	1.28	1.47	1.74	2.10	3.35
Div'd Decl'd per sh	--	--	--	--	.01	.01	.01	.03	.05	.08	.13	.16	.24	.31	.38	.43		.50	.80
Cap'l Spending per sh	--	1.26	1.27	.42	1.20	1.01	.62	1.01	1.24	.82	.77	2.02	1.01	2.30	3.46	5.79	5.59	6.70	9.00
Book Value per sh	--	1.26	1.27	1.33	1.44	1.60	1.82	2.01	2.11	2.36	2.60	3.05	4.38	6.72	7.70	9.95	11.03	17.60	19.50
Common Shs Outst'g	19.66	20.75	21.32	21.73	22.0	21.48	20.34	20.29	22.09	22.41	25.60	35.84	45.70	56.02	58.67	65.10	69.46	12.60	90.00
Avg Ann'l P/E Ratio	33.9	24.3	18.0	22.0	13.3	5.2	3.0	4.1	5.0	6.6	8.8	8.6	14.1	11.5	13.6	13.7	13.7		18.0
Relative P/E Ratio	2.06	1.74	1.15	1.51	1.31	.73	.40	.52	.65	.90	1.27	1.14	1.71	1.27	1.15	1.21			1.50
Avg Ann'l Div'd Yield	--	--	--	--	.5%	1.3%	1.8%	2.6%	3.1%	3.0%	3.1%	2.6%	1.7%	2.1%	1.9%	1.8%			1.3%

1987-89 PROJECTIONS

	Price	Gain	Ann'l Total Return
High	75	(+240%)	38%
Low	50	(+125%)	25%

© Value Line, Inc.

CAPITAL STRUCTURE as of 5/31/84

Total Debt $976.5 mill. Due in 5 Yrs $580.0 mill.
LT Debt $946.5 mill. LT Interest $97.0 mill.

(LT interest earned: 3.8x; total interest coverage: 3.7x)

Incl. $84.0 mill., 9% sub. debs. ('06), each cv. into 40.32 shares at $24.80; $103.0 mill., 12¾% sub. debs. ('01), each cv. into 36.08 (Continued on Chart) (55% of Cap'l)

Leases, Uncapitalized Annual rentals $31.0 mill.
Pension Liability None vs. None in '83

Pfd Stock None

Common Stock 69,464,901 shs. (45% of Cap'l)

CURRENT POSITION ($mill.)

	5/31/82	5/31/83	5/31/84
Cash Assets	151.0	282.1	95.0
Receivables	219.0	279.8	378.0
Inventory (FIFO)	44.4	50.6	60.0
Other	8.5	14.4	21.0
Current Assets	422.9	626.9	554.0
Accts Payable	66.3	90.8	128.0
Debt Due	20.7	28.4	30.0
Other	121.3	147.8	194.0
Current Liab.	208.3	267.0	352.0

												(A)	
Revenues ($mill)	75.0	95.2	116.1	159.3	210.8	279.5	610.8	892.4	1167.1	1764.7	2065.0	2450	4500
Operating Margin	19.2%	17.3%	16.2%	16.0%	16.3%	16.0%	15.7%	17.3%	17.9%	17.5%	17.8%	19.0%	20.0%
Depreciation ($mill)	2.6	3.4	3.8	5.3	7.7	7.7	15.5	25.0	38.0	66.3	83.6	110	225
Net Profit ($mill)	3.5	4.1	5.4	6.9	9.8	13.8	29.5	51.8	75.2	92.9	121.3	150	300
Income Tax Rate	48.3%	48.3%	47.3%	42.1%	43.6%	46.9%	45.7%	46.2%	43.5%	44.2%	43.8%	44.0%	44.0%
Net Profit Margin	4.7%	4.3%	4.7%	4.3%	4.7%	5.0%	4.8%	5.8%	6.5%	5.3%	5.9%	6.1%	6.7%
Working Cap'l ($mill)	7.2	9.2	13.4	18.1	24.0	27.9	74.8	156.0	214.6	359.9	202.0	200	350
Long-Term Debt ($mill)	66.9	79.3	98.5	110.6	109.7	131.7	258.5	282.6	475.2	849.0	946.5	1200	2000
Net Worth ($mill)	37.0	40.8	46.7	52.9	66.6	114.2	205.3	381.3	457.0	648.0	766.2	920	1750
% Earned Total Cap'l	5.8%	6.3%	6.5%	7.2%	8.5%	7.8%	9.2%	10.3%	10.7%	9.0%	9.7%	10.0%	10.5%
% Earned Net Worth	9.4%	10.0%	11.6%	13.0%	14.7%	12.1%	14.4%	13.6%	16.5%	14.3%	15.8%	16.5%	17.0%
% Retained to Comm Eq	8.9%	9.5%	10.4%	11.1%	11.9%	9.0%	11.3%	10.2%	12.6%	10.6%	12.0%	12.5%	13.0%
% All Div'ds to Net Prof	6%	5%	10%	15%	19%	29%	24%	26%	25%	26%	24%	24%	24%

(A) Fiscal year ends May 31 of cal. yr. (B) Primary earnings. Next earn'gs rep't due mid-Oct. Includes a nonoperating gain: 12¢ in '82. Est'd current cost egs./sh.: '84, $1.35. (C) Next div'd meet'g about Oct. 26. Goes ex about Nov. 18. Div'd paym't dates: 15th of Mar., June, Sept. & Dec. ■ Div'd reinvestment plan av'ble. (D) Incl. in-tangibles. In '84: $213.0 mill., $3.07/sh. (E) In millions, adjusted for stock splits and dividends.

Company's Financial Strength	B
Stock's Price Stability	35
Price Growth Persistence	100
Earnings Predictability	90

Factual material is obtained from sources believed to be reliable but cannot be guaranteed.

421

period, long-term debt increased twelve times (from $79 to $947 million) and net worth almost nineteen times (from $41 to $766 million). See Exhibit 4 for a summary of financial data and a 1984 assessment of NME for investment purposes. Exhibit 5 gives a breakdown of revenues and operating profits by lines of business.

1984 Organizational Restructuring

During 1983 and early 1984, NME's operations were organized into four major business units. The Hospital Group comprised acute-care hospitals (inpatient) and alternative care (outpatient) clinics. The Long-Term Health Care Group included convalescent care, rehabilitative services, and medically supported retirement housing. Psychiatric and Substance Abuse Services included psychiatric hospitals and chemical dependency centers (to deal with drug and alcohol dependency problems). And the Health Products and Services Group comprised home-care products, equipment, and services; respiratory, anesthesia, and cardiopulmonary equipment and supplies; and general contracting services.

In June 1984, NME reorganized its operations, creating three new groups. The Health Care Systems and Services Group was assigned rsponsibility for managing NME's growing involvement with HMOs, PPOs, and freestanding clinics—activities theretofore under the aegis of the Hospital Group. This move reflected management's desires to give these businesses more visibility and freedom of action than they might receive as part of the established hospital operations. For similar reasons, home-care services were spun off from the Health Products and Services Group. See Exhibit 6 for the company's organizational structure as of September 1984.

Leonard Cohen (age fifty-nine), to whom the seven operating units reported in his capacity as president and chief operating officer, saw his role as an adviser. He explained, "I don't want to interfere with the business operations. If the group presidents need help framing an acquisitions deal or with public relations, fine. Otherwise I'll be looking to them for exciting ideas and sound operations."

The reorganization came at a time when NME's hospital census (capacity utilization) was declining. It was also a time when competition for investment funds was increasing in the hospital care field in general as well as among NME's business groups.

Hospital Group

"The centerpiece of our company is the acute-care hospital operation. But despite its past accomplishments, or maybe because of them, this division had begun to lose some of its zip." Scott Gross well understood the nature of the critical job he had been given in taking over NME's largest and most profitable group in July 1984. He went on to describe the task as follows: "One of my

Exhibit 5 Revenues and operating profits by lines of business ($ millions).

Years Ended May 31	1980	1981	1982	1983	1984
Operating Revenues					
Acute and primary care	$ 465.3	$ 710.6	$ 927.4	$1,208.8	$1,357.1
Long term care	205.7	252.4	318.0	507.3	651.9
Psychiatric and substance abuse services	—	—	—	182.4	205.7
Health products and services	70.5	96.2	144.8	249.2	309.3
	$ 741.5	$1,059.2	$1,390.2	$2,147.7	$2,524.0
Operating Revenues % of Total					
Acute and primary care	62.8%	67.1%	66.7%	56.3%	53.8%
Long term care	27.7	23.8	22.9	23.6	25.8
Psychiatric and substance abuse services	—	—	—	8.5	8.1
Health products and services	9.5	9.1	10.4	11.6	12.3
	100.0%	100.0%	100.0%	100.0%	100.0%
Operating Profits					
Acute and primary care	$ 58.0	$ 89.4	$ 101.7	$ 134.0	$ 151.8
Long term care	14.9	21.5	27.2	45.2	67.3
Psychiatric and substance abuse services	—	—	—	30.1	37.5
Health products and services	6.5	7.6	17.8	18.4	28.8
	$ 79.4	$ 118.5	$ 146.7	$ 227.7	$ 285.4
Operating Profits % of Total					
Acute and primary care	73.1%	75.4%	69.3%	58.8%	53.2%
Long term care	18.8	18.1	18.6	19.9	23.6
Psychiatric and substance abuse services	—	—	—	13.2	13.1
Health products and services	8.1	6.5	12.1	8.1	10.1
	100.0%	100.0%	100.0%	100.0%	100.0%

Three psychiatric hospitals, owned before the acquisition of Psychiatric Institutes of America, are included in acute and primary care for 1982 and earlier years.

Exhibit 6 Company organizational chart, September 1984.

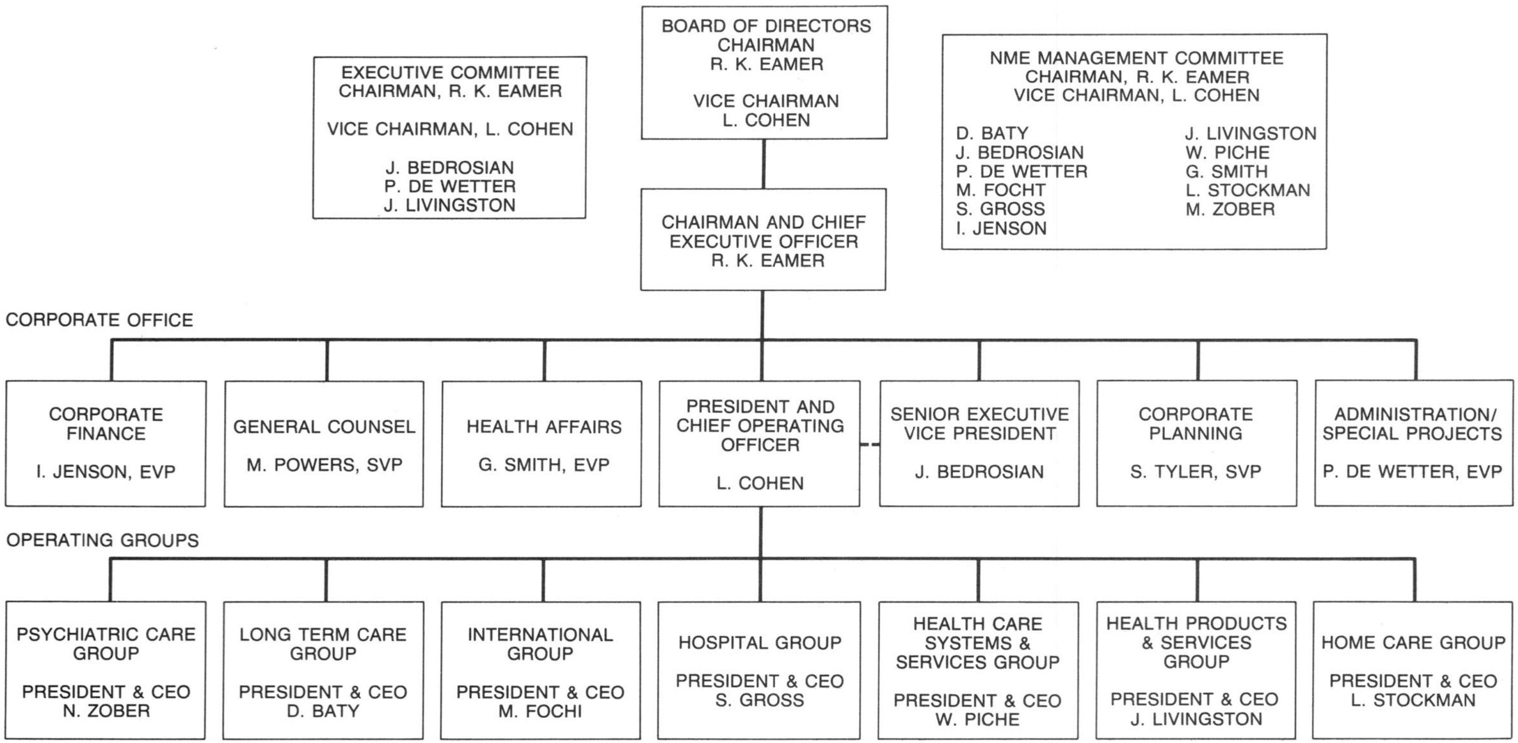

CORPORATE OFFICE

EXECUTIVE COMMITTEE CHAIRMAN, R. K. EAMER
VICE CHAIRMAN, L. COHEN
J. BEDROSIAN P. DE WETTER J. LIVINGSTON

BOARD OF DIRECTORS CHAIRMAN R. K. EAMER
VICE CHAIRMAN L. COHEN

NME MANAGEMENT COMMITTEE CHAIRMAN, R. K. EAMER VICE CHAIRMAN, L. COHEN
D. BATY   J. LIVINGSTON J. BEDROSIAN   W. PICHE P. DE WETTER   G. SMITH M. FOCHT   L. STOCKMAN S. GROSS   M. ZOBER I. JENSON

CHAIRMAN AND CHIEF EXECUTIVE OFFICER R. K. EAMER

CORPORATE FINANCE I. JENSON, EVP	GENERAL COUNSEL M. POWERS, SVP	HEALTH AFFAIRS G. SMITH, EVP	PRESIDENT AND CHIEF OPERATING OFFICER L. COHEN	SENIOR EXECUTIVE VICE PRESIDENT J. BEDROSIAN	CORPORATE PLANNING S. TYLER, SVP	ADMINISTRATION/ SPECIAL PROJECTS P. DE WETTER, EVP

OPERATING GROUPS

PSYCHIATRIC CARE GROUP PRESIDENT & CEO N. ZOBER	LONG TERM CARE GROUP PRESIDENT & CEO D. BATY	INTERNATIONAL GROUP PRESIDENT & CEO M. FOCHI	HOSPITAL GROUP PRESIDENT & CEO S. GROSS	HEALTH CARE SYSTEMS & SERVICES GROUP PRESIDENT & CEO W. PICHE	HEALTH PRODUCTS & SERVICES GROUP PRESIDENT & CEO J. LIVINGSTON	HOME CARE GROUP PRESIDENT & CEO L. STOCKMAN

biggest challenges is to change the group culture. That requires changing the structure as well as the way decisions are made."

On September 5, he announced major changes to the group's organizational structure and operating philosophy. Key elements of the new approach included a restructuring of the hospital groupings and the way the units would be managed, continued support for the cost-control information system under development, and increased emphasis on both business development and marketing.

Hospital Operations

In Scott Gross's judgment, the Hospital Group's earlier regional organization failed to recognize the different managerial challenges and opportunities connected with large versus small hospital units. To provide the special management attention called for by NME's eight largest hospitals (over 200 beds), he grouped them in a new Medical Center Division. The smaller, acute-care hospitals (eighty-seven in all), continued to be grouped and run on a regional basis.

Accompanying the organizational restructuring, Gross introduced the concept of "guided autonomy." He explained the new approach in reporting relationships and the reasons for it:

> Our major competitors are the free-standing, not-for-profit hospitals serving the communities in which our units are located. Years ago, these hospitals were not very competitive, but as pressures on them have mounted, they have become increasingly aggressive and innovative. As new opportunities arose in the community, by the time an NME hospital manager was able to get regional and group headquarters' approval, the local competition had already made the decision and moved on it. We were becoming a lumbering giant.
>
> To my mind, the local unit has to have more say in deciding competitive moves. I want us to realize that the role of group headquarters is to give guidance, to make funds available, and to provide technical assistance to the local level with respect to negotiations, advertising, management systems, and the like.
>
> The guidance part of the formula has to do with limits. Controls have to be in place so that a St. Mary's hospital, on its own, cannot just go out and buy an expensive piece of equipment.

Some colleagues saw limits on Gross's freedom to employ the concept of guided autonomy. As one executive noted, "Delegation requires subordinates capable of handling it. The hospital CEOs are not used to such independence, and some of the people Scott inherited may not be up to much responsibilities."

In Scott Gross's view, an essential element for the success of guided autonomy was providing managers, at all levels, with timely information. He noted, "We need good information, so that we can spend less time reacting and improvising and more time managing ahead." A major new effort to develop a computerized management information system for hospitals gave testimony to this view.

Hospital MIS

Early in 1984, the Hospital Group data processing staff was given the assignment to improve hospital and financial data reporting. According to Don Amaral, chief financial officer for the Hospital Group, "Not long ago, hospital information systems were in the dark ages. Tying clinical information with financial data was considered impossible, or at least impractical. DRG's discipline on fees has changed all that. Now a hospital has to integrate treatment and costs in its management of operations."

Soon after Scott Gross took charge, the MIS assignment was broadened to include clinical, as well as financial, data. By October, a proposal to develop a system capable of providing the following information was being prepared.

1. Hospital financial data
2. Admittance, discharge, and outpatient registration
3. Pharmacy information (make medical checks with respect to possible adverse side effects for each individual patient; generate labels and medication ministration schedule; record charges)
4. Medical records information (trace a patient's chart and abstract a patient's experience for quality control)
5. Order-entry information (order and schedule initial clinical tests for incoming patients; record charges)

The proposed system, which envisaged locating eight IBM System 38 minicomputers in larger NME hospitals across the country to serve as hubs for collecting data daily from forty-five facilities, would require an investment of $25 to $30 million over three years. (The normal data-processing annual budget was about $12 million.) The most important benefit expected from such a system was that patients would be moved in and out of a hospital faster. As one executive explained, "With a DRG fixed-price arrangement, hospitals can no longer afford to have patients sitting around waiting for tests and diagnosis. There is pressure to compress the patient's stay as much as possible within the bounds of good medical treatment."

Another benefit of the system would be in selecting the optimal DRG for each patient. A particular set of patient symptoms quite often could be associated with more than one DRG. Since each DRG had its own reimbursement ceiling, the selection could affect hospital revenues.

Business Development

Henry Mordoh, a senior vice president who had headed the Hospital Group's Northwest Region, returned to headquarters to take over the newly created job of business development. He explained the significance of this move. "In the past we had a strong operational bias. We basically focused on adding and running acute-care hospitals. My new assignment reflects on important changes in management's thinking." As of late 1984, Mordoh had initiated four primary efforts. The first of these was the development of rehabilitation facilities. The kinds of services under study included simple rehabilitation for postoperative patients, stroke-patient rehabilitation, chemical imbalance (drug and alcohol) rehabilitation, major trauma (e.g., spinal-cord injury) rehabilitation, and surgical trauma rehabilitation. Mordoh explained his views on the project: "These rehabilitation patients are now dispersed in hospitals in an indiscriminate manner. We are looking at developing rehabilitation as a special new line of business for the Hospital Group."

The second effort involved joint ventures with doctors to offer out-patient services. Mordoh explained:

> As fees have been reduced, doctors, in looking for other means of earning an income, have increasingly become involved in setting up independent out-patient facilities to provide health care treatment formerly handled in hospitals. Surgicenters, for minor surgery, are a good example. By collaborating with the doctors, we see a way of averting this threat with an opportunity for growth. NME can provide legal, management, and financial expertise in return for a share of the profits and access to the patient. By working with doctors not connected with our hospital network, we can broaden our patient base. These activities also provide us with a way to enter new areas of health care.

An organized system for assimilating new acquisitions into NME was the third of Mordoh's developments. The task of assimilating each new hospital into the NME system had been the responsibility of regional managers. Mordoh planned to have headquarters' management team take over this function. He explained the reasons for the move:

> By their very nature, the pressing requirements connected with assimilating a new hospital acquisition distracted the regional executive from managing ongoing operations. Moreover, since it was a job they didn't do every day, they tended to handle these situations in a disorganized fashion . . . and the results were sloppy at times, despite our efforts and good intentions. By dealing with new acquisitions on a systemwide basis, we can professionalize the job and at the same time reduce the disruption to our important ongoing operations.

The final of the four efforts was a model hospital project. This undertaking represented a systematic effort to define effective and efficient hospital procedures and policies. It was intended to cover all aspects of hospital operations. As an illustration of its scope, Mordoh noted:

> We are trying to lay out ideal approaches to each and every aspect of hospital operations. Attention must obviously be given to such important considerations as patient care, pharmaceutical operations, laboratory operations, and the like, but small things are also important. For example, a

patient's impression of his or her hospital experience tends to be strongly affected by the last person with whom he or she deals. If the discharge staff person is not attuned to the patient's needs, you miss out on an opportunity for good public relations. And so we are focusing attention on this typically overlooked administrative duty.

University Medical Center

In 1984, negotiations were under way with the University of Southern California to develop a major medical complex to serve as the medical school's primary teaching facility. This venture—to include an acute-care hospital, an ambulatory care center, a research building, and a hotel for visitors—would require an investment of about $100 million for which NME would be responsible.

NME would operate the facility and would bear the full financial risk of the venture. Dallas Riddle, a principal negotiator for NME, noted, "The venture, if concluded, will add significantly to NME's prestige in the medical community. It also could serve as a prototype for similar future undertakings with other universities. What's more, we expect it to make a profit."

Marketing

Increasing hospital utilization (census) was the primary task for the newly created marketing function. Nathan Kaufman explained how he viewed his new job, "As you might expect, we are developing TV and print ad campaigns to promote our facilities with the public. Our principal focus, however, is directed at the physicians. They are really our primary customers because they are the ones who refer most patients to the hospital. So an important part of my job is to make NME increasingly attractive to the physician."

Pressures to cut health care costs both aided and complicated Kaufman's job. He saw opportunities for NME to enter into new arrangements with physicians that could strengthen the bonds between these two parties. The joint ventures being developed by Mordoh were cited as a case in point. On the negative side, NME's entry into HMO and PPO arrangements were viewed with disfavor by many physicians who saw them as potential threats to their practices. Since the Hospital Group operations were affected in one way or another by activities in other NME units, Kaufman, and Scott Gross on a broader scale, had to work across divisional lines to deal with these developments.

Relations with Other NME Units

In early years, acute-care hospital operations not only dominated NME's activities, they were also largely independent of the company's other ventures. The increase in the size and diversity of NME's other health care operations, the general emergence of new approaches to health care, and the recent declines in acute-care census all served to increase the Hospital Group's dependency on other NME units. The need for interaction occurred in two principal ways.

The more straightforward form of collaboration had to do with the use of related health care services to support and enhance the hospitals' operations. For example, an empty hospital wing might be devoted to substance-abuse treatment for people suffering from alcohol and drug dependencies. This health care activity would be handled by the Psychiatric Group. Convalescent facilities represented another area involving divisional interaction. As cost-cutting pressures required early discharge from hospitals, the need for available convalescent facilities increased. Since there was a general shortage of such facilities, especially in California, the Hospital Group sought to have the Long Term Care Group locate convalescent facilities near NME hospitals.

More complex was the problem of coordinating the Hospital Group's needs with the new developments taking place in the Health Care Systems and Services Group. The HMO, PPO, and free-standing clinic programs all held great potential for affecting Hospital Group results. Kaufman gave one indication of the impending impact, "Traditionally, patient flow in hospitals has been physician directed. Third party payors, industry HMOs and PPOs, will increasingly control this vital element." Since these health care arrangements were all still relatively new developments for NME, the Hospital Group management had little experience to fall back on as it tried to influence the evolution of these new activities.

Reflecting on the diverse activities of his group, and its relationship to other groups, Scott Gross saw all efforts as directed toward one shared goal: "Anything that we do is ultimately designed to get more utilization of our facilities." Though acute-care hospitals were critical to NME's continued success, Gross realized that from 1979 to 1984 they had contributed a decreasing share to overall earnings. Vital new businesses were growing rapidly within NME, and the need for intragroup cooperation and coordination became imperative. Gross was particularly attuned to those currents of change within the company.

Health Care Systems and Services Group

As the new general manager of a newly created division, Bill Piche soon found himself confronting a variety of knotty issues. The more salient of these included decisions on how to develop the new health care activities he had inherited, managing the independent-minded physicians who headed several of the ventures, working out a proper relationship with the Hospital Group, and defining the role HCSSG was to play within NME. While Piche had already been involved with the group's ventures before his move from the Hospital Group, his expanded duties as group president left him with little time to reflect with leisure on these matters.

The HCSS Group was responsible for four principal business operations. The largest and most complex of these was the insurance-related subgroup of activities, including both PPO and HMO ventures. Piche explained how NME had first entered this field, "In 1983, as cost-cutting pressures mounted in California, it soon became obvious to us that negotiations between hospitals and

private insurance companies would become a one-way street. The insurance companies were playing off the hospitals one against the other to push down rates. The providing organizations also had to be organized."

In March 1984, NME introduced Health Pace, a fully underwritten "preferred provider organization" health care plan (PPO), in Southern California, with intentions to move subsequently to selected markets throughout the United States. NME was responsible for establishing and administering the preferred-provider network. A national insurance brokerage firm, Corroon & Black, had been engaged to market and service Health Pace through independent brokers and agents, and New York Life Insurance Company was the underwriter for the plan.

While moving ahead in the development of the PPO program, NME management was also interested in gaining experience with health maintenance organizations (HMOs). In June 1984, the company acquired Av-Med, Inc., a Florida-based corporation operating federally qualified prepaid health plans with 75,000 subscribers and a provider network of more than 1,100 physicians and thirty-five hospitals in the Miami and Tampa regions. NME took over 80 percent of the ownership; the founding physician retained a 20 percent ownership share.

Three independent clinic groups constituted HCSSG's other businesses. In October 1983, NME acquired an 80 percent share of Instant Care Centers of America, an owner and operator of fourteen free-standing urgent-care centers in Louisiana, California, Texas, and Florida. The purpose of the acquisition, as reported in the annual report, was to facilitate establishing a national network of such ambulatory-care centers. The founding physician retained 20 percent ownership.

In March 1984, NME acquired the Stein Women's Center, a small clinic in St. Petersburg, Florida. The unit was viewed as a possible base for creating a chain of gynecological clinics throughout the U.S. The remaining HCSSG business operation was to manage six occupational health care clinics in California. This activity had been organized in 1980.

In describing the Health Care Systems and Services Group's operations, the 1984 annual report concluded, "These highly competitive health care distribution alternatives, consolidated into a national program under a new operating group, will reinforce utilization of NME hospitals while creating a new product to market to employers and health care insurers." A careful reading of this statement revealed some of the ambiguities Piche faced in defining the role his unit was to play. The group had been formed with several goals in mind: to conduct experimentation and program development for NME; to feed patients to existing hospital units; and to create profitable new growth businesses. Deciding on the right balance among these somewhat conflicting aims was viewed by Piche as one of the most pressing strategic issues he faced. Several operational problems were certain to influence the outcome of his consideration.

One problem concerned the mixed feelings of hospital administrators and physicians about the impact such programs would have on the hospitals' financial performance. While these parties welcomed the additional patients HMOs

and PPOs might provide, they were less favorably disposed to the reduced-fee features of these programs. The resulting trade-off between additional patients versus any loss of revenue associated with full-paying patients transferring to the contract service was difficult to predict.

The net effect of the free-standing clinics on hospital patient loading was also difficult to predict. These clinics potentially could enlarge the patient base available to feed the acute-care hospitals, but they also promised to compete with these hospitals for outpatient and emergency care. One executive noted wryly, "The introduction of PPOs, HMOs, and alternative health care facilities is like a bad-tasting medicine for the physicians. They know that they need to take it, but they want to put it off as long as possible."

For Piche, physician resistance to the introduction of alternative health care arrangements touched on a broader strategic issue. He remarked:

> Why should I have to force a PPO on to an NME hospital that doesn't want it when there are plenty of other hospitals eager for it? Beyond ease of entry, there is also a question of profitability. Should the group establish an HMO or PPO in support of NME hospitals in an area with profit potential limited by demographics versus moving into more attractive locales? And even in areas where NME hospitals are located, an HMO or PPO will probably have to include competing hospitals in the plan in order to create a sufficiently large provider network to secure a viable membership base. For example, were we to set up an HMO in the Boston area, it would be necessary to include hospitals in the city and the suburbs to provide an effective health care network. Selecting our initial PPO and HMO targets is going to require some careful thinking and probably some hard negotiating with the Hospital Group and top management.

Such negotiations were complicated by the ownership structures for the new health-care ventures. Av-Med (HMO), Instant Care Centers of America (urgent care centers), and Stein Women's Center (gynecological clinics) were each owned 20 percent by the founding physician. Each of these entrepreneurs had joined NME with the expectation of achieving rapid profitable growth, and consequently they held aggressive priorities for their particular units. Piche faced a problem in getting these key people to back a strategy aimed primarily in support of NME hospitals. As one executive pointed out, "We are already encountering internal strife between the venture leaders and the hospital-related advisory board of physicians." According to Piche, a related problem was whether NME would approve the business-development expenditures that each of the entrepreneurial physicians wanted and expected.

Entrepreneurship and Synergy

One outcome of the reorganization was the installation of a new generation of group presidents. These men were young, energetic, and eager to prove themselves. Just as Scott Gross had set out to expand and improve hospital operations, and Bill Piche to introduce and develop new approaches to health care,

the other group executives were actively implementing promising growth opportunities for NME.

As an indication of these opportunities, the 1984 annual report stated in
connection with the Long Term Care Group:

> The accelerating growth of a longer-living elderly population, coupled
> with a new emphasis on cost-effective alternative care settings for all age
> groups, has made long-term care the fastest growing segment of the U.S.
> health care industry. . . .
>
> In addition to expansion of its network of skilled nursing facilities, de-
> velopment of retirement complexes and rehabilitation centers was acceler-
> ated, and special care units for the treatment of Alzheimer's Disease were
> established.
>
> Of particular significance to the emerging market for long-term care ser-
> vices are the economic incentives to reduce lengths of stay at acute-care
> hospitals. . . . Another factor fueling the growth of the long-term care mar-
> ket is the increasing economic independence of the emerging elderly popu-
> lation.

Along with the acquisition in 1984 of forty-nine additional long-term care
facilities with a total of 5,366 beds, the Long Term Care Group had also opened
four special care units for the treatment of Alzheimer's Disease and were developing seven more. In addition, a new subsidiary—Cadem Corporation—
had been formed to develop retirement complexes, rehabilitation centers, long-
term care hospitals, and other health facilities. The group's president, Don
Baty (age forty), had a reputation as a hard-driving and profit-oriented executive.

Psychiatric care also offered NME major growth opportunities. Under the
new leadership of Norman Zober (age forty-one), the Psychiatric Group planned
to accelerate its expansion of diagnostic and treatment facilities. With more
than ten out of every 100 employees and more than 3 million teenagers dependent on alcohol or drugs, a special emphasis was to be placed on chemical-
abuse treatment, with an expansion of both free-standing and in-hospital facilities. And with the statement, "The home health market is at the threshold of
a new era of growth," NME's annual report also recognized the Home Care
Group as another contender for investment funds.

With opportunities beckoning in every direction and with the size of meaningful NME ventures becoming ever larger, the future availability of funds was
of growing concern to a number of group executives. As one observed, "Given
its size and ambitions, the company is beginning to encounter capital constraints. The problem of who gets money is beginning to surface. Since NME
has not had any problem raising funds, we don't really have a system for
allocating capital, nor do we have any experience along these lines. In the old
days, if you wanted something, you got it. Now you have to justify it."

A competition for funds among groups promised to unsettle the traditional
laissez-faire character of divisional relationships. Sidney Tyler, senior vice president for corporate planning, described the company's dilemma, "We expect
the future of health care to involve long-term mental, home, and primary treat-

ments in some integrated fashion. Putting them all together under a health care plan and learning how to get the different lines of business to talk to each other and to feed each other will present a major challenge to our management. This is one of the downsides in having an entrepreneurial setup. You're not rewarded for building bridges to each other."

Other senior officers echoed concern with the organizational dilemma described by Tyler. Peter de Wetter, executive vice president and member of the board, referred to the compensation system to illustrate the problem: "A group CEO can earn up to $250,000 with a 40 percent annual incentive bonus opportunity. This incentive is based on group and personal performance. If we want these executives to increase focus on total corporate performance, we will obviously have to strengthen our long-term incentive program, but this has to be balanced with our corporate culture, which stresses entrepreneurial autonomy."

John Bedrosian, senior executive vice president and member of the board, emphasized the importance of individuals and was inclined to prefer people selection over organizational restructuring as a response. He argued, "People are very important around here. You need structure, but more importantly, you need people who will work well together." Leonard Cohen, NME president, made clear the full force of the dilemma as the need for restructuring argued by some clashed with the entrepreneurial climate prized by others: "In the past we have been able to fit the pieces together on an informal basis. It would be foolish for me to say that this approach will necessarily continue to work in the future."

Management's concerns with synergy were clearly connected to another concern as to just how many ventures NME should pursue. Bedrosian explained the pressure to diversify: "The reason that NME is involved in so many aspects of health care is that there is uncertainty as to where the industry is going. We want to be sure that we are in position when the market changes."

As chief operating officer with responsibility for operational performance, Cohen advanced a note of caution to this strategy: "We are moving into a lot of businesses we know little about. Sometimes I worry that we are trying to juggle too many balls at one time and that bothers me. Obviously, the company needs to keep its options open. Sometimes we're afraid that we might be missing something. But there's an important distinction between doing a million things and doing them well."

Serving as a reference point to management in its analysis of these issues was Richard Eamer's overarching vision of health care:

> There are things we should keep in mind. First, we are in a simple business. Basically, we are in the business of delivering patient care. Acute, long-term psychiatric and home care are all part of this business. People will want an integrated package of total health care from birth to death.
>
> Second, very little really changes in our business. Ninety percent of what you do this year, you will do next year. People focus too much on the 10 percent change. Changing this business is like turning the S.S. *Queen Elizabeth.* . . . . It takes a lot of time.

Glossary

Acute-care facilities. Traditionally referred to as hospitals.

Average Length of Stay. Average period that inpatients spend during a reporting period. Derived by dividing the number of inpatient days by the number of admissions.

Blue Cross/Blue Shield. A not-for-profit third-party insurer.

Capitation. A payment plan based on the number of patients seen over a specified time.

Census. Occupancy rate in an acute-care hospital.

Diagnostic Related Groups (DRGs). Federally defined categories of medical services and procedures that apply to the fixed amount a hospital will receive as reimbursement for services rendered to Medicare patients.

Fee-for-Service. The traditional system of payment in specified amounts for services rendered by physicians.

Health Maintenance Organizations (HMOs). Organized system of health care that assure the delivery of comprehensive, continuous preventative and treatment services to members. Subscribers pay a predetermined flat fee and are entitled to specified health care services as needed.

Medicaid. Federally supported health insurance for the indigent.

Medicare. Federally supported health insurance for the elderly.

Preferred Provider Organization (PPO). A group of health care providers—including hospitals, physicians, dentists, optometrists and so on—who agree to provide medical services to members on a discount fee-for-service schedule.

Third-party insurers. Insurance companies who provide health care insurance. (e.g., Blue Cross/Blue Shield, Traveler's Insurance Company).

Nike in China

In April 1980 Nike, the leading sports-footwear company in the United States, submitted a business proposal to the People's Republic of China. In his letter of transmittal, Nike founder and president Phil Knight laid out the project's objectives and rationale:

> Primary among our objectives is to establish the means by which we would buy a finished shoe product from the People's Republic of China. We presently target a goal of 100,000 pair per month in the first phase, with growth to 1,000,000 pair per month, or US$30 million per year, by the mid-1980s.
>
> We feel that the People's Republic of China, with its long tradition of excellence in this field of manufacture, would be an ideal additional source for our product. We see immediate benefits to be derived by each party in this business relationship with even more important long-term benefits in the future.

Five months later the first production supply contract was signed; by October 1981 shoe production had begun. The rapidity with which Nike had maneuvered through the Chinese bureaucracy was hailed in the business press as "dazzling."

By late 1984, however, production had reached only 150,000 pair per month. Many unforeseen problems had been encountered, leading Knight to comment: "China has got to be about the toughest place in the world to do business." Nike was also facing a significant slowdown in the rapid growth of the sports-shoe market and a concomitant increase in competition. The market decline had caused a drop in volume and major cutbacks in Nike's orders from its suppliers in Korea and Taiwan (which provided 86 percent of its shoes).

David Chang, a Nike vice president and a key player in the China project from its beginning, reflected on the experience and future options. "Unfortunately, China has not come on-stream as we expected. Although there have recently been encouraging changes in the government's policies, with our earnings going down there is pressure to get out of China." Given the importance of Nike's global sourcing strategy to its past and future success, Chang felt it was time to review the China experience and make recommendations on future actions.

Company Background

From a $1000 investment and a small importing business in 1964, Nike had by 1984 grown into America's leading sports-shoe company with sales approaching $1 billion. Return on equity averaged 46 percent over the 1978–82 period. During these years the business went public, but Knight remained the major stockholder and chief executive officer.[1]

Nike's product line proliferated as the fitness boom created new market opportunities. From high-performance racing shoes, Nike expanded into other sports (soccer, football, basketball, tennis), other user segments (joggers, non-athletes, and children), and other product lines (leisure shoes and apparel). The number of basic footwear models increased from 63 in 1978 to 185 in 1983. Including model variations, the total number of products was 340. Footwear accounted for almost 90 percent of Nike's 1982 revenues, with running shoes 34 percent, court shoes 30 percent, children's shoes 15 percent, cleated shoes 2 percent, and leisure shoes 2 percent. Exports added another 6 percent, and apparel sales were 10 percent of total revenue.

From its inception the company had sourced almost all its shoes from off-shore producers. Eventually, the original Japanese suppliers were replaced by South Korean contract factories that provided 70 percent of Nike's needs. Other important suppliers were Taiwan (16 percent) and Thailand and Hong Kong. The remaining 7 percent were produced in Nike's own U.S. production and research facilities. China was the most recent supplier. The Philippines had been phased out due to its political uncertainties. Brazil was no longer considered cost competitive. Nike owned a factory in Ireland that supplied the European Common Market 15,000 pairs of shoes per month in 1984, half its earlier peak. Nike had also built a rubber factory in Malaysia, which in 1984 had significant excess capacity.

Nike held a commanding lead in the U.S. athletic footwear market, with a 30 percent share. Its strong R&D capacity, high quality, economic offshore sourcing, dependable delivery, and outstanding brand image lay behind its success. Its major competitor, West Germany's Adidas, had a 19 percent share in the U.S. and led in the world with $2 billion in sales, of which 40 percent was in apparel. In contrast to Nike's emphasis on importing and marketing, Adidas developed as a manufacturer. It had its own and contract plants throughout the world, including in the Soviet Union, where it had opened a factory in 1979. Converse held the next largest share with 9 percent; it manufactured 70 percent of its shoes in the U.S. and sourced the rest from the Far East. Puma, a spin-off from Adidas, and Keds, a leader in children's sneakers, accounted for 7 percent each. Several other smaller companies specialized in certain categories. New Balance, for example, had 15 percent of the running-shoe submarket. Exhibit 1 provides a more detailed breakdown of competitor shares and market-segment information.

---

1. This description is based primarily on data from the Nike (A)-(E) case series, Harvard Business School, 1984, prepared by Senior Research Associate David C. Rikert and Professor C. Roland Christensen.

Exhibit 1 Leading competitors' market shares of the branded athletic footwear submarkets (1982).

Racquet 35%		Running 30%		Basketball 15%		Field 15%		Other 5%
Nike	40%	Nike	50%	Converse	35%	Puma	30%	Hiking and walking: Small but growing, as older people discover walking.
Adidas	20%	New Balance	15%	Puma	30%	Adidas	20%	
Tretorn	6%	Adidas	10%	Nike	20%	Hyde	10%	
Common for street use; tennis has not been growing but may in coming years.		Growth of 6% to 8% expected, depending on how long people continue to run and how many are diverted to home exercise.		Beginning to decline; fewer teens; Title IX[a] bulge over.		Team sports, dependent on increase in industrial leagues; soccer will grow but at expense of football.		Leisure: Moderate growth unless a model captures imagination of young people.

a. Title IX, a federal statute, required that educational institutions provide athletic programs and facilities for women similar to those provided for men.

Note: Data based on sales in athletic specialty and sporting goods channels *only*.

Source: NIKE (A), Harvard Business School Case 385–025, 1984.

437

The rapid market growth during the 1970s began to taper off in the 1980s. Some felt that a shift from a seller's to a buyer's market was in process and that pricing would become more aggressive. The proliferation of shoe models accelerated; their life cycle in the marketplace shortened. Nike's basic models were expected to rise from 196 in 1984 to 430 by 1986. Seasonality of sales emerged: about 65 percent of company sales were in the spring and during the August-September back-to-school period. In the past, Nike had maintained level production year-round.

With faltering demand, Nike cut back its orders significantly (from Korean factories by a third) and closed a U.S. factory. It posted a $2.2 million net loss for the second fiscal quarter ending November 30, 1984. Industry observers projected a 6–8 percent growth rate for the rest of the 1980s.

Nike shifted its attention to the apparel line. The Nike name and swoosh logo were believed to be transferable, but apparel, a very different business than footwear, was presenting new problems. Knight commented:

> Adidas sells $700 million in apparel. We should get a portion of this, but with U.S. customs quotas, sourcing is a tough business. The quota on shoes is not so hard on us, because we can get it better than our competitors due to our bargaining power with foreign suppliers. This is not true for clothes. Factories prefer to sell ski apparel rather than running warmups in their quota because of the higher value. In footwear we source 90 percent from abroad, but in apparel only 50 percent. Our apparel sales are growing: in 1984 they grew from $110 million to $180 million, but profit margins are lower this year. We would like to source apparel from China, but their quota is used up through 1987.

China

Before the Chinese government embarked upon its open-door policy in 1978, it had relied on a "lean to one side" (toward the USSR) policy. Then Mao had instituted the Cultural Revolution, which stressed self-sufficiency, isolationism, and anti-intellectualism. After Mao's death in 1976 and the imprisonment of the Gang of Four, the government under Deng Xiaoping concluded that to modernize, China needed to tap Western technology, management, and capital. In 1979 Foreign Trade Minister Li Qiang described the break with old policy:

> We have made great changes in our trade practices and adopted various flexible policies. Not long ago we still had two important "forbidden zones" in our dealings with other countries. One, we would not accept government-to-government loans. We would accept only commercial loans between banks. Two, we would not consider foreign investments. Recently we have decided to break down these "forbidden zones." By and large we now accept all the common practices known to world trade.

In 1981, Premier Zhao Ziyang described the rationale for the new strategy:

> By linking our country with the world market, expanding foreign trade, importing advanced technology, utilizing foreign capital and entering into different forms of international economic and technological cooperation, we can.use our strong points to make up for our weak points through international exchange on the basis of equality and mutual benefit. Far from inspiring our capacity for self-reliant action, this will only serve to enhance it. In economic work, we must abandon once for all the ideal of self-sufficiency, which is a characteristic of the natural economy. All ideas and actions based on keeping our door closed to the outside world and sticking to conventions are wrong. . . . Ours is a sovereign socialist state. In accordance with the principle of equality and mutual benefit foreigners are welcome to invest in China and launch joint ventures in opening up mines and running factories or other undertakings, but they must respect China's sovereignty and abide by her laws, policies, and decrees.[2]

Foreign investment flow into China in 1981 rose to an estimated $1.2 billion.

Also in Nike's favor was China's shift in emphasis from heavy to light industry, by which it hoped to meet consumer demands and raise its standard of living closer to that of its neighbors. By exporting consumer goods, China would also earn foreign currency needed to achieve its goals of modernization before the year 2000.

China's Economic System

As a centrally planned economy, China did not rely on market mechanisms as the major tool for resource allocation. Rather, development priorities were set at the highest levels of party and government decision making, which then instructed the State Planning Commission to implement these policies through a series of economic plans. Plans were first defined as national programs to meet long-range objectives and were later specified in short-run local directives and development targets, based on the various economic units' capacities. The commission allocated resources to ministries and provinces according to these plans. Ministries, organized by economic sector, controlled all important national economic units. Provinces, based on geographic divisions, ran their own economic activities like small nations. The commission had centralized control over the ministries; decentralized power was granted at the provincial level.

The bureaucracy tended to be vertical. Ministries were connected horizontally only by the State Planning Commission. As a result, production sometimes was disconnected, uncoordinated, and difficult to control.

Prices were not based on market needs and demands, but were arbitrarily set by the State Planning Commission to realize national goals. For example, food prices were kept low to meet consumption needs, and luxury items were

---

2. Quoted in David G. Brown, "Sino-Foreign Joint Ventures: Contemporary Developments and Historical Perspective," *Journal of Northeast Asian Studies*, vol. 1, no. 4 (December 1982), p. 27.

priced high. Because output was geared to annual targets regardless of market demand, many goods became scarce and others were in oversupply.

Before the 1978 reforms, the Chinese had an "iron rice bowl" system whereby everyone was guaranteed a job and equal pay regardless of performance. Promotions were mostly based on seniority or politics. With no tools to measure performance, workers had few incentives to produce more. Although the 1978 reforms provided bonuses to workers based on their performance, they were still limited. Factory cadres able to institute rewards for their workers had little motivation to do so, because they had few incentives for their own performance.

The Chinese Footwear Industry

Most shoes produced in China in the past had been manually made. The Chinese had experience in the autoclave production technique for manufacturing canvas and rubber court shoes, but the process for making more expensive jogging shoes was almost unknown to them. The government had neglected the footwear industry.

Workers in Chinese shoe factories generally had had only an elementary school education. Also, Chinese factory managers lacked managerial training. For example, in the Nike factories, most managers had begun as workers about twenty years earlier and advanced to managerial levels only because of seniority or politics.

Infrastructure

The transportation and communication infrastructure was quite outmoded. The government had recently begun to rebuild port facilities to handle larger ships, and many new roads were under construction. Only the Beijing-Tianjin highway was close to U.S. standards. There was no direct-dialing telephone system between major cities; capacity within the cities was severely strained.

Cultural Environment

Trust and reliability were important components of business relationships in China. While trust could be important for any business relationship in the world, it took on special meaning in China, where a formal legal system had yet to be completely institutionalized, and channels for the free flow of information were often obstructed. Because of past experience with untrustworthy foreigners, the Chinese were reluctant to do business with strangers. "Friend of China" had a special meaning implying trust, patience, and understanding. The Chinese insisted that foreigners doing business with them treat them as equals and with respect.

Nike's Entry Strategy and Negotiations

Nike saw sourcing from China as a logical next stage in its global production strategy. It had shifted to Korea and Taiwan from Japan when rising wages and the value of the yen pushed costs up. As costs in Korea and Taiwan rose, Nike signed small production contracts in 1980 and 1981 with suppliers in the Philippines (250,000 pair), Thailand (250,000), Malaysia (75,000), and Hong Kong (50,000). A company study on future sourcing indicated India and China as the long-term, lowest-cost suppliers; the PRC won out. (Appendix A provides a brief chronological summary of Nike's involvement in China during 1980–83.)

The company's director of Far East operations, Neal Laurinson, was the first Nike official to visit China when he went, or tried to go, to the Canton Trade Fair in October, 1979. Knight, deeply interested in Asia and China, waited in Hong Kong two weeks for a visa that never came. Like many other foreign companies, Nike at first found the Chinese bureaucracy impenetrable. To gain access, management hired David Ping-Ching Chang as a consultant.

A Princeton-educated architect, Chang was born in China but had left in 1941 at age ten. He was still a favored guest of the PRC and held a rare, multiple-entry visa. His father had been the Kuomintang government's ambassador to Czechoslovakia, Portugal, and Poland in the 1930s. The Chinese communists held ancestry in high regard and also saw political value in dealing with their former class enemies. Before his work with Nike, Chang had helped arrange a deal between a Chinese factory and a U.S. auto-parts company. His experience, contacts, language ability (he spoke Chinese but did not read or write it), and personality facilitated Nike's entry.

Chang described the entry period:

> One of the keys to Nike's success so far has been determining ongoing economic sources of supply. The president of the company had determined that China was the last major untapped source for a relatively labor-intensive product. We had to go. It was not a market; it was a production source. But we couldn't help but notice the two billion feet.
>
> Success in China depends on common sense. The first thing we did was write a proposal to the Chinese, outlining the long-term nature of our commitment, the scope that would indicate to them that we were not just coming in to buy 100,000 pair of rack shoes and then heading over the hill. And we had the common sense to have the proposal translated into Chinese. This probably got our document to the top of the bureaucrats' stack. We wrote the proposal in April 1980 and got an invitation in July to come and hold a seminar. We were directed to the Ministry of Light Industry, which supervises the footwear industry. Our group of six visited 20–30 factories in Tianjin and Shanghai.

Negotiations continued in September and November 1980. The Nike team (Chang, the corporate counsel, and production and finance people) met daily with their Chinese counterparts, who numbered between twenty and thirty, depending on the issues discussed. Supply contracts were signed between two factories each in Tianjin, Guangzhou (formerly Canton), and Fujian province, and one in Shanghai. Ten trips over twelve months were required to complete negotiations involving the ministries of Light Industries, Chemistry (which controlled the rubber supply), and Foreign Trade and the provincial and municipal officials where the factories were located.

Christopher Walsh, Nike's first resident managing director in China, who had worked for two years in Korea and three in Taiwan, stated:

> The negotiations were some of the most strenuous exercises I have ever participated in. The major issues we faced . . . were issues that we did not expect to arise. The Chinese were not familiar with the standard exclusivity clauses within our contracts. We wanted exclusive rights to these particular factories. We do not have difficulties enforcing these clauses in our other Asian countries, and so we tried to institute them in China.
>
> The second issue was B-grade production. The Chinese will package almost 100 percent of what they make. There are certain standards that had to be adhered to which they were not familiar with, so that was a stumbling block for us.
>
> The third issue was defective returns. A great deal of Nike's success today comes from standing behind its product. The Chinese could not accept that particular concept. . . . They felt that once a shoe had been put in the container and was on its way to the U.S., that was the end of the production agreement. In Taiwan or Korea that particular clause is long-standing and not questioned whatsoever. What we were able to procure from the Chinese was that they will guarantee the shoes for only nine months after they depart China. This virtually eliminates that clause, for nine to twelve months will have passed by the time the shoes reach the consumer.

Pricing was another key issue in the negotiations. Chang described the company's approach: "One of the first things we told the Chinese was that their prices had to be more than competitive with our other Far East sources because the cost of doing business in China was so enormous. We opened our books to them and showed what we were paying our other suppliers." Walsh commented on the results of the price negotiations:

> I think a lot of American corporations are misled in that you go to China expecting to pay much lower prices because people are earning $40 per month. However, the foreign trade corporations are of the opinion that since the standards are the same for them as for Nike in Korea or Taiwan, they deserve equal prices. We gave the Chinese a break on the first pricing round to get started, but we have to be more adamant in the future. The hope is for a 20 percent price advantage over Korea.

All contract agreements were negotiated with the ministries' staffs and the factory managers and were based on specific shoe models' price, volume, delivery, and specifications. Since the factories had no foreign currency to purchase equipment, Nike entered into compensation-trade arrangements whereby equipment was paid for in shoes. Nike would purchase B-grade shoes at a 20 percent discount during the first two years, then at a 40 percent discount. The agreements stipulated that factories could not sign contracts with Nike's competitors; they also granted Nike trademark protection.

Nike agreed to pay for purchases directly to the Ministry of Foreign Trade or its local offices. The factories would then receive Chinese currency at exchange rates higher than the fixed rate, as subsidies from the foreign trade unit (the only organization in China authorized to pay higher exchange rates). In Guangzhou the contracts were signed through the municipal government; new contracts were to be negotiated directly with the factory managers.

Operating Experiences

Walsh recounted the original production plans:

> In July 1981 we established forecasts for 10,000 pair per month in the initial twelve-month period, with the gradual increase over fifteen months to 100,000 pair. In retrospect those expectations were far too high. In the first nine months we were able to export a total of only 35,000 pair. Not until 1984 did we reach 100,000 pair per month. We originally thought we would be producing a million pair a month by now.

The annual production figures were 140,000 pair in 1982, 263,000 in 1983 (nine models), and about 700,000 in 1984 (twelve models).

Nike had to deal with a multitude of problems in technology transfer, materials, quality control, inventory control, production flexibility, worker and manager motivation, transportation, pricing, plant location, expatriate staffing, and government relations.

Technology transfer. Walsh described the transfer process:

> During the start-up period we had to arrange for technology transfer. The Chinese are looking for something in return. In the footwear industry the machinery was very antiquated; they expected us not only to import machines, but to provide them with technical designs to help them get away from the cottage industry that had existed in China. Normally they would sit in small rooms and do most of the work by hand. A South Korean factory that makes 100,000 pair a day has good systems, so we brought those to China.
>
> We ran into difficulties, however. We did not really recognize what lay ahead for us. There's a lot of things that will evolve in these relationships with the Chinese that simply cannot be foreseen from overseas. It takes an on-site presence to get a feeling for the situation. As a result, six individuals and I located in Shanghai. We visited the factories daily. We attempted to institute inventory and transportation strategies. We assessed what these people could actually accomplish relative to our expectations.
>
> Communication is one of the chief liabilities in entering the Chinese market, and we went to great lengths to develop a communications system enabling us to identify on-site problems and provide solutions to problems that arose in those factories. Only two Nike residents spoke Chinese, and no one at the factory spoke English, so we had to use interpreters.

Managers from the Fuzhou factory visited Nike headquarters in Beaverton, Oregon, in May 1981 and the Hong Kong factory in July 1983; managers from the Tianjin No. 2 factory visited Nike's Thailand producer in December 1982; and those from the Guangzhou and Quanzhou (Fujian) factories traveled to the facilities in the Philippines and Thailand in November 1983.

Nike considered bringing native managers from South Korea and Taiwan to teach the Chinese advanced technology. However, the Taiwan factories were much smaller than those in China, and the managers were unwilling or unable for diplomatic and political reasons to go to China. South Korean factories were similar in size to those in China, and the Korean managers were willing to cooperate.

Chang approached the Chinese about the possibility of bringing Korean managers to China to help in training. The Chinese leaders agreed, but only if the Koreans obtained U.S. passports. The Chinese remained obstinate on this issue because of its political sensitivity. Unable to arrange entry for the Koreans, Nike finally resorted to using videotapes of how the Koreans operated different equipment. Walsh concluded:

> The biggest problem is that we are buyers and they have to do it our way. It is difficult to convince them to use our processes and not theirs. For example, the factories need conveyor systems which are not now there. Our shoes, although simple, require a lot of preplanning and coordination on procurement. But their systems can't be changed overnight. There was give and take on processing methods. You have to be flexible.

Materials. The factories continually lacked local materials. Nylon, canvas, rubber, and chemical compounds were essential components in shoe production. Only about a third of Nike's needs were available locally, and even these were sometimes difficult to obtain. Even when Nike offered the Chinese foreign currency for domestically produced supplies, they were still not forthcoming due to bureaucratic obstacles. For example, there was sufficient canvas in Shanghai for all Nike factories, but to ship it to Tianjin required prior approval of at least six ministries. Nike thus found it easier to import canvas from Taiwan and Korea; they also had to import nylon. However, the suppliers were ambivalent about providing their competitor with materials: Shipments often arrived deliberately damaged. This created strain between Nike and its Korean and Taiwanese suppliers.

Walsh reflected on this aspect of the materials-sourcing problem:

> The Taiwan issue went back and forth. Some months Beijing would turn its back on the issue, and some months they would lobby heavily to increase the trade via indirect avenues such as Hong Kong, Tokyo, or wherever, which increased our transport costs. South Korea was another issue. We did not really recognize the posture that the Chinese had on South Korea. The Chinese knew very clearly that South Korea was our base for expansion and R&D in the Far East, and that we had to utilize these sources. However, when we brought in material and machinery that was marked properly and said "Republic of South Korea" on the outside, it just incurred a lot of wrath from the customs officials, and fines were assessed. But the major difficulties were the resultant delays. These were sixty to ninety days, depending on the moods of customs people.

Quality Control. Nike had established a worldwide policy for B-grade shoes: they could not constitute more than 5 percent of a supplier's total production during the first year or 3 percent thereafter. B-grade shoes had cosmetic defects but were structurally sound. Nike sold them as promotional items or in discount stores; their price was at a 40 percent discount. However, because of quality-control difficulties in China, Nike offered a 20 percent discount for the first two years and initially lowered its quality specs. After four years, still only 80 percent of the Chinese shoes were A-grade. Nike and the Chinese argued constantly about the proper discount for B-grade shoes and the standard measurements for A-grade. Nike felt that Chinese managers used more energy arguing than improving production quality.

Walsh commented on the quality problem:

> The Chinese don't understand the brand concept. They couldn't grasp why C-grade shoes had to be destroyed and not sold locally or in another country. In fact, one batch of these was shipped to Australia without our knowledge.
>
> We are educating factory managers that Korean, Taiwanese, and Chinese shoes are sold as equals and must, therefore, meet international standards. We are also getting the China Trading Company to understand the Nike production and marketing concept. The trading company staff and factory managers don't communicate enough with each other. Nike's people are physically in each of the factories almost daily. Our role is quality control, but we're looked on as educators. We prepared lots of manuals to define our methods.

Nike hired one Chinese inspector for each factory through the Foreign Services Company, which it paid $300 a month per inspector. The inspectors were paid $60 monthly by the services company. They monitored quality, production volume, new model development, and shipping documentation.

One cause of the quality problem was the high level of dust in the cities and factories, which impeded the glueing of insoles to soles. All the Tianjin factory windows had to be shut to keep dust out. However, this made the work area too hot; since air conditioning was too expensive, the factory had to stop production during the summer. The cleaning procedure was to blow dust off the soles with a squeeze bulb, but workers tended not to do this. Nike took factory managers to the Thailand plants, where they saw the conditions and results of a less dusty environment and process. Dust-control procedures improved significantly after the visit.

Nike's national accounts, such as J. C. Penney, had been reluctant to take PRC shoes because of their presumed inferior quality. These buyers had at first been similarly reluctant when Taiwan began producing for Nike.

Inventory Control. Since some shoe materials could not be bought locally, Nike was responsible for imports of unavailable materials. Ordering took six weeks. To guarantee normal production schedules, Nike had to know in advance what needed to be imported and when. Chinese managers, however, were unable to relay this information, because they did not keep adequate inventory records. Planners did not recognize the importance of the time factor. In the Long March Factory in Guangzhou, the large storage room was on the top floor of the production building. A woman at the door checking materials in and out functioned more as a doorkeeper than as a recordkeeper: She did not know what materials were needed for next month's production schedule and did not regularly coordinate her records with the planners. The planning staff responsible for ordering materials from Nike kept their own records based on a guess method of expected usage; very rarely did they check what materials actually remained in storage.

To remedy this, the Nike staff tried to keep track of materials needed for forthcoming contracts and to coordinate these needs with the supply-room records to ensure that supplies were available. They also began teaching Chinese workers how to store the materials correctly to prevent damage.

Production Flexibility. The primary characteristic of South Korea and Taiwan that allowed Nike to expand production quickly was their flexibility. These factories were able to develop shoe models from written specifications. Chang remarked on the contrasting situation in China: "Decisions in China are cast in concrete. You can't tell them, 'Stop making that shoe next month and start making this one.' Forget it! It's another round of meetings."

To increase flexibility, Nike hoped that the Chinese would:

- build sample rooms enabling them to produce new models from patterns and specifications. This would require some new advanced equipment, about nineteen more people, and an investment equal to about 2 percent of sales. The Chinese were unwilling to make such an investment.
- produce, rather than import, lasts, molds, dies, and small tools necessary for the construction of each model. The initial investment could cost over $10 million, but individual factories had the authority to invest only $100,000. The Chinese were thus unwilling to accept small orders for different styles requiring different equipment. It was safer and easier for the Chinese managers to import materials than to try to develop or purchase local materials. Local suppliers tended to charge high prices, because they did not want to incur losses; under the government's new policies, losing factories risked being closed.
- obtain more cooperation from the factory managers. But these managers felt that as yet there was no real commitment from Nike. Furthermore, Nike's efforts to negotiate further price and quantity reductions had antagonized the managers.

Worker and Manager Motivation. Walsh described the basic (and unexpected) motivational problems encountered:

> We set out more or less to emulate the South Korean and Taiwan factories. We wanted to get Chinese factories up to where they could compete from development, pricing, and quality standpoints. We didn't realize the problems we would run into from the system. It's a planned economy: There

are quotas in all sorts of different areas, and pricing stipulations are established in Beijing. But most of all, there's the "iron rice bowl" concept that has long been a thorn in the side of the economy. It is hard to break. The factories are often poorly run, because there is just no background in managing factory facilities.

By dangling big numbers we thought it would entice these people. It did not. We'd approach factories at midday, and our production would be at a total standstill, and they still had quotas to reach for that particular month. There was no motivation or incentive to increase the production.

A big problem is adhering to schedules. We've brought in graphics outlining schedules, and they don't grasp this. Partially the problem is related to the lack of incentives. There is no difference in pay if they produce more shoes sooner. There is also a lack of talent on production scheduling. The talented business people are in the trading companies.

What we did was to institute our own incentive program. We lined up criteria based on productivity, quality, and delivery. We virtually put money on the table. If they could satisfy our demands, we would reward them with cash bonuses given to the factories. This concept was presented to Vice Premier Huan Lee in November 1981, and he was receptive to the idea. We instituted it in our first year there with mixed results. We saw a great leap forward for about sixty days. After that it was back to the same lack of motivation.

Transportation. In Korea, where Nike had dockside factories, the products could be loaded directly into containers and shipped to world markets. In contrast, the PRC shoes had to be trucked to the nearest harbor and shipped to Kobe, Japan, where they were transferred into container vessels. A Japanese trading company, Nissho-Iwai (Nike's primary supplier of working capital), handled all the company's exporting logistics from the Far East.

In Guangzhou, the two factories were close to each other and to the port. They had enough space for containerized trucks to drive in and out. In Fuzhou, however, the factory was on the main street; containerized trucks could not approach the entrance. The factory in Fujian, halfway between Fuzhou and Xiamen on a well-maintained road, also had no access for container vehicles. The dock was outmoded and could not be used on rainy days, causing many loading delays.

Pricing. Tensions in the initial pricing negotiations continued to exist. The Chinese partners were used to the stable prices of a central planning system. Because of unexpectedly high overhead, the initial price had to be reduced by 25 percent after two years. Although Nike had to pay extra dollars due to inefficiencies and scarcities in the Chinese system, the Chinese felt that the costs for foreign firms to do business in China were still lower than in Korea or Taiwan, because of lower food and transportation costs. They also disagreed about which side should benefit from the dollar's relative strength. The Chinese felt Nike should first reduce its own costs before asking them to lower theirs. For example, they felt that Nike could reduce costs if their employees were to live and eat right at the factories. Managers of one factory were dissatisfied because a price agreement reached with Nike's Shanghai representatives was later rescinded by Nike headquarters.

None of the Chinese participants in price negotiations (staff from the foreign trade bureau, factory directors, and local production bureau leaders) had authority to make price decisions. Everything had to be relayed to authorities in Beijing. Thus, compared to Korea or Taiwan, negotiations were slow. The lack of a cost-accounting system and of market prices also made estimating actual costs very difficult. The amount of the government subsidy became a key factor in the costing.

Knight commented on the pricing process: "China has such a cumbersome bureaucracy. In our price negotiations, four ministries were involved. Three said yes, but the fourth wouldn't. Therefore, the agreement was delayed ninety days. In a market that's changing, you can't do this." A further complicating fact in Nike's eyes was that the Chinese did not consider variations in the exchange rate in the price negotiations.

Plant Location. By 1983 Nike concluded that its original plant locations were not optimal. Walsh remarked: "We were more or less forced to go to Tianjin and Shanghai. We were new to China and did not know which areas would give us the best opportunity and the greatest degree of cooperation. We followed the government's recommendations."

In Shanghai and Tianjin, a major problem was the length of negotiation periods. In Shanghai there was little support from the municipal authorities, who were more interested in larger industrial projects. In Tianjin there was support from the mayor, but product quality was low.

Nike terminated its supply arrangement in 1983 with the Shanghai factory and was attempting the same for Tianjin. In Shanghai the company had to make a small compensation payment to close. In Tianjin officials were quite disgruntled about the original five-year agreement's early termination and, in May 1984, sent a strong letter of protest to Nike (see *Appendix B*). Nike risked not being able to recover all its equipment investment.

In the same period, Nike opened two new factories in the south. The Guangzhou and Fujian factories were located in Special Economic Zones, where there was more decentralized authority for decision making and less red tape.

Expatriate Staffing. In September 1981 Nike opened its residential headquarters in Shanghai with a staff of six. In their twenties and thirties, the personnel all had previous experience in Nike's other Asian operations. The Beijing office was closed in December 1983 because it was deemed no longer necessary and because housing was scarce. Walsh commented on the expatriates:

> It's always been Nike's production philosophy to assign expatriates to foreign communities for control purposes. I think that has a great deal to do with our success in the Far East. The expatriate community for Nike in Asia is eighty to ninety people. In Shanghai we represent 20 percent of the American community. Most of the people are from the State Department,

but two other U.S. joint ventures are there. The Americans are a very small, but close-knit community.

Shanghai was considered the best place in China for foreigners to live. It was China's commercial center, and transportation and communications facilities were relatively more advanced than elsewhere in China. But there were few western movies, and TV consisted almost entirely of programs in Chinese and only from 5 to 10 P.M. It was rumored that the Shanghai city government wanted Nike to remove its office from the city because it had closed the factory. Meanwhile, the Guangzhou and Fuzhou city governments were trying to persuade Nike to move their offices south, but Nike employees resisted because of inferior living conditions and weather.

Instead, the Nike staff flew to the factories in the south on Mondays and stayed for three or four days, returning to their families in Shanghai on Thursdays. More than half the staff brought their families to China. They lived in Western-style apartments built in the 1940s. Nike paid their living expenses and a 30 percent salary supplement for working abroad. The staff also received a week's vacation every two months, when they could go anyplace with their families, fully paid by Nike. The staff usually rotated every two years.

Government Relations. From the beginning, Nike tried to establish a positive relationship with the government through contributions to the country's sports activities, e.g., holding sports clinics and equipping the national 1984 Olympic team. Nike also hosted various Chinese officials visiting the United States.

China received Nike with great hospitality. During banquets the staff met many high-level leaders who listened carefully to its problems. However, this interchange did not resolve anything. The Chinese leaders seemed more intent on persuading Nike to sign joint-venture agreements.

Nike often did not know with whom they should talk to solve their problems. The combination of decision makers for different problems was always changing, and it was not always apparent who was in charge of what. Sometimes officials failed to show up for appointments. The local Nike staff often felt it was necessary for high-level managers from headquarters to come to China to get the attention and access of higher-level officials. When the mayor of a city gave a banquet for the Nike staff, one factory manager remarked that he was very happy to see so many leaders for the first time.

The company sent a report to First Vice Premier Wan Li reviewing Nike's progress and problems in the 1980–83 period. An excerpt from Knight's letter of transmittal indicates the company's approach to dealing with the government:

> In my country there is an old belief that in order for any relationship to grow and to develop there must be a mutually candid and beneficial relationship. In our co-equal partnership effort in China, I feel that I should, representing Nike, mention in candor, some of the problems we must face and resolve together if our long-term goals are to be met.[3]

3. See Appendix C for the complete text of the letter.

Many factory managers had negative feelings about the $7 million Nike contributed to support the Chinese national sports teams. They felt that such extravagant PR expenses did nothing to solve Nike's production problems and only increased Nike's overhead. They felt that a Nike joint-venture agreement would be stronger evidence of Nike's commitment to China's modernization program, and at a fraction of the cost. The managers felt the PR program attracted the attention of only the national leaders and that Nike put more effort into fostering good relationships at the top level than at the local level. They also noted that the Chinese Olympic team was criticized in the Hong Kong media for wearing Nike apparel rather than Chinese-made clothing.

Chang reflected on Nike's approach to relations with China:

> China historically has been exploited for so long by the West. I, as a Chinese, am perhaps more aware of the sensitivity of the Chinese to the past exploitation. So I want to do everything that we can to come across, for lack of a better term, as good guys. We don't want to be the rapers and plunderers of colonial days, because the Chinese are very, very sensitive to any possible reemergence of that kind of attitude.[4]
>
> You talk about international diplomacy. We are really doing something with the Chinese, not just talking about it. We're pressing the flesh; we're down in the trenches. We're doing every bit as much as the politicians.[5]

Future Strategic Considerations

As Chang deliberated on possible recommendations for Nike's future course of action regarding China, he focused on six areas: the situations of Nike's other suppliers, recent changes in the business environment in China, joint ventures, new factory locations in China, the domestic China market, and Nike's competitors.

Other Suppliers

Chang compared Chinese factories with Nike's primary suppliers using several criteria:

1. *Development and production start-up time*. The time from when the factory received the shoe model's technical package to the point of shoe production was four months in Korea and eight in China (see Exhibit 2).
2. *Quality*. The A-grade to B-grade ratio was 99:1 in Korea, 98:2 in Taiwan, and 80:20 in China.
3. *Quantity*. Taiwan produced 1 million pair a month, Korea 2.25 million (with installed capacity sufficient to double output), and China 100,000 (with current capacity for 180,000).

4. "Nike Builds Firm Foothold in China," *Los Angeles Times*, February 16, 1982.
5. Charles Humble, "China Connection," *Oregon Journal*, December 23, 1981.

Exhibit 2 Current models' development timelines.

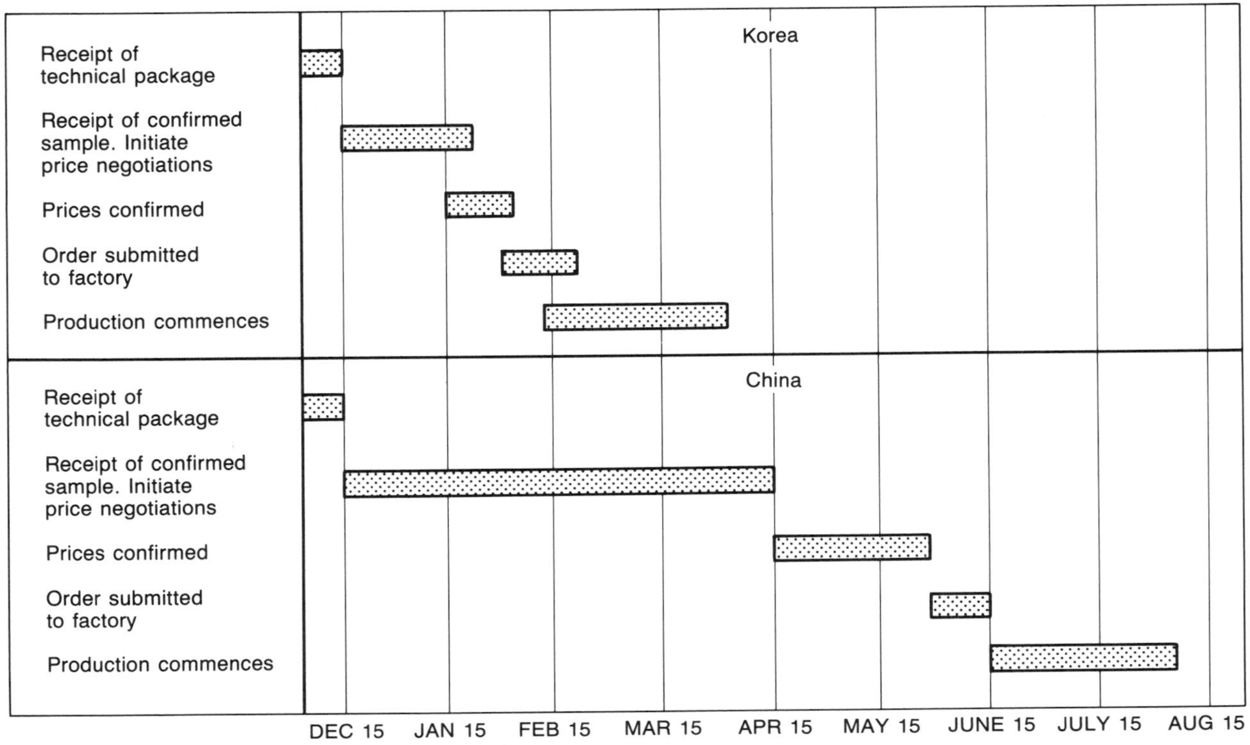

| | DEC 15 | JAN 15 | FEB 15 | MAR 15 | APR 15 | MAY 15 | JUNE 15 | JULY 15 | AUG 15 |

Korea

- Receipt of technical package
- Receipt of confirmed sample. Initiate price negotiations
- Prices confirmed
- Order submitted to factory
- Production commences

China

- Receipt of technical package
- Receipt of confirmed sample. Initiate price negotiations
- Prices confirmed
- Order submitted to factory
- Production commences

451

Table A   Landed cost comparison.

	Korea	PRC
Price paid at factory	$6.36	$6.36
Interest	.37	.47
Freight	.23	.45
Duty	.54	.79[a]
Commission	.25	.25
Nike local office overhead	.11	1.55
Total	$7.86	$9.87
Retail price needed to maintain equal margins	$18.75	$23.50

a. Higher duty due to importation of rubber products.

4. *Raw-material sourcing.* The Taiwanese and South Koreans sourced 100 percent of their raw materials domestically; the Chinese imported 70 percent.
5. *Financing.* South Korea and Taiwan provided their own financing and had a straight trading arrangement with Nike; China required compensation trade.
6. *Transportation.* Shipping time from Taiwan and Korea was 20–25 days and 35–40 days from Shanghai.
7. *Labor costs.* For the factories, labor costs as a percentage of total costs were about 30 percent in Korea, 20 percent in Taiwan, and 10 percent in China.
8. *Landed costs.* Table A shows that the landed costs for a pair of shoes from Korea were $7.86; from the PRC they were $9.87. Nike estimated it was losing $1.00 on each pair of Chinese-made shoes.

The Korean shoe manufacturers had been encountering rising labor cost. As shown in Exhibit 3, the unit labor cost rose by more than 300 percent between 1972 and 1979 and was still rising in late 1984. In addition, the Korean

Exhibit 3   Comparative changes in unit labor cost.

	1972	1973	1974	1975[a]	1976	1977	1978	1979
Korea	65.4	71.1	85.5	100.0	126.7	149.0	173.2	196.9
Taiwan	65.2	70.5	100.9	100.0	95.3	94.8	90.1	94.3
Singapore	—	71.4	90.7	100.0	99.7	120.4	—	—
USA	74.6	76.7	84.9	100.0	100.7	107.3	115.7	123.2
Japan	59.8	62.0	80.4	100.0	99.4	104.0	102.0	99.1

a. 1975 = 100 in national currency.

Source: *Financial Times.*

government discontinued in 1981 all its support, mostly financial, for the shoe industry. One Korean government official said: "We believe that our shoe industry is now fully developed to compete internationally. Our limited resources for support should be directed to higher-growth-potential industries such as heavy, chemical, and high-tech industries."[6]

About rising labor costs, an executive of one of the largest Korean shoe exporting firms (and a Nike supplier) said:

> In the athletic shoe industry, labor cost must not exceed 24 percent of total cost to maintain international competitiveness. As of 1984, our proportion of labor costs is between 22 percent and 24 percent. This is about 30 percent higher than in Taiwan. To cope with this problem, we recently modified our production facilities; we reduced the capacity for cheap products (canvas/vinyl shoes) by 25 percent and increased capacity for more expensive products (nylon/leather shoes). In simple and cheap products, we cannot compete with Taiwan and other countries with cheaper labor such as China, Sri Lanka, Thailand, and the Philippines. Moreover, in response to recent decreases in orders for canvas shoes, we are concentrating in the high-end products such as aerobic shoes. Whatever market segments we may concentrate on, however, I do not think that our international competitiveness with large-scale production can last more than five to ten years from now. We have to get out of this sunset industry successfully and as soon as possible.[7]

In 1983 and 1984 Korea exported $928 million and $1 billion worth of footwear; Taiwan exported about 50 percent more than Korea. About 70 percent of both countries' footwear exports went to the United States. As of late 1984, most Taiwanese footwear products cost in the $3 to $4 range; the Korean products were about a dollar higher.

Most Korean footwear firms were large, employing up to 17,000 people. This size gave advantages in dealing with large foreign buyers, rather than technical economies of scale. Almost all companies exported their footwear under foreign brand names.[8]

Chang remembered, "when we first went to China, Korea and Taiwan saw their meal leaving the table." He wondered now if it should be brought back, and if other newer suppliers should be expanded. The two Thai factories' output was up to 260,000 pair a month with a capacity for 400,000. The A:B-grade ratio was 97:3. Delivery time from Bangkok was 30 days. Price negotiations took two weeks. Thailand had been able to reduce its raw material imports to 40 percent for canvas and nylon shoes; however, it would not be able to supply locally significant quantities of leather if these shoe types were to be manufactured there. Knight looked at Thailand positively but wondered if "it might turn into West Vietnam," given the political dynamics in Southeast Asia. India and Sri Lanka could also be reconsidered for future sourcing.

6. Direct interview by Research Assistant Seok Ki Kim in 1984.
7. *Ibid.*
8. Yung Whee Rhee, Bruce Ross-Larson, Garry Pursell, *Korea's Competitive Edge: Managing the Entry into World Markets* (Baltimore: Johns Hopkins University Press, 1984).

China's Changing Business Environment

Deng Xiaoping, the eighty-year-old leader, continued to accelerate the country's opening to the West. In December 1984 he proclaimed, "China is a good place to invest. China keeps its commitments." He asserted that the PRC would remain open to foreign investors for at least the next seventy years. A proclamation in October 20, 1984, stated that "factory workers will enjoy free enterprise incentives, including the freedom to change jobs, and a wage scale keyed to the real difficulties of their jobs."[9] *The People's Daily* in Beijing also published an editorial stating that the country could not rely on Marx and Lenin's doctrines to solve all present problems. This ideological shift was favorable to private and foreign investors, but many traditionalists within the Communist Party were reportedly disturbed by it. In late 1983 they had mobilized a campaign against "spiritual pollution" caused by the mounting Western presence.

Joint Ventures. The joint-venture form of foreign investment was increasingly favored by PRC authorities: About twenty involving $20 million had been mounted by 1981, and the number increased significantly by 1984. Under the 1979 law, the foreign investor's participation could not be less than 25 percent, technology contributed was to be "truly advanced and appropriate to China's needs," and exports were encouraged. However, joint-venture companies were allowed to sell their products in China. State subsidies were available to joint ventures, and the foreign partner could screen workers and require new employees to pass skill examinations. Presumably workers could be fired for violating work rules. But some existing joint ventures had met difficulties in exercising these management prerogatives. Salaries were about 20 percent higher than in local factories.

Such joint ventures, if undertaken by Nike, were estimated to require an investment of $500,000 per factory, which could reduce Nike's flexibility in later shifting production sites if necessary.

New Factory Location. Shenzhen was the most advanced of the Special Economic Zones (SEZs). By October 1984 it had signed 3,316 agreements and contracts with overseas firms involving a total investment of 6 billion yuan (US$1 = 2.8 yuan). These SEZs were intended to attract foreign investment, particularly in light manufacturing industries catering to export markets. The Chinese government provided special facilities (infrastructure and services) and preferential tax treatment. Because Shenzhen was administered directly by the provincial authorities, the bureaucracy was simplified, and foreign trade and investment were granted broad latitude to protect investors' legitimate rights and privileges. Other special privileges included favorable consideration in land rent, choice of land sites, corporate income tax (15 percent—half the normal rate), and import duties (waived on production inputs). There were also favorable personal income tax laws for foreigners working in the SEZs. About 85 of

9. Hobart Rowen, "Deng's Private-Enterprise Initiative," *The Washington Post*, December 16, 1984, p. L1.

the nearly 100 joint ventures in Shenzhen made profits, with an average rate of 15 percent. Considerable construction was under way to remedy Shenzhen's remaining infrastructure inadequacies with telephones, power, water, housing, and hotels.

Domestic Market. Visions of two billion feet still floated in Chang's mind. The numbers held inevitable market magnetism, but he was not optimistic about selling Nike shoes locally. The product was made for an affluent consumer; the Chinese were interested in Nike's exporting rather than selling locally. But still, two billion feet.

Competitors. Finally, Chang wondered about the possible reactions of Nike's competitors:

> Puma, New Balance, Adidas, and Bata have visited China; none are sourcing from there yet. Dunlop has been buying canvas court shoes from the PRC, but we don't consider them to be a significant competitor. We are the point man for the industry. They are observing closely our experience and moves.

The China project had been what brought Chang into Nike. He had made a heavy personal and professional investment in the project. However, he was now well-established in the firm and in charge of the company's apparel division. He believed it was important to analyze the China situation objectively and make recommendations that would best further Nike's success. He remembered Knight's words: "Winning is ultimately defined by the scorecard which is financial results, but in the long run. We've had success but have to keep looking forward."

Appendix A: Chronological Summary of Nike in China, 1980–83

April 1980	Nike submits "A Business Proposal Between BRS, Inc., and the People's Republic of China," which outlines Nike's plans to trade with China.
July 1980	A Nike delegation including President Philip H. Knight visits the PRC for the first time for the purpose of entering into a long-term trade agreement with China.
September 1980	Second Nike delegation, headed by Vice President Robert J. Strasser, negotiates and signs the first supply agreements between Nike and factories in Tianjin, Beijing, and Shanghai.
November 1980	Nike delegations return for further discussions with Sports Shoe Factory No. 2 in Tianjin. Agreements call for a total of about 1.5 million pairs of shoes in the first year of production. Nike also signs an agreement with China Sports Service to equip Chinese national men's and women's basketball teams with shoes and apparel. Plans are begun for registering offices in Beijing, Tianjin, and Shanghai, and for establishing long-term residence for Nike quality-control managers in China.

March 1981	Nike's vice president, David Chang, hosts Luo Xin, first secretary of the Chinese embassy in Washington, D.C., at Nike's research and development facilities in Exeter, New Hampshire, and Saco, Maine. Nike signs basketball contract with China Sports Service at head office of Nike in Beaverton, Oregon.
May 1981	Fuzhou factory delegation visits Nike's operations in Beaverton, Oregon.
July 1981	Nike signs supply agreement with Shanghai #4 factory to begin production.
August 1981	Nike resident teams selected for China under direction of Christopher Walsh, managing director, China operations. Nike sends three U.S. basketball coaches to Shanghai to conduct a clinic and assist in training Chinese athletes. China sends representatives of China National Light Industrial Products Import and Export Corporation to U.S. and to visit Nike.
September 1981	Nike sends three U.S. marathoners to participate in First International Beijing Marathon (placed 7th, 16th, and 25th in a field of 75). Nike China office established at 65 Yanan West Road, Shanghai. Nike signs supply agreement with Shanghai No. 5 Rubber Shoe Factory.
October 1981	Nike's One-Line shoe production begins.
November 1981	Nike president Philip Knight heads delegation including David Chang, vice president, and Richard Holbrooke, former U.S. assistant secretary of state and Nike special counsel, to Beijing and Shanghai to hold high-level discussions concerning Nike's long-term plans for China and to commemorate first "Made in China" shoes. Delegation was received by Vice Premier Wan Li at the Great Hall of the People in Beijing. Nike signs agreement with Quanzhou Rubber Shoe Factory to begin manufacturing canvas court (tennis) shoes for export. Ribbon-cutting ceremony held in Tianjin by Knight for first production of Nike One-Line (nylon running shoes).
January 1982	Production schedules mutually agreed upon calling for over three million pairs of athletic shoes to be produced in China by the end of 1983.
February 1982	First workers' cash-incentive plan begun in Tianjin. Other similar workers programs are planned.
May 1982	Nike signs supply agreement with Long March Rubber Shoe Factory in Guangzhou and Fuzhou No. 1 Shoe Factory.
June 1982	Nike signs track and field agreement with China Sports Service, wherein Nike agrees to endorse, equip, and help in training Chinese national men's and women's track and field teams.
July 1982	Nike hosts delegation of ten Chinese coaches to attend clinics held at Washington State University.
August 1982	Nike coaches conduct a ten-day clinic in Qunming.
September 1982	Nike sends three U.S. marathoners to participate in the second International Beijing Marathon (placed 6th, 10th, and 15th). Three U.S. coaches sponsored by Nike conduct track and field clinics in Nanjing, Shanghai, and Beijing.
November 1982	China's national track and field and basketball teams participate in the Asian Games in New Delhi and capture overall title in Nike apparal and shoes. Nike hosts special trip for Shanghai No. 4 factory personnel to inspect Nike's production facilities in the Philippines.

December 1982	Nike hosts special trip for Tianjin No. 2 factory personnel to inspect Nike sources in Thailand.
January 1983	First shoes manufactured in PRC arrive in U.S. from Quanzhou factory. Second shipment of shoes made in China also arrives in U.S. from Tianjin factory.
March 1983	Nike signs supply agreement with Nan Fang factory in Guangzhou.
June 1983	Vice president David Chang meets Zhang Wen Jin, Chinese ambassador to the U.S., at the Tenth Anniversary Banquet of the National Council for U.S./China Trade. Former President Richard Nixon is keynote speaker. Zhu Jian Hua, in Nike shoes, breaks the world high-jump record of 2.37 meters at China's Fifth National Games at the Beijing Worker's Stadium.
July 1983	Delegation from Fuzhou factory inspects Nike operations in Hong Kong. Ron Nelson, vice president for production for Nike, visits factory sources in China with senior executives in charge of all shoe production scheduling and sales forecasting.
August 1983	Nike sponsors Nike China Summit for Foreign Trade Corporation meeting in Shanghai to discuss common problems and seek solutions. At meeting are twenty-four individuals selected from Nike's source cities of Beijing, Tianjin, Fuzhou, Quanzhou, and Shanghai. High-jumper Zhu Jian Hua captures bronze medal in the World Track & Field Championship Games in Helsinki.
September 1983	Nike chairman Knight visits new factory sources in Guangdong and Fujian provinces and attends 3rd Annual International Beijing Marathon and a meeting of board of directors of National Council for U.S./China Trade in Beijing.
November 1983	Guangzhou and Quanzhou factory personnel visit Nike's operations in Thailand and the Philippines.

Appendix B: Letter from a Tianjin Official to Scott Thomas

May 10, 1984

Scott Thomas
Managing Director,
NIKE, INC.
Shanghai International Club,
65 Yanan West Road, RM. 304 SHANGHAI,
PEOPLE'S REPUBLIC OF CHINA

Dear Mr. Scott Thomas,

We have read your letter of May 2, 1984 and wish to reply as below: Tianjin and Nike have been cooperating for shoe production for three years. Although we are still behind our designated goal, we have been making progress all the time both in quality and quantity of the products. Now, let us take the last 90 days evaluation period—Jan. 1 to March 31, 1984 as a case in point. The goal was 1,200 pairs of shoes per day for quantity and over 90 percent of A Grade shoes for quality while the daily output of TJ2 was over 1,000 pairs and A grade shoes was around 90 percent by the end of March 1984. This means we have created the conditions for further cooperation.

On April 11, 1984 in Tianjin, you talked about the market changes and raised the subjects of price, new models, etc. We clearly expressed our willingness to consider your requests, meaning the prices would be lower and adoption faster for future new models. Our relative department already said we would set up specialized factories to make moulds and materials for large-scale production and quick adoption of new and varied models of NIKE shoes.

However, we must not be divorced from the present reality while considering things in future. In your letter, you definitely asked us to reduce the prices of the present models by 26 percent and specified the prices of different sizes of all the three models. You asked TJ2 to develop eight new models in September 1984, one new model per month from September to February and two per month after February 1985. Finally, you said that price and adoption of new models were the two prerequisites of our cooperation. If we accept them, our cooperation will continue. Otherwise, you will come to talk with us to cancel the supply agreement. May we ask, even if we accept your requirements on these two points, would you raise further points or put forward higher criteria two months later? We therefore cannot but feel doubtful about your sincerity in the cooperation.

We signed the five-year supply agreement in September 1980. In the spirit of that agreement, we signed the first sales contract for about 80,000 pairs of ONE LINE shoes for which you supplied some of the necessary materials unavailable locally in China. Later on, you said you would not supply the materials and asked us to do the import. That was a great change. But in consideration of our long-term business, we agreed to do so and imported part of the materials enough for the production of 300,000 pairs of shoes. After two years of cooperation, the factory is actually producing only two models— OCEANIA and OLLIE OCEANIA. Production for the third model—DYNO is not started yet. Now you ask the factory to develop eight new models in about four or five months (from May to September). Is this a realistic attitude towards continued cooperation with Tianjin? On more than one occasion, your people said: NIKE is recession proof (not affected by recession) and that your business is expanding very fast while many others in this line collapse because of market changes. With this in mind, we were all very surprised when you said that your inventory of shoes was very high and that you had more shoes than you could sell at the recent FUZHOU Conference held in March this year. During our talk in Tianjin on April 11, you again said the prices must be reduced since the market was not good. We said we were ready to cooperate relating to the prices of future new models and even to a certain extent for those of the present three models for which prices have been fixed. You should not refuse to let us have orders for the models already in production such as OCEANIA and OLLIE OCEANIA and DYNO of which prices were just confirmed in February. You must be responsible for the losses arising from the suspension of production. So far we have not received any fresh orders from you after P.O.#84-3-5-TJ while in your letter you asked to reduce all the prices for OCEANIA, OLLIE OCEANIA, and even DYNO. For more than one reason, TJ2 has suffered heavy losses owing to the long suspension and abnormal situation of production. For Nike production, TJ2 has set up new buildings and purchased special equipments and are heavily in debts now. How can a sudden reduction of prices by 26% be possible? Do you really think this is a responsible request? The prices of DYNO were just confirmed in Feb. 1984 by your Shanghai Liaison Office, but you also asked to reduce them two months later on April 11. We expressed on the spot it was not a right way of business while you said it was the decision or instruction of your American Head Office. If your Shanghai Office did not represent your head office and prices confirmed or decision made by your Shanghai Office could be negated by your American Head Office, it would be very difficult for us to accomplish things.

In your letter of May 2, 1984, you put forward two prerequisites for continued cooperation with Tianjin, i.e., reduce FOB prices by 26% and develop eight new models in September 1984. If we are not able to accept them, you will come to talk with us to cancel the supply agreement. Does it mean that you are ready to stop NIKE-TIANJIN cooperation? Finally, we wish to advise that we should cherish our mutual relations already established and abide by the signed agreement. We should have further negotiations on prices, new models, etc. on the principles of mutual understanding and accommodations and in consideration of the market changes and actual situation of the factory so as to reach an agreement on main issues to let our cooperation continue. Cancellation of the supply agreement will be good to neither party, especially to NIKE's reputation. If you intend to terminate the agreement unilaterally by not giving fresh order to the factory while TJ2 has made preparations for the production, you will be held responsible for any loss of the factory arising from the suspension of production, etc.

It is hoped that you will carefully consider the above frank opinions and the five points mentioned by Mr. Li Guang Zeng of Tianjin Second Light Industry Bureau at our last meeting. Please come to Tianjin soon so that we may talk further in detail.

cc: Philip H. Knight of NIKE Beaverton head office, U.S.A.
      David Ping-Ching Chang of NIKE Beaverton head office, U.S.A.

China National Light Industrial Products
Import and Export Corporation
Tianjin Stationery and Sporting Goods Branch
General Manager, LI YANJI

Appendix C: Transmittal Letter from Philip Knight to First Vice Premier Wan Li

September 2, 1983

First Vice Premier Wan Li
Beijing
People's Republic of China

Dear Mr. Vice Premier:
Three years ago, I came to China with some of my senior officers on what was for us a first trip to your country. For all of us, myself in particular, this trip represented the culmination of a long-term desire to include China in the "NIKE family" of countries around the world with whom we engage in mutually beneficial and cooperative trade.

NIKE has been fortunate in its growth, and in this last fiscal year we have become a nearly billion-dollar (U.S.) company, engaged in the manufacture and sale of both athletic footwear and apparel. We have production sources in 20 countries and market in over 60. Our nearly 100 expatriates living around the globe include six who reside in China. Our original enthusiasm and commitment toward making China an important member of the "NIKE family" of nations continues undiminished.

As you are aware, today, after 3 years in China, we have agreements with seven factories, ranging from Tianjin to Guangzhou, and are receiving regular shipments of athletic shoes from factories in Quanzhou and Tianjin. Our present plans are to export over a million pairs of these shoes to the U.S. in 1984. Our long-term plans are more ambitious still and we expect China to represent a significant portion of the over 50 million pairs of shoes we make annually worldwide in the near future.

In my country there is an old belief that, in order for any relationship to grow and to develop, there must be a mutually candid and beneficial relationship. In our co-equal partnership effort in China I feel that I should, representing NIKE, mention in candor some of the problems we must face and resolve together if our long-term goals are to be met.

First, we continue to face problems with availability of local materials for manufacturing our athletic footwear. Nylon, canvas, rubber, and chemical compounds are the essential components of our product. After 3 years, we continue to need to import a majority of our materials, to the detriment of your economic goals and to ours.

Second, it is essential that we see improvement in terms of the shipping and transportation of our finished product from factory to dockside. A major portion of our sales is booked six months in advance, and these sales include guaranteed delivery dates to our customers. We know of your efforts to develop more dock facilities in cities such as Xiamen and Fuzhou in addition to your presently overburdened terminals in Shanghai and Tianjin, and urge you to press on with these plans.

Third, we must work together even harder to ensure that China produces quality products. For a nation historically associated with fine silks, art treasures, and craftsmanship, to be less than best would be unthinkable. And yet, in candor, I believe I speak for other American manufacturers as well when I say there is a growing perception in my country that manufactured goods from China are not consistently of high quality. It would be tragic to demean your proud tradition.

Fourth, and perhaps most important, is the need to develop even further a sense of motivation and commitment on the part of your workers. I remember well when we first met two years ago in the Great Hall of the People and, at that time, discussed the subject of incentives among workers. The group representing NIKE, including myself, was delighted to hear you say that we should try an incentive-reward system in our factories. We have done this with mixed results. We shall continue in our efforts to instill a sense of motivation among the workers in our factories, but we feel that the major portion of creating any attitudinal change must come from you, our host and partner.

I look forward to the honor of a second meeting with you on my impending trip and to our having another open and candid discussion as old friends.

Sincerely and with best personal regards,

Philip H. Knight
Chairman of the Board

Nike in China: 1985

"We've made a lot of progress this past year," noted Scott Thomas, Nike's managing director, People's Republic of China operation. "Pricing negotiations are no longer the serious problem they once were. The same goes for quality. The Chinese have also come to accept the need for flexibility in model changes, although their ability to execute such changes is still limited. And the problems we've had with raw materials supplies and inventories have largely been resolved."

"My number one problem today is getting the factories to double output this year from about 120,000 pairs per month. You'd think that any manufacturer would jump at such an opportunity. But not in China. Expansion means getting all sorts of official approvals, and that's quite a hassle."

"We are also discussing a possible joint-venture arrangement with our Nan Fang factory," he continued. "Investing in overseas production facilities runs counter to Nike's general policy, but a joint venture seems to be a necessary condition for foreign companies to have access to the Chinese domestic market. An opportunity to shoe two billion feet would seem to warrant an exception to our normal practice."

Nike's Situation in China

By mid-1985, Nike's production base in China comprised four factories in two regions: two in Fujian province, in Fuzhou and Quanzhou, and two on the outskirts of Guangzhou (Canton). Plans were under way to add a small operation in a Shanghai shoe plant. Exhibit 1 contains a map showing the plant locations.

Four Americans made up the Nike management team in China. (See Exhibit 2 for an organization chart.) Their offices and families were located in Shanghai. Steve Roth typically flew on Monday to Guangzhou to oversee the manufacturing operations there and returned to Shanghai on Thursday. Peter Nickerson did the same for the two factories in Fujian province. Nike's on-location presence in each plant also included an overseas Chinese person to oversee quality control.

Scott Thomas's outlook for Nike's future in China was one of cautious op-

Exhibit 1   Partial map of coast of China.

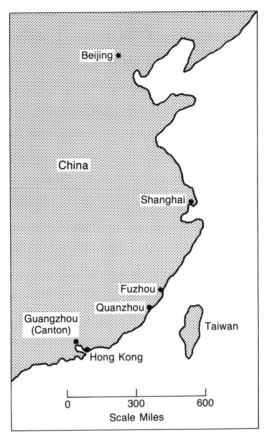

timism. Over five years and after several changes in plants, Nike management had developed a good working relationship with the managers and government officials with whom it had to deal. Chinese industrial policies continued to move in favorable directions and were taking hold deeper in the governmental hierarchies. And evidence was mounting that the potential demand for Nike shoes in China was substantial.

Chinese Policies

China's turn toward an open-door policy under the leadership of Deng Xiaoping took a major step toward a supply-and-demand economy in late October 1984, when the Communist Party Central Committee approved a landmark economic plan to dismantle heavy-handed central control. The move was reported in the *Wall Street Journal* (on November 8 and 26, 1984):

> Over the next few years, more than a million state-run enterprises and factories will be freed to make more of their own manufacturing, price and

Exhibit 2 Nike organization for China, June 1985.

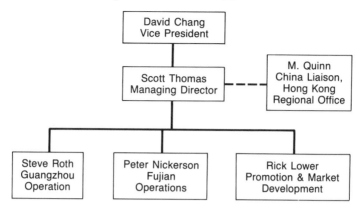

Scott Thomas, 29, BA political science, U.N.H. 1976. Joined Nike
January 1978 as shipping clerk. Experience in Q.C., production
control (U.S. 1978-1980), production management (Korea 1980-
1982, logistics (Hong Kong 1982-1983), operations director
(China 1983 —).

Steve Roth, 30. Nike shipping (U.S. 1977-1978), technical manager
(U.S. 1978-1981, Korea 1981-1982), production manager (China
1983 —).

Pete Nickerson, 28, BA political science, minor Chinese, U. Oregon
1980. Training (Taiwan 1981), production manager (China
1982 —).

Rick Lower, 32, BS, MS sports medicine U. Colorado 1974, MA Ball
State Teachers. Nike R&D manager (U.S. 1977-1979), soccer shoe
division (U.K. 1979), production manager (Korea 1979-1981, China
1981-1984), Chinese language (1984), marketing (China 1985 —).

All four men were active in athletics. Only Roth and Lower were
considered runners.

marketing decisions. But they will lose government subsidies that kept inefficient and money-losing plants operating; factories that can't make it on
their own will be allowed to close. . . .

China plans to increase the autonomy of local governments and factories
by giving them more hard currency to buy foreign technology and goods.

China has plenty of cash. . . . The country's foreign exchange reserves
ballooned to $16.48 billion at the end of June from . . . only $2.26 billion in
1980. The rapid growth has been fueled by trade surpluses, increased tour-
ism and remittances from overseas Chinese.

While optimism reigned in the flurry of press accounts about China's new
economic policies, a note of caution was also sounded in a February 18, 1985
Fortune article.

The People's Republic is still far from a capitalist's paradise. "Anyone
coming here for quick gain is mistaken," says an experienced American in
Peking. For all the government's intent to change, China remains a poor
socialist economy that's tough and expensive to crack. No one, including
Deng Xiaoping, the 80-year old leader who is orchestrating China's swing

away from doctrinaire Marxism, can be certain the new policies will stick. Deng is shrewdly installing younger men who think more or less as he does, but China has a history of sudden ideological swings.

Scott Thomas attested to the difficulties associated with operating in China:

> The policy changes are really positive steps, although some are vague, with hidden qualifications. The problem is, even with widespread agreement in principle, when you try to take action, you run into a barrier of clarifications on specifics in dealing with the lower-level officials. Part of the difficulty is that the guys on the firing line are trying to figure out what the top people really want. On top of that, there is still a reluctance by the people in the middle to take responsibility. Basically, it's a problem of bureaucracy. There are still too many people involved in making decisions.

The Chinese Market for Running Shoes

While China's "two billion feet" were a strong lure for any shoe manufacturer, the potential market for Nike seemed more illusory than real. With most urban employees—workers, engineers, and even managers—earning between 80 and 120 yuan per month (about $30 to $45 U.S. at the official exchange rate) and most rural workers far less, management had to question the number of people who could afford or who would choose to buy high-quality running shoes.

In 1984, Nike received a clearly positive signal when a Hong Kong firm obtained permission from Chinese officials to import running shoes from Taiwan. The flashy white shoes with an Italian name, priced at 28 yuan, were an instant hit. Three million pairs were sold before import restrictions reduced sales volumes.

The significance of this event was not lost on Nike. Rick Lower rejoined the Nike China team in January 1985 with primary responsibility for developing Nike's market on the mainland. He assessed the situation as follows:

> The success of the Pacino shoes was impressive, especially since their quality was not very high. What this told us was that the Chinese want and are able to buy attractive nonessential consumer items when they're available. The way I see it, while income is low, the opportunities for spending money are also limited. As a result, there seems to be plenty of money saved up and available for such purchases.
>
> If we could gain access to the Chinese market, we could do a lot better than Pacino. For one thing, we would offer a superior product, in terms of design and quality materials, at the same price. For another, Nike has developed a brand awareness in China for quality shoes through its sponsorship of Chinese teams, earlier with the Olympics and basketball and now with track and field.

Lower described his efforts to develop channels of distribution as still very early in the exploratory stage. He described the uncertainty connected with his assignment: "We would love to move fast into the Chinese market. However, as far as I understand, selling Chinese-made shoes in China will require a joint-venture arrangement, and those discussions are still pretty much up in the air. Until that gets settled, there is really little I can do."

With that avenue blocked, at least temporarily, Lower had also begun to look into the possibilities of importing Nike shoes for sale in China. Nike had received permission to bring in a 30,000-pair shipment of grade B shoes, but Lower considered this arrangement only a one-shot affair. Other possible arrangements under investigation were the import of Taiwanese-produced shoes (which benefited from being subject to a 30 percent import duty, compared with the normal 80 percent) and the sale of locally produced models using imported Taiwanese materials.

The Chinese Views

Nike had to deal with myriad parties in conducting business in China, from managers and Communist Party secretaries at the plants to officials from various national ministries, provincial agencies, and municipal governments. Exhibit 3 shows the principal relationships among these official parties. The most heavily involved and directly concerned with Nike were the four plants and the Ministry of Foreign Trade in Fujian Province.

Fujian Footwear and Headwear Branch, Ministry of Foreign Trade

With its ready access to the sea and rugged, mountainous terrain, Fujian province had traditionally been more closely linked with the outside world than with China proper. During more than three decades of Chinese isolation, the region had languished economically. As China opened its doors to the West, Fujian was marked for special economic development.

The Ministry of Foreign Trade bore major responsibility for the development of Fujian exports. In this capacity, the Ministry's Fujian Footwear and Headwear Branch served as the intermediary between Nike and the two factories in the province. Nike paid the branch office for all shoe purchases. The factories then received Chinese currency at a higher-than-official exchange rate as a subsidy. In addition, the branch had set up a business arrangement in Hong Kong to supply the Fujian factories with all the imported raw materials and equipment necessary for Nike shoes. (In all its other Chinese locations—current and discontinued—Nike had had to make these purchases.)

Mao Gui Rong, director of the Fujian Footwear and Headwear Branch, described her views of the Nike arrangement:

> We began over twenty years ago to export low-cost shoes to overseas Chinese. Our first direct shipment to the U.S. occurred in 1971. Eventually, we began to realize that we would be unable on our own to reach beyond the small ethnic niche we were serving. To gain access to the mainstream Western markets, we would have to go through the big foreign shoe-trading companies. It became clear that we would have to change our approach if we were to make Fujian province the leading supplier of export shoes in China.
>
> We assessed our strengths and weaknesses. On the positive side, we had plenty of intelligent, hard-working people to provide low-cost labor.

Exhibit 3 Chinese governmental organization for industry, 1985 (partial).

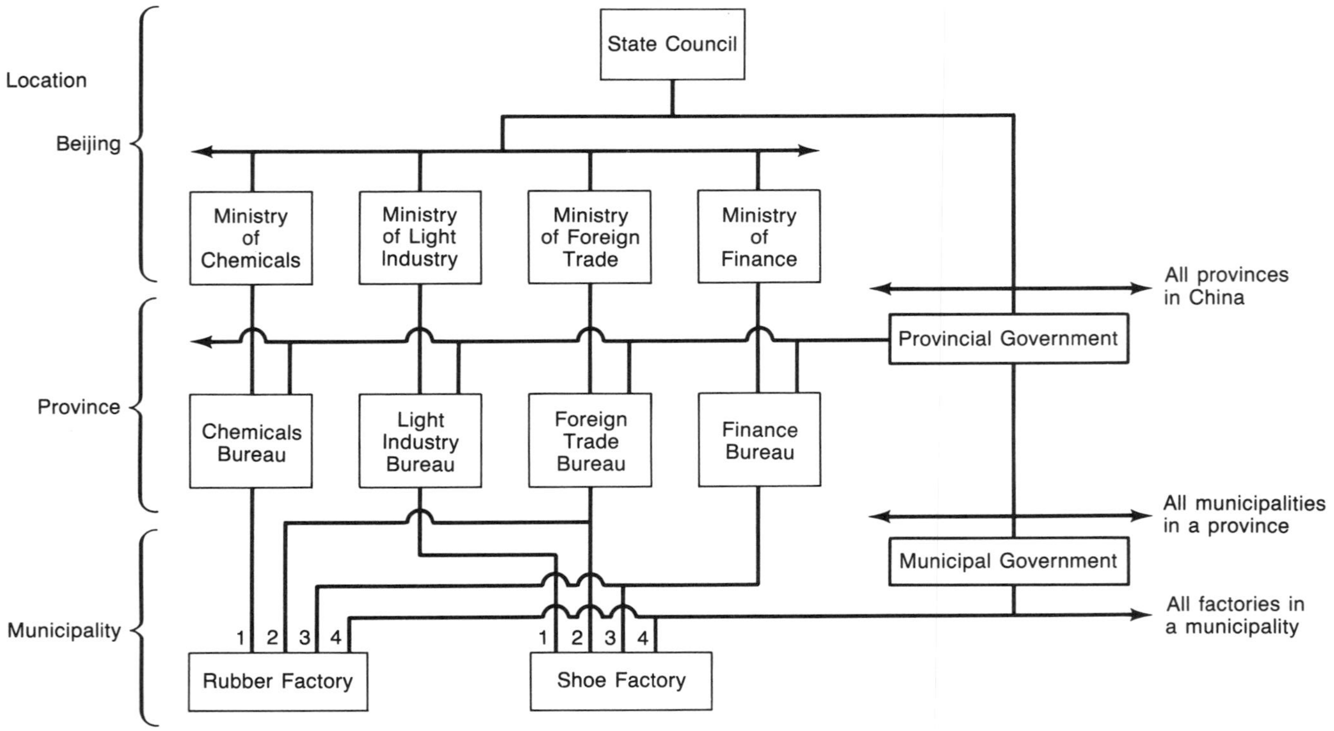

Responsibilities: (1) technology, production planning, investment, domestic sales
(2) foreign trade, foreign currency
(3) financial performance
(4) administration: personnel policies, salary, hours, health care, etc.

And we had a will to succeed. On the negative side, we didn't know the markets, we didn't have distribution, our quality wasn't good enough, our technology was antiquated, raw materials were limited in quality and availability, and we had a poor reputation in the trade.

So you can see, we were more than happy to cooperate with Nike when it first approached us. And the results to date have been gratifying. Nike has contributed importantly to our objectives in helping our factories to develop the skills and operations needed to manufacture quality running shoes. We have made and continue to make gains in capabilities, productivity, quality, and flexibility as a result of this relationship. Our association with Nike has also greatly helped us to improve our reputation abroad as shoe manufacturers.

Today, Fujian Province is the largest exporter of quality shoes in China. Moreover, we have developed a favorable support system. Our factories can obtain foreign currencies for purchasing raw materials and equipment, enough energy to keep the equipment in operation, and capital for investments. Moreover, this office is sending its people abroad to visit our customers and our markets so that we can better understand their needs and be more and more responsive. For example, Jian-Zhong Chen (a young branch official who worked with the Quanzhou plant), will spend a month next fall in the United States, visiting Nike facilities, major outlets, and so forth. Min Sheng Yu (a young branch official who worked with the Fuzhou plant) made a similar trip last year.

Mao went on to discuss her thinking about Nike's request to double output:

Nike wants us to double our output but will not give us any commitments to purchase these shoes. This puts all the risk on our shoulders. So, we conducted a feasibility study to assess the situation. On the demand side, we examined Nike's sales, its inventory position, its commitments to other suppliers, and the like. On the supply side, we checked on how much output could be expanded through increased productivity of the existing lines and by converting equipment used for other shoes. Once we were satisfied with the numbers, we gave both plants permission to double their Nike production lines.

Under this arrangement, we will invest about $400,000 in foreign currency for equipment and raw material stocks. I must explain that when Beijing moved to make factories more autonomous, we established a corporation under the branch to enable us to join forces with the factories. In effect, we shifted our focus from the central office to a more local perspective. We now have 50–50 joint venture ownership with forty-six export shoe factories in Fujian province, including the two involved with Nike. In the Nike case, the industrial ministries to which the factories report are to supply several million yuan in the form of mortgage loans for the new buildings and will continue to have responsibility for technical assistance and domestic sales.

What happens if Nike should fail to provide orders for the expanded facilities? In the short run, the factories would fail to meet their quotas, and no one, including our people, would get any bonus. We would have to help the factories to make their mortgage payments during this time. In the long run, we would develop other markets for our shoes—domestic as well as international.

> We believe that Nike has made some moral commitment in asking us to expand. However, one thing we've come to learn: Unlike Chinese tradition, for U.S. businessmen, "Friend is friend, and business is business."

Mao, a vivacious woman in her forties, had spent four years in France and Morocco and spoke English and French fluently. Scott Thomas had a high regard for her abilities and her commitment to her task. She, in turn, held Nike in high regard. Nonetheless, while conceding the need for continuing improvement on the Chinese side, she also saw room for improvement on Nike's side:

> Nike still needs to improve its understanding of the Chinese system, especially in knowing what to discuss with different offices. For example, the Nike people would raise price issues with the ministry's headquarters in Beijing. That's inappropriate. They should address broad issues—such as future exports, investments, domestic sales, etc.—at that level and talk with us on the specific details. They believe that they were able to set up the Fujian arrangement as a result of their discussions with the Ministry of Foreign Trade in Beijing. The truth is that we went to the head office after them and convinced the top people to support us in terms of investments, subsidies, and overseas sourcing so that we could work with Nike.
>
> In fact, one of my branch's most critical jobs is to secure appropriations from the limited funds available in Beijing. We have to convince ministry headquarters that the expansion of shoe production in Fujian is more in the national interest than expansion of another product or in another region.

Scott Thomas countered Mao's views on the manner in which the Nike-Fujian relationships were initially arranged:

> Whether the Fujian Footwear Corp.'s follow-up or Nike's persistence solved our problems is an interesting question. The head office in Beijing claims all credit for the "special arrangement" (subsidized prices, low interest loans, etc.) in Fujian, implying in turn that if Nike has any problems or questions they are both able and willing to assist. Madam Mao's interpretation and Nike's differ not only to the extent we represent a foreign perspective but also to the extent we are willing to try options not historically accepted as "correct."

Fujian Factories

In July 1985, the two Fujian factories produced about 80 percent of Nike's output in China. The Fuzhou factory, which had manufactured inexpensive footwear for domestic consumption before its association with Nike, reported to the Ministry of Light Industry. By 1984, the old multistory plant, located in the heart of a city with one-half million inhabitants, had phased out all other products to devote itself to Nike production. The three assembly lines and supporting operations spilled over from the production floor to fill every nook and cranny. Inventory and supplies cluttered the corridors, and materials flow was complicated by the small size of the main manufacturing lofts. The normal work-force complement of 750 workers was swelled by some 250 additional persons who were in training to man future expanded operations.

Mao Huang Kue, director of the Fuzhou Sportshoes Factory, gave the following account of the Nike arrangement:

> We have a good working relationship with Nike. Our productivity so far has been somewhat limited for several reasons: We've had raw-material supply problems; models keep changing; and we're still learning the new techniques. We are now producing about 50,000 pairs of Nike shoes per month and hope to raise that to 60,000 pairs.
>
> One of our greatest difficulties this year has been Nike's severe price cuts. We had just reduced costs about 15 percent when Nike demanded another price reduction of 26 percent. That seemed to us to be an unrealistic demand, but at Nike's insistence, we had no choice but to swallow the reduction.
>
> We are committed to doubling our capacity. To do this, we plan to build a new plant about a kilometer in distance from here and to install three more assembly lines.

The Quanzhou (pronounced Chuenzo) factory, a rubber-products manufacturer reporting to the Ministry of Chemicals, began shoe operations under Nike supervision. Located in a quiet, provincial city with 200,000 inhabitants, the factory comprised multiple one-story buildings comfortably spread out on several acres of land. The three assembly lines and the supporting rubber-manufacturing operations for Nike shoes were physically and organizationally separated from the manufacture of other rubber products.

Zhen Xie Jin, factory manager for Quanzhou Rubber Shoes Factory, was a young and dynamic individual, eager to build his business in size and capability. To compensate for Quanzhou's relative inaccessibility—the city, which had reputedly been China's largest port in the time of Marco Polo, lay 200 kilometers and four hours' hard driving distance from Fuzhou, with its major airport—Zhen had an apartment built on the second floor of the warehouse to house a Nike representative and his family. Although spacious and attractive by Chinese standards, with Western toilet facilities, it failed to attract any Americans from Shanghai.

Zhen's comments about the Nike arrangement generally mirrored those of his counterpart in Fuzhou. In discussing the price cuts, Zhen raised the issue of Nike's overhead costs.

> Nike has very high overhead costs in China. Its location in Shanghai, with the high cost of space and the need to travel so often back and forth by air, adds a lot of unnecessary costs. I don't think it's right for Nike to ask us to make up for all those extra expenses by lowering prices below our costs. They could go a long way to reducing cost pressures if they were willing to tighten their own operations.

Zhen was committed to doubling his factory's shoe-manufacturing capacity in response to Nike's request. For this purpose a separate building to house three additional assembly lines would be constructed on the factory's grounds. He estimated a total investment of about 5 million yuan and a payback period of about five years.

Guangzhou Factories

Unlike the arrangement in Fujian, Nike dealt directly with the two factories in Guangzhou. For Nike, this arrangement greatly simplified negotiations by eliminating the third-party intermediary. One disadvantage was the absence of subsidy payments from the Ministry of Foreign Trade. Moreover, Nike was responsible for supplying all imported equipment and raw materials. Guangzhou's proximity to Hong Kong, however, did enable Nike to use trucks to move raw materials in and finished goods out, greatly simplifying the logistics.

Long March Shoe Factory

Of the four factories with which Nike collaborated, it had had the longest working relationship with the Long March Shoe Factory, located on the outskirts of Guangzhou. Formal agreements were concluded in October 1982 with a plan to install six assembly lines in three equal stages. In May 1983, two assembly lines with a combined capacity of 30,000 pairs per month began operations.

In November 1984, unable to reach agreement on prices, Nike discontinued the purchase of shoes form Long March. On June 17, 1985, with Nike's two lines lying idle under dusty plastic covers, Huh Gua Chang, director of Long March Shoe Factory, met with Scott Thomas and Steve Roth to find a way of putting the equipment back into operation. Following this meeting, Huh described some of the problems that had led to the present situation:

> We were very attracted to Nike with its reputation, with the orders it could place, and with its ability to supply us with new technology, raw materials and management skills. And, at the time, the purchase price for completed shoes was a good one. At the end of our first year, Nike told us that we were potentially their best factory and even included our workers in a bonus payment which some of their more established factories received. Then the problems began.
>
> Price was the most serious problem. Nike would ask us to reduce price again and again. It seemed strange to us that Nike would claim to be losing money and at the same time be giving out a bonus. Now, I can understand a price cut in connection with volume gains or with lowered material costs. But our volume never even reached 800 pairs per day [20,000 pairs per month] and our raw material costs remained high. What was happening was that Nike was trying to cover exhorbitant overhead costs by cutting its contract prices. The lavish accommodations for the American representatives inflicted us with an oppressive burden.
>
> In the two years of operations, we produced only 110,000 pairs of shoes. While normal start-up difficulties accounted in part for this low number, supply problems were largely at fault. Quite often we did not receive the imported raw materials on time and the lines would be idled. Supplies of

domestic materials were also difficult to count on, and what's worse, their quality was not always up to the required standards.

And speaking of quality, probably the most vexing problem had to do with quality grading. We found the basis for deciding whether a shoe was an A or a B grade to be rather arbitrary. Every Nike employee seemed to have his own view of what made a shoe B grade. Each day it would be something different. The problem for us was that we would receive only 60% of the price for grade B shoes. With the low prices to begin with, we calculated a break-even with 85% grade A shoes. With our average A grade output having reached about 90%, our margins were very low, leaving little room for further price reduction. We suggested that we sell the grade B shoes in China as a way of increasing our income, but Nike rejected that proposal.

At least in our experience, the opportunity to work with Nike turned out to be, to use a Chinese expression, better for looking at than for eating.

In the June meeting, Huh proposed that Long March produce Nike shoes for the Chinese market, using local materials. In response, Scott suggested that Long March produce some representative models as a basis for further discussion.

Nan Fang Rubber Factory

Nan Fang Rubber Factory first came to Nike's attention in its role as supplier of rubber soles to the Long March factory. Attracted by the large, relatively new, three-story factory building, its location near the Long March factory, and the quality of management, Nike explored the possibility of manufacturing shoes in Nan Fang, reaching an agreement in March 1983. Operations began in September 1984. By June 1985, two assembly lines with a capacity of more than 60,000 pairs per month were producing about 25,000 pairs per month. A third line was scheduled for completion by July 1985 and plans were to add two more lines by December 1985, bringing capacity up to 165,000 pairs per month.

Steve Roth, who had been responsible for developing Nan Fang's shoe operations, described the important role this factory was to play in Nike's future plans.

I'm very pleased with what we have been able to accomplish in Nan Fang. This plant will become a model for Nike's Chinese operations. It is spacious enough to set up efficient production lines, and management does a good job maintaining quality. We are looking to expand these operations over the next year or so to eight lines. That would increase output to 250,000 pairs per month, or 3 million pairs per year.

By early 1985, Scott Thomas had also opened discussions concerning the possibility of establishing a joint venture with Nan Fang. Access to the Chinese domestic market was the principal incentive for such an arrangement. While terms of such an agreement still had to be worked out, his initial thinking was for Nike to invest several hundred thousand dollars in equipment and raw materials stock in exchange for 50 percent ownership of the factory's shoe operations. The possibility of involving the Ministry of Foreign Trade in order to get favorable foreign-exchange rates was also being looked into.

Si Shao, director of Nan Fang Rubber Factory, expressed his views about the proposed joint venture.

> We are very interested in developing a joint venture with Nike for our shoe operations. However, there are several problems for us in this connection. One is to figure out how best to separate shoes from the factory's rubber-products operations. We are considering divisionalizing the organization to separate managerial responsibilities. More difficult will be to figure out how to reconcile two different pay scales in a single plant. Our Nike shoe workers receive a higher income than do our rubber-products workers. It hasn't been too big a problem so far because of the modest size of the Nike operations [the rubber products operations were about four to five times as large as the shoe operations in mid-1985]. But with larger Nike operations, we could create serious morale problems.
>
> Another major problem is how to treat Nike's employees. Their pay and expenses are so far out of line with those for their Chinese counterparts that it will be difficult to reconcile the two in a single venture. This is already a problem for us. Nike wants us to reduce our price 30 percent. But we are only making a 10 percent profit on our adult shoes and no profits on children's shoes. Chinese labor is cheap, but it is also inefficient. Nike's overhead expenses place too heavy a burden on pricing at the current low-volume level of production.

Nike's Views

In 1984, Nike's China operation resulted in a net loss for the company of close to $1 million. Scott Thomas explained the problem:

> Our operating loss comes from the low volume of shoes produced in China. We need to increase output to one million pairs per month to be cost-effective. So you can see why we're pushing so hard to double output this year.
>
> The Fujian plants could probably increase their output by almost 50 percent on existing equipment with some effort, but they favor adding plant and equipment. The problem for us with that approach is that it might take a year or more to add the capacity by the time all the necessary agreements and clearances are completed. So, to get things moving faster, we're now trying to accelerate our expansion at Nan Fang.

With softening demand in Nike's established markets, domestic sales in China had become increasingly important in Thomas's plan to increase volume to a profitable level. Since access to this market required a joint-venture arrangement, Thomas placed a high priority on these negotiations. He described the status of his efforts:

> We would really like to move ahead quickly and button down the venture this year. But with all the red tape that we have to go through, we'll be lucky to complete the negotiations by the end of 1986.

The problem is not at the local level. Each of our factories would love to become our partner. A joint venture with a foreign firm raises the factory manager's status and gives him a greater degree of freedom from central control. The problem is in getting all the ministries involved to come to terms and to give the necessary clearances.

In a July 29, 1985 article on joint ventures in China, *Forbes* described some of the administrative difficulties faced by foreign firms:

> Dozens of U.S. corporations are setting up shop in China. Pity the lawyers who draft those joint-venture contracts, however. They aren't easy.
> "There is little substantive common law, so you have to pay great attention to detail in writing the contract with your Chinese partner," says Dennis Slattery, senior counsel of First Interstate Bancorp. . . . Foreign firms have had to cope with restrictions on technology transfer, bringing in expert management, access to foreign exchange and the freedom to arbitrate disputes anywhere outside China.

Even more serious was the possibility of at least a partial reversal in the government's joint-venture policy, as reported in the *Wall Street Journal* on July 23, 1985:

> Peking is clearly having a hard time with its urban reforms, issuing confusing directives only to rescind them. A year ago, for example, the government allowed fourteen coastal cities to contract for foreign investments and promised to open more cities as special economic zones. Last week, however, Peking pulled back. It cut the number to four and said that all joint ventures would have to be weighed carefully in view of a fall in China's foreign-exchange reserves.

In line with Nike's growing involvement with the Nan Fang factory, plans were under way to move the office and domiciles from Shanghai to Guangzhou in August 1985. The Nike office was to be located in a modern, luxury hotel and the families quartered in a related apartment complex. Scott Thomas, who would continue to be in charge of the Chinese operation, would move to Hong Kong to enable him to tie China more closely to Nike's other Far Eastern operations (i.e., Korea, Taiwan, Thailand, Malaysia, Singapore, and the Philippines.)

Thomas described his long-term strategy for Nike in China:

> My key goal is to make China a bigger force in the company. Even if we join with Nan Fang in a joint venture, we shall continue to rely on Fujian as a major source of our shoes. This commitment would include shoes for the domestic market, assuming that we can arrange to have the Fujian factories work through the joint venture as subcontractors.

According to current plans, Nike's China operation would at best take several years to show operating profits and would require sizable investments in the meantime. As a result, Scott Thomas was sensitive to possible concerns the Chinese might have with respect to Nike's commitment in light of the company's poor overall financial showing in 1985:

When you're looking at down quarters back to back, you have to look at an operation like China with a bit of skepticism, especially for the short term. But we're not here for the short-term pay-off.

We're lucky to have a chairman, Phil Knight, who has a long-range vision about Nike in China.

Nike's recent quarterly financial results are shown below:

| | 1983 | | 1984 | | | | 1985 |
	Aug.	*Nov.*	*Feb.*	*May*	*Aug.*	*Nov.*	*Feb.*
($ millions)							
Sales	270	169	224	257	285	184	221
Profit after taxes	22.7	5.7	6.4	6.0	7.8	(2.2)	(2.2)

Source: Nike, Inc., 10K report.

Richardson Hindustan Limited

Two projects of major potential interest to the Richardson Vicks Inc. (RVI) Indian subsidiary were very much on the mind of Gurcharan Das, president of Richardson Hindustan Limited (RHL), as he reviewed his company's strategic plan in early 1984. The first would take the Indian firm into products not included among the parent company's worldwide offerings. The second would set up RHL as a supplier of a key raw material for RVI's global operations. Both propositions went counter to existing corporate policies and practices, which stressed products capable of being transferred to markets around the world and which favored investments in marketing over manufacturing. A recent forced reduction of RVI's ownership from 55 percent to 40 percent was sure to affect corporate management's thinking about these two ventures, as well as about a host of other activities and expectations that defined the relationship between parent and its distant subsidiary.

"Balancing the requirements of headquarters and those of the local organization in a way which serves the long-term interests of both is clearly one of the most critical parts of my job," noted Das. "RHL is a loyal subsidiary, yet it has a kindred spirit of its own. As a result, I have to promote RHL's interests at headquarters and then turn around to promote RVI's interests in Bombay. Luckily, I am dealing with excellent people at both ends, or the job would not be much fun."

RVI and RHL

Richardson-Vicks, Inc., was a leading worldwide marketer of branded consumer products for health care, personal care, home care, and nutritional care. The company's product line could be traced to 1905, when Lunsford Richardson, a North Carolina pharmacist, formed a company to sell Vicks VapoRub, which he had developed "especially for children's croup or colds." The company experienced rapid growth following World War II with the addition of new products and the expansion of overseas operations.

In management's view, marketing had been the key to RVI's success. The 1982 annual report described RVI's corporate strategy as follows:

> The company seeks leadership positions for each of its brands by developing products that meet distinct consumer needs. It then produces them

under high manufacturing standards to ensure high performance and consumer acceptance. Finally it supports them with outstanding advertising,
promotion and distribution.

In 1983, RVI had revenues of $1.1 billion based on the sales of such prod-
ucts as Vicks VapoRub (cold product), Oil of Olay (skin care), Clearasil (acne
medication), Vidal Sassoon (hair care), Vicks Throat Drops (cough drops), Sinex (nasal spray), NyQuil (nighttime cold medication), and Homer Formby
(home-care products). According to company records, one out of every four
dollars spent in the U.S. on cold remedies went to purchase a Vicks product.
Overseas sales had grown even faster than domestic and in 1983 accounted for
more than half the company's total sales and profits. Exhibit 1 shows financial
information for RVI.

RHL was one of more than thirty subsidiaries in the Richardson-Vicks
worldwide network. The Indian company was founded in 1964 to oversee the
construction of a pharmaceutical plant and to take over the marketing efforts
then being handled by a small RVI branch operation. Upon completion of the
plant in 1966, 45 percent of RHL's equity was sold to the Indian populace
through a public stock offering. RVI retained 55 percent ownership.

Starting from annual sales of $2.5 million in its first year of operation (1966–
67 fiscal year), RHL posted a record sales volume of $23 million in 1983 and
had become an important unit to the parent company. Its facilities in 1984
included headquarters in Bombay, a modern 160,000-square-foot factory on a
sixteen-acre site at Kalwa (twenty miles north of Bombay), and a menthol-
distillation center at Bilaspur (150 miles north of Delhi).

Gurcharan Das at Richardson Hindustan Limited

When Das returned to his native India in January 1981 to head RHL after working in different parts of the world for thirteen years (see Exhibit 2 for details of
his career), he found a company in trouble. He recounted his initial impressions:

> I was very excited to go back home as head of the company where I had
> started as a trainee eighteen years earlier. But what I found when I got there
> was a real mess. The company was cash poor, morale was low, labor was
> hostile, labor-management relations were adversarial, and turnover in the
> management ranks was very high. Because of governmental price controls,
> management for years had stressed volume, selling at any price and pro-
> ducing at any cost. I can tell you, it was a difficult homecoming for me.

Das, together with RVI management, quickly mapped out a strategy to turn
around the situation. He explained the resulting priorities and actions:

> The top priority was to increase profitability. We raised prices wherever
> we could, reduced inventories and accounts receivable, cut low-yielding sales
> and distribution activities, and got the sales force to push the more profita-
> ble lines. RHL suffered some decline in volume, but not as much as the
> marketing people had predicted in resisting these moves. The cash flow
> improved dramatically.

Exhibit 1   Richardson-Vicks Inc. financial summary, 1979–83 ($ millions).

| | *Year Ended June 30* | | | | |
Summary of Operations	*1983*	*1982*	*1981*	*1980*	*1979*
Sales	$1,116	$1,116	$1,088	$929	$829
Investment, royalty, and other income	9	17	16	14	8
Total Income	1,125	1,133	1,104	943	837
Cost of products	444	433	428	360	329
Selling, advertising, and administrative	517	502	485	408	362
Research	35	32	29	22	19
Interest	21	23	14	11	9
Other	10	29	13	11	20
Total costs and expenses	1,027	1,019	969	812	739
Earnings before taxes	98	114	135	131	98
Income taxes	46	47	52	56	50
	$52	$67	$83	$75	$48
Discontinued operations	—	—	(4)	9	15
Earnings for the year	$52	$67	$79	$84	$63
Earnings per common and common equivalent share	$2.10	$2.74	$3.31	$3.56	$2.66
Key Statistical Data					
Cash	$119	$91	$106	$109	$142
Tangible net assets	265	395	361	461	373
Working capital	245	225	198	290	268
Current ratio	2.0	2.1	1.8	2.0	2.2
Long-term debt	168	41	13	18	19
Stockholders' equity	471	486	452	550	498
Property, plant, and equipment (net)	242	247	209	184	209
Expenditures for property, plant, and equipment	34	58	49	53	48
Depreciation	21	19	16	13	12
Advertising and promotional expenditures	278	276	268	230	206
Average common and common equivalent shares (in thousands)	24,511	24,448	23,982	23,678	23,706
Cash dividends paid per-share common	$1.48	$1.48	$1.32	$1.20	$1.06
Number of employees	10,700	11,000	10,800	15,000	15,000
Stock price					
High	32.5	30.9	42.5	27.0	31.0
Low	22.4	20.5	22.3	17.5	19.8

Source: Annual reports.

Exhibit 2 Gurcharan Das' career.

June 1963	Graduated from Harvard University, A.B. cum laude
July 1963	Joined Richardson-Merrell Inc., as a management trainee in New York
December 1963	Marketing Trainee—Vicks, Bombay
January 1966	Product Manager—Richardson Hindustan Ltd., Bombay
December 1968	Group Product Manager—Vicks, Latin America/Far East, New York
January 1971	Marketing Manager—Mexico
July 1971	Marketing Manager—Richardson Hindustan Ltd.
April 1972	Marketing Controller—Richardson Hindustan Ltd.
February 1974	Marketing Director—Richardson Hindustan Ltd.
February 1976	General Manager, Nutritional Division, Richardson-Merrell S.A. de C.V. Mexico
January 1980	Assistant General Manager, General Foods, Spain
January 1981	President, Richardson Hindustan Ltd.
May–June 1982–83	91st Advanced Management Program, Harvard Business School

Gurcharan Das, born in Punjab, India, in 1943, was the author of several plays which were successfully produced and published. *Larins Sahib,* a prize-winning play about the British in India, was produced in Bombay and by the BBC in London, and published by Oxford University Press in England. *Mira* was staged in New York to critical acclaim and had long and successful runs in many cities in India. A Spanish version was performed in Mexico City and Madrid. In 1984 Das was completing a novel about an Indian family. He is married and has two sons.

> Next, I dealt with the labor situation. Labor relations could be characterized as bitterly adversarial. Management advocated the approach of "stick it to the workers," and the workers, I am sure, would have happily done the same back.
>
> I set out to convince the workforce that we had a problem which could only be worked out together. To help change the prevailing hostile attitudes, we mounted an attitude-change program—first for managers, then for supervisors, and finally for workers. In October, 1981, the old personnel manager was replaced by someone who shared my views on how to work with labor instead of against it. A year later we succeeded in signing a three-year contract that made sense to both sides.
>
> The final step was to identify and commit to new opportunities for future growth. I tend to favor participative management and have found the strategic-planning process to be a splendid vehicle for involving and motivating young managers throughout the organization.

As a result of the turnaround, profits had almost doubled, return on equity employed had increased from 22.6 percent to 30.5 percent, accounts receivable had been reduced from seventy days outstanding to thirty, and headcount had been reduced from 750 to 675 with a sales-volume increase of close to 50 percent. In tune with these results, RHL stock prices had more than doubled. (See Exhibit 3 for the RHL financial results.)

Das summed up his assessment of RHL's situation as of mid-1984: "Given the results for 1983 and the situation today, the company has more than met the objectives I had set in 1981. Profits are good, relations with the government have improved greatly, labor is happy, and management is enthusiastic—not one key manager has left the company in the past eighteen months. The central challenge for us now is profitable growth."

Strategy for Profitable Growth

RHL's five-year growth objectives were to double sales revenues and to triple profits by 1988. (See Exhibit 4 for the company's key financial projections.)

An expansion and extension of RHL's core product lines was to serve as the basis for this sales growth. The company planned to launch twelve new products and relaunch one other product during this period. Entry into two new businesses had also been proposed to serve as a base for future growth.

Expansion and Extension of Core Product Lines

RHL prided itself on its marketing skills; its advertising programs and extensive distribution system were the primary engines for sales growth. Arun Bewoor, General Sales Manager, explained the company's approach:

> About 75 percent of the Indian population live in some 526,000 rural communities. That's a potential market of almost one-half billion people. And RHL has built the largest rural distribution structure in our field. We do grass-roots marketing and draw upon Indian culture for unique campaign ideas. India is a country with many people outside the monied economy, so we sell small tins of Vicks for fifteen cents. Television is still in its infancy, so we advertise through the movie halls. Our market research showed that people had colds in the rainy season as well as winter, so we started to do intensive market promotion during the monsoons. The land and people are heterogeneous, so we segment our advertising based on language, economic development, and market development.

Colds Care and Casual Therapeutics

Colds care and casual therapeutics products accounted for about 80 percent of RHL's 1983 total sales, and Vicks VapoRub for the greater part of these. The strategic plan aimed to continue the company's dominance in these market segments in order to generate funds for new-product expansion.

VapoRub was the single largest product in its category and its dominance was expected to continue. However, competition was intensifying from lower-

Exhibit 3 RHL financial highlights (table in lakhs: units of 100,000 rupees)[a] (1983 financial details in $ millions).

Summary of Operations	1983	1982	1981	1980	1979	1978	1977	1976	1975	1974
Sales	2,330	2,000	1,919	1,656	1,335	1,389	1,247	1,086	889	738
Earnings before taxes	390	229	159	174	96	201	185	125	124	57
Income taxes	297	155	103	123	71	156	132	85	92	36
Earnings after taxes	92	74	56	51	25	45	53	40	32	21
Dividends	54	36	36	30	18	36	26	26	26	11
Retained profits	39	38	20	21	7	9	27	14	6	10

Years Ending June 30

Profit and Loss Account for Year Ended June 30, 1983

Sales	$23.3
Expenses	19.7
Raw and packaging materials	8.0
Wages	2.7
Operations	5.5
Sales and excise taxes	3.3
Other	0.2
Profit before taxes	3.9
Profit after taxes	0.9

Balance Sheet as of June 30, 1983

Inventories	$5.3
Current assets	7.2
Fixed assets	3.0
Total assets	$10.2
Current liabilities	5.6
Long-term debt	1.0
Deferred payment credits	0.2
Equity	3.4
Total liabilities	$10.2

a. The exchange rate as of late 1983 was approximately 10 rupees to one U.S. dollar.

Source: Richardson Hindustan Limited annual report.

Exhibit 4 Key financial objectives (comparison to industry average).

	Industry Average[a] (1982)	Our Company	
		Actual 1982–83	Objective 1987–88
Sales growth (5-year compound)	15.2	10.7	20.0
Operating profit (% sales)	NA	[b]	[b]
Earnings before tax (% sales)	9.8	19.1	22.3
Earnings growth (5-year compound)	9.2	14.2	23.9
Earnings after tax (% sales)	3.9	4.6	7.5
ROI (%)	19.0	19.6	29.2
Debt/Equity	0.43	0.33	0.30
Net working capital (% sales)	20.0	7.7	7.0
Return on shareholders equity (%)	21.8	27.1	36.0
Price earnings multiple	8.1	9.6	10.0

Our financial performance for 1982–83 compares favorably with industry average on all financial indicators. Our financial ratios are expected to further improve by 1987–88. The most dramatic improvement is expected in the PAT ratio, which will rise as a result of our plan to invest in tax-designated areas. Our tax rate would come down to 48 percent as a result and PAT ratio go up to 11.6 percent. In the interest of producing a conservative plan, we have not projected the full benefit of tax incentives and have shown tax rate at 66.4 percent (v. 76 percent today).

a. Industry average is based on the performance of the following companies. Industries sales figures include excise tax (10–15%) which ours do not. (1) Warner Hindustan, (2) Pfizer, (3) Abbott Laboratories, (4) Parke-Davis, (5) Colgate-Palmolive, (6) Beechams (HMM), (7) Cadbury, (8) Ponds, (9) Nicholas, (10) Nestle (FS), (11) Brooke Bond, (12) German Remedies, (13) May & Baker, (14) Cyanamid.
b. Deleted.

Source: RHL Strategic Plan, August 1983.

priced regional "look-alike" brands. According to Arun Bewoor, "We have a lot of problems with mushroom competitors. These are small, fly-by-night manufacturers who make copies of VapoRub, sell them for a month or two, and then disappear, only to reappear somewhere else later. When RHL raised its price on the popular five-gram tin from one rupee to two rupees, we brought these hit-and-run outfits out in droves."

The colds-care line also included the following products: Formula 44 cough liquid; Formula 44 Disc cough lozenges; and Action-500 cold tablets, which was scheduled to be relaunched with an aromatic formulation, new packaging, and premium pricing, and eventually extended with an antihistamine formula (Action-500 Plus). Vicks Sinex Nasal Spray was also scheduled to be introduced as a new product.

Dominant in the casual-therapeutics line of products was Vicks Cough Drops, which accounted for about 20 percent of RHL's total sales. It held a 40 percent national market share, followed by Boots' Strepsils (23 percent) and Halls (17 percent). Arun Bewoor noted, "Cough drops has big growth potential, and Halls is a big threat as it moves more aggressively in the north and south of

India from its strong base in Bombay. It was Hall's successful growth which prompted us to launch a single-portion twist-wrapped candy throat drop to combat their successful offering of this product type."

The first results of RHL's test marketing of the Vicks Herbal twist-wrapped throat drop were considered very positive. As a result, the company planned to launch this product nationally in July 1984.

Vicks Inhalers, which dominated its small but growing market, were also included in the casual therapeutic line.

Personal Care

In management's judgment, Clearasil was synonymous with pimple care in India and overwhelmingly dominated the acne-remedy market. According to market studies, although only about 24 percent of young urban pimple sufferers used acne medication, increasing urbanization, literacy, social interaction, and spending power would make young people more and more conscious of their skin problems. For this reason, management considered the young people's skin-care market segment as ready for a major takeoff. The strength of the Clearasil franchise was reflected in its ability to hold sales volume while its price tripled to almost $1 per tube. To capitalize on this potential, the company planned to introduce related Clearasil products (soap, medicated cleanser, and super-strength lotion).

Future Business Climate

RHL's plans were to unfold in an expected climate of steady business growth. The strategic plan reported that the economy and consumer spending would continue to grow at 3–4 percent; the country would become increasingly self-reliant in petroleum; the rupee would gently weaken (5–8 percent per annum versus the U.S. dollar) as the trade gap widened; and per capita income for the top 20 percent of the population would continue a modest growth. Population was projected to grow at a 2.2 percent rate; as a result, 16 million people (the equivalent of the population of Australia) would be added to India's population each year.

Entry into New Business Areas

Clearly labeled in the RHL strategic plan as a hedge against the possible underachievement of the projected sales growth for core products were two new business ventures. Each in its own way was considered by Gurcharan Das as important to his goal of rapid profitable growth.

Ayurvedics

Das and Dr. Victor Moreno, vice president of research and development for Vick Americas/Far East division, had been intrigued for some time with the possible opportunity to commercialize the supply of herbal medicines that had been widely popular in India for some 2,000 years. Das characterized ayurvedic, or natural (herbal) medicines as safe, slow, and long acting, and therefore ideally suited for chronic diseases. Dr. T. G. Rajagopalan was hired in 1982 to develop an ayurvedic line of products. Rajagopalan had received an M.S. in biochemistry from the University of Madras and a Ph.D. in the same field from Duke University and had worked in Ciba Geigy's laboratories as a biochemist for fifteen years.

Rajagopalan described his approach to this challenge:

> To decide on the best initial target areas, we began with a broad study of twelve areas of medicine, such as skin, liver, hair/teeth, respiratory, etc. With the help of a consultant and several university students, we collected over 7,000 ayurvedic recipes and had them translated from Sanskrit. These recipes included anywhere from one to ninety plants. Since the plant names were only in Sanskrit, it was a task to find the equivalent botanical names.
>
> We next developed a computer program to categorize the pharmacological properties of the plants, as well as the vehicles for administering the medication. Since we wanted to meet Western pharmacological and toxicity standards, we screened the products to show toxicity based on reports in Western literature published from 1905 to 1982. The data bank we have on herbal plants is unique. Nobody has done this before.

Opinions about RHL's entry into ayurvedic products differed widely. Das saw great commercial possibilities in India and eventually abroad from ayurvedic medications and personal-care products. Bharat V. Patel, vice president of marketing for RHL, was much less enthusiastic about its market potential, viewing the effort as more of a move to gain favor with the Indian government by promoting indigenous medicinal practices. Lou Mattis, with line responsibility for RHL as general manager for Vick Americas/Far East, was undecided as to the project's profit potential, but willing to give it a try.

Patel questioned RHL's ability to devise an ayurvedic product that could compete with the efficacy of a Western drug:

> I am opposed to the idea of our introducing a serious drug for several reasons. First, such a drug would take us into a domain where doctors hold sway. RHL does not have expertise in this arena; our strength is in over-the-counter products. Second, ayurvedics will never be able to provide the quick relief that people want in this day and age. Finally, such a product does not fit into our specialty of casual therapeutics for minor ailments.
>
> If we do come out with such a product, the company should not project it as an ayurvedic drug. It should be offered with modern packaging emphasizing its attributes rather than its natural herbal content.

Somewhat in line with Patel's thinking, RHL management had as its objective to offer proprietary medicinal products that could be advertised and sold over the counter. Furthermore, introducing ayurvedic toiletries was seen as easier than introducing herbal medicinal products, because of the latter's more stringent requirements for quality consistency (difficult to achieve with natural plants).

In 1984, RHL was committed to constructing an R&D facility for developing ayurvedic products. Construction was estimated at $275,000, and initial equipment orders would run about $330,000. Das estimated these investments would increase to a total of $1 million in two years and to $2 million in five years. (Figures disguised.)

Dextromethorphan-Hydrobromide

As a way of increasing exports and of making a high-technology basic drug to comply with government pressures, RHL management began looking into the possibility of producing dextromethorphan-hydrobromide, an antitussive ingredient used in products to counter cough symptoms. RVI was reportedly the world's largest consumer of dextro with its annual purchases of almost $9 million (figure disguised), at the 1983 price of $285 per kilogram, from two established suppliers. RHL proposed to become a global source of dextro for RVI, producing the same quality product at a lower price with the aim of making a profit and of gaining important goodwill with the government.

The person pushing the dextro-manufacturing venture was B. K. Patney, RHL's vice president of manufacturing. His plan was to import the intermediate materials and produce the dextromethorphan at a cost 20 percent below RVI's current price. Although he preferred to license the process in Italy or even to develop his own version, Patney proposed to license from one of the current suppliers, despite the higher cost, so as more readily to gain headquarters' approval.

Tax savings were also an important element in the dextro proposal. In this case, the company would qualify for a duty draw-back and cash incentive if the intermediate chemicals were imported into a duty-free site and at least 30 percent value added. Moreover, by being based in a trade-free zone, RHL would have its profits from this operation tax free for seven years. Overall, the investment in dextro facilities would total about $2.2 million (figure disguised); the payback for this investment was calculated to be less than two years.

Notwithstanding RHL's enthusiasm for the dextro project, RVI's response was seen by Das as unenthusiastic. He recognized several reasons for headquarters' reluctance. Perhaps most important was RVI's general policy of focusing its resources on marketing investments and keeping down its investments in manufacturing plant. Moreover, dextromethorphan-hydrobromide was a complicated chemical compound requiring special processes with which RVI had had no direct experience.

RHL's failure to deliver on an earlier promise to produce low-cost menthol exports possibly provided some people with further grounds for opposing the project. In the 1960s, RHL management had proposed to grow the mentha arvensis plant in India, both as a means of import substitution and as a source of low-cost menthol for the parent company. For a variety of agricultural reasons, the costs of producing menthol in India turned out to be much higher than had been anticipated when compared to production in Brazil.

On the positive side, Das felt that RHL's strong financial performance over the past two years had done much to improve its credibility at headquarters. Patney's successful track record in manufacturing also went a long way in having headquarters take the dextro project seriously. He had developed a reputation as a person who submitted carefully prepared capital-investment proposals and who had successfully implemented each approved project within a typically tight budget limit.

Despite these strong pluses for the dextro project, Das recognized their limits, "RHL is 10,000 miles from the home office in Wilton, Connecticut. And so there is still a healthy dose of skepticism there as to what RHL can do."

Building and Balancing Constituency Relationships

Notwithstanding his deep interest and involvement in products and markets, Das saw as a special part of his job that of serving several important RHL constituencies. The most important of these constituencies were the parent company, the RHL employees, the Indian government, and the Indian shareholders. For the most part, the requirements and expectations among these parties were different and often in direct conflict. Not only was it important for Das to figure out what balance to strike with respect to specific decisions; it was also vital to convince each party to accept the concessions it might perceive itself making. His ability to argue each case on its own merits was limited where RHL was viewed as only a small element in a total picture, such as might be the case for an RVI headquarters executive or even more so for an Indian government official.

RVI Headquarters

As a worldwide marketer of branded consumer products, RVI followed a strategy of developing or acquiring a brand leader in one market and then transferring its experience to other markets around the world. Each of the operating divisions was relatively autonomous and had complete responsibility for its product line. The corporate level organization structure is shown in Exhibit 5.

Louis Mattis, president and general manager of the Vick Americas/Far East division since 1982, was responsible for thirteen country managers and twenty-six countries with sales of $232 million in 1983. He had joined the company in 1979 from Warner-Lambert Co. At the age of forty-two, he had established a reputation as a hard-driving and successful consumer-product manager who encouraged and expected high-level performance from his people. Lou Mattis was to become an executive vice president of RVI and a member of a newly formed corporate strategic-planning committee, along with the company's other two executive vice presidents, as of January 1, 1985. With this promotion, he would also gain responsibility for RVI's nutritional care products in the United States.

Mattis described the evolution of corporate/divisional relations as follows:

Exhibit 5 Richardson-Vicks, Inc., corporate and divisional organization structure, February 1983.

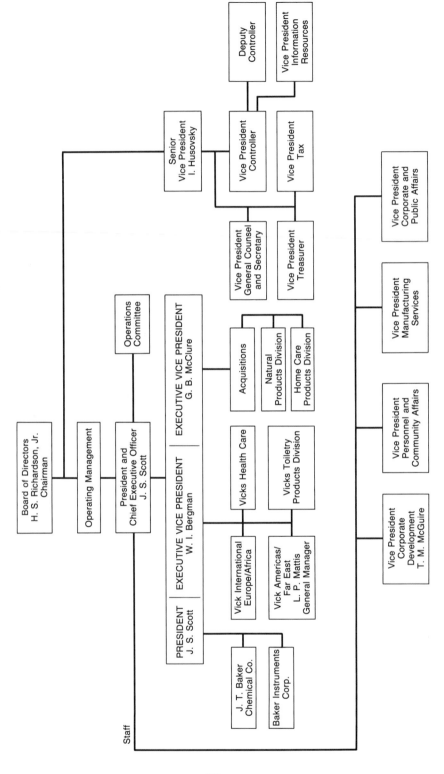

We've gone through several stages of evolution in dealing with our multicountry operation. In the 1960s we said, "Young man, go do your thing." We had a very small home-office staff and exercised loose control. In the 1970s, the pendulum swung to the other end, and the division was centralized very tightly in terms of home-office control. Staff was set up in every function—manufacturing, personnel, finance, policy. The staff became decision makers, and the field were implementers.

My predecessor made some really good decisions and business did very well in the 1970s. . . . But the control system had an impact on the country managers. They became upward looking, bureaucratic and procedural oriented.

In the last four years, we have given country managers independence with financial controls. We still use a continuous planning and review system, but staff executives don't have to concur on the line manager's decisions before they can be implemented, as was true earlier.

To achieve decentralization, four areas had been created (namely, Mexico, Japan, Canada and South America, and Australia and the Far East) with an area director in charge of each. As Mattis described it:

We've put line responsibility and authority with the area directors. The staff is a resource to the countries and to me. The way our process works, the country managers first discuss their ideas and then budget with their area director and then with the home-office staff. Only then do the country managers come with their area director to me for approval. My review is for each country, not for an areawide budget.

Capital expenditures require corporate approval, and so I get involved. I also get into plans for products that are new to the entire division. If a product is new to a country but is already in the division, it is the area director's concern.

Area Director. Don Glover was area director for Australia and the Far East, an area that covered eleven countries and some miscellaneous South Pacific islands. Eight of these countries had independent companies. The area director's staff consisted of a marketing research director, a personnel director, and a finance director.

He described his role as follows, "The work of the area director is not to be a policeman. It's a link between the country manager and the home office and between countries. We look for similarities and common problems, so that we can avoid reinventing the wheel."

Country Manager. Under Mattis, the country manager played a pivotal role with full responsibility for the bottom line of the subsidiary company. RVI's manager's guide defined the main role of the country manager as follows: "To ensure that the market strategic and operational objective and standards set and implemented are the most advantageous for the market environment and are consistent with area and division plans and policies."

With this purpose in mind, the manager's guide defined a set of nine key result areas by which country managers were to be evaluated:

- Market strategic plans
- Profitability
- Today's products and markets
- Tomorrow's products and markets
- Organizational effectiveness
- Corporate responsibilities
- Social responsibilities
- Supply of product
- Asset protection and utilization

A typical career path for a country manager was to start in marketing, move on to marketing director, next to general manager in a small country with no manufacturing operations, then to a small country with integrated operations (marketing and manufacturing), and finally to head up a major national organization.

As for RHL, Das had been rerecruited from General Foods to take on the job of country manager and subsequently worked closely with Mattis and Glover in his efforts to turn around this troubled subsidiary. Both men were generally pleased with RHL's progress and performance and had a high regard for Das' abilities and accomplishments.

RHL Organization

Gurcharan Das' philosophy and style of management set the tone for the RHL organization. His stress on people was clearly signaled in a letter accompanying the first annual report, "Our success over the years is a result of the development of our people. . . . We seek the best qualified individuals we can find for every job. Employment, training, advancement, and compensation are on the basis of merit."

The following year, the introductory letter was devoted exclusively to the subject of "people excellence." In it, Das stated:

> My main job today is to create an environment where new ideas thrive and people develop their full potential. Otherwise good people do not stay. At RHL, we are working hard to create a climate which fosters innovativeness and encourages risk taking.
>
> Our philosophy of growth through people excellence is based on the following tenets:
> 1. A basic belief that people can grow.
> 2. To help people grow, we need to invest in them.
> 3. We believe that a consultative and participative management style is more effective than an authoritarian or paternalistic one.
> 4. We believe the best form of motivation is through achievement.

In practice, Das spoke softly, listened well, smiled often, and had an air of enjoying his work. He interacted frequently with his managers individually and in groups, encouraging debate and seeking new ideas. Clearly, he was respected and well liked by his subordinates. Exhibit 6 contains an organizational chart for RHL.

Exhibit 6 Richardson Hindustan Limited organizational structure, 1983.

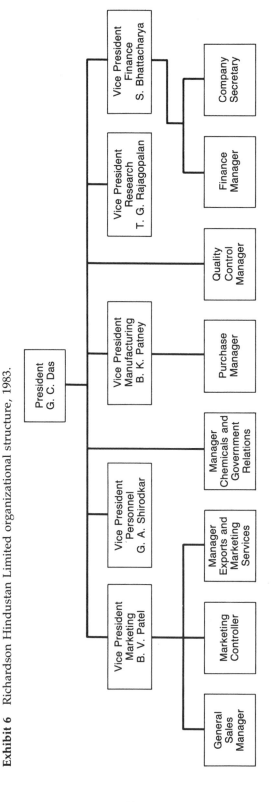

Ginil Shirodkar, vice president-personnel, saw RHL as being in transition from a task-oriented organization to one concerned with task *and* people. In an organizational development plan, the earlier managerial atmosphere was described as one characterized by "jockeying for power, functional empires, interfunctional conflicts, low morale, legalistic management style, low mutual trust, and high management turnover." Faced with this company culture, he set out to replace it with one reflecting the philosophy Das had articulated.

To help change attitudes, Shirodkar developed a training and development program for people at all levels of the organization. One of the most important elements in this program, in his view, was a series of top management workshops in team building and sensitivity training held in March and September, 1982, and February, 1983. The objectives for these sessions were to build management teamwork, to set new goals, and to instill the new RHL values. Other elements in the overall program included a ten-day residential workshop for field sales supervisors and managers focused on people-management and selling skills; a one-week residential program for senior middle managers with emphasis on developing general management skills; a personal growth laboratory for union leaders, workers, supervisory staff, and executives; and a team-building workshop for manufacturing managers.

The training program was connected with a formal appraisal system. Shirodkar described the procedure: "At the start of each year, every manager and his or her immediate superior agree on several major objectives for the junior manager. At the end of the year, both of them rate the assessee's performance. It is mandatory for the appraisal interview to last for at least two hours. It may go on for six hours. The discussion of the junior manager's strengths and weaknesses forms the basis on which the senior manager prepares a report identifying the training needs of the assessee."

Subsequently, the assessee and the appraiser individually charted a career path for the assessee. These were compared and the objectives for the next year set by agreement. To ensure objectivity, a second appraiser then made an independent assessment of the appraisee's performance potential and charted a career path. For the "high fliers" in each division, Shirodkar would meet with Das and the relevant functional director to chart a separate five-year career path.

A growing concern for Shirodkar had to do with the second-class status nonmarketing managers perceived themselves to have in RHL. In an in-house management seminar held in January, 1984, several middle-level managers in manufacturing and finance voiced unhappiness with the limitations of their careers, because of the importance Das attached to the marketing function. This strong focus on marketing was evident in a remark made on another occasion by Patney: "This is a consumer marketing-oriented company. Everything else must fall in line. It's very difficult to talk to top management about manufacturing or the need to invest there. They will spend $5 million on advertising at the drop of a hat, but will study to death a $50,000 capital investment for plant."

Das acknowledged this bias and was puzzled as to how he might deal with it: "This company will live or die on its marketing. I would like all of our managers to gain first-hand experience in marketing, but so far I have not had much success in getting my managers in finance or manufacturing to transfer to a marketing position."

Indian Government

Taxes, price controls and licenses made the government a significant factor in the business planning for any company operating in India. As a low-technology, high-return, foreign-owned consumer-product company, RHL was particularly vulnerable to governmental restrictions and penalties.

Most of the company's decisions with respect to products, markets and investments attempted to reduce this vulnerability and to build good will by being a "good citizen." This approach reflected the parent company's deep-seated commitment to conducting a sound business in an ethical manner. In management's thinking, everyone involved—the consumer, the host country, and RVI—had to benefit for the business to be sound.

Patel, summed up the company's situation, saying, "Selling our kind of products in India is not difficult. The real problem is to get the government's permission to sell it and to do so profitably, given the complex and tough tax structure."

Taxes. Faced with an effective tax rate of 76 percent, management viewed the reduction of taxes as the most important element in its plan to improve RHL's profitability. The target was to reduce the tax rate to 48 percent by 1987–88.

RHL paid high taxes because of its low capital base, high advertising expenditure, and high profitability. These taxes included a basic corporate income tax of 55 percent; a surcharge levied on the resulting profit after taxes exceeding 15 percent of net worth (bringing taxes up to 70 percent); a disallowance of 20 percent of advertising expenditures as a deduction for tax purposes; a federal excise tax of 105 percent of sales price for toiletry items; and various state and city taxes (e.g., 4 percent for Bombay and 15 percent sales tax for Maharashtra, the state in which Bombay is located).

Basically, RHL's approach to reducing taxes was to utilize in a responsible manner the variety of tax incentives offered by the Indian government as a means of directing business investments for purposes of social and economic improvement. For example, the company planned to introduce toiletries based on natural herbs in line with India's policy of favoring the sale of such products by excusing them from excise tax. To reduce corporate taxes, RHL planned to construct a satellite plant in an industrially backward area. The tax incentive for a new manufacturing unit was an eight- to ten-year tax holiday on 25 percent of the profits; locating in a backward area qualified an additional 20 percent for the tax holiday. In addition, Das was also actively engaged in working with industry associations to convince the government to eliminate the advertising disallowance.

The tax consequences at times played an important role in RHL's efforts to obtain headquarters' approval for new investments. Sumit Bhattacharya, vice president-finance, noted, "Last year the government imposed a heavy tax on advertising [the 20 percent disallowance]. Investments in R&D, however, could serve as a tax set-off. This certainly helped RHL to get approval for additional R&D expenditures."

Along these same lines, Patney remarked:

> Over the years, I've learned the need to justify my requisitions for plant and equipment investments for other than manufacturing reasons. Let me give you an example. With the introduction of the new herbal drops, the plant needed additional capacity. Any request for added capacity based on a straightforward manufacturing rationale would have been hard to sell. Headquarters would probably have urged me to squeeze more production out of my existing plant. My approach, therefore, was to emphasize the tax advantages we could obtain from setting up new equipment. The tax savings alone would pay for the equipment in eight to nine months. Since the equipment has to be installed within a year from the time the product is introduced, I received approval in record time.

Das noted in connection with this new capacity investment, "Here's a good case in point where a tax incentive benefited everyone involved. RHL got needed additional capacity; RVI got an attractive investment; and India got new, efficient facilities for a new product."

Overview. In light of the importance of governmental actions to business, RHL's strategic plan contained an analysis of the political and regulatory outlook. The report predicted political stability: Democracy would continue; Mrs. Gandhi would return to power in 1985; and regional problems (e.g., Punjab and the Sikhs) would be contained, but with a greater devolution of power and funds to the states. It also predicted that "pragmatic socialism" would continue to be the ideology of the government, with a high degree of bureaucratic control. With respect to regulation and taxes, the report predicted the continuing decontrol of prices, except for essential and life-saving drugs, and the unlikelihood of dramatic change in indirect and direct taxes, except for an expected discontinuation of the advertising disallowance in 1985.

Taking into account business-government relations in India as a whole, Das noted:

> The environment in India is generally not supportive of business and certainly not of multinational corporations operating in India. The private sector and the market mechanism are constantly questioned. The government evaluates business with respect to the extent to which it can help the country to achieve national social objectives. As a result of this situation, RHL's credentials are constantly challenged, making it important for us to prove that we are contributing to Indian society. The proposals to increase exports and to develop products with a social benefit, such as an ayurvedic remedy for chronic pain, are good examples of how RHL is attempting to strengthen its national franchise by helping to solve Indian problems.

Shareholders

The Indian government's regulations also led to a change in RHL's shareholders structure in 1983.

Recent expansion had been impossible because as a company with greater than 40 percent foreign equity, RHL came under the Foreign Exchange Regulation Act (FERA). Manufacture and sale by all industrial companies in India had to be carried out in accordance with an industrial license issued by the Indian government. Since many companies, including RHL, were outgrowing their industrial license, the Indian government had been obliged from time to time to grant both general increases in production in excess of licensed capacity, as well as specific requests for such increases. As had been the case with all FERA companies, however, RHL's request for grants of specific increased production had been rejected. For Das, this situation presented serious limits to growth.

Then in the late 1970s, the Indian government began to push for reducing foreign ownership to no more than 40 percent in all companies except those involved in high technology or those primarily in export. Das described his experience in dealing with this challenge to RVI, with its 55 percent equity share of RHL:

> A number of the corporate executives were strongly opposed to any dilution of RVI's holdings in RHL. For one thing, RVI has 100 percent ownership of most of its subsidiaries and does not hold a minority position in any. For another, the sale of shares would incur a book loss. Major devaluations in the rupee resulted in RVI's investment being overvalued on the balance sheet.
>
> Whatever the merits of individual cases, the Indian government was committed to the electorate for reducing foreign ownership in Indian companies. RHL's management tried to get an exception on the grounds that its pioneering work in developing a strain of mentha arvensis sufficiently drought and disease resistant to be grown in India qualified the company as involved in high technology. The Indian government rejected this claim on the basis of the low manufacturing technology involved in producing RHL's products.

While battling the Indian government for an exception to the new requirement for foreign ownership, Das was at the same time trying to convince headquarters of the advantages attached to reducing its ownership to 40 percent. This reduction in foreign ownership would remove the company from the severe FERA restrictions to growth. Das explained:

> I tried to make clear that RVI would do better owning a smaller share of a larger operation than a larger share of a smaller one. In any event, the company might have been able to delay the equity restructuring for another year or two by dragging out the dispute in the courts, but eventually it would have been compelled to reduce its ownership. By agreeing to reduce the foreign ownership when we did, we were able to gain some recognition as a high-tech company for our agricultural research. This recognition enabled

us to avoid being placed in the same category as Colgate and Ponds, who are viewed as manufacturers of nonessential items.

A senior executive at RVI headquarters provided further perspective to management's thinking:

> To start with, there was a major split in headquarters on whether or not to reduce RVI's ownership to a minority position. It was not a matter of being unwilling to share the profits or to open our affairs to scrutiny. After all, Indian investors already owned 45 percent of RHL. Rather it was a reluctance to lose positive control of a business with our good name on it. RVI holds its managers to high standards of behavior as well as of performance. And there were those of us who opposed any possible impairment of our ability to ensure that these standards be met. After all, our name and reputation mean a lot to us.

Following RVI's decision to reduce its ownership to 40 percent, Das made every effort to reassure headquarters of his intentions to continue his dedication to RVI. The strategic plan stated:

> Our objective will be to continue to get full and continuing access to RVI products, technology, and ways of working. In turn we will manage the Indian business in order to maximize RVI's interest and continue to add value to RVI through transfer of management people to RVI subsidiaries.

With the reduction in ownership to 40 percent, RVI was obliged by U.S. accounting regulations to remove RHL's figures from its consolidation and to carry it as an "investment in an affiliate." Since the 40 percent ownership could be presumed to control the financial results of RHL, RVI would have to employ "equity accounting," which required it to adjust its investment each year to show any gain or loss in RHL's new worth. To reflect these accounting changes, the RHL plan indicated a change in strategy: "After deconsolidation focus should shift from Operating Profit to Profit after Tax. Strategy is to maximize PAT even at expense of O.P."

Notwithstanding these efforts to maintain former allegiances, there were signs of some change in the parent-subsidiary relationship. Glover, the area director, described his views about the change: "With the equity divestment, my role will change to balancing RVI's interests with those of local shareholders. And my responsibilities will change. I won't have the same kinds of controls to play with. It'll be a more entrepreneurial role, and I'll act as a conduit through which new market ideas and opportunities are communicated."

Das also recognized that the new shareholder structure might put RHL at some disadvantage as compared to before: "If I was at headquarters, I probably wouldn't invest as much in India as before. If I had to make a choice between solving a serious manufacturing problem in Japan or in India, I would probably go to the subsidiary where I had the greatest ownership. In other words, the reduced equity might give us reduced leverage for attention."

As of late 1984, the make-up of the Indian share ownership was as follows:

Total Indian ownership	1,485,000 shares
	(60 percent of total)
Number of Indian shareholders	approximately 8,750
Average holding of individual Indian	
shareholders	approximately 100 shares
Largest shareholders:	
Government-owned financial	
institutions	264,600 shares
Mr. S. C. Banta, RHL chairman	147,700 shares

The 1984 shareholders' annual meeting, held in a theater, was attended by some 1,200 shareowners.

*   *   *   *   *   *

It was in this new context that Gurcharan Das had to try to move ahead with his proposals to introduce thirteen new products, to develop an ayurvedics business, and to gain RVI support for the dextro manufacturing and export project.

Index